The Design of Interactive Computer Displays

The Design of Interactive Computer Displays

A Guide to the Select Literature

Kate McGee
Catherine Matthews
Compiling Editors

Eileen Williams
Research Associate

Judith K. Kroeger
Project Coordinator

the Report Store

910 Massachusetts St., Suite 503
Lawrence, Kansas 66044

Printed in the United States of America

Published by The Report Store, 910 Massachusetts St., Suite 503, Lawrence, Kansas 66044-2975 U.S.A.

Kate McGee and Catherine Matthews, Compiling Editors

Eileen Williams, Research Associate

Judith K. Kroeger, Project Coordinator

Design and production by Publication Management Services

Credits for illustrations on cover (top to bottom):

View of the rising earth as photographed by the Apollo 8 astronauts. National Aeronautics and Space Administration.

"Nevada Geology," Douglas Lora, Los Alamos National Laboratory.

"Moth Eaten Butterfly," Melvin L. Prueitt, Motion Picture Group, Los Alamos National Laboratory, author of *Art and the Computer,* McGraw-Hill, 1984.

"Orthognathic Modeling Sequence," Robert A. Sternberg, Arctan Graphic Arts Inc., Rochester, New York.

Image of a recently discovered complete minimal surface without self-intersections. Mathematical existence established by David Hoffman, Univ. of Massachusetts, Amherst, and William Meeks III, Rice Univ. Image generated using the VPL programming language developed by James T. Hoffman, Univ. of Massachusetts; processed by the Digital Image Analysis Laboratory and printed by the Computer Science Department, both at U. Mass., Amherst.

Library of Congress Cataloging in Publication Data

McGee, Kate
    The design of interactive computer displays.

    Includes indexes.
      1. Information display systems—Bibliography.
2. Computer graphics—Bibliography.   3. Interactive
computer systems—Bibliography.   I. Matthews, Catherine.
II. Title
Z5642.2.M395 1985 [TK7887.8.T4]   016.00164′43   85-60627
ISBN 0-916313-08-5

Contents

Preface   *vii*

Acknowledgments   *xi*

Introduction   *xiii*

Quick Reference List   *xvii*

Capsule Review Description   *xxviii*

Section I

Capsule Reviews   3

Section II

Appendices

   Recommended Basic Library   587
   Design Guidelines   589
   Graphic Standards   591
   Recommended Readings on VDT
      Health and Safety   592

Section III

Author Index   595

Section IV

Subject Index   605

Preface

The most prevalent form of human-computer interaction—both today and no doubt for many years to come—is mediated by means of visual displays. *The Design of Interactive Computer Displays: A Guide to the Select Literature* is a reference tool for practicing display designers—both those concerned with hardware and those working in software development. It provides a comprehensive guide and quick reference to a diverse collection of pertinent, high quality literature brought together from many disciplines. It will help designers become informed of work outside their own particular specialties and will ensure that they have access to the full range of significant sources of information, expertise, and ideas.

Such a reference book meets a widespread and increasingly urgent need, as the topic is one of rapidly growing commercial, economic, and social importance. Display design has become a subject of critical concern for the computer industry. In today's computer marketplace, the video display often accounts for the strongest source of differentiability between competing systems. Except for the quality of their displays—the user's window to the system—computers often *appear* similar, even though in functionality and application they may be quite different.

In addition, consumer-oriented systems such as videotex which aim to supplant the printed word as a medium for information distribution require enhanced display capabilities if they are to be successful. Most major PCs now offer graphics programs and color monitors, and future product enhancement for small systems will be focused on increased processing power and on making high-resolution, full-color screens economically viable. At the same time, the growing demand for portable, space-efficient displays is driving a strong research effort on flat panel systems. Display engineers will soon have a variety of cost-effective non-CRT technologies from which to choose.

The design of display-based human-computer interaction is thus increasing in complexity as it is increasing in importance. Computer graphics applications are growing dramatically in diversity and in volume, ranging from computer-aided design and manufacturing (CAD/CAM) to business graphics and executive/professional workstations. Graphics functions which formerly required dedicated mini-computer systems are now being housed in the read-only memories of "dumb" terminals. Bit-mapped displays which support the extensive use of windowing and icons are gaining acceptance and popularity.

As the technological options are becoming more numerous and complex, the importance of user considerations, or human factors, is also increasing. The display is not just the most visible part of a computer system; it is the part with which the interactive user spends the greatest amount of time. A well-designed screen layout can greatly increase the user's productivity, while a poorly designed display can confuse the user, encourage mistakes, impede performance, and generally inhibit the usefulness of the computer system itself. At worst, a badly designed display can contribute to visual fatigue and general stress for the user.

With regard to the latter, it should be noted that research continues concerning the effects on users of intensive, near visual work at computer workstations. There is general agreement that workplace and workstation design, of which screen design is a part, are critical components of the user environment.

Apart from such issues, however, the economics of computer usage—the low cost of computing power, the large and growing number of computer users representing a significant fraction of the population—is orienting the design process as much toward improving human effectiveness as toward enhancing technological efficiency. Despite this recognized need, little effort has been expended in developing a comprehensive, multidisciplinary ergonomics of visual systems which would include not only "traditional" human factors and sensory, psychological, and human performance data, but also such application-driven fields as the graphic arts, cartography, and statistical graphics, and such theoretical fields as semiotics.

Design practitioners and researchers alike have almost no agreed upon guidelines or information sources which coordinate the diverse data and principles from the array of disciplines relevant to display design for interactive systems. Various reputable handbooks and human factors guidelines exist, but no single book or expert can encompass the full range of relevant scientific, technical, and professional fields. Independent work has been conducted for years in separate research disciplines and application domains with little cross-fertilization of ideas and, in many cases, without workers' even being aware of one another's activities. Further, because knowledge of the principles governing the visual presentation of information is highly specialized, it is often inaccessible to those with responsibility for display design.

In fact, much scientific and professional work with either practical or theoretical relevance to the design of displays is available, but little of it is well known. The relevant work originates in different disciplines and circulates through limited dissemination channels. Few designers of interactive computer displays are aware of the wealth of information which has been accumulated—indeed, few professionals in any field can have in-depth expertise in more than one or two technical areas. Given the difficulty of accessing or becoming aware of useful information, many individuals with the responsibility for designing displays must work completely intuitively.

In sum, the tasks of those responsible for the design of computer displays, and whose decisions ultimately determine the conditions of end use, are becoming more difficult even as they are becoming more critical. Display designers receive little or no information support concerning such matters as the anatomical and physiological limits of the human visual processing system, the established human factors considerations and rules, issues concerning health and safety, and the applicable principles from the graphic arts. The product manager, the display engineer, the icon designer, the R & D manager, the human factors specialist, the programmer, the systems analyst, the data processing manager, all are caught between a growing demand for broad-based expertise and an inadequate supply of information. For product managers and R & D managers in particular, lack of access to recent, reliable, pertinent information sources creates an unacceptably high risk in today's scientific and commercial environment.

The Design of Interactive Computer Displays: A Guide to the Select Literature was conceived and designed to meet these information needs. It is intended for personal use by all engineering and design professionals involved in or interested in any aspect of the design of displays for interactive computer systems. It should also be useful for those in management positions in organizations concerned with the quality of computer displays. We believe it to be the only reference tool of its kind in the domain of electronic displays generally. Thus, human factors researchers, perceptual psychologists, students, and graphics professionals will also find it a useful and time saving tool—as will all those wishing to explore the seemingly endless possibilities for computer-generated displays.

This volume is the first of several publications intended to provide information support for professionals concerned with the design of interactive computer displays. Subsequent titles will include a guide to relevant and useful periodicals; a collection of proceedings from conferences, association meetings, and professional gatherings; and an information update emphasizing the 1985 literature.

Acknowledgments

The editors wish to thank John Poggio, who helped design the questionnaire that was sent to artists, designers, and teachers, and to express their appreciation to all those who responded to the questionnaire. Their comments and suggestions were invariably constructive and helped to focus the direction of the collection.

The editors are also grateful to Colette Bangert, Richard Branham, Aaron Marcus, George McCleary, and Sherrie Sparks, all of whom assisted in the initial selection and refining of the title list. They were particularly helpful in developing an awareness of the resources available in art, design, and cartography.

For taking the time to examine and critique the title list, and for helping to identify additional sources of information, the editors gratefully acknowledge Robert Beaton, Herbert W. Franke, Paul Lefrere, Harry L. Snyder, Michael Twyman, Victoria Jane Willis, and P.A.M. Wright.

Introduction

This book is a guide to information about the design of display-based human-computer interaction—a guide to information about the *visual presentation* of information. It is the product of a special compilation process which brings together related material from the several disciplines and professional specialties where work relevant to display design is being conducted. It is intended to help a technical audience eliminate or substantially reduce the need for time-consuming literature searches.

Included are unpublished technical and research reports (the "gray literature"), government documents, reference works, books, journal special issues, a selection of conference proceedings, and material pertaining to national and international standards activities (because of their general availability, individual journal articles are not listed). For each title complete bibliographic data, an original abstract, and full table of contents are provided. An ancillary document delivery service offers access to all available titles.

The Compilation Process:
Producing a Consensus Bibliography™

This work is a consensus bibliography,™ a new kind of reference tool developed specifically to meet the information needs of professionals in multidisciplinary technical fields. It was designed to help such professionals access useful literature from the range of relevant sources quickly and efficiently.

Consensus bibliographies are produced by means of a specialized process of literature analysis analogous to the literature search an individual might ideally conduct if he or she had access to unlimited time and resources. The first step in the process is to identify the constituent disciplines by analyzing applicable index terms and the language used to discuss the research issues. Second, and at the heart of the process, is the generation of a primary list of titles that have been cited as useful and important by subject experts in papers appearing in refereed publications in the targeted fields. The process then builds upon the primary title list by analysis of the citation and reference patterns within those titles. The list expands to include related works by authors who have been frequently cited, and expands further by extrapolation from these authors' citations. Less frequently cited but significant titles are identified by qualitative analysis, which evaluates the content of the citations.

This approach not only maps a research community, but also registers trends in the development of knowledge, such as the convergence of separate disciplines around related problems. By allowing the literature to, in effect, speak for itself, it accurately reflects the operative assumptions and biases of the field and serves both as a reliable indicator of current areas of activity and an index to those areas where research is slowing or lacking.

A collection of "select" literature compiled by these means represents the collective judgment of active researchers and practitioners in a given field as to 1) what work is or is becoming significant in their field, and 2) what literature is representative of that work and most likely to be useful. For the user of the collection, the result—at a fraction of the expense and in a fraction of the time that a formal review process or DELPHI technique would require—is access to information of demonstrated usefulness and quality.

Display Design: Development of the Collection

Preliminary research for this collection indicated that while there were scattered guidelines for such things as type legibility, there were no works which brought together relevant information from the diverse fields bearing on display design. To identify those fields, the editors first analyzed the applicable index terms and the language used to discuss display design issues in the published record. Then, beginning with review papers and the review portions of a variety of scientific and technical documents, they systematically analyzed the citation patterns of critical works in all pertinent fields. Citation threads were traced across disciplinary boundaries (where indexing terms often are misleading because of differences in word usage). This procedure filled out the list of disciplines or research communities involved and led directly to the relevant parts of the various specialized, disciplinary literatures.

Further research revealed that because artists and designers rarely write about what they do, much useful information was not available through conventional research paths. It was therefore decided to augment the material identified through citation analysis by canvassing working artists, designers, and teachers. Titles targeted by consulting designers and teachers were added to those derived from citation analysis, and the master list was circulated to a selected sample of professionals in the areas of information design and presentation, who were asked to rate the titles in terms of their usefulness and to identify titles they felt should be added or deleted.

The results of the survey, moderated by the judgment of the editors, formed the core of the collection. Other titles were identified through extended citation analysis, which pinpointed individuals whose work is central to ongoing research in fields related to display design. The final compilation represents a synthesis of both implicit (derived through literature analysis) and explicit (derived through direct survey) expert opinion.

Focus and Scope of the Collection

The focus of this collection is information applicable to the design of interactive computer displays—more specifically, to one or more of three aspects of display-interface design: the equipment and its limits and potentials, the information itself, and the user's constraints and capabilities. The primary sources of the collection are the literatures of engineering technology, computer graphics, graphic arts, cartography, mathematics, statistical graphics, human factors, human engineering, and perceptual and cognitive psychology, each of which brings a particular perspective to bear on design issues.

Engineering Technology and Computer Graphics

The work included here from engineering technology and computer graphics is primarily basic technical information on the operating characteristics of display devices. For computer graphics there are, as well, several widely used texts, reports from workshops, and a number of dissertations which are regularly cited in the literature. Both fields are subject to active research with advances in one fueling effort in the other.

Graphic Arts, Cartography, Mathematics and Statistical Graphics

The selections from four information disciplines—graphic arts, cartography, mathematics, and statistical graphics—address the issue of information presentation. A number of works from the graphic arts deal with the presentation of complex information in a combined picture-text or picture format (while there is some evidence that what is effective on paper may not transfer to the display screen, the techniques developed by graphic artists for attracting, holding, and focusing attention should prove useful in display design). The titles from cartography approach the problem of presenting large amounts of abstract data in a concise and readily comprehensible form. The texts on statistical graphics deal specifically with the analysis of data and its presentation in tabular, chart or graph form. The works on mathematics are of two kinds: some, such as the titles on fractals and hypergraphics, describe material which forms the basis of many graphics algorithms; others, such as those by Stevens, Kim, and Abelson and diSessa, have been included because they stimulate visual thinking or because they can be used to generate graphics algorithms.

Human Factors, Human Engineering, Perceptual and Cognitive Psychology

Works included here from human factors, human engineering, and perceptual and cognitive psychology treat user capabilities and constraints as these relate to the design of the interface. Since displays are visual interfaces, the titles selected emphasize visual perception and processing and task performance in response to visual stimulation. In addition to standard works on vision, a number of technical reports in the collection describe research projects on displays and visual performance. Largely owing to military interest in the outcome, research interest in this area is increasing and may be expected to result in an experimentally based foundation for visual ergonomics.

How to Use this Book

For a rapid scan of the contents, consult the Quick Reference List. It provides a summary of selected titles and allows for the easy location of capsule reviews within the volume.

The Capsule Reviews section offers a basis for the selection of relevant materials. The capsule reviews include full bibliographic information, original abstracts prepared by staff editors, and tables of contents—all materials essential to the accurate evaluation of reviewed work.

The Subject Index guides the reader to titles pertinent to his or her area of interest. Owing to the multidisciplinary nature of the material, multiple entry points (drawn from the contributory disciplines) are provided.

The Author Index allows for the location of a title by the name of the primary author or authors, or by the name of any contributing author. Contributing authors are listed in the tables of contents included in the Capsule Reviews section.

The appendices provide listings of titles for four specialized collections: a basic recommended library for display design; guidelines, handbooks, and other references for display design; standards materials; and health and workplace issues related to VDT design and use.

Quick Reference List

ID	First Author	Title	Page
1	Abelson, Harold	Turtle Geometry: The Computer as a Medium for Exploring Mathematics, 1981	3
	Abramson, Sandra R.	*SEE UNDER ID 255*	
2	Albers, Josef	Interaction of Color, 1971	8
3	Alexander, Christopher	Notes on the Synthesis of Form, 1964	9
	Almagor, Maier	*SEE UNDER ID 248*	
4	American Institute of Graphic Arts	Symbol Signs, 1981	10
	American National Standards Institute	*SEE UNDER ID 99, 100*	
5	Angell, Ian O.	A Practical Introduction to Computer Graphics, 1981	12
6	Applegate, Sheldon L.	The Use of Interactive Raster Graphics in the Display and Manipulation of Multidimensional Data, 1981	13
7	Arnheim, Rudolf	Visual Thinking, 1969	15
8	Arnheim, Rudolf	Art and Visual Perception: A Psychology of the Creative Eye (rev. ed.), 1974	18
9	Artwick, Bruce A.	Applied Concepts in Microcomputer Graphics, 1984	21
10	Badre, Albert	Directions in Human/Computer Interaction, 1982	26
11	Bailey, Robert W.	Human Performance Engineering: A Guide for System Designers, 1982	28
12	Banks, William W.	Human Engineering Design Considerations for Cathode Ray Tube-Generated Displays, 1982	33
13	Banks, William W.	Human Engineering Design Considerations for Cathode Ray Tube-Generated Displays, Volume II, 1983	35
14	Barmack, Joseph E.	Human Factors Problems in Computer-Generated Graphic Displays, 1966	37
	Beaton, Robert J.	*SEE UNDER ID 256*	
15	Beatty, John C.	Tutorial: Computer Graphics (2ed.), 1982	39
16	Beck, Jacob	Organization and Representation in Perception, 1982	43
17	Belady, L.A.	DESIGNPAD: Computer Graphics for Block Diagram Problems, 1970	47
	Benjamin, Moshe	*SEE UNDER ID 212*	
18	Bennett, John	Visual Display Terminals: Usability Issues and Health Concerns, 1984	47
19	Berbaum, Kevin S.	Design Criteria for Reducing "Popping" in Area-of-Interest Displays: Preliminary Experiments, 1983	49
20	Bergqvist, Ulf	Video Display Terminals and Health: A Technical and Medical Appraisal of the State of the Art, 1984	50
21	Bertin, Jacques	Graphics and Graphic Information-Processing, 1981	52
22	Bertin, Jacques	Semiology of Graphics: Diagrams, Networks, Maps, 1983	54
23	Biberman, Lucien M.	Perception of Displayed Information, 1973	56
24	Biberman, Lucien M.	Photoelectronic Imaging Devices, Volume 2: Devices and Their Evaluation, 1971	58

	Blackman, Harold S.	SEE UNDER ID 285, 286	
25	Blinn, James F.	Computer Display of Curved Surfaces, 1979	63
26	Borgefors, Gunilla	An Improved Version of the Chamfer Matching Algorithm, 1983	65
27	Bosman, I.D.	Modern Display Technologies and Applications, 1982	66
28	Boyce, P.R.	Lighting and Visual Display Units, 1981	69
29	Braunstein, Myron L.	Depth Perception through Motion, 1976	70
30	Brinton, Willard C.	Graphic Methods for Presenting Facts, 1980	72
31	Brisson, David W.	Hypergraphics: Visualizing Complex Relationships in Art, Science and Technology, 1978	73
32	Britton, Edward G.	A Methodology for the Ergonomic Design of Interactive Computer Graphic Systems, and Its Application to Crystallography, 1977	75
33	Brodlie, K.W.	Mathematical Methods in Computer Graphics and Design, 1980	77
34	Buckler, Andrew T.	A Review of the Literature on the Legibility of Alphanumerics on Electronic Displays, 1977	78
	Burke, James J.	SEE UNDER ID 251	
35	Bylander, E.G.	Electronic Displays, 1979	78
36	Caelli, Terry	Visual Perception: Theory and Practice, 1981	81
37	Cakir, Ahmet	Visual Display Terminals: A Manual Covering Ergonomics, Workplace Design, Health and Safety, Task Organization, 1980	83
38	Campbell, J. Olin	Instructional Systems Development Model for Interactive Videodisc: Final Report, 1983	86
39	Card, Stuart K.	Psychology of Human-Computer Interaction, 1983	88
40	Carlbom, Ingrid	High-Performance Graphics System Architecture: A Methodology for Design and Evaluation, 1984	89
	Carlson, Curtis R.	SEE UNDER ID 54	
41	Carterette, Edward C.	Handbook of Perception: Volume I, Historical and Philosophical Roots of Perception, 1974	91
42	Carterette, Edward C.	Handbook of Perception: Volume III, Biology of Perceptual Systems, 1974	96
43	Carterette, Edward C.	Handbook of Perception: Volume V, Seeing, 1975	100
44	Carterette, Edward C.	Handbook of Perception: Volume IX, Perceptual Processing, 1978	103
45	Castner, Henry W.	Dot Area Symbols in Cartography: The Influence of Pattern on Their Perception, 1969	106
46	Catmull, Edwin	A Subdivision Algorithm for Computer Display of Curved Surfaces, 1974	107
47	Chambers, John M.	Graphical Methods for Data Analysis, 1983	108
48	Chasen, Sylvan H.	Geometric Principles and Procedures for Computer Graphic Applications, 1978	111
	Cheng, Patricia W.	SEE UNDER ID 213	
49	Clark, David R.	Computers for Imagemaking, 1981	113
50	Cleveland, William S.	The Elements of Graphing Data, 1985	114
51	Cohen, Roger W.	Image Descriptors for Displays, 1975	118
52	Cohen, Roger W.	Image Descriptors for Display, 1976	120
53	Mezrich, Joseph J.	Image Descriptors for Displays, 1977	122
54	Carlson, Curtis R.	Visibility of Displayed Information, 1978	124
55	Collins, Belinda L.	The Development and Evaluation of Effective Symbol Signs, 1982	127
	Computer Graphics	SEE UNDER ID 101	
56	Conrac Corporation	Raster Graphics Handbook, 1980	129
57	Cornog, Douglas Y.	Legibility of Alphanumeric Characters and Other Symbols I: A Permuted Title Index and Bibliography, 1964	130

58	**Cornog, Douglas Y.**	Legibility of Alphanumeric Characters and Other Symbols II: A Reference Handbook, 1967	130
59	**Damodaran, Leela**	Designing Systems for People, 1980	131
60	**de Beaugrande, Robert**	Text Production: Toward a Science of Composition, 1984	133
61	**Dent, Borden D.**	Principles of Thematic Map Design, 1985	134
62	**Derefeldt, Gunilla**	Color Coding of Displays, Maps and Images, 1981	141
63	**Derefeldt, Gunilla**	Colour Order Systems for Computer Graphics I: Transformation of NCS Data into CIELAB Colour Space, 1984	142
64	**Doblin, Jay**	Perspective: A New System for Designers, 1956	143
65	**Dondis, Donis A.**	A Primer of Visual Literacy, 1973	145
66	**Downs, Roger M.**	Maps in Minds: Reflections on Cognitive Mapping, 1977	146
67	**Dudek, C.L.**	Human Factors Design of Dynamic Visual and Auditory Displays for Metropolitan Traffic Management: Volume 1, Summary Report, 1982	148
68	**Eades, Craig A.**	CHART: A Graphic Display and Analysis System, 1981	150
69	**Easterby, Ronald S.**	Information Design: The Design and Evaluation of Signs and Printed Material, 1984	151
70	**Elworth, Charles**	Instructor/Operator Display Evaluation Methods, 1981	153
71	**Engel, Stephen E.**	Guidelines for Man/Display Interfaces, 1975	154
72	**Ergonomics Research Society**	The Visual Presentation of Technical Data, 1973	155
73	**Farley, Willard W.**	Digital Image Processing Systems and an Approach to the Display of Colors of Specified Chrominance, 1980	156
74	**Feldman, Laurence A.**	Computer Graphics for Scientific Applications, 1982	157
75	**Fertig, Janet A.**	An Inquiry into Effective Design of Graphicolingual Displays for Systems Engineering, 1980	158
76	**Fisher, Howard T.**	Mapping Information: The Graphic Display of Quantitative Information, 1982	160
77	**Fleming, Malcolm L.**	Instructional Message Design: Principles from the Behavioral Sciences, 1978	163
78	**Foley, James D.**	The Human Factors of Graphic Interaction: Tasks and Techniques, 1981	166
79	**Foley, James D.**	Fundamentals of Interactive Computer Graphics, 1982	169
80	**Franke, Herbert W.**	Computer Graphics--Computer Art, 1971	173
81	**Freeman, Herbert**	Tutorial and Selected Readings in Interactive Computer Graphics, 1980	175
82	**French, Thomas E.**	Graphic Science and Design (4ed.), 1984	178
	Friedell, Mark	*SEE UNDER ID 138*	
83	**Frutiger, Adrian**	Type, Sign, Symbol, 1980	179
84	**Fu, King Sun**	Picture Engineering, 1982	181
85	**Gagalowicz, André**	Synthesis of Natural Textures on 3-D Surfaces, 1983	183
86	**Galitz, Wilbert O.**	Handbook of Screen Format Design (2ed.), 1985	184
87	**Gates, David**	Type, 1973	189
88	**Geissler, Hans-Georg**	Modern Issues in Perception, 1983	190
89	**Gerstner, Karl**	Compendium for Literates: A System of Writing, 1974	195
	Gertman, David I.	*SEE UNDER ID 283*	
90	**Getty, David J.**	Three-Dimensional Displays: Perceptual Research and Applications to Military Systems, 1982	196
91	**Giloi, Wolfgang K.**	Interactive Computer Graphics: Data Structures, Algorithms, Languages, 1978	198
92	**Glinert, Ephraim P.**	PICT: Experiments in the Design of Interactive, Graphical Programming Environments, 1985	200

93	Gnanamgari, Sakunthala	Providing Automatic Graphic Displays through Defaults, 1980	203
94	Gombrich, Ernst H.	The Sense of Order: A Study in the Psychology of Decorative Art, 1979	203
95	Gombrich, Ernst H.	The Image and the Eye: Further Studies in the Psychology of Pictorial Representation, 1982	206
96	Gorrell, E.L.	A Human Engineering Specification for Legibility of Alphanumeric Symbology on Video Monitor Displays (rev.), 1980	207
97	Gouraud, Henri	Computer Display of Curved Surfaces, 1979	208
98	Grandjean, Etienne	Ergonomic Aspects of Visual Display Terminals, 1980	209
99	American National Standards Institute	Computer Graphics Metafile for the Storage and Transfer of Picture Description Information (draft proposal), 1984	213
100	American National Standards Institute	Graphical Kernel System (draft proposal), 1984	217
101	Computer Graphics	Computer Graphics: Status Report of the Graphic Standards Planning Committee, 1979	220
102	International Organization for Standardization (ISO)	Graphical Kernel Systems (GKS) Functional Description, 1984	223
103	Guedj, Richard A.	Methodology in Computer Graphics: Seillac I, 1979	227
104	Guedj, Richard A.	Methodology of Interaction: Seillac II, 1980	229
105	Hopgood, F. Robert A.	Introduction to the Graphical Kernel System (GKS), 1983	232
106	McKay, Lucia	GKS Primer, 1984	235
107	Van Deusen, Edmund	Graphics Standards Handbook, 1985	237
108	Greenberg, Donald	The Computer Image: Applications of Computer Graphics, 1982	239
109	Gregory, Richard L.	The Intelligent Eye, 1970	240
110	Gregory, Richard L.	Concepts and Mechanisms of Perception, 1974	241
	Guedj, Richard A.	*SEE UNDER ID 103, 104*	
111	Gutmann, James C.	Displaying Colors of Specified Chrominance on a Color Graphics Display, 1982	244
112	Hardesty, George K.C.	NAVSHIPS Display Illumination Design Guide, Section I: Introduction to Light and Color, 1973	245
113	Harrington, Steven	Computer Graphics: A Programming Approach, 1983	250
114	Hartley, James	Designing Instructional Text, 1978	254
115	Harvard University Laboratory for Computer Graphics and Spatial Analysis	Management's Use of Maps: Commercial and Political Applications, 1979	256
116	Harvard University Laboratory for Computer Graphics and Spatial Analysis	Mapping Software and Cartographic Data Bases, 1979	256
117	Harvard University Laboratory for Computer Graphics and Spatial Analysis	Urban, Regional and State Applications: Plus a Special Section on Cadastral Systems, 1979	256
118	Harvard University Laboratory for Computer Graphics and Spatial Analysis	Computer Mapping in Natural Resources and the Environment: Including Applications of Satellite-Derived Data, 1979	257
119	Harvard University Laboratory for Computer Graphics and Spatial Analysis	Computer Mapping in Education, Research and Medicine, 1979	257

120	**Harvard University Laboratory for Computer Graphics and Spatial Analysis**	Thematic Map Design, 1979	
			257
121	**Harvard University Laboratory for Computer Graphics and Spatial Analysis**	Management's Use of Maps: Including an Introduction to Computer Mapping for Executives, 1980	
			257
122	**Harvard University Laboratory for Computer Graphics and Spatial Analysis**	Cartographic and Statistical Data Bases and Mapping Software, 1980	
			258
123	**Harvard University Laboratory for Computer Graphics and Spatial Analysis**	Computer Graphics Hardware, 1980	
			258
124	**Harvard University Laboratory for Computer Graphics and Spatial Analysis**	Computer Mapping of Natural Resources and the Environment: Including Applications of Satellite-Derived Data, 1980	
			258
125	**Harvard University Laboratory for Computer Graphics and Spatial Analysis**	Urban, Regional, and State Government Applications of Computer Mapping: Plus Computer Mapping in Education, 1980	
			258
126	**Harvard University Laboratory for Computer Graphics and Spatial Analysis**	Management's Use of Computer Graphics, 1981	
			259
127	**Harvard University Laboratory for Computer Graphics and Spatial Analysis**	Cartographic Data Bases and Software: Plus Cadastral Data Bases, 1981	
			259
128	**Harvard University Laboratory for Computer Graphics and Spatial Analysis**	Computer Graphics Hardware, 1981	
			259
129	**Harvard University Laboratory for Computer Graphics and Spatial Analysis**	Computer Mapping of Natural Resources and the Environment: Plus Satellite Derived Data Applications, 1981	
			259
130	**Harvard University Laboratory for Computer Graphics and Spatial Analysis**	Computer Mapping Applications in Urban, State and Federal Government: Plus Computer Graphics in Education, 1981	
			260
131	**Harvard University Laboratory for Computer Graphics and Spatial Analysis**	How to Design an Effective Graphics Presentation, 1981	
			260
132	**Harvard University Laboratory for Computer Graphics and Spatial Analysis**	Bibliography and Index: Part I, Authors Index, 1982	
			260
133	**Harvard University Laboratory for Computer Graphics and Spatial Analysis**	Bibliography and Index: Part II, Bibliographic and KWIC Indexes, 1982	
			260

134	Heglin, Howard J.	NAVSHIPS Display Illumination Design Guide, Section II: Human Factors, 1973	261
135	Hemingway, Peter W.	Study of Symbology for Automated Graphic Displays, 1979	264
136	Herdeg, Walter	Graphis Diagrams: The Graphic Visualization of Abstract Data (5ed.), 1983	266
137	Herot, Christopher F.	Spatial Management of Data, 1979	267
138	Friedell, Mark	Spatial Data Management System, 1979	269
139	Kramlich, David	Spatial Data Management System, 1979	270
140	Herot, Christopher F.	Spatial Data Management System: Final Report, 1980	271
141	Herot, Christopher F.	*USS Carl Vinson* SDMS: Final Report, 1983	273
142	Hess, Stanley	The Modification of Letterforms, 1972	274
143	Hildreth, Ellen C.	The Measurement of Visual Motion, 1984	275
144	Hills, Philip	The Future of the Printed Word: The Impact and the Implications of the New Communications Technology, 1980	276
145	Hollister, Walter M.	Advancement on Visualization Techniques, 1980	278
	Hopgood, F. Robert A.	*SEE UNDER ID 105*	
146	Hubbard, Stuart W.	The Computer Graphics Glossary, 1983	279
147	Huggins, A.W.F.	Display-Control Compatibility in Three-Dimensional Displays: Final Report, 1984	280
148	Huggins, William H.	Iconic Communication: An Annotated Bibliography, 1974	281
149	Hurlburt, Allen	Layout: The Design of the Printed Page, 1977	282
150	Hurlburt, Allen	The Grid: A Modular System for the Design and Production of Newspapers, Magazines, and Books, 1978	283
151	**IBM Human Factors Center**	Human Factors of Workstations with Visual Displays (3ed.), 1984	285
	International Organization for Standardization (ISO)	*SEE UNDER ID 102*	
152	Itten, Johannes	The Elements of Color, 1970	288
153	Jarett, Irwin M.	Computer Graphics and Reporting Financial Data, 1983	289
154	Jarosz, Christopher J.	Evaluation of Map Symbols for a Computer-Generated Topographic Display: Transfer of Training, Symbol Confusion, and Association Value Studies, 1982	290
155	Johnsson, Bengt	The Human-Computer Interface in Commercial Systems: Investigations of Dialogue Design Factors and Usability with Alphanumeric Display Terminals, 1981	292
156	Jonassen, David H.	The Technology of Text: Principles for Structuring, Designing, and Displaying Text, 1982	294
157	Judd, Deane B.	Color in Business, Science and Industry (3ed.), 1975	296
158	Julesz, Bela	Foundations of Cyclopean Perception, 1971	298
159	Kantowitz, Barry H.	Human Factors: Understanding People-System Relationships, 1983	301
160	Kazan, Benjamin	Advances in Image Pickup and Display, Volume 1, 1974	305
161	Kazan, Benjamin	Advances in Image Pickup and Display, Volume 2, 1975	307
162	Kazan, Benjamin	Advances in Image Pickup and Display, Volume 3, 1977	308
163	Kazan, Benjamin	Advances in Image Pickup and Display, Volume 4, 1981	310
164	Kazan, Benjamin	Advances in Image Pickup and Display, Volume 5, 1982	311
165	Kazan, Benjamin	Advances in Image Pickup and Display, Volume 6, 1983	313
166	Keates, J.S.	Cartographic Design and Production, 1973	314
167	Kim, Scott	Inversions: A Catalog of Calligraphic Cartwheels, 1981	319
168	King, Jean C.	The Designer's Guide to Text Type, 1980	320
169	Kmetz, A.R.	Nonemissive Electrooptic Displays, 1976	321
170	Knuth, Donald E.	TEX and METAFONT: New Directions in Typesetting, 1979	323
171	Knuth, Donald E.	The TEXbook, 1984	325

172	**Kolers, Paul A.**	Processing of Visible Language 1, 1979	327
173	**Kolers, Paul A.**	Processing of Visible Language 2, 1980	329
	Kramlich, David	*SEE UNDER ID 139*	
174	**Kronauer, Richard**	Quantification of Interference and Detectability Properties of Visual Stimuli for Optimal Display Design, 1983	332
175	**Küppers, Harald**	Color: Origin, Systems, Uses, 1973	332
176	**Lachman, Roy**	Cognitive Psychology and Information Processing: An Introduction, 1979	334
177	**Leavitt, Ruth**	Artist and Computer, 1976	337
178	**Levens, Alexander**	Graphics in Engineering Design (3ed.), 1980	339
179	**MacGregor, Annette J.**	Graphics Simplified: How to Plan and Prepare Effective Charts, Graphs, Illustrations, and Other Visual Aids, 1979	340
180	**Mandelbrot, Benoit B.**	The Fractal Geometry of Nature, 1982	341
181	**Marr, David**	Vision: A Computational Investigation into the Human Representation and Processing of Visual Information, 1982	343
182	**Marsh, Patrick O.**	Messages That Work: A Guide to Communication Design, 1983	345
183	**Massaro, Dominic W.**	Letter and Word Perception: Orthographic Structure and Visual Processing in Reading, 1980	346
184	**McCormick, Ernest J.**	Human Factors in Engineering and Design (5ed.), 1982	349
	McKay, Lucia	*SEE UNDER ID 106*	
185	**McLean, Ruari**	The Thames and Hudson Manual of Typography, 1980	351
186	**McLendon, Charles B.**	Signage: Graphic Communications in the Built World, 1982	353
	Mezrich, Joseph J.	*SEE UNDER ID 53*	
187	**Monkhouse, Francis J.**	Maps and Diagrams: Their Compilation and Construction (3ed.), 1971	355
188	**Monmonier, Mark S.**	Maps, Distortion, and Meaning, 1977	357
189	**Monmonier, Mark S.**	Computer-Assisted Cartography: Principles and Prospects, 1982	359
190	**Moore, Martha V.**	The Educational Effectiveness of Graphic Displays for Computer Assisted Instruction, 1978	361
191	**Moore, Martha V.**	The Instructional Effectiveness of Three Levels of Graphics Displays for Computer-Assisted Instruction, 1979	362
192	**Moroze, Michael L.**	The Ability to Process Abstract Information, 1983	363
193	**Muckler, Frederick A.**	Human Factors Review: 1984, 1984	365
194	**Muehrcke, Phillip**	Thematic Cartography, 1972	366
195	**Müller-Brockmann, Josef**	Grid Systems in Graphic Design: A Visual Communication Manual for Graphic Designers, Typographers and Three Dimensional Designers, 1981	367
196	**National Research Council. Committee on Vision**	Video Displays, Work, and Vision, 1983	368
197	**National Technical Information Service**	Signs and Display Systems: Graphic Design and Human Engineering (citations from the NTIS database, 1964-March 1982), 1982	373
198	**National Technical Information Service**	Interactive Display Devices: Citations from the NTIS Database (June 1970-September 1983), 1983	373
199	**National Technical Information Service**	Interactive Display Devices: Citations from the U.S. Department of Energy Database (June 1976-August 1983), 1983	373
200	**Nawrocki, Leon H.**	Alphanumeric versus Graphic Displays in a Problem-Solving Task, 1972	374
201	**Nelson, Roy P.**	The Design of Advertising (3ed.), 1977	375
202	**Neurath, Otto**	International Picture Language/Internationale Bildersprache, 1980	382
203	**Newcomb, John**	The Book of Graphic Problem-Solving: How to Get Visual Ideas When You Need Them, 1984	383

204	Newman, Richard L.	Operational Problems Associated with Head-Up Displays during Instrument Flight, 1980	384
205	Newman, William M.	Principles of Interactive Computer Graphics (2ed.), 1979	388
206	NIOSH	Potential Health Hazards of Video Display Terminals, 1981	392
207	Okoshi, Takanori	Three-Dimensional Imaging Techniques, 1976	393
208	Overheim, R. Daniel	Light and Color, 1982	395
209	Somers, Patricia	Interference among Sources of Information in Complex Integrated Displays, 1977	400
210	Somers, Patricia	Perceptual Interaction between Stimulus Dimensions as the Basis of Dimensional Integrality, 1978	401
211	Pachella, Robert G.	A Psychophysical Approach to Dimensional Integrality, 1980	402
212	Benjamin, Moshe	The Effect of Complexity in Integrated Multidimensional Displays, 1980	402
213	Cheng, Patricia W.	A Psychophysical Approach to Form Perception: Incompatibility as an Explanation of Integrality, 1980	403
214	Pachella, Robert G.	The Development and Utilization of Integrated Multidimensional Displays: Final Report, 1981	405
215	Pankove, Jacques I.	Display Devices, 1980	405
216	Park, Chan S.	Interactive Microcomputer Graphics, 1985	409
217	Pavlidis, Theo	Algorithms for Graphics and Image Processing, 1982	412
	Petersen, Rohn J.	*SEE UNDER ID 284*	
218	Phillips, Arthur H.	Handbook of Computer-Aided Composition, 1980	419
219	Piantanida, Thomas P.	Perception of Spatial Features with Stereoscopic Displays, 1981	421
220	Poulton, E.C.	Tracking Skill and Manual Control, 1974	422
221	Prueitt, Melvin L.	Art and the Computer, 1984	427
222	Reading, Veronica M.	Visual Aspects and Ergonomics of Visual Display Units, 1978	429
223	Refioglu, H. Ilhan	Electronic Displays, 1984	430
224	Rehe, Rolf F.	Typography: How to Make It Most Legible (rev. ed.), 1984	436
225	Resnick, Elizabeth	Graphic Design: A Problem-Solving Approach to Visual Communication, 1984	437
226	Reynolds, Linda	Presentation of Data in Science, 1981	438
227	Robinson, Arthur H.	Elements of Cartography (5ed.), 1984	444
228	Rock, Irvin	The Logic of Perception, 1983	445
229	Rogers, David F.	Procedural Elements for Computer Graphics, 1985	446
230	Rogers, David F.	Mathematical Elements for Computer Graphics, 1976	449
231	Rookledge, Gordon	Rookledge's International Typefinder: The Essential Handbook of Typeface Recognition and Selection, 1983	452
232	Rosenfeld, Azriel	Digital Picture Processing (2ed.) 2 vols., 1982	453
233	Rosinski, Richard R.	Effect of Projective Distortions on Perception of Graphic Displays: Final Report, 1982	456
234	Samet, Michael G.	Development of Innovative Graphic Symbology for Aiding Tactical Decision Making, 1983	457
235	Schachter, Bruce J.	Computer Image Generation, 1983	458
236	Schiekel, Manfred	Rasteranzeigeschirm in Gasentladungstechnik, 1982	460
237	Schmid, Calvin F.	Statistical Graphics: Design Principles and Practices, 1983	461
238	Schmid, Calvin F.	Handbook of Graphic Presentation (2ed.), 1979	462
239	Schweitzer, Dennis L.	Interactive Surface Visualization Using Raster Graphics, 1983	463
240	Scott, Joan E.	Introduction to Interactive Computer Graphics, 1982	465
241	Sekuler, Robert	Sourcebook of Temporal Factors Affecting Information Transfer from Visual Displays, 1981	467

242	Shahnavaz, Houshang	VDU-Operators' Preferred Environmental Conditions in a Telephone Information Centre, 1982	469
243	Sherr, Sol	Electronic Displays, 1979	470
244	Sherr, Sol	Video and Digital Electronic Displays: A User's Guide, 1982	471
245	Sidner, Candace L.	Requirements for Natural Language Understanding in a System with Graphic Displays, 1983	472
246	Smith, Sidney L.	Design Guidelines for User-System Interface Software, 1984	473
247	Snyder, Harry L.	Visual Search and Image Quality: Final Report, 1976	475
248	Almagor, Maier	Spatio-Temporal Integration in the Visual System, 1979	476
249	Snyder, Harry L.	An Evaluation of the Effect of Spot Wobble upon Observer Performance with Raster Scan Displays, 1980	478
250	Snyder, Harry L.	Human Visual Performance and Flat Panel Display Image Quality, 1980	480
251	Burke, James J.	Quality Metrics of Digitally Derived Imagery and Their Relation to Interpreter Performance: I, Preparation of a Large-Scale Database, 1982	482
252	Snyder, Harry L.	Quality Metrics of Digitally Derived Imagery and Their Relation to Interpreter Performance: II, Effects of Blur and Noise on Hard-Copy Interpretability, 1982	484
253	Snyder, Harry L.	Quality Metrics of Digitally Derived Imagery and Their Relation to Interpreter Performance: III, Subjective Scaling of Hard-Copy Digital Imagery, 1982	486
254	Snyder, Harry L.	Quality Metrics of Digitally Derived Imagery and Their Relation to Interpreter Performance: VIII, Final Report, 1983	488
255	Abramson, Sandra R.	Operator Performance on Flat-Panel Displays with Line and Cell Failures, 1984	489
256	Beaton, Robert J.	A Human-Performance Based Evaluation of Quality Metrics for Hard-Copy and Soft-Copy Digital Imaging Systems, 1984	491
	Somers, Patricia	*SEE UNDER ID 209, 210*	
257	Spencer, Herbert	The Visible Word (2ed.), 1969	492
258	Spoehr, Kathryn T.	Visual Information Processing, 1982	494
259	Steinbeck, Jürgen	Flachanzeigeschirm mit Flussigkristallen, 1980	496
260	Steinberg, Esther R.	Teaching Computers to Teach, 1984	498
261	Stevens, Peter S.	Handbook of Regular Patterns: An Introduction to Symmetry in Two Dimensions, 1980	500
262	Stevenson, George A.	Graphic Arts Encyclopedia (2ed.), 1979	502
263	Talcott, Noel A., Jr.	The Use of Interactive Graphic Displays for Interpretation of Surface Design Parameters, 1981	503
264	Tannas, Lawrence E., Jr.	Flat-Panel Displays and CRTs, 1985	503
265	Teichner, Warren H.	Color Research for Visual Displays, 1977	513
266	Teicholz, Eric	Computer Graphics and Environmental Planning, 1983	514
267	Thiel, Philip	Visual Awareness and Design: An Introductory Program in Conceptual Awareness, Perceptual Sensitivity, and Basic Design Skills, 1981	518
268	Tillitt, David N.	Performance and Design Requirements for a Graphics Display Research Facility, 1982	519
269	Tinker, Miles A.	Legibilty of Print, 1963	521
270	Tinker, Miles A.	Bases for Effective Reading, 1965	522
271	Treurniet, W.C.	Display of Text on Television, 1981	523
272	Trumbo, Bruce E.	A Theory for Coloring Bivariate Statistical Maps, 1980	524
273	Tschichold, Jan	Asymmetric Typography, 1967	525
274	Tufte, Edward R.	The Visual Display of Quantitative Information, 1983	526

275	Turnbull, Arthur T.	The Graphics of Communication (4ed.), 1980	527
276	Tzeng, Ovid J.L.	Perception of Print: Reading Research in Experimental Psychology, 1981	530
277	Ullman, Shimon	The Interpretation of Visual Motion, 1979	532
278	Ullman, Shimon	Image Understanding 1984, 1984	533
279	Ullner, Michael K.	Parallel Machines for Computer Graphics, 1983	535
280	University of Reading. Department of Typography and Graphic Communication	Graphic Communication through ISOTYPE (2ed.), 1981	537
281	U.S. Joint Army-Navy-Air Force Steering Committee	Human Engineering Guide to Equipment Design (rev. ed.), 1972	538
282	U.S. Nuclear Regulatory Commission	Human Factors Acceptance Criteria for the Safety Parameter Display System, 1981	539
283	Gertman, David I.	CRT Display Evaluation: The Multidimensional Rating of CRT-Generated Displays, 1982	541
284	Petersen, Rohn J.	An Empirical Examination of Evaluation Methods for Computer Generated Displays: Psychophysics, 1982	542
285	Blackman, Harold S.	Noninteractive Simulation Evaluation for CRT-Generated Displays, 1983	544
286	Blackman, Harold S.	CRT Display Evaluation: The Checklist Evaluation of CRT-Generated Displays, 1983	545
287	Uttal, William R.	A Taxonomy of Visual Processes, 1981	546
288	Uttal, William R.	Visual Form Detection in Three-Dimensional Space, 1983	549
	Van Deusen, Edmund	*SEE UNDER ID 107*	
289	Vaughan, W.S., Jr.	Vision-Perception Research and Analyses Relevant to Display Design for Underwater Applications, 1980	550
290	Vickers, Douglas	Decision Processes in Visual Perception, 1979	552
291	Waern, Yvonne	Reading Text from Visual Display Units, 1982	553
292	Wertheim, Alexander H.	Tutorials on Motion Perception, 1982	554
293	Weston, George F.	Alphanumeric Displays: Devices, Drive Circuits and Applications, 1983	558
294	White, Jan V.	Editing by Design: A Guide to Effective Word-and-Picture Communication for Editors and Designers (2ed.), 1982	561
295	White, Jan V.	Mastering Graphics: Design and Production Made Easy, 1983	566
296	White, Jan V.	Using Charts and Graphs: 1000 Ideas for Visual Persuasion, 1984	570
297	Wickens, Christopher D.	Engineering Psychology and Human Performance, 1984	572
298	Winkler, Robert E.	Readability of Electronic Displays, 1979	575
299	Wong, Wucius	Principles of Two-Dimensional Design, 1972	576
300	Wong, Wucius	Principles of Three-Dimensional Design, 1977	577
301	Wyszecki, Günter	Color Science: Concepts and Methods, Quantitative Data and Formulae (2ed.), 1982	578

Description of Capsule Review Listings

A sample Capsule Review is shown below. The numbered items are explained in the numbered descriptive paragraphs which follow.

Titles within the Capsule Reviews section are arranged alphabetically by first author except in the case of titles grouped logically as members of a set or series. Such instances are treated by a cross-reference at the place where the author's name would otherwise appear. The occurrence of a set or series is indicated by a brief listing of the set title with appropriate bibliographic and descriptive data. In some cases the set title appears, along with the total number of volumes in the set, even though not all volumes were selected for inclusion in the collection.

Special types of documents are classified, and identified in the Capsule Reviews section, as follows: technical report, proceedings, reference, collection, and journal special issue. Where no designation appears, the title is a monograph. Where ISBNs occur, parentheses around the ISBN number indicate a softbound volume.

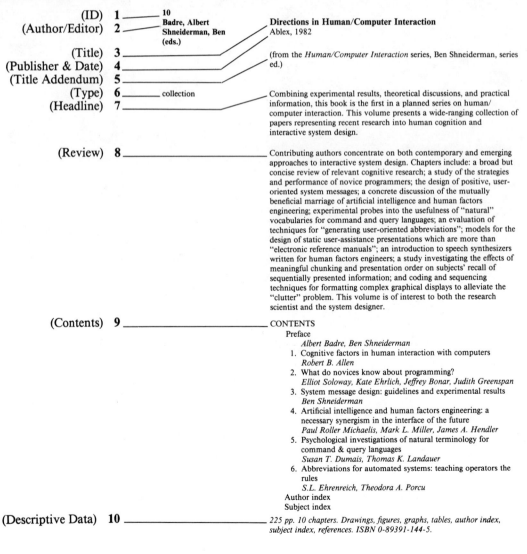

(ID) **1** 10

(Author/Editor) **2** Badre, Albert
Shneiderman, Ben
(eds.)

Directions in Human/Computer Interaction
Ablex, 1982

(Title) **3**

(Publisher & Date) **4**

(Title Addendum) **5**

(from the *Human/Computer Interaction* series, Ben Shneiderman, series ed.)

(Type) **6** collection

(Headline) **7**

Combining experimental results, theoretical discussions, and practical information, this book is the first in a planned series on human/computer interaction. This volume presents a wide-ranging collection of papers representing recent research into human cognition and interactive system design.

(Review) **8**

Contributing authors concentrate on both contemporary and emerging approaches to interactive system design. Chapters include: a broad but concise review of relevant cognitive research; a study of the strategies and performance of novice programmers; the design of positive, user-oriented system messages; a concrete discussion of the mutually beneficial marriage of artificial intelligence and human factors engineering; experimental probes into the usefulness of "natural" vocabularies for command and query languages; an evaluation of techniques for "generating user-oriented abbreviations"; models for the design of static user-assistance presentations which are more than "electronic reference manuals"; an introduction to speech synthesizers written for human factors engineers; a study investigating the effects of meaningful chunking and presentation order on subjects' recall of sequentially presented information; and coding and sequencing techniques for formatting complex graphical displays to alleviate the "clutter" problem. This volume is of interest to both the research scientist and the system designer.

(Contents) **9**

CONTENTS
Preface
   Albert Badre, Ben Shneiderman
  1. Cognitive factors in human interaction with computers
    Robert B. Allen
  2. What do novices know about programming?
    Elliot Soloway, Kate Ehrlich, Jeffrey Bonar, Judith Greenspan
  3. System message design: guidelines and experimental results
    Ben Shneiderman
  4. Artificial intelligence and human factors engineering: a necessary synergism in the interface of the future
    Paul Roller Michaelis, Mark L. Miller, James A. Hendler
  5. Psychological investigations of natural terminology for command & query languages
    Susan T. Dumais, Thomas K. Landauer
  6. Abbreviations for automated systems: teaching operators the rules
    S.L. Ehrenreich, Theodora A. Porcu
Author index
Subject index

(Descriptive Data) **10**

225 pp. 10 chapters. Drawings, figures, graphs, tables, author index, subject index, references. ISBN 0-89391-144-5.

1   **Identification Number.**

2   **Author(s)** or **Editor(s):** Reviews are arranged alphabetically by this field.

3   **Title:** Subtitles (if any) follow a colon.

4   **Publisher** and **Year of Publication:** Technical reports list year of publication only, not publisher.

5   **Title Addendum:** (optional) This section provides additional descriptive information about the work. Title addenda (TAs) are given for volumes in a series, technical reports, and proceedings.

A *volume in a series TA* indicates series name and, when known, series editor(s). An example is shown.

A *technical report TA* indicates the sponsoring organization, performing organization, and, when available, the monitoring organization. Any available identification numbers are also included. An example:

    (a technical report for the Defense Advanced Research Projects Agency [DOD], performed by Carnegie-Mellon University, CMU CS 79-144)

A proceedings TA indicates the type of meeting, place of meeting, date(s) of meeting, and additional information. An example:

    (proceedings of the scientific symposium conducted on the occasion of the Fifteenth Anniversary of the Science Center Heidelberg of IBM Germany; Heidelberg, Federal Republic of Germany; 18 March 1983; vol. 150 in the *Lecture Notes in Computer Science* series, G. Goos and J. Harmanis, series eds.)

6   **Type of Document.** In the absence of a type-of-document label, the title may be assumed to be a book which does not fall into the following categories: technical report, collection, proceedings, journal special issue or reference work.

Some capsule reviews carry the designation "Overview" because the works they discuss are a set or series that has been deemed especially significant. Overview reviews comment on the set's plans, goals, and methods and may discuss the writers or editors of the works. Volumes in the set are then discussed individually.

7   **Headline Statement:** This brief section highlights the document's purpose and significance. It may include information about potential audience.

8   **Review:** This section specifies topics the work discusses, its place in the discipline's canon, the author's area(s) of expertise, and so on. It may also comment on the methods, strengths, and weaknesses of the work.

Proceedings usually receive an expanded headline statement rather than a review.

9   **Table of Contents:** For all documents except certain technical reports, the table of contents is provided to supplement the review.

10   **Descriptive Data:** This section includes additional descriptive information: the number of pages, the arrangement of the material within the book, the specific non-text items used by the author (such as illustrations, formulae, figures), and the type of support provided (notes, references, appendices). Parentheses enclosing the International Standard Book Number (ISBN) indicate paperback edition.

Section I

Capsule Reviews

1
Abelson, Harold
diSessa, Andrea A.

Turtle Geometry: The Computer as a Medium for Exploring Mathematics
The MIT Press, 1981

(from *The MIT Press Series in Artificial Intelligence*, Patrick H. Winston, Mike Brady, series eds.)

This textbook uses computation, first to teach geometry, and second to encourage an exploratory learning experience which can be applied to many areas.

Students are taught to write computer programs to move a "turtle," or display indicator, in various geometric patterns across a display screen. The teaching strategy employed here is learning by doing, and students are encouraged to develop and test their own hypotheses as well as to explore new phenomena. The authors emphasize that their approach to teaching mathematics is unusual and they feel that their computational approach influences both the nature of students' experiences and the ideas covered in the curriculum. The programming language used here is very close to LOGO, and the MIT LOGO Group had much to do with establishing the foundations of the work presented here. The topics covered in the text include basics of writing turtle geometry programs, comparisons between turtle and coordinate geometries, topology of curves in a plane, and the geometry of curved surfaces. The turtles are moved off of the two dimensional display screen in three chapters devoted to cubes, spheres, and piecewise flat surfaces. The final chapter demonstrates how turtle geometry can be used to explain Einstein's general theory of relativity. The textbook includes many projects and exercises of varying difficulty. In keeping with the "student as discoverer" approach to the book, three exercise solution sections are included at the back of the book, though one section provides hints rather than answers. Two appendices show computer language notation and an implementation of turtle commands in BASIC. Access to an interactive computer is preferable for using this book, but much of the work can be utilized with simply paper and pencil. The material in the text has been developed, modified, and used over a number of years in math courses at MIT as well as in special summer institutes for high school students at MIT. This book is written primarily for high school and undergraduate students, but is also directed at educators who are considering using computers in teaching or who are involved in curriculum reforms. The innovative approach to geometry pursued here supports a style of visual thinking which the authors feel more accurately represents what we know about figures than such non-visual explanations as Cartesian equations. Thus, this work will interest anyone who is concerned with thinking about seeing.

CONTENTS

Preface

Preliminary Notes

1: INTRODUCTION TO TURTLE GEOMETRY

1.1: Turtle Graphics
    1.1.1. Procedures
    1.1.2. Drawing with the turtle
    1.1.3. Turtle geometry versus coordinate geometry
    1.1.4. Some simple turtle programs
    Exercises for section 1.1

1.2: POLYs and Other Closed Paths
    1.2.1. The closed-path theorem and the simple-closed-path theorem
    1.2.2. The POLY closing theorem
    Exercises for section 1.2

1.3: Looping Programs
    1.3.1. The looping lemma
    1.3.2. Examples of looping programs
    1.3.3. More on the looping lemma
    1.3.4. Technical summary
    1.3.5. Nontechnical summary
    Exercises for section 1.3

1.4: Symmetry of Looping Programs
    1.4.1. The symmetry of POLY
    1.4.2. Common divisors
    Exercises for section 1.4

2: FEEDBACK, GROWTH, AND FORM

2.1: The Turtle as Animal
    2.1.1. Random motion
    2.1.2. Directed motion: modeling smell
    2.1.3. Modeling sight
    Exercises for section 2.1

2.2: Turtles Interacting
    2.2.1. Predator and prey
    2.2.2. Following and chasing
    Exercises for section 2.2

2.3: Growth
    2.3.1. Equiangular spirals
    2.3.2. Branching processes: a lesson in recursion
    Exercises for section 2.3

2.4: Recursive Designs
    2.4.1. Nested triangles
    2.4.2. Snowflakes and other curves
    2.4.3. Space filling designs
    Exercises for section 2.4

3: Vector Methods in Turtle Geometry

3.1: Vector Analysis of Turtle Programs
    3.1.1. Vector operations: scalar multiplication and addition
    3.1.2. Vector representations of closed paths
    3.1.3. POLY revisited: rotations and linearity
    3.1.4. MULTIPOLYs: another application of vector analysis
    3.1.5. Unexpectedly closed figures

Exercises for section 3.1

3.2: Coordinates for Vectors
3.2.1. Vector operations in coordinates
3.2.2. Rotation in coordinates: the linearity principle
Exercises for section 3.2

3.3: Implementing Turtle Vector Graphics on a Computer
3.3.1. Turtle state
3.3.2. State-change operators
Summary: a vector-based turtle implementation
Exercises for section 3.3

3.4: Maneuvering a Three-Dimensional Turtle
3.4.1. Rotating the turtle
3.4.2. Rotation out of the plane
3.4.3. The state-change operators, in summary

3.5: Displaying a Three-Dimensional Turtle
3.5.1. Parallel projection
3.5.2. Dot product: another application of linearity
3.5.3. Parallel projection in coordinates; generalizations
3.5.4. Perspective projection
3.5.5. Outline of a three-dimensional turtle project
Exercises for section 3.5

4: TOPOLOGY OF TURTLE PATHS

4.1: Deformations of Closed Paths
4.1.1. Turtle paths: pictures and programs
4.1.2. Correlating pictures and programs
4.1.3. Topological classification of closed paths
Exercises for section 4.1

4.2: Local and Global Information
4.2.1. Escaping from a maze
Exercises for section 4.2

4.3: Deformation of Curves and Planes
4.3.1. Proof of the deformation theorem
Exercises for section 4.3

4.4: Correctness of the Pledge Algorithm
4.4.1. Unfair mazes
4.4.2. The body of the proof
4.4.3. Looping and finite-state processes
Exercises for section 4.4

5: TURTLE ESCAPES THE PLANE

5.1: Turtle Geometry on a Sphere
5.1.1. Turtle lines
5.1.2. Turtle turning and trip turning
5.1.3. Angle excess
5.1.4. Excess is additive
5.1.5. Excess and area
Exercises for section 5.1

5.2: Curvature
5.2.1. Curvature density
5.2.2. Total curvature
5.2.3. Cylinders
5.2.4. Cones
5.2.5. Curvature for curves and surfaces

Exercises for section 5.2

5.3: Total Curvature and Topology
    5.3.1. Dents and bends
    5.3.2. Concentrated curvature
    5.3.3. Cutting and pasting
    Exercises for section 5.3

6: EXPLORING THE CUBE

6.1: A Computer Cube
    6.1.1. Internal representation
    6.1.2. Permutations
    6.1.3. Crossing edges using dot products
    6.1.4. Implementing the state-change operators
    6.1.5. Displaying the cube; capitalizing on linearity
    6.1.6. Summary outline of the cube program
    6.1.7. Comments on the cube program
    Exercises for section 6.1

6.2: Observations and Questions About Cubes
    6.2.1. Monogons
    6.2.2. POLY
    6.2.3. Other gons
    6.2.4. Lines and distance
    6.2.5. More projects
    6.2.6. Things to think about

6.3: Results
    6.3.1. The monogon problem
    6.3.2. Headings for monogons
    6.3.3. POLYs and other looping programs
    6.3.4. Another representation
    6.3.5. Another representation revisited
    6.3.6. More distance

6.4: Conclusion

7: A SECOND LOOK AT THE SPHERE

7.1: A Computer Simulation
    7.1.1. Internal representation
    7.1.2. Display
    7.1.3. Distances and angles

7.2: Exploring
    7.2.1. POLY
    7.2.2. Symmetry types
    7.2.3. Circles
    7.2.4. Distances
    7.2.5. Two new views of sphere

7.3: Results
    7.3.1. The FORWARD-LEFT symmetry
    7.3.2. Net rotation of a POLY step
    7.3.3. The spherical Pythagorean theorem
    7.3.4. Exact formula for θ
    7.3.5. Results for circles
    7.3.5. Proof of net rotation theorem
    Exercises for chapter 7

8: PIECEWISE FLAT SURFACES

8.1: A Program for Piecewise Flat Surfaces
    8.1.1. Internal representation
    8.1.2. Maintaining the display
    8.1.3. Implementing the FORWARD command
    8.1.4. Starting to explore: surfaces with only one face
    Exercises for section 8.1

8.2: Orientations
    8.2.1. Nonorientable surfaces
    8.2.2. A program for nonorientable surfaces
    Exercises for section 8.2

8.3: Curvature and Euler Characteristics
    8.3.1. Curvature of piecewise flat surfaces
    8.3.2. Euler characteristic
    Exercises for section 8.3

9: CURVED SPACE AND GENERAL RELATIVITY

9.1. Wedge Representations
    9.1.1. A parable: at the edge of a wedge
    9.1.2. Symmetric wedge maps
    9.1.3. A computer simulation
    Exercises for section 9.1

9.2: Phenomena of Curved Space and Time
    9.2.1. Curved space
    9.2.2. Curved spacetime
    9.2.3. The four curvature effects
    Exercise for section 9.2

9.3: The General Theory of Relativity
    9.3.1. Gravity as curvature
    9.3.2. Rotating world lines
    9.3.3. Understanding Lorentz rotations
    Exercises for section 9.3

9.4: A Simulator for General Relativity
    9.4.1. The coordinate system
    9.4.2. Turning and leaping
    9.4.3. The program
    9.4.4. Help with units
    Exercises for section 9.4

Appendix A: Turtle Procedure Notation

Appendix B: Writing Turtle Programs in Conventional Computer Languages

Hints for Selected Exercises

Answers to Selected Exercises

Index

477 pp. 9 chapters. Drawings, figures, algorithms, abstract formalisms, models, general index, appendices. ISBN 0-262-01063-1.

Abramson, Sandra R.   *SEE UNDER ID 255*

2
Albers, Josef

Interaction of Color
Yale University Press, 1971

(text of the original edition with selected plates)

A theoretical and practical work on color interactions designed to teach the reader with assigned exercises.

Albers believes that art has lacked a basic step-by-step approach to education. In this volume he presents a studio course in color designed to develop the student's creativity. Confronted with the basic problems of color, the student is asked to solve these in a logical order. Self-expression is firmly discredited as a method of art training. Albers' approach to color training focuses on providing the student extensive experience with color problems and an opportunity to compare his own approach to a color problem with other solutions. Color is explained as the most relative medium in art ("what we see is not what we see"): colors influence and transform adjoining colors. Two colors may look alike or one color may appear to be two different colors, or two colors may blend together to become a third. Some theory is discussed, and various color phenomena such as after-image are illustrated using color plates. Exercises investigate color deception, and the interdependence of color with: form, placement, quantity, number, and pronouncement. The reader should be prepared to perform the suggested exercises to receive the greatest benefit from the book. This slim volume includes the full text but contains only ten of the 150 illustrations from the original edition of Albers' work. (The size and cost of the original edition made it prohibitive for most classroom uses.) This is a valuable book for all who would work with color media. Albers' rigorous, rule-oriented approach may be particularly suited to graphics designers who are working with computer graphics in color but who have limited formal color training.

CONTENTS

Preface

Introduction

I: Color Recollection—Visual Memory

II: Color Reading and Contexture

III: Why Color Paper—Instead of Pigment and Paint

IV: A Color Has Many Faces—the Relativity of Color

V: Lighter and/or Darker—Light Intensity, Lightness
  Gradation studies—new presentations
  Color intensity—brightness

VI: 1 Color Appears as 2—Looking Like the Reversed Grounds

VII: 2 Different Colors Look Alike—Subtraction of Color

VIII: Why Color Deception?—After-Image, Simultaneous Contrast

IX: Color Mixture in Paper—Illusion of Transparence

X: Factual Mixtures—Additive and Subtractive

XI: Transparence and Space-Illusion
  Color boundaries and plastic action

XII: Optical Mixture—After-Image Revised
XIII: The Bezold Effect
XIV: Color Intervals and Transformation
XV: The Middle Mixture Again—Intersecting Colors
XVI: Color Juxtaposition—Harmony—Quantity
XVII: Film Color and Volume Color—2 Natural Effects
XVIII: Free studies—A Challenge to Imagination
    Stripes—restricted juxtaposition
    Fall leaf studies—an American discovery
XIX: The Masters—Color Instrumentation
XX: The Weber-Fechner Law—the Measure in Mixture
XXI: From Color Temperature to Humidity in Color
XXII: Vibrating Boundaries—Enforced Contours
XXIII: Equal Light Intensity—Vanishing Boundaries
XXIV: Color Theories—Color Systems
XXV: On Teaching Color—Some Color Terms
    Explanation of color terms
    Variants versus variety

74 pp. 25 chapters. Figures, color plates. ISBN 0-300-01474-0. (ISBN 0-300-01473-2)

3
Alexander, Christopher

Notes on the Synthesis of Form
Harvard University Press, 1964

A classic theoretical work on architectural design methods, this book is a combination of simple common sense and fairly complex theory.

The preface to the 1971 paperback edition of this 1964 book helps to place the work in context and emphasizes that the theory of diagrams, not the method used to obtain them, is the most valuable concept in this work. Alexander studied mathematics at Cambridge before turning to architecture and that background forms the basis for his early approaches to the problems inherent in finding the best possible solution to designing anything, from a tea kettle (a frequently used example in *Notes*), to buildings or whole towns. In his introduction, the author discusses the process of design and introduces the thesis that mathematics and logic can be valuable tools in design, a process which most designers think of as intuitive. The book is divided into two parts. The first deals with the nature of design problems and ways in which they have been solved in the past, both in primitive and civilized cultures. The contrast between the two methods leads Alexander to his method of representation and resolution. For him the object of design is to find a form which fits its context in frictionless co-existence with all forces (social, environmental, economic) that must be taken into consideration by the designer. He describes this form as having "goodness of fit." In the second, more theoretical, part of the book,

Alexander proposes the use of set theory to analyze the design problem. The text is accessible to those with little mathematical background, and non-mathematical application examples are presented alongside their mathematical counterparts. There are two appendices. The first is a worked example (a reorganization of an agricultural village in India) of the method, including Alexander's diagrams; the second is a mathematical treatment of decomposition of the graph that is produced during the synthesis. Related works of potential interest are Lionel March and Philip Steadman's *The Geometry of the Environment* and Alexander's own *A Pattern Language*.

CONTENTS

    1. Introduction: the need for rationality

Part One

    2. Goodness of fit

    3. The source of good fit

    4. The unselfconscious process

    5. The selfconscious process

Part Two

    6. The program

    7. The realization of the program

    8. Definitions

    9. Solution

    Epilogue

    Appendix 1. A worked example

    Appendix 2. Mathematical treatment of decomposition

    Notes

216 pp. 9 chapters in 2 parts. Drawings, mathematical formulae, abstract formalisms, references, appendices. ISBN 0-674-62750-4. (ISBN 0-674-62751-2)

Almagor, Maier   *SEE UNDER ID 248*

4

American Institute of Graphic Arts

Symbol Signs

Hastings House, 1981

(a symbol development project sponsored by the U.S. Department of Transportation; from the *Visual Communication Books* series)

Presents a standardized set of fifty symbols designed to communicate basic transportation related messages to speakers of any language at travel facilities around the world. The symbol set has been developed by the American Institute of Graphic Arts (AIGA) in cooperation with the United States Department of Transportation.

The first section of the book describes four general message areas (public services, concessions, processing activities, and regulations) identified by the Department of Transportation as needing symbols. Altogether a need for about fifty symbols was assessed. A symbol set was developed by first collecting 300 symbols used in twenty-eight symbol systems around the world and then evaluating each symbol according to semantic, syntactic, and pragmatic value. The semantic evaluation rated how well the symbol represented the message, the syntactic how well the symbol and its parts related to other symbols, and the pragmatic the ease with which a person could recognize the sign. From these evaluations a favored symbol was selected or else a new symbol developed based on the critique of the old symbols. The second section of the book presents figures showing all 300 symbols originally collected, together with the evaluation of each. The third section of the book presents whole page illustrations of each of the official symbols selected and developed by AIGA. These illustrations are designed to be easily copied to promote widespread use. A final section discusses guidelines for transforming the symbols into useful signs including legibility criteria, using a grid, lettering, foreign language translation, and using directional arrows. An appendix presents the entirety of the twenty-eight symbol systems that were evaluated as a basis for the development of the current symbol set. The symbol set developed in this book has been carefully designed and thirty-four of the symbols have already undergone extensive testing in the field since their original development in 1974. Already in use in parts of the United States, the Middle East, Australia, and England, the symbol set is not copyrighted because the developers hope that it will be adopted for widespread international usage. This book should be useful for designers, students, architects, business corporations, local authorities, or anyone who needs a sign system. The writing in the book is easy to read, and the illustrations are clear.

CONTENTS
Introduction
Thomas H. Geismar
1: Inventory
Message areas
2: Analysis/Evaluation
Organization
Methods of evaluation
Symbol concept evaluation sheet
Basis of evaluation
Recommendations
Symbol source abbreviations
Symbol sources
3: Recommended Symbols
Considerations in drawing the symbols
4: Guidelines
Introduction
Legibility criteria
Symbol/lettering size relationships
Use of grid
Lettering
Symbol presentation
Foreign language translations
Suggested directional arrow
Fabrication
Examples

Location signs
Uni-directional signs
Multi-directional signs
Door signs
Curb side signs
Exit symbol
Terminology
Alternate symbol formats
Figure without a symbol field
Figure in a reversed symbol field
Figure in a circular symbol field
Summary
5: Appendix
Symbol sources inventory
Bibliography

240 pp. 4 chapters. Drawings, bibliography, appendix. (ISBN 0-8038-6777-8)

American National Standards Institute

SEE UNDER ID 99, 100

5
Angell, Ian O.

A Practical Introduction to Computer Graphics
John Wiley and Sons, 1981

A beginner's course in computer graphics which progresses from programs for simple shapes to complex three-dimensional designs, utilizing a variety of appropriate exercises and projects for the reader.

This short beginning handbook of computer graphics assumes a working knowledge of FORTRAN IV and Cartesian coordinate geometry. Beginning with the concept of matrix representation with two-dimensional graphics, geometry and space, the author proceeds to the coordinate geometry and matrix transformation of three-dimensional space and matrix representation, and the problem of the hidden line algorithm. The book includes a chapter on computer movies. Demonstration projects are given throughout the work, because the author believes that "the only way to understand . . . computer science completely is to study and write large numbers of programs; that is why the format . . . is that of 'understanding through worked examples.' " To serve as guides to learning, over seventy program segments are included, as well as a series of projects with hints to solutions.

CONTENTS
Preface
  1. An informal introduction to two-dimensional graphics
  2. An introduction to two-dimensional geometry
  3. Transformations of two-dimensional space; matrix representation

4. Clipping and covering
5. The coordinate geometry of three-dimensional space
6. Matrix transformation of three-dimensional space; orthographic projections
7. Perspective and stereoscopic views
8. Hidden line algorithms
9. Setup techniques
10. Computer movies
11. Projects
12. Conclusion: What next?
Index

146 pp. 12 chapters. Drawings, figures, graphs, algorithms, abstract formalisms, general index. (ISBN 0-470-27251-1)

6

Applegate, Sheldon L.

technical report

The Use of Interactive Raster Graphics in the Display and Manipulation of Multidimensional Data
1981

(report number N82-21920; Purdue University; sponsored by NASA Ames Research Center; August 1981)

Discusses raster graphics techniques for the review, display, and manipulation of multi-dimensional/scalar data.

This NASA report on the use of raster graphics consists of the 1981 doctoral dissertation of Sheldon L. Applegate. Applegate's study of raster graphics techniques for multi-dimensional data display and manipulation begins with a lengthy and general survey of state-of-the-art computer graphics trends before addressing the specific goal of his thesis: the development of an engineering raster graphics package for the review of large quantities of numerical information. To do this the author discusses in detail raster graphics applications to the display of empirical and theoretical technical data, including depiction of functions of one, two, and three variables as well as bivariate data types. In his treatment of the problems of interactive data display the author develops a package that emphasizes speed over display quality and also provides the analyst with access to displayed data without corrupting the information on the screen. He shows that shaded displays of three-dimensional geometries with color data representation viably convey complex information even when the display is "degraded" for the sake of efficient interaction. The package also includes isarithmic color-to-data correspondence and continuous tone correspondence for the interactive representation of complex information. The thesis concludes with a summary of the broad areas of application for the techniques developed in the preceding chapters and a reiteration of the author's preference for speed over display quality. A useful work for advanced display designers. (Note: An inaccurate table of contents misrepresents the work's actual pagination.)

CONTENTS

Abstract

Introduction
    Computers and graphics
    Research objectives

Classes of Data and Their Display
    Functions of a single variable
    Functions of two variables
    Functions of three or more variables
    Restricted functions of three variables

Hardware and Software Environment
    UNIX, C, and GRAFIC
    Color spaces

Interactive Data Display
    Coordinate transformations
    Raster considerations
    Hidden surface algorithms
    Description of geometries
    Displaying data with a geometry
    Interactive control of a geometry display
    Focusing the display on a section of interest
    Clipping planes
    User orientation
    Screen accoutrements
    Saving viewing parameters
    Split screen viewing
    Handling large geometries

Interactive Data Manipulation
    Highlighting geometry elements

The Display of Bivariate Data
    The topographical display of bivariate data
    Hue and intensity displays of bivariate data

Organizational Overview of Interaction
    Methods of interaction

Practical Considerations
    Possible extensions of a data display package

Conclusions

List of References

Appendices
    Appendix A: Command descriptions
    Appendix B: Geometry file format
    Appendix C: Data file format

Vita

124 pp. 9 chapters. Photographs, figures, mathematical formulae, references, appendices.

7
Arnheim, Rudolf

Visual Thinking
University of California Press, 1969

Addresses how the mind gathers and processes information and emphasizes the unity of sensory perception and reasoning.

This theoretical exploration draws on major disciplines and thinkers, from ancient and modern times, to craft an argument for the systematic training of visual perception as a tool of the intellect. The author deplores the declining attention paid to the arts and the senses as children begin their formal education, and calls for a "rebuilding [of] the bridge between perception and thinking." He establishes a hierarchy of the senses, calling vision "the primary medium of thought" and urging that art be freed from its "unproductive isolation." In a subtle but persistent manner, the author advocates a more conscious use of perceptual abstraction in teaching. His apt verbal examples, complemented by useful figures, demonstrate an encyclopedic familiarity with philosophy, physics, education, photography, and, especially, psychology and psychiatry. Convinced of the superiority of the human senses and the human mind, the author emphasizes machines' ultimate dependence on human programmers. "The computer can be made to see but not to perceive," he asserts in this book which predates contemporary strides in artificial intelligence. He distinguishes active from passive perception, intuitive from intellectual cognition, and builds patiently from physical sight to discernment, comparison, abstraction, distortion, memory, imagination, numbers, and words as he makes his case. The book is for educators at all levels but will be illuminating for artists, writers, inventors, psychologists, and others involved in problem solving. Those wishing to learn more about Arnheim's views on the psychology of perception are referred to his earlier volume, *Art and Visual Perception*.

CONTENTS

1: Early Stirrings
    Perception torn from thinking
    The senses mistrusted
    Plato of two minds
    Aristotle from below and above

2: The Intelligence of Perception (i)
    Perception as cognition
    Perception circumscribed
    Exploring the remote
    The senses vary
    Vision is selective
    Fixation solves a problem
    Discernment in depth
    Shapes are concepts
    Perception takes time
    How machines read shape
    Completing the incomplete

3: The Intelligence of Perception (ii)
    Subtracting the context
    Brightness and shape as such
    Three attitudes
    Keeping the context
    The abstraction of shape
    Distortion calls for abstraction
    Permanence and change

4: Two and Two Together
    Relations depend on structure
    Pairing affects the partners
    Perception discriminates
    Perception compares
    What looks alike?
    Mind versus computer

5: The Past in the Present
    Forces acting on memory
    Percepts supplemented
    To see the inside
    Visible gaps
    Recognition

6: The Images of Thought
    What are mental images like?
    Can one think without images?
    Particular and generic images
    Visual hints and flashes
    How abstract can an image be?

7: Concepts Take Shape
    Abstract gestures
    A pictorial example
    Experiments with drawings
    Thought in visible action

8: Pictures, Symbols, and Signs
    Three functions of images
    Images to suit their functions
    What trademarks can tell
    Experiences interacting with ideas
    Two scales of abstraction

9: What Abstraction Is Not
    A harmful dichotomy
    Abstraction based on generalization
    Generality comes first
    Sampling versus abstraction

10: What Abstraction Is
    Types and containers
    Static and dynamic concepts
    Concepts as highspots
    On generalization

11: With Feet on the Ground
    Abstraction as withdrawal
    The extraction of principle
    Against the grain
    In love with classification
    In touch with experience

12: Thinking With Pure Shapes
    Numbers reflect life
    Quantities perceived
    Numbers as visible shapes
    Meaningless shapes make trouble
    Self-evident geometry

13: Words in Their Place
    Can one think in words?
    Words as images
    Words point to percepts
    Intuitive and intellectual cognition
    What words do for images
    The imagery of logical links
    Language overrated
    The effects of linearity
    Verbal versus pictorial concepts

14: Art and Thought
    Thinking in children's drawings
    Personal problems worked out
    Cognitive operations
    Abstract patterns in visual art

15: Models for Theory
    Cosmological shapes
    The nonvisual made visible
    Models have limits
    Figure and ground and beyond
    Infinity and the sphere
    The stretch of imagination

16: Vision in Education
    What is art for?
    Pictures as propositions
    Standard images and art
    Looking and understanding
    How illustrations teach
    Problems of visual aid
    Focus on function
    The burden of it all

Notes

Bibliography

Index

345 pp. 16 chapters. Drawings, photographs, figures, models, general index, bibliography, chapters notes. ISBN 0-520-01378-6. (ISBN 0-520-01871-0)

8
Arnheim, Rudolf

Art and Visual Perception: A Psychology of the Creative Eye (rev. ed.)
University of California Press, 1974

Surveys the formal mechanisms of seeing, relating art theory to work on the psychology of perception.

This is the 1974 revision of the book first published in 1954 and contains many revisions and modifications to the material presented in the first edition, based on study, developments, and research which occurred during the decades between editions. In writing this book Arnheim states that, in a certain sense, the visual experience cannot be reduced to words. However, suitable categories can further communication about art. Through his discussion of vision, Arnheim hopes not only to educate the reader but also to help reawaken the eye to an understanding of art. This is a book about art and vision, about experimental findings on perception, and about categories for organizing and understanding what we see. The author's orientation, and main body of experimental evidence, is derived from gestalt theory; his examples are drawn from art history. The visual elements of art are analyzed as shape, form, light, motion, expression, color, balance, space, and dynamics. Throughout the book, the dynamic nature of art is stressed. A chapter on children's art discusses different theories regarding intellectual maturation and the successive development of types of artistic representation. Analogies drawn between children's art and primitive art are used to point out principles influencing the artistic creations of adults. Points are well-illustrated with figures and works of art. This book is a useful text for graphic artists, psychologists, and others interested in both the visual arts and the perception of visual images.

CONTENTS

Preface to the New Version

Introduction

I: Balance
The hidden structure of a square
What are perceptual forces?
Two disks in a square
Psychological and physical balance
Why balance?
Weight
Direction
Patterns of balance
Top and bottom
Right and left
Balance and the human mind
Madame Cézanne in a yellow chair

II: Shape
 Vision as active exploration
 Grasping the essentials
 Perceptual concepts
 What is shape?
 The influence of the past
 Seeing shape
 Simplicity
 Simplification demonstrated
 Leveling and sharpening
 A whole maintains itself
 Subdivision
 Why the eyes often tell the truth
 Subdivision in the arts
 What is a part?
 Similarity and difference
 Examples from art
 The structural skeleton

III: Form
 Orientation in space
 Projections
 Which aspect is best?
 The Egyptian method
 Foreshortening
 Overlapping
 What good does overlapping do?
 Interplay of plane and depth
 Competing aspects
 Realism and reality
 What looks lifelike?
 Form as invention
 Levels of abstraction
 La source
 Visual information

IV: Growth
 Why do children draw that way?
 The intellectualistic theory
 They draw what they see
 Representational concepts
 Drawing as motion
 The primordial circle
 The law of differentiation
 Vertical and horizontal
 Obliqueness
 The fusion of parts
 Size
 The misnamed tadpoles
 Translation into two dimensions
 Educational consequences
 The birth of form in sculpture
 Sticks and slabs
 The cube and the round

V: Space
>   Line and contour
>   Contour rivalry
>   Figure and ground
>   Depth levels
>   Application to painting
>   Frames and windows
>   Concavity in sculpture
>   Why do we see depth?
>   Depth by overlapping
>   Transparency
>   Deformations create space
>   Boxes in three dimensions
>   Help from physical space
>   Simple rather than truthful
>   Gradients create depth
>   Toward a convergence of space
>   The two roots of central perspective
>   Not a faithful projection
>   Pyramidal space
>   The symbolism of a focused world
>   Centrality and infinity
>   Playing with the rules

VI: Light
>   The experience of light
>   Relative brightness
>   Illumination
>   Light creates space
>   Shadows
>   Painting without lighting
>   The symbolism of light

VII: Color
>   From light to color
>   Shape and color
>   How colors come about
>   The generative primaries
>   Addition and subtraction
>   Generative complementaries
>   A capricious medium
>   The quest for harmony
>   The elements of the scale
>   Syntax of combinations
>   The fundamental complementaries
>   Interaction of color
>   Matisse and El Greco
>   Reactions to color
>   Warm and cold

VIII: Movement
>   Happenings and time
>   Simultaneity and sequence
>   When do we see motion?
>   Direction
>   The revelations of speed

Stroboscopic movement
Some problems of film editing
Visible motor forces
A scale of complexity
The body as instrument
The kinesthetic body image

IX: Dynamics
Simplicity is not enough
Dynamics and its traditional interpretations
A diagram of forces
Experiments on directed tension
Immobile motion
The dynamics of obliqueness
Tension in deformation
Dynamic composition
Stroboscopic effects
How does dynamics come about?
Examples from art

X: Expession
Traditional theories
Expression embedded in structure
The priority of expression
Symbolism in art

Notes

Bibliography

Index

508 pp. 10 chapters. Drawings, photographs, figures, general index, bibliography, chapter notes. ISBN 0-520-02327-7. (ISBN 0-520-026136)

9
Artwick, Bruce A.

Applied Concepts in Microcomputer Graphics
Prentice-Hall, 1984

A useful reference book and guide to computer graphics systems; emphasizes microcomputer graphics and practical aspects of computer graphics. Software, hardware, and mathematical bases for computer graphics are covered.

Several introductory chapters discuss and illustrate basics of equipment, display generation, hardware, and peripheral graphic devices. The author suggests that these first few chapters contain the information that would be covered in an introductory course in computer graphics. The book goes on to discuss computer-human interfaces and computer-assisted design and simulations. In a long chapter dealing with more difficult mathematical concepts, the reader is first introduced to basic matrix arithmetic. The concepts become more complex as the author progresses to discussions of transformations, instancing, and image surfaces. The coverage here is fairly detailed, includes helpful figures, and is generally easy to follow. The next chapter focuses on the special problems and procedures for producing high performance graphics and animation on microcomputers. Since the processor speed and memory size of microcomputers are limited, the "special techniques" and "imaginative gimmicks" discussed in detail in this chapter are needed to attain good quality microcomputer graphics. A final chapter briefly discusses common uses of graphics in business and their implementation. Appendices cover foreign video standards and graphics specifications on the Apple II and IBM personal computers. This well written, organized, and illustrated book should prove useful for people wanting an in-depth introduction to computer graphics or seeking a handy reference on computer graphics. The author provides very basic and easily understood introductory information, but is able to take the novice on to a fairly complex understanding of concepts and practical uses of computer graphics. The mathematical coverage is admirably readable and not intimidating to the novice.

CONTENTS

PREFACE

CHAPTER 1: APPLICATIONS OF MICROCOMPUTER GRAPHICS

Types of Graphic Displays
    Graphs and charts
    Status and control displays

Computer-Aided Design

Simulating with Graphics

CHAPTER 2: DISPLAY GENERATION BASICS

Coordinate Systems and Conventions
    Cartesian coordinates
    Polar coordinates
    Other coordinate systems
    Coordinate system mapping

Display Generation, Resolution, and Aspect Ratio

Point Manipulation
    Point plotting
    Point readback

Line Generation Concepts
    Line geometry
    Differential line generation methods
    Analog line generation methods
    Absolute vs. relative line graphics

Coordinate System Boundary Conflicts
    Wraparound
    Saturation methods
    Clipping

Restricted-Area Displays
    Viewports
    Windows

Display Contol
   Panning
   Roaming
   Scrolling
   Rotation
   Scaling and zoom
   Display erase and fill
   Cursors
Graphics Data Compression
   Cell-organized displays
   Chained lines
   Shape tables
Alphanumerics Generation
   Cell definition
   Vector definition
Practical Ways of Using Graphics
   Graphics calls
   Display files
   Language for graphics
CHAPTER 3: WORKING WITH DISPLAY GENERATION
HARDWARE
Raster-Scan CRT displays
Interlace
   Raster generation using bitmaps
   Display memory mapping
   Multilevel displays and gray shades
   Color displays
   Display memory organization
   Monochrome video signals
   Color video signals
   Video noise
   Graphic display generators
   Raster-scan monitors
Vector Refresh Displays
Storage-Tube Displays
Static-Matrix Displays
   Plasma panels
   LED, LCD, and incandescent matrixes
CHAPTER 4: AN INTRODUCTION TO PERIPHERAL GRAPHIC
DEVICES
Input Devices
   Switches and keyboards
   Potentiometers and paddles
   Control sticks
   Track balls
   Graphics tablets
   Light pens
   Touch panels
   Automatic digitizers

Performance-Boosting Peripherals
    Graphic function microprocessors
    Arithmetic processors
    Matrix multipliers and array multipliers
    Clipper dividers
Hard-Copy Output Devices
    Matrix printers
    Pen plotters
CHAPTER 5: INTERACTIVE DESIGN ELEMENTS AND INTELLIGENCE
Design Elements and Their Submittal
    Straight lines
    Squares and rectangles
    Circles and ellipses
    Partial circles and ellipses
    Spiral segments
    Curves
    Text symbols
    Symbols, cells, and subpictures
Locating and Deleting Elements
    Finder system
    Element deletion
Display Intelligence
    Tagging
    Keys within tags
    Tag access methods and links
CHAPTER 6: DESIGN AND SIMULATION SYSTEM INTERACTION
Design System Interaction
    Design aids
    Automatic geometric construction
    Area patterning
    Viewing and movement in space
    Design files and access
    Design system software structure
Simulation System Interaction
    Interactive control
    Simulation software structure
    Improving simulation performance
CHAPTER 7: MATHEMATICS AND TRANSFORMS FOR ADVANCED GRAPHICS
Matrix Representation of Graphic Operations
    Vector matrix arithmetic
    Rectangular matrix arithmetic
    2D graphics transforms
    3D graphics transforms
    3D to 2D conversion and projection
Instancing
    Instance transforms
    Nested instancing
    Instancing precision
    Direct raster screen cells

Wire-Frame Element Generation
    Point plotting
    Geometric configurations
    Circle fitting and fillets
    Ellipse and parabola fitting
    Arc segment joining
Blending Techniques
    The blending operation
Image Surfaces
    Surface definition
    Surface clipping
    Surface area calculation
    Surface area filling
    Hidden surface elimination

CHAPTER 8: HIGH-PERFORMANCE GRAPHICS AND ANIMATION

Frame Considerations in Animation
    Frame refreshing
    Discontinuity and flicker
    Flicker reduction

Display Generation Time Analysis

Transformation—Computation Speed Improvement
    Arithmetic type considerations
    Integer arithmetic techniques
Image Generation Speedup Techniques
    Fast erase
    Speed and resolution tradeoffs
    Resolution truncation mapping problems
    High-speed vector generation
Improving Image Quality
    Edge smoothing
    Surface shading based on normals
    Vertical blanking synchronization
Special-Case Software Performance Boosters
    Frame synthesis and movement extrapolation
    Clipping without dividing
    Text transform speedup
    Artificial screen memory readback
    Incremental fill
    Reserved points
    Space framing and 3D interpolation
Boosting Performance with Special Hardware
    Scroll and zoom displays
    Multipliers and arithmetic processors
    High-performance microprocessors
    Bit-sliced microprocessors

CHAPTER 9: BUSINESS GRAPHICS

Charts and Graphs
    Software characteristics
    Software implementation

Mixed Graphics and Text
Presentation Graphics
Intelligent Graphics Data Bases
Office Automation
APPENDIX A: FOREIGN AND DOMESTIC TELEVISION DATA
APPENDIX B: GRAPHICS ON THE APPLE II MICROCOMPUTER
Mode Control and Memory Areas
Text and Low Resolution Memory Mapping
High-Resolution Mode
480 Horizontal Resolution
Orange Squeezeout
Fast Erase
Screen Ping-Ponging
APPENDIX C: GRAPHICS ON THE IBM PERSONAL COMPUTER
Memory Areas
Mode Controls
Memory Mapping
Using the Display Modes
Nonstandard Modes
Screen Ping-Ponging
RGB Compatibility
INDEX

374 pp. 9 chapters. Drawings, photographs, figures, charts, graphs, tables, mathematical formulae, algorithms, general index, appendices. ISBN 0-13-039322-3.

10
Badre, Albert
Shneiderman, Ben
(eds.)

collection

Directions in Human/Computer Interaction
Ablex, 1982

(from the *Human/Computer Interaction* series, Ben Shneiderman, series ed.)

Combining experimental results, theoretical discussions, and practical information, this book is the first in a planned series on human/computer interaction. This volume presents a wide-ranging collection of papers representing recent research into human cognition and interactive system design.

Contributing authors concentrate on both contemporary and emerging approaches to interactive system design. Chapters include: a broad but concise review of relevant cognitive research; a study of the strategies and performance of novice programmers; the design of positive, user-oriented system messages; a concrete discussion of the mutually beneficial marriage of artificial intelligence and human factors engineering; experimental probes into the usefulness of "natural" vocabularies for command and query languages; an evaluation of techniques for "generating user-oriented abbreviations"; models for the design of static user-assistance presentations which are more than "electronic reference manuals"; an introduction to speech synthesizers written for human factors engineers; a study investigating the effects of meaningful chunking and presentation order on subjects' recall of sequentially presented information; and coding and sequencing techniques for formatting complex graphical displays to alleviate the "clutter" problem. This volume is of interest to both the research scientist and the system designer.

CONTENTS

Preface
 Albert Badre, Ben Shneiderman
1. Cognitive factors in human interaction with computers
 Robert B. Allen
2. What do novices know about programming?
 Elliot Soloway, Kate Ehrlich, Jeffrey Bonar, Judith Greenspan
3. System message design: guidelines and experimental results
 Ben Shneiderman
4. Artificial intelligence and human factors engineering: a necessary synergism in the interface of the future
 Paul Roller Michaelis, Mark L. Miller, James A. Hendler
5. Psychological investigations of natural terminology for command & query languages
 Susan T. Dumais, Thomas K. Landauer
6. Abbreviations for automated systems: teaching operators the rules
 S.L. Ehrenreich, Theodora A. Porcu
7. Models for the design of static software user assistance
 M.L. Schneider
8. A human factors engineer's introduction to speech synthesizers
 Paul Roller Michaelis, Richard H. Wiggins
9. Designing chunks for sequentially displayed information
 Albert N. Badre
10. Information highlighting on complex displays
 Beverly G. Knapp, Franklin L. Moses, Leon H. Gellman
Author index
Subject index

225 pp. 10 chapters. Drawings, figures, graphs, tables, author index, subject index, references. ISBN 0-89391-144-5.

11
Bailey, Robert W.

Human Performance Engineering: A Guide for System Designers
Prentice-Hall, 1982

A textbook on human factors for design engineers. This guide
introduces basic aspects of human performance engineering and
investigates ways to improve human performance.

Commissioned and with a final review by a committee of Bell
Telephone Laboratories human factors supervisors, this text considers
issues in improving human performance, including: motivation; design
of work and interfaces; testing; and preparation of training, instructions,
and performance aids. Of particular interest to the engineer with a
limited background in psychology, it discusses how humans "sense,
process information, and respond." Courses at Columbia University
and Stevens Institute of Technology, as well as internal Bell Labs
courses, were used as sources of material and criticism. The work is
divided into sections which cover: the human user, the activity-basic
design, the activity-interface design, the activity-facilitator design, the
context (environment), tests, and studies. It contains a 23-page reference
section, and each chapter includes suggestions for further reading. A
straightforward, wide-ranging text created by industry/business and
geared for use in that sphere.

CONTENTS

Preface

INTRODUCTION

1: Psychology and Systems
    Performance or behavior
    Focusing on performance
    Performance defined
    Establishing standards
    Performance examples
    Measuring human performance
    Human vs. system performance
    Human performance model
    People in systems
    Human performance engineering
    Making informed design decisions
    For more information

2: History of Human Performance
    Introduction
    Motivation
    Training
    Selection (testing)
    Human-oriented design

THE HUMAN (USER)

3: Human Limits and Differences
    The concept of limits
    Cognitive processing limits

4: Sensing
    Stimuli
    Sensors and receptors
    Sensory limits
    Sensing and performance
    Vision
    Audition
    Cutaneous senses
    Taste
    Smell
    Kinesthetic sense
    Sensory adaption
    Sensory interaction
    For more information

5: The Body and Performance
    Body dimensions
    Average person fallacy
    Anthropometric measures
    Range of movement
    Strength
    For more information

6: Cognitive Processing and Performance
    Introduction
    Stage processing
    Processing stages and skills
    Processing levels
    Processing levels and skill
    For more information

7: Perception, Problem Solving and Decision Making
    Perception and perceptual skills
    Intellectual processing
    Intellectual skill
    Problem solving
    Decision making
    For more information

8: Memory
    Introduction
    Sensory memory
    Short-term memory
    Long-term memory
    Sensory-related characteristics
    Memory skill
    For more information

9: Motivation
    Introduction
    Internal vs. external motivation
    Differences in users
    Instincts, drives, and motives
    Motivating system users
    Motivation vs. satisfaction
    For more information

THE ACTIVITY - BASIC DESIGN

10: Designing for People
    Systems
    Total system design
    System development stages
    For more information

11: Basic Design
    Introduction
    Function allocation
    Performance requirements
    Task analysis
    Facilitating human performance
    Beginning early
    For more information

THE ACTIVITY - INTERFACE DESIGN

12: Displays, Controls, and Workplace Design
    Introduction
    User expectations
    Visual displays
    Auditory displays
    Controls
    Controls/displays
    Workplace design
    For more information

13: Speech Communication
    A major disaster
    Intelligibility testing
    Speech transmission systems
    Evaluating speech transmission
    Speech interference levels
    Language considerations
    For more information

14: Human/Computer Interface
    Introduction
    Computer users
    General interface guidelines
    Human-to-computer
    Computer-to-human
    For more information

15: Forms and CRT Screen Design
    Display design steps
    General considerations
    Additional considerations
    CRT screen guidelines
    Form design guidelines
    For more information

16: Code Design
    Introduction
    Codes
    Types of codes
    Coding errors
    Error control

User characteristics
Activity characteristics
Response considerations
Formats
Guidelines

THE ACTIVITY - FACILITATOR DESIGN

17: Supporting Human Performance
Dosage level example
Determining requirements
Developing facilitators
Balancing facilitators
Selecting personnel
Developing performance aids
Developing written instructions
Developing training
Making tradeoffs

18: Selection Criteria
Determining qualifications
Statement of qualifications
Proposing tests
Skills, knowledge and attitudes
Matching existing people
For more information

19: Printed Instructions
Introduction
Verbal and written instructions
Meaningful instructions
Writing style and grammar
Writing for a specific user
Developing instructions
Presenting instructions
Formatting instructions
Translating foreign instructions
Instructions as programs
Computer-based documentation
Readability measures
Writer's workbench
For more information

20: Performance Aids
Introduction
Types of performance aids
The need for performance aids
General considerations
Human (user) characteristics
Activity characteristics
Context characteristics
Performance aid development
Effectiveness assessment

21: Training Development
Introduction
Learning vs. training
Developing skills
Using reinforcement
Motivating trainees
Training development
Computers and training
Computer-based training
For more information

THE CONTEXT (ENVIRONMENT)

22: Physical and Social Environments
Introduction
An altered environment
Environmental design
Human-environment interaction
Adaption
Environmental components
Physical environment
The social environment
For more information

TESTS AND STUDIES

23: Data Collection
Studies and tests
Data collection considerations
Sampling
Developing questionnaires
Conducting interviews
Observation
Other techniques
For more information

24: Performance Testing
Introduction
Achieving acceptable performance
The test program
Predicting human performance
Preparing for a test
Example of a work module test
Validity of work module tests

25: Conducting Comparison Studies
Common sense vs. fact finding
Study design and statistics
Stastical methods
For more information

Appendices
A. Statistical tables
B. Human performance engineering resources
C. Code design tables

References

Index

656 pp. 25 chapters in 7 parts. Drawings, figures, graphs, tables, mathematical formulae, general index, references, appendices. ISBN 0-13-445320-4.

12
Banks, William W.
Gertman, David I.
Petersen, Rohn J.

Human Engineering Design Considerations for Cathode Ray Tube-Generated Displays
1982

technical report

(report number NUREG/CR-2496; EG&G Idaho, Inc.; sponsored by U.S. Nuclear Regulatory Commission; April 1982)

This report investigates the validity of various standards in CRT-generated displays, their relevance for human performance, and related hardware. The authors conclude that further human factors research is needed to develop valid standards.

The first of a two-volume report to the U.S. Nuclear Regulatory Commission on human-computer interaction, this work addresses major hardware aspects of workstation design by examining the validity of current standards in CRT-displays and their positive or negative effects upon human performance. The authors review and discuss sets of standards from sources including the Technical University of Berlin, the German Standards Organization, the Swedish Board of Health, the University of London, and IBM, as well as papers from the French Society of Ergonomics and U.S. government and military standards documents. The authors select and review in detail twenty-two display variables such as symbol size, contrast and luminance, image distortion, display height, and a variety of keyboard factors. Their analysis leads to the conclusion that further human factors research is needed in order to establish valid standards for CRT displays that would ensure improved human performance. Research is especially needed in the areas of image distortion, display format, work-surface light reflection, cognitive fidelity, response time, and phosphor types. Volume I ends with an extensive, helpful summary and user's guide which contains information, analyses, and recommendations to aid in the design or procurement of imagery interpretation equipment. Due to this feature, this is an especially useful and comprehensive survey of CRT design effects on human performance and should be of interest to systems analysts and designers, as well as anyone involved in human factors research.

CONTENTS

ABSTRACT

SUMMARY

FOREWORD

INTRODUCTION

SOURCES REVIEWED

DISPLAY VARIABLES

FINDINGS

Symbol Contrast

Symbol Luminance

Acceptable Color

Image Polarity

Minimum Refresh Rate

Phosphor Recommendations

Glare Control

Display Viewing Distance

Symbol Size

Percent Active Area

Character Format

Character Line/Column Spacing

Image Distortions

Screen Orientation

Height of Display

Ambient Light Levels

Reflectivities of Work Station Surfaces

Keyboard Factors
     Keystroke feedback
     Key actuation force
     Key travel
     Key spacing
     Keytop dimensions
     Numeric block
     Keyboard height
     Keyboard slope

Work Station Dimensions

Color for Information Coding
     Intensity
     A guide for color design decision

Response Time
ALTERNATE DATA ENTRY DEVICES
Isometric Joysticks
Ball Control
Free-Moving X-Y Controller
Light Pen
Touch Panel
REFERENCES
APPENDIX A - GLOSSARY
APPENDIX B - EXCERPTS FROM DESIGN HANDBOOK FOR
IMAGERY INTERPRETATION EQUIPMENT

243 pp. 5 sections. Drawings, figures, graphs, tables, references, glossary, appendices.

13
Banks, William W.
Gilmore, Walter E.
Blackman, Harold S.
Gertman, David I.

technical report

Human Engineering Design Considerations for Cathode Ray Tube-Generated Displays, Volume II
1983

(report number NUREG/CR-3003; EG&G Idaho, Inc.; sponsored by U.S. Nuclear Regulatory Commission; July 1983)

This second volume of a report on CRT displays and human factors focuses on display screen design guidelines and examines the data used to support or criticize particular display designs.

The second volume of a report to the U.S. Nuclear Regulatory Commission. Volume one is primarily focused on major hardware aspects of human-computer interaction and the validity of standard hardware guidelines. This volume concentrates on software issues. The authors define software in this context as "all programs, routines, codes, and other written information for use with computers." They investigate the following software variables relating to the design of display screens: screen organization, screen structures, coding visual displays, dynamic display characteristics, system feedback, and system-induced viewing abnormalities. The authors define and comment in detail on each of these variables; review the guidelines for each area; discuss the guidelines' rationale; and conclude that while many of the guidelines are empirically derived and relevant to human performance, some are based on insufficient data and require further research. The work ends with a succinct discussion of specific research recommendations for the six variables discussed in the main body of the report. This is a well-organized survey of interrelated software issues which can be employed on its own or in conjunction with volume one of the report. The work is of use to beginning and advanced systems analysts and designers.

CONTENTS

ABSTRACT

EXECUTIVE SUMMARY

FOREWORD

INTRODUCTION

Problem and Approach

Organization of the Document

DISPLAY ISSUES

Screen Organization
    Grouping
    Format

Screen Structures
    Labels
    Messages

Coding Visual Displays
    Symbolic and pictographic coding
    Highlighting
    Alphanumeric coding
    Cognitive fidelity

System Feedback
    Display update rate
    Display status indication

Dynamic Display Characteristics
    Display (animated) motion

System-Induced Viewing Abnormalities
    Display distortion
    Chromatic display aberration

SUMMARY OF RESEARCH RECOMMENDATIONS

Grouping

Format

Screen Structure
    Labeling
    Messages

Coding of Visual Displays
    Symbolic and pictographic coding
    Highlighting
    Alphanumeric coding
    Cognitive fidelity

System Feedback
    Display update rate
    Display status indication

Dynamic Display Characteristics
    Display (animated) motion

System-Induced Viewing Abnormalities
    Display distortion
    Chromatic display aberration

REFERENCES
APPENDIX A: A SUMMARY OF ADDITIONAL INFORMATION
RELATING TO CRT DESIGN BY RAMSEY AND ATWOOD
102 pp. 3 sections. Photographs, figures, tables, references, appendix.

14
Barmack, Joseph E.
Sinaiko, H. Wallace

technical report

Human Factors Problems in Computer-Generated Graphic Displays
1966

(report number STUDY-S-234/ARPA-15; Institute for Defense Analyses; sponsored by Advanced Research Projects Agency; April 1966)

The intent of this early study was to identify shortcomings of then-existing computer generated display and input devices and to learn what features might be incorporated into future developments.

The information in this report, processed for the Defense Documentation Center and the Defense Supply Agency, is based on: extensive interviews and site visits to fourteen institutions (including Bell Laboratories, IBM, the Federal Aviation Agency, the RAND Corporation, Stanford Research Institute, and the University of Michigan); examinations of in-use equipment; and a search of relevant literatures. Computer designers, programmers, and design engineer-users with and without programming experience were interviewed. Most of the equipment studied was designed for use by people with extensive experience in its concept and operation. The five sections cover introductory matter, displays, input devices, general system properties and requirements, methods of enhancing computer-user interaction, a review of contemporary cognitive theory in the psychological literature, and a brief section on research recommendations. While the specific technology investigated has developed dramatically since this study was conducted, this report is still of interest for the information it provides about one of the earliest studies to use such an extensive on-site visit and user interview model, and for its review of cognitive theory, an area which has received little attertion in graphics research.

CONTENTS
I: INTRODUCTION
II: DISPLAYS
A: Introduction
B: CRT Displays
    1. CRT display size
    2. CRT brightness
    3. Console design
    4. Cluttered displays
C: Display Coding
    1. Color-coding
    2. Shape coding
    3. Alphanumeric coding
    4. Size coding
    5. Intermittency coding

  6. Depth coding

  7. Other modes of coding

D: Effects of Flicker or Intermittent Light

E: Three-Dimensional Considerations

  1. Uses of three-dimensional displays

  2. Producing three-dimensionality

F: Design of Numbers, Letters, and Symbols

  1. Scale markings

  2. Counters, pointers, and labels

G: Research and Development Recommendations

  1. Display characteristics

  2. Display component evaluation

III: INPUT DEVICES

A: Operand Inputs (Alphanumeric Data)

  1. Standard typewriter keyboards

  2. Experimental typewriter keyboards

  3. Multiple press keyboards

  4. Character recognition systems

  5. Speech recognition systems

  6. Cathode ray tube, command lists and light pen

  7. Requirement for a bulk data input device

B: Operand Inputs (Graphic Data)

  1. Light pens

C: Operator Inputs

  1. Toggle switches, push buttons and rocker buttons

  2. Potentiometer activating devices

D: Recommendations

IV: GENERAL SYSTEM PROPERTIES AND REQUIREMENTS

A: Introduction

B: Current Practices

C: Needed Research

D: A Prospective Input-Output Console

E: Training

F: Reliability and Delay Time

G: Cost Effectiveness Evaluation

H: Languages

I: Summary

J: Research Recommendations

V: ENHANCING CREATIVE EFFORT

A: Theories of Computer-User Interaction

B: Cognition Simulation and Information Processing Theories

C: Contemporary Cognitive Theory in the Psychological Literature

  1. The nature of the perceptual input

  2. Filtering systems

  3. Set structuring

  4. Intensity

  5. States of activation

D: Human and Computer Differences

E: Implications for Computer Development

F. Research Recommendations
    References

116 pp. 5 chapters. Photographs, figures, references.

Beaton, Robert J.   *SEE UNDER ID 256*

15
Beatty, John C.
Booth, Kellogg S.
(eds.)

collection

Tutorial: Computer Graphics (2ed.)
IEEE Computer Society Press, 1982

This collection is a self-contained tutorial on the subject of computer graphics.

The editors have selected articles which provide an overview to state-of-the-art materials in the field. Additional text introduces important subfields such as visible surface processing, computer animation, hardware, software, and interactivity and human engineering. This second edition also includes a new section devoted entirely to raster graphics. Each of the eight sections has an introduction highlighting the articles which follow and placing them in a broader context. Intended for use as an introductory anthology of the field's literature, this volume will be valuable to both experienced and inexperienced students of graphics, "although more experienced readers will, of course, find the material more meaningful." It is liberally illustrated with photographs, drawings, and models; the work also contains an extensive bibliography and sources of additional material for the reader who wants to go beyond the level of the material presented. Though some of the papers are out of date, this book is a thorough overview of the computer graphics field, of interest to a wide range of graphics users and designers, from advanced hobbyists to experienced professionals.

CONTENTS

Preface

Part I: Introduction to Computer Graphics
    Computer displays
        I.E. Sutherland
    (*Scientific American*, June 1970)
    A brief, personal history of computer graphics
        C. Machover
    (*Computer*, November 1978)
    Interactive computer graphics: poised for takeoff?
        W. Myers

(*Computer Graphics, Proceedings of the 4th Annual Conference on Computer Graphics and Interactive Techniques*, 1977)
Computer graphics, interactive techniques, and image processing 1970-1975: a bibliography
   U.W. Pooch
(*Computer*, August 1976)
Survey—computer graphics: a keyword-indexed bibliography for the years 1976, 1977, and 1978
   G.F. Schrack
(*Computer Graphics and Image Processing 14*, 1980, pp. 24-79)
A guide to sources of information about computer graphics
   C. Machover
(*IEEE Computer Graphics and Applications*, January 1981)

Part II: Hardware for Computer Graphics
On the design of display processors
   T.H. Myer, I.E. Sutherland
(*Communications of the ACM*, June 1968)
An overview of directed beam graphics display hardware
   A.P. Lucido
(*Computer*, November 1978)
Storage CRT display terminals: evolution and trends
   R.B. Preiss
(*Computer*, November 1978)
Plasma displays
   H.G. Slottow
(*IEEE Transactions on Electron Devices*, July 1976)
Head-mounted display terminal
   D.L. Vickers
(*Proceedings of the 1970 IEEE International Computer Group Conference*, 1970)
Graphics displays
   C. Machover, M. Neighbors, C. Stuart
(*IEEE Spectrum*, August 1977, pp.24-32)
Graphics displays: factors in systems design
   C. Machover, M. Neighbors, C. Stuart
(*IEEE Spectrum*, October 1977)
Excerpts from *The Focal Encyclopedia of Film and Television Technology*
   The Focal Encyclopedia of Film and Television Technology
(Hastings House, NY, 1969)

Part III: Raster Graphics
Raster graphics
   J.F. Blinn
(*Computer Graphics*, 1979)
Color table animation
   R.G. Shoup
(*SIGGRAPH 79*, August 1979)
Using ordered dither to display continuous tone pictures on an AC plasma display
   C.N. Judice, J.F. Jarvis, W.H. Ninke
(*Proceedings of the S.I.D., Fourth Quarter*, 1974)
The use of grayscale for improved raster display of vectors and characters

F.C. Crow
(*SIGGRAPH 78 Proceedings*)
A tutorial on compensation tables
E. Catmull
(*SIGGRAPH 79*, 1979)

Part IV: Software for Computer Graphics
An approach to graphics systems design
W.M. Newman, R.F. Sproull
(*Proceedings of the IEEE*, April 1974)
Three dimensional transformations and projections
D.F. Rogers, J.A. Adams
(*Mathematical Elements for Computer Graphics*, 1976)
Reentrant polygon clipping
I.E. Sutherland, G.W. Hodgman
(*Communications of the ACM*, January 1974)
Clipping using homogeneous coordinates
J.F. Blinn, M.E. Newell
(*Computer Graphics*, August 1978)
A simply extended and modified batch environment graphical
system (SEMBEGS)
J.W. Wendorf
(*Communications of the ACM*, November 1978)
Hierarchical geometric models for visible surface algorithms
J.H. Clark
(*Communications of the ACM*, October 1976)
A tutorial on satellite graphics systems
J.D. Foley
(*Computer*, August 1976)

Part V: Interactive Graphics—The Human Factor
The art of natural graphic man-machine conversation
J.D. Foley
(*Proceedings of the IEEE*, April 1974)
One-point touch input of vector information for computer displays
C.F. Herot, G. Weinzapfel
(*Computer Graphics*, August 1978)
Computer displays optically superimposed upon input devices
K.C. Knowlton
(*The Bell System Technical Journal*, March 1977)
Special session on vision
F.S. Montalvo
(*SIGGRAPH 79*, 1979)
Color vision
R.P. Feynman, R.B. Leighton, M. Sands
(*The Feynman Lectures on Physics*, 1977)
Contour and contrast
F. Ratliff
(*Scientific American*, June 1972)

Part VI: Visible Surface Algorithms
A characterization of ten hidden-surface algorithms
I.E. Sutherland, R.F. Sproull, R.A. Schumacker
(*Computing Surveys*, March 1974)
Shadow algorithms for computer graphics
F.C. Crow

(*Computer Graphics*, Summer 1977)
Illumination for computer generated pictures
    B.T. Phong
(*Communications of the ACM*, June 1975)
Texture and reflection in computer generated images
    J.F. Blimm, M.E. Newell
(*Communications of the ACM*, October 1976)
A hidden-surface algorithm with anti-aliasing
    E. Catmull
(*SIGGRAPH 78*, 1978)
Scan line methods for displaying parametrically defined surfaces
    J.M. Lane, L.C. Carpenter, T. Whitted, J.F. Blinn
(*Communications of the ACM*, January 1980)

Part VII: Computer Animation
Shaded computer graphics in the entertainment industry
    F.C. Crow
(*Computer*, March 1978)
The problems of computer assisted animation
    E. Catmull
(*Computer Graphics*, August 1978)
Paint
    A.R. Smith
Interactive skeleton techniques for enhancing motion dynamics in key frame animation
    N. Burtnyk, M. Wein
(*Communications of the ACM*, October 1976)
Digital video display systems and dynamic graphics
    R. Baecker
(*SIGGRAPH 79*, 1979)

Part VIII: Applications of Computer Graphics
Computer graphics in archeticture
    D.P. Greenberg
(*Scientific American*, May 1974)
Computer graphics in urban and environmental systems
    R.L. Phillips
(*Proceedings of the IEEE*, April 1974)
Computer graphics and art
    C. Csuri
(*Proceedings of the IEEE*, April 1974)

570 pp. 46 papers in 8 parts. Drawings, photographs, maps, mathematical formulae, algorithms, models, references. (ISBN 0-8186-0425-5)

16
Beck, Jacob
(ed.)

collection

Organization and Representation in Perception
Lawrence Erlbaum Associates, 1982

(based on a conference on Processes of Perceptual Organization and Representation, funded by the National Science Foundation and the Consiglio Nazionale Ricerche of Italy; Abano, Italy; June 1979)

Examines perceptual organization and representation using the alternate approaches of Gestalt theory and information processing theory. Intended for psychologists, this collection also has important implications for the perceptual problems often faced by computer scientists.

Eighteen edited papers which apply Gestalt theory and information processing theory to focus on those unresolved issues relating to perceptual organization and representation. The editor points out in his introduction the shared assumption of the two theories, specifically that "perception is mediated by an underlying representation that can be studied through modeling." The papers themselves focus on the fundamentally different approaches of the two theories and how those approaches can: "reflect current theorizing concerning the problems of organization and representation;" clarify "fundamental problems, indicating new directions for research;" and focus attention on advances in theoretical understanding. Papers contain numerous figures and are written in technical language. Jacob Beck works in the Department of Psychology at the University of Oregon in Eugene.

CONTENTS

Introduction
   Jacob Beck
   References

1: Prägnanz and Soap Bubble Systems: A Theoretical Exploration
   Fred Attneave
   Introduction
   A soap bubble system
   References

2: Coding Theory as an Integration of Gestalt Psychology and
Information Processing Theory
   Frank Restle
   Coding theory
   Coding theory and Gestalt laws
   Neo-Gestalt theory
   Ecological perception
   Information processing
   Conclusions
   References

3: Metrical Aspects of Patterns and Structural Information Theory
   Emanuel Leeuwenberg
   Introduction
   Müller-Lyer illusion
   Discussion
   Appendix

References

4: The Perceiver as Organizer and Geometer
   D.N. Perkins
   Introduction
   The perceiver as organizer
   The perceiver as geometer
   Toward a model of good form perception
   The kind of Gestalt theory this is
   References

5: Symmetry, Transformation, and the Structure of Perceptual Systems
   Stephen E. Palmer
   Introduction
   Preliminary remarks
   A transformational theory of perceptual structure
   Relation to perceptual phenomena
   Concluding remarks
   References

6: Relaxation Processes for Perceptual Disambiguation in Computer Vision
   Azriel Rosenfeld
   Computer vision
   Classification problems
   Relaxation
   Discussion
   References

7: What Is Involved in Surface Perception?
   James J. Gibson
   Introduction
   Persisting and nonpersisting surface properties
   Fluctuation in the ambient optic array
   The ecological level of reality
   References

8: Contrasting Emphases in Gestalt Theory, Information Processing, and the Ecological Approach to Perception
   Eleanor J. Gibson
   The ecological approach
   References

9: Amodal Completion: Seeing or Thinking
   Gaetano Kanizsa, Walter Gerbino
   Seeing and thinking: just a phenomenal dichotomy?
   Amodal presence: a phenomenon to be revalued
   Functional effects of amodal completion
   A tool for analysis
   Concluding remarks
   References

10: How Big Is a Stimulus?
   Julian Hochberg
   Introduction
   The whole does not determine the appearance of the part: local depth cues and other local features
   The limits on any direct theory of surface perception

Implications of spatial and temporal limits on the pickup of higher-order variables

Perceived shapes and objects are not merely loci of points, but they are not themselves forms or objects, either

References

11: Some Characteristics of Gestalt-Oriented Research in Perception
Fabio Metelli
Introduction
The importance of phenomenological observation
Aggregation versus structure
Past experience versus perceptual laws
Quality versus quantity
Fact versus theories
References

12: The Effect of Perceived Depth on Phantoms and the Phantom Motion Aftereffect
Naomi Weisstein, William Maguire, Mary C. Williams
Experiment 1: Effect of binocular viewing on phantoms
Experiment 2: Binocular viewing at zero and non-zero disparities
Experiment 3: Relation between phantoms and the phantom motion aftereffect
General discussion
Conclusions
References

13: Figure Organization and Binocular Interaction
Mario Zanforlin
Introduction
Case I
Case II
Case III
Conclusion
References

14: Some Observations in the Auditory Field
Giovanni B. Vicario
Introduction
Phenomenal dependence
Embedded figures
Embedded elements
Objects in auditory field
Amodal completion
References

15: Textural Segmentation
Jacob Beck
Introduction
Empirical findings
A model for textural segmentation
Concluding remarks
References

16: Analysis of Discrete Internal Representations of Visual Pattern Stimuli
David H. Foster
Introduction
Discrete internal pattern representations
Pattern discrimination determined by probability differences
Analysis by parameterized pattern perturbation
An attribute designating the collinearity or noncollinearity of points in a pattern
An attribute designating the acuteness or obtuseness of an angle between two lines
General application of the pattern perturbation technique
Relationship to experiments on categorical identification and discrimination
Summary
Appendix
References

17: The Two Modes of Processing Concept and Some Implications
Herschel W. Leibowitz, Robert B. Post
Introduction
Dissociation
Implications for evaluation of vision
Plasticity, learning, and development
Perceptual constancies
Transportation safety
Orientation and disorientation
Height vertigo
General comments
References

18: Illumination, Color, and Three-Dimensional Form
Sten Sture Bergström
The vector model
Illumination borders and reflectance borders
Predictions and tests
Experiment 1
Experiment 2
Experiment 3
Discussion
References
Author index
Subject index

387 pp. 18 papers. Drawings, figures, tables, mathematical formulae, abstract formalisms, models, author index, subject index, references, appendices. ISBN 0-89859-175-9.

17
Belady, L.A.
Blasgen, M.W.
Evangelisti, C.J.
Tennison, R.D.

technical report

DESIGNPAD: Computer Graphics for Block Diagram Problems
1970

(report number RC-3128; IBM Watson Research Center; 28 October 1970)

Describes an experimental computer graphics system designed by IBM researchers more than a decade ago. In 1970, when the report was written, work on this system had been suspended following a partial implementation of the modeling subsystem.

Addressed to the research community, the report points out the need for two-dimensional man-machine interfaces. DESIGNPAD exemplifies an integrated graphics system applied to problems that can be represented by labeled block diagrams. It encompasses facilities for interactive structuring of these diagrams. The system functions through a time-sharing arrangement in which the user at a small satellite computer ties into a large, host computer. Complex block diagrams, many times larger than the screen of a VDT, can be constructed using the added capabilities of the host computer. The system includes a modeling subsystem, a drawing package, and a data structure. DESIGNPAD was to be used for processing large design problems.

29 pp. Drawings, figures, references, appendices.

Benjamin, Moshe

SEE UNDER ID 212

18
Bennett, John
Case, Donald
Sandelin, Jon
Smith, Michael
(eds.)

collection

Visual Display Terminals: Usability Issues and Health Concerns

Prentice-Hall, 1984

A collection that explores issues related to the design, development, and implementation of visual display terminals (VDTs).

This collection provides a knowledge base for designing and implementing VDTs. The articles deal with issues from cognitive psychology, ergonomics, and principles of human engineering. Each article has its own introduction, summary, and list of references. The first of the two sections addresses the question: What should a designer or implementor know about people's thought processes, skills, attitudes, and work to provide VDTs that are both useful and usable? The authors agree that VDTs bring a dramatic change to the office organization. The obvious usefulness of VDTs, however, does not mean users will find them usable or tolerate the change they introduce. Section two identifies potential health risks associated with the use of VDTs. Possible causes are explained and guidance is given on how to reduce or eliminate these risks. The book's uncluttered presentation and consistently clear writing make comprehension of the material easy, even pleasant. Numerous illustrations aid in further clarification of the contents. This volume should benefit anyone involved with the design or implementation of VDTs.

CONTENTS
Preface
Author profiles

SECTION ONE

Developing and Implementing VDT-Based Systems: Usability Issues
Introduction
The VDT as an agent of change
Peter G.W. Keen
The concept of usability
Brian Shackel
Designing the VDT interface for human-computer productivity
James H. Bair
Human limits and the VDT computer interface
Stuart K. Card
Managing to meet usability requirements: establishing and meeting software development goals
John L. Bennett

SECTION TWO

Using Visual Display Terminals: Health Concerns
Introduction
Health issues in VDT work
Michael J. Smith
Visual fatigue and the VDT workplace
Lawrence W. Stark, with the editorial assistance of Phyllis Grey Johnston
Health considerations at the information workplace
O. Bruce Dickerson, Walter E. Baker
Index
Afterword: The horseless carriage
About this book

297 pp. 8 papers in 2 sections. Drawings, photographs, figures, graphs, abstract formalisms, general index, references. ISBN 0-13-942482-2.

19
Berbaum, Kevin S.

technical report

Design Criteria for Reducing "Popping" in Area-of-Interest Displays: Preliminary Experiments
1983

(report number 81-C-0105-8; Canyon Research Group; sponsored by Naval Training Equipment Center; September 1983)

Research directed toward solving the problem of visual material or details appearing to "pop" suddenly into view in eye-coupled area-of-interest displays.

This report examines the possible causes and methods for correcting the problem of visual material "popping" suddenly into view in scenes presented through a computer-generated, eye-coupled, helmet-mounted display designed for the Navy's pilot training program. Popping is explained as "the compelling phenomenal appearance of new scene content" as it moves from low levels of detail in the background to higher levels within the area of interest. This computer-generated imagery is displayed through two projectors, a target projector and a background projector, both of which are slave to the observer's eye. Where the eye fixates, the target projector provides a high level of detail. Discontinuous changes in the level of detail along with popping were deemed unacceptable. This research explores the visual mechanisms involved in the perception of popping and investigates approaches designed to minimize or eliminate the effect. One set of experiments reported here dealt with contrast sensitivity as a function of retinal eccentricity, rate of pattern motion, or temporal modulation. The second set of experiments involved the notion of varying the temporal contrast modulation of the test patterns. Detection and subjective impressions of popping were studied as a function of spatial frequency and temporal wave form; this approach was thought to produce the most significant results. Other experiments examined other possible factors influencing this problem. The author makes suggestions for methods of suppressing the popping phenomenon and recommends directions for further research. This research would most interest those involved with research and design of eye-coupled systems, display designers, and perceptual researchers.

CONTENTS

Summary
Section I: General Introduction
Section II: Experiment 1
    Introduction
    Method
    Results
    Discussion
Section III: Experiment 2
    Introduction
    Method
    Results and discussion
Section IV: Experiment 3
    A demonstration of adaptation to popping

Section V: Experiment 4
   The affect of attentional load on popping

Section VI: Recommendations
   Further research on throughput delay and color

References

Appendix A—Preliminary Experiments

Appendix B—Size and Temporal Waveform Experiments

Appendix C—Adaptation

Appendix D—Attention

61 pp. 6 chapters. Figures, graphs, tables, references, appendices.

20
Bergqvist, Ulf

Video Display Terminals and Health: A Technical and Medical Appraisal of the State of the Art
National Board of Occupational Safety and Health, Sweden, 1984

(special issue of the *Scandinavian Journal of Work, Environment and Health*, vol. 10, supplement 2, 1984; also available as part of the NORD series published by the Nordic Council of Ministers)

This ambitious report presents a comprehensive summary and evaluation of current knowledge about virtually all aspects of the effects of VDTs on the health of users.

The author identifies three causal group distinctions for rating VDT involvement in adverse health effects: direct VDT use, implication of VDT use along with the presence of certain other factors, and no implication of VDT use. In addition, he identifies two "modes" of emphasis in the studies cited, "machine-centered" (hardware originated) and "people-centered" (environmental and psychosocial factors related to the introduction of VDTs). Based on this the report is divided into a section on technical occupational hygiene and one on medical-epidemiological aspects. At some points these two sections discuss the same topics. The first section treats in detail such topics as electromagnetic radiation, and display and lighting characteristics. Workstation design, task design, and task environment are also considered. The second section discusses specific complaints, including eye problems, headaches and stress, skin problems, muscular problems, and adverse pregnancy outcome. This extensively researched, copiously referenced report provides a thorough and balanced presentation which will be invaluable for manufacturers, physicians, designers, managers, legislative bodies, and any other group concerned with VDT health issues. This report was also included in the NORD series published by the Nordic Council of Ministers.

CONTENTS

Introduction

Section I: Technical and Occupational Hygiene Aspects of Video Display Terminals

1. General description of a video display terminal
2. Electromagnetic radiation and fields
3. Ionizing radiation
4. Optical radiation
5. Hertzian radiation and fields
6. Electrostatic fields
7. Sound and noise
8. Display characteristics and readability of text
9. The operator and workstation design
10. Office environment
11. Job design and psychosocial factors

Section II: Medical and Epidemiologic Aspects of Work with Video Display Terminals

12. General comments on performed epidemiologic studies and field surveys
13. Asthenopia and eye strain symptoms
14. Effects of work with video display terminals on measures of eye functions
15. Pathological changes in the eyes
16. Headaches and epilepsy
17. Stress and psychological effects
18. Skin rashes
19. Muscular discomfort
20. Adverse pregnancy outcome

Summary
U.O.V. Bergqvist, B.G. Knave
Technical and occupational hygiene aspects of video display terminals
Medical and epidemiologic aspects of work with video display terminals

References

Appendix 1: Some Relations between the Electromagnetic Measurement Units Used in This Report
Measures related to the energy of a photon
Measures of the electric field strength (E) and the magnetic field strength (B) (or the magnetic field H)
Radiation quantities for ionizing radiation
The relationship between the electrostatic charge and the field
Measurements of optical radiation
References

Appendix 2: A Model Study on the Occurrence of Adverse Pregnancy Outcomes in Clusters of Workers Using Video Display Terminals
Definition of the problem
Model assumptions
Spontaneous abortion
Congenital defects
References

Appendix 3: A Model Study on an Epidemiologic Cohort, Examining Some Complications Due to Temporal Factors

Definition of the problem
Application to an actual study
Model assumptions
Calculations and results
Variations in the assumptions
Conclusions
References

87 pp. 20 chapters in 2 parts. Figures, graphs, tables, references, appendices. (ISSN 0355-3140)

21
Bertin, Jacques

Graphics and Graphic Information-Processing
Walter de Gruyter, 1981

(transaltion by William J. Berg and Paul Scott of Bertin's *La Graphique et le Traitement Graphique de l'Information,* 1977)

This volume uses practical and topical examples to show how data becomes more meaningful, yields a higher level of information, and leads to better decision making when presented in graphic form. Intended for students and professionals in graphic design, but can be very useful for anyone designing computer-generated displays.

Bertin's book examines the potential and limitations of graphic constructions, looks at graphics as a sign system, and presents a matrix analysis of a problem. The text: gives step-by-step instructions in permutation matrices, reorderable networks, ordered tables, and ordered networks in topography and cartography; discusses and illustrates the specificity of graphics, the basis of graphics, differential variables, and the law of visibility; introduces matrix analysis; discusses the apportionment table; and gives applications of matrix analysis. Bertin discusses the uses and limitations of graphic constructions and presents criteria for the evaluation of graphic designs. Through the use of several examples (including maps, matrices, scalograms, image files, arrays, and collections of tables) he implies many of the possibilities for communication using graphics, especially the efficiency of graphic presentation. It is extensively illustrated with figures which clearly show the process from presentation of data to finished graphic presentation of information. The translators have succeeded in creating a smoothly flowing, highly readable book with a useful index, which supplies the French term for each item. Readers, whether novice or expert, should find the questions, suggestions, and recommendations useful.

CONTENTS

A: POSTMORTEM OF AN EXAMPLE

1: The Stages of Decision-Making

2: The Aim of Graphics: A Higher Level of Information

2.1. Useful information
2.2. Information levels
2.3. Measurement of useless constructions

3: The Three Successive Forms of Graphic Application
   3.1. The matrix analysis of a problem
   3.2. Graphic information-processing
   3.3. Graphic communication
   3.4. Outline of work

B: GRAPHIC CONSTRUCTIONS

1: A "Synoptic" of Graphic Constructions

2: Permutation Matrices
   2.1. The reorderable matrix
   2.2. The weighted matrix
   2.3. The image-file
   2.4. The matrix-file
   2.5. The array of curves

3: Ordered Tables
   3.1. Tables with 1, 2 or 3 characteristics
   3.2. Superimpositions and collections of tables

4: Reorderable Networks

5: Ordered Networks: Topography and Cartography
   5.1. Information provided by a map
   5.2. The base map
   5.3. Cartography with one ordered characteristic
   5.4. Cartography with several characteristics

C: THE GRAPHIC SIGN SYSTEM (A SEMIOLOGICAL APPROACH TO GRAPHICS)

1: Specificity of Graphics

2: The Bases of Graphics

3: Variables of the Image: the Plane, Size and Value

4: Differential Variables

5: The Law of Visibility

6: Summary

D: THE MATRIX ANALYSIS OF A PROBLEM AND THE CONCEPTION OF A DATA TABLE

1: The Apportionment Table

2: The Homogeneity Schema

3: The Pertinency Table

4: Applications of Matrix Analysis

CONCLUSION

273 pp. 4 chapters. Photographs, figures, graphs, tables, general index. ISBN 3-11-008868-1. (ISBN 3-11-006901-6)

22
Bertin, Jacques

Semiology of Graphics: Diagrams, Networks, Maps
University of Wisconsin Press, 1983

(translation by William J. Berg of Bertin's *Sémiologie graphique,* 1973)

Investigates the sign-systems of graphic design by a detailed examination of the x, y, and z components of a graph. Bertin then discusses the xyz construction of the graphic image from the perspective of image variables, and also studies the permutations of the rows and columns of the xyz matrix, the visual form of information processing.

This work presents a comprehensive theory of the sign-systems used in graphic representation and the functions of such systems in graphic design. Approximately one-half of the text presents the theoretical framework for the author's approach to graphics, and the remainder examines applications of his semiological system. This recent (1983) English translation of Bertin's 1967 *Sémiologie graphique* was sparked by widening interest in semiology. In that tradition, Bertin's book is a highly theoretical, structuralist work, based implicitly on the structuralist belief in universally applicable "deep structures" in the human mind and on McLuhan's famous dictum that "the medium is the message." In part I, Bertin proceeds from this theoretical perspective and poses several fundamental questions on the nature of the graphic representation of information in the computer age. Graphic representation, specifically the "reorderable matrix," the permutable graphic construction xyz, is the answer. The author explains the power and applicability of the reorderable matrix in his "matrix theory of graphics," and defines graphics in terms of the construction. Bertin maintains that human logic is based on the visual properties afforded only by the xyz construction which represents the natural and immediate perception of the relationships among three dimensions. With his theoretical foundations meticulously examined and explicated, Bertin turns in part II to the applications of the graphic sign-system analyzed in part I. The author covers problems associated with multiple-component diagrams and graphic information processing, briefly treats complex networks, and ends the work with a lengthy chapter on one- and multiple-component maps, including detailed discussion of projections, scales, accuracy in graphic representation, ways to avoid graphic error, and the cartographic problems of multiple-component maps. Despite the challenges posed by the theoretical nature of part I, the author's penetrating insights justify the difficulties. Part II applies Bertin's principles with admirable lucidity and scope. More than half of the book consists of judiciously chosen and well-produced illustrations which delineate both the theoretical and applied aspects of Bertin's semiological approach. Ambitious in design and execution, the entire work should be of interest to graphic artists and designers, including computer users, as well as cognitive psychologists.

CONTENTS
    Foreword
        Howard Wainer
    Preface to the English edition
        Jacques Bertin

PART ONE: SEMIOLOGY OF THE GRAPHIC SIGN-SYSTEM
General theory
Definition of graphics
Annotated table of contents to part one:
I. Analysis of the information
II. The properties of the graphic system
III. The rules of the graphic system

I: Analysis of the Information
A. The invariant and the components
B. The number of components
C. The length of the components
D. The level of organization of the components

II: The Properties of the Graphic System
A. The scope of the graphic system
B. The plane
C. The retinal variables
Table of properties of the retinal variables

III: The Rules of the Graphic System
A. The basic graphic problem
B. Image theory: efficiency
C. Three functions of graphic representation
D. General rules of construction
E. General rules of legibility (or rules of separation)
Summary of the rules of legibility

PART TWO: UTILIZATION OF THE GRAPHIC SIGN-SYSTEM
Classification of graphic problems

I: Diagrams
A. Diagrams involving two components
B. Diagrams involving three components
C. Problems involving more than three components

II: Networks
Construction and transformation of a network
Application of networks to classifications
Trees
Areas, inclusive relationships
Perspective drawings

III: Maps
A. External geographic identification
B. Internal geographic identification
C. Maps involving one component (the geographic component)
D. Maps involving two components
E. Cartographic problems involving more than two components

Appendix: Area-Radius Table-Graph

Index

415 pp. 6 chapters in 2 parts. Drawings, charts, maps, graphs, general index, appendices. ISBN 0-299-09060-4.

23
Biberman, Lucien M.
(ed.)

collection

Perception of Displayed Information
Plenum, 1973

(from the *Optical Physics and Engineering* series, William L. Wolfe, series ed.)

A collection which attempts to formulate a theory about how information is transferred from a visual source to an observer.

This volume presents a method to calculate user perception. It provides a survey of the perception of displayed information and a review of the literature which covers seven decades. Topics discussed are: image quality and observer performance; signal-to-noise ratio; image sampling (one- and two-dimensional); and display systems. The editor provides an introduction to each chapter that relates it to previous chapters and to material yet to be presented. The final chapter summarizes the work of all contributors. It also furnishes psychophysical evidence to support the consolidated theory concerning information transfer from displays to the user. The text is accessible to advanced undergraduate students in electrical engineering, human engineering, and psychology, as well as to practicing electro-optical system designers.

CONTENTS

CHAPTER 1: INTRODUCTION
  Lucien M. Biberman

CHAPTER 2: IMAGE QUALITY
  Lucien M. Biberman

2.1: Editor's Introduction

2.2: The Quality of Continuous Tone Images
  2.2.1. Concepts and definitions
  2.2.2. Factors related to geometrical and physiological optics
  2.2.3. Experimental programs for studying the informative content of images

2.3: Line-Scanned Imagery
  2.3.1. Definitions, confusions, and general problems
  2.3.2. Human factors experiments with line scan imagery

2.4: Scale and Time

2.5: Bibliography

CHAPTER 3: IMAGE QUALITY AND OBSERVER
PERFORMANCE
  Harry L. Snyder

3.1: Editor's Introduction

3.2: Notation

3.3: Photometric Display Quantification

3.4: Human Performance Evaluation Considerations

3.5: Individual Display Parameters and Observer Performance

3.6: The Modulation Transfer Function Area

3.7: Evaluation of the MTFA for Photographic Imagery

3.8: The MTFA and Raster-Scan Displays

3.9: Conclusions and Cautions

3.10: Editor's Postscript

CHAPTER 4: ANALYSIS OF NOISE-REQUIRED CONTRAST AND
MODULATION IN IMAGE-DETECTING AND DISPLAY
SYSTEMS
   Alvin D. Schnitzler

4.1: Introduction

4.2: Historical Review of the Signal-to-Noise Ratio Theory of Visual
Performance

4.3: The Ideal Photon Counter Model of an Image-Detecting System
   4.3.1. Elementary decision theory
   4.3.2. Output signal-to-noise ratio
   4.3.3. Detective quantum efficiency
   4.3.4. Noise-required input contrast
   4.3.5. Noise-required input contrast of the visual system

4.4: Modifications of the Ideal Photon Counter Model
   4.4.1. Fourier analysis of spatial dispersion
   4.4.2. Noise-required input modulation

4.5: Noise Power Density Spectral Analysis

4.6: Editor's Postscript

CHAPTER 5: RECENT PSYCHOPHYSICAL EXPERIMENTS AND
THE DISPLAY SIGNAL-TO-NOISE RATIO CONCEPT
   F.A. Rosell, R.H. Willson

5.1: Editor's Introduction

5.2: Introduction

5.3: The Elementary Model

5.4: Effects of Finite Apertures

5.5: Levels of Discrimination

5.6: Psychophysical Experimentation—Aperiodic and Periodic Images

5.7: Psychophysical Experiments; Recognition and Identification

5.8: Prediction of Electrooptical Sensor Resolution

5.9: Editor's Postscript

CHAPTER 6: IMAGE REPRODUCTION BY A LINE RASTER
PROCESS
   Otto H. Schade, Sr.

6.1: Editor's Introduction

6.2: Notation

6.3: Raster Processes
   6.3.1. Raster constant and frequency
   6.3.2. Carrier wave and line structure
   6.3.3. System response to sine wave test patterns

6.4: Raster Line Frequencies and MTF Combinations for Low Spurious Response

6.5: System Design

6.6: Noise in a Raster Process

6.7: Cathode Ray Tubes for Visual Display of TV Images

    6.7.1. The Gaussian spot

    6.7.2. The composite spot of CRT's

    6.7.3. Measured MTF's of high-resolution CRT's

    6.7.4. Specifications for display CRT's

    6.7.5. Flicker

    6.7.6. System requirements for long-persistence picture displays

    6.7.7. MTF measurements of long-persistence phosphors

CHAPTER 7: THE ALIASING PROBLEMS IN TWO-DIMENSIONAL SAMPLED IMAGERY

    Richard Legault

7.1: Introduction

7.2: A Brief Review of One-Dimensional Sampling

7.3: Electrooptical Sampled Image Systems

7.4: Analytic Representation of Two-Dimensional Image Sampling

7.5: Effects of Aliasing on Sampled Images

7.6: Best Sampling Lattices

7.7: System Design Considerations for Sampled Image Systems

Appendix

CHAPTER 8: A SUMMARY

    Lucien M. Biberman

8.1: An Overview of Image Quality

8.2: A Few Last Remarks

REFERENCES

INDEX

345 pp. 8 chapters. Drawings, photographs, figures, charts, graphs, tables, mathematical formulae, models, general index, references. ISBN 0-306-30724-3.

24

**Biberman, Lucien M.
Nudelman, Sol
(eds.)**

collection

Photoelectronic Imaging Devices, Volume 2: Devices and Their Evaluation

Plenum, 1971

(from the *Optical Physics and Engineering* series, William L. Wolfe, series ed.)

Describes the characteristics and operation of photoelectronic devices as well as methods for the laboratory evaluation of these devices.

This volume opens with a discussion of low-light video-imaging systems, followed by a description of image-intensifier units. These units provide an image of a scene which is superior to that perceived by the eye alone. Other topics discussed in this volume include: principal sensor parameters and their measurement; image converters and direct-viewing devices; special sensors; and an evaluation of tube performance in video cameras. A number of signal-generating devices are reviewed: cascade photoelectric, x-ray, and image orthicon tubes; new image isocon tubes; tubes using high-gain, electron-imaging, charge-storage targets; tubes using silicon-diode arrays; vidicon and return-beam vidicon tubes; plumbicon tubes; and multi-element self-scanned mosaic sensors. Intended for researchers and students in photoelectronics. The first volume of this two volume set presents discussions of the fundamental principles and electronic processes involved in the operation of photoelectronic image-forming sensors and describes the optical conditions under which they operate.

CONTENTS

Contributors

Preface

Contents of Volume 1

Chapter 1: Introduction
Lucien M. Biberman, Sol Nudelman
Organization of volume II
References

PART I: PRINCIPAL SENSOR PARAMETERS AND THEIR MEASUREMENT

Chapter 2: The Television Camera Tube as a System Component
A. Danforth Cope, Sidney Gray, Edwin C. Hutter
I. The camera tube as a system component
II. Properties and functions of the television camera tube
References

Chapter 3: Evaluation of Direct-View Imaging Devices
J.A. Hall
I. Introduction
II. Photocathode responses
III. Spectral response
IV. Brightness gain and background
V. Radiation sources for image-quality tests
VI. The modulation transfer function
VII. Conclusion
References

Chapter 4: Evaluation of Signal-Generating Image Tubes
J.A. Hall
I. Introduction
II. The camera tube and its system
III. Measurement of photoelectric response
IV. Signal versus irradiance
V. Measurements of internal gain
VI. Measurement of signal-to-noise ratio
VII. Measurement of a spatial modulation transfer function for camera tubes
VIII. Measurement of response to changing scenes
IX. Relation between objective and subjective measurements
References

PART II: IMAGE INTENSIFIERS, CONVERTERS, AND DIRECT-VIEWING DEVICES

Chapter 5: Cascade Image Intensifiers
   G.A. Morton, A.D. Schnitzler
   I. Foreword - History of the development of image intensifiers (up to about 1960)
   II. Cascade image intensifiers
   References

Chapter 6: Photoelectric Image Intensifiers
   J.D. McGee
   I. Introduction
   II. Electron-image recording
   III. Photocathode-phosphor cascade image intensifier
   IV. The cascade intensifier tube
   V. The number of cascade intensifier stages
   VI. Electrostatic focusing tubes
   VII. TSE image multiplier
   References

Chapter 7: X-Ray Image Intensifiers
   B. Combée, P.J.M. Botden, W. Kuhl
   I. X-ray radiology to date
   II. X-ray intensifiers today and tomorrow
   References

Chapter 8: The Channel Image Intensifier
   C.E. Catchpole
   I. Introduction
   II. Discrete dynode electron multipliers
   III. The continuous-resistive-strip channel multiplier
   IV. Channel-multiplier manufacturing techniques
   V. Operating parameters of single-channel multipliers
   VI. Uses of single-channel multipliers
   VII. Uses of microchannel plates in imaging
   References

PART III: SIGNAL-GENERATING IMAGE TUBES

Chapter 9: The Image Orthicon
   R.W. Redington
   I. Introduction
   II. Image section
   III. Reading beam
   IV. Storage target
   V. Possibilities for improving low light level performance

Chapter 10: The New Image Isocon—Its Performance Compared to the Image Orthicon
   E.M. Musselman
   I. Introduction
   II. Beam separation
   III. Image isocon setup and adjustment
   IV. Performance of the image isocon
   V. Conclusion
   References

Chapter 11: Camera Tubes Employing High-Gain Electron-Imaging
Charge-Storage Targets
 G.W. Goetze, A.B. Laponsky
 I. Introduction
 II. Physics of the SEC layer
 III. Application of the SEC target to television camera tubes
 IV. Special experiments with the SEC target
 V. Applications of the SEC camera tubes
 VI. Summary
 Appendix—Condensed data on five SEC camera tubes

Chapter 12: Early Stages in the Development of Camera Tubes
Employing the Silicon-Diode Array as an Electron-Imaging Charge-
Storage Tube
 G.W. Goetze, A.B. Laponsky
 I. Introduction
 II. The silicon diode array target
 III. Silicon-diode array target
 IV. Conclusions
 References

Chapter 13: Introduction to the Vidicon Family of Tubes
 R.W. Redington
 I. Introduction
 II. Response
 III. Response time
 IV. Transfer characteristics
 V. Resolution
 References

Chapter 14: The Plumbicon
 E.H. Stupp, R.S. Levitt
 I. Physical properties of the Plumbicon
 II. Operating characteristics of the Plumbicon
 References

Chapter 15: The Silicon-Diode-Array Camera Tube
 Merton H. Crowell, Edward F. Labuda
 I. Introduction
 II. Operating principles of the diode-array camera tube
 III. Sensitivity and resolution capabilities of a diode-array target
 IV. Modifications of the basic target structure
 V. Resistive sea structure
 VI. Miscellaneous topics
 VII. Conclusion
 References

Chapter 16: Electron Optics and Signal Readout of High-Definition
Return-Beam Vidicon Cameras
 Otto H. Schade, Sr.
 I. Introduction
 II. Electron optics and modulation transfer functions
 III. Modulation transfer functions of camera components
 IV. The readout electron optic
 V. Operational characteristics of high definition cameras
 VI. Conclusion
 References

Chapter 17: Theory Operation and Performance of High-Resolution Return-Beam Vidicon Cameras—A Comparison with High-Resolution Photography

> *Otta H. Schade, Sr.*
> I. Introduction
> II. Modulation transfer functions (MTF)
> III. Current limits
> IV. Signal-transfer functions
> V. The readout transfer function
> VI. Signal-to-noise ratios (SNR)
> VII. Overall transfer functions of television camera
> VII. Photographic film
> IX. Comparison of high-definition vidicon camera and photographic film
> X. Detection efficiency
> XI. Conclusions
> References

Chapter 18: The High-Resolution Return-Beam Vidicon with Electrical Input

> *M.J. Cantella*
> I. Introduction
> II. Operation as a scan converter
> III. Conclusions
> References

Chapter 19: Multielement Self-Scanned Mosaic Sensors

> *P.K. Weimer, W.S. Pike, G. Sadasiv, F.V. Shallcross, L. Meray-Horvath*
> I. Introduction
> II. Principles of digital scanning of sensor arrays
> III. A 256 × 256 element thin-film image sensor with integrated decoders
> IV. A novel self-scanned photodiode array
> V. Summary and conclusions
> References

PART IV: SPECIAL SENSORS

Chapter 20: Special Sensors

> *James A. Hall*
> I. Introduction
> II. The thermicon
> III. Directly viewed infrared sensor
> IV. Far-vacuum-UV sensor
> V. The image dissector
> VI. Electronography
> References

Chapter 21: The Spectracon

> *J.D. McGee*
> I. Introduction
> II. The spectracon
> References

PART V: EVALUATION

Chapter 22: Television Camera Tube Performance Data and Calculations

Frederick A. Rosell
I. Introduction
II. Image intensifiers
III. Lead oxide vidicons
IV. The vidicon
V. The SEC camera tube
VI. The image orthicon
VII. The image isocon
VIII. The silicon-EBIR camera tube
IX. Low-light-level camera comparisons
Index

584 pp. 22 chapters in 4 parts. Photographs, figures, graphs, tables, mathematical formulae, general index, references. ISBN 0-306-37082-4.

Blackman, Harold S.   *SEE UNDER ID 285, 286*

25
Blinn, James F.   **Computer Display of Curved Surfaces**
University Microfilms International, 1979

(Ph.D. dissertation, Department of Computer Science, University of Utah, 1978)

Discusses a scan line based algorithm for rapidly generating computer images and examines models for enhancing image realism.

The scan line based algorithm is most significantly characterized by its ability to reduce the computation time required for generating computer images. It accomplishes this by calculating the intensity values of a few strategic points—rather than of all points—and then interpolates the intensities between them. The mathematics required for understanding these algorithms are discussed in chapters two through four. Specific topics covered in these chapters include the geometric operations necessary for surface representations, a review of bivariate functions, the operations necessary for drawing parametrically defined surfaces in a scan line fashion, and a review of some standard numerical methods for solving the necessary equations. The algorithm itself is discussed in chapter five, along with a slower but more accurate method that finds the values of all picture elements. Methods that use more accurate models of light reflection, and thus enhance image realism, are covered in chapter six; chapter seven examines a technique for simulating roughened surfaces (such as an orange peel). Here, developments in digital image systhesis are discussed in terms of their application to the production of more realistic images of textured surfaces. The concluding chapter offers the author's summary of the discussed methods, and provides his observations on the future of image realism. Because this thesis discusses methods that both improve performance and enhance realism of computer generated images, most graphics programmers concerned with simulating three-dimensional images would find it of interest.

CONTENTS

Abstract

Chapter 1: Introduction
    Methods for rendering curved surfaces
    Surface property simulation
    Rastering effects

Chapter 2: Mathematical Basis of Curves and Surfaces
    Types of surface representation
    Geometrical operation necessary for drawing
    Examples
    Properties of bivariate functions

Chapter 3: Scan Line Based Algorithms
    Overview
    Polygon based algorithms
    Quadratic surface algorithms
    Parametric surface algorithm (introduction)
    Summary

Chapter 4: Useful Numerical Algorithms
    Finding zeros in a function
    Finding local maxima of functions

Chapter 5: Scan Line Parametric Surface Algorithm
    Accurate algorithm
    Fast algorithm
    Interpolation schemes

Chapter 6: Intensity Calculations
    Simulation of surface reflective properties
    Lighting models

Chapter 7: Elimination of Rastering Effects
    Mathematical background
    Image filtering
    Texture filtering

Chapter 8: Summary and Conclusions
    Scan line curved surface algorithm
    Texture mapping
    Simulation of surface reflection properties
    Lighting models
    Future frontiers of realism .

167 pp. 8 chapters. Photographs, figures, mathematical formulae, algorithms, abstract formalisms, models, references.

26
Borgefors, Gunilla

technical report

An Improved Version of the Chamfer Matching Algorithm
1983

(report number FOA-C-30344-E1; National Defense Research Institute, Linkoping, Sweden; November 1983)

Chamfer matching is a method of "finding the best fit between the edges in the two different images." This report discusses modifications and extensions of the original implementation.

This report details chamfer matching. The original work on the process is discussed and an explanation of the advantages of this technique over more traditional methods is provided. Among these advantages are easy implementation, relatively fast processing time, and high resistance to noise. The technique is useful in a variety of areas including the analysis of remote-sensor and satellite data, map and terrain matching, navigation, photointerpretation, target detection, and precision analysis. Three new versions—Chamfer 34, Euclidean, and City Block—are discussed and analyzed relative to each other and the "standard" chamfer algorithm. Chamfer 34 is viewed as providing markedly better results. This report provides a variety of useful information for the researcher in the fields of pattern matching and visual processing. The text is clear and all points are amply illustrated and diagrammed. An excellent extension of chamfer matching theory.

CONTENTS

Document sheet, English

Document sheet, Swedish

1: Introduction

2: Preprocessing
    2.1. Preprocessing of the map
    2.2. Preprocessing of the aerial photograph

3: Methods Used
    3.1. Distance metrics
    3.2. Averages

4: Comparison between the Methods
    4.1. Two parameters
    4.2. Three parameters

5: Comparison with Human Matching

6: Further Comparison between the Methods

7: Conclusions

8: References

36 pp. 8 chapters. Figures, tables, algorithms, references.

27
Bosman, I.D.
(ed.)

technical report

Modern Display Technologies and Applications
1982

(report number AGARD-AR-169; Avionics Panel of AGARD; sponsored by Advisory Group for Aerospace Research and Development; October 1982)

This report from the Advisory Group for Aerospace Research and Development (AGARD) to NATO outlines the state of the art of both emerging and established display technologies and assesses their applicability to military avionics.

Assembled from the efforts of an international working group, this paper reviews the major display methods from established technologies using cathode-ray tubes (CRTs) to the more experimental electrochemical designs. For each type of visual display the authors discuss history, principles of operation, physical and visual characteristics, addressing/driving and system interface solutions, and the maturity of current applications. Increasing sophistication and speed of miltary aircraft necessitates an increasing information load on the pilot. The goal stated here is to synthesize and display electronic sensor input in a form that is within human perceptual limits and "matches the pilot's inner representation of the aircraft," without distorting the original data. Environmental and human factors in cockpit design, such as viewing angle and elimination of toxic materials from display panels, are also discussed. Specific design factors such as helmet-mounted vs. panel-mounted displays and design considerations for entire mission management systems are briefly considered.

CONTENTS

PREFACE

CHAPTER 1: INTRODUCTION TO THE REPORT
     D. Bosman

References Chapter 1

CHAPTER 2: AN ENGINEERING VIEW ON VISION AND DISPLAYS
     D. Bosman

2.1: The Technical Factors Affecting the Perception of Displayed Data
          2.1.1. Optical factors
          2.1.2. Contrast definitions
          2.1.3. Spatial frequency response of optical systems
          2.1.4. Spatial frequencies, frame rate and video bandwidth

2.2: Sampling and Addressing
          2.2.1. The cathode ray tube
          2.2.2. The matrix display
          2.2.3. Line at a time addressing
          2.2.4. Other addressing schemes

2.3: Human Factors Affecting Display Design and Use
          2.3.1. Resolution, MTF
          2.3.2. Scanning
          2.3.3. Spatial and temporal luminance variations
          2.3.4. Legibility
          2.3.5. Environmental effects on legibility

2.4. Color in Display
    2.4.1. The value of color in displays
    2.4.2. Color characteristics of displays
References Chapter 2
CHAPTER 3: TECHNOLOGIES
3.1: Cathode Ray Tubes
    G. Hunt
    3.1.1. Historical survey
    3.1.2. Principles of operation
    3.1.3. Physical characteristics
    3.1.4. Addressing/driving
    3.1.5. System interface
    3.1.6. Visual characteristics
    3.1.7. State of development
    3.1.8. Special CRTs
References Chapter 3.1.

3.2: Vacuum-Fluorescent Tubes
    G. Hunt
    3.2.1. Historical survey
    3.2.2. Principles of operation
    3.2.3. Physical characteristics
    3.2.4. Addressing/driving and system interface
    3.2.5. Visual characteristics
    3.2.6. State of development
References Chapter 3.2

3.3: Liquid Crystal Displays
    B. Gurman
    3.3.1. Historical survey
    3.3.2. Principles of operation
    3.3.3. Other physical characteristics
    3.3.4. Addressing/driving of non-smectic displays
    3.3.5. Visual characteristics
    3.3.6. State of development
    3.3.7. Summary
References Chapter 3.3

3.4: Large Area Gas Discharge Displays or Plasma Displays
    J.P. Michel
    3.4.1. Historical survey
    3.4.2. General principles of operation
    3.4.3. AC plasma displays
    3.4.4. DC plasma displays
References Chapter 3.4

3.5: Light Emitting Diodes
    D. Price, K. Burnette
    3.5.1. Introduction
    3.5.2. Principles of operation
    3.5.3. Physical characteristics
    3.5.4. Addressing/driving
    3.5.5. System interface
    3.5.6. Visual characteristics
    3.5.7. State of development

References Chapter 3.5

3.6: Electroluminescent Displays
   B. Gurman
   3.6.1. Historical survey
   3.6.2. Principles of operation
   3.6.3. Physical characteristics
   3.6.4. Addressing/driving
   3.6.5. System interface
   3.6.6. Visual characteristics
   3.6.7. Other EL devices
   3.6.8. State of development

References Chapter 3.6

3.7: Electrochemical Displays
   G. Meier
   3.7.1. Historical survey
   3.7.2. Principles of operation
   3.7.3. Addressing
   3.7.4. Visual characteristics
   3.7.5. State of development

References Chapter 3.7

3.8: Other Display Technologies
   G. Meier
   3.8.1. Ferroelectric displays with PLZT
   3.8.2. Ferroelectric displays with KDP
   3.8.3. Magneto-optic displays
   3.8.4. Magnetic particle displays

References Chapter 3.8

CHAPTER 4: APPLICATIONS
   W. Hollister

4.1: Classifications
   4.1.1. Video
   4.1.2. Vector-graphic
   4.1.3. Message
   4.1.4. Discrete

4.2: Head-Up Displays (HUD)

4.3: Head-Down Displays (HDD)

4.4: Helmet Mounted Systems

4.5: Mission Management Displays (MMD)

4.6: Keyboard Displays

4.7: Alphanumeric Modules

4.8: Summary

References Chapter 4

CHAPTER 5: MODERN DISPLAY TECHNOLOGY ASSESSMENT
   W. Hollister

5.1: Measures of Performance
   5.1.1. Maximum luminance
   5.1.2. Maximum reflectance ratio
   5.1.3. Contrast
   5.1.4. Efficiency
   5.1.5. Dimming ratio

5.1.6. Typical resolution

5.1.7. Maximum number of pixels per picture height

5.1.8. Gray scales

5.1.9. Viewing angle

5.1.10. Current color capability

5.1.11. Storage temperature range

5.1.12. Uncompensated operating temperature range

5.1.13. Current system cost (per pixel)

5.1.14. Projected cost (per pixel)

5.1.15. Operating life

5.2: Capability of Technology

5.3: Requirements for Applications

5.4: Technology Potential

5.5. Summary

Glossary of Terms

List of Abbreviations

Appendix 1: List of Working Group Members

218 pp. 5 chapters. Drawings, photographs, figures, tables, glossary, appendix.

28

Boyce, P.R.

technical report

Lighting and Visual Display Units
1981

(report number ECRC/M1448; Electricity Council Research Centre; June 1981)

A study of lighting problems encountered in VDU environments and possible methods of alleviating such problems.

This brief study identifies the most common aspects of the visual environment which often cause operator's complaints. These complaints are classified by symptoms which are: ocular, visual, systemic or behavioral. The causes of such complaints are grouped into those types which are: inherent in the VDU; associated with the environment of the VDU; or related to the operators. The author follows classification of problems with a discussion of the cause of and solutions to each of the identified problem areas. Though brief, this study offers incisive suggestions for elimination of actual and potential VDU environment problems.

15 pp. 6 chapters. Photographs, figures, references.

29
Braunstein, Myron L.

Depth Perception through Motion
Academic Press, 1976

(from the *Academic Press Series in Cognition and Perception*, Edward C. Carterette, Morton P. Friedman, series eds.)

A technical review of research on depth perception through motion.

The first chapter presents a general introduction on depth perception in philosophy and some of the early discoveries in perception of depth through motion. The work attempts to explain how the three-dimensional perception of depth is acquired, in spite of the retinal image itself being only two-dimensional. Two concepts which allow an explanation are cue and gradient, which are described in some detail. The geometrical considerations necessary in the study of depth perception in dynamic environments are discussed next, using graphic rather than mathematical illustrations. Some of the mathematics are included in the appendix. This highly accessible background material is designed to introduce the nonspecialist to the concepts presented in the following research-oriented chapters. The book next covers the major research areas and the current knowledge base: "dynamic factors leading to perception of depth, slant judgements in dynamic displays and factors affecting the accuracy of perceived direction of rotary motion." This includes both static and dynamic slant perception and a model of the perception of rotary motion. The conclusion presents a new theoretical approach to perceptual processing, wherein perception is related to other human problem solving skills and perceptual processes are regarded as heuristic processes. Each chapter includes a summary, along with conclusions drawn from the information presented. Many of the stimulus materials used in the author's research used computer animation techniques. An appendix, with mathematical formulae and actual programming examples, is provide for researchers who wish to produce the materials themselves. The text is fairly technical in nature and is primarily intended for use by researchers and graduate students interested in depth perception in dynamic environments. It is also of interest to specialists in other fields in which depth perception is a concern.

CONTENTS
Preface

1: The Paradox of Depth Perception
    The eye-camera analogy
    Other problems with the analogy
    The cue concept
    Conclusion

2: Early Observations: Illusion of Motion in Depth
    The windmill and fan illusions
    The rotating trapezoid
    Lissajous figures
    The stereokinetic effect
    Conclusion

3: The Optic Array
    The projection plane
    Perspective gradients
    Rigid motions in three-dimensional space
    Conclusion

4: Transformations Leading to the Perception of Depth
    Rotations about the x or y axis
    Rotations about the z axis
    Translations along the x and y axes
    Translations along the z axis
    Conclusion

5: Slant Perception
    Static slant perception
    Dynamic slant perception
    Conclusion

6: Perceived Direction of Rotary Motion
    Shadow and computer projections
    Direct observation of rotating figures
    Combining the two lines of research
    A model of the perception of rotary motion
    Evaluation of the model
    Conclusion

7: Heuristic Processes in Perception
    Perception as problem solving
    Heuristic processes in problem solving
    Reasons for using heuristic processes
    Heuristics and logical consistency
    Heuristic processes in depth perception
    Heuristic processes in the perception of rotary motion
    Relationship to other theories
    Conclusion

Appendix: Computer Animation
    Graphic displays
    Setting up an animation laboratory
    Computational procedures
    Programming example
    References
    Index

200 pp. 7 chapters. Drawings, photographs, figures, graphs, tables, models, general index, references, appendix. ISBN 0-12-127950-2.

30
Brinton, Willard C.   **Graphic Methods for Presenting Facts**
Ayer Company, 1980

(reprint of the 1914 edition published by Engineering Magazine
Company in their *Works Management Library* series, currently from
the *Dimensions of Accounting Theory and Practice* series, Richard P.
Brief, advisory ed.)

A handbook (reprinted from the 1914 edition) intended for use by the
non-technical reader as a guide to the preparation of graphs or charts to
represent information.

Seventy years old, this text is of historical as well as current interest.
The techniques and methods presented here are timeless and the text is
highly readable, addressing a wide audience. Intended for use as a
handbook, material is organized to be accessible. Each chapter covers a
specific type of chart and provides a complete guide for the preparation
of a chart representing detailed facts or data. Numerous examples of
illustrations are provided. Anyone who represents facts graphically will
find this book valuable, especially those in government, business,
advertising, natural sciences, engineering, or statistics. Statistical
techniques have been deliberately omitted from the work. The
sophisticated user will want to consult more recent works such as
Cleveland's *Elements of Graphical Data*, Tufte's *Visual Display of
Qualitative Information* or *Graphical Methods of Data Analysis* by
Chambers et al.

CONTENTS
Chapter I. Component parts
Chapter II. Simple comparisons
Chapter III. Simple comparisons involving time
Chapter IV. Time charts
Chapter V. Curve plotting
Chapter VI. Curve plotting continued
Chapter VII. Comparison of curves
Chapter VIII. Component parts shown by curves
Chapter IX. Cumulative or mass curves
Chapter X. Frequency curves. Correlation
Chapter XI. Map presentations
Chapter XII. Maps and pins
Chapter XIII. Curves for the executive
Chapter XIV. Records for the executive
Chapter XV. Corporation financial reports
Chapter XVI. General methods
Chapter XVII. A few cautions

*371 pp. 17 chapters. Drawings, photographs, figures, charts, maps,
graphs, general index. ISBN 0-405-13504-1.*

31
Brisson, David W.
(ed.)

Hypergraphics: Visualizing Complex Relationships in Art, Science and Technology
Westview Press, 1978

collection

(based in part on a symposium held at the annual conference of the American Association for the Advancement of Science; Washington, D.C.; February 1978; vol. 24 in the *AAAS Selected Symposia Series*)

A collection of papers by hypergraphic "enthusiasts": artists, sculptors, mathematicians, and computer scientists. Some of the authors in this volume have shown their works, including computer-generated films, at various symposia, particularly the hypergraphics exhibit featured at the 1978 AAAS meeting.

This collection represents an interesting cross-fertilization of ideas from professional groups that would not ordinarily have much contact. The authors' common interest is in exploring nontraditional visual design—in particular, "the visual, basically geometrical transformation of information"—and in exploring hypergraphics as a method of "seeing" the non-visualizable. The first paper outlines descriptive geometry from its first applications by the ancient Egyptian and Greek builders and engineers. Next, aspects of dimensionality as a part of the space-time continuum are discussed by a metallurgist. The third paper focuses on the application of hypergraphics to problems in urban and regional planning, where variables related in a complex fashion can be better mapped onto curved hypersurfaces and higher dimensional Euclidean spaces than the conventional Cartesian coordinates. An architect then considers the evolution of human consciousness and aesthetic sense as rooted in the symmetries of nature, from bilateral to spherical. Brisson's and Noll's presentations, originally offered with slides and movies, explore four-dimensional visualization. The use of real-time computer graphics which show three-dimensional slices of hypercubes in various rotations is presented as a means of exploring the topology of 4-space. An artist follows linguistic theory in generating a visual syntax and exploring the perceptual process through 2-d representations of 3-d structures in which ambiguous information creates illusion. The construction of 4-d analogs of the impossible triangle and the false assumptions that allow optical illusions to work as visual puns are explained. The topics treated in this volume demonstrate the use of computer and high-tech construction methods to explore the far fringes of visual experience. Despite the mathematical treatment, this is a useful work for the mathematically naive.

CONTENTS

About the Editor and Authors

Introduction
David W. Brisson

1: Geometry in Applied Science and Engineering
Steve M. Slaby

2: Speculations on Dimensionality, Valence and Aggregation
Cyril Stanley Smith
Abstract
Introduction
On things and environments
Polyhedra don't exist
Dimensionality
Dimensionality with interlock
Crystals
On stability
On time
References

3: Algorithms, Structures and Models
Arthur L. Loeb

4: Complex Relations in Urban and Regional Planning: An Application of Hypergraphics
C. Ernesto S. Lindgren
Introduction
The basic problem
First method
Second method
Third method
Conclusion
References

5: Seeing Order: Systems and Symbols
Anne Griswold Tyng

6: Visual Comprehension of *n*-Dimensions
David W. Brisson

7: Displaying *n*-Dimensional Hyperobjects by Computer
A. Michael Noll
Introduction
Rotation
Projection
Hyperobjects
Computer technique
Examples
Discussion
References

8: Real-Time Computer Graphics Analysis of Figures in Four-Space
Thomas F. Banchoff, Charles M. Strauss

9: Randomness and Order in Sculptural Form
Harriet E. Brisson

10: Ambiguous Structures
J.M. Yturralde

11: An Impossible Four-Dimensional Illusion
Scott E. Kim
Introduction
The impossible triangle
Elements of construction
The 3-d cube
Vision
The 4-d cube

Elements of construction
The impossible skew quadrilateral
Conclusions
Bibliography

239 pp. 11 chapters. Drawings, photographs, algorithms, models, references. ISBN 0-89158-292-4.

32
Britton, Edward G.

technical report

A Methodology for the Ergonomic Design of Interactive Computer Graphic Systems, and Its Application to Crystallography
1977

(report number UNC-TR-77-011; Department of Computer Science, University of North Carolina; 30 November 1977)

Details a methodology for the ergonomic design of graphic system interfaces and presents a system for determining the structures of macromolecules developed using these methods.

This dissertation presents a systematic approach to the development of man-machine interfaces. Roughly half of the work deals with specific implementations which use the principles discussed. The remaining portions of the text deal with the methodology used and the theory behind it. Linguistic and psychological principles receive thorough treatment within the framework of designs for graphic system and simple system interfaces. Details discussed include action syntax and vocabulary, picture syntax and vocabulary, frustration, confusion, boredom, panic, and discomfort. System interface design procedures which take these various factors into account are discussed in light of the sample system. Useful for anyone interested in the methodic design of system-user interfaces, the methodology presented in this work will be especially helpful to designers of expert systems and system "tools"—complex library programs for the non-programmer. While the sample interface design describes a graphic system of limited interest, applications are possible in any area requiring human-computer interaction.

CONTENTS
1: INTRODUCTION
2: CRYSTALLOGRAPHY
2.1: Scope and Orientation
2.2: Overview of Diffraction and Refinement
    2.2.1. Diffraction data
    2.2.2. The phase problem
    2.2.3. Refinement
2.3: Trial Structure Determination
    2.3.1. Iterative fitting
    2.3.2. Molecular model
    2.3.3. Contour maps
    2.3.4. Viewing map and molecule together
    2.3.5. Viewbox

2.3.6. Fitting a residue
2.3.7. Summary of trial structure determination

3: OTHER CRYSTALLOGRAPHY SYSTEMS

4: GRAE ARCHITECTURE

4.1: Introduction

4.2: Devices

4.3: Command Organization

4.4: FILE Mode

4.5: EXEC Mode
    4.5.1. The stack
    4.5.2. Molecules
    4.5.3. Viewbox
    4.5.4. Contour maps
    4.5.5. Fitting

4.6: STOP Mode

4.7: Summary

5: GRAE IMPLEMENTATION

5.1: Deviations

5.2: Resources

5.3: Implementation

5.4: Use

6: METHODOLOGY FOR ERGONOMIC DESIGN

6.1: Methodology

6.2: Paradigm of Graphics

6.3: Linguistic Principles
    6.3.1. Semantics
    6.3.2. Action syntax
    6.3.3. Action vocabulary
    6.3.4. Picture syntax
    6.3.5. Picture vocabulary

6.4: Psychological Principles
    6.4.1. Frustration
    6.4.2. Confusion
    6.4.3. Boredom
    6.4.4. Panic
    6.4.5. Discomfort

6.5: Iterative Design

7: CONCLUSIONS AND SUGGESTIONS

REFERENCES

252 pp. 7 chapters. Photographs, figures, tables, references.

33
Brodlie, K.W.
(ed.)

collection

Mathematical Methods in Computer Graphics and Design
Academic Press, 1980

(based on the conference of the same name, organized by the Institute of Mathematics and its Applications; University of Leicester, Leicester, U.K.; 28 September 1978; from *The Institute of Mathematics and its Applications Conference Series*)

Six papers from a conference which arose out of the perceived need to bring together developing graphics algorithms and the likely users of these products.

Over 200 representatives from academia, private industry, and government research groups attended this conference. Speakers included specialists in numerical analysis, computer graphics, and computer-aided design. The papers cover a somewhat diverse number of subjects within the genre. Discussions were not included in the collection, but responses were made to many of the questions and comments submitted by the conference participants. In cases where papers were not re-written to address the questions participants asked, the questions are included, along with the authors' replies, at the end of the papers. The papers are clearly written and should prove useful to those developing computer graphics algorithms and software.

CONTENTS

Preface
1. A review of methods for curve and function drawing
   K.W. Brodlie
2. Contouring over rectangular and skewed rectangular grids - an introduction
   D.C. Sutcliffe
3. Contouring - a review of methods for scattered data
   M.A. Sabin
4. Interpolation methods for erroneous data
   D.H. McLain
5. Recent work on geometric algorithms
   A.R. Forrest
6. Stepwise construction of polyhedra in geometric modelling
   I.A. Stroud

Subject index

149 pp. 6 papers. Drawings, figures, graphs, mathematical formulae, subject index, references. ISBN 0-12-134880-6.

34
Buckler, Andrew T.

technical report

A Review of the Literature on the Legibility of Alphanumerics on Electronic Displays
1977

(report number TM-16-77; U.S. Army Human Engineering Laboratory; May 1977)

A report containing reviews of the available literature.

The purpose of this report is to identify the important parameters of legibility and to summarize previous findings. An effort is made to determine the acceptability of principles derived from conventional media for applications with electronic displays. New problems and questions with electronic displays are discussed. Although brief, this is a very good discussion and set of guidelines on both the principles from previous media and on new questions of electronics. The issues covered are: generation technique, symbol subtense, resolution, percent active area, contrast, font, symbol-width-to-height, stroke-width-to-height, spacing, viewing angle, edge displayed symbology, and color.

14 pp. 12 sections. Figures, tables, references.

Burke, James J.

SEE UNDER ID 251

35
Bylander, E.G.

Electronic Displays
McGraw-Hill, 1979

(from the *Texas Instruments Electronics Series*)

This book about applications of digital displays is for practicing engineers. It is designed to provide interfaces between the display designer and 1) the manufacturer, 2) the end user (or engineer user), and 3) the circuit designer.

Various display specifications are discussed including pleasing appearance, reliability, cost effectiveness, and efficiency. The book begins by describing display choices (with a section on how to compare digital display technologies), typical display applications, and general display considerations (font, legibility, size). This is followed by a chapter on human factors considerations (visibility, legibility). The rest of the book is devoted to an exploration of display types. One chapter each is devoted to a discussion of gas discharge displays, visible light-emitting diode displays, vacuum fluorescent displays, and liquid crystal displays. Incandescent and cathode-ray-tube displays are treated together in the last chapter. This book is simply written, and an abundance of tables very effectively depict, at a quick glance, the information in the text. Bylander is a practicing engineer with the Opto-Electronics Department of Texas Instruments, Inc.

CONTENTS

PREFACE

CHAPTER 1: INTRODUCTION TO ELECTRONIC DISPLAYS

1.1: Introduction

1.2: Survey of Display Types

1.3: Applications

1.4: The Electronic Display Symbols

CHAPTER 2: ELECTRONIC DISPLAY FUNDAMENTALS

2.1: Specifying Displays
    Introduction
    Major design factors

2.2: Comparison Methods

2.3: Addressing Methods

2.4: Connectors and Mounting

2.5: General Test Methods
    Test philosophy
    Test parameters

Appendix 2.1: Multiplexing of Matrix Displays

CHAPTER 3: DISPLAY HUMAN FACTORS

3.1: Introduction to Display Human Factors

3.2: Visibility
    Definitions of contrast
    Photometry
    Contrast enhancement
    Color contrast
    Human factors: minimum contrast
    Summary

3.3: Legibility
    Character size and proportion
    Sharpness and blur
    Summary

3.4: Temporal Factors

Appendix 3.1: Photometric Units: A Glossary of Terms

Appendix 3.2: Conversion of Candelas to Footlamberts

CHAPTER 4: GAS DISCHARGE DISPLAYS

4.1: Introduction

4.2: Gas Discharge Fundamentals
    Gas discharge geometry
    Current-voltage relationships of the discharge
    Applications to the display
    Fill gases
    Light emission
    AC plasma display

4.3: The Gas Discharge Display
    Gas discharge display applications
    Construction techniques
    Forming
    Failure mechanisms and temperature considerations
    Special provisions and requirements
4.4: DC Drive Circuits
    Anode drivers
    Segment driver circuit
4.5: AC Drive Circuits
Appendix 4.1: Analysis of Multiplexed Multiple-Segment Tube
Appendix 4.2: Parameter Estimation
CHAPTER 5: THE VISIBLE LIGHT-EMITTING DIODE DISPLAY
5.1: Introduction
5.2: Principles of Operation
    VLED material
    Diode operation
    Color
    VLED brightness
5.3: The VLED Display
    Display configurations
    Fabrication
    Reliability and environmental considerations
    Special considerations
5.4: Drive Circuit Requirements
    General driving requirements
    Multiplexed displays
Appendix 5.1: Microprocessor Interfacing
CHAPTER 6: VACUUM FLUORESCENT DISPLAY
6.1: Introduction
6.2: Principles of Operation
    Tube display configuration
    Tube operation
    Phosphor principles
6.3: The VF Display
    Fabrication methods
    Reliability and environmental considerations
    Special considerations
6.4: Drive Circuits
Appendix 6.1: Calculation of Tube Currents
CHAPTER 7: LIQUID CRYSTAL DISPLAYS
7.1: Introduction
7.2: Liquid Crystal Principles
    LCD materials
    Optics
    Failure modes
7.3: Liquid Crystal Display
    Operating parameters
    Special considerations

7.4: Multiplexing Principles
    LC MUX properties

Appendix 7.1: An Optimum Set of Multiplexing Voltages

Appendix 7.2: Pulse Design

CHAPTER 8: THE INCANDESCENT DISPLAY AND THE
CATHODE-RAY-TUBE DISPLAY

8.1: The Incandescent Display
    Introduction
    Operation
    Construction
    Reliability and environmental considerations
    Multiplex operation

8.2: The Cathode-Ray-Tube Display
    Introduction
    Cathode-ray-tube considerations
    Notes on character display

Appendix 8.1: Incandescent Display Parameter Estimation

Index

175 pp. 8 chapters. Drawings, figures, charts, graphs, tables, mathematical formulae, models, general index, references, appendices. ISBN 0-07-009510-8.

36
Caelli, Terry

Visual Perception: Theory and Practice
Pergamon, 1981

This introduction to the multidisciplinary field of visual perception reviews current technologies, processes, mathematical techniques, and their applications to clarify various languages used by vision researchers.

In an effort to unify the areas of vision research and close the communication gap between humanities researchers and scientific researchers, this work defines the central issues and questions in visual perception. The book is divided into two parts. Part one discusses recent technologies and models of visual functions. Part two reviews visual information processing theories which use these technologies. Necessary background in visual research is briefly introduced and specific titles for in-depth information on certain topics are mentioned within the text. In addition, references follow each chapter summary. The book is well organized and easy to follow. The author's aims are to facilitate understanding among the various disciplines currently involved in visual research, to demonstrate that no one technology can adequately explain any one perceptual phenomenon, and to point out similarities in findings achieved by, and thus defined by, different disciplinary languages. Though the work includes ample use of mathematics, it is addressed to readers with limited technical backgrounds.

CONTENTS

1: Introduction: Languages, Processes, and Perception
   References
PART I: TECHNOLOGY RELEVANT TO VISUAL PERCEPTION
2: Light and Introductory Optics
   2.1. On the nature of light
   2.2. Common light sources in vision research
   2.3. Introductory optics
   2.4. Some optical systems
   2.5. Conclusions
   References
3: Convolutions and Fourier Methods
   3.1. Introduction
   3.2. Fourier series and Fourier transform
   3.3. The discrete Fourier transform
   3.4. Linear systems, modulation transfer functions and filtering
   3.5. Digital image processing and the Fourier transform
   3.6. Convolutions, autocorrelations, and other transforms
   3.7. Fourier transform routines
   3.8. Summary and conclusions
   References
4: Network Theory and Systems
   4.1. Introduction to networks
   4.2. Networks in vision
   4.3. Statistical and probability analyses of systems
   4.4. Summary
   References
5: Introduction to Geometric Structures
   5.1. Introduction
   5.2. Projective and affine geometries
   5.3. Vector analysis and metrics
   5.4. Some properties of curves
   5.5. Properties of surfaces
   5.6. Transformations of curves and surfaces
   5.7. Special topics
   5.8. Conclusions
   References
PART II: APPLICATIONS AND CURRENT APPROACHES TO VISUAL PERCEPTION
6: Spatial Vision
   6.1. Introduction
   6.2. Contrast and intensity perception
   6.3. Texture preception
   6.4. Contours and illusions (mechanisms)
   6.5. Spatial equivalences and perceptual invariants
   References
7: The Perception of Motion
   7.1. Introduction
   7.2. Psychophysics of real motion perception—relativistic perception
   7.3. Transformations and analysis in motion perception—depth effects

7.4. Apparent motion
7.5. Conclusions
References
8: Specific Issues in Vision
    8.1. Colour vision
    8.2. Stereopsis
    8.3. Conclusion
    References
9: Conclusion
    References
    Index

197 pp. 9 chapters in 2 parts. Drawings, figures, tables, mathematical formulae, algorithms, general index, references. ISBN 0-08-024420-3. (ISBN 0-08-024419-X)

37
Cakir, Ahmet
Hart, D.J.
Stewart, T.F.M.

Visual Display Terminals: A Manual Covering Ergonomics, Workplace Design, Health and Safety, Task Organization
John Wiley and Sons, 1980

(originally prepared for the Inca-Fiej Research Association)

The first treatment of the health and human factors, the technology, and the functions of visual display terminals (and still one of the most useful).

Written by leading British and European authorities in occupational health and machine design, *Visual Display Terminals* is a direct response to widespread concerns of operators faced with the prospect of working regularly with computers. The authors' premise—based on their own extensive research as well as the work of many others—is that, while VDTs in themselves pose no threats to health or safety, neglect of ergonomic factors in design, selection, installation, or usage can lead to significant new operator tensions as well as visual and other physical problems. Within that context, the book examines five major topics: how a VDT works and how it fits into a large system, the basics of light and vision, terminal design, workplace design, and the health of operators as affected by the foregoing. As the first major book to treat both the human and hardware specifications for functional systems, this volume is essential reading for anyone concerned with office automation.

CONTENTS

Foreword
Preface
CHAPTER 1: VDT BASICS
How a VDT works
The CRT Display
    Beam scanning
    Distortion control
    The phosphor
    Character generation

The Keyboard
    The alphanumeric keyset
    Auxiliary numeric keyset
    Function keyset
    Cursor control keys
    From the keystroke to the screen
Other Considerations
    VDT cooling
    Voltage stability
    Implosion safeguards
Radiation
    Radio frequency radiation
    Microwave radiation
    Infrared radiation
    Ultraviolet radiation
    X-radiation
    Background radiation
    Occupational exposure to X-radiation
    X-ray sources in VDTs
    X-ray absorption in CRTs
    X-radiation measurements on VDTs
The VDT as a Systems Component
    The intelligent terminal
Communication
    Data transmission
    Transmission mode
    Transmission rate
    Address, error and parity checking
    System response time
Terminal Configuration
    On-line vs off-line
    Portable terminals
    Stand-alone terminals, terminal clusters
    Point-to-point coupling
    Multiplexing
    Concentration
CHAPTER 2: LIGHT, VISION AND THE OPTICAL
CHARACTERISTICS OF VISUAL DISPLAYS
Light and Vision
    The human eye and vision
    Eye movements
    The sensitivity of the eyes to light
    Adaptation
    Age and vision
    The measurement of light
Light Emitting vs Illuminated Characters
    The optical characteristics of visual displays
    The optical characteristics of source documents
    Subjective evaluation of the readability of source documents and
    CRT displays
Glare
    Reflected glare

Screen Reflections
    The disturbing effects of screen reflections
    The use of screen filters
    Subjective evaluation of screen filters
    Summary
CHAPTER 3: ERGONOMIC REQUIREMENTS FOR VDTs
The Visual Display
    Legibility specifications
    Legibility and readability
    Character formation
    Display capacity
    Image stability
    Display format
    Display coding
    Enhancement coding
    Cursors
    The keyboard
    Typing and keyboarding
    Key and keyboard design
    Keyboard layout
Summary of Recommendations
CHAPTER 4: ERGONOMIC REQUIREMENTS FOR VDT
WORKPLACES
Workplace Ergonomics
    Importance of the VDT task
    Types of VDT working area
    General workplace considerations
    Anthropometric aspects of VDT workplaces
Working Environment
    Lighting
    Lighting installation
    Windows and curtains
    Air conditioning
    Noise
    Anti-static precautions
Summary of Recommendations
CHAPTER 5: THE HEALTH, SAFETY AND ORGANISATIONAL
ASPECTS OF WORKING WITH VDTs
Postural Discomfort
    Working procedure
    Matching posture with the visual task
    Equipment design and the reduction of postural loading
Visual Discomfort
    The causes of visual discomfort
    Defective vision
    On the question of visual 'damage'
    Eye tests for VDT operators
    Cataracts
    Visually precipitated epilepsy

Problems Related to Air Conditioning
    Temperature
    Relative humidity
    Air circulation
    Air conditioning of VDT workrooms
Psychological Aspects
    The study of mental work load
    Alienation
    Fatigue and monotony
    Job satisfaction
    Workload and time pressure
    Job organisation and physical demand
    Ergonomic requirements of VDTs and activation
    On the subject of rest pauses
APPENDIX I: ERGONOMIC CHECKLIST FOR VDTs AND VDT
WORKPLACES
APPENDIX II: EYE TEST FOR VDU OPERATORS - A
DISCUSSION DOCUMENT
APPENDIX III: BIBLIOGRAPHY
APPENDIX IV: GLOSSARY OF TERMS

319 pp. 5 chapters. Drawings, photographs, figures, graphs, bibliography, glossary, appendices. ISBN 0-471-27793-2.

38
Campbell, J. Olin
Tuttle, David M.
Gibbons, Andrew S.

technical report

Instructional Systems Development Model for Interactive Videodisc: Final Report
1983

(report number RN-83-53; WICAT, Inc.; sponsored by U.S. Army Research Institute for the Behavioral and Social Sciences; December 1983)

The final report from a three year research project in which a methodology for the authoring and production of interactive videodiscs was developed based upon the Interservice Procedures for Instructional Systems Developement (IPISD).

This final report summarizes the work done during the three year project, with particular emphasis on the third year's work. The report describes in detail the production of two job training and simulation program videodiscs. Each is an interactive program that provides a user with a much more engaging training experience than a training manual or ordinary videotape could. In the first year a system for producing videodiscs was developed. In the second year a trial videodisc was made and revised. In the third year the procedure for producing videodiscs was taught to some military personnel who produced a second videodisc. The procedures were revised somewhat based upon the experiences of the makers of the second videodisc. The U.S. Army hopes to be able to use interactive videodiscs like these as training instruments for high technology jobs that require complex skills. An additional result from this research project was the modification and expansion of some aspects of the Interservice Procedures for Instructional Systems Development. These are described in the report. The procedure for making videodiscs is not in itself described in this final report, but is available separately. The primary focus here is on the videodiscs that were created, and on methodology and research findings. This research project was sponsored by the U.S. Army Research Institute for the Behavioral and Social Sciences. While the work of this research project represents a substantial contribution to this developing new field, the report is technical and poorly organized. Persons involved in research, development, and training either of videodisc production or in areas which have the potential of effectively using videodisc technologies would find this report of interest.

CONTENTS

DD1473

Interactive Videodisc: Background

Project Summary
    Purpose and outcomes
    Yearly summaries

Design and Production Considerations
    IPISD additions and tryouts
    Interactive videodisc techniques
    Hardware tryout
    Personnel changes for interactive videodisc
    Videodisc mastering and programming
    Costs
    Evaluation

Revisions to the Interservice Procedures for Instructional Systems Development (IPISD)
    Analyze
    Design
    Develop instruction
    Implement
    Control (evaluate and revise)

The "Call for Fire" Program
    Packing procedures
    Training extension course (TEC) lessons
    Skill qualification tests (SQT's)
    Videotape productions
    Simulations and games
    Executive review
    Authoring guide
    Voice and keypad inputs

The RT 524 Alignment Simulation Program
    Training army personnel
    Delivery system hardware
    Authoring system
    Evaluation results

Conclusions

References

List of Figures

48 pp. 7 chapters. Figures, references.

39
Card, Stuart K.
Moran, Thomas P.
Newell, Allen

Psychology of Human-Computer Interaction
Lawrence Erlbaum Associates, 1983

Perhaps the most important recent book in the field, summarizing more than a decade of research at Xerox's Palo Alto Research Center, it presents specific models of user behavior (emphasizing human response times), relates these to an overall model of human information-processing, and shows how they can be used in the design of interactive computer systems.

The text is divided into four main sections which: present a basic model of the human information-processor, useful as a design tool and grounded in current research; provide a detailed examination of text-editing as a prototypical example of human-computer interaction (including the development of a model for the behavior of users with an editing system based on the users' employment of goals, operators, methods and selection rules—the GOMS analysis—to accomplish an editing task); focuses on the simplification of the GOMS analysis to provide practical models for predicting the time required by users to perform a specific task (this covers simplifications made both at the level of individual keystrokes and at a more complex level of behavior); and applies this analysis to new task domains and discusses in general terms how a basic understanding of cognitive skill can be applied in computer system design. Finally, the authors offer ten specific principles for user-interface design. The authors' thesis is that because human-computer interface design is vital to all future developments in the computer field, computer system designers must learn to incorporate the relevant psychological principles into their original designs.

CONTENTS
    Preface
1: An Applied Information-Processing Psychology
SCIENCE BASE
2: The Human Information-Processor

TEXT-EDITING

3: System and User Variability

4: An Exercise in Task Analysis

5: The GOMS Model of Manuscript Editing

6: Extensions of the GOMS Analysis

7: Models of Devices for Text Selection

ENGINEERING MODEL

8: The Keystroke-Level Model

9: The Unit-Task Level of Analysis

EXTENSIONS AND GENERALIZATIONS

10: An Exploration into Circuit Design

11: Cognitive Skill

12: Applying Psychology to Design

13: Reprise
   Symbol glossary
   Bibliographic index
   Subject index

469 pp. 13 chapters in 4 parts. Drawings, figures, graphs, abstract formalisms, models, subject index, appendices. ISBN 0-89859-243-7.

40

Carlbom, Ingrid

High-Performance Graphics System Architecture: A Methodology for Design and Evaluation
UMI Research Press, 1984

(revision of the author's thesis, Brown University, 1980; vol. 21 in the *Computer Science: Systems Programming* series, Harold S. Stone, series ed.)

Provides a methodology for the evaluation and design of high-performance vector graphics systems.

This revision of the author's master's thesis is based on a functional model and a set of performance modeling techniques aimed at developing evaluation and design methodologies for the hardware, firmware, and software of complex graphics system architectures. Intended primarily for electrical engineers, programmers, researchers, and designers, it presupposes a fundamental grasp of the mathematics, techniques, and terminology of graphics systems programming. Primarily for calculating processing times and estimating overall delay and lag, the functional model developed in the book is used to illustrate the similarities and differences between the Vector General 3400 and the Evans and Sutherland Picture System 2, two existing high-performance systems. From this functional model, performance modeling techniques are derived that identify design trade-offs and quantitative cutoff points between the two systems. The author concludes by listing several areas where the research presented in the study might be extended, including its application in evaluating medium- and low-performance devices.

CONTENTS

1: Introduction
    1.1. Subject area of the study
    1.2. The problem and its importance
    1.3. The approach to the problem
    1.4. Contributions
    1.5. Outline of the study

2: Related Research

3: Functional Model
    3.1. Representations, processes, and input in the functional model
    3.2. Output in the functional model
    3.3. Input in the functional model
    3.4. Case studies

4: Performance Modeling Techniques
    4.1. Macro instructions
    4.2. Hardware parameters of a performance model
    4.3. Performance measures

5: Application of the Performance Modeling Techniques
    5.1. Macro instructions
    5.2. Activity flows
    5.3. Timing sequence diagrams
    5.4. Applications of delays
    5.5. Composite macro instructions

6: Comparisons of Graphics Systems
    6.1. General methodology of comparison
    6.2. Introduction to the case study
    6.3. A macro instruction subset
    6.4. Composite macro instructions for E&S PS2 and VG3400
    6.5. Results of the comparison

7: Methodology for Hardware and Software Design
    7.1. General methodology of design
    7.2. User instruction set design
    7.3. Summary

8: Graphics Software
    8.1. Introduction
    8.2. Theseus—a graphics system access method

9: Conclusion
    9.1. Summary of research
    9.2. Future extensions

Appendix A: Summary of Graphics System Capabilities
Appendix B: System Timings
Appendix C: Theseus
Notes
Bibliography
Index

172 pp. 9 chapters. Figures, abstract formalisms, models, general index, bibliography, appendices. ISBN 0-8357-1595-7.

Carlson, Curtis R.

SEE UNDER ID 54

Carterette, Edward C.
Friedman, Morton P.
(eds.)

overview

Handbook of Perception
Academic Press, 1974-78

A ten-volume treatise on the various aspects of perception, i.e., "all processes by which the organism transforms, organizes and structures information arising from the world, either in sense data or in memory." This set of works is primarily intended for psychologists and natural scientists, although its writers' intention is that "it should serve as a basic source and reference work for all in the arts or sciences." Each volume addresses a specific aspect of perception, examining various findings, theories and viewpoints. Included in the set are works on psychological, physiological, philosophical, historical, and psychophysical aspects of perception; language and speech; vision; hearing; chemical perceptions; the tactile senses; and perceptual ecology. This is a valuable collection of some of the finest papers on perception. Individually and collectively, these volumes "summarize the fundamental facts and concepts and provide comprehensive references to the literature."

41
Carterette, Edward C.
Friedman, Morton P.
(eds.)

collection

Handbook of Perception: Volume I, Historical and Philosophical Roots of Perception
Academic Press, 1974

The introductory volume in a ten-volume treatise that consists of a wide range of experimental and theoretical papers on perception.

This collection serves to introduce a ten-volume treatise on perception. The intention of the authors is that the *Handbook* serve as a basic source and reference book, not only for psychologists and natural scientists, but for everyone in the arts and sciences. This first volume explores the historical development of current theories of perception, examining various modes of thought and the current theory which has evolved from them. Aspects of perception covered include attention, perceptual structuring, information processing, cognition and knowledge, and learning theory. The list of contributing authors to the introductory volume of this important set includes psychologists and philosophers from Canada, France, West Germany, England, and Australia, as well as the United States. Extensive references are included.

CONTENTS

Foreword

Contents of Other Volumes

PART I: PHILOSOPHICAL ROOTS

Chapter 1: Sense Experience
  Roderick Firth
  I. The epistemological problem of perception
  II. Cartesianism and its critics
  References

Chapter 2: Some Philosophical Problems of Perception
  R. M. Yost
  I. Introduction
  II. General schema of a common kind of philosophical problem of perception
  III. Preliminary clarification of the ordinary concept of perception
  IV. Inconsistent sets of sentences that constitute philosphical problems of perception
  V. Four prima facie solutions to problems constituted by the inconsistent sets; each solution rejects one or more of the three general presuppositions
  References

Chapter 3: Epistemology
  Gilbert Harman
  I. Radical skepticism
  II. The appeal to meaning
  III. The revolt against meaning
  IV. Psychologism
  V. Sense data and unconscious inferences
  VI. Knowledge and inference
  References

Chapter 4: Some Questions in the Philosophy of Mind
  Max Deutscher
  I. Introduction
  II. Some general considerations about the mind/body distinction
  III. Main sources of philosophical problems about mind
  IV. Physicalism
  V. Religion and mind
  VI. Free will
  VII. Describing, reporting, and expressing one's thoughts and feelings
  References

PART II: HISTORICAL BACKGROUND OF CONTEMPORARY
PERCEPTION

Chapter 5: The Problem of Perceptual Structure
Michael Wertheimer
I. Introduction
II. Recognition of the problem
III. Solving the problem by ignoring it
IV. Recognition that ignoring the problem doesn't make it go away
V. A proposed solution: a new element
VI. Another proposed solution: empiricism
VII. Turning the problem right side up
VIII. Beginnings of a quantitative solution
IX. Beginnings of a physiological solution
X. Summary and conclusion
References

Chapter 6: Association (and the Nativist-Empiricist Axis)
Bruce Earhard
I. Philosophical background
II. Empiricism, association, and perception
III. Opposition and alternatives to empiricism: the rise of nativism
IV. Nativism and empiricism: data
V. Epilogue: What is learned?
References

Chapter 7: Consciousness, Perception, and Action
Wolfgang Metzger
I. The concepts of consciousness, perception, and stimulus
II. Judgement hypotheses
III. Act hypotheses
IV. The role of bodily activities
References

Chapter 8: Attention
D.E. Berlyne
I. The prebehaviorist period
II. The interwar period
III. The postwar period
References

Chapter 9: Cognition and Knowledge: Psychological Epistemology
Joseph R. Royce
I. Introduction and overview
II. Three ways of knowing
III. Cognitive structure
IV. Toward a psychology and philosophy of the *Weltanschauung*
References

PART III: CONTEMPORARY VIEWS OF PERCEPTION: A.
MODERN CLASSICAL TRADITION

Chapter 10: Organization and the Gestalt Tradition
Julian Hochberg
I. The Gestalt approach to the problem of organization
II. Other approaches to perceptual organization
III. In summary and assessment
References

Chapter 11: The Learning Tradition
    Wm. W. Rozeboom
    I. The historical structure of learning theory
    II. Perceptual commitments of learning theory
    III. Learning-theoretic acknowledgments of perception
    References

PART III: CONTEMPORARY VIEWS OF PERCEPTION:
B. CURRENT PSYCHOLOGICAL EMPHASES

Chapter 12: The Historical and Philosophical Background of Cognitive
Approaches to Psychology
    W.J. Dowling and Kelyn Roberts
    I. History of philosophical theories
    II. Purposiveness
    III. Creativity
    IV. Structure
    V. Conscious experience
    VI. Epilogue
    References

Chapter 13: Choosing a Paradigm for Perception
    Richard L. Gregory
    I. Introduction
    II. The selection of paradigms by data
    III. Perceptual facts to challenge paradigm candidates
    IV. Summary of the questions
    V. The paradigm candidates challenged by questions
    VI. The candidates' scores
    VII. Conclusions
    References

Chapter 14: The Visual System: Environmental Information
    R.M. Boynton
    I. Introduction
    II. Historical notes
    III. The eye as a camera
    IV. The relation of geometrical optics to ecological optics
    V. Contour
    VI. Useful properties of light
    VII. The dense network of rays
    VIII. The stationary convergence point
    IX. A magic cube
    X. Point sources and point sinks
    XI. The pickup device
    XII. Summary
    References

Chapter 15: A Note on Ecological Optics
    James J. Gibson
    Text
    References

Chapter 16: Information Processing
  Ralph Norman Haber
  I. Origins of information processing approaches
  II. The unity of sensation, perception, memory, retrieval,
      cognition, and knowledge
  III. Specification of stages
  IV. Definition of information
  V. Types of information processing models
  VI. Conclusion
  References

Chapter 17: Automata
  Patrick Suppes, William Rottmayer
  I. Introduction
  II. Perceptrons
  III. Automata and line drawings
  IV. Picture-parsing grammars
  V. Learning
  References

Chapter 18: The Developmental Emphasis
  Eliane Vurpillot
  I. Association or the Gestalt theory
  II. Does the baby perceive as soon as it is born?
  III. Interaction between maturation and exercise
  IV. The role of action in perceptual development
  V. Conclusion
  References

Chapter 19: Phenomenology
  Dagfinn Føllesdal
  I. A general survey of phenomenology
  II. The phenomenological theory of perception
  References
  Supplementary reading

Chapter 20: Transactional and Probabilistic Functionalism
  Kent Dallet
  I. Transaction
  II. The Ames demonstration
  III. Brunswik's "lens model" of perception
  IV. Perceptual learning and development
  V. Perception and other knowledge
  VI. Probabilism and representative design
  VII. Persons as stimulus objects
  VIII. Current status
  References

Author Index

Subject Index

*431 pp. 20 chapters in 3 parts. Drawings, photographs, figures, tables,
abstract formalisms, models, footnotes, author index, subject index,
references. ISBN 0-12-161901-X.*

42

Carterette, Edward C.
Friedman, Morton P.
(eds.)

collection

Handbook of Perception: Volume III, Biology of Perceptual Systems
Academic Press, 1974

The papers describe the basic properties of perception and the elements of sensory physiology, focusing mainly on the structure and function of sensory systems.

This volume includes papers written by specialists in psychology, physiology, anatomy, zoology, and environmental medicine. All types of organic sensory systems are discussed. The first chapter examines what a sensory organ does, i.e., what is detected and, in general, how it is detected. Subsequent chapters address the role of the nervous system in perception, the evolution of sensory organs, ethology and perception, recognition, chemoreception, taste and smell, tactile perception, the spatial senses, vision, and audition. Among the specific topics addressed in the volume are: the functioning of sense organs, the stimulus-response relationship, the brain-body correspondence, psychological functioning at birth, control of behavior by genes and by the environment, and perceptual learning. This book should serve the needs of researchers and graduate students interested in the functional and psychological aspects of perception.

CONTENTS

Foreword

Preface

Contents of Other Volumes

Chapter 1: Energy, Transducers, and Sensory Discrimination
  T.D.M. Roberts
  I. Introductory summary
  II. Sensory experience
  III. Receptors
  IV. Stimuli
  V. Responses
  VI. Special cases
  VII. Conclusion
  References

Chapter 2: Neuronal Properties
  Charles F. Stevens
  I. Structural basis for nervous system functioning
  II. The nerve impulse
  III. Synaptic function
  IV. Neural integration
  V. Encoding information
  VI. Special properties
  VII. Summary
  VIII. Guide to the neurophysiological literature
  References

Chapter 3: Integration in Nervous Systems
G. Adrian Horridge
I. Coding
II. Synapses
III. Integration
IV. Fields of sensitivity
V. Convergence and complex fields
VI. Summation versus discrimination
VII. Physiological pathways and anatomic connections
VIII. The problem in historical perspective
IX. Reflexes
X. Eccles' explanatory contribution
XI. Back to anatomy
XII. Other developments
XIII. The splintering field
XIV. Centrally determined sequences
XV. Computers as models of brains
XVI. Circuits of restricted locality
XVII. Toward more identified cells
XVIII. Constancy of synaptic connections
XIX. Prospect
References

Chapter 4: Primordial Sense Organs and the Evolution of Sensory Systems
Lawrence Kruger, Barry E. Stein
I. Introduction
II. The variety of sense organs
III. Primitive "eyes"
IV. Specialization in vertebrates
V. The vertebrate central nervous system
VI. Mammalian evolutionary trends
VII. Cerebral cortex
VIII. Neural organization and perception
References

Chapter 5: Behavioral Embryology
Colwyn B. Trevarthen
I. Introduction
II. The embryonic nervous system
III. The fetus
IV. The neonate: postnatal behavior growth
V. Conclusion
References

Chapter 6: Ethology
Wolfgang M. Schleidt
I. Introduction
II. Basic concepts of ethology
III. An ethological approach to the study of perception
References

Chapter 7: Genetic Control
Karla Butler Thomas
I. Objectives and methods of behavior-genetic analysis
II. Research findings
III. General conclusions
References

Chapter 8: Object Recognition
N.S. Sutherland
I. Introduction
II. Facts
III. Theory
References

Chapter 9: Chemoreception
Bernice M. Wenzel
I. Introduction
II. Morphology of chemoreceptors
III. Electrophysiology
References

Chapter 10: Tasting and Smelling
Bernice M. Wenzel
I. Introduction
II. Sensitivity
III. Preferences
IV. Dietary and metabolic factors
V. Chemical communication and pheromones
References

Chapter 11: Cutaneous Mechanoreceptors
Paul R. Burgess
I. Criteria for classification of cutaneous mechanoreceptive
   neurons
II. Mechanoreceptors in hairy skin
III. Mechanoreceptors in glabrous skin
IV. Mechanoreceptors associated with sinus hairs, teeth, and claws
V. Conclusion
References

Chapter 12: Tactual Perception of Texture
M.M. Taylor, S.J. Lederman, R.H. Gibson
I. Introduction
II. Experiments related to texture perception
III. Toward a conceptual model of texture perception
IV. General discussion and conclusion
References

Chapter 13: The Spatial Senses
I. P. Howard
I. Auditory localization
II. Joint receptors
III. Muscle spindles and tendon organs
IV. The vestibular system
References

Chapter 14: Orientation and Motion in Space
I.P. Howard
I. The topology of the sensorimotor system
II. Kinesthesis
III. The body schema
IV. Gravitational orientation
V. Egocentric orientation
VI. Geographic orientation and navigation
VII. Sensori-motor coordination
References

Chapter 15: Temperature Reception
Herbert Hensel
I. Thermal sensations
II. Neurophysiology of thermoreception
III. Comparison of various approaches to temperature reception
References

Chapter 16: Vision
Israel Abramov, James Gordon
I. Light
II. Photopigments
III. Anatomy
IV. Electrical responses—retina
V. Electrical responses—CNS
References

Chapter 17: Seeing
Israel Abramov, James Gordon
I. Psychophysics
II. Psychological correlates
References

Chapter 18: Hearing: Central Neural Mechanisms
Bruce Masterson, Irving T. Diamond
I. The evolution of the vertebrate auditory system
II. The evolution of sound reception
III. The contribution of central auditory structures to hearing
References

Chapter 19: Audition
Douglas B. Webster
I. Nonmammalian auditory systems
II. Mammalian auditory systems
III. Summary
References

Author Index

Subject Index

521 pp. 19 chapters. Drawings, figures, graphs, tables, models, author index, subject index, references. ISBN 0-12-161903-6.

43

Carterette, Edward C.
Friedman, Morton P.
(eds.)

collection

Handbook of Perception: Volume V, Seeing
Academic Press, 1975

Focuses on the technical aspects of sight, visual perception, and pattern recognition.

The six parts of this volume encompass a group of related problems and topics associated with seeing. Part one provides a brief but thorough look at the history of vision research. Also included in part one are papers on measurement of visual stimuli and contemporary problems, both of which are well-written and serve as excellent transitions to the papers in part two—the neural basis of seeing. Part three examines spatial and temporal factors in perception and how the "problems" associated with each are resolved by the nervous system. Part four discusses how objects are recognized as being distinct and how color is perceived. Space and motion (visual, non-kinesthetic) perceptions are examined in part five. Part six is an abstraction of *Optics, Painting, and Photography* (Cambridge University Press, 1972) by its author, M.H. Pirenne. This particular volume will be most useful to those interested in human perception and how motion, space, and objects can be simulated graphically, e.g. display designers; the work will also interest designers or researchers working with visual perception systems. (Note: Volume 10 in this series, *Perceptual Ecology*, contains several chapters of a less technical, but equally relevant nature. These include: Chapter 6—Aesthetics; Chapter 10—Art and Perception; and Chapter 11—Perception of Motion Pictures.)

CONTENTS

List of Contributors

Foreword

Preface

Contents of Other Volumes

PART I: HISTORY, MEASUREMENT, AND CONTEMPORARY PROBLEMS

Chapter 1: History of Research on Seeing
   Yves Le Grand
   I. Light and vision
   II. Dioptrics of the eye
   III. The retina
   IV. The visual pathway
   V. Visual function
   References

Chapter 2: Measurement of the Visual Stimulus
   Yves Le Grand
   I. Light and radiation
   II. Sources of radiant energy
   III. The visual receptor
   References

Chapter 3: Contemporary Theoretical Problems in Seeing
   P.C. Dodwell
   I. Introduction
   II. Physiological bases of seeing
   III. The nature-nurture controversies
   IV. Levels of functioning
   V. Levels of explanation
   References

PART II: THE NEURAL BASIS OF SEEING

Chapter 4: Receptive Fields: Neural Representation of the Spatial and
Intensive Attributes of the Visual Image
   J.G. Robson
   I. Introduction
   II. The retinal image and its analysis
   III. Retinal ganglion cells—receptive fields
   IV. Maintained activity of cells and the signaling of illumination
   V. Quantitative aspects of retinal ganglion cell behavior
   VI. Geniculate nucleus
   VII. Visual cortex
   VIII. Orientation specificity in the visual cortex
   IX. Binocular interactions and stereopsis
   X. Spatial frequency analysis of the visual system
   References

Chapter 5: Neural Coding of Color
   Russell L. De Valois, Karen K. De Valois
   I. Introduction
   II. Neurophysiology of color systems
   III. Relation to color vision
   References

PART III: TEMPORAL AND SPATIAL RESOLUTION

Chapter 6: Temporal Factors in Visual Perception
   Leo Ganz
   I. Introduction
   II. Bloch's law of temporal summation
   III. Temporal summation with double pulses
   IV. Linear systems analysis of the response to temporal transients
   V. Visual persistence
   VI. The perception of succession
   VII. Visual numerosity
   VIII. Homogeneous light masking
   IX. Metacontrast
   X. Visual noise masking
   XI. Spatio-temporal interactions
   References

Chapter 7: Spatial Resolution and Spatial Interaction
   James P. Thomas
   I. Spatial resolution
   II. Spatial interaction
   References

PART IV: PATTERN, OBJECT, AND COLOR

Chapter 8: Pattern and Object Perception
   P.C. Dodwell
   I. Introduction
   II. Organization and form
   III. Perceptual stability and clarity
   IV. Perceptual constancies
   V. Perceptual illusions
   VI. Developmental and cross-cultural evidence
   VII. Information processing
   VIII. Attentional and emotional aspects of pattern perception
   IX. Conclusion
   References

Chapter 9: Color, Hue, and Wavelength
   Robert M. Boynton
   I. Introduction
   II. Basic concepts
   III. Subjective description and ordering of colors
   IV. Physical basis of the ordering of spectral colors
   V. Psychological ordering of spectral colors
   VI. Principle of univariance and the cone photopigments
   VII. Appearance of the spectrum: physiological basis
   VIII. Saturation
   IX. Color metrics
   References

PART V: SPACE AND MOTION PERCEPTION

Chapter 10: Visual Space Perception
   Whitman Richards
   I. Egocentric coordinates
   II. Stereopsis
   III. Fixation reflexes and disparity tuning
   IV. The horopter
   V. Dynamic stereopsis
   VI. Motion parallax
   VII. Perspective and gradients: contextual cues
   VIII. Interposition and shadow
   References

Chapter 11: Visual Motion Perception
   Robert Sekuler
   I. Introduction
   II. A general orientation to motion perception
   III. Direction-specific mechanisms
   IV. A code for perceived motion
   V. Velocity and spatio-temporal modulation
   VI. Motion varies with retinal location
   VII. Movement, orientation, and spatial frequency
   VIII. Oculomotor influences on motion perception
   IX. Suprathreshold direction-specific effects
   X. Binocular aspects of motion perception
   XI. The variety of motion
   References

PART VI: PAINTING AND PHOTOGRAPHY

Chapter 12: Vision and Art
  M.H. Pirenne
  I. Introduction
  II. Natural perspective
  III. Linear perspective
  IV. Trompe l'oeil
  V. Deformation of three-dimensional illusions viewed from the wrong position
  VI. Ordinary pictures seen with both eyes
  VII. What is a painting?
  VIII. Stability of ordinary paintings
  IX. The painter's task
  X. Effects of irradiation
  References

Author Index

Subject Index

527 pp. 12 chapters in 6 parts. Drawings, photographs, figures, graphs, tables, author index, subject index, references. ISBN 0-12-161905-2.

44
Carterette, Edward C.
Friedman, Morton P.
(eds.)

collection

Handbook of Perception: Volume IX, Perceptual Processing
Academic Press, 1978

The ninth of a ten-volume treatise, this handbook addresses perceptual processing. Directed particularly at psychologists and, more generally, to natural scientists.

The scope of this work includes attention/selection, pattern processing, and perceptual illusions and disorders. Research which covers the mechanisms, schemes, and theories of these topics is presented and analyzed to allow generalizations about perceptual processing and perceptual anomalies. Several chapters stress newer, more contemporary research; one on pattern recognition theories and another on perceptual processing in reading have their bases in recent research. Similarly, newer research on the auditory modality to counterbalance a past emphasis on vision is presented in a review of perceptual learning. Chapter outlines and a preface enhance the book's value as a reference handbook. Because the work addresses how humans translate data into information for storage in knowledge structures, this book should assist the researcher attempting to model vision systems and feedback mechanisms for applications in the fields of cybernetics and robotics.

CONTENTS

List of Contributors

Foreword

Preface

PART I: ATTENTION AND SELECTION

Chapter 1: Mechanisms of Attention
   Steven W. Keele, W. Trammell Neill
   I. Introduction
   II. Two kinds of processing limitations
   III. Illustrative difficulties for single-channel theory
   IV. Processing multiple signals
   V. Elaborations of attention theory
   VI. The final model
   References

Chapter 2: Perceptual Structure and Selection
   David E. Clement
   I. Introduction
   II. Measurement of structure
   III. Ontogeny of perceptual selection
   IV. General discussion and conclusions
   References

Chapter 3: Sorting, Categorization, and Visual Search
   Patrick Rabbitt
   I. Introduction
   II. Neisser's experiments reevaluated
   III. Learning and remembering the target set
   IV. Categorization in terms of critical perceptual distinctions
   V. Discriminations between classes of letters and digits:
       categorization independent of naming
   VI. Semantic class and visual search
   VII. The use of acoustic properties of letter names to separate target
       and background categories in visual search
   VIII. The bases of word superiority effects in visual search for
       individual letters
   IX. Rapid serial visual presentation of displays for visual search
   X. Control processes in self-paced visual search and scanning of
       text
   XI. Conclusions
   References

PART II: PATTERN PROCESSING

Chapter 4: Schemes and Theories of Pattern Recognition
   Stephen K. Reed
   I. Introduction
   II. Template theories
   III. Feature theories
   IV. Structural theories
   V. Analysis by synthesis
   VI. Topological theories
   VII. Prototypes
   VIII. Overview
   References

Chapter 5: Perceptual Processing in Letter Recognition and Reading
   W.K. Estes
   I. Some strategic considerations
   II. Properties of the visual system basic to reading
   III. Perception of individual letters
   IV. Perception of multiple-letter displays
   V. Target-background relationships and category effects
   VI. Parallel versus serial processing
   VII. Linguistic factors in letter recognition
   VIII. Afterthoughts
   References

Chapter 6: Eye Movements and Visual Perception
   Geoff D. Cumming
   I. Introduction
   II. Types of eye movement
   III. Measurement of eye position
   IV. The value of eye movements for perception
   V. Problems introduced by eye movements
   References

Chapter 7: Perceptual Learning
   Richard D. Walk
   I. Introduction
   II. Examples of perceptual learning
   III. Development and perceptual learning
   IV. Theoretical and research issues
   V. Conclusion
   References

Chapter 8: Size, Distance, and Depth Perception
   Walter C. Gogel
   I. Introduction
   II. Instances of stimulus ambiguity
   III. Theories of the resolution of stimulus ambiguity
   IV. Résumé
   References

PART III: ILLUSIONS AND DISORDERS

Chapter 9: Illusions and Hallucinations
   Richard L. Gregory
   I. Introduction
   II. Processes of perception
   III. Physiological and cognitive illusions
   IV. The theory of inappropriate constancy scaling
   V. Concluding remarks
   References

Chapter 10: Disorders of Perceptual Processing
   Francis J. Pirozzolo
   I. Introduction
   II. Lesions of the visual pathways
   III. The concept of agnosia
   IV. Visual agnosia
   V. The somatosensory system and tactile agnosia
   VI. Nociception and "asymbolia for pain"
   VII. Lesions of the auditory pathways

VIII. Sensory aphasia

IX. Auditory agnosia

X. Related disorders

XI. The chemical senses

XII. Developmental disorders of perceptual processing

XIII. Conclusions

References

Author Index

Subject Index

404 pp. 10 chapters in 3 parts. Drawings, photographs, figures, graphs, tables, models, author index, subject index, references. ISBN 0-12-161909-5.

45

Castner, Henry W.
Robinson, Arthur H.

Dot Area Symbols in Cartography: The Influence of Pattern on Their Perception

American Congress on Surveying and Mapping, 1969

(technical monograph number CA-4)

This technical monograph is a summary of the literature on map symbols and their visual and communicative objectives through 1969. The results of tests, in which subjects were asked to describe their visual responses to a map's dot patterns, are analyzed and discussed.

Citing a scarcity of basic research in the field (compared to applied research) the authors attempt to cover only a small part of the large subject of cartographic design, i.e., the role of pattern in cartographic symbology. Rather they attempt to contribute to the understanding of how map readers visually respond to commonly used dot symbols. The stated aim is to lay the groundwork for more extensive and sophisticated investigations. The three major sections discuss: 1) the identification of six characteristics of dot patterns—form, size, spacing, arrangement, orientation, and reflectance density; 2) the results and limitations of tests designed to study and analyze whether or not map readers actually perceive dot patterns in different ways and, if so, whether this is a function of the texture, dot size, dot spacing, and/or the "grayness" of the pattern; and 3) summary and conclusions. While they acknowledge connections to the literature from psychology, physiology, lithography and optics, one observation of the study is the lack of clear connections between other (especially perceptual) disciplines and cartography. A valuable initial study of an important area for researchers and cartographers.

CONTENTS

Foreword

Introduction

Part I: The Characteristics of Dot Patterns and Their Perception

    1. The form of the dots

    2. The size of the dots

    3. The spacing of the dots (texture)

    4. The arrangement of the dots

    5. The orientation of the dot pattern

6. The pattern-value of dot patterns

Part II: The Testing Program and Its Results
1. The logic of the tests
2. The development of the test maps
3. The tests and the subjects
4. The test results: texture
5. The test results: dot size
6. The test results: dot spacing
7. The effect of guessing
8. The test results: pattern-value

Part III: Summary and Conclusions
1. Response to value and pattern
2. The discrimination of contrast

Footnotes

Appendix A: Glossary

Appendix B: The Tests

Appendix C: Supplementary Tables: Dot Patterns and Test Responses

Bibliography

78 pp. 3 parts. Maps, tables, bibliography, references, glossary, appendices.

46

Catmull, Edwin

technical report

A Subdivision Algorithm for Computer Display of Curved Surfaces
1974

(report number UTEC-CSC-74-133; Department of Computer Science, University of Utah; sponsored by Defense Advanced Research Projects Agency; December 1974)

A method using curved patches to produce computer shaded images of three-dimensional objects is discussed.

This report presents an algorithm for establishing the correspondence between a curved patch and the raster elements of a CRT display. The described method is distinguished from other methods in that three-dimensional curved patches are used, rather than the polygons used in more conventional methods. In general, this approach allows for the accurate representation and shading of curved surfaces and objects displayed on a CRT. Though the author stresses that the algorithm is not limited in application to bicubic patches, the greater part of this report focuses on such surfaces. Of particular importance is a detailed description of a method for fast subdivision of bicubic patches. Two dominant causes of visual distortion, rastering and aliasing, are described and steps that can be taken to reduce these distortions are discussed, with emphasis given to the subdivision algorithm. By using the author's method, texture may also be added to computer generated pictures by mapping photographs onto the patches. Other topics discussed are the hidden surface problem, and methods used for obtaining the appropriate intensity for the corresponding point. Four appendices include a discussion of generating bicubic patches with the bicubic equation, an analysis of how correction factors can be used to help find the Bezier control points, and a description of how to "approximate the quintic normal equation with a bicubic equation." Pictures made on a high-precision CRT at the University of Utah have also been included, though they are not reproduced well in the paper. This report will be of interest to researchers and practitioners in computer display design, particularly those interested in hidden surface problems.

CONTENTS
Chapter 1. Introduction
Chapter 2. A general algorithm for displaying curved patches
Chapter 3. Subdividing a cubic curve
Chapter 4. Extension of cubic subdivision to surfaces
Chapter 5. The hidden surface problem
Chapter 6. Intensity
Chapter 7. Sampling, rastering, and aliasing
Chapter 8. Conclusion
Appendix A. The bicubic equation
Appendix B. Relationship of correction factors to Bezier control points
Appendix C. Approximating the bicubic normal equation
Appendix D. Pictures
References

83 pp. 8 chapters. Drawings, photographs, figures, algorithms, abstract formalisms, references, appendices.

47
Chambers, John M.
Cleveland, William S.
Kleiner, Beat
Tukey, Paul A.

Graphical Methods for Data Analysis
Wadsworth, 1983

(from *The Wadsworth Statistics/Probability Series*, Peter J. Bickel, William S. Cleveland, Richard M. Dudley, series eds.)

Provides effective methods for graphing and analyzing data. Most can be implemented through standard computer operations or with pencil and paper.

Going beyond the pie and bar graphs commonly seen in business reports, the authors present a variety of methods for the visual presentation of quantitative data. The work stresses the ability of graphical displays to reveal the "structure of data"; in keeping with this perspective, they show the range or graphical applications that run from plotting data to analyzing it. Chapter two explores methods—including quantile plots, one-dimensional scatter plots, box plots, stem-and-leaf diagrams, and density traces—for exhibiting the distribution of a single set of data. Chapter three focuses on how to compare distributions of several data sets. Graphical methods that analyze the relationship between two variables are dealt with in chapter four, while chapter five explores the same topic with multi-dimensional data. Also examined are the more technical probability plots (these assess distributional assumptions for the data), and graphical methods for regression. The concluding chapter provides an excellent set of guidelines and principles to follow when creating a graph. An appendix contains the complete data sets used in the graphs throughout the text. This volume assumes some background information in statistics, though much of the material would be accessible to any interested reader. The list of readings and practice exercises included in each chapter provide further help. Data analysts, business managers, executives, science researchers, and anyone else who works with quantitative data on a regular basis would potentially be interested in this work.

CONTENTS

1: Introduction
    1.1. Why graphics?
    1.2. What is a graphical method for analyzing data?
    1.3. A summary of the contents
    1.4. The selection and presentation of materials
    1.5. Data sets
    1.6. Quality of graphical displays
    1.7. How should this book be used?

2: Portraying the Distribution of a Set of Data
    2.1. Introduction
    2.2. Quantile plots
    2.3. Symmetry
    2.4. One-dimensional scatter plots
    2.5. Box plots
    2.6. Histograms
    2.7. Stem-and-leaf diagrams
    2.8. Symmetry plots and transformations
    *2.9. Density traces
    2.10. Summary and discussion
    2.11. Further reading
    Exercises

3: Comparing Data Distributions
    3.1. Introduction
    3.2. Empirical quantile-quantile plots
    3.3. Collection of single-data-set-display
    *3.4. Notched box plots
    *3.5. Multiple density traces
    *3.6. Plotting ratios and differences
    3.7. Summary and discussion
    3.8. Further reading
    Exercises

4: Studying Two-Dimensional Data
    4.1. Introduction
    4.2. Numerical summaries are not enough
    4.3. Examples
    4.4. Looking at the scatter plots
    4.5. Studying the dependence of y on x by summaries in vertical strips
    4.6. Studying the dependence of y on x by smoothing
    4.7. Studying the dependence of the spread of y on x by smoothing absolute values of residuals
    4.8. Fighting repeated values with jitter and sunflowers
    4.9. Showing counts with cellulation and sunflowers
    *4.10. Two-dimensional local densities and sharpening
    *4.11. Mathematical details of lowess
    4.12. Summary and discussion
    4.13. Further reading
    Exercises

5: Plotting Multivariate Data
    5.1. Introduction
    5.2. One-dimensional and two-dimensional views
    5.3. Plotting three dimensions at once
    5.4. Plotting four and more dimensions
    5.5. Combinations of basic methods
    5.6. First aid and transformation
    *5.7. Coding schemes for plotting symbols
    5.8. Summary and discussion
    5.9. Further reading
    Exercises

6: Assessing Distributional Assumptions About Data
    6.1. Introduction
    6.2. Theoretical quantile-quantile plots
    6.3. More on empirical quantiles and theoretical quantiles
    6.4. Properties of the theoretical quantile-quantile plot
    6.5. Deviations from straight-line patterns
    6.6. Two cautions for interpreting theoretical quantile-quantile plots
    6.7. Distributions with unknown shape parameters
    6.8. Constructing quantile-quantile plots
    *6.9. Adding variability information to a quantile-quantile plot
    *6.10. Censored and grouped data
    6.11. Summary and discussion
    6.12. Further reading
    Exercises

7: Developing and Assessing Regression Models
    7.1. Introduction
    7.2. The linear model
    7.3. Simple regression
    7.4. Preliminary plots
    7.5. Plots during regression fitting
    7.6. Plots after the model is fitted
    7.7. A case study
    *7.8. Some special regression situations
    7.9. Summary and discussion
    7.10. Further reading

Exercises

8: General Principles and Techniques

    8.1. Introduction

    8.2. Overall strategy and thought

    8.3. Visual perception

    8.4. General techniques of plot construction

    8.5. Scales

References

Appendix: Tables of Data Sets

Index

    *An elementary course can omit Chapters 7 and 8, starred sections in other chapters, and starred exercises; a more advanced course can include all of the material. Starred sections contain material that is either more difficult or more specialized than other sections.

395 pp. 8 chapters. Figures, graphs, mathematical formulae, abstract formalisms, models, general index, references, appendix. ISBN 0-534-98052-X.

48

Chasen, Sylvan H.

Geometric Principles and Procedures for Computer Graphic Applications

Prentice-Hall, 1978

Presents a concise introduction to the geometric ideas which form the basis of computer graphics, and to the practical application of these ideas in computer graphic design.

Sylvan E. Chasen of the Lockheed-Georgia Company offers an introductory text on the geometric bases of computer graphic design and the practical application of such designs. This concise and well-organized work covers the fundamentals and problems of displaying equations, the creation and selection of appropriate mathematical formulae for particular data constraints, and the elements and applications of 3-D geometry in computer graphics. Within the context of these topics, the author provides a detailed and clear discussion of least squares, polynomials, Bezier curves, a long section on conics, and curves. The text is supplemented throughout with mathematical formulae, geometrical figures, and illustrations. The general approach is one of real world applications of the geometric concepts discussed. Seven brief appendices offer useful formulae and equations for easy reference. It would be of use to graphic designers as well as systems programmers or analysts, and is suitable as an introductory or reference text, although limited by an extremely brief general index. The work includes a judiciously selected bibliography.

CONTENTS

FOREWORD

INTRODUCTION

CHAPTER I: DISPLAYING EXISTING EQUATIONS

CHAPTER II: CREATING A MATHEMATICAL FORMULATION TO MATCH KNOWN OR DESIRED DATA CONSTRAINTS

A: Least Squares
  1. Manually derived least squares fit
  2. Mathematical least squares (2-D)
  3. Mathematical least squares (linear in N dimensions)
  4. Least squares, two interdependent variables

B: Polynomial Fitting

C: Splines

D: Local Axis Principles

E: Parametric Techniques

F: Bezier Curves

G: Conics
  1. Parabolas
  2. Circles
  3. Ellipses
  4. Generalized ellipses
  5. General conics
  6. Combination of conics

H: Examples of Other Basic Functions
  1. Exponential curves
  2. Normal curves
  3. Trigonometric curves

CHAPTER III: THREE-DIMENSIONAL GEOMETRY

A: Three-Dimensional Primitives

B: Distinction between 3-D Drawings and 3-D Primitives

C: 3-D Boundary Curves for Surfaces
  1. Space curves
  2. Curves in a general plane

D: Surfaces Formed from Four Space Curves—At Least Two in a Principal Coordinate Plane

E: Surfaces Formed from Four General Space Curves

F: Variable Interpolation for Flexible Surface Development

G: Surface Intersections

H: Lengths of Curves, Areas, and Volumes

APPENDICES

A: Derivation of Formulas to Define a Circle, of Given Radius, Tangent to Two Other Circles

B: Finding the Equation of a Circle Inscribed in a Triangle

C: Finding the Equation of a Circle That Is Tangent to Two Other Circles and Passes through a Given Point

D: Derivation of Input Slope Limit to Derive an Elliptic Equation for an Ellipse in Standard Position

E: Derivation of the Equation of an Ellipse in Standard Position with Center on the Y-Axis

F: Lines That Meet Given Constraints
G: Sample Programs for Bezier Curve Generation
BIBLIOGRAPHY
INDEX

241 pp. 3 chapters. Drawings, photographs, figures, graphs, mathematical formulae, general index, bibliography, appendices. ISBN 0-13-352559-7.

Cheng, Patricia W.   *SEE UNDER ID 213*

49
Clark, David R.
(ed.)

collection

Computers for Imagemaking
Pergamon, 1981
(vol. 2 in the *Audio-Visual Media for Education and Research Series*)

This book features eight papers which provide information on the generation of images by computer for the non-expert user.

The topics covered in this collection include: a comparison and contrast of computer imagemaking theories and their applications; a discussion of human image perception; a description of the advantages and disadvantages of the various modes of computer imaging (including interesting supplemental information and commentary); a discussion of the difficulty in achieving artist-quality computer animation due to unresolved artificial intelligence problems encountered in substituting machines for people; a description of three facilities with which the public may contract for the production of computer-generated images; a discussion which recognizes the development of computer imagemaking for use by professionals in disciplines other than computing (architects and engineers, for example) as bringing a powerful problem-solving tool to users; an examination of computer graphics in television which suggests great educational potential and a need for understanding of the interactive roles of human perception and visual presentation; and an assessment of computer imagemaking as a device which allows humans to expand their views of the world, and should be identified as "an aid to comprehending the universe," because it enables a range of visual representations from the smallest to largest known objects, atomic particles to galaxies. (Note: Much of the material is quite technical for the non-expert, but the illustrations are excellent, doing much to clarify difficult concepts.)

CONTENTS
    Chapter 1. The technical foundations of computer imagemaking
        David R. Clark
    Chapter 2. Seeing hypotheses
        Richard L. Gregory
    Chapter 3. Matching the system to the goals or TV or not TV

Tom DeFanti, Dan Sandin
Chapter 4. Computer character animation - is it possible?
Edwin Catmull
Chapter 5. Facilities
  New York Institute of Technology
  Computer-Aided Design Centre
  Computer Image Corporation
Chapter 6. Problem solving on a centralized interactive computer graphics system
Yehonathan Hazony
Chapter 7. Combining computer animation and television presentation: a case study - the Open University mathematics course
John C. Gilbert, John Richmond
Chapter 8. Computer animation as an aid to comprehending the universe
Ken Knowlton
Appendix A: Films
Appendix B: Further reading
Appendix C: Addresses of manufacturers of equipment
Appendix D: Some facilities companies
Index

156 pp. 8 chapters. Drawings, photographs, figures, charts, graphs, general index, appendices. ISBN 0-08-024058-5. (ISBN 0-08-024059-3)

50
Cleveland, William S.

The Elements of Graphing Data
Wadsworth, 1985

An introduction to the technique of graphical data analysis (GDA) and presentation, emphasizing applications in science and technology.

Because he believes that graphical procedures will raise the effectiveness of scientific data analysis, the author has written this book for the general scientific community. The work is intended as an introduction to GDA and its only prerequisites are a basic understanding of probability and statistics. Those sections which require this background are not integral to comprehension of the remaining sections. Little coverage is given to computer graphics, although all of the original illustrations in the book are computer-generated. "The basic ideas, the methods, and the principles of the book transcend the medium used to implement them, but . . . [the computer] is the medium of the present for many and of the future for almost all." Only those methods with wide application in the sciences and technology are included in the book, e.g., sunflowers; jittering; juxtaposition; point, box, and percentile graphs; dot charts; time series; and high-interaction graphical methods. A separate chapter on graphical perception pulls theory and application together. An essential work for the scientist, engineer, or business analyst interested in accurately and effectively representing and analyzing data graphically. (This work is scheduled for publication in the fall of 1985; information provided here is based on prepublication materials provided by the publisher and the author.)

CONTENTS

Note: The following table of contents is based on a prepublication draft

PREFACE

Contents

The Book Within the Book

Computer Graphics

Examples

CHAPTER 1: PROLOGUE: POWER AND IMPROVEMENT

The Power of Graphs

Improving and Expanding Graphical Data Display in Science and Technology

Principles of graph construction

Graphical methods

Graphical perception

Examples of Improved Graphs

Scottish granite

The !Kung birth interval

Body and brain

Playfair's imports and exports

Summary

CHAPTER 2: PRINCIPLES OF GRAPH CONSTRUCTION

Terminology

Clear Vision

Make the data stand out.

Avoid superfluity.

Use visually prominent graphical elements to show the data.

Use four scale lines. Make the data region the interior of the rectangle formed by the scale lines. Put tick marks on all scale lines and keep the ticks outside of the data region.

Do not clutter the data region.

Do not overdo the number of tick marks.

Use reference lines to guide the eye when appropriate, but do not let them interfere with the data.

Avoid putting written explanations, keys, and markers in the data region. Put keys and markers just outside the data region and put written explanations in the legend or in the text.

Overlapping plotting symbols must be visually resolvable.

Superposed data sets must be readily discriminated.

Put labels in the data region only when they aid identification and provide information not easily gotten otherwise.

Visual clarity must be preserved under reduction and reproduction.

Clear Understanding

Make legends comprehensive and informative.

Put a factor on the horizontal scale and a response on the vertical scale.

Error bars should be clearly explained.

When logarithms of a variable are graphed, the scale label should correspond to the tick labels.

Proofread graphs.

Scales

Choose the range of tick marks to include or nearly include the range of the data.

Subject to the constraints that scales have, choose the scales so that the data fill up as much of the data region as possible.

Choose appropriate scales when graphs are being compared.

Be sensible about including zero on a scale.

Use a logarithmic scale when it is important to understand percent change or multiplicative factors.

Showing data on a logarithmic scale can improve resolution.

Use a scale break only when necessary. If a break cannot be avoided, use a full scale break. Take great care in allowing graphical elements to cross a break.

Graphical Style

Put major conclusions into graphical form.

You can pack a lot of information into a small region.

Do not hesitate to make two or more graphs of the same data when it is needed.

Strive for clarity.

CHAPTER 3: GRAPHICAL METHODS

Resolution

Moving

Sunflowers

Jittering

Circles

Logarithms

Residuals

Superposed symbols in black and white

Superposed curves in black and white

Juxtaposition

Color

Logarithms

Distributions

Point graphs

Percentile graphs

Box graphs

Percentile graph with summary

Histograms

Percentile comparison graph

Dot Charts

Factors and Responses

Box graphs for summarizing distributions of repeat measurements of responscs

Strip summaries using box graphs

Smoothing factor-response graphs

Time Series and Other Single-Valued Response Cases

Connected symbol, symbol, connected, and vertical line graphs

Other cases of a single-valued response with an equally spaced factor

Step function graphs and Hershey bars

Three or More Variables
  Framed-rectangle graphs
  Scattergraph matrices
Variation
  Empirical distribution of the data
  Sample-to-sample variation of a statistic
  A hard look at the one standard error bar
  An alternate to the convention of showing sample-to-sample
  variability
  Non-normal population distributions
A View of the Future: High-Interaction Graphical Methods
  High interaction graphical methods
  Brushing a scattergraph matrix
CHAPTER 4: GRAPHICAL PERCEPTION
Introduction
Principles of Data Display Based on an Ordering of Graphical-
Perception Tasks
  The tasks and an order based on the accuracy of visual decoding
  A basic principle of data display
  Graphing rate of change
  Length judgments
  Angle judgments
  Distance and detection
  Detection and superposed curves
  Area
  Volume, color saturation, and color hue
  Shading and statistical maps
  Differences and residuals
  Dot charts and bar charts
Graphical Perception: Theory and Experimentation
  Weber's law
  Stevens' law
  Angle judgments
  The angle contamination of slope judgments
  Experiments in graphical perception
  Summation
CHAPTER 5: AN INTERVIEW
Prologue
  Graphs in statistics
  Graphs in quality control
Principles
  Standards
  Arbitrary inflexibility
  Tick marks and grid lines
  Grid marks
  Tick marks for logs
Methods
  What to graph
  Computers
  Color
  Ducks
  Histograms

Smoothing noisy data
Graphical Perception
   The paradigm
   Experimentation
   Goals
   Cognitive studies
Peroration
REFERENCES

350 pp. 5 chapters. Figures, graphs, references. ISBN 0-534-03729-1.
(ISBN 0-534-03730-5)

Cohen, Roger W.

overview

Image Descriptors for Displays
1975-78

In these reports, Cohen and Carlson and their associates describe a four
year research project intended to develop a series of measures, or
descriptors, for quantifying what an observer sees in a visual display.
Such measures would provide design engineers with a tool for matching
display and human visual performance. In the course of the work, the
authors also develop a nonlinear signal detection model of visual
functioning. These reports are quite technical and assume a working
knowledge of perceptual psychology as well as mathematics and
statistics (especially Fourier analysis). Although more than five years
old, these studies remain definitive. Extension of this work may be
found in Carlson and Cohen's contributions to *Photographic Science
and Engineering Journal*, Vol. 22, 1978, the *SID International
Symposium Digest of Technical Papers* for 1978 and 1979, and *SID:
Proceedings of the Society for Information Display*, Vol. 21, 1980. The
interested reader will also want to refer to the overviews for Snyder,
"Cognitive Studies of Complex Displays," and Pachella, "Visual
Performance in Display Design."

51
Cohen, Roger W.
Gorog, Istvan
Carlson, Curtis R.

technical report

Image Descriptors for Displays
1975

(report number ONR-CR213-120-1; RCA Laboratories; sponsored by
Office of Naval Research; March 1975)

This technical report describes the second year's progress in a research
project which is developing and experimentally testing a mathematical
model for image descriptors in human-display systems.

The mathematical model developed by these researchers covers both
analog and sampled displays. Four image descriptors are essential to the
model. Three of these have been included from the beginning (visual
capacity, perceived signal-to-noise ratio, total information capacity); a
correlation fidelity descriptor has been added to the model in this

report. Correlational fidelity is the measure of how closely a reproduced (displayed) scene corresponds to the original. After a brief introduction, this report devotes a section to describing correlational fidelity, presenting a mathematical explanation of this descriptor, and discussing the relationships between correlational facility and the other three descriptors. These descriptor relations are often monotonic, but sometimes the requirements for obtaining good correlational facility can differ greatly from requirements of total information capacity and call for a very different display design strategy. A third section covers hardware related imperfections in matrix displays. Section four covers the two-dimensional characteristics of displays and the human visual process. A final section discusses experimental research on the human contrast sensitivity function. Psychophysical measurements of the two-dimensional sine wave human response are given as this response relates to visual angle, brightness of display, and background brightness. This well-written and well-organized report subsumes most of the material from the first report as well as adding new information. Although quite technical and mathematical, the burden on the reader is eased somewhat by a placement of mathematical derivations in appendices rather than the text. A great deal of data is presented in this report, much of it conveyed through graphs and presented for the benefit of vision psychologists. The authors stress the interdisciplinary nature of their research and much of the early research in television; this research is relevant to the work of the display design professional and the perceptual psychologist.

CONTENTS

SYMBOLS EMPLOYED IN FORMULAS AND TEXT

I: INTRODUCTION

II: STATISTICAL PROPERTIES OF NATURAL SCENES

III: THEORY OF ONE-DIMENSIONAL SAMPLED DISPLAYS

A: Assumptions and Limitations

B: General Formulation of the One-Dimensional Sampling Scene Problem

C: Separation of the Perceived Intensity into Signal and Noise Components

D: Two-Descriptors: The Visual Capacity and the Perceived Signal-to-Noise Ratio
    1. The visual capacity
    2. The perceived signal-to-noise ratio

E: The Total Information Capacity—A Combined Perceivable Information Descriptor

VI: TWO-DIMENSIONAL ANALOG DISPLAYS - THE VISUAL CAPACITY

A: Mathematical Formulation

B: Properties of $C^T_{v_2}(r)$
    1. Far-field viewing
    2. Near-field viewing
    3. Maximum visual capacity

C: A Calculated Example

D: Summary

V: OPTICAL BLOCK PROCESSOR

VI: VISUAL PROCESSING OF COMPLEX TWO-DIMENSIONAL GRATINGS

A: Background

B: Statement of the Problem

C: Experimental Approach

D: Experimental Studies Design

E: Calibration

F: Experimental Procedure

G: Results and Discussion

REFERENCES

154 pp. 6 chapters. Photographs, figures, graphs, mathematical formulae, abstract formalisms, references.

52
Cohen, Roger W.
Carlson, Curtis R.
Cody, George D.

technical report

Image Descriptors for Display
1976

(report number ONR-CR213-120-2; RCA Laboratories; sponsored by Office of Naval Research; May 1976)

Presents experimental findings and psychophysical theory as they apply to the development of image quality descriptors that can predict and enhance performance of display systems for the human viewer.

This is the first report of a several year research project which used linear systems analysis and the methodology of statistical communications theory to develop image descriptors. A brief introductory section opens this report. Following sections cover: a spectral analysis of the information content of natural scenes as produced by off-the-air television signals on VHF channels; a mathematical description of a one-dimensional sampled display system, including visual capacity and perceived signal-to-noise ratio; development of a third descriptor—the total information capacity descriptor—that combines both components; a discussion of experimental work with the visual capacity of and need for two-dimensional analog displays; a description of the optical block processor used in this research; and a long section on experimental work on one- and two-dimensional sine wave responses in human visual perception. The two-dimensional data collected here is, according to the authors, the first available and "is in general agreement with predictions based on previously obtained one-dimensional data," suggesting that the linear analysis used in the study may be methodologically permissible. The research reported here is complex and requires a knowledge of mathematics, statistics, human perception, and image descriptors. The authors provide little introductory material, assuming most of the readers to be other experts in the field with large working vocabularies in these areas. This report includes many illustrations, primarily graphic reports of experimental findings. Mathematical equations and derivations are also included in the text.

CONTENTS

SYMBOLS EMPLOYED IN FORMULAS AND TEXT

I: INTRODUCTION

II: THE CORRELATION FIDELITY

A: Descriptors for Information Transmission and for Image Fidelity

B: The Correlation Fidelity

C: Optimum Modulation Transfer Functions

    1. Noisy analog displays

    2. Sampled displays

D: The Block-Sampled Display

E: The Bilevel Matrix Display

III: THEORY OF IMPERFECT MATRIX DISPLAYS

A: Introduction

B: Luminance Fluctuations in Matrix Displays

C: Cell Position Fluctuations in Matrix Displays

IV: THEORY AND APPLICATION OF TWO-DIMENSIONAL DESCRIPTORS

A: Two-Dimensional Descriptors

B: The Two-Dimensional Power Spectrum of Natural Scenes

C: Noisy Analog Displays

D: Subjective Effects of Two-Dimensional Noise - The Experiments of Huang

E: Improved Array Configurations for Matrix Displays

V: EXPERIMENTAL RESULTS IN VISUAL PROCESSING OF SINE-WAVE LUMINANCE GRATINGS

A: Introduction

    1. Objective

    2. The contrast sensitivity function

    3. Linear processing in the human visual system

B: Experimental Facility and Procedure

    1. Experimental facility

    2. Experimental procedure

    3. Estimation of total experimental accuracy

C: Effects of Display Size on the Contrast Sensitivity Function

    1. Introduction

    2. Experimental apparatus

    3. Experimental procedure

    4. Results and discussion

D: Two-Dimensional Sinusoidal Luminance Grating Experiments

    1. Introduction

    2. Problem statement

    3. Experimental apparatus

    4. Experimental procedure

    5. Results and discussion

E: Effects of Surround Brightness on the Visual Contrast Sensitivity Function
1. Introduction
2. Experimental apparatus
3. Experimental procedure
4. Results and discussion

F: Individual Variations in the Contrast Sensitivity Function
1. Introduction
2. Experimental apparatus
3. Experimental procedure
4. Results and discussion

G: Two-Dimensional Adaption Experiments
1. Introduction
2. Experimental apparatus and procedure
3. Results and discussion

H: Relation of Contrast Sensitivity Function to Signal-to-Noise Characteristics of the Visual System

I: Conclusions

APPENDICES

A: Expressions for Image Descriptors Used to Evaluate Block-Sampled Displays

B: Derivation of Equations (25) and (26)

C: Derivation of Equation (37)

D: Derivation of Equations (39) and (40)

E: Derivation of Equations (49) and (50)

F: Derviation of the Expression for the Perceived Noise Power N_2^2

G: Calculation of the Expression for the Two-Dimensional Perceived Signal-to-Noise Ratio

REFERENCES

247 pp. 5 chapters. Photographs, figures, graphs, mathematical formulae, abstract formalisms, references, appendices.

53
Mezrich, Joseph J.
Carlson, Curtis R.
Cohen, Roger W.

technical report

Image Descriptors for Displays
1977

(report number ONR-CR213-120-3; RCA Laboratories; sponsored by Office of Naval Research; February 1977)

The third annual research report of a U.S. Navy sponsored research project; describes expansions in the author's work developing image descriptors for human-display systems, including theoretical and empirical work on chrominance information and color.

The research program focuses on empirical work dealing with the role of color in pattern recognition. One of the findings was that color is involved in shape recognition when color and shape dimension are integral rather than separate and when a stimulus is locally rather than globally processed. The results indicate that the role of color in pattern recognition is a complex one. The second major thrust of the research was the development of a new descriptor for the total channel capacity of the display-observer system, which takes chrominance information into account. This descriptor is developed from a model of a visual system having one luminance channel and two channels for chrominance information. This new descriptor has a non-linear basis, unlike the linearly based earlier descriptors developed by the researchers. Additional empirical work on a previously developed descriptor for visual capacity or sharpness is described in this report. Specifically, the relationships between visual capacity and subjectively judged sharpness of displayed images were examined. The results suggest the importance of edge transitions "in determining image sharpness in pictorial scenes." This research report, technical and with complex mathematical content and numerous graphic presentations of empirical findings, should be of interest to display design professionals as well as researchers in human perception.

CONTENTS

LIST OF NOTATIONS

I: INTRODUCTION

II: EFFECT OF COLOR ON PATTERN RECOGNITION

A: Introduction to Experiments
1. Overview
2. Instrumentation and procedures

B: Influence of Color in Letter and Word Recognition
1. Introduction
2. Experimental procedure
3. Results

C: Status of Color as a Shape-Independent Stimulus Feature
1. Introduction
2. Experimental procedure
3. Results

D: Intrusion of Color into Shape-Recognition Decision Processes in Steadily Viewed Displays
1. Introduction
2. Experimental procedure
3. Results

E: Conclusions

III: STATISTICAL PROPERTIES OF THE LUMINANCE AND CHROMINANCE VARIATIONS IN NATURAL SCENES

A: Introduction

B: Measurement Techniques

C: Results
1. Average rms modulation depth for luminance information
2. Luminance power spectral density measurements
3. Average rms modulation depth for chrominance information
4. Chrominance power spectral density measurements

D: Summary of Results

IV: SUBJECTIVE SHARPNESS OF DISPLAYED IMAGES

A: Introduction

B: Experimental Apparatus

    1. Introduction

    2. Diffuser display

    3. Scene characteristics

    4. Scene modulation transfer functions

    5. Observer modulation transfer functions

C: Experimental Procedure

D: The Perceived Edge-Gradient Content

E: Results

F: Summary of Conclusions

V: STATISTICAL THEORY OF DISPLAY DESCRIPTORS

A: Introduction

B: The Distribution of Perceivable Sine-Wave Luminance Levels

    1. Signal-detection model

    2. Number of perceivable contrast levels

C: The Luminance Channel Capacity

    1. Formalism

    2. Properties of the luminance channel capacity

D: The Chrominance Channel Capacity

    1. Independent channel capacity

    2. Chrominance contrast-sensitivity functions and equivalent rms chrominance modulation

    3. Application of the chrominance channel capacity

REFERENCES

DISTRIBUTION LIST

142 pp. 5 chapters. Figures, graphs, mathematical formulae, abstract formalisms, models, references.

54
Carlson, Curtis R.
Cohen, Roger W.

technical report

Visibility of Displayed Information
1978

(report number ONR-CR213-120-4F; RCA Laboratories; sponsored by Office of Naval Research; July 1978)

This final report of a four year U.S. Navy sponsored research project addresses the problem of predicting what an observer viewing a display will see. The predictions suggested by the nonlinear luminance signal-detection visual model developed in this research project are empirically tested and the results reported, along with some theoretical discussions of the model.

The nonlinear signal-detection model utilized here is the second visual model developed by this research project and it is considered by the researchers to be far more powerful than the linear model originally developed. The present nonlinear model is based on recent discoveries in the psychophysics of vision and takes into account a variety of display parameters, including modulation transfer, noise, sampling processes, scene content, mean luminance, and display size. The empirical findings of the study are presented as graphic figures referred to as Discriminable Difference Diagrams (DDDs). These diagrams convey information about "the total amount of perceived image structure at different retinal frequencies, and also the perceptual effect that results from changes in the system MTF" (Modulation Transfer Function). One hundred DDDs are presented in the report across parameters such as signal-to-noise ratio, mean luminance, and display size. Section one of the report provides a short introduction to the research project. Sections two and three are a handbook of DDDs, including introductory material, examples, and graphic data presentation. The final section and the appendices describe "the theory and experimental verification behind the DDDs." This report is technical and requires a strong mathematical and statistical background as well as a good understanding of display design and the psychology of perceptual issues. The reader is expected to have prior knowledge of modulation transfer functions and Fourier analysis. This report builds upon the earlier work in the research project; familiarity with the previous three reports of the project is helpful.

CONTENTS

LIST OF SYMBOLS

I: INTRODUCTION

II: THE USE OF DISCRIMINABLE DIFFERENCE DIAGRAMS: A GUIDE

A: Overview and Summary

B: Application of the DDDs to Analog Displays
    1. Introduction
    2. Examples
       a. Predicting a discriminable difference in image structure (or sharpness)
       b. Perceptually perfect display
       c. Effect of display luminance on perceived image structure
       d. Effect of the viewing distance parameter r/w on perceived image structure
       e. Comparison of the sharpness of NTSC and PAL systems

C: Application of the DDDs to Sampled and Raster Displays
    1. Introduction
       a. Parameters for the sampled/raster display problem
       b. Discriminable difference diagrams for sampled/raster displays
    2. Examples
       a. Perception of raster lines in a white field
       b. Elimination of aliasing
       c. Effect of increasing the display modulation transfer function
       d. Effect of prefiltering on signal and noise jnd's
       e. Change in sampling frequency required to produce an improvement in perceived image quality

III: COMPUTED DISCRIMINABLE DIFFERENCE DIAGRAMS

A: Index

B: Analog Display DDDs

C: Sampled and Raster Display DDDs

IV: MODEL EMPLOYED FOR THE COMPUTATION OF DISCRIMINABLE DIFFERENCE DIAGRAMS

A: Introduction

B: Quadratic Signal-Detection Model
  1. Discrimination of changes in sine-wave contrast
  2. Discrimination model for complex scenes
  3. Equivalent sine-wave contrasts for signals and noise
  4. Number of distinguishable contrast levels

C: Model Parameters for $m_T(v)$ and $k(v)$
  1. Sine-wave threshold contrast sensitivity $m_T(v)$
  2. Weber's fraction $k(v)$

D: Some Properties of Images
  1. Power spectrum of pictorial scenes
  2. The importance of luminance edge transitions
  3. Distribution of luminance levels in pictorial scenes

E: Parameters and Assumptions Used in Computing the DDDs

F: Combining jnd's from Several Channels
  1. Probability summation among independent frequency-specification channels
  2. Comparison of different approaches

G: Application of the Contrast Detection Model to Anisotropic MTFs

H: Experimental Verification of the DDDs
  1. Introduction
  2. MTF discrimination experiments: sequential presentation
  3. Results and discussion: sequential presentation
  4. MTF discrimination experiments: simultaneous presentation
  5. Results and discussion: simultaneous presentation
  6. Conclusions

APPENDICES

A: Power Spectra for Various Signals

B: Equations for Sampled and Raster Displays

C: Noise Visibility: Three Issues

D: Image Quality and the DDDs

E: Derivation of the Equation for the Total Number of Discriminable Contrast Levels

REFERENCES

274 pp. 4 chapters. Figures, graphs, abstract formalisms, models, references, appendices.

55
Collins, Belinda L.

technical report

The Development and Evaluation of Effective Symbol Signs
1982

(report number NBS-BSS-141; National Bureau of Standards, NBS
Building Science Series 141; May 1982)

This report, sponsored by the National Bureau of Standards, reviews
research and discusses issues of importance in developing and
evaluating symbols used as signs, with a special emphasis on symbols
that communicate safety information.

The author points out the growing need for developing effective
symbolic signs due to such factors as increased international travel and
high illiteracy rates. Effective symbol signs are defined as symbols in
which the message sent by the sign's creator is the same as the message
received by the user. An introductory section defines some symbol
terminology and gives background information on the history of
symbols and symbol standardization. The remainder of the report
considers "pictorial" and "abstract concept-related" symbol types. The
paper discusses advantages and disadvantages of symbol use and
outlines some important graphical considerations for creating and
producing symbol signs. Three case studies are discussed in which
symbols are subjected to a graphics review. The limitations of a
graphics review by itself are noted and the importance of evaluation of
symbols by users is stressed. A third section focuses on experimental
evaluations of symbols with particular emphasis on the methodology of
evaluation studies and on research findings. Five particular application
areas are reviewed. Most of the research investigated understandability
of symbols, but detection, discrimination, recognition, attention, and
ability of symbol signs to alter behavior were also studied. The author
stresses the need for future research to examine these evaluation
dimensions more fully. The concluding section of the paper emphasizes
the need for further research into developing and evaluating symbol
signs and suggests the directions that research should take. Specific
issues covered here include: good graphic design, characteristics of user
groups, shape and color of graphics visibility, realism of symbols,
legibility, durability, and placement. The coverage of the topic area of
this report is thorough and the writing is competent. The reproduction
of the report (and its accompanying figures) is poor and in places
interferes directly with readability.

CONTENTS

ABSTRACT

LIST OF FIGURES

LIST OF TABLES

SI CONVERSION UNITS

1: INTRODUCTION

1.1: Overview

1.2: Definition of Graphic Symbols

1.3: Symbol History and Standardization

2: DEVELOPMENT OF EFFECTIVE SYMBOLS

2.1: Advantages of Symbol Use

2.2: Limitations of Symbols

2.3: Design Considerations
2.3.1. Graphic concerns
2.3.2. Application of perceptual principles to symbol design

2.4: Case Studies of Design Evaluation

2.5: Need for Evaluation of Effectiveness

3: EXPERIMENTAL EVALUATION OF SYMBOL EFFECTIVENESS

3.1: Requirements for Communication

3.2: Highway Symbol Research
3.2.1. Reaction time to word and symbol signs
3.2.2. Glance legibility assessment of understandability
3.2.3. Direct assessment of meaningfulness
3.2.4. Comparison of laboratory and behavioral data
3.2.5. Visibility of highway symbols

3.3: Automotive and Machinery Symbols
3.3.1. Machine symbol evaluation
3.3.2. Automotive symbol evaluation
3.3.3. Automotive symbol production
3.3.4. Orientation of symbols

3.4: Public Information Symbols for Buildings

3.5: Hazard Warning Symbols for Products

3.6: Safety Symbols for Buildings

3.7: Categorization of Previous Research

3.8: Concerns for Future Research

4: SUMMARY

4.1: Overview of the Literature

4.2: Issues in the Development and Standardization of More Effective Symbols

REFERENCES

96 pp. 4 chapters. Figures, tables, references.

Computer Graphics   *SEE UNDER ID 101*

56
Conrac Corporation

Raster Graphics Handbook
Conrac Corporation, 1980

A handbook providing an overview of the hardware, software, and system design issues related to raster graphics.

The term *raster graphics* includes almost every type of computer-processed or computer-generated display, encompassing alphagraphic, vectorgraphic, and continuous-tone imagery. This handbook gives a broad overview of state-of-the-art technology and outlines developments likely to influence the future of graphics. Prepared with the help of the Conrac engineering staff, and based on Conrac's extensive experience as producer of approximately three-quarters of all broadcast and teleproduction studio monitors, this handbook attempts to pull together television and computer display technologies. While attempting to facilitate the interchange between the technologies of television and computer science, this book addresses issues in the design, selection, and utilization of a raster graphics system. It may also be used to evaluate currently available systems. Areas covered include: the functions of a graphics system; the processing required to convert source data to a graphic display; the SIGGRAPH Core System (a standard graphics package for viewing systems); the distribution of graphics intelligence between processing centers; controller characteristics; system interfaces; and the selection and evaluation of monitors. In a discussion of human factors relevant to graphics design, this book takes into account the capabilities and limitations of the human eye, pointing out that ultimately the purpose of a graphics system is to communicate information to the human observer. One appendix summarizes Electronic Industries Association (EIA) display signal standards, while another discusses factors in color programming. This handbook presumes a knowledge of computer technology and, while the work is aimed at those who are actively involved in the design of raster graphics systems, its extensive glossary also makes the handbook accessible to the newcomer. A second edition of this text has been published, but was not available for examination.

CONTENTS
    Purpose and scope of handbook
    Display principles and technologies
    Functions and tasks
    Raster-display software
    Distributing the intelligence
    Accessories and peripherals
    Designing the graphics controller
    The monitor interface
    Monitor evaluation and selection
    The human interface
    Appendix

347 pp. 10 chapters. Drawings, figures, charts, mathematical formulae, general index, references, glossary, appendices. (ISBN 0-9604972-0-X)

Cornog, Douglas Y.
Rose, F. Clayton
Walkowicz, Josephine L.
overview

Legibility of Alphanumeric Characters and Other Symbols
U.S. Government Printing Office, 1964-67

These two volumes comprise a reference handbook intended for use as a guide to the literature in basic human factors and psychological, technical, and scientific legibility literature. Though each is complete in itself, they are designed to be used together. This extensive, yet selective, handbook provides summaries and extracts of information from most major psychological findings and data on the legibility of alphanumeric characters and other symbols (particularly those used in radar displays). Three editorial criteria govern the selection of material: literature must focus on legibility, readability, perceptibility, visibility or other closely related concepts; research should emphasize post-1940 information; and research should emphasize psychological, quantitative experimentation. The 203 entries are indexed in three ways: "(1) a matrix cross-reference index (article versus functional variables - environmental typographical), (2) author indexes (alphabetical and chronological), and (3) a character-face-name-index." A glossary of matrix index terms is included. From the material presented here, the reader should be able to ascertain whether or not the original source of information will be of value.

57
Cornog, Douglas Y.
Rose, F. Clayton
Walkowicz, Josephine L.

reference

Legibility of Alphanumeric Characters and Other Symbols I: A Permuted Title Index and Bibliography
U.S. Government Printing Office, 1964

(National Bureau of Standards Miscellaneous Publication 262-1)

CONTENTS
Introduction
Permuted title index
Cross reference: Accession numbers
to entry identification
Bibliography
Author index

100 pp. 5 sections. Author index, bibliography.

58
Cornog, Douglas Y.
Rose, F. Clayton

reference

Legibility of Alphanumeric Characters and Other Symbols II: A Reference Handbook
U.S. Government Printing Office, 1967

(National Bureau of Standards Miscellaneous Publication 262-2)

CONTENTS
Introduction
Reference information extracts
Appendix A: Author indexes (alphabetical and chronological)
Appendix B: Character face name index
Appendix C: Character face samples

Appendix D: Glossary of matrix index terms
Appendix E: Matrix subject index

460 pp. 7 sections. Figures, tables, appendices.

59
Damodaran, Leela
Simpson, Alison
Wilson, Paul

Designing Systems for People
NCC Publications, 1980

(sponsored by the National Computing Centre and the research group on Human Sciences and Advanced Technology [HUSAT] of Loughborough University of Technology)

Intended for practicing systems analysts and others concerned with implementing office systems, this concise handbook combines principles from applied ergonomics with precepts from practical experience to help design and implement computer systems for "non-expert" users.

This handbook is intended to advise designers and recommend specific approaches in systems design. The result of a collaboration between human scientists and computer specialists, this book will inform the system designer and will introduce the user, the employer, and the trade union to specific issues in systems design and to the human aspects of technology. The bulk of the book deals with selection, installation, and use of terminal equipment. Workplace design and user support are also addressed. Nearly fifty pages of appendices—one-fourth of the text—include: checklists; human aspects criteria for video display units and keyboards; a sample data definition sheet; VDU workplace design factors; and VDU eye-test record sheets. While it is quite specifically not a text on human science or systems analysis/design, a briefly annotated bibliography to source books in these areas is provided. An easy-to-read, no-nonsense companion for anyone involved in the efficient use of computer installations.

CONTENTS

Preface

Introduction

1: Planning the Development
    Setting up lines of communication
    Planning the design strategy
    Planning for disruption

2: Systems Analysis—User Aspects
    Introduction
    Work situation appraisal
    User identification
    Task demands
    Work role analysis
    User readiness

3: Equipment Selection
    Equipment survey
    Criteria for equipment selection
    Mechanics of the selection process
4: Systems Design—User Aspects
    Job design
    Activity feedback
    Dialogue design
    Designing procedures for faults and breakdowns
5: Workplace Design
    Collection of environmental data
    Workstation design
    Lighting
    Room climate
    Noise
    Room layout
    Upkeep of equipment, workstations and workplaces
6: User Support
    Planning user support
    Training
    Documentation
    Human support
    Change mechanisms
    Continuing user support
Appendices
    1. Checklists
    2. Human aspects criteria (VDUs and keyboards)
    3. Completed data definition sheet
    4. VDU/keyboard assessment for workstation design
    5. Manuscript holder recommendations for VDU tasks
    6. VDU workstation design factors
    7. VDU eye test record sheets
    8. Office space availability measurement
    9. Terminal identification record sheet
    10. Stock control clerk training needs
    11. Bibliography
Index

193 pp. 6 chapters. Figures, tables, subject index, bibliography, appendices. ISBN 0-85012-242-2.

60
de Beaugrande, Robert

Text Production: Toward a Science of Composition
Ablex, 1984

(vol. 11 in the *Advances in Discourse Processes* series, Roy O. Freedle, series ed.)

A book on the many factors influencing the process of producing compositions, including a review of theoretical and experimental work in this area.

Concerned about public literacy and literacy education, de Beaugrande calls for more research in the area of text production, stating that it is essential that we learn how people develop compositions. Research, prior theories, personal experience, original speculation, and approximately 500 examples of every day discourse all find their way into the author's search to establish a framework for a science of composition. De Beaugrande pulls together thirty-nine pages of references from works in linguistics, education, English, psychology, and philosophy. Emphasizing the importance of a comprehensive model of the mental processes involved in text production, the author points out that texts and discourses are dynamic events and that researchers must study how items are chosen and used in real contexts. The book discusses memory, attention, and other factors that influence the processes of text development, and proposes seven principles of linearity to account for the arrangement of compositions. Different levels of text processing, phases of text production, issues related to style, work on spelling and on grammar are all included. The author examines different models of text production and offers criteria for evaluating these; problems with research and research design are also scrutinized. New terms are introduced in block capitals and defined in everyday language. While this work is directed foremost to the educator, there is much to interest the researcher in cognition and the composition process.

CONTENTS

Preface to the Series

Introductory Note

0: Plan of the Book

I: The Context of Communication
    1. A "science" of composition?
    2. Literacy: critique of a crisis
    3. Evaluation and grading
    4. Text and discourse as events

II: Scientific Precursors
    1. Structuralism and linguistics
    2. Physicalism and behaviorism
    3. Mentalism and transformational grammar

III: The Procedural Approach
    1. Designing a model
    2. The phases of text production
    3. The resources of text processing

IV: The Linearity of Text Production
  1. Temporality versus spatiality
  2. Seven principles of linearity
  3. Linearity and the motives for punctuating
V: Writing vs. Spelling, Grammar, and Speech
  1. Spelling: rules, regularity, or randomness?
  2. Grammar made operations
  3. Speaking versus writing
VI: Style, Stages, and Steps Toward Progress
  1. Style
  2. The stages of discourse
  3. Theory and practice: a common cause
References
Abbreviations
Name Index
Subject Index
About the Author

400 pp. 6 chapters. Figures, tables, footnotes, subject index, references, name index. ISBN 0-89391-158-5. (ISBN 0-89391-159-3)

61
Dent, Borden D.

Principles of Thematic Map Design
Addison-Wesley, 1985

This introductory cartography textbook focuses on the design of thematic maps, otherwise known as "special purpose" or "statistical" maps. The integration of cartographic theory and practice is a priority of the text.

The text is composed of eleven chapters that focus on material to be learned and four "design interludes" that focus on design issues and "attempt to inspire students' creative impulses." The first six chapters present basic information about design, mapping, and geography. The coverage here, of major concepts in geography and their relationship to cartography, is not commonly found in textbooks. The final five chapters each focus on one major type of thematic mapping: choropleth maps (which present quantitative information through the use of shading); dot maps; proportional symbol maps; isarithmic maps (which map "real or conceptual three-dimensional geographic volume" using "quantitative line symbols"); and value-by-area cartograms. The four design interludes cover map composition, organizing maps according to "visual hierarchies" so that important features are more noticeable, lettering, and color theory. Throughout the text the role of students as map designers is stressed. Computer mapping is very minimally discussed, but the principles discussed apply to any form of mapping. Glossaries of important terms and suggestions for further reading are included. Numerous well constructed example maps and figures, nearly all of which are originals created for this textbook, demonstrate concepts treated in the text. One of the appendices provides information about where to obtain many varieties of maps produced by the U.S. government. This textbook is written at the introductory undergraduate level. Although the book is easy to read and understand, the author is still able to provide thorough coverage of the subject matter. The book should be useful for professional cartographers and graphic artists as well as students.

CONTENTS

Preface

CHAPTER 1: INTRODUCTION TO THEMATIC MAPPING

Preview

The Realm of Maps
    The map defined
    What is cartography?
    Kinds of maps
    Map scale
    Map communication

Cartographic Abstraction and Generalization
    Classification
    Simplification
    Symbolization
    The art in cartography
    The quantitative mapping process

Thematic Map Design
    What is map design?
    The design process
    Map elements for design consideration
    Notes
    Glossary
    Readings for further understanding

CHAPTER 2: THE ROUND EARTH TO FLAT MAP: MAP PROJECTIONS FOR DESIGNERS

Preview

Size and Shape of the Earth

Coordinate Geometry for the Cartographer
    Plane coordinate geometry
    Earth coordinate geometry
    Principle geometric and mathematical relationships of the Earth's coordinate grid

An Introduction to Map Projections for the Designer
    The map projection process
    Surface transformation and map distortion
    Determining deformation and its distribution over the projection
    Patterns of deformation
    Notes
    Glossary
    Readings for further understanding

CHAPTER 3: EMPLOYMENT OF PROJECTIONS AND THEMATIC BASE MAP COMPILATION

Preview

Employment of Map Projections
World projections
Projections for mapping continents
Mapping large and small countries at mid-latitudes
Mapping at low latitudes
The selection of projections for individual states
Unique solutions to the employment of projections

Base Map Compilation
Compilation and generalization
Compilation sources
Methods of compilation
Copyright
Notes
Glossary
Readings for further understanding

CHAPTER 4: GRAPHIC TOOLS OF MAP PRODUCTION AND REPRODUCTION

Preview

Printing Technology for Cartographers
Brief history of map printing
Modern photolithography

Map Production Techniques
Two manual techniques
Technique
Computer-generated maps

The Artwork Plan
Getting started
Making a flow chart
Map editing
Preparing copy for the printer
Proofing completed art
Notes
Glossary
Readings for further understanding

DESIGN INTERLUDE 1: ELEMENTS OF MAP COMPOSITION

Preview

Design Levels on the Map

The Map's Design Elements

The Composition Process
Visualization
Experimentation

Elements of Map Composition
Purpose of map composition
Planar organization of the visual elements
Figure and ground organization
Contrast
Visual acuity
Notes

Glossary

Readings for further understanding

CHAPTER 5: THE NATURE OF GEOGRAPHICAL PHENOMENA
AND THE SELECTION OF THEMATIC MAP SYMBOLS

Preview

Geography and Geographical Phenomena
Geography defined
Major themes in geographical research
Key concepts in geography

Measurement in Geography
Spatial dimensions of geographical phenomena
Measurement scales
Measurement error
Data sources
The geographical areal unit

The Multidimensional Characteristics of Thematic Map Symbols
Symbol types and visual dimensions: qualitative and quantitative mapping
Characteristics of geographical phenomena and symbol selection

Enumeration Data, Geographical Units, and Census Definitions
The United States Census
The Census of Canada
Notes
Glossary
Readings for further understanding

CHAPTER 6: PREPROCESSING GEOGRAPHICAL DATA:
COMMON MEASURES USEFUL IN THEMATIC MAPPING

Preview

Need for Data Preprocessing

Mathematical and Statistical Methods
Ratio, proportion, and percent
Variables, values, and arrays
Frequency distributions and histograms

Summarizing Data Distributions
Nominal scale: the mode and the variation ratio
Ordinal scale: the median and percentiles
Interval and ratio scales: the arithmetic mean and the standard deviation

Measures of Areal Concentration and Association
The coefficient of areal correspondence
Areal means
Two measures of point clustering
Measuring spatial association by regression methods

Data Classification
Classification is more
Groups based on similarities
Notes
Glossary
Readings for further understanding

CHAPTER 7: MAPPING ENUMERATION DATA: THE
CHOROPLETH MAP

Preview

Selecting the Choropleth Technique
    Mapping rationale
    Data appropriateness
    When to use the choropleth map
    Preliminary considerations in choropleth mapping

Data Classification Techniques
    The importance of classification
    Methods of data classification
    Constant intervals
    Variable intervals
    Different maps from the same data
    Unclassed choropleth maps

Legend Design, Areal Symbolization, and Base Map Design
    Sources of map reading error and the need for accurate design
      response
    Symbol selection for choropleth maps
    Providing adequate base information
    Notes
    Glossary
    Readings for further understanding

DESIGN INTERLUDE 2: TOTAL MAP ORGANIZATION, THE
VISUAL HIERARCHY, AND THE FIGURE-GROUND
RELATIONSHIP

Preview

Visual Hierarchy Defined
    Customary positions of map elements in the hierarchy

Achieving Visual Hierarchy
    Fundamental perceptual organization of the two-dimensional visual
      field: figure and ground
    Perceptual grouping principles
    Figure formation and closure
    Using texture to produce figures
    Strong edges and figure development
    The interposition phenomenon
    Figures and grounds in the map frame

The Special Case of Land-Water Contrast
    Vignetting for land-water differentiation
    Notes
    Glossary
    Readings for further understanding

CHAPTER 8: MAPPING POINT PHENOMENA: THE COMMON
DOT MAP

Preview

Mapping Technique
    A classification of dot maps
    Advantages and disadvantages of dot mapping
    The mapping activity
    Dot map production

Visual Impressions of Dot Maps
    Numerousness and density
    Rescaling dot maps

Computer-Generated Dot Maps
    Notes
    Glossary
    Readings for further understanding

CHAPTER 9: FROM POINT TO POINT: THE PROPORTIONAL SYMBOL MAP

Preview

Conceptual basis for proportional point symbol mapping
    When to select the method

A brief history of proportional point symbols
    A variety of choices
    Three-dimensional symbols

Proportional Symbol Scaling
    Psychophysical examination of quantitative thematic map symbols
    Range-grading: a probable solution

Graphic Design Considerations for Proportional Point Symbol Maps
    The nature of the data
    Overloaded proportional point symbol
    Graphic treatment of the proportional symbols
    Computer maps
    Notes
    Glossary
    Readings for further understanding

DESIGN INTERLUDE 3: MAKING THE MAP READABLE THROUGH INTELLIGENT USE OF TYPOGRAPHY

Preview

Functions of Map Lettering

Elements of Type
    Typeface characteristics
    Letter and word spacing
    Typeface classification
    Personalities of typefaces
    Legibility of type

Thematic Map Typography and Design
    Lettering practices
    Experimental studies

Production of Cold Type Map Lettering
    Hand lettering
    Pressure-sensitive materials
    Photographic image production
    Notes
    Glossary
    Readings for further understanding

CHAPTER 10: CAPTURING GEOGRAPHICAL VOLUMES: THE ISARITHMIC MAP

Preview

The Nature of Isarithmic Mapping
    Fundamental concepts
    Isarithmic forms and terminology
    Basis of isarithmic construction
    A brief history of isarithmic mapping
    When to select the isarithmic method

Isarithmic Practices
    Elements of isarithmic mapping
    Sources of error in isarithmic mapping

Preparing the Finished Isarithmic Map
    Design elements
    Production methods
    Notes
    Glossary
    Readings for further understanding

CHAPTER 11: VALUE-BY-AREA MAPPING

Preview

Value-by-Area Cartogram
    Basic history of the method
    Two basic forms emerge
    Mapping requirements

Communicating with Cartograms
    Recognizing shapes
    Estimating areas
    A communication model
    Two-variable value-by-area cartogram

Cartogram Construction
    Manual methods
    Computer solutions
    Notes
    Glossary
    Readings for further understanding

DESIGN INTERLUDE 4: PRINCIPLES FOR COLOR THEMATIC MAPS

Preview

Color Perception
    The human eye
    Physical properties of color production
    Color dimensions
    Color interaction
    Subjective reactions to color
    Advancing and retreating colors

Color Specification Systems
    Munsell color solid
    Ostwald color solid
    The ISCC-NBS method
    CIE color specification
    Printing color specifications

Color in Cartographic Design
> The functions of color in design
> Design strategies for the use of color
> Notes
> Glossary
> Readings for further understanding

APPENDIX A: GEOGRAPHICAL TABLES
APPENDIX B: CENSUS GEOGRAPHY DEFINITIONS
APPENDIX C: MAP SOURCES
INDEX

398 pp. 15 chapters. Drawings, photographs, figures, maps, tables, general index, references, appendices, color graphics, chapter glossaries. ISBN 0-201-11334-1.

62
Derefeldt, Gunilla

technical report

Color Coding of Displays, Maps and Images
1981

(report number C-53003-H9; Foersvarets Forskningsanstalt, Stockholm; February 1981)

Surveys research on color coding of displays, maps, and pictures as a means of improving human performance in visual tasks.

The author provides a review of applied color coding research in the areas of symbolic display, maps, and pictures. The survey of research on color coding of symbols stresses, in addition to the advantages of color coding, the importance of display density, display variety, and symbol size. Her discussion of work on color coding of maps emphasizes the importance of carefully chosen color schemes. The author's survey of color use in sonar CRT display notes that the merits of color codes in this area have more to do with harmonious color combinations than with individual color "conspicuousness." Her review of the literature on color coding of pictures raises a number of important questions about the many factors that must be considered in measuring color code effectiveness which have yet to be investigated thoroughly: how, for example, do the spacing and combination of colors used in a code affect performance and subjective preference? While it brings attention to important questions, the review of works on color coding provides the author with a basis for only some very general conclusions and a "first guide to the use of color." Although long, the reference list is somewhat dated with some citations from the ninteenth century (i.e., mostly of historical value). The majority of citations are from the mid-1970s or earlier. Numerous tables and figures used for clarification and illustration are, unfortunately, found at the very end of the work, causing much cross referencing; further, they are not especially well reproduced. This report is useful as a bibliography and as the beginning point for more detailed research; it will be of greatest interest to display designers and cognitive psychologists.

CONTENTS

Abstract

Sammanfattning

1: Introduction

2: Color Coding of Symbols

    2.1. Color coding and identification accuracy

    2.2. Color coding and search

    2.3. Maximum gain or loss in using color coding

    2.4. Identification of unidimensional color stimuli

    2.5. Identification of multidimensional color stimuli

    2.6. Color schemes and colored backgrounds

    2.7. Color schemes and complex target patterns

    2.8. Color schemes and lighting conditions

    2.9. Color schemes and symbol size

3: Color Coding of Maps

    3.1. Color coding and map reading performance

    3.2. Color schemes for maps

4: Color Coding of Sonar Data

5: Color Coding of Pictures

    5.1. Natural color representation (true-color coding)

    5.2. Psuedo-color coding

6: Subjective Preference for Color Coding

7: Recommendations

References

Tables

Figures

78 pp. 7 chapters. Drawings, figures, graphs, tables, references.

63
Derefeldt, Gunilla
Sahlin, Christer

technical report

Colour Order Systems for Computer Graphics I: Transformation of NCS Data into CIELAB Colour Space
1984

(report number FOA-C-53013-H2; Foersvarets Forskningsanstalt, Stockholm; January 1984)

This paper describes efforts to identify "analytical relations" between two color order systems designated specifically for computer graphics: the Natural Color System (NCS), and the CIE 1976 (l*a*b*) system (CIELAB).

The functions delineating individual colors in NCS—defined by three variables: hue, chromaticness (chromaticity), and blackness—were mapped onto the CIELAB color space. The NCS color atlas, developed by the Swedish Institute of Standards, is reproduced with tristimulus values and the corresponding l*a*b* CIELAB values in an appendix. However, some systematic distortion appears in transforming colors between the two systems. The NCS hue-circle projection is equidistant between colors but the CIELAB hue-circle tends to constrict near yellow and expand near blue. Triangle projections of NCS colors in CIELAB space do not remain equilateral, and blackness plots show distortion. Curve-fitting techniques used to obtain relationships between chroma and chromaticness and blackness and lightness are briefly described. The authors suggest that additional correction factors might remove the systematic shifts in some values. The authors assert that, at the present, CIELAB is most suitable for displaying small color differences, and the NCS for larger color differences. Highly technical, this report would be of greatest interest to designers and practitioners concerned with the quality of color graphics displays.

90 pp. 4 chapters. Figures, graphs, mathematical formulae, references, appendices.

64
Doblin, Jay

Perspective: A New System for Designers
Watson-Guptill, 1956

Describes the role of perspective in the graphic arts, especially as it relates to industrial design.

This work is dominated by illustrations which provide examples of such things as linear perspective, parallel perspective, three-point perspective, and mechanical perspective. Succinct and to the point, the text focuses on the demonstration of working methods for constructing perspective drawings. The author contrasts his approach to those of various traditional systems, listing the advantages and disadvantages of each system. He then discusses ways in which the cube (the basic form in perspective) may be constructed according to different perspectives. Concise instructions provide a step-by-step description of the drafting process, such as that involved in the construction of a 30-60 degree view of the cube or the construction of a cube in a parallel perspective. This discussion is extended to relate to the creation of drawings that are more complex. The industrial orientation of this text is evident in its many illustrations, which include electric shavers, vending machines, trucks, and airplanes. The work will be of interest to industrial designers, but graphic artists from various orientations will also find this book useful, as would anyone whose work involves an understanding of perspective.

CONTENTS
BAS
    Basic principles of linear perspective
REV
    Review of existing systems
45°
    Introduction to 45° perspective
45°
    Construction of a cube in 45° perspective
45°
    Example of the use of 45° perspective

ERR
>   Two types of error

ERR
>   The curved diagonal

ERR
>   The control of error

30-60°
>   Construction of the cube in 30-60° perspective

30-60°
>   Example of the use of 30-60° perspective

PARA
>   Construction of the cube in parallel perspective

PARA
>   Example of the use of parallel perspective

DEV
>   Developing a drawing—view

DEV
>   Developing a drawing—size and scale, multiplication and division

DEV
>   Examples showing the development of a drawing

CIRC
>   Construction of a circle in perspective

CIRC
>   Choice of methods for drawing perspective circles

CIRC
>   Rotation and simple geometric forms

CIRC
>   Compound forms

3-PT
>   Introduction to three-point perspective

3-PT
>   Construction of the cube in three-point perspective

3-PT
>   Special cases of three-point perspective

EYE
>   Use of the trained eye in perspective drawing

EYE
>   Violation of normal perspective

FREE
>   Practice in drawing freehand cubes

FREE
>   View, scale, and size in freehand drawing

FREE
>   Complex forms in freehand drawing

FREE
>   Excercise in freehand drawing

AID
>   Drawing aids—true scale

AID
Mechanical drawing aids
67 pp. 30 chapters. Drawings. ISBN 0-8230-7419-6.

65
Dondis, Donis A.

A Primer of Visual Literacy
The MIT Press, 1973

The author explains why he feels visual expression differs from written language in that it need not be decoded because the visual message is experienced directly and immediately.

Dondis believes that the visual mode has the same potential as written language for the composition and transmission of messages on multiple levels, an opinion he utilizes in the organization of this book. Visual literacy is defined as the ability to use visual components "for learning, recognizing, making and understanding visual messages that are negotiable by all people." The first chapters describe the basic elements of visual communication: the dot, the line, shape, direction, tone, color, texture, scale, dimension and motion. Later chapters discuss the techniques and strategies of visual design and the psychophysiological effects of good composition. The last chapters examine the special characteristics of several visual media. The book closes with a discussion of ways to achieve a universal visual literacy. Dondis argues that "visual intelligence" is a skill which can be developed and which can convey simple or complex information rapidly and efficiently. The book itself is a good exemplar of Dondis' point of view. The text and illustrations complement each other well. Although his prose lapses into overembellished discussion while covering aesthetics and meaning, his descriptions of visual elements and techniques are clear and well organized. Much of what he says may be basic review for the experienced artist or designer, but the book should still provide a good reference for these people, as well as a primer for the neophyte and visually inexperienced.

CONTENTS
Preface
1. The character and content of visual literacy
2. Composition: the syntactical guidelines for visual literacy
3. The basic elements of visual communication
4. The anatomy of a visual message
5. The dynamics of contrast
6. Visual techniques: the communication strategies
7. The synthesis of visual style
8. The visual arts: function and message
9. Visual literacy: how and why
Bibliography
Illustration Credits
Index

194 pp. 9 chapters. Drawings, photographs, figures, general index, bibliography, illustration credit list. (ISBN 0-262-54029-0)

66
Downs, Roger M.
Stea, David

Maps in Minds: Reflections on Cognitive Mapping
Harper and Row, 1977

(from the *Harper and Row Series in Geography*, D.W. Meinig, series advisor)

An introduction to cognitive maps and "inner space" for a general audience.

The authors define a cognitive map as "the representation of the geographical environment as it exists within a person's mind." By exploring and analyzing this topic they seek to illuminate such abstract matters as how we know the world and what we mean by the ability to know the world, as well as such practical matters as how we design our built environment or our school curriculum. Preferring a popular approach to an academic one, Downs and Stea draw a great deal of supporting material from newspapers, magazines, ads, and fiction. After the introduction, in which the authors explain their attitudes toward the material and preview the rest of the book, following chapters: examine the way the cognitive map influences external behavior; clarify the internal process by considering separately the notions of "mapping" and "cognitive"; offer examples of cognitive maps and the real environments which inspired them; discuss how daily lives are affected by cognitive mapping; and explore changes in cognitive mapping ability throughout the lifespan. The final chapter reviews some of the applications of cognitive mapping theory to environmental design. While the book is intended to introduce elements of cognitive theory to a large audience, and is therefore written at a somewhat general level, many of the lessons learned and principles offered would apply to professionals in cognitive and design disciplines.

CONTENTS
Preface
Chapter 1: Senses of Place
Introduction
Cognitive mapping and maps
Why is cognitive mapping important?
The organization of the book
Chapter 2: Spatial Problem Solving
Introduction
What are spatial problems?
Knowing
Whereness
Whatness and whenness
What are the ways of solving spatial problems?
Cognitive mapping as spatial problem solving
Chapter 3: The Meaning of Cognitive Mapping
Introduction
What do we mean by "mapping"?
The objectives of cognitive mapping
Cognitive mapping as an interactive process
The selectivity of cognitive mapping

Making sense out of the world

Chapter 4: The World in the Head
 Introduction
 The accuracy and similarity of cognitive maps
 Whatness and whenness
 Whereness
 Conclusion

Chapter 5: A Tale of Two Places
 Puluwat: the art of navigation
 Two views of Boston

Chapter 6: The Genesis of Cognitive Mapping
 Introduction
 Cognitive mapping and the functioning of the brain
 The evolutionary record
 The development of cognitive mapping
 An attempt at integration

Chapter 7: Learning: How Environments Get Mapped
 Introduction
 Learning a new city
 The process of environmental learning
 Conclusions

Chapter 8: Cognitive Mapping in Everyday Life
 Introduction
 The design of urban spaces
 You can't get there from here
 Games
 The worlds of fantasy and imagination
 Conclusion

Bibliography
Name index
Place index
Subject index

284 pp. 8 chapters. Drawings, figures, maps, author index, subject index, bibliography, place index. (ISBN 0-06-041733-1)

67
Dudek, C.L.
Huchingson, R.D.

technical report

Human Factors Design of Dynamic Visual and Auditory Displays for Metropolitan Traffic Management: Volume 1, Summary Report
1982

(report number FHWA-RD-81-039; Texas Transportation Institute, Texas A&M University; sponsored by U.S. Department of Transportation; May 1982)

Reports the results of a series of experiments that evaluated design characteristics of dynamic visual displays used in traffic control, and characteristics of highway advisory radio messages.

The extensive research program reported here included laboratory and field research as well as controlled field studies in which subjects drove experimental cars which were equipped to measure certain responses in actual traffic situations. The dynamic visual displays examined were "changeable message signs in which the display elements appear to move." These changing visual displays were evaluated by five visual factors: message factors included content, format, load, and presentation rate; character factors included font style, size of matrix, and upper or lower case letters; accentuation factors included flashing lines, color variation, and special character type; dynamic factors included sequenced or run-on messages, and "blanking time"; and the final visual factor was visibility. The extensive findings of the studies include numerous suggestions for length of exposure time for messages; most effective font style legibility; and visibility comparisons of bulb matrix and disk matrix messages. The studies of highway advisory radio messages also looked at five dimensions: brevity of language style, amount of information presented, message redundancy, descriptions of alternate routes and turns, and presence of road signs directing motorists to tune their radios to the broadcast. In these studies the radio messages informed drivers of a diversion route to avoid a traffic situation that would slow their progress. Findings included: most effective language styles; percentages of drivers who noticed an advance warning sign (to tune in the radio); and percentages of drivers who noticed an advisory sign and did listen to the highway advisory broadcast. The present report is a summary report and is the first volume in a three volume series; all volumes report upon the same research program. This report presents brief methodologies, extensive result reports, and recommendations based on the studies. Some diagrams and pictures are included, but these are poorly reproduced. The authors have provided enough background information and term definitions to make their research comprehensible, but a reader of this report will not develop a broad understanding of these experiments. Designers of large format electronic displays and public information signage will find the results presented here to be of interest.

CONTENTS
1: MESSAGE FACTORS
Traffic Control Abbreviations
Message Format and Types of Sequencing
Message Load and Exposure Rate
Trade-Off of Message Repetition and Exposure Rate
Exposure Rate
2: CHARACTER FACTORS
Optimum Font Style for Dot Matrix Character Recognition
Optimum Size for Dot Matrix Character Recognition
Comparison of the Composite and Rounded 4 x 7 Font Styles
Relative Legibility of Upper and Lower Case Characters
3: ACCENTUATION FACTORS
Line Accentuation by Color, Flashing, and Double Stroke
4: DYNAMIC FACTORS
Update Methods
Blanking Time at End of Message
5: VISIBILITY FACTORS
Legibility of Bulb and Disk Matrix CMSs
Recognition of Cycling Message Lines on Disk CMSs
Margins on Bulb Matrix CMSs
6: INTRODUCTION TO HAR STUDIES
Objectives
Background
In-Situ Studies
Field Studies
    Study site
    HAR hardware system
    FCC license
7: HAR IN-SITU STUDIES
Information Load and Language Style
    Results - information load
    Conclusions and recommendations - informations load
    Results - language style
    Conclusions and recommendations
External vs. Internal Redundancy
    Results
    Discussion
    Conclusions and recommendations
Route Descriptors
    Results
    Conclusions and recommendations
Turn Descriptors for Familiar Drivers
    Results
    Conclusions and recommendations
Advance Signs
    Results and discussion
    Conclusions and recommendations

149

8: HAR FIELD STUDIES
Background
    Study site
    Diversion route
Method
    HAR system
Results
    Driver response
    Summary of questionnaire results
REFERENCES
APPENDIX A
APPENDIX B

1113 pp. 8 chapters. Figures, graphs, tables, references, appendices.

68
Eades, Craig A.

technical report

CHART: A Graphic Display and Analysis System
1981

(report number PUB-3015; Lawrence Berkeley Laboratory, University of California; sponsored by U.S. Department of Energy; 19 February 1981)

A manual that describes how to use CHART, a computer program for performing graphical data analysis and designing attractive, useful graphics.

CHART is an interactive program which allows the user to try out different graphic data displays before selecting a preferred display. Data is entered into this program in numerical tabular format either from a terminal or via a previously prepared script. A group of commands called GROUP I are used for data entry. The program permits temporary modification of the entered table so that different portions of the table can be made visible on the screen or the data itself can be manipulated through ranking or arithmatic calculations. GROUP II commands are used for these data manipulations. The program produces bar charts, line graphs, pie charts, tabular reports, or combinations of these as directed by the user via GROUP III commands. Various display enhancement commands are available so that titles can be added to the graph as well as borders, marks, and shading. Thus, portions of the graph can be highlighted. It is possible to display more than one graph on a page. GROUP IV commands are used for these display adjustments. This manual is clearly written, easy to follow, easy to understand, and easy to use. The manual has an introductory section and is then divided into four sections that cover the four groups of commands. At least a page of the manual is devoted to each command and many examples are given of the actual output a specified command will produce. The program yields clear, easily comprehensible charts and graphs. This user manual and program are highly recommended.

102 pp. 4 chapters. Drawings, figures, glossary.

69
Easterby, Ronald S.
Zwaga, Harm J.
(eds.)

collection

Information Design: The Design and Evaluation of Signs and Printed Material
John Wiley and Sons, 1984

(based on the NATO Conference on Visual Presentation of Information; Het Vennenbos, The Netherlands; September 1978)

Intended "to bring [the work of] cognitively oriented psychologists, ergonomists, human factors researchers and practitioners together with [that of] engineers, typographers and designers so that they could begin to understand and learn from one another."

The 1978 NATO Conference on the Visual Presentation of Information was conceived of and organized by the editors of this volume and this book is a fine testament to the success of their interdisciplinary goal. Contributions by leading professionals in all of the above fields are collected in the work. The common bond drawing them together is the fact that information display affects all areas of contemporary life. There is also an awareness that much of the work currently being done is widely dispersed in the professional literature. Some of the most recent research in the theory and practice of information design is included in the collection, which is divided into six parts. The first two deal with theory and method and the remainder examine the various applications for sign systems, road traffic signs, consumer/safety signs, and printed material. The diversity of topics, combined with coherent organization, makes this an enjoyable, informative, and useful work. Readability, applications, evaluations, checklists, color coding, pictograms, and fault diagnosis are among the many topics addressed and interrelated through the papers in the collection. This is an excellent group of papers and is highly recommended for all those who have an interest in presenting information visually.

CONTENTS

List of contributors
Foreword
Preface

1: Theory and Method in Design Evaluation
1. Theory and application in visual displays
   Alan Welford
2. Tasks, processes and display design
   Ronald Easterby
3. Representation and understanding in the use of symbols and pictograms
   Phil Barnard, Tony Marcel
4. Methods of evaluation of traffic signs
   Robert Dewar, Jerry Ells
5. The use of signal detection theory in the evaluation of information displays
   Don McNicol
6. Recognition memory: implications for visual information presentation

Peter Hecht, Joseph Juhasz
7. Optimising legibility for recall and retention
   Robert Swezey
8. Information display in process control training
   Ed Marshall, Keith Duncan

2: Design Parameters
9. Letter size and legibility
   Sidney Smith
10. The legibility of printed scientific and technical information
    Linda Reynolds
11. Research for evaluating visual display codes: an emphasis on colour coding
    Richard Christ
12. Natural associations between symbols and military information
    Franklyn Moses, Richard Maisano, Philip Bersh

3: Applications: Sign Systems
13. Way-finding and signposting: penance or prosthesis?
    David Canter
14. Graphic design of building sign systems
    Katherine Selfridge
15. Developing effective symbols for public information
    Harm Zwaga, Ronald Easterby
16. The presentation of information about bus services
    Dave Bartram
17. Some factors affecting spatial memory for route information
    Anthony Wetherell

4: Applications: Road Traffic Signs
18. The practical and graphic problems of road sign design
    Jock Kinneir
19. A users' guide to positive guidance in highway control
    Gerson J. Alexander, Harold Lunenfield
20. Visual information path definition: delineation of the roadway ahead
    Thomas J. Triggs

5: Applications: Consumer/Safety Signs
21. Visual alerts to machine hazards: a design case study
    Fred Robinett, Al Hughes
22. Issues in the design of safety sign systems
    Simon Hakiel, Ronald Easterby
23. Factors affecting the comprehension of pictographic instructions
    Carl Szlichcinski

6: Applications: Printed Material
24. Design principles for instructional materials
    Jorge Frascara
25. Readability and comprehension
    George Klare
26. Space and structure in instructional text
    James Hartley
27. Applications of instructional design principles to nuclear power plant operating procedures manuals

Ekhard Bohr
28. Transaction structures and format in form design
   Robert B. Miller
29. Informed design for forms
   Patricia Wright

588 pp. 29 chapters in 6 parts. Drawings, photographs, figures, graphs, tables, general index, references. ISBN 0-471-10431-0.

70
Elworth, Charles

technical report

Instructor/Operator Display Evaluation Methods
1981

(report number AFHRL-TR-79-41; Boeing Aerospace Company; sponsored by Air Force Human Resources Laboratory; March 1981)

The report of an effort to develop techniques for evaluating CRT and other devices used in flight simulators to display flight information to the instructor/operator.

Five basic flight maneuvers—climb, descent, level turn, climbing turn, and descending turn—were recorded. Questions were then designed for each maneuver to assess the comprehensiveness of the subject's observations during replay. The subjects, twenty experienced pilots, were advised to watch the display and to answer a set of questions about their observations. Each pilot was tested using two display types: digital readouts and repeat instruments. Though the intent was to evaluate the methodology rather than compare the displays themselves, it was noted that in some cases answers to questions related to pitch, airspeed, and vertical velocity proved more accurate with the repeater display. This report is difficult to read in many places due to poor photocopying. While the report is, on the whole, somewhat dated, it may be of some interest to display designers and human factors engineers, particularly those working with cockpit displays.

CONTENTS
    I. Introduction
    II. Background
    III. Research methodology
    IV. Experimental design
    V. Procedure
    VI. Results and Discussion
    VII. Conclusions and recommendations
    Appendix A. Instructions to subjects
    Appendix B. Test conditions and raw data
    Appendix C. Test questions
    Appendix D. Strip chart recordings of the six flight parameters
    Appendix E. Presentation order for flight segments and questions
    Appendix F. Observer pilot information form
    Appendix G. Initial exploration study
    Appendix H. Literature survey abstracts
    Appendix I. Test questions

Appendix J. Test conditions and data
Appendix K. Test IP briefing
Appendix L. Data summary by maneuver and indication
Appendix M. Learning effects

192 pp. 7 chapters. Figures, tables, bibliography, appendices.

71
Engel, Stephen E.
Granda, Richard E.

technical report

Guidelines for Man/Display Interfaces
1975

(report number TR-00.2720; IBM Poughkeepsie Laboratory; 19 December 1975)

An excellent set of general guidelines for designers of interactive software and, to a lesser extent, hardware.

This report covers display frame layout, frame content, command languages, error prevention and recovery, response times, and behavioral principles. While some conclusions are controversial (e.g., the joystick is the "best" cursor control device), they are well reasoned and sufficiently well explained to allow the guidelines to be used in a thoughtful, informed fashion. A good deal of information is presented in a relatively short, easily readable form. While these guidelines were developed primarily for interfaces using visual displays, many of the guidelines dealing with consistency of presentation, information presentation, and labeling are applicable across a wide range of person/terminal interfaces. Illustrations of proposed layouts are given.

CONTENTS
1.0: Introduction
    1.1. Methodology
    1.2. Interface topic areas
2.0: Display Formats
    2.1. Highlighting
    2.2. Data presentation
    2.3. Screen layout and structuring
3.0: Frame Content
    3.1. Feedback to user action
    3.2. Labeling
    3.3. Messages
    3.4. Interface considerations
4.0: Command Language
    4.1. Abbreviations
    4.2. Prompting and structuring
5.0: Recovery Procedures
6.0: User Entry Techniques
    6.1. Hardware control methods
    6.2. Entry stacking
    6.3. Implicit prompting/entry definition
7.0: Principles ·
8.0: Response Time

9.0: Summary
10.0: Bibliography

42 pp. 9 chapters. Tables, bibliography.

72
Ergonomics Research Society

collection

The Visual Presentation of Technical Data
University of Reading, Department of Typography, 1973

(papers from the joint meeting of the Ergonomics Research Society and the Society of Industrial Artists and Designers; London, U.K.; 21 November 1972)

Five articles which describe ergonomic considerations in the visual presentation of technical data.

These papers discuss the visual presentation of technical data from the perspective of human factors research. Hartley, Burnhill, and Fraser summarize their research on the spatial problems of textual matter and how these impact learning. Pointing out that maps are far more complex than most display types for which ergonomic guidelines are available, Hopkin discusses issues related to the design and evaluation of maps. Methodological problems in legibility research form the basis for Shaw's article while Spencer discusses work aimed at improving information presentation in engineering drawings. Wright's article on tabular displays reviews principles of display design which facilitate understanding of the material presented. Each of these brief articles is well-written and easily understood. In most cases, references guide the reader to more detailed treatments of these subjects. These papers will be of interest to designers of print displays in cartography and engineering, to anyone concerned with issues of legibility, and to designers of computer displays wishing to include sound ergonomic principles in their designs, especially for cartographic and tabular displays.

CONTENTS
Typography, communication and learning: a progress report
James Hartley, Peter Burnhill, Susan Fraser
Human factors in the design of maps
V.D. Hopkin
Some methodological problems in legibility research
Alison Shaw
Presentation of information on engineering drawings
John Spencer
Understanding tabular displays
Patricia Wright

32 pp. 5 papers. Figures, graphs, tables, references. (ISBN 0-7049-0139-0)

73
Farley, Willard W.
Gutmann, James C.

technical report

Digital Image Processing Systems and an Approach to the Display of Colors of Specified Chrominance
1980

(report number HFL-80-2/ONR-80-2; Department of Industrial Engineering and Operations Research, Virginia Polytechnic Institute and State University; sponsored by Engineering Psychology Programs, Office of Naval Research; 1 August 1980)

Describes an approach to developing the capability to display colors using a color digital image processing system.

This report covers the major design considerations for developing measurement techniques and developing software to display colors of known chromaticity. Color visual displays are being used to convey information in an increasing number of fields. Thus, research on workers' perception of color contrasts and the effects of different levels of color contrast on workers' performance is a priority. Determining a metric of color contrast has predictive value and would be useful to display designers. This research is quantitative by nature and the report relies heavily on mathematical relationships to present information on chromaticity and luminance. The authors have developed a technique that will make priority research on color contrasts a reality.

CONTENTS

OVERVIEW

Equipment Description
    Digital image system
    Spectroradiometric measurement system

MEASUREMENT SYSTEM SOFTWARE

Acquisition of Radiometric Data
    Calibration
    Scanning
    Radiometric data collection

Analysis of Radiometric Data

Measurement Considerations

DISPLAY SYSTEM SOFTWARE

System Characterization

Display Software

Display Stability

CONCLUSIONS

APPENDIX A: LINEAR EQUATIONS RELATING BITS TO CHROMATICITY COORDINATES

APPENDIX B: ONE JND ELLIPSE CALCULATIONS

REFERENCES

36 pp. 4 sections. Figures, graphs, mathematical formulae, references, appendices.

74
Feldman, Laurence A.
Rapagnani, Nazareno L.

Computer Graphics for Scientific Applications
1982

technical report

(report number AFWL-TR-80-138; Air Force Weapons Laboratory; sponsored by Air Force Weapons Laboratory; February 1982)

This report presents a survey of computer graphics applications in engineering and scientific data analysis, including discussion of two- and three-dimensional dynamic simulations, algorithm shading, and the writing of a multi-dimensional animation graphics package (SCAN).

The authors offer a survey of computer graphics applications to data analysis which would be of interest to engineers who are familiar with computer modeling but not with computer graphics techniques. They briefly survey the areas of computer hardware, physics, numerics, and software development, but concentrate on computer graphics. Discussions of appropriate mainframe selection, advantages and disadvantages of line plotting and raster scan graphics devices, and the variety of software techniques are followed by an examination of real and simulated engineering data which provides detailed mathematical analysis of dimensionality and numerical simulation problems. An introduction to the authors' software package for analysis of multi-dimensional scientific data (SCAN) follows. The authors then turn to applications of the various techniques available on the SCAN system for surface and line plotting (contours, 3-D surface mapping, vectors, trace particles), followed by a brief discussion of the nature of computer animation and real time and their value for analysis of physics. A short, general summary of future trends in computer graphics ends the report. Sparse footnotes and a brief list of references are included, along with a helpful but elementary glossary. Intended for the computer graphics novice, this helpful introduction to computer visualization techniques will be of little interest to advanced designers and analysts.

CONTENTS
SECTION I: INTRODUCTION
SECTION II: COMPUTER GRAPHICS
1: Selecting a Host Computer for Computer Graphics
2: Selecting a Graphics Device
3: Software Techniques
SECTION III: CATEGORIZING ENGINEERING DATA
1: Dimensionality
2: Numerical Simulation
SECTION IV: SOFTWARE OBJECTIVES
SECTION V: BUILDING BLOCKS OF A GRAPHICS SOFTWARE PACKAGE
1: Graphics Tools for Line Plotting
    a. Contouring
    b. Topography
    c. Modeling a 3-D scene
    d. Vectors
    e. Tracer particles

2: Graphics Tools for Surface Plotting (Shade, Color)
    a. Visible surface problem
    b. Shading
    c. Realism
SECTION VI: ANIMATION AND REAL TIME
SECTION VII: FUTURE TRENDS IN COMPUTER GRAPHICS
REFERENCES
GLOSSARY

78 pp. 7 chapters. Drawings, photographs, figures, tables, algorithms, abstract formalisms, footnotes, references, glossary.

75
Fertig, Janet A.

An Inquiry into Effective Design of Graphicolingual Displays for Systems Engineering
University Microfilms International, 1980

(Ph.D. dissertation, School of Engineering and Applied Science, University of Virginia, 1980)

Research performed to determine more effective designs of graphicolingual displays.

This dissertation discusses the results of research done to determine ways to improve the effectiveness of graphicolingual displays used as communication tools in large scale systems engineering projects. The research covered why graphics may be valuable in systems engineering, how graphics may be designed more effectively, and in what way objective measures of display design correlate with subjective judgments of display clarity. A review of the literature of display design highlights work done by experts not only in display design but in human factors engineering and cognitive psychology. The author includes a discussion of structure and symbols. The dissertation is carefully organized and well-structured, and the author presents a series of relevant definitions before proceeding with the discussion of the research. Reports on three experiments of effective display design are included, along with typology of graphicolingual displays and many effective charts and diagrams. While the intended audience is primarily those involved in systems engineering, the dissertation is valuable for all display users. It is well written and an excellent resource tool.

CONTENTS
CHAPTER I: INTRODUCTION
Graphics and Engineering
Investigating Display Effectiveness
Assumptions and Limitations
Definitions
Dissertation Organization
CHAPTER II: PORTRAYING STRUCTURE
The Concept of Structure
Structure and Systems Engineering
Symbol Systems for Portraying Structure
    Symbol systems
    Language
    Mathematics
    Graphics
Graphics for Structuring in Systems Engineering
Summary
CHAPTER III: GRAPHIC DESIGN CONSIDERATIONS
Design Aspects
First Aspect: Predesign Considerations
    Purpose
    Audience
Second Aspect: Capabilities of Individuals
    Cognitive processes
    Visual perception
    Display coding
    Legibility
Third Aspect: Circumstances of Use
    Display media
    Group viewing of displays
Fourth Aspect: Display Format
Summary
CHAPTER IV: EXPERIMENTAL INVESTIGATION OF
DIAGRAPH-BASED DISPLAYS
Introduction
Readability
Experiments
    Independent variables
    Dependent variables
    Preliminary findings
Method
    Subjects
    Materials
    Design
    Procedure
Results
    Rating phase
    Choice phase
    Comparison of rating and choice

Discussion

CHAPTER V: ILLUSTRATIVE EVALUATION OF THE STRUCTURAL MODELING GRAPHICS SYSTEM

Interpretive Structural Modeling

Structural Modeling Graphics System
    Hardware
    SMGS software design requirements and assumptions
    Operation of SMGS

Evaluation of SMGS
    Hardware evaluation
    Software evaluation

Recommendations for an Interpretive Structural Modeling Graphics System
    Hardware recommendations
    Software recommendations

CHAPTER VI: SUMMARY AND RECOMMENDATIONS

REFERENCES

APPENDICES

A: Glossary

B: Definitions of Some Basic Graph-Theoretic Terms

C: Experimental Procedure and Instructions

D: Diagrams for Simple Structures

E: Diagrams for Large Structure

236 pp. 6 chapters. Drawings, figures, charts, graphs, tables, algorithms, abstract formalisms, models, references, glossary, appendices.

76
Fisher, Howard T.

Mapping Information: The Graphic Display of Quantitative Information
Abt Books, 1982

This work demonstrates how to take rough spatial information and quantitative facts and translate them into maps using effective graphic techniques. It presents topics in increasing degrees of complexity and draws from textbook, encyclopedia, and manual formats to create a "hybrid" format.

This work, by the late Howard T. Fisher, provides an excellent introduction to thematic cartography. It was edited by Jacqueline Cohen after the author's death and represents the culmination of Fisher's career in mapping. The book is divided into four parts. The first part explains the difference between General Reference Cartography and Thematic Cartography. The second part introduces cartographic language and describes: how to choose a base map, how to create effective titles, how to describe the "study space" which may exist in the physical world or may be conceptual, and ends with a chapter on values which may be positive, negative, or a combination of both. The third part of the book, comprising over half the text, is concerned with the actual creation of the display. This begins with choosing an appropriate symbolism, starting with the seven basics of circles, bars, planes (both flat and raised), spot count, dots and sectors. The symbolism becomes increasingly complex as the chapter progresses, but lucid descriptions and excellent illustrations make these concepts accessible even to the completely uninitiated. Part three also contains chapters on: value classing, single-subject mapping, and multi-subject mapping. The fourth part of the book is concerned with aesthetics, the use of gray scales, and the use of color for quantitative differentiation. The book concludes with eight appendices ranging from procedures (with extensive tables) for using reciprocal curve classing and classing by specific mathematical curves, to hand contouring and traditional dot mapping. This is an excellent text for both specialists and non-specialists and will be of interest not only to cartographers and geographers but also to city and regional planners, architects, statisticians, graphic designers, and all those interested in computer display technology. Fisher created the first computer mapping system, SYMAP, which is still the most commonly used system. He was also the founder and first director of Harvard University's Laboratory for Graphics and Spatial Analysis.

CONTENTS

Tables

Figures

Foreword

Preface

Biographical Notes

PART I: INTRODUCTION

Chapter 1: Beginning Spatial Analysis
    What is a map?
    What is thematic cartography?
    Function and form in map design
    The sponsor's role

Chapter 2: A Dialogue Between a Sponsor and a Designer

PART II: THE GIVEN INFORMATION

Chapter 3: Introduction to Cartographic Language

Chapter 4: Base Maps

Chapter 5: "A Dialogue" Revisited: Subjects and Titling
    Differentiating single- and multi-subject maps
    Creating effective titles

Chapter 6: The Study Space and Locations
    Describing the study space
    Assignment to locations

Chapter 7: Values
    Addable and nonaddable values
    Nominal and ordinal values
    Intralocational variability
    Interpolation

PART III: CREATING THE DISPLAY

Chapter 8: Steps in the Design Process
    Step 1. Symbolism
    Step 2. Study space assignment
    Step 3. Location assignment
    Step 4. Value classing
    Other considerations
    Figure and ground

Chapter 9: Varieties of Symbolism: The Foursquare Study
    The study space: locations and values
    Introduction to graphic symbolisms
    Seven basic symbolisms
    Interpolated symbolisms
    Contouring
    The validity of interpolation
    Collaborative symbolisms
    Choosing the best symbolism
    Value keys

Chapter 10: Value Classing
    Introduction to classing
    Why class?
    How many classes
    Value positions and value curves
    Equal classing and subclassing
    Rounding
    Unequal classing

Chapter 11: Single-Subject Mapping
    Procedure
    Sparse France: a problem with alternative solutions
    Dense France
    All France

Chapter 12: Multi-Subject Mapping
    A note on procedure
    Appropriateness and limitations
    Symbolisms

PART IV: PRACTICAL AESTHETICS

Chapter 13: Designing in Black-and-White
    Gray scales and dot screens
    Elements of effective symbolism

Chapter 14: Color for Quantitative Differentiation
    Introduction to color
    Dominance
    Hue
    Darkness
    Intensity
    Selecting quantitative color schemes

APPENDICES
Appendix 1: Using Reciprocal Curve Classing
Appendix 2: Classing by Specific Mathematical Curves
Appendix 3: Classing for Value Curves with Major Reversal
Appendix 4: Classing Charts
Appendix 5: Hand Contouring by Linear Interpolation
Appendix 6: Hand Contouring Form
Appendix 7: Constructing Proximal Maps
Appendix 8: Traditional Dot Mapping by Hand
Bibliography
Index

384 pp. 14 chapters in 4 parts. Figures, maps, graphs, tables, general index, bibliography, appendices. ISBN 0-89011-571-0.

77
Fleming, Malcolm L.
Levie, W. Howard

Instructional Message Design: Principles from the Behavioral Sciences
Educational Technology Publications, 1978

A detailed, lucidly written, and well-organized guide to some basic principles of human psychology and how to apply these principles to message design.

Based on recent research in the behavioral sciences, this work attempts "to narrow the gap between research and practice in instructional message design." It recognizes messages as sign patterns (words/ pictures) which attempt to change human behavior, and design as an intellectual process distinct from application. Both of these definitions are easily applied to graphic displays. The work is especially appropriate for the designer interested in the development of computer aided instruction systems, including those involving interactive graphics. After a brief introduction, four areas of behavioral science are outlined: memory, concept learning, perception, and attitude change. Within this framework the authors discuss in detail: problems of temporal and spatial perception, the effects of motion on perception, and how a knowledge of such factors can enhance the presentation of information and thus cognition; the human memory's capacity for remembering concrete words and pictures, and its poorer capacity to retain abstractions; the utility of conjunctive concepts and criterial attributes in the design of effective concept presentation; and the principles of message content and structure and their role in creating a persuasive (i.e., attitude-changing) message. Throughout the text the authors provide numerous examples to illustrate the principles under discussion and encourage feedback on their efficacy from readers. Of great value to display and message designers in various print and electronic media, this work would also be of interest to communication theorists, cognitive psychologists, and educators. Readers are assumed to be familiar with instructional design techniques and problem analysis.

CONTENTS

PREFACE

INTRODUCTION

CHAPTER 1—PERCEPTION PRINCIPLES

Basic Principles
    Summary of basic principles of perception

Attention and Preattention
    Summary of principles of attention and performance

Perceptual Elements and Processing
    Perceiving brightness and color
    Perceiving elemental features

Perceiving Figures: Objects, Pictures, and Words
    Signs vs. modality
    Modalities
    Signs: words and pictures
    Summary of perceiving figures: objects, words, and pictures

Perceptual Capacity
    Single channel capacity
    Two-channel capacity
    Summary of perceptual capacity

Perceptual Distinguishing, Grouping, Organizing
    Distinguishing and grouping
    Relating and organizing
    Summary of perceptual distinguishing, grouping, organizing

Perception of Size, Depth, Space, Time, and Motion
    Space and depth
    Space, time, and motion

Perception and Cognition

References

Sources for Principles

CHAPTER 2—MEMORY PRINCIPLES

Basic Principles of Memory

Acquisition of Associative Learning
    Modality effects and side-type effects
    Cues and prompts
    Unit size, spacing and pacing
    Organization, pattern, and relationship
    Learner activity, strategy

Consolidation of Associative Learning
    Knowledge of correct responses, reinforcement
    Practice, application, and review

Discrimination Learning
Observational and Motor Learning
References
Sources of Principles
CHAPTER 3—CONCEPT LEARNING PRINCIPLES
Types of Concepts
Selection of Examples and Non-examples
Prerequisites and Instructions
Presentation of Examples and Definitions (Rules)
Sequencing of Examples and Definitions (Rules)
Consolidation and Confirmation of Concept Learning
Problem Solving and Creativity
References
Sources for Principles
CHAPTER 4—ATTITUDE CHANGE PRINCIPLES
The Concept of Attitude
The Source
    Source credibility
    Attractiveness
    Credibility vs. attractiveness
    The source-receiver relationship
Message Content—WHAT to Say
    Information about the source
    The needs of the receiver
    The values of the receiver
    Introducing opposing arguements
    Stating vs. not stating the conclusion
    The extremity of the position advocated
Message Structure—HOW to Say It
    Sequencing variables
    Appeals to emotions or reason
    Attitude change via behavioral change
    Miscellaneous flamboyant technique
The Channel
    Media types
    Media attributes
    Direct experience with attitude objects
The Receiver
    Topic-specific factors
    Demographic characteristics
    Aptitudes and personality characteristics
    Characteristics related to the adoption of innovations
    Group influences
Final Comments
References
Sources for Principles
Author Index
Subject Index

289 pp. 4 chapters. Drawings, figures, charts, graphs, author index, subject index, references. ISBN 0-87778-104-4.

78
Foley, James D.
Wallace, Victor L.
Chan, Peggy

technical report

The Human Factors of Graphic Interaction: Tasks and Techniques
1981

(Dept. of Electrical Engineering and Computer Science, George Washington University, and Dept. of Computer Science, University of Kansas; sponsored by U.S. Army Research Institute; January 1981)

An important—perhaps seminal—human factors analysis by well-known computer graphics experts which focuses on the selection and design of user techniques to promote effective and responsive interaction interfaces.

These techniques are selected at the final "lexical" stage of interaction design. The authors determine the quality of interaction design according to three primary criteria: speed, accuracy, and pleasurability. Eight secondary criteria are also identified: learning time, recall time, short-term memory load, long-term memory load, error susceptibility, fatigue susceptibility, naturalness, and boundedness. Proper technique selection will minimize the workload of perceptual, cognitive, and motor processes involved in human performance. Various interaction techniques are described in detail, including experiments used in technique selection. Controlled techniques transform objects by a process of contour modification. The authors recommend research to develop a model of user-computer interaction which can serve as a technique selection guide for both new and skilled users. The sixty pages of appendices include interaction technique diagrams, experiment summaries, recommendations for experimental design, and an annotated bibliography. This report fills a gap in the human factors literature in general and in interactive graphic systems research in particular. It is intended for software and hardware systems designers and for human factors researchers and practitioners.

CONTENTS

1: INTRODUCTION

1.1: Scope

1.2: Interaction Tasks

1.3: Psychological and Physiological Foundations
    1. The perceptual process
    2. The cognitive process
    3. The motor process

1.4: Reference Sources

2: MEASURES OF ERGONOMIC QUALITY

2.1: Primary and Secondary Criteria
    1. Learning, recall and memory
    2. Memory load
    3. Fatigue and error
    4. Naturalness

2.2: The Effect of Context

2.3: The Effect of User Experience and Knowledge

3: INTERACTION TASKS AND TECHNIQUES

3.1: Interaction Tasks: Types and Requirements
1. Select
2. Position
3. Orient
4. Path
5. Quantify
6. Text
7. Summary

3.2: Controlling Tasks
1. Stretch
2. Sketch
3. Manipulate
4. Shape

3.3: Organization of Interaction Techniques
1. Techniques and their variations
2. Technique parameters

4: INTERACTION TECHNIQUES

4.1: Selection Techniques
1. Command selection
2. Operand selection
3. Discussion of selection techniques

4.2: Positioning Techniques
1. Continuous translation
2. Discrete translation
3. Discussion of positioning techniques

4.3: Orienting Techniques
1. Continuous orientation
2. Discrete orientation
3. Discussion of orienting techniques

4.4: Pathing Techniques
1. Discussion of pathing

4.5: Quantifying Techniques
1. Continuous quantifying
2. Discrete quantifying
3. Discussion of quantifying techniques

4.6: Text Entry Techniques
1. Discussion of text entry

5: CONTROLLED TECHNIQUES

5.1: Stretching Techniques
1. Stretched lines
2. Rubber figures

5.2: Sketching Techniques

5.3: Manipulating Techniques
1. Dragging
2. Twisting
3. Scaling

5.4: Shaping Techniques
    1. Adjustable curves
    2. Adjustable surfaces

6: CONCLUSIONS

6.1: Summary

6.2: Research

APPENDICES

A: Interaction Technique Diagrams
    A.1. Basic elements and symbology
    A.2. Functional steps and control flows
    A.3. The making of interaction techniques diagrams

B: Experiment Summaries and Reviews
    B.1. An evaluation of devices for text selection (Card et al.)
    B.2. A comparison of selection techniques (Earl and Goff)
    B.3. A comparison of selection devices (English et al.)
    B.4. Valuation and selection techniques (Fields et al.)
    B.5. Chord keyboard command entry method (Gallo and Levine)
    B.6. A comparison of selection techniques (Goodwin)
    B.7. Sketching techniques (Irving et al.)
    B.8. Locator techniques (Mehr and Mehr)
    B.9. Command selection techniques (Morrill et al.)

C: Recommendations for Experimental Design
    C.1: Selection of interaction techniques to be evaluated
    C.2. Identification and placement of monitoring tasks
    C.3. Selection of subjects
    C.4. Criteria for evaluation
    C.5. Form of reporting experimental procedures and findings

D: Interaction Devices
    D.1. Selection devices
    D.2. Positioning and orienting devices
    D.3. Quantifying Devices
    D.4. Text devices

E: References and Bibliography

148 pp. 6 chapters. Figures, charts, graphs, tables, bibliography, references, appendices.

79
Foley, James D.
van Dam, Andries

Fundamentals of Interactive Computer Graphics
Addison-Wesley, 1982

(from the *Addison-Wesley Systems Programming Series*, IBM Editorial Board, consulting eds.)

Both a tutorial and a basic reference for those interested in all aspects of modern interactive graphics, including materials on hardware, software data structures, mathematical manipulation graphics, the user interface, and fundamental implementation algorithms.

Interactive graphics provides pictorial communication, a natural and efficient facilitator of man/machine interaction. Early in the book a complete graphics application program in Pascal, using the new CORE System of standard graphic subroutines, is presented. Also included is a comprehensive discussion of color theory and practice, with a section of color plates illustrating descriptions of color models. Clearly focused on good human factors and user-friendly interactive dialogue design, chapters are devoted to raster and vector displays, the development of 3-D geometrical transforms, graphics modeling, and other aspects of interactive computer graphics. The sequencing of subjects allows the reader to begin programming projects quickly while studying hardware and software issues in parallel. The structure is designed to introduce the reader to the generally applicable fundamentals of computer graphics, then move to more complex, specialized subjects. Exercises for self-testing are provided at the end of each chapter. While no background in graphics is needed, a basic background in programming, data structure, and computer architecture is assumed. This volume is a wealth of information about interactive computer graphics and is of value as a introduction to an "extremely versatile, aesthetically pleasing and instructive medium."

CONTENTS

Preface

Chapter 1: What Is Interactive Graphics?
    1.1. Introduction
    1.2. Image processing as picture analysis
    1.3. Advantages of interactive graphics
    1.4. Some representative uses of computer graphics
    1.5. Classification of applications
    1.6. Interactive graphics in the future: the normal mode of interaction
    1.7. Brief history of computer graphics
    1.8. Overview of the programmer's model of interactive graphics
    Exercises

Chapter 2: Basic Interactive Graphics Programming
    2.1. Models, picture description, and interaction
    2.2. Introduction to the simple graphics package
    2.3. Graph plotting
    2.4. Windows and clipping
    2.5. Segmentation

2.6. Simple graph
2.7. Viewports
2.8. Character strings
2.9. Summary of SGP's picture-making facilities
2.10. Interactive graphics program—layout of symbols
2.11. Generating a picture from the data structure
2.12. Interactive programming
2.13. Mainline using buttons for function invocation
2.14. Using a menu for function invocation
2.15. Defining a title
2.16. Adding symbols to the data structure
2.17. Deleting symbols
2.18. Changing view by panning and zooming
2.19. Adding solid areas for raster displays
2.20. Alternative implementation
2.21. Summary
Exercises
Chapter 3: Graphics Hardware
3.1. Output-only technology
3.2. Display technologies
3.3. Random-scan display processing unit
3.4. Input devices for operator interaction
3.5. Raster-scan display processing unit
Exercises
Chapter 4: Implementation of a Simple Graphics Package (SGP)
4.1. Overview of SGP
4.2. Viewing operation
4.3. DPU program code generation
4.4. CPU-DPU synchronization
4.5. Interaction handling
4.6. Segmented DPU programs for other devices
4.7. Error handling
4.8. Device-independent graphics
4.9. Summary
Exercises
Chapter 5: Interaction Devices and Techniques
5.1. Logical classes of devices and techniques
5.2. Physical interaction devices
5.3. Techniques for simulating logical devices
5.4. Interaction techniques
Exercises
Chapter 6: The Design of User-Computer Graphic Conversations
6.1. The language analogy
6.2. The language model
6.3. Design principles
6.4. The design process
Exercises
Chapter 7: Geometrical Transformations
7.1. 2D transformations
7.2. Homogeneous coordinates and matrix representation of 2D transformations
7.3. Composition of 2D transformations
7.4. Efficiency considerations

7.5. Matrix representation of 3D transformations
7.6. Composition of 3D transformations
7.7. Transformation as a change of coordinate systems
Exercises
Chapter 8: Viewing in Three Dimensions
8.1. Projections
8.2. The mathematics of planar geometric projections
8.3. Specifying an arbitrary 3D view
8.4. Calculating the planar geometric projections
8.5. Clipping against a canonical view volume
8.6. Image transformations
8.7. 3D viewing in simple graphics package (SGP)
8.8. Summary
Exercises
Chapter 9: Modeling and Object Hierarchy
9.1. What is a model?
9.2. Geometric models and object hierarchy
9.3. Object placement and instance transformations
9.4. Transforming objects with the current transformation matrix
9.5. Generalizing to two-level and *n*-level hierarchies
9.6. How can hierarchy be encoded?
9.7. Multilevel correlation
9.8. Passing attributes
9.9. Pre- and postmultiplication
9.10. Combining model traversal with the viewing operation
9.11. Clipping in master coordinates
9.12. Extents
9.13. Object windows and instance rectangles
9.14. Summary
Exercises
Chapter 10: Advanced Display Architecture
10.1. Introduction
10.2. Background
10.3. The simple refresh display
10.4. Vector transformations and clipping in image space
10.5. High-performance displays with modeling transformations and viewing operation
10.6. Functional model for high-performance architectures
10.7. The Evans & Sutherland PS300—another turn on the wheel
10.8. Extensions for raster graphics—Megatek 7200
10.9. Multiprocessor and host-satellite graphics
Summary
Exercises
Chapter 11: Raster Algorithms and Software
11.1. Introduction
11.2. Scan-converting lines
11.3. Scan-converting characters
11.4. Scan-converting circles
11.5. Region filling
11.6. Polygon clipping
11.7. Scan-converting polygons
11.8. Unsegmented graphics subroutine package with temporal priority

11.9. Segmented graphics subroutine package with priority
Exercises

Chapter 12: Display Architecture
12.1. Introduction
12.2. A simple raster display system
12.3. Programming the raster display
12.4. The image display system
12.5. Alternative raster display architectures
12.6. Raster architecture for personal computers
Exercises

Chapter 13: Representation of 3D Shapes
13.1. Introduction
13.2. Polygon meshes
13.3. Consistency of polygon mesh representations
13.4. Plane equations
13.5. Parametric cubic curves
13.6. Parametric cubic surfaces
13.7. Transforming curves and patches
13.8. Calculation of points on a bicubic surface
Exercises

Chapter 14: The Quest for Visual Realism
14.1. Introduction
14.2. Techniques for displaying depth relationships
14.3. Stereopsis
14.4. Approaches to visual realism

Chapter 15: Algorithms for Removing Hidden Edges and Surfaces
15.1. Introduction
15.2. Simplifying depth comparisons: the perspective transformation
15.3. Avoiding depth comparisons: extents
15.4. The depth-sort algorithm
15.5. The z-buffer algorithm
15.6. Scan-line algorithms
15.7. Area-subdivision algorithms
15.8. Algorithm efficiency
15.9. Algorithms for curved surfaces
Exercises

Chapter 16: Shading Models
16.1. Introduction
16.2. Diffuse reflection and ambient light
16.3. Specular reflection
16.4. Polygon mesh shading
16.5. Shadows
16.6. Light-transmitting surfaces
16.7. Surface detail
Exercises

Chapter 17: Intensity and Color
17.1. Introduction
17.2. Achromatic color: intensity
17.3. Chromatic color
17.4. Color models for raster graphics
17.5. Reproducing color hard copy

17.6. Color harmony
17.7. Using color in interactive graphics
Exercises
Bibliography
Index

664 pp. 17 chapters. Drawings, photographs, figures, tables, mathematical formulae, algorithms, models, general index, bibliography. ISBN 0-201-14468-9.

80
Franke, Herbert W.

Computer Graphics—Computer Art
Phaidon, 1971

(translation by Gustav Metzger of Franke's *Computergraphik— Computerkunst,* 1971)

An early (1971) classic work by a major theorist of the computer's impact on the arts and aesthetics, offering "a comprehensive survey of the new phenomenon of computer art."

This English language version of an early work by W.G. Franke, the German computer-art theoretician and practitioner, presents a survey of computer art, which the author defines as "any aesthetic formation which has arisen on the basis of the logical or numerical transposition of given data with the aid of electronic mechanisms." Divided into three major sections, the book begins with a lucid, basic introduction to computer structure, languages/programs, memory, graphic and electronic output devices, picture processing, and the creation of computer sculpture and music. A succinct but thorough history of computer art forms follows, including discussion of the development of computer graphics, texts, films, dance, theater, architecture, and multi-media. The brief final section deals with the aesthetics of computer art, emphasizing contemporary German work on the theoretical foundations of exact and information aesthetics. The work concludes with an outlook on the future of computer art, and with brief biographies of prominent computer artists and theoreticians. The author's discussion is complemented throughout by a particularly judicious choice of illustrations. His conclusions have been confirmed not only by contemporary developments but also by his own continued work on the relations between art and science, which includes a recent interest in visual languages and the increasing impact of visual information media on human thought processes ("Observations Concerning Practical Visual Languages," *Visible Language* 11:2, 1977; "The New Visual Age: the Influence of Computer Graphics on Art and Society," *Computer Graphics Forum* 2:2-3, 1983). However, the first edition remains a standard practical and theoretical introduction to this rapidly developing, controversial field, and should be of lasting, though primarily historical, interest to graphic artists, display designers, aestheticians and critics. A second edition of this volume will be available in the spring of 1985, and will be substantially revised and expanded, including all new illustrations. According to information supplied by prepublication materials, several topics of current interest (CAD/CAM, computer-aided process control, picture processing, text processing, animation, and simulation, among others) will be examined, and the preface clearly demonstrates that this influential author has continued to be active in the field of display design. The new edition of this classic is likely to join the original as a standard work. It will be published in German and English (through Springer Verlag) simultaneously.

CONTENTS

Preface

Installations and Methods
1. The computer and aesthetic processes
2. The analogue computer
3. The digital computer
4. Structure of the computer
5. Programs
6. Memory
7. Output devices
8. Organization of digital computing processes
9. Graphic output
10. Mechanical drawing devices
11. Electronic output devices
12. Printing devices
13. Random processes
14. Figurative computer graphics
15. Picture processing
16. Other forms of computer art

History of Computer Art
1. The move to computer graphics
2. The beginning of computer graphics
3. International exhibitions
4. Publications on computer art
5. Recent developments in computer graphics
6. Computer sculpture
7. Computer film
8. Computer texts
9. Computer music
10. Theater, dance, multi-media
11. Computer architecture

Theoretical Foundations of Computer Art
1. Computer art and art criticism
2. Exact aesthetics
3. Experimental aesthetics
4. The random as the generative impulse

Outlook—The Future of Computer Art

Biographies

Bibliography

Index

134 pp. 4 chapters. Drawings, photographs, general index, bibliography, color graphics. ISBN 0-7148-1503-9.

81
Freeman, Herbert
(ed.)

collection

Tutorial and Selected Readings in Interactive Computer Graphics
IEEE Computer Society Press, 1980

(initially presented at the twentieth IEEE Computer Society International Conference, Compcon 80; San Francisco, California; 25-28 February 1980)

A collection of historical and current articles for the computer graphics student.

This collection of forty-four articles on computer graphics comprises a basic text for use by college level students and a reference material source for practicing engineers and computer scientists. It provides a balance of historical background and current trends in computer graphics. Computer image processing, computer-aided design, and display systems technology are not dealt with specifically. They are viewed as being related to computer graphics, but not a central part of the field. The work is drawn from articles assembled for use in a course in computer graphics taught by the editor and reflects the change in emphasis in the field, from the hardware used to the algorithms which generate graphic displays. In each section the editor introduces papers carefully selected to reflect the changes which have occurred in the field. All are well written. The historical perspective includes the seminal (1963) paper on computer graphics by Ivan Sutherland. In addition to individual author reference lists for the papers included in the work, Freeman includes a selected bibliography.

CONTENTS

Preface

Introduction

Part I: Graphics Systems
    Overview
    Sketchpad, a man-machine graphical communication system
        I.E. Sutherland
    Sketchpad III, a computer program for drawing in three dimensions
        T.E. Johnson
    Multi-function graphics for a large computer system
        C. Christensen, E.N. Pinson
    A clipping divider
        R.F. Sproull, I.E. Sutherland

Part II: Graphics Facilities
    Overview
    An introduction to computer graphic terminals
        M.H. Lewin
    The Adage graphics terminal
        T.G. Hagan, R.J. Nixon, L.J. Schaefer
    A plasma-panel interactive graphics system
        D.L. Fulton
    The PLATO IV student terminal
        J. Stifle

Intermixing refresh and direct view storage graphics
   N. Thanhouser
A scan conversion algorithm with reduced storage requirements
   B.W. Jordan, Jr., R.C. Barrett
A practical approach to implementing line printer graphics
   J.R. Rumsey, R.S. Walker
Part III: Algorithms for Line and Curve Generation
Overview
Algorithm for computer control of a digital plotter
   J.E. Bresenham
An improved algorithm for the generation of nonparametric curves
   B.W. Jordan, Jr., W.J. Lennon, B.D. Holm
On circle generation algorithms
   W.L. Chung
Free drawing of curves for computer display
   D. Cohen, T.M.P. Lee
A new curve fitting method using a CRT computer display
   F. Yamaguchi
Part IV: Graphics Languages and Data Structures
Overview
A general purpose graphics language
   H.E. Kulsrud
Display procedures
   W.M. Newman
LG: a language for analytic geometry
   J. Raymond
The synthesis of solids bounded by many faces
   I.C. Braid
GLIDE: a language for design information systems
   C. Eastman, M. Henrion
Graphic and relational data base support for problem solving
   D. Weller, R. Williams
Part V: Hidden Line Removal Algorithms
Overview
BE VISION, a package of IBM 7090 FORTRAN programs to draw
orthographic views of combinations of plane and quadric surfaces
   R.A. Weiss
A notion of quantitative invisibility and the machine rendering of
solids
   A. Appel
A solution to the hidden-line problem for computer-drawn
polyhedra
   P.P. Loutrel
A procedure for generating visible-line projections of solids
bounded by quadric surfaces
   P. Woon, H. Freeman
A solution to the hidden surface problem
   M.E. Newell, R.G. Newell, T.L. Sancha
Reentrant polygon clipping
   I.E. Sutherland, G.W. Hodgman
Sorting and the hidden surface problem
   I.E Sutherland, R.F. Sproull, R.A. Shumacker

Raster-scan hidden surface algorithm techniques
  G. Hamlin, Jr., C.W. Gear
The perspective representation of functions of two variables
  B. Kubert, J. Szabo, S. Giulieri
A two-space solution to the hidden line problem for plotting functions of two variables
  T.J. Wright
Part VI: Generation of Halftone Images
  Overview
  A procedure for generation of three-dimensional half-toned computer graphics presentations
    W.J. Bouknight
  Continuous shading of curved surfaces
    H. Gouraud
  Computer display of curved surfaces
    E. Catmull
  Models of light reflection for computer synthesized pictures
    J.F. Blinn
  A new technique for displaying continuous tone images on a bilevel display
    J.F. Jarvis, C.S. Roberts
Part VII: Computer Animation
  Overview
  Picture-driven animation
    R.M. Baecker
  Animator: an on-line two-dimensional film animation system
    P.A. Talbot, J.W. Carr III, R.R. Coulter, Jr., R.C. Hwang
  Computer generated animation of faces
    F.I. Parke
  ANIMA II: 3-D color animation system
    R.J. Hackathorn
Part VIII: Freeform Surfaces
  Overview
  Surfaces for computer-aided aircraft design
    S.A. Coons, B. Herzog
  On Coons and other methods for the representation of curved surfaces
    A.R. Forrest
  Visual interaction with Overhauser curves and surfaces
    J.A. Brewer, D.C. Anderson
Bibliography
  Books
  Journals and conference proceedings
  Bibliographies
  Supplementary references
Author Index
Subject Index

415 pp. 44 papers in 8 parts. Drawings, photographs, figures, charts, maps, graphs, tables, mathematical formulae, algorithms, abstract formalisms, models, author index, subject index, bibliography, references. ISBN 0-8186-0266-X.

82
French, Thomas E.
Vierck, Charles J.
Foster, Robert J.

Graphic Science and Design (4ed.)
McGraw-Hill, 1984

This work presents a comprehensive introduction to the basic concepts and applications of engineering graphics and graphic design.

Designed as an introductory textbook in engineering graphics and graphics science, this fourth edition (formerly titled *Graphic Science*) succinctly and thoroughly examines the basic elements of graphics. The text is divided into four major sections: basic graphics, space geometry, graphic solutions and applied graphics in design. The authors emphasize graphic and space geometry and their use before turning to a consideration of graphics instruments and the role of empirical data in constructing graphic solutions. The applications of numerous chart, graph, and diagram types are discussed in detail, along with the mathematical techniques employed in their design. Design phases, machine tools, and specific types of drawings used for various manufacturing processes are also treated. The text includes an extensive survey of the elements of computer graphics, computer graphics applications, and examples. A selection of problems follows each of the four major sections of the book, and a final chapter presents professional design problems drawn from a variety of engineering fields which deal with projections, structures and components, graphic solutions, and the design process. This edition represents a substantial review of the third edition, and incorporates ANSI standards, metric units, and a chapter on computer graphics, while at the same time condensing the overall text. While this is not specifically dedicated to computer graphics, the general principles presented provide a useful reference for display designers. Similarly, while not directly intended for draftsmen, many of the techniques described are essential to that field. An informative, lucid introduction of interest to beginning students of engineering graphics and graphic design.

CONTENTS

Preface

Part One: Basic Graphics

1. Introduction
2. Using modern instruments
3. Constructional geometry and curved surfaces
4. Orthographic drawing and sketching
5. Pictorial drawing and sketching
6. Sectional views in practice
7. Dimensioning and tolerancing

Part Two: Space Geometry

8. Fundamental analyses of lines and planes: true length; edge view; true surface
9. Further explorations of lines and planes: parallelism; perpendicularity; curved lines
10. Relationships between lines and planes

11. Intersections in space
12. Developments: utilizing revolution; development of flat and curved surfaces
13. Vector analysis

Part Three: Graphic Solutions
14. Empirical data: presenting and analyzing
15. Graphic solutions of equations
16. Graphic calculus

Part Four: Applied Graphics and Design
17. Introduction to design
18. Working drawings for manufacture
19. Elements of computer graphics
20. Professional problems

Addendum: Assembly Elements: Threaded Fasteners, Keys, Rivets, Springs

Appendixes

Index

692 pp. 20 chapters in 4 parts. Drawings, photographs, figures, tables, mathematical formulae, general index, appendices. ISBN 0-07-022307-6.

Friedell, Mark   *SEE UNDER ID 138*

83
Frutiger, Adrian

Type, Sign, Symbol
Hastings House, 1980

Describes the author's ideas about type, colorfully illustrating the concepts with many practical examples from his widely varied work in developing typefaces, logotypes, public signs, digital typefaces, and communicative sculpture.

The author views type as relevant for many applications beyond the printed page and much of this book describes his work with various media such as public signs or cathode ray tube (CRT) displays. He sees type as a "human problem" despite the many changes in technology that have drastically altered printing and display methodologies over the centuries. He believes in fully accepting new technologies, rather than resisting change, but thinks that new techologies should be encountered "on the basis of the past." He views the development of new typefaces as a blend of creative desire and utilization of technological advances. The author's type-faces are designed so that they are "readable," "technically practical," and subtly novel. The book covers a variety of areas related to type, logotypes, signs, and symbols. History of typeface is discussed as well as the development of new typeface, with a particular focus on the sans serif typefaces the author sees as prototypically modern. New technologies influencing typeface are discussed, including type to be read by computers and typefaces for computer display. The author discusses his work on the development of OCR-B, the computer typeface that has been a world standard since 1973. Many pictorial examples of different typefaces are given in a discussion of typeface legibility. Issues relevant to the creation of public signs, including computer display signs, are focused on and signs are viewed as an important part of the environment that can significantly diminish or enhance environmental appearance. Designs of trademarks, non-lettered pictorial signs used as communicative symbols, and sculptures as three-dimensional graphics for communication are discussed. Excellent illustrations are an integral part of the work. The written text is presented in three languages throughout the book: English, German, and French. Anyone who is involved with the printed word and the creative and effective use of design would benefit from this book.

CONTENTS
About this book
The development of script
Why New Typefaces?
The nature of sanserif and the significance of Univers (E. Ruder)
Why Univers was designed and how it developed
New possibilities for designers
Typefaces and printing techniques: Meridien
Constructivism in type design: on Serifa (E. Ruder)
On the planning of a typeface: Serifa as example
New Techniques, New Craftsmanship
Type as a worldwide means of communication
The graphology of the centuries
Specific phototype faces for offset and gravure
Typewriter composition as a new possibility: Univers on the IBM Composer
Type Recognised by the Computer
OCR-B: a typeface for the automatic (optical) reading of texts
The computer as aid to drawing
The limits of the automatic modification of typefaces
Typefaces and Their Legibility
Type in the Environment and in Architecture
Lettering for the Paris Metro
The EDF-GDF alphabet
Lettering system for Paris (Charles de Gaulle) Airport
Digital typeface design for movable indicators
Scripts of Foreign Cultures
Can the sacred script of India be modernized?
Work on the Devanagari script
Work on the Tamil script
Logotypes
How a logotype is designed
From logotype to company image

Signs and Symbols
    Signs for the Air France timetable
    Non-figurative vignettes for the Koran
    Symbolic pictures or pictorial symbols
    Symbolic expression through the transformation of a sign
    Developments
    Symbolic vignettes
    Symbolic interpretations of the theme of Love, Life and Death
    Symbols of western dualism
Artistic Creation with Matter and Light
    On free graphic representations (Maurice Besset)
    Woodcut sequence: "Genesis"
    "Urgarten": a marble relief
    Concrete lettering at the railway station of Roissy (H.R. Schneebeli)
Biography

151 pp. 9 chapters. Drawings, photographs, color graphics. ISBN 0-8038-7221-6.

84
Fu, King Sun
Kunii, Tosiyasu L.
(eds.)

collection

Picture Engineering
Springer-Verlag, 1982

(vol. 6 in the *Springer Series in Information Sciences*, King Sun Fu, Thomas S. Huang, Manfred R. Schroeder, series eds.)

Examines picture engineering, presenting it as a new discipline for handling picture processing.

This book focuses on pictorial database management, picture representation, picture computer architecture, office automation, computer-aided design, and computer art. The chapters on database management include a data model for building a picture database computer, a discussion of computer system organization for handling pictorial data, and a methodology for pictorial indexing and encoding. The section on "Picture Representation" contains papers on picture analysis and the design of three-dimensional objects, as well as a unique approach to surface construction and 3-D analysis by means of "structure lines." Picture computer architecture covers techniques of picture engineering in hardware. Two sections examine picture engineering for automation in business and engineering offices. There are papers on color graphic report generation, image editing and filing techniques, a multiple microprocessor system for office image processing, and computer-aided design. The book closes with a discussion of computer generated art. Several papers are drawn from a 1981 symposium on picture engineering held in Japan. The three contributions on computer architecture come from a 1981 workshop at Hot Springs, Virginia. Among the many figures throughout this work are five pages of color photographs illustrating computer visual design. This highly specialized work is aimed at electrical and computer engineers, computer scientists, and information systems researchers.

CONTENTS

Part I: Pictorial Database Management
PICCOLO: a data model for picture database computers
K. Yamaguchi, T.L. Kunii
(with 10 figures)
Computer system organization for pictorial data
A. Klinger
(with 3 figures)
A methodology for picture indexing and encoding
S.-K. Chang
(with 3 figures)

Part II: Picture Representation
A general (syntactic-semantic) approach to picture analysis
K.S. Fu
(with 7 figures)
Shape design, representation and restoration with splines
Y. Ikebe, S. Miyamoto
(with 23 figures)
Computer-aided design of 3-D objects using polar spline representations
L.L. Schumaker
(with 2 figures)
Application of structure lines to surface construction and 3-dimensional analysis
H. Enomoto, N. Yonezaki, Y. Watanabe
(with 26 figures)

Part III: Picture Computer Architecture
A configurable micro array computer for signal and image processing
W.K. Giloi, R. Bruening
(with 3 figures)
A multiprocessor system for dynamic scene analysis
D.P. Agrawal, R. Jain
(with 8 figures)
VLSI array architecture for picture processing
P.S. Liu, T.Y. Young
(with 10 figures)

Part IV: Office Automation
High-level programming support for color/graphics reports
K. Saigusa, T. Takeshita
(with 18 figures)
An approach to image editing and filing
Y. Takao
(with 7 figures)
A multiple microprocessor system for office image processing
L.M. Ni, K.Y. Wong, D.T. Lee
(with 7 figures)

Part V: Computer-Aided Design
   Logic diagram editing for interactive logic design
      H. Hiraishi, S. Yajima
   (with 17 figures)
   Extended graphic functions of the A-IDAS system for visual design
      H. Matsuka, S. Uno, K. Sugimoto, J. Takama
   (with 15 figures)
Part VI: Computer Art
   Towards an intelligent computer art system
      M.K. Sasaki, T. Sasaki
   (with 7 figures)
   Index of contributors

303 pp. 16 papers in 6 parts. Drawings, photographs, figures, graphs, tables, mathematical formulae, references. ISBN 3-540-11822-5.

85
Gagalowicz, André
De Ma, Song

Synthesis of Natural Textures on 3-D Surfaces
1983

technical report

(report number AFOSR-TR-84-0176; Computer Vision Laboratory, University of Maryland; sponsored by Air Force Office of Scientific Research; November 1983)

Presents a new method of synthesizing texture on 3-D surfaces which avoids some of the problems of current techniques.

The authors offer computer graphics programmers a new method of synthesizing natural textures on three-dimensional surfaces. The one technique previously reported in the literature by others is faulted as too complex, requiring significant computer time, and possibly presenting aliasing effects and continuity problems at the edge of curved templates. The authors believe that they have solved these problems with a relatively simple, quick procedure requiring only one set of second order statistics to develop a texture on any surface, at any distance. As the synthesis is achieved sequentially, point by point, there are no problems with aliasing or edge effects. Any kind of texture may be reproduced. Samples of texture quality representing surfaces such as natural and artificial paper, wool, and rattan are shown in figures which, unfortunately, did not reproduce well. The authors have previously published work on planar textures and this technique represents and extention of that procedure. This report is intended for other professional computer graphics programmers.

25 pp. Figures, abstract formalisms, bibliography.

86
Galitz, Wilbert O.

Handbook of Screen Format Design (2ed.)
Q.E.D. Information Sciences, 1985

Provides materials to assist designers in developing an effective screen
interface between a program and its users (i.e., a screen product that is
easily used and visually clear). Only simple programming concepts
necessary to accomplish this objective are introduced.

Intended as a ready reference source for all screen design, this handbook
is an effort to document a useful set of guidelines. The author draws
from human factors and psychological principles, experimental studies
in the behavioral disciplines, documents for people-machine interfaces,
and his own experience. Each chapter contains a series of important
points, concepts, or guidelines presented in highlighted checklist format,
followed by a narrative providing further detail. There are numerous
illustrations and examples. The contents include: design consistency and
design tradeoffs; a review of the considerations integral to the design
process; data collection or data entry screens; inquiry screens;
interactive screens; use of color in screen design; guidelines for source
document design; and a step-by-step illustrated review of the design
steps necessary to define, design, and lay out a typical data entry screen.
This well-respected handbook has been expanded and revised in this
new edition. Many of the criticisms of the first edition have been
addressed. Explanatory text has largely been expanded, figures are more
pleasantly designed, and the formal typesetting of this edition is a vast
improvement over the computer print-out style of the first edition. A
significant chapter on systems considerations has been added. (Portions
of earlier chapters from the original have been incorporated into this
section.) Overall, this edition has been improved in readability,
thoroughness, and appearance, which should make it even more useful
than the original.

CONTENTS
CHAPTER 1: INTRODUCTION
An Historical Review
Handbook Objectives
Handbook Scope
Types of Screens
Overview
How to Use This Handbook
Topic Organization and Illustrations
A Final Word
CHAPTER 2: SYSTEM CONSIDERATIONS
Why People Have Trouble with Computer Systems
Responses to Poor Design
Friendly Systems
The Desirable Qualities of a System
Natural Language Dialogues

Current Directions and Guidelines
    Consistency
    Design tradeoffs
    Log-on
    Initiative
    Flexibility
    Complexity
    Power
    Information load
    Control
    Command languages
    Command language arguments
    Assistance
    Feedback
    Recovery
    Function keys
    Control functions
    Error management
    Response time
    Specific response times
CHAPTER 3: CONSIDERATIONS IN SCREEN DESIGN
Human Considerations
    Most wanted features of screens
    Human characteristics important to screen design
    Screen format and content
    Where to put information on a screen
    What information to put on a screen
How to Place Information on a Screen
    General
    Fonts
    Text and illustrations
    Field captions/data fields
    Messages
Hardware Considerations
Software Considerations
    Field characteristics
    Field types
    Defining field characteristics
    Common field definitions
    Monochromatic display features
    Edit requirements
    Storage capabilities
Application Considerations
CHAPTER 4: DATA ENTRY SCREENS
Section 4-1: Data Entry Screens - General
    Information grouping techniques
    Transaction organization
    Keying procedures
    Data structure
    Data editing

Section 4-2: Data Entry Screens Used with a Dedicated Source
Document
    Screen organization
    Captions
    Entry fields
    Field alignment
    Spacing
    Headings
    Messages & instructional information
    Title
    Screen number
    Examples

Section 4-3: Data Entry Screens Used without a Dedicated Source
Document
    Screen organization
    Captions
    Entry fields
    Field alignment
    Field justification
    Spacing
    Headings
    Messages and instructional information
    Title
    Screen number
    Examples

CHAPTER 5: INQUIRY SCREENS

Screen Organization

Captions
    Structure & size
    Formatting

Data Fields

Data Organization

Field Alignment

Field Justification

Headings
    Field group headings
    Section headings
    Subsection headings

Spacing
    Vertical spacing
    Horizontal spacing - single fields
    Horizontal spacing - multiple occurrence fields

Messages & Instructional Information

Title

Screen Numbers

Examples

CHAPTER 6: MULTIPURPOSE SCREENS

Implementation

CHAPTER 7: QUESTION AND ANSWER SCREENS

Transaction Development Rules

Field Formatting

Field Characteristics

Title

Examples

CHAPTER 8: MENU SCREENS

Structure

Organization

Item Captions
    Item caption alignment and justification
    Item identification

Item Identification Code Positioning

Item Selection Techniques

Combining Identification and Selection Techniques

Item Identification Techniques

Category Headings

Spacing
    Vertical spacing
    Horizontal spacing - between columns of items

Messages & Instructional Information

Title

Screen Number

Examples

CHAPTER 9: COLOR IN SCREEN DESIGN

Color Uses

Cautions Using Color

Color as a Formatting Aid

Color as a Visual Code

Choosing Categories of Data for Color

Choosing Colors to Display
    Terminal color capabilities
    Consistency
    Compatibility with expectancies
    Discriminability
    Frequency of use & importance
    Relevance & confusion

CHAPTER 10: GRAPHICS

Symbols

CHAPTER 11: SOURCE DOCUMENTS

General Design Criteria

Design Considerations

Source Data Collection

Design Consistency

Alternative Design Concepts

Document Physical Characteristics
  Size
  Margins
  Type style
  Type size
  Line rules
  Turns
  Colors

Document Organization

Document Content
  Captions
  Fill-in areas
  Coding techniques - alternatives
  Coding techniques - design
  Coding aids

Other Considerations
  Title
  Completion instructions
  Section headings
  Fill-in area alignment

CHAPTER 12: SCREEN DESIGN STEPS

Review Screen Design Documentation & Services

Identify System Inputs and Outputs

Identify Unique User Requirements

Describe Data Elements

Develop Transaction
  Summarize design requirements affecting screen design
  Specify data elements which will comprise a transaction
  Organize transaction data elements into sections
  Identify and layout screens

Define Paper Screen

Define Computer Screens

Test Screens

Implement Screens

Evaluate Screens

BIBLIOGRAPHY

225 pp. 12 chapters. Figures, bibliography. (ISBN 0-89435-119-2)

87
Gates, David

reference

Type
Watson-Guptill, 1973

This compendium of typefaces presents over 850 fonts. Arranged by categories and indexed by name, this oversized, spiral-bound reference is designed for convenient use by display designers and graphic artists.

CONTENTS

Alphabetical Index of Typefaces

Introduction

Part One
One-line showings of over 850 typefaces arranged according to style category. Each style category is fully described in regard to historical background and development, structural system employed and characteristic details.

Part Two
Complete alphabets of selected typefaces. Organization of alphabets is by style category. Typefaces of major importance are shown in all sizes from 72 point to the smallest machine sizes. Other typefaces are shown in one or more display sizes.

Rules, Borders, and Ornaments

Linotype Character Count Chart

Proofreaders' Marks

STYLE CATEGORIES

Old Style

Transitional

Modern

Square Serif
Two-weight
One-weight
Reversed weight

Sans Serif
Old style proportions
Even-width proportions
Straight-sided
Engraved
Novelty

Calligraphic

Gothic

Titling and Inscriptional

Swash Capitals

Script
Engraved
Formal
Informal

Latin (Triangular) Serif
Stencil
Typewriter
Outline, Inline, Open, Shaded
Ornamented, Novelty

207 pp. 7 chapters. Index of typefaces, proofreaders' marks. (ISBN 0-8230-5522-1)

88
Geissler, Hans-Georg (ed.)

collection

Modern Issues in Perception
North-Holland, 1983

(based on the Twenty-second International Congress of Psychology; Leipzig, German Democratic Republic; July 1980; vol. 11 in the *Advances in Psychology* series, G.E. Stelmach, P.A. Vroon, series eds.)

This collection of fifteen papers covers "perception" in the broad sense, that is, as a process by which outside information becomes part of inner mental processes.

Invoking Fechner's nineteenth century idea of an exact science of mind-body relations, which included "higher mental activities," the editors have attempted a dialectic across the different schools of thought to give a complete picture of the field, ranging from the Gestalt school to contemporary goal-related information-processing. Rather than a simple aggregate of papers, the result is a progressive unfolding of the concepts and experimental results, building upon the basic theoretical underpinnings. The editors have organized part one around structural information theory, which describes the structure and organization of perceptual events, and defines suitable units of measure for those events and the relations between them, such as primitive code and the elementary operations. The remainder of the first section takes up the internal representation of information that is not so simply classified: fuzzy concepts and three-dimensional versus linear orderings. Part two, organized around information integration theory, is concerned with the more qualitative aspects of perceptual measurements, and attempts to define the mathematical laws covering them, the so-called cognitive algebras. This section also deals with the problems of scaling, i.e., psychological measurement. A paper on information integration theory provides a basic introduction to the rationale behind this theory and what is termed functional measurement. Issues of perceptual versus judgmental integration are discussed and individual weighing is investigated by cross-task comparisons. Cognitive algebras as a means of investigating intuitive physics (psychophysics) in animals and humans are explored. The final paper is an interesting attempt to discern the operative rules of synesthetic metaphors. Although the American participants edited these papers for fluency, some unusual word choices in the translation render the text occasionally clumsy. This volume provides a good overview of the field, although the highly technical language and the mathematical emphasis make this collection primarily of interest to those in disciplines closely related to perceptual psychology.

CONTENTS
    Preface
    General introduction
        Hans-Georg Geissler
PART I: PERCEPTUAL ORGANIZATION AND CLASSIFICATION PROCESSES
    Introduction
        Hans-Georg Geissler
1: An Outline of Coding Theory. Summary of Some Related Experiments
    Emanuel Leeuwenber, Hans Buffart
    1. Introduction
    2. Relations within patterns
    3. Relations between patterns: context
    4. Discussion
    References
2: Structural Information Theory
    Hans Buffart, Emanuel Leeuwenber
    1. Formal aspects of the language
    2. Theory of human interpretation
    3. Measurement of human interpretation
    4. Extension to perceptual inference
    Appendix 1. A. Primitive code
    Appendix 2. B. Code
    References
3: Pattern Cognition and the Processing of Transformational Structures
    Shiro Imai
    1. Psychophysical judgment of configuration
    2. Transformational structure of configurations
    3. Cognitive judgments and transformation structures of configurations
    4. Perceptual classification of configurations
    5. Discussion
    6. Conclusion
    References
4: The Inferential Basis of Classification: From Perceptual to Memory Code Systems
    Hans-Georg Geissler, Martina Puffe
    Part 1: Theory
        Hans-Georg Geissler
    1. Introduction
    2. Outline of a theoretical framework
    3. Organization of inference
    Part 2: Experiments on discrete feature processing
        Hans-Georg Geissler, Martina Puffe
    4. General design and hypothesis
    5. Experiment 1: effects of feature layout
    6. Experiment 2: effects of category composition
    7. Concluding remarks
    References

5: Representation of Ill-Defined Perceptual Categories
   Peter Quaas, Winfried Hacker
   1. Introduction
   2. Competing models of internal categorical representation
   3. Material and design of the experiments
   4. Experimental results on the classification of ill-defined
      perceptual categories
   5. Discussion and consequences
   References

6: Three-Dimensional Orderings and Text Representation
   Werner Krause, Fritz Wysotzki
   1. The internal representation of one-dimensional orderings
   2. The internal representation of three-dimensional orderings
   3. The analysis of the internal representation by comparison of
      reaction times for text and picture-like presentation of
      information
   4. The analysis of the internal representation through strategy
      analysis of "inference process" by means of eye fixation
      measurements
   5. The influence of instruction on the construction of an internal
      representation
   6. Concluding remarks
   References

7: A Systems Approach to Parallel-Serial Testability and Visual Feature
Processing
   James T. Townsend, Ronald Evans
   Introduction
   1. Mental processing and reaction time studies
   2. Introduction to system concepts
   3. Stochastic systems approach to the parallel-serial equivalence
      problem
   4. Methods and testing using second guessing
   References

8: The Conceptual Reflex Arc: A Model of Neural Processing as
Developed for Colour Vision
   E.N. Sokolov, Ch. A. Izmailov
   Description of colour vision in terms of the conceptual reflex arc
   1. The analyser of equally bright colour signals: the spherical
      model
   2. Output responses: the performing subsystem
   3. The switching block
   4. Conclusion
   References

9: The Spatial Frequency Basis of Internal Representation
   Lewis O. Harvey, Jr., Jonathan O. Roberts, Martin J. Gervais
   1. Experiment I—letter identification
   2. Experiment II—picture identification
   3. Discussion
   References

PART II: INTEGRATION AND TRANSFORMATION OF
STIMULUS INFORMATION
   Introduction
      Hans-Georg Geissler

10: Cognitive Algebra in Intuitive Physics
   Norman H. Anderson
   Integration-theoretical approach to intuitive physics
   Stimulus integration
   Integration diagram
   Cognitive algebra
   Functional measurement
   Parallelism theorem
   Linear fan theorem
   Galilean experiment
   Graphic response method
   Observation of physical events
   Studies with a collision task
   Related studies with the inclined plane
   Cognitive algebra
   Intuitive physics
   Intuitive mathematics
   Developmental analysis
   Intuitive physics and psychophysics
   Task structure and knowledge structure
   Physicalist and cognitive views
   Psychological measurement
   Integration rules
   Cognitive units
   The cognitive approach
   Learning
   Knowledge functions
   Information-reinforcement schedules
   References

11: Common Components in Information Integration Tasks: Individual Differences Investigation
   Peter Petzold
      1. Experiment I: Halo effect
      2. Experiment II: Stereotyping
      3. Summary
   References

12: Category Ratings and the Relational Character of Judgment
   Allen Parducci
   The method of single stimuli
   Phenomenal character of relational judgements
   The subjective range
   Equalizing stimulus frequencies
   Range-frequency compromise
   Tests of the range-frequency model
   Defining the context
   Anchoring
   Range vs. frequency
   Relational vs. absolute character of judgement
   References

13: A Comparison of "Frame of Reference" Paradigms in Human and Animal Psychophysics

Barbara Zoeke, Victor Sarris

1. Introduction and overview
2. Major "frame of reference" conceptions in human psychophysics
3. Some special "frame of reference" problems in animal psychophysics
4. Summary and general conclusions

References

14: Scale Convergence as a Principle for the Study of Perception

Michael H. Birnbaum

Algebraic models of perception and judgement
EMMERT's law extended
Comprehensive theory of D is lacking
Scale convergence for subjective distance
Scale convergence as a constraint
Outcomes of model tests
Brief review of studies of scale convergence
Impression formation
Contextual effects in ratings
"Ratios" and "differences" of numbers
Psychophysical "averaging"
"Ratios" and "differences"
Extension of ratio-difference problem
Reverse or inverse attributes
Contextual effects in comparison
Concluding comments
References

15: Categories of Perceptual Experience: A Psychophysicist Peruses Synthetic Metaphors

Lawrence E. Marks

Cross-modality matching
Synesthetic perception
Characteristics of synesthesia
Synesthesia and language
Psychophysics of synesthetic metaphor
Quantifying meaning
Metaphors of brightness and loudness
Metaphors of brightness and pitch
Children's comprehension of synesthetic metaphors
Categories of perception and meaning
References

List of Contributors

Author Index

361 pp. 15 chapters in 2 parts. Drawings, figures, graphs, tables, mathematical formulae, abstract formalisms, models, author index, references. ISBN 0-444-86632-9.

89
Gerstner, Karl

Compendium for Literates: A System of Writing
The MIT Press, 1974

(translation by Dennis Q. Stephenson of Gerstner's *Kompendium for Alphabeten: Systematik der Schrift*

An elegant little book by one of Europe's foremost typographers.

This esoteric work, while not for everyone, is an enjoyable experience for those who come to it with the sense of excitement and enthusiasm that the author conveys throughout. Gerstner sees this book as an attempt at a systematic analysis of the possibilities raised by the art of typography at its best, namely, as a powerful visual expression of moods, ideas, and feelings, as well as of information. All the basics are here: type size and face, spacing, use of color and texture, figure/ground, margins, configuration, and the importance of uniformity and form. Gerstner calls these the "atomic components" of the typographer's art, components with which "letter pictures" are created. Throughout the work the author takes care to establish a historical perspective of writing and present a prescriptive analysis of current implications and future applications. His bibliography extends from Mallarmé, Lévi-Strauss, and Saussure to McLuhan, Tinker, and Cage. This book is highly recommended, not only for its intelligent synthesis, but also because it is quite simply an excellent example of the typographer's art. [Those interested in this work may also wish to read Gerstner's *Designing Programs* (Arthur Niggli, 1968). Although the text is cryptic and difficult to follow, the collection of essays contains Gerstner's major design ideas.]

CONTENTS
1: WRITING AND LANGUAGE
Alphabet
Direction of Reading
Mode of Writing
2: CRAFT
Process
Repetition
PICTURE
Letter Picture
Word Picture
    Spacing
    Size
    Proportion
    Thickness
    Configuration
    Color
    Color chord
    Value
    Texture

Composition Picture
    Dimension
    Leading
    Figure
    Ground
    Placement
    Unity
Morphological Boxes
4: FUNCTION
5: EXPRESSION
Coordinate
Articulate
Display
Arrange
Underline
Derive
Visualize
Play
LITERATURE

180 pp. 5 chapters. Bibliography. ISBN 0-262-07061-8.

Gertman, David I.   *SEE UNDER ID 283*

90
Getty, David J.
(ed.)

technical report

Three-Dimensional Displays: Perceptual Research and Applications to Military Systems
1982

(National Academy of Sciences-National Research Council, Committee on Human Factors; sponsored by Naval Air Systems Command; monitored by Office of Naval Research; 30 September 1982)

A collection of papers which contains the edited proceedings of a symposium which convened to review what was known about three-dimensional display systems, to decide what issues in that field most required research, and to discuss military applications of the technology.

The first section of this report presents five basic research projects in three-dimensional display. The areas covered are: how the interactions between parts of visual stimuli affect perception response performance in tasks requiring an operator to re-orient three-dimensional images to each other or to himself; whether binocular images create the retinal experience of depth more completely than do monocular images; the way viewing conditions, especially point of view, can distort depth perception, and techniques for compensating for such distortion; and a description of five separate experiments which reveal the effects of temporal and spatial variations in dot and line stimuli. The second section of the report transcribes a panel discussion on "Critical Research Issues" in three-dimensional display. These issues include cockpit applications, stereo-rangefinders, evaluating three-dimensional display, and undersea application of three-dimensional display systems. The third section transcribes a panel discussion about military applications of three-dimensional displays, including airborne display systems, air-traffic control, and explosive ordnance disposal. Though this report is written for a professional audience, neither its mathematics nor its terminology is too advanced for other readers. The report does focus on military applications of three-dimensional display technology, but its material generally remains broad enough to support non-military purposes.

CONTENTS

Introduction: Three-Dimensional Displays
David J. Getty

Part I: Basic Perceptual Research
1. The effect of depth position on stimulus interaction
Robert Fox
2. Display-control compatibility in 3-D displays
W.H.F. Huggins, David J. Getty
3. Stereopsis has the "edge" in 3-D displays
Thomas P. Piantanida
4. Effects of projective distortion on perception of graphic displays
Richard R. Rosinski
5. Dot and line detection in stereoscopic space
William R. Uttal, Mark Azzato, John Brogan

Part II: Panel Discussion: Critical Research Ideas in 3-D Displays
6. Critical research issues on cockpit applications of 3-D displays
Kenneth R. Boff
7. A stereo-rangefinder experience
George S. Harker
8. Issues in the evaluation of 3-D display applications
John O. Merritt
9. Visual perception research at Naval Ocean Systems Center
Ross L. Pepper

Part III: Panel Discussion: The Applicability of 3-D Display Research to Military Operational Needs
10. The applicability of 3-D display research to airborne display systems
James H. Brindle
11. Airborne and air-traffic-control applications of 3-D display systems
Roger P. Neeland
12. The applicability of 3-D display research to explosive ordnance disposal
John J. Pennella

192 pp. 12 papers in 3 parts. Drawings, photographs, figures, graphs, tables, references.

91
Giloi, Wolfgang K.

Interactive Computer Graphics: Data Structures, Algorithms, Languages
Prentice-Hall, 1978

This textbook teaches general concepts of interactive computer graphics. The book emphasizes data structures suitable for computer graphics applications, algorithms for picture generation and transformation, and appropriate language constructs for the generation of graphic objects.

Part one of the book focuses on data structures and algorithms. Specific topics covered include: representations of data structures in a computer, construction principles for data management systems, picture structures and transformations, the CORE concept of a universal graphic programming system, curve and surface interpolation, and the hidden-surface problem. Part two covers language constructs and specifically discusses interaction handling, hardware aspects of computer display systems, implementational aspects of display files and picture files, and high and intermediate level programming languages. The final chapter presents the Graphic Procedures for Instructional Purposes (GRIP) model and discusses implementation of this model in existing high level languages including FORTRAN, Pascal, and ALGOL 60. An appendix written by Steven L. Savitt presents a sample implementation of the GRIP concept. Study exercises are included at the end of each chapter. This is a theoretical text and always emphasizes general solutions and concepts, including specific implementations only as examples to clarify discussion of underlying concepts. The book is a complex college textbook that should also be useful to graphics applications programmers, graphics system programmers and designers, and computer-aided design applications programmers. In his preface Giloi presents the organization of the book, detailing which chapters will prove most significant to each of these audiences.

CONTENTS

Preface

PART I: DATA STRUCTURES AND ALGORITHMS

1: Introduction
    1.1. What is computer graphics?
    1.2. The motivation for interactive computer graphics
    1.3. Model of interactive graphics systems
    1.4. The display file
    1.5. The necessity of a dual representation of graphic objects
    1.6. The problem of picture transformations
    1.7. Taxonomy of display systems
    1.8. Stand-alone versus satellite systems
    Exercises

2: Data Structures, Data Bases, and List Handling
    2.1. Formal definition of data structures
    2.2. Representation of data structures in a computer
    2.3. Data models and data base organization
    2.4. List handling
    Exercises

3: Picture Structure and Picture Transformations
    3.1. Picture structure
    3.2. Domain transformations
    3.3. Geometric transformations
    3.4. The perspective representation of three-dimensional objects
    3.5. The "4 × 4-matrix" for rotation, scaling, translation, and perspective
    3.6. A standard transformation system
    Exercises

4: Interpolation and Approximation of Curves and Surfaces
    4.1. Introductory remarks
    4.2. Classical methods: Lagrange and Hermite interpolation
    4.3. Interpolation with *B*-splines
    4.4. Bézier approximation of curves
    4.5 General principles of surface construction
    Exercises

5: Rendering of Surfaces and Solids
    5.1. The hidden-surface problem
    5.2. The set of transition functions {PM,IS,CT,DT,VT}
    5.3. Description of four hidden-surface algorithms
    5.4. Comparison
    5.5. Sorting
    Exercises

PART II: LANGUAGES AND THEIR INTERPRETERS

6: Interaction Handling
    6.1. Interactive input devices
    6.2. Device independence
    6.3. Attention handling
    Exercises

7: The Display Processor
    7.1. The display console
    7.2. The display generator
    7.3. The display controller
    7.4. High-performance display systems
    7.5. Low-cost displays
    Exercises

8: Display File and Picture File Organization
    8.1. Data base and display file revisited
    8.2. Display file without subpicture calls
    8.3. Display file with subpicture calls
    8.4. Display file and picture file
    Exercises

9: Language Concepts for Interactive Computer Graphics
    9.1. High-level graphic programming languages
    9.2. High-level graphic languages: two cases in point
    9.3. L^4-an intermediate language for device-independence and intra system communication

10: High-Level Language Implementation of Display Programming Systems

    10.1. Tasks of a graphical programming package

    10.2. Language structures

    10.3. Interaction handling routines

    10.4. GRIP (Graphic Procedures for Instructional Purposes)

    10.5. The instant of object creation

    10.6. Command languages

    10.7. Implementation of the GRIP philosophy in existing high-level languages

    Exercises

BIBLIOGRAPHY

Appendix: Implementation of the GRIP Concept

    A.1. General considerations

    A.2. Terminal graphics software

    A.3. High-level graphic programming packages

Index

354 pp. 10 chapters in 2 parts. Drawings, figures, tables, algorithms, abstract formalisms, models, general index, bibliography, appendix. ISBN 0-13-469189-X.

92

Glinert, Ephraim P.

PICT: Experiments in the Design of Interactive, Graphical Programming Environments
1985

technical report

(report number TR-85-01-01; Department of Computer Science, University of Washington; January 1985)

This dissertation describes a programming system called PICT that uses icons (small pictorial images) instead of textual symbols for its "language."

Visually oriented programming systems such as PICT represent radical departures from the typical word-oriented programming system. The author believes that visually oriented systems can alleviate some of the problems many would-be programmers experience in their attempts to use text-based systems, problems based in part in the one-dimensional, static, verbal, procedural nature of the textual system. PICT does not require a user to "learn" a language; a user can develop programs in PICT using visual images he or she is familiar with after only a short training session. A program can be written, edited, and run with one "simple, consistent command structure," Furthermore the execution of the program can be viewed by the programmer enabling him or her to see bugs as they occur. This report is composed of: a literature survey of earlier non-textual (iconic) programming systems; the philosophy behind PICT; a precise formal definition of iconic versus textual programming systems; and a description of a series of simple experiments in which the PICT/D system for programming simple numeric calculations was tested on college students having varying degrees of familiarity with computer programming. The study suggests that PICT/D can be easily and quickly learned and is popular with users. The issues raised in the experiments about the successful design and implementation of iconic systems are discussed. Metrics are presented that "provide a means for quantitatively comparing alternative visual programming environments to one another, as well as for comparing programs written in a given visual environment." This report requires some background in programming for a reader to achieve full comprehension of its material. The programming system described here is an intriguing one.

CONTENTS

1: INTRODUCTION

1.1: The Motivation for This Work

1.2: The Contributions of Our Research

1.3: An Overview of the Dissertation

2: SURVEY OF PREVIOUS WORK

2.1: Classifications for Programming Environments

2.2: Graphical Extensions to Conventional Programming Languages
    2.2.1. Graphical extensions to Pascal
    2.2.2. Graphical extensions to Lisp

2.3: Early Iconic Systems
    2.3.1. The work of Ivan and William Sutherland
    2.3.2. Newman's *Reaction Handler*
    2.3.3. Ellis *et al.*'s *GRAIL*
    2.3.4. Christensen *et al.*'s *AMBIT* languages and Denert *et al.*'s *PLAN2D*

2.4: More Recent Iconic Systems
    2.4.1. Smith's *Pygmalion*
    2.4.2. Curry's *Programming by Abstract Demonstration (PAD)*
    2.4.3. Borning's *ThingLab*
    2.4.4. Finzer and Goulde's *Programming by Rehearsal*

2.5: Iconic Systems in the Office and the Home

3: THE PICT ENVIRONMENTS

3.1: The PICT Philosophy

3.2: The PICT Prototypes

3.3: PICT's Facade: System Data Structures and Modes of Operation
    3.1.1. Programming mode
    3.1.2. Erasing mode
    3.1.3. Icon editing mode
    3.1.4. User library mode
    3.1.5. Program execution mode

3.4: A Session with PICT/D

3.5: Notes on the Implementation of PICT/D
    3.5.1. The major PICT/D data structures
    3.5.2. The path generation subsystem

4: USER RESPONSE TO PICT/D

4.1: Description of the Experiments

4.2: Discussion of Methodological Issues

4.3: First Conclusions: Primary Directions for Future Work

5: ICONIC VS. TEXTUAL ENVIRONMENTS

6: ISSUES IN THE DESIGN OF ICONIC PROGRAMMING ENVIRONMENTS

6.1: On Alternatives to the Flowchart Metaphor

6.2: On the Allocation of Limited Space

6.3: On the Choice of Input Device(s)

6.4: On the Use of Color

6.5: On the Iconic Representation of Data Structures and Variables

6.6: On the Menu Hierarchy and its Display

6.7: On the Provision of On-line *HELP*

6.8: On Left vs. Right Handedness in the Display

6.9: On the Need for the Clear Demarcation of Screen Windows

6.10: Can Icons Be Unintentionally Suggestive?

6.11: On User Acceptance of PICT as a Function of Sex and Age

6.12: Ease of Use is Critical

7: SOFTWARE METRICS FOR VISUAL PROGRAMMING

7.1: Survey of Previous Work

7.2: A Metric for Visual Programming Environments
    7.2.1. Development of a general method for devising evaluation schemes
    7.2.2. Comparison of PICT with other visual programming environments

7.3: Some Metrics for Iconic Programs

7.4: Possible Experiments to Validate Our Metrics

8: PICT AND THE FUTURE

9: SUMMARY

BIBLIOGRAPHY

POCKET MATERIAL:

Thirty Slides of a Session with PICT/D (see Section 3.4)

Ten Slides Illustrating a Possible Alternative to the Flowchart Metaphor (see Section 6.1)

204 pp. 9 chapters. Figures, tables, abstract formalisms, footnotes, bibliography.

93
Gnanamgari, Sakunthala
Badler, N.I.
Morgan, H.L.
Webber, Bonnie L.

Providing Automatic Graphic Displays through Defaults
1980

technical report

(report number 80-03-09; Department of Decision Sciences, The Wharton School; sponsored by Office of Naval Research; April 1980)

This short report discusses a method for implementing a default system to provide automatic graphic displays for computer users who have limited experience using graphics.

The article discusses the providing of defaults for selecting the type of graph appropriate for a set of data and for selecting attributes for the graph such as color, size, or orientation. In order to determine appropriate defaults several factors need to be taken into account: the data to be displayed graphically, the device on which the display will be presented, and the users who will view the display. In addition, five properties of data that affect the selection of a graphic representation are identified (continuity, totality, cardinality, multiplicity, and units). The authors develop a formalism using these properties. Examples of how the proposed system selects particular graphic displays for different sets of data are given. The authors also discuss user modification of the graphic display provided by the default system. Useful figures clarify concepts throughout the text. A poor quality reproduction of the entire report does impair the impact of the figures, however, as well as the overall readability of the text. This highly theoretical report is directed at practitioners involved in the development of computer graphics programs and displays. The work reported here makes an important addition to the field of computer graphics; the authors report that their system is the first default system for computer graphics display to be developed.

8 pp. Drawings, graphs, bibliography.

94
Gombrich, Ernst H.

The Sense of Order: A Study in the Psychology of Decorative Art
Cornell University Press, 1979

(from *The Wrightsman Lectures* series)

Lectures which continue Gombrich's earlier work, here emphasizing the perception of patterns through an investigation of ornamental or decorative art.

The chapters in this volume are revised and expanded versions of the author's Wrightman Lectures, delivered under the auspices of the NYU Institute of Fine Arts in 1970. Gombrich continues the line of inquiry he began with *Art and Illusion* (1960), but here he applies perceptual theory to the history of ornamentation and fluctuation of "taste," rather than to representational art. Admittedly speculative, this volume proceeds from a discussion of pattern-making in nature, through a discussion of the human drive for mastery over materials, and the development of motifs from guardian images and floral sources, to the outline of the psychology of style. This volume's organization parallels that of the earlier *Art and Illusion* (which dealt with figurative art), thus inviting their complementary use. The 1982 work on perception of images, *The Image and the Eye*, also falls naturally into the sequence of the author's work. All three volumes will be of interest to both historians and psychological theorists in the fields of art and perception. Profusely illustrated with both black and white figures and color plates.

CONTENTS

PREFACE

INTRODUCTION

Order and Purpose in Nature
1. Order and orientation
2. The Gestalt theory
3. The patterns of nature
4. Man-made orders
5. The geometry of assembly
6. Monotony and variety
7. Order and movement
8. Play and art

PART ONE: DECORATION: THEORY AND PRACTICE

I: Issues of Taste
1. The moral aspect
2. Classic simplicity
3. Polemics around the Rococo
4. Design and fashion

II: Ornament as Art
1. The menace of the machine
2. Pugin and the reform of design
3. John Ruskin and Expressionism
4. Gottfried Semper and the study of function
5. Owen Jones and the study of form
6. The Japanese
7. The new status of design
8. Adolf Loos: 'Ornament and Crime'
9. Ornament versus abstraction

III: The Challenge of Constraints
1. Realities of pattern-making
2. The mastery of the material
3. Laws and orders
4. The limits of foresight
5. Tools and samples

PART TWO: THE PERCEPTION OF ORDER

IV: The Economy of Vision
1. Varieties of vision
2. The selective focus
3. Loss of definition
4. Testimonies of art
5. Visual information

6. Expectation and extrapolation
7. The probable and the surprising
8. Breaks as accents
9. Order and survival
10. Global perception

V: Towards an Analysis of Effects
1. The limitations of aesthetics
2. Restlessness and repose
3. Balance and instability
4. Waves and vortices
5. From form to meaning
6. Colour
7. Representation
8. Form and purpose

VI: Shapes and Things
1. The kaleidoscope
2. Repetition and meaning
3. 'Fields of force'
4. Projection and animation
5. Decoration
6. Modifying the body

PART THREE: PSYCHOLOGY AND HISTORY

VII: The Force of Habit
1. Perception and habit
2. Mimicry and metaphor
3. The language of architecture
4. The etymology of motifs
5. Invention or discovery?

VIII: The Psychology of Style
1. Riegel's perceptual theory of style
2. The pervasiveness of style
3. Heinrich Wölfflin
4. Focillon and the 'life of forms'
5. 'Purity' and 'decadence'
6. The logic of situations
7. The Rococo: mood and movements

IX: Designs as Signs
1. Motifs and meanings
2. Marks of distinction
3. Heraldic symbolism
4. Symbol and setting
5. The transformation of the flourish
6. The symbolic potential
7. The sign of the cross

X: The Edge of Chaos
1. A zone of licence
2. Protective spells
3. 'A great dragon force'
4. The elusive mask
5. The migration of monsters
6. Domesticated demons
7. The revival of the grotesque

8. The dissolution of form
EPILOGUE
Some Musical Analogies
    1. The claims of music
    2. The rivalry of the arts
    3. Song and dance
    4. Nature and artifice
    5. Form, rhyme and reason
    6. Elementary effects
    7. From fields of force to worlds of sound
    8. New media
NOTES
PLATES
FULL TITLES OF BOOKS CITED
LIST OF ILLUSTRATIONS
INDEX

411 pp. 10 chapters in 3 parts. Drawings, photographs, figures, general index, chapter notes. ISBN 0-8014-1143-2.

95
Gombrich, Ernst H.

The Image and the Eye: Further Studies in the Psychology of Pictorial Representation
Phaidon, 1982

A volume of essays on image perception, delivered as lectures or included in various publications over a fifteen year period. It is intended to amplify and clarify the ideas on the psychology of art presented in *Art and Illusion* (1960).

Aimed at a wide spectrum of readers, this collection covers a variety of topics reflecting the current emphasis on the perception of images: visual discovery and the difference between recognition and recall; how movement and action are expressed in pictorial art; the contrast between portraiture, caricature, and the likeness achieved in a snapshot; and, particularly, the visual image as information. This work is closely allied to other works by the author, and certain essays summarize and then expand specific arguments from prior publications. As a result, these essays provide an excellent introduction to Gombrich's work. In addition, the author has not included some of his most technical work, making this even more accessible as an introduction. Interested readers may also wish to read the companion volume *The Sense of Order,* which emphasizes "patterns rather than images" in the study of perception. Detailed with many black and white illustrations.

CONTENTS
    Preface
    Visual discovery through art
    Moment and movement in art
    Ritualized gesture and expression in art
    Action and expression in western art

The mask and the face: the perception of physiognomic likeness in
life and in art
The visual image: its place in communication
'The sky is the limit': the vault of heaven and pictorial vision
Mirror and map: theories of pictorial representation
Experiment and experience in the arts
Standards of truth: the arrested image and the moving eye
Image and code: scope and limits of conventionalism in pictorial
representation
Notes
Bibliographical note
Sources of photographs
Index

*320 pp. 11 chapters. Drawings, photographs, general index, bibliography,
chapter notes. ISBN 0-7148-2245-0.*

96
Gorrell, E.L.

**A Human Engineering Specification for Legibility of
Alphanumeric Symbology on Video Monitor Displays (rev.)**
1980

technical report

(report number DCIEM-80-R-26; Defence and Civil Institute of
Environmental Medicine, Canada; sponsored by Directorate Computer
Systems Engineering and Maintenance; June 1980)

Discusses legibility specifications for electronic displays, emphasizing
specifications based on user performance criteria.

This report takes the view that conventional (technology-based) human
engineering specifications for electronic displays can be either too
general or too restrictive, causing adequate displays to be rejected, or
inadequate displays to be accepted. The suggestion is made that these
problems can be resolved by using specifications based on performance
criteria of users in test situations. The conventional legibility
specifications for electronic displays (symbol size, symbol luminance,
contrast ratio, font, dot matrix dimensions, and pixel active areas) are
surveyed, followed by a thorough analysis of test procedures used to
obtain performance-oriented legibility specifications. Specific legibility
test procedures examined are subject selection, environmental controls,
video monitor setup, the design and presentation of the test material,
and the tasks to be performed by the subject. Minimum acceptable
criteria for both conventional and user performance specifications are
given. The revised version of this report differs from its earlier version
in that fewer Minimum Conventional Legibility Criteria have been
proposed, and an appendix that describes a method for calculating
contrast ratios and measuring CRT symbol luminances has been added.
Although this report contains no new original research material, the
revisions to the original conclusions should interest ergonomists and
electronic display engineers for the practical information it brings
together on legibility test specifications and display design.

CONTENTS

Abstract

Introduction

Conventional Human Engineering Specifications for Electronic Displays

Legibility Testing

Proposed Legibility Specification for Video Monitors
    Part A. Minimum Conventional Legibility Criteria
    Part B. Legibility test performance criteria
    Part C. Legibility test specification

References

Appendix:A standardized procedure for measuring CRT symbol
    luminances and calculating contrast ratios

27 pp. 3 chapters. Figures, abstract formalisms, references, appendix.

97
Gouraud, Henri

Computer Display of Curved Surfaces
Garland, 1979

(from the *Outstanding Dissertations in the Computer Sciences* series)

This dissertation discusses the display of curved surfaces on a CRT. The central topic is a shading technique that enhances realism by giving the surface displayed a smooth appearance.

Gourard begins by discussing the limitations of previous methods used to display curved surfaces with a computer. He shows how polygon approximations improve upon the line drawing method by removing the hidden parts of the reproduction. An undesirable visual effect is created, however, by the discontinuities between the adjacent polygons. Gourard shows that simply increasing the number of polygons does not lead to the desired smooth appearance. A visual phenomena called the Mach band effect, discussed in the text, explains "why the planar polygon approximation . . . 'looks' worse than expected." He also posits the solution, the creation of a smooth appearance by using a shading technique to remove the discontinuous intensity values between the polygons. A shading function that accomplishes this is discussed in detail. Other topics included are the hardware and software implementation of this function, and a discussion of how to choose the points defining the surface. Some concluding observations are made on how the shading technique might be applied. The most striking example involves the author's attempt to reproduce his wife's face as part of a larger project to simulate a dancer. Photographs showing the results of both the polygon approximation method and the smooth shading technique demonstrate the advantages of the smooth shading method. Three appendices conclude the text. A method of representing three-dimensional curves, the Bezier Patch, is discussed here. The contents of this dissertation should interest graphics programmers, simulation designers, and other interested in the display of three-dimensional objects on a CRT. Numerous photographs are included to illustrate the methods discussed.

CONTENTS
Abstract
I. Introduction
II. Limitations of existing techniques
III. The Mach band effect
IV. Computing the shading on a curved surface
V. Computing the shading at the verticıes
VI. Choosing the points defining the surface
VII. Hardware implementation
VIII. Conclusion and future research
IX. References
Appendix A. Statistics on the figures
Appendix B. Description of the Bezier patch
Appendix C. Finite differences for the Bezier patch
Vita

81 pp. 9 chapters. Photographs, figures, models, references, appendices.
ISBN 0-8240-4412-6.

98
Grandjean, Etienne
Vigliani, Emilio
(eds.)

proceedings

Ergonomic Aspects of Visual Display Terminals
Taylor and Francis, 1980

(proceedings of the international scientific workshop on ergonomic aspects of VDUs; Milan, Italy; 17-19 March 1980)

These papers, from one of the most important conferences of recent years, examine problems (among others, postural, visual, and psychosocial) encountered by users of visual display terminals (VDTs) and attempt to develop guidelines based on practical experience with VDTs.

CONTENTS
Preface
    E. Grandjean
Introductory Paper
    Ergonomics of VDUs: review of present knowledge
        E. Grandjean
Section 1: Physical Characteristics of VDTs
    Electromagnetic radiations emitted by visual display units
        T. Terran, F. Merluzzi, E. Guidici
    The concept of contrast. A short note and a proposal
        H.H. Bjørset, B. Brekke
    Resolution model for a VDU-based person/machine interface: an overview
        N.D. Lubart
Section 2: Visual Functions
    Ophthalmological aspects of work with display work-stations
        H. Krueger
    Accommodation and visual fatigue in display work
        O. Östberg
    Worker strain related to VDUs with differently coloured characters

M. Haider, M. Kundi, M. Weissenböck
Dioptric problems in connection with luminance-brightness relationship on VDUs
Lucia R. Ronchi, G. Cicchella
Tasks involving contrast resolution, spatial and temporal resolution presented on VDU screen as a measuring technique of visual fatigue
J.H.W. Kalsbeek, F.W. Umbach

Section 3: Visual Impairments
Visual impairments and their objective correlates
Paule Rey, J.J. Meyer
Visual impairments in VDU operators related to environmental conditions
Th. Läubli, W. Hünting, E. Grandjean
Visual fatigue in VDT operators
M.J. Dainoff

Section 4: Performance at VDTs
Visual reading processes and the quality of text displays
H. Bouma
Visual work recognition as a function of contrast
H. Timmers, F.L. van Nes, F.J.J. Blommaert
Information selection from visual display units
F.L. Engel
Experimental investigations for optimal presentation-mode and colours of symbols on the CRT-screen
G.W. Radl
Improving the legibility of visual display units through contrast reversal
D. Bauer, C.R. Cavonius
Error detection at visual display units
S. Bagnara
Method of calculating inspection time of samples on visual display by measurement of eye movement
K. Noro, K. Tsuchiya
Application of SAINT for the analysis of visual performance and workplace layout
K.-F. Kraiss
Design of VDU operator tasks
Enza Tintori Pisano

Section 5: Postural Problems
Postural reactions related to activities on VDU
A. Laville
Constrained postures of VDU operators
W. Hünting, Th. Läubli, E. Grandjean
Field study in newspaper printing: a systematic approach to the VDU operator strain
A. Grieco, G. Molteni, B. Piccoli, R. Perris
User-adjusted VDU parameters
C.R. Brown, D.L. Schaum

Section 6: Psychosocial Aspects
Job stress in video display operations
M.J. Smith, L.W. Stammerjohn, Barbara G.F. Cohen, Nina R. Lalich
Investigations in operators working with CRT display terminals; relationships between task content and psychophysiological alterations
R. Elias, F. Cail, M. Tisserand, M. Christmann
Study on subjective symptomatology of fatigue in VDU operators
S. Binaschi, G. Albonico, E. Gelli, M.R. Morelli di Popolo
Collection of subjective opinions on use of VDUs
L. Ghiringhelli
Section 7: Practical Experiences
Practical experiences in solving VDU ergonomics problems
T.F.M. Stewart
Trade union aspects and experiences with work on VDUs
F. Margulies
CRT-keyboard VDUs—implementing the solutions that already exist
D. Doran
Practical implications of the interest in ergonomic aspects of VDUs
D.J. Wheatley, B.M. Drake
NCR: From the first computer in Italy. to the 1980s. Research and development on VDUs connected to EDP systems
G. Bassani
Can VDU operation cause dermatitis?
H. Tjønn
Section 8: Ergonomic Design and Guidelines
Ergonomic design principles of alphanumeric displays
H. Schmidtke
Visual display units: present status in ergonomic research and applications in the Federal Republic of Germany
K. Buhmann
Ergonomic and medical requirements in VDU workplaces and corresponding rules within the Federal Republic of Germany
K. Buhmann
Ergonomic design of a workplace for VDU operators
L. Bandini Buti, G. Cortili, F. de Nigris, E. Moretti
Ergonomics in the design, evaluation and application of the Philips PTS 6000 terminal system
N. Claridge
Name index
Subject index

300 pp. 40 papers in 8 sections. Photographs, figures, graphs, tables, general index, references, name index. ISBN 0-85066-211-7.

Graphics Standards

overview

Graphics Standards

Although the need for a graphics standard is unquestioned, its required features are hotly debated. Current controversy is focused on the relative merits of the Core System and the Graphics Kernel System (GKS). In 1974 SIGGRAPH-ACM chartered the Graphics Standards Planning Committee whose job was to develop a standards proposal based on accepted practice. In 1976, the International Federation of Information Processors sponsored an international workshop on graphics standards, commonly referred to as Seillac I, which developed four methodological themes to guide the development of a standard; SIGGRAPH's Planning Committee incorporated the workshop's results into the first draft for the Core System. This draft, pubished in 1977 in *Computer Graphics*, was distributed worldwide with a request for debate and criticism. The planning committee reviewed all comments and, in 1979, published a larger, extensively revised draft which included a proposal for a graphics metafile and draft extensions for raster devices and distributed systems. This second draft was sent to the American National Standards Institute for finishing touches and became the informal standard for many users and vendors, although it was never formally voted on or forwarded to the International Standards Organization for consideration. Meanwhile, the Europeans were working on the Graphic Kernel System which, after several revisions, was accepted by the ISO as its operating standard. In 1982, ANSI voted to support GKS over the Core System and published its own draft for GKS. It is important to note that the two standards are remarkably similar; the technical differences are such that GKS has the edge in some applications while the Core System works better for others. Both standards are currently supported by the computer graphics industry; some of the debate stems from economic concern that the industry cannot profitably support two standards. Regardless of the merits of the two standards, the debate often obscures two points. First, GKS and the Core System are not the only graphics standards in existence. There are seven standards which have been developed for a variety of applications. If a single standard is sought, it must be compatible with specialized applications and with the interface standards being developed. Second, considering the expanding capabilities of graphics systems driven by technical advances, any standard should be considered a temporary solution. The chances are that both GKS and the Core System, as now written, will be obsolete within the decade. In this overview collection, we have included the 1979 draft for the Core System and both the ANSI and ISO drafts for GKS along with two introductory texts on GKS. Also present are the proceedings of Seillac I and the follow-up conference on the methodology of interaction referred to as Seillac II and the ANSI draft for the Computer Graphics Metafile. The reader who wants a current, more succinct reference to the standards drafts will want to consult the 1985 edition of the *Graphics Standards Handbook*. This volume contains the most recent drafts of the various graphics standards accompanied by text explaining the differences and applications.

99
American National
Standards Institute

technical report

Computer Graphics Metafile for the Storage and Transfer of Picture Description Information (draft proposal)
1984

(report number ISO/DIS-8632; Computer Graphics Committee, Information Processing Systems, American National Standards Institute; 1984)

This draft proposal of ANSI for an American National Standard for Computer Graphics describes a set of basic elements—the computer graphics metafile (CGM)—which provides a file format for the storage and retrieval of picture information.

The file format elements described in this proposal are designed to be compatible between different system architectures and devices of different design. CGM is based on the Core System, and the name of the proposed standard was changed from virtual device metafile (VDM) to CGM in June 1984. The current proposal stresses CGM's easy implementation and device independence. The standard defines the form/syntax and functional behavior/semantics of the eight classes of CGM elements: delimiter, metafile descriptor, picture descriptor, control, graphical primitive, attribute, escape, and external. The volume also includes detailed but diffuse descriptions of the file format using an abstract syntax; character encoding; binary encoding; and clear text encoding. In this draft proposal, CGM "draws extensively for its model on a graphics system of GKS." However, while both standards are presently restricted to 2-D graphics, CGM does not exclude a future extension to 3-D elements. GKS does not mention this possibility, though it discusses segmentation in detail, which CGM mentions only as a future extension. The CGM standard, as presented in this draft proposal, is unwieldy and diffuse in comparison to *The GKS Primer*'s presentation of GKS.

CONTENTS

PART 1: FUNCTIONAL SPECIFICATION

0: Introduction
    0.1. Purpose
    0.2. Reasons for this standard
    0.3. Design requirements
    0.4. Design criteria
    0.5. Access to a metafile
    0.6. Generation and interpretation of metafiles
    0.7. Distinction between formal specification and encodings
    0.8. Relationship to other ISO standards
    0.9. Status of annexes

1: Scope and Field of Application

2: References

3: Definitions and Abbreviations
    3.1. Definitions
    3.2. Abbreviations

4: Concepts
    4.1. Introduction
    4.2. Delimiter elements
    4.3. Metafile descriptor elements
    4.4. Picture descriptor elements
    4.5. Control elements
    4.6. Graphical primitive elements
    4.7. Attribute elements
    4.8. Escape elements
    4.9. External elements
    4.10. Conceptual state diagrams
    4.11. Registration

5: Abstract Specification of Elements
    5.1. Introduction
    5.2. Delimiter elements
    5.3. Metafile descriptor elements
    5.4. Picture descriptor elements
    5.5. Control elements
    5.6. Graphical primitive elements
    5.7. Attribute elements
    5.8. Escape elements
    5.9. External elements

6: Metafile Default
    6.1. Default values

7: Conformance
    7.1. Forms of conformance
    7.2. Functional conformance of metafiles
    7.3. Full conformance of metafiles
    7.4. Conformance of other bindings

A: Formal Grammar of the Functional Specification
    A.1. Introduction
    A.2. Notation used
    A.3. Detailed grammar
    A.4. Terminal symbols

B: Guidelines for Private Encodings

C: Reference Models

D: Guidelines for Metafile Generators and Interpreters
    D.1. Introduction
    D.2. General guidelines
    D.3. Guidelines specific to element classes
    D.4. Minimum suggested capability list

PART 2: CHARACTER ENCODING

0: Introduction
    0.1. Purpose of the character encoding
    0.2. Objectives
    0.3. Metafile characteristics
    0.4. Relationship to other standards
    0.5. Status of annexes

1: Scope and Field of Application
    1.1. Scope
    1.2. Field of application

2: References
3: Notational Conventions
    3.1. 7-bit and 8-bit code tables
    3.2. Code extension techniques vocabulary
4: Entering and Leaving the Metafile Environment
    4.1. Implicitly entering the metafile environment
    4.2. Invoking the CGM coding environment from ISO 2022
5: Method of Encoding Opcodes
6: Method of Encoding Parameters
    6.1. Coding integers
    6.2. Coding real numbers
    6.3. Coding VDCs and points
    6.4. Coding point list parameters
    6.5. Colour specifiers
    6.6. Colour index lists
    6.7. String parameters
    6.8. Enumerated parameters
    6.9. Index and colour index parameters
    6.10 Data record parameters
7: Character Substitution
8: Representation of Each Element
    8.1. Delimiter elements
    8.2. Metafile descriptor elements
    8.3. Picture descriptor elements
    8.4. Control elements
    8.5. Graphical primitive elements
    8.6. Attribute elements
    8.7. Escape elements
    8.8. External elements
9: Defaults
10: Conformance
PART 3: BINARY ENCODING
0: Introduction
    0.1. Purpose of the binary encoding
    0.2. Objectives
    0.3. Relationship to other standards
    0.4. Status of annexes
1: Scope and Field of Application
    1.1. Scope
    1.2. Field of application
2: References
3: Notational Conventions
4: Overall Structure
    4.1. General form of metafile
    4.2. General form of pictures
    4.3. Data structures
5: Primitive Data Forms
    5.1. Signed integer (symbol SI)
    5.2. Unsigned integer (symbol UI)
    5.3. Character (symbol = C)
    5.4. Fixed point real (symbol = FXR)

5.5. Floating point (symbol = FPR)

6: Representation of Abstract Parameter Types

7: Representation of Each Element
    7.1. Method of presentation
    7.2. Delimiter elements
    7.3. Metafile descriptor elements
    7.4. Picture descriptor element
    7.5. Control elements
    7.6. Graphical primitive elements
    7.7. Attribute elements
    7.8. Escape elements
    7.9. External elements

8: Defaults

9: Conformance

A: Formal Grammar

B: Examples
    B.1. Example 1: BEGIN METAFILE 'Example 1'
    B.2. Example 2: BEGIN PICTURE 'Test'
    B.3. Example 3: POLYLINE from 0,2 to 1,3 to 2,1 to 0,2
    B.4. Example 4: TEXT 'Hydrogen' at 0,1
    B.5. Example 5: 'Text with more than 23 characters' at 1,2
    B.6. Example 6: Partitioned POLYLINE with 50 points
    B.7. Example 7: METAFILE DEFAULT REPLACEMENT
    linewidth 0.5
    B.8. Example 8: Application data 'Record 1' with 10Kbytes of data

List of Binary Encoding Metafile Element Codes

PART 4: CLEAR TEXT ENCODING

0: Introduction
    0.1. Purpose of the clear text encoding
    0.2. Primary objectives
    0.3. Secondary objectives
    0.4. Relationship to other standards
    0.5. Status of annexes

1: Scope and Field of Application
    1.1. Scope
    1.2. Field of application

2: References

3: Notational Conventions

4: Metafile Format
    4.1. Character repertoire
    4.2. Separators
    4.3. Encoding of parameter types
    4.4. Forming names

5: Encoding the CGM Elements
    5.1. The ELEMENT production
    5.2. Encoding delimiter elements
    5.3. Encoding metafile descriptor elements
    5.4. Encoding picture descriptor elements
    5.5. Encoding control elements

    5.6. Encoding graphical primitive elements
    5.7. Encoding attribute elements
    5.8. Encoding escape elements
    5.9. Encoding external elements
6: Clear Text Encoding Defaults
7: Clear Text Encoding Conformance
A: Clear Text Encoding-dependent Formal Grammar
B: Clear Text Encoding Example

330 pp. 33 chapters in 4 parts. Figures, tables, models.

100
American National
Standards Institute

technical report

Graphical Kernel System (draft proposal)
1984

(report number X3H3/83-25R3; Computer Graphics Committee, Information Processing Systems, American National Standards Institute; 5 January 1984)

This draft proposal of the American National Standards Institute (ANSI) describes a set of basic functions for computer graphics programming, the Graphical Kernel System (GKS).

GKS is "a basic graphics system that can be used by the majority of applications that produce computer generated pictures." The basic capabilities of the system include: outputting graphical primitives; appearance control of primitives (using attributes); controlling graphical workstations, transformations, and co-ordinate systems; generating and controlling segments; obtaining graphical input; metafile manipulation; supporting inquiry into capabilities and states of the graphics system; and handling errors. It is important to note that this ANS GKS differs from the internationally prominent GKS originally developed in West Germany (ISO GKS) as follows. The ANS GKS: defines a new minimal output level; contains proposed standards not present in ISO GKS (bindings of GKS functions to program languages); offers a less restrictive conforming program and implementation in place of the ISO GKS conformance statement; modifies several ISO GKS Annexes and changes the word Annex to Appendix; uses INDIVIDUAL as the default; and defines data records for INPUT. As a manual, this suffers by comparison to *The GKS Primer*. Though it is better organized than both the VDM and CGM draft proposals, it is lengthy, and, therefore, does not facilitate an overview of the proposed standard. While a better piece of work than earlier proposals, this GKS draft proposal still falls far short of the lucidity and succinctness of the more widely accepted ISO GKS.

CONTENTS
PART 1: LANGUAGE INDEPENDENT SPECIFICATION
0: Introduction
    0.1. Conformance

1: Scope and Field of Application

2: References

3: Definitions

4: The Graphical Kernel System
    4.1. The standard
    4.2. Introduction
    4.3. Concepts
    4.4. Graphical output
    4.5. Workstations
    4.6. Coordinate systems and transformations
    4.7. Segments
    4.8. Graphical input
    4.9. GKS metafile interface
    4.10. GKS levels
    4.11. States of GKS and inquiry functions
    4.12. Error handling
    4.13. Special interfaces between GKS and the application program

5: GKS Functions
    5.1. Notational conventions
    5.2. Control functions
    5.3. Output functions
    5.4. Output attributes
    5.5. Transformation functions
    5.6. Segment functions
    5.7. Input functions
    5.8. Metafile functions
    5.9. Inquiry functions
    5.10. Utility functions
    5.11. Error handling

6: GKS Data Structures
    6.1. Notation and data types
    6.2. Operating state
    6.3. GKS description table
    6.4. GKS state list
    6.5. Workstation state list
    6.6. Workstation description table
    6.7. Segment state list
    6.8. GKS error state list

A: Function Lists
    A.1. Alphabetic
    A.2. Order of appearance
    A.3. Ordered by level
    A.4. Ordered by state
    A.5. Applicability to workstation groups

B: Error List
    B.1. States
    B.2. Workstations
    B.3. Transformations
    B.4. Output attributes
    B.5. Output primitives
    B.6. Segments
    B.7. Input

B.8. Metafiles

B.9. Escape

B.10. Implementation dependent

B.11. Other errors

C: Interfaces

C.1. Language binding

C.2. Implementation

D: Allowable Differences in GKS Implementations

D.1. Global differences

D.2. Workstation dependent differences

E: Metafile Structure

E.1. Metafile based on dpANS VDM

E.2. Metafile based on ISO DIS7942

E.3. Generation of metafiles

E.4. Interpretation of metafiles

E.5. Control items

E.6. Items for output primitives

E.7. Items for output primitive attributes

E.8. Items for workstation attributes

E.9. Items for transformations

E.10. Items for segment manipulation

E.11. Items for segment attributes

E.12. User items

F: GKS Functions Summary

F.1. Control functions

F.2. Output functions

F.3. Output attributes

F.4. Transformation functions

F.5. Segment functions

F.6. Input functions

F.7. Metafile functions

F.8. Inquiry functions

F.9. Utility functions

F.10. Error handling

G: Differences between ANS GKS and ISO GKS

PART 2: LANGUAGE SPECIFIC BINDINGS: GKS BINDING IN FORTRAN

1: FORTRAN Binding

1.1. Principles

1.2. Abbreviations in generating subroutine names

1.3. Data types

1.4. Enumeration types

1.5. List of the GKS function names and levels

1.6. GKS errors specific to the FORTRAN binding

1.7. The GKS function interface

1.8. Control functions

1.9. Output functions

1.10. Output attributes

1.11. Transformation functions

1.12. Segment functions

1.13. Input functions

1.14. Metafile functions

1.15. Inquiry functions
1.16. Utility functions
1.17. Error handling
1.18. Utility functions not defined in GKS

A: FORTRAN Examples

396 pp. 7 chapters in 2 parts. Figures, charts, tables, glossary, appendices.

101
Computer Graphics

Computer Graphics: Status Report of the Graphic Standards Planning Committee
Association for Computing Machinery, 1979

(vol. 13, no. 3, August 1979; ACM order number 428791)

A special volume of SIGGRAPH-ACM proceedings proposing the revised (as of 1979) Core System as a draft graphics standard.

Included are a brief history of the Core System's development; detailed and lucid discussion of design changes in the Core System; sections on methodology and functional specifications, stressing Core's program portability, device independence, and functional capabilities; an overview of Core's five output primitives; discussion of retained and temporary segments; explanations of primitive, segment, static and dynamic attributes; outlines of 2-D and 3-D viewing operations and co-ordinate transformations; discussion of logical input devices as the central feature of Core's input facilities; rules for control of the picture-generation process and error handling; and interfaces for accessibility to the Core System in more than one programming language—though implementation of the Core System "will still be somewhat dependent on the programming language being used." A lengthy chapter on issues considered since 1977 concludes the volume. This is by far the best organized (and most clearly reproduced) presentation of the Core System. Subsequent versions and surveys (VDM, CGM) are reduced in value due to poor planning and print reproduction. Easy accessibility to 3-D is a useful feature, since the GKS standard is for 2-D graphics, but by the time the more recent Core surveys appeared, the system was already being envisioned as a metafile of GKS and draws extensively on GKS (see notes on VDM and CGM).

CONTENTS

PART I: SYNOPSIS OF THE CORE SYSTEM CHANGES SINCE GSPC 77

1: Introduction

2: Output Primitives

3: Picture Segmentation and Naming

4: Attributes

5: Viewing Operations and Coordinate Transformations

6: Input Primitives

7: Control
    7.1. Initalization and termination
    7.2. View surface initialization and selection
    7.3. Picture change control (formerly batching of updates)
    7.4. Frame control7.5. Error handling

8: Special Interfaces

PART II: GENERAL METHODOLOGY AND THE PROPOSED CORE SYSTEM (REVISED)

Chapter 1: Methodology
    1. Introduction
    2. Philosophy

Chapter 2: Functional Specification for a Core System Graphic System
    1. Introduction
    2. Output primitives
    3. Picture segmentation and naming
    4. Attributes
    5. Viewing operations and coordinate transformations
    6. Input primitives
    7. Control
    8. Special interfaces between the Core System and the application program
    9. Philosophy of interfacing the Core System with its environment

Chapter 3: Issues Considered Since GSPC 77
    1. Introduction
    2. Output primitives
    3. Picture segmentation and naming
    4. Attributes
    5. Viewing operations and coordinate transformations
    6. Input primitives
    7. Control
    8. Special interfaces between the Core System and the applications program

Appendix A. Functions available by level

Appendix B. Error severity

References

PART III: RASTER EXTENSIONS TO THE CORE SYSTEM

Part 1: Raster Extensions
    1. Introduction
    2. Raster device models
    3. Raster extensions

Part 2: Reference Manual
   2. Output primitives
   4. Attributes
   7. Control

Part 3: Raster Issues
   2. Output primitives
   4. Attributes
   7. Control

Appendix A. Introduction to raster graphics

Appendix B. Color model conversion algorithms

References

PART IV: THE GSPC METAFILE PROPOSAL

Introduction

The GSPC Metafile in a Graphics System

Metafile Format

Pictures

Coordinate Precision

Description of Metafile Commands
   Positioning commands
   Non-positioning commands

Summary of Metafile Commands

Metafile Defaults

Issues

References

PART V: DISTRIBUTED GRAPHICS SYSTEMS (DRAFT REPORT)

1: Introduction

2: Categories of Intelligent Terminals
   2.1. Locally controlled terminals
   2.2. Software-controlled terminals
   2.3. Programmed terminals

3: Issues of Distributed Processing and Intelligent Terminals

References

274 pp. 5 parts. Figures, charts, algorithms, references. (ISSN 0097-8930)

102
International Organization
for Standardization (ISO)

technical report

Graphical Kernel Systems (GKS) Functional Description
1984

(report number ISO/DIS-7942; International Organization for
Standardization; October 1984)

This International Standard manual specifies a set of functions for the
Graphics Kernel System (GKS), "a basic graphics system for
applications that produce computer generated two-dimensional pictures
on line graphics or raster graphics output devices."

Well-organized and very detailed, this manual provides a useful list of
GKS definitions at the outset, and then describes: the standard; its
concepts; output primitives and attributes; workstations;
transformations; segments; graphical input; metafiles; and GKS levels,
functions, and data structures. Supplemental information on GKS
functions, an error list, a description of allowable differences in GKS
implementations, and sample programs can be found at the end of the
work. Though not as succinct as the GKS Primer, this manual provides
a considerably more detailed survey of GKS functions, applications, and
advantages. The amount of detail does not seriously vitiate the work's
clarity and should increase the manual's usefulness. As a lengthy GKS
manual this is markedly superior in format and information
accessibility to the ANSI Draft Proposal. One critical weakness of the
ISO manual is the print reproduction, which is distracting and of
uneven quality. The reproductions of figures is, in general, of slightly
higher quality.

CONTENTS

0: INTRODUCTION

1: SCOPE

2: REFERENCES

3: DEFINITIONS

4: THE GRAPHICAL KERNEL SYSTEM

4.1: The Standard
    4.1.1. Specification
    4.1.2. Registration

4.2: Introduction

4.3: Concepts

4.4: Graphical Output
    4.4.1. Output primitives
    4.4.2. Output primitive attributes
    4.4.3. Polyline attributes
    4.4.4. Polymarker attributes
    4.4.5. Text attributes
    4.4.6. Fill area attributes
    4.4.7. Cell array attributes
    4.4.8. Generalized drawing primitive attributes
    4.4.9. Colour

4.5: Workstations
    4.5.1. Workstation characteristics
    4.5.2. Selecting a workstation
    4.5.3. Deferring picture changes
    4.5.4. Clearing the display surface
    4.5.5. Elimination of primitives outside segments
    4.5.6. Sending messages to a workstation

4.6: Coordinate systems and transformations
    4.6.1. Normalization transformations
    4.6.2. Clipping
    4.6.3. Workstation transformations
    4.6.4. Transformation of locator input
    4.6.5. Transformation of stroke input

4.7: Segments
    4.7.1. Introduction to segments
    4.7.2. Segment attributes
    4.7.3. Segment transformations
    4.7.4. Clipping and WDSS
    4.7.5. Workstation Independent Segment Storage
    4.7.6. WISS functions and clipping

4.8: Graphical Input
    4.8.1. Introduction to logical input devices
    4.8.2. Logical input device model
    4.8.3. Operating modes of logical input devices
    4.8.4. Measures of each input class
    4.8.5. Input queue and current event report
    4.8.6. Initialisation of input devices

4.9: GKS Metafile Interface

4.10: GKS Levels
    4.10.1. Introduction
    4.10.2. The level structure
    4.10.3. Level functionality

4.11: States of GKS and Inquiry Functions
    4.11.1. Description of states
    4.11.2. Inquiry functions

4.12: Error Handling

4.13: Special Interfaces between GKS and the Application Program

5: GKS FUNCTIONS

5.1: Notational Conventions

5.2: Control Functions

5.3: Output Functions

5.4: Output Attributes
    5.4.1. Workstation independent primitive attributes
    5.4.2. Workstation attributes (representations)

5.5: Transformation Functions
    5.5.1. Normalization transformation
    5.5.2. Workstation transformation

5.6: Segment Functions
    5.6.1. Segment manipulation functions
    5.6.2. Segment attributes

5.7: Input Functions
    5.7.1. Initialisation of input devices
    5.7.2. Setting the mode of input devices
    5.7.3. Request input functions
    5.7.4. Sample input functions
    5.7.5. Event input functions

5.8: Metafile Functions

5.9: Inquiry Functions
    5.9.1. Introduction
    5.9.2. Inquiry function for operating state value
    5.9.3. Inquiry functions for GKS description table
    5.9.4. Inquiry functions for GKS state list
    5.9.5. Inquiry functions for workstation state list
    5.9.6. Inquiry functions for workstation description table
    5.9.7. Inquiry functions for segment state list
    5.9.8. Pixel inquiries
    5.9.9. Inquiry function for GKS error state list

5.10: Utility Functions

5.11: Error Handling

6: GKS DATA STRUCTURES

6.1: Notation and Data Types

6.2: Operating State

6.3: GKS Description Table

6.4: GKS State List

6.5: Workstation State List

6.6: Workstation Description Table

6.7: Segment State List

6.8: GKS Error State List

A: FUNCTION LISTS

A.1: Alphabetic

A.2: Order of Appearance

A.3: Ordered by Level
    A.3.1. Level 0a
    A.3.2. Level 0b
    A.3.3. Level 0c
    A.3.4. Level 1a
    A.3.5. Level 1b
    A.3.6. Level 1c
    A.3.7. Level 2a

A.4: Ordered by State
    A.4.1. Functions allowed in state GHSL
    A.4.2. Functions allowed in state GKOP
    A.4.3. Functions not allowed in state WSOP
    A.4.4. Functions not allowed in state WSAC
    A.4.5. Functions not allowed in state SGOP

A.5: Applicability to Workstation Groups

B: ERROR LIST

B.1: Implementation Dependent

B.2: States

B.3: Workstations

B.4: Transformations

B.5: Output Attributes

B.6: Output Primitives

B.7: Segments

B.8: Input

B.9: Metafiles

B.10: Escape

B.11: Miscellaneous

B.12: System

B.13: Reserved Errors

C: INTERFACES

C.1: Introduction

C.2: Language Binding

C.3: Implementation

D: ALLOWABLE DIFFERENCES IN GKS IMPLEMENTATIONS

D.1: Introduction

D.2: Global Differences

D.3: Workstation Dependent Differences

E: METAFILE STRUCTURE

E.1: Metafiles
    E.1.1. Introduction
    E.1.2. ISO 8632
    E.1.3. Metafile designed for GKS

E.2: File Format and Data Format

E.3: Generation of Metafiles

E.4: Interpretation of Metafiles
    E.4.1. Introduction
    E.4.2. Control items
    E.4.3. Output primitives
    E.4.4. Output primitive attributes
    E.4.5. Workstation attributes
    E.4.6. Transformations
    E.4.7. Segment manipulation
    E.4.8. Segment attributes

E.5: Control Items
E.6: Items for Output Primitives
E.7: Items for Output Primitive Attributes
E.8: Items for Workstation Attributes
E.9: Items for Transformations
E.10: Items for Segment Manipulation
E.11: Items for Segment Attributes
E.12: User Items
F: SAMPLE PROGRAMS
G: GKS FUNCTIONS SUMMARY
G.1: Control Functions
G.2: Output Functions
G.3: Output Attributes
    G.3.1. Workstation independent primitive attributes
    G.3.2. Workstation attributes (representations)
G.4: Transformation Functions
    G.4.1. Normalization transformation
    G.4.2. Workstation transformation
G.5: Segment Functions
    G.5.1. Segment manipulation functions
    G.5.2. Segment attributes
G.6: Input Functions
    G.6.1. Initialisation of input devices
    G.6.2. Setting the mode of input devices
    G.6.3. Request input functions
    G.6.4. Sample input functions
    G.6.5. Event input functions
G.7: Metafile Functions
G.8: Inquiry Functions
G.9: Utility Functions
G.10: Error Handling
TABLES
FIGURES

282 pp. 6 sections. Figures, charts, tables, references.

103
Guedj, Richard A.
Tucker, Hugh A.
(eds.)
proceedings

Methodology in Computer Graphics: Seillac I
North-Holland, 1979

(based on the IFIP workshop of the same name organized by IFIP Working Group 5.2, CAD; Seillac, France; 23-26 May 1976)

Papers and discussions intended to provide direction in the creation of a methodology of computer graphics, with the long-range goal of developing standards in the field. Presented papers were invited to provide background. Much of the work of the conference took place during discussions; notes of these discussions are included here, along with working documents of the sub-groups.

CONTENTS
    Preface

Chapter I: Invited and Submitted Papers Plus Notes of Discussions
Introduction
A. Some methodological remarks for the workshop
R.A. Guedj
B. Is a graphics standard possible?
F.R.A. Hopgood
C. What might be computer graphics?
J.P. Crestin, M. Lucas
D. Computer graphics - a projection for the future
E.A. Warman, E. Hermans, K. Bø
E. Software interfaces for graphics
M. Sabin
F. Recommendations on methodology in computer graphics
J. Encarnação, G. Nees
G. Considerations for methodology
R.M. Dunn
H. Standardization through a metalanguage
P.R. Bono
I. Realistic objectives leading to a graphics standard
M.E. Newell
J. Picture naming and modification: an overview
J.D. Foley
K. Output primitives
J.D. Foley
L. Guidelines for the IFIP workshop on graphics methodology
T.L. Sancha
M. Design criteria
T.L. Sancha
N. Preliminary proposals for graphics functions
T.L. Sancha

Chapter II: Working Documents of the Sub-Groups
Introduction
A. The core approach
B. On a methodology for deriving program structures
C. A standardized approach to the design of graphics systems
D. Miscellaneous topics
E. The conceptual framework and related issues. (Editors notes on last session)

Chapter III:
Report of the workshop to IFIP W.G. 5.2
Guidelines and recommendations

Appendix 1: Information about Continuing Activities

206 pp. 21 papers in 3 parts. Drawings, figures, charts, graphs, tables, references, appendix. ISBN 0-444-85301-4.

104
Guedj, Richard A.
ten Hagen, Paul J.W.
Hopgood, F. Robert A.
Tucker, Hugh A.
Duce, David A.
(eds.)

proceedings

Methodology of Interaction: Seillac II
North-Holland, 1980

(based on the IFIP workshop of the same name organized by IFIP Working Group 5.2, CAD; Seillac, France; May 1979)

Position papers, invited presentations, group reports, and edited discussions from a workshop which considered computer graphics. Emphasizes the need to understand the problems associated with input and its relationship to the output of graphics, and is especially concerned with interaction, both graphic and non-graphic.

CONTENTS
Preface
PART I: INVITED PRESENTATIONS
1: Introduction
    1.1. Goals of the workshop
        R.A. Guedj
2: Control Structures
    2.1. SMALLTALK
        A. Kay
    2.2. Interactive control
        R.F. Sproull
    2.3. Discussion
3: Syntactic Structures
    3.1. Interaction and syntax
        P.J.W. ten Hagen
    3.2. Discussion
4: Cognitive Psychology
    4.1. Introduction
        T. Moran
    4.2. Cognitive psychology and interaction
        J. Hayes
    4.3. Systems design
        T. Moran
    4.4. Discussion
5: Visual Communication
    5.1. Visual communication and interaction
        N. Negroponte
    5.2. Discussion
PART II: WORKING GROUPS
6: Presentations
    6.1. Introduction
    6.2. Control structure model for interaction
        R.M. Dunn
    6.3. Discussion
    6.4. Methodology of interaction
        J. Foley

6.5. Discussion

6.6. Proposal for working groups
W. Newman

6.7. Discussion

6.8. Programming environment
M.E. Newell

6.9. Discussion

7: Working Groups

7.1. Introduction

7.2. Working groups

7.3. Discussion

PART III: GROUP REPORTS

8: Group Reports

8.1. Definition of interaction

8.2. Discussion

8.3. Models of interaction

8.4. Discussion

8.5. Methodology for designing interactive programs

8.6. Discussion

8.7. Specification of dialogues and interactive programs

8.8. Discussion

8.9. Program environment

8.10. Discussion

8.11. Portability and device independence

8.12. Discussion

8.13. Questions raised at Seillac II

8.14. Musings and restatements of motherhood

8.15. The future

8.16. Discussion

9: Summary

9.1. Postscript

9.2. An open list of statements

PART IV: POSITION PAPERS

10: Position Papers

10.1. The semantics of graphical input
E. Anson

10.2. Towards an effective characterization of graphical interaction
R. Baecker

10.3. Problems of the 80's in man/machine communication
K. Bø

10.4. High-level graphics input tools and their semantics
J. van den Bos

10.5. Towards semantics for graphical interactions
J.P. Crestin, C. Queinnec

10.6. A philosophical prelude to methodology of interaction
R.M. Dunn

10.7. A paradigm for task-oriented man-computer interaction
W. Dzida, S. Herda, W.D. Itzfeldt

10.8. Specification of graphics systems
R. Eckert

10.9. The input and manipulation of complex, structured graphical objects
 J. Encarnação

10.10. Interactive requirements of knowledge based consultant programs
 C. Engelman

10.11. The structure of interactive command languages
 J.D. Foley

10.12. Remarks on some aspects of man-machine interaction
 R.A. Guedj

10.13. A conceptual basis for graphical input and interaction
 P.J.W. ten Hagen

10.14. A production system approach to interactive program design
 F.R.A. Hopgood, D.A. Duce

10.15. A framework for the integration of graphics and pattern recognition
 P. Klint, M. Sint

10.16. On computer problem-solving interaction
 G. Krammer

10.17. A framework for studying human-computer interaction
 T.P. Moran

10.18. Graphic input specification in a general purpose interactive graphics system
 S.P. Mudur

10.19. The metaphysics of television
 N. Negroponte

10.20. Towards a design methodology for interactive systems
 M.E. Newell

10.21. Some notes on user interface design
 W. Newman

10.22. Sites, modes and trails: telling the user of an interactive system
 J. Nievergelt, J. Weydert

10.23. Towards intelligent interactive systems
 S. Ohsuga

10.24. Models of interactive graphics software
 D.S.H. Rosenthal

10.25. The design of graphically interactive systems
 T.L. Sancha

10.26. On the specification of graphics command languages and their processors
 A.C. Shaw

10.27. Man-machine communication in process control
 C. Tozzi

PART V: BIBLIOGRAPHY

11: Bibliography

408 pp. 10 chapters in 5 parts. Drawings, figures, charts, tables, algorithms, models, bibliography, references. ISBN 0-444-85479-7.

105
Hopgood, F. Robert A.
Duce, David A.
Gallop, Julian R.
Sutcliffe, Dale C.

Introduction to the Graphical Kernel System (GKS)
Academic Press, 1983

(vol. 19 in the *A.P.I.C. Studies in Data Processing* series, Fraser
Duncan, general ed.)

An informal manual and introduction to the Graphical Kernel System
(GKS) accepted as a draft international standard (DIS) by the
International Organization for Standardization (ISO). GKS is a graphic
system that produces and manipulates many kinds of pictures and that
can be implemented across numerous graphic devices and programming
languages.

The authors of this book are the editors of the GKS document, and
have written the book to give examples and to present a more
descriptive introduction to GKS than the document provides. The book
has two parts. The first section describes the development of GKS and
introduces the essential concepts of the system. Output primitives are
described together with their attributes and the coordinate systems in
which they are specified. Segments and segment attributes that permit
the saving, re-use, and modification of pictures and sub-pictures are
explained. Graphical input facilities are described. A discussion of the
workstation concept that allows for specification of different graphic
devices and promotes program portability completes the first section.
Part two describes special features of GKS that are likely to be required
by graphics programming specialists. Each chapter in this part stands
independent of the others. The topics covered include initialization of
GKS, data structures, level structures, error handling, control of input
devices, advanced segmentation facilities, GKS metafile, and additional
output primitives and attributes. All examples in the book are given in
FORTRAN 77. An appendix specifies a language binding of
FORTRAN 77 to GKS. The ISO GKS described in this book is very
similar to the American National Standards GKS presently under
review for adoption as the draft standard. The few differences are as
follows. An additional output level (labeled m) defined in ANS GKS
has four output levels and three input levels for a total of twelve levels
of complexity of implementation. ANS GKS specifies official bindings
of programming languages to GKS while ISO GKS is independent of
programming language. Another difference appears where ANS GKS
specifies INDIVIDUAL (global attributes) as the default for the
ASPECT SOURCE FLAG statement that specifies class of GKS
primitive attributes, and ISO GKS does not specify whether the default
is INDIVIDUAL or BUNDLED, but permits each implementation to
specify the default. A final difference is that ANS GKS specifies a GKS
function for inputting data (INPUT DATA RECORD). In ISO GKS
formats and contents of input data are specified by a programming
language routine. Although information on conformity to ISO GKS
standards is not included in *Introduction to the Graphical Kernel System
GKS*, the ANS GKS and ISO GKS actual documents differ in the
restrictiveness of their conformance statements such that ANS GKS has

a less restrictive statement. Written for applications programmers, this work assumes no knowledge of GKS, but does assume that readers have a good understanding of programming and some understanding of computer graphics. The book is well-written, well-organized, and should prove a useful tool for programmers.

CONTENTS

Preface

Notation

PART I

1: Introduction
    1.1. The changing scene
    1.2. Seillac I
    1.3. Developments
    1.4. The ISO graphics working group
    1.5. The GKS review
    1.6. The future
    1.7. References

2: Graphical Output
    2.1. Introduction
    2.2. Polyline
    2.3. Polyline representation
    2.4. Polymarker
    2.5. Fill area
    2.6. The duck
    2.7. Text
    2.8. Primitives and attributes

3: Coordinate Systems
    3.1. Introduction
    3.2. User and world coordinates
    3.3. Normalized device coordinates
    3.4. Window to viewport transformation
    3.5. Multiple normalization transformations
    3.6. Graphical annotation
    3.7. Clipping
    3.8. Normalization transformation 0

4: Segments and Their Attributes
    4.1. Introduction
    4.2. Creating and deleting segments
    4.3. Segment attributes
    4.4. Renaming segments

5: Graphical Input Devices
    5.1. Introduction
    5.2. REQUEST mode
    5.3. LOCATOR
    5.4. PICK
    5.5. CHOICE
    5.6. VALUATOR
    5.7. STRING
    5.8. STROKE

6: Styles of Interaction
   6.1. Interaction modes
   6.2. Mode setting
   6.3. REQUEST mode
   6.4. Status
   6.5. SAMPLE mode
   6.6. EVENT mode
   6.7. Mixed modes

7: Workstations
   7.1. Introduction
   7.2. Workstations
   7.3. Workstation selection
   7.4. Workstation transformations
   7.5. Polyline representation
   7.6. Colour table
   7.7. Polymarker representation
   7.8. Fill area representation
   7.9. Text representation
   7.10. Segment storage on workstation
   7.11. Deferring picture changes
   7.12. Input devices

PART II

8: GKS Environment
   8.1. Initialisation
   8.2. Operating states
   8.3. GKS state lists
   8.4. Inquiry functions
   8.5. Error handling
   8.6. Levels

9: Control of Input Devices
   9.1. Introduction
   9.2. An interaction in GKS
   9.3. Initialising an input device
   9.4. Further control of the input queue

10: Segment Storage
   10.1. Introduction
   10.2. Workstation independent segment storage
   10.3. WISS functions

11: Metafiles
   11.1. Introduction
   11.2. Metafile output
   11.3. Metafile input

12: Further Output
   12.1. Introduction
   12.2. Cell array
   12.3. Drawing
   12.4. ESCAPE

13: Individual Attributes
   13.1. Introduction
   13.2. Unbundled attributes
   13.3. Switching modes

Appendices
  A. Abbreviations
  B. Language binding

Index

200 pp. 13 chapters in 2 parts. Drawings, figures, tables, general index, appendices. ISBN 0-12-355570-1.

106
McKay, Lucia

GKS Primer
Nova Graphics International, 1984

This work presents an introduction to the Graphical Kernel System (GKS), a graphics programming tool which is rapidly becoming the international standard for computer graphics.

Addressed to "anyone interested in the possibilities and power of graphics, whether for business, scientific, artistic, or educational purposes," this primer explains on a basic level what the GKS ("a proposed international standard for two-dimensional Computer Graphics") does and how it functions. Ten brief chapters provide an overview of GKS, emphasizing its important advantages of software portability and simplified program development. Topics discussed include: the relationships among various standards; the four main GKS primitives; picture-programming; attribute specification; text generation; coordinate systems for graph production; segment creation, transformation and deletion; and the compatibility of GKS with a variety of workstation devices. A list of GKS sub-routines and a detailed glossary are also included. A well-organized, lucid presentation.

CONTENTS

CHAPTER ONE: EAGLE'S EYE VIEW OF THE GRAPHICAL KERNEL SYSTEM

Graphics Hardware
  Output
  Input

Graphics Software—GKS
  Virtual devices
  The workstation concept
  The importance of a standard

CHAPTER TWO: OVERVIEW OF GRAPHICS STANDARDS
Graphics Standards
Relationships Between Standards
CHAPTER THREE: THE GKS PRIMITIVES
Definitions
Polyline Attributes
Polymarker Attributes
Fill Area Attributes
CHAPTER FOUR: PROGRAMMING A PICTURE
Specifying the Data
Polyline Linetypes
Fill Area
CHAPTER FIVE: Specifying Attributes
Unbundled Attributes
Bundled Attributes
Bundle Table
Linewidth Scale Factor
Specifying Colour
Setting Attributes Individually
Steps for Bundled Attributes
CHAPTER SIX: PRODUCING TEXT
Geometric and Non-Geometric Attributes
Character Spacing and Expansion
Text Font and Precision
CHAPTER SEVEN: TRANSFORMING GRAPHS
Coordinates
Windows and Viewports
Coordinate Systems
Aspect Ratio
The Unit Square
Multiple Normalization Transformations
Panning and Zooming
Examples of Panning and Zooming
Clipping
CHAPTER EIGHT: SEGMENTS
Creating a Segment
Segment Transformations
Clipping and Segment Transformations
Segment Attributes
Visibility
Highlighting
Priority
CHAPTER NINE: WORKSTATIONS
Logical Input Devices
Metafiles

Generalized Drawing Primitives
ESCAPE
Levels
Workstation Segment Storage
CHAPTER TEN: SUBROUTINES
Control Functions
Output Functions
Output Attributes
    Workstation independent primitive attributes
    Workstation attributes (representations)
Transformation Functions
    Normalization transformation
    Workstation transformation
Segment Functions
Input Functions
Metafile Functions
Inquiry Functions—General
Inquiry Functions for GKS Description Table
Inquiry Functions for GKS State List
Inquiry Functions for Workstation State List
Inquiry Functions for Workstation Description Table
Other Inquiry Functions
    Inquiry functions for segment state list
    Pixel inquiries
    Inquiry function for GKS error state list
Utility Functions
Error Handling
CHAPTER ELEVEN: FURTHER READING
CHAPTER TWELVE: GLOSSARY

106 pp. 12 chapters. Drawings, figures, glossary.

107
Van Deusen, Edmund
(ed.)

reference

Graphics Standards Handbook
CC Exchange, 1985

Seven proposed graphics standards systems are currently in wide use. This work presents in a convenient, compact form the actual standards for virtually all of them.

This handbook, presented in familiar user documentation style, brings together the seven graphics standards systems currently vying for acceptance. Its purpose is to clarify the capabilities of each in order to both assist in the selection of products and increase understanding of the various systems in order to facilitate the development of a true "standard." The systems included are: the CORE system and the GKS (Graphics Kernel System), both of which have been competing for acceptance as the primary graphics-application interface standard; PHIGS (Programmer's Hierarchical Interactive Graphics Standard), which is also a graphics-application interface standard; IGES (Initial Graphics Exchange Specification) and CGM (Computer Graphics Metafile, formerly called Virtual Device Metafile), both graphics storage and transmittal standards; CGI (Computer Graphics Interface, previously called Virtual Device Interface), a universal graphics-device software interface standard; and NAPLIPS, the only currently adopted ANSI standard for graphics-device software interfaces. This is a useful, well-organized tool which will be useful not only as a reference for display designers and engineers but also as an overview of the current standards in this volatile area.

CONTENTS

Section 1: Overview

Section 2: Core

    Core introduction

    Core overhead functions

    Core transformation/viewing functions

    Core primitive functions

    Core attribute functions

    Core input functions

    Core inquiry functions

    Core error list

Section 3: GKS

    GKS introduction

    GKS overhead functions

    GKS transformation/viewing functions

    GKS primitive functions

    GKS attribute functions

    GKS input functions

    GKS inquiry functions

    GKS description tables

    GKS state lists

    GKS error list

    GKS-3D extensions

    GKS-3D transformation/viewing functions

    GKS-3D primitive functions

    GKS-3D attribute functions

    GKS-3D input functions

    GKS-3D inquiry functions

    GKS-3D tables and lists

Section 4: PHIGS

    PHIGS introduction

    PHIGS overhead elements

    PHIGS transformation/viewing functions

    PHIGS primitive elements

    PHIGS attribute elements

    PHIGS input elements

    PHIGS inquiry elements

    PHIGS description tables

    PHIGS state lists

    PHIGS error lists

Section 5: IGES
  IGES introduction
  IGES geometry entities
  IGES annotation entities
  IGES structure and definition entities

Section 6: CGM
  CGM introduction
  CGM overhead elements
  CGM primitive elements
  CGM attribute elements

Section 7: CGI
  CGI introduction
  CGI overhead elements
  CGI transformation/viewing elements
  CGI primitive elements
  CGI attribute elements
  CGI input elements
  CGI inquiry elements
  CGI description tables, state lists, reports

Section 8: NAPLIPS
  NAPLIPS introduction
  NAPLIPS C sets
  NAPLIPS G sets
  PDI overhead opcodes
  PDI primitive opcodes
  PDI attribute opcodes

Section 9: Glossary

438 pp. 9 sections. Figures, glossary. ISBN 0-939078-01-5.

108
Greenberg, Donald
Marcus, Aaron
Schmidt, Allan H.
Gorter, Vernon

The Computer Image: Applications of Computer Graphics
Addison-Wesley, 1982

(from the *Addison-Wesley Microbooks Popular Series*, Thomas A. Bell, sponsoring ed.)

Contents cover existing computer graphics technology, demonstrating the diversity, complexity, and potential of the subject. Explanations are clear and applications practical.

This collection by four computer graphics specialists is useful for a wide audience—the consumer, educators, businessmen, and designers, as well as those in high technology areas. It is assumed that the reader has little or no previous knowledge of the subject. Color plates present scenes from computer animated cartoons, computer art, synthetic landscapes, models of molecules, computer-aided design, remote sensing, and astronomy. Practical suggestions are given on the use of color as a tool for computer graphics communication. The subject of computer-aided business graphics is discussed, demonstrating current applications and describing hardware, software, and databases. Ways of getting started are suggested, and future uses in business, government, education, and the home are predicted. A section on Polaroid instant photography explains basic principles of the computer graphing camera and its operation, and shows how it produces a high quality image.

CONTENTS

An overview of computer graphics
Donald Greenberg
Images from the computer: a selection
Computer art
Scenes from computer animated films
Synthetic landscapes
Models of molecules
Computer-aided design
Remote sensing
Astronomy
Color: a tool for computer graphics communication
Aaron Marcus
Computer-aided business graphics
Allan H. Schmidt
Polaroid instant photography in the computer graphics camera
Vernon Gorter
Glossary
Bibliography
Index

128 pp. 5 chapters. Drawings, figures, graphs, general index, bibliography, glossary, color graphics. ISBN 0-201-06192-9.

109
Gregory, Richard L.

The Intelligent Eye
McGraw-Hill, 1970

In this classic work R.L. Gregory, one of Britain's most renowned psychologists, offers a highly readable synopsis of the psychology of visual perception.

This book originated as a series of six lectures which Gregory, a professor of bionics at the University of Edinburgh, gave for the Royal Institution in 1967-68. The lectures, which were televised by the BBC, covered a wide field in cognitive and perceptual psychology. Although many of the demonstrations around which the lectures were structured cannot be reproduced in book form, the author strives to involve his audience by including 3-D glasses and two disks that can be rotated on a record-player turntable to produce different visual effects. The nine chapters each deal with a different visual aspect of visual perception. The subject matter includes discussions of the following: Rubin's work with figure/ground; Ames' work with distorted perspective; M.C.

Escher's paradoxical (impossible) engravings; figure distortion and after-images; Müller-Lyer's optical illusion figures; man's perception of the universe; two- and three-dimensional drawing; pictographs; hieroglyphics and interconnections between pictures, symbols, thought and language; and a look at how we perceive the functional significance of complex systems like computers. Gregory's conclusion is that as technology advances, man must learn to adapt to the world he has created without cutting himself off from his biological past, and that he must avoid the danger of creating a world he cannot see. There are two appendices, seven pages of notes, an excellent bibliography, and a general index. This book is highly recommended.

CONTENTS

Foreword
Directions for viewing the 3-D pictures and performing the experiments in this book
1. Objects and pictures
2. The peculiarities of pictures
3. Ambiguous, paradoxical and uncertain figures
4. Distorting figures
5. Scaling the universe
6. Drawing in two-dimensional space
7. Drawing in three-dimensional space
8. Pictures, symbols, thought and language
9. Seeing how things work
Appendix A: Stereoscopic projection and drawing in 3-D
Appendix B: An instrument for improving disturbed images
Notes
Bibliography
Index

188 pp. 9 chapters. Drawings, photographs, figures, graphs, models, general index, bibliography, appendices. ISBN 0-07-024664-5.

110
Gregory, Richard L.

Concepts and Mechanisms of Perception
Duckworth, 1974

Drawn predominantly from a variety of scientific and technical journals, this collection of papers by R.L. Gregory represents his research and his comments on research in perceptual psychology between 1950 and 1973.

Selected by Gregory himself as those "that still seem to me to be of interest," these papers are grouped in three categories—experimental studies of perceptual systems, the design of specialized experimental equipment, and philosophical essays on problems of understanding perception and brain function. Each paper is introduced by a section written specifically for this volume in which background information on the project and additional data and discussion, where appropriate, are provided. The inclusion of papers on equipment design may seem inappropriate in a work on perception, but Gregory argues that knowing how much and what sort of aid is provided by tools and instruments permits inference about otherwise hidden processes. He writes with skill and humor, discussing complex arguments and phenomena in an easily followed manner. Seen from the perspective of the 1980s, the papers on perceptual systems and equipment design may appear dated and unsophisticated, but they are models of good writing and careful thought. For example, the paper "Social Implications of Intelligent Machines," although fifteen years old, is particularly interesting in light of the attention currently devoted to artificial intelligence research. The real virtue of this collection lies in the Pretext and the philosophical papers. Although writing specifically about perceptual psychology, Gregory's implicit focus is on the equally difficult problems of knowledge and understanding and on the promise and limitations of science in the twentieth century. Would serve well as background and model for researchers and practitioners in psychology in general and perceptual areas in particular.

CONTENTS
Preface
Pretext

Part One: Experiments
1. Sensory processes
2. Human perception
3. Recovery from early blindness: a case study
4. Blinking during visual tracking
5. Variations in blink rate during non-visual tasks
6. Colour anomaly, the Rayleigh equation and selective adaptation
7. A statistical information theory of visual thresholds
8. Increase in 'neurological noise' as a factor in sensory impairment associated with ageing
9. A theory of nerve deafness
10. A note on summation time of the eye indicated by signal/noise discrimination
11. Is the Weber fraction a function of physical or perceived input?
12. Arm weight, adaptation and weight discrimination
13. Weight, illusions and weight discrimination - a revised hypothesis
14. Eye-movements and the stability of the visual world
15. A blue filter technique for detecting eye-movements during the autokinetic effect
16. The origin of the autokinetic effect
17. The after-effect of seen motion: the role of retinal stimulation and of eye-movements
18. Influence of stroboscopic illumination on the after-effect of seen movement
19. The effect of touch on a visually ambiguous three-dimensional figure
20. An auditory analogue of the visual reversible figure
21. Stereoscopic shadow-images
22. Changes in the size and shape of visual after-images observed in complete darkness during changes of position in space

23. Measuring visual constancy for stationary or moving objects
24. Visual constancy during movement: effects of S's forward and backward movement on size constancy
25. Visual constancy during movement: size constancy, using one or both eyes or proprioceptive information
26. Visual perception in simulated space conditions
27. Seeing in depth
28. Distortion of visual space as inappropriate constancy scaling
29. Comments on the inappropriate constancy scaling theory of distortion illusions and its implications
30. Perceptual illusions and brain models
31. Illusion and depth measurements in right-angular and parallel line figures
32. The curious eye of *Copilia*

Part Two: Instruments
33. A multi-channel printing chronograph
34. A printing chronograph for recording data
35. Master patent specification for printing chronograph
36. Patent specification for 'Little Brother'
37. A device for giving a histogram of time-intervals
38. An optical micro-stimulator for the human retina
39. A single-flash rotary disk optical shutter
40. The solid image microscope
41. The solid image microscope: a more technical description
42. Patent specification for a heterochròmatic photometer
43. Patent specification for apparatus for visual researches
44. Patent specification for 3-D drawing machine
45. A technique for minimizing the effects of atmospheric disturbance on photographic telescopes

Part Three: Philosophy
46. A speculative account of brain function in terms of probability and induction
47. On physical model explanations in psychology
48. The two psychologies
49. The brain as an engineering problem
50. Models and localization of function in the central nervous system
51. Köhler's perception
52. On how so little information controls so much behaviour
53. The evolution of eyes and brains—a hen-and-egg problem
54. The speaking eye
55. The grammar of vision
56. Social implications of intelligent machines
Bibliography
Name index
General index

669 pp. 56 papers in 3 parts. Drawings, photographs, figures, graphs, tables, mathematical formulae, general index, bibliography, name index. ISBN 0-7156-0556-9.

Guedj, Richard   *SEE UNDER ID 103, 104*

111
Gutmann, James C.
Rogers, Steven P.

technical report

Displaying Colors of Specified Chrominance on a Color Graphics Display
1982

(report number DVAA-TR-81-0089-4; Anacapa Sciences, Inc.; sponsored by U.S. Army Communications-Electronics Command; monitored by U.S. Army Avionics R&D Activity; December 1982)

Describes a simple technique for displaying colors of specified chrominance on cathode ray tubes (CRTs).

The research reported here is part of an ongoing research and development program in avionics in which computer generated topographic display (CGTD) systems that use color displays are being developed for use by U.S. Army aviators. The present research represents a first step in developing procedures for displaying colors of known chrominance using standard color coordinates (CIEXYZ of the Commission de l'Eclairage). The technique developed here uses models of color CRT bits-to-luminance transfer functions and linear color mixing equations to find color graphic system bit values that will yield colors of specified chrominance. In order to develop this technique the researchers examined the general form of the relationship between bits and luminance and found the relationship to be monotonic, non-linear, and increasing. The General Linear Model of the Statistical Analysis System (SAS) was used to fit second order polynomials to the bit-to-luminance relationship. The most accurate predictions of luminance came from a two-part model or spliced fit approach. A major advantage of the technique developed here is its simplicity. Earlier researchers accomplished similar ends using spectroradiometric equipment, and the present technique requires only a photometer to measure luminance of display. The usefulness of this technique is not only limited to color CRTs, and can be used for other displays provided that the CIE color coordinates of the display system color mixing primaries do not vary as a function of luminance output. One appendix to the report describes in detail the measurement procedures used with the photometer (a PR-1600 model). This is a complex and technical report for readers who already have a thorough background in the mathematical and technical aspects of computer graphics display.

CONTENTS

Foreword

Introduction
    Displaying colors of known chrominance
    Overview of the report

Method
    Apparatus
    Procedure

Results
    Characterizing the luminance measurements
    Models of the bits-to-luminance relationship

Discussion
    Color mixing using a CRT
    Limitations and assumptions of the technique
    Summary
References
Appendix A
Appendix B

53 pp. 4 chapters. Graphs, tables, mathematical formulae, references, appendices.

112
Hardesty, George K.C.
Projector, Theodore H.

technical report

NAVSHIPS Display Illumination Design Guide, Section I: Introduction to Light and Color
1973

(sponsored by Naval Ship Research and Development Center; monitored by J. Todd McLane, NAVSHIPRANDCEN; February 1973)

A summarized treatment of material and concepts to be addressed in greater detail in subsequent sections of the *Guide*.

The overall *Guide* deals with some of the special optical systems developed for the internal illumination of indicating instruments and control panels and their color-coded signal devices. This volume presents working concepts and quantities rather than rigorous formal definitions. Some of the areas addressed in this work are: the nature of light and color, the control of light, light sources, and photometric concepts and units. Applications and implications are provided in appendix form. Military systems or equipment specification writers, contractors, project engineers, and inspectors would find this useful. Other sections of the *Guide* offer detailed, instrument-supported evaluation procedures.

CONTENTS
PREFACE
CHAPTER I: THE NATURE OF LIGHT AND COLOR
Radiant Energy and the Eye
The Physical Correlates of Color
The Eye and Color
The Specification of Chromaticity
Chromaticity Computation for Light Sources
Chromaticity Computation for Reflecting or Transmitting Materials
Light Sources, Color Temperature and Correlated Color Temperature
Fluorescence
Luminous Efficacy
Dark Adaptation
List of Figures

CHAPTER II: PHOTOMETRIC CONCEPTS AND UNITS

Flux and Intensity

Illuminance

Luminance (Photometric Brightness)
Point sources, extended sources, and the eye
Optics, illuminance, and luminance
The possibility of increasing luminance optically
Geometry and photometric quantities

Contrast

List of Figures

List of Tables

CHAPTER III: PHOTOMETRIC MEASUREMENTS

The Eye as a Photometer
The Bunsen photometer
The Lummer-Brodhun photometer
Flicker photometers

Photovoltaic Cells (Barrier-Layer Photocells)
"Zero resistance" circuits
Correction of spectral response
Photometric response of photocells
Electronic circuitry

Vacuum Phototubes and Photomultipliers

Photoconductors, Photodiodes, and Phototransistors

Illuminometers
The point source in illuminance measurements

Luminance Meters
Baffle-tube luminance sensors
The Macbeth "illuminometer"—a visual baffle-tube luminance
meter
Image-forming luminance meters
Visual image-forming luminance meters
Photoelectric image-forming luminance meters
Stray light in luminance meters

Total Flux Measurements

Polarized Light

Calibration
Standards of horizontal intensity
Color temperature standards
Luminance standards
Standards of flux
Color correction of standards

List of Figures

CHAPTER IV: THE CONTROL OF LIGHT

Regular Reflection and Transmission
Regular (specular) reflection
Regular transmission
Multiple reflection and transmission
Retroreflectors (reflex reflectors)

Diffuse Reflection and Transmission
    Nonspecular reflection
    Non-regular transmission
    Lambertian and perfect diffusers
    Quantitative concepts and measurements

Polarization
    Basic concepts
    Reflection and transmission
    Polarizing materials

The Control of Light
    Contrast
    Shielding
    Control of glare reflection by diffusion
    Anti-reflection interference coatings
    Reflection control with plane polarized light
    Control of contrast with filters
    Reflection control with circularly polarized light

List of Figures

CHAPTER V: LIGHT SOURCES

Introduction

Thermal Radiators
    Blackbody radiators
    Color temperature
    Emissivity
    Incandescent lamps
    Fluorescent lamps
    Electroluminescent lamps
    Glow lamps
    Light emitting diodes
    Radioactive light sources

Bibliography

List of Figures

ADDENDUM

Abstract

PART I: MAXIMUM LUMINOUS EFFICIENCY CONTOUR CHARTS FOR COLORED MATERIALS

Introduction

Supporting Theory

Uses of Maximum Luminous Efficiency Contours

List of Figures

Bibliography

Abstract

PART II: CHROMATICITY COMPUTATIONAL FORMS FOR SOURCES FROM 1600° TO 3200° K INCLUDING 2854° K (SOURCE A) AND SOURCES B, C, AND D_{6500} (16, 20, AND 40 ORDINATES)

Introduction
    General
    Limited coverage of colorimetry theory

Sources of Empirical Data Used for Computations of Chromaticity Coordinates
    Spectrophotometric analyses—transmittances
    Spectrophotometric analyses—reflectance
    Spectrophotometric analyses—of light emitting devices
    Derivation of numerical values used in forms
    Examples of use of computational forms

Comparison of Chromaticities Computed with 16, 20, and 40 Ordinate Forms

Some Comments on the Use of Chromaticity Specifications

List of Figures

List of Tables

Appendixes
    Appendix A—Computational forms for 16, 20, and 40 ordinate data for courses from 1600° to D_{6500}
    Appendix B—Bibliography and acknowledgments

Abstract

PART III: THE COMPUTATION AND USE OF CONE-TO-ROD RATIO SPECIFICATIONS

Introduction

Characteristics of the Eye

Spectral Luminous Efficiency

Cone-to-Rod Ration (CRR)

The Use of Computational Forms with Spectral Transmittance Data

Differences To Be Expected when the 1951 Scotopic Observer Is Applied

Correlation of Old and New Bases

Working with Spectroradiometric Data

Variation of CRR's with Color Temperature of Source

Discussion

List of Figures

List of Tables

Appendixes
    Appendix A: Forms
    Appendix B: Bibliography

Abstract

PART IV: THE APPLICATION OF A COLOR-CORRECTION FACTOR IN THE PHOTOMETRY OF COLORED SIGNAL AND INDICATOR DEVICES

Introduction
    Purpose and scope
    Experimental verification of procedures

Technical Coverage

General Procedure
    Quantities measured
    Conditions of test
    Test equipment for SED measurements

Part One: Chromaticity Determinations
    Test procedure
    Computations

Part Two: The Application of Color-Correction Factors in Photometry
    Background considerations
    Basic considerations of photometer response
    Enabling instrumentation
    Derivation of color correction factor, "C"
    Actual procedure
    Application of color-correction factor
    Abridged computations of correction factors
    Further examples of abridged computations

Discussion

List of Figure

List of Tables

Bibliography

Abstract

PART V: SPECTROPHOTOMETRIC CURVES AND RADIANT TRANSMITTANCES, LUMINOUS TRANSMITTANCES, AND CHROMATICITIES OF A SET OF REFERENCE FILTERS (AS COMPUTED FOR SOURCES OF PRACTICAL COLOR TEMPERATURES)

Introduction
    Basis for data presented in this part
    Tabular data—origin of
    Functional description of the filters
    Physical uses of reference filters
    Precautions in use of tabular data

List of Figures

Bibliography

Explanation for Material in This Part

PART VI: LABORATORY SETUPS OF PHOTOMETRIC AND SPECTRORADIOMETRIC EQUIPMENT

General Considerations
    Practical color temperatures

List of Figures
   Photographs
   Curves

400 pp. 5 chapters. Drawings, photographs, figures, charts, graphs, mathematical formulae, bibliography, addenda.

113
Harrington, Steven

Computer Graphics: A Programming Approach
McGraw-Hill, 1983

Presenting the basic concepts of interactive computer graphics in a clearly written, easily followed style, this book is an excellent introductory text.

Written as a hands-on guide, this text is a highly effective learning tool. Because it presents material at a lower level than previous graphics texts, the work is suitable for undergraduate use. Each chapter introduces a new topic related to interactive graphics and the level of complexity builds as the text progresses. The work begins with an elementary review of analytic geometry which may initially lead one to believe the book is dealing with material too basic to be worth reading. Yet, as computer graphics are dealt with more fully, the material becomes more difficult, but still remains comprehensible. Topics covered in the work include: line- and character-drawing; display device/system interfaces; the CORE system; raster graphics; translation, scaling, and rotation transformations; display file management; intelligent graphics terminals; windowing; clipping; interactive techniques; detailed two- and three-dimensional graphics; hidden lines and hidden surfaces; curve generation; and shading. This would be an ideal text for use in a graphics course for college sophomores or juniors, as well as a good introductory text for anyone wanting to understand how graphics work.

CONTENTS

Preface

Chapter 1: Geometry and Line Generation
   Introduction
   Points and lines
   Planes and coordinates
   Line segments
   Perpendicular lines
   Vectors
   Pixel and frame buffers
   Vector generation
   Character generation
   Displaying the frame buffer
   Bibliography
   Exercises
   Programming problems

Chapter 2: Graphics Primitives
   Introduction
   Display devices
   Primitive operations
   The display-file interpreter
   Normalized device coordinates
   Display-file structure
   Display-file algorithms
   Display control
   Text
   The line-style primitive
   An application
   Bibliography
   Exercises
   Programming problems
Chapter 3: Polygons
   Introduction
   Polygons
   Polygon representation
   Entering polygons
   An inside test
   Polygon interfacing algorithms
   Filling polygons
   An application
   Bibliography
   Exercises
   Programming problems
Chapter 4: Transformations
   Introduction
   Matrices
   Scaling transformations
   Sin and cos
   Sum of angles identities
   Rotation
   Homogeneous coordinates and translation
   Rotation about an arbitrary point
   Other transformations
   Transformation routines
   Display procedures
   An application
   Bibliography
   Exercises
   Programming problems
Chapter 5: Segments
   Introduction
   The segment table
   Segment creation
   Closing a segment
   Deleting a segment
   Renaming a segment
   Visibility
   Image transformation
   Revising previous transformation routines

Saving and showing segments
Other display file structures
Some raster techniques
An application
Bibliography
Exercises
Programming problems

Chapter 6: Windowing and Clipping
Introduction
The viewing transformation
Viewing transformation implementation
Clipping
The clipping of polygons
Adding clipping to the system
Avoiding division
Generalized clipping
Position relative to an arbitrary line
Multiple windowing
An application
Bibliography
Exercises
Programming problems

Chapter 7: Interaction
Introduction
Hardware
Input device - handling algorithms
Event handling
Sampled devices
The detectability attribute
Simulating a locator with a pick
Simulating a pick with a locator
Echoing
Interactive techniques
Bibliography
Exercises
Programming problems

Chapter 8: Three Dimensions
Introduction
3D geometry
3D primitives
3D transformations
Rotation about an arbitrary axis
Parallel projection
Perspective projection
Viewing parameters
Conversion to view plane coordinates
The 3D viewing transformation
Special projections
An application
Bibliography
Exercises
Programming problems

Chapter 9: Three-Dimensional Clipping
Introduction
When to clip
Clipping volumes
Clipping planes
Establishing clipping parameters
Clipping against a plane
3D clipping algorithms
Further modifications
An application
Bibliography
Exercises
Programming problems

Chapter 10: Hidden Surfaces and Lines
Introduction
Section one
Back-face removal
Back-face algorithm
Section two
The painter's algorithm
Collection of polygons
Remembering the style
The hidden surface check
Decomposition into triangles
Comparing two triangles
The minimax test
Overlapping edges
Containment of a point
Finding a point in the triangle plane
Containment of the entire triangle
Establishing depth order
Geometrical sorting
Linked lists
Sorting the triangles
Section three
Hidden line removal
How triangles obscure lines
Dividing a line
Hidden line checking for all sides of the triangle
Section four
Generalization to concave polygons
Bibliography
Exercises
Programming problems

Chapter 11: Shading
Introduction
Diffuse illumination
Point-source illumination
Specular reflection
Shading algorithms
Transparency and shadows
Bibliography
Exercises

Programming problems

Chapter 12: Curves
Introduction
Curve generation
Interpolation
Interpolating algorithms
Interpolating polygons
B splines
B splines and corners
An application
Bibliography
Exercises
Programming problems

Appendixes
A Pidgin Algol
B The CORE graphics system
C Graphics on a normal terminal
D Interfacing to PLOT10
E Interfacing to CALCOMP Routines
F Graphics on the Compucolor II
G Graphics on the Apple II
H Graphics on the Commodore Pet

Index

448 pp. 12 chapters. Drawings, figures, charts, mathematical formulae, algorithms, general index, appendices, chapter bibliographies. ISBN 0-07-026751-0.

114
Hartley, James

Designing Instructional Text
Nichols, 1978

Discusses the elements involved in the typographical layout of instructional materials. The text itself is an excellent example of the principles of graphic design as they relate to this process.

This book emphasizes the importance of planning and clarity of presentation in the creation of educational documents. The first five chapters review basic points of typography, identifying and illustrating practices that hinder comprehension. Chapters six through nine deal with general issues relating to the composition of textual information and to the use of graphic aids. The remainder of the book focuses on more specific issues, such as what makes one questionnaire better than another and how textbooks may be evaluated in terms of teaching effectiveness. Graphically illustrated and practically oriented, this book is intended for writers of instructional materials, as well as typographers, printers and educators. The Social Science Research Council provided financial assistance for several years of research on which this publication is based. Portions of the text were previously published in a pamphlet prepared by UNESCO, an educational organization connected with the United Nations.

Preface and acknowledgements
Chapter 1. Page-size
Chapter 2. Basic planning decisions
Chapter 3. Typesize and spacing
Chapter 4. Typefaces
Chapter 5. Theory into practice
Chapter 6. The role of illustrations
Chapter 7. Tables, graphs, diagrams and symbols
Chapter 8. Prose and some alternatives
Chapter 9. Programmed textbooks
Chapter 10. Lecture handouts, worksheets and writing books
Chapter 11. Forms and questionnaires
Chapter 12. Listed information: the layout of bibliographies, indexes and references
Chapter 13. Evaluating instructional text
Appendix: An annotated bibliography

125 pp. 13 chapters. Drawings, figures, tables, general index, bibliography, appendix. ISBN 0-89397-034-4.

Harvard University Laboratory for Computer Graphics and Spatial Analysis

Harvard Library of Computer Graphics Mapping Collection
Laboratory for Computer Graphics and Spatial Analysis, 1979-81

overview

The Harvard Laboratory for Computer Graphics and Spatial Analysis was established in 1965 within the Graduate School of Design at Harvard; its purpose is to conduct research on the definition and analysis of spatial structures and processes and to design and develop software for the analysis and display of spatial data. To date, most of the research and development has had predominantly geographic applications—in particular, computer mapping and the development and maintenance of cartographic and demographic databases. Research is published in several series of technical papers. The software is available to research and educational agencies. The Laboratory also sponsors short courses, seminars, and conferences on topics related to their research and development activities. The Harvard Library of Computer Mapping, listed with this overview, is composed of three sets of papers which were written for a conference sponsored by the Laboratory. At the conference a variety of professionals illustrated various applications of computer mapping techniques using specially designed case studies. The first six volumes comprise twenty-eight case studies selected from the conference and constitute the 1979 Mapping Collection. In 1980, Patricia A. Moore assumed general editing responsibilities for the series. The 1980 (volumes 7-11) and 1981 (volumes 12-17) Mapping Collections present updates and new material on the themes presented in the 1979 papers. Most papers were prepared specifically for this series and have not been published elsewhere. An author and subject index for the whole Library of Computer Mapping appears in volumes 18 and 19. Because much of the material in these volumes is directed to specific cartographic applications of computer mapping techniques, we have chosen to reproduce here only the titles of the individual volumes; the interested reader may request abstracts and tables of contents for any or all volumes from The Report Store. We do, however, direct the reader's attention to volume 17, *How to Design an Effective Graphics Presentation*. The papers in this volume represent the cartographer's art applied to the visual presentation of data. In particular, George McCleary's contribution (also titled "How to Design an Effective Graphics Presentation") has become a classic; versions of the paper have been presented at the National Computer Graphics Association annual conference and in the journal *IEEE Computer Graphics and Applications*.

19 volumes.

115

Harvard University Laboratory for Computer Graphics and Spatial Analysis

collection

Management's Use of Maps: Commercial and Political Applications
Laboratory for Computer Graphics and Spatial Analysis, 1979

(vol. 1 in the *Harvard Library of Computer Graphics Mapping Collection*)

64 pp. 8 papers. Figures, maps, models, bibliographies. (ISBN 0-89866-010-6)

116

Harvard University Laboratory for Computer Graphics and Spatial Analysis

collection

Mapping Software and Cartographic Data Bases
Laboratory for Computer Graphics and Spatial Analysis, 1979

(vol. 2 in the *Harvard Library of Computer Graphics Mapping Collection*)

240 pp. 28 papers. Figures, charts, maps, graphs, models, references. (ISBN 0-89866-011-4)

117

Harvard University Laboratory for Computer Graphics and Spatial Analysis

collection

Urban, Regional and State Applications: Plus a Special Section on Cadastral Systems
Laboratory for Computer Graphics and Spatial Analysis, 1979

(vol. 3 in the *Harvard Library of Computer Graphics Mapping Collection*)

195 pp. 16 papers in 2 sections. Drawings, figures, maps, tables, bibliography, references. (ISBN 0-89866-012-2)

118
Harvard University
Laboratory for Computer
Graphics and Spatial
Analysis

collection

Computer Mapping in Natural Resources and the Environment:
Including Applications of Satellite-Derived Data
Laboratory for Computer Graphics and Spatial Analysis, 1979

(vol. 4 in the *Harvard Library of Computer Graphics Mapping*
Collection)

138 pp. 14 papers. Figures, charts, maps, graphs, tables, models,
bibliographies. (ISBN 0-89866-013-0)

119
Harvard University
Laboratory for Computer
Graphics and Spatial
Analysis

collection

Computer Mapping in Education, Research and Medicine
Laboratory for Computer Graphics and Spatial Analysis, 1979

(vol. 5 in the *Harvard Library of Computer Graphics Mapping*
Collection)

112 pp. 13 papers. Drawings, figures, maps, bibliographies. (ISBN
0-89866-014-9).

120
Harvard University
Laboratory for Computer
Graphics and Spatial
Analysis

collection

Thematic Map Design
Laboratory for Computer Graphics and Spatial Analysis, 1979

(vol. 6 in the *Harvard Library of Computer Graphics Mapping*
Collection)

134 pp. 8 papers. Drawings, figures, maps, tables, bibliographies.
(ISBN 0-89866-015-7)

121
Harvard University
Laboratory for Computer
Graphics and Spatial
Analysis

collection

Management's Use of Maps: Including an Introduction to
Computer Mapping for Executives
Laboratory for Computer Graphics and Spatial Analysis, 1980

(vol. 7 in the *Harvard Library of Computer Graphics Mapping*
Collection, Patricia A. Moore, series ed.)

103 pp. 13 papers. Charts, maps, graphs, tables, models, color graphics.
(ISBN 0-89866-016-5)

122
Harvard University
Laboratory for Computer
Graphics and Spatial
Analysis

collection

Cartographic and Statistical Data Bases and Mapping Software
Laboratory for Computer Graphics and Spatial Analysis, 1980

(vol. 8 in the *Harvard Library of Computer Graphics Mapping Collection*, Patricia A. Moore, series ed.)

265 pp. 21 papers in 3 parts. Drawings, photographs, figures, maps, graphs, tables, abstract formalisms, models, references. (ISBN 0-89866-017-3)

123
Harvard University
Laboratory for Computer
Graphics and Spatial
Analysis

collection

Computer Graphics Hardware
Laboratory for Computer Graphics and Spatial Analysis, 1980

(vol. 9 in the *Harvard Library of Computer Graphics Mapping Collection*, Patricia A. Moore, series ed.)

80 pp. 11 papers. Drawings, photographs, figures, charts, maps, graphs, tables, models, references. (ISBN 0-89866-018-1)

124
Harvard University
Laboratory for Computer
Graphics and Spatial
Analysis

collection

Computer Mapping of Natural Resources and the Environment: Including Applications of Satellite-Derived Data
Laboratory for Computer Graphics and Spatial Analysis, 1980

(vol. 10 in the *Harvard Library of Computer Graphics Mapping Collection*, Patricia A. Moore, series ed.)

131 pp. 15 papers. Photographs, figures, charts, maps, tables, abstract formalisms, models, references. (ISBN 0-89866-019-X)

125
Harvard University
Laboratory for Computer
Graphics and Spatial
Analysis

collection

Urban, Regional, and State Government Applications of Computer Mapping: Plus Computer Mapping in Education
Laboratory for Computer Graphics and Spatial Analysis, 1980

(vol. 11 in the *Harvard Library of Computer Graphics Mapping Collection*, Patricia A. Moore, series ed.)

232 pp. 26 papers. Drawings, figures, maps. (ISBN 0-89866-020-3)

126
Harvard University
Laboratory for Computer
Graphics and Spatial
Analysis

collection

Management's Use of Computer Graphics
Laboratory for Computer Graphics and Spatial Analysis, 1981

(vol. 12 in the *Harvard Library of Computer Graphics Mapping Collection*, Patricia A. Moore, series ed.)

128 pp. 16 papers. Figures, charts, maps, graphs, models, footnotes, color graphics. (ISBN 0-89866-021-1)

127
Harvard University
Laboratory for Computer
Graphics and Spatial
Analysis

collection

Cartographic Data Bases and Software: Plus Cadastral Data Bases
Laboratory for Computer Graphics and Spatial Analysis, 1981

(vol. 13 in the *Harvard Library of Computer Graphics Mapping Collection*, Patricia A. Moore, series ed.)

176 pp. 19 papers in 3 parts. Figures, maps, graphs, tables, abstract formalisms, bibliographies. (ISBN 0-89866-022-X)

128
Harvard University
Laboratory for Computer
Graphics and Spatial
Analysis

collection

Computer Graphics Hardware
Laboratory for Computer Graphics and Spatial Analysis, 1981

(vol. 14 in the *Harvard Library of Computer Graphics Mapping Collection*, Patricia A. Moore, series ed.)

79 pp. 11 papers. Drawings, figures, tables. (ISBN 0-89866-023-8)

129
Harvard University
Laboratory for Computer
Graphics and Spatial
Analysis

collection

Computer Mapping of Natural Resources and the Environment: Plus Satellite Derived Data Applications
Laboratory for Computer Graphics and Spatial Analysis, 1981

(vol. 15 in the *Harvard Library of Computer Graphics Mapping Collection*, Patricia A. Moore, series ed.)

180 pp. 21 papers in 2 parts. Photographs, figures, charts, maps, graphs, tables, models, color graphics. (ISBN 0-89866-024-6)

130

Harvard University Laboratory for Computer Graphics and Spatial Analysis

collection

Computer Mapping Applications in Urban, State and Federal Government: Plus Computer Graphics in Education
Laboratory for Computer Graphics and Spatial Analysis, 1981

(vol. 16 in the *Harvard Library of Computer Graphics Mapping Collection*, Patricia A. Moore, series ed.)

140 pp. 18 papers in 2 parts. Drawings, figures, maps, graphs, tables, abstract formalisms, models, bibliographies. (ISBN 0-8122-1196-0)

131

Harvard University Laboratory for Computer Graphics and Spatial Analysis

collection

How to Design an Effective Graphics Presentation
Laboratory for Computer Graphics and Spatial Analysis, 1981

(vol. 17 in the *Harvard Library of Computer Graphics Mapping Collection*, Patricia A. Moore, series ed.)

86 pp. 6 papers. Figures, charts, maps, graphs, references. (ISBN 0-89866-026-2)

132

Harvard University Laboratory for Computer Graphics and Spatial Analysis

reference

Bibliography and Index: Part I, Authors Index
Laboratory for Computer Graphics and Spatial Analysis, 1982

(vol. 18 in the *Harvard Library of Computer Graphics Mapping Collection*, Patricia A. Moore, series ed.)

73 pp. (ISBN 0-89866-027-0)

133

Harvard University Laboratory for Computer Graphics and Spatial Analysis

reference

Bibliography and Index: Part II, Bibliographic and KWIC Indexes
Laboratory for Computer Graphics and Spatial Analysis, 1982

(vol. 19 in the *Harvard Library of Computer Graphics Mapping Collection*, Patricia A. Moore, series ed.)

99 pp. 2 parts. (ISBN 0-89866-028-9)

134
Heglin, Howard J.

technical report

NAVSHIPS Display Illumination Design Guide, Section II:
Human Factors
1973

(report number NELC-TD-223; Naval Electronics Laboratory Center;
sponsored by Naval Ship Research and Development Center; July 1973)

Details the tradeoffs between ambient illumination, local illumination
for design areas, and self-emanating and projected displays.

Human factors guidelines are provided, supported by data, graphs,
charts, and tables for reference and application specifications by
designers concerned with display illumination. The author assumes that
the reader is familiar with basic vision anatomy and physiology. The
twelve chapters cover: human vision capabilities and limitations;
illumination, layout, and visual displays; cathode ray tube displays;
single observer television displays; group viewing of television displays;
coding; optical projection devices; legibility; general specifications for
displays; coding, legend, and labeling specifications; layout
specifications; and ambient illuminance specifications. The bibliography
lists over 300 references and a separate section lists all pertinent
military specifications and standards such as MIL-M-18012 B. This
would be a good source for those needing to meet the listed standards,
as well as human factors and display illumination professionals.

CONTENTS
    Preface
    Administrative information
Chapter I: Human Vision Capabilities and Limitations
    "Vision"
    Accommodation
    Intensity relationships
    Acuity
    Other features of seeing
    Color
    Psychophysical relations
    List of figures
    List of tables
Chapter II: Illumination, Layout, and Visual Displays
    Illumination and layout considerations
    Use and control of natural daylight
    Problems of glare
    Panel layout
    Panel finish treatment and panel illumination
    Visual display applications
    Indicator lights—legend
    Warning lights
    Indicator detail
    Readouts
    Pictorial indicators
    Combined displays
    Graphic panels
    Automatic printers and graphic recorders

Navy UYA-4 standard console
Underwater display illumination
List of figures
List of tables
Chapter III: Cathode Ray Tube Displays (PPI)
Introduction
How large should the scope be?
How large should the pip be?
How persistent should the pip be?
What is the most desirable scanning rate?
What is the most desirable viewing distance?
What is the most desirable viewing angle?
Luminance
Visibility, CRT bias, and gain
Noise effects
Target symbols
Ambient illumination
Phosphors
Operator performance characteristics
Equipment considerations
List of figures
List of tables
Chapter IV: Random Position and Television Type Displays (Single Observer Viewing)
Introduction
Symbol resolution
Symbol size
How to determine the number of symbols that can be presented
Geometric distortion
Effect of signal bandwidth on symbol identification
Viewing distance
Symbol characteristics
Aspect ratio
Variations in TV quality
Ratio of active to inactive elements
Light/dark contrast
Display format
Viewing angle
Exposure duration
Flicker
The effects of surround luminance on visual comfort
The effects of signal-to-noise ratio
List of figures
List of tables
Chapter V: Television Displays for Group Viewing
Introduction
Symbol size
Viewing angle
Resolution
Bandwidth
Choosing the maximum viewing distance from the screen
Response time
Luminance

Ambient illumination
Registration accuracy
List of figures
Chapter VI: Coding
Introduction
Advantages and disadvantages of available codes
Design analysis
How much improvement in observer performance can one expect
with coding?
Additional factors to be considered
Color coding
Other relationships
Alphanumeric coding
Shape (geometric figures) coding
Other codes
List of figures
List of tables
Chapter VII: Optical Projection Devices
Introduction
Symbol size
Aspect ratio
Viewing distance
Viewing angle
Image luminance
Direction of light/dark contrast
Contrast ratio
Projection screen types
Audience seating
Summary of TV and projected display data
List of figures
List of tables
Chapter VIII: Display Legibility
Definitions
Preferred gothic styles
Design of transilluminated numerals and letters
Experimental psychology findings
Low levels of illumination and contrast
Legibility at great distance or with small-size characters
Width-to-height ratio
Comments on some proposed styles
Experimental methods
Specifications
List of figures
List of tables
Chapter IX: Visual Displays—General Specification Requirements
General
Transilluminated displays
Cathode ray tube (CRT) displays
Large-scale displays
Other displays
List of figures
List of tables

Chapter X: Coding, Legend, and Labeling Specifications
    Coding
    Legend switches
    Labeling
    List of figures
    List of tables

Chapter XI: Layout Specifications
    Standing operations
    Seated operations

Chapter XII: Ambient Illuminance Specifications
    List of tables

Military Reference Documents (for Chapters IX through XII)

References and Bibliography

Appendix A: Situational and Environmental Effects of Vision and Display Viewing, with Design Implications

Appendix B: Visual Acuity and Contrast Effects—Display Design Considerations

Appendix C: Display Viewing Dynamics

Index

282 pp. 12 chapters. Drawings, figures, graphs, tables, mathematical formulae, general index, references, appendices.

135
Hemingway, Peter W.
Kubala, Albert L.
Chastain, Garvin D.

technical report

Study of Symbology for Automated Graphic Displays
1979

(report number TR-79-A18; Human Resources Research Organization; sponsored by Headquarters TCATA; monitored by U.S. Army Research Institute for Behavioral and Social Sciences; May 1979)

Presents the results of a literature review and investigation on alternative symbol ranking for use in the development of more effective automated graphic displays used in tactical information systems.

This report focuses on visual display factors which affect user requirements and performance. Factors affecting the performance of users of interactive display devices include: display size, character size, type of display, brightness, contrast, resolution, viewing distance, viewing angle, type of character, information coding, character/background relationship, number of characters on a display, and frame change rate. While these factors may influence display legibility, the user acts upon an interpretation of the entire display. The authors conclude that a new symbology is needed for use with computer generated tactical displays but note that there is little agreement on what kind of symbol set is needed. The authors review the literature on display technique including questions concerning the use of geometrics, color, flash rate, and alphanumerics in coding systems, as well as associated advantages and problems. A section of this report reviews studies dealing with symbol size and proportion. The authors performed a study to determine symbol preferences of naive users in assigning symbols to represent military units commonly displayed on the CCIDES system. The authors found that current automated graphic display equipment and technology such as the CCIDES system appear to be capable of handling the display requirements for investigating many alternative and/or supplemental symbologies and that alternative symbology forms appear to appeal to naive subjects when they are similar to the concept symbolized. Intended for military audiences and data processing specialists.

CONTENTS

Chapter 1: Background

Chapter 2: Review of the Literature
    Graphic coding
    Historical development of graphic symbologies
    Applied research in graphic symbology
    Color coding
    Alphanumeric coding
    Symbol size and proportion
    Flash rate coding

Chapter 3: An Investigation of Symbol Preferences
    Research problem and design
    Results and conclusions

Chapter 4: Overview and Conclusions

References

Appendixes
    A. The symbol preference form
    B. Table B-1. Results of Nemenyi Pairwise Comparisons Test

Figure
    1-1. CCIDES configuration for intelligence analysis workshop

Tables
    1-1. Activities that use information displays
    2-1. Classes of objects used within the four dimensions (after Eriksen)

56 pp. 4 chapters. Tables, footnotes, references, appendices.

136
Herdeg, Walter
(ed.)

Graphis Diagrams: The Graphic Visualization of Abstract Data (5ed.)
Graphis Press, 1983

The fifth edition of this anthology presents graphic design as a conveyer of abstract information. Over 400 examples of the designer's skills are applied to a variety of problems, from organizational charts of international firms to the carbon dioxide/oxygen cycle in plants and animals.

Except for a foreword by the editor and an introduction by Leslie A. Segal (a specialist in corporate reports), the text is restricted to cutline notes which provide publication details and a brief description for each illustration. The notes are presented in German, French, and English in this Swiss publication. The examples are culled from an international selection of publications, with emphasis on promotional booklets, brochures, textbooks, corporate annual reports, and technical publications. The material is organized into statistical diagrams, charts, functional diagrams, tabulations, maps and design elements, and computer illustrations. Of particular interest are the functional diagrams and illustrations presenting information such as metabolic and drug pathways for pharmaceutical companies and the mining of oil and minerals by energy companies—all processes which are unavailable to the eye without the artist's help. The final chapter presents diagrams used as design elements for cover art and other decorative uses. This edition adds a supplement with new materials from corporate reports and other sources, including illustrations of oil field exploration, drilling techniques, and computer-drawn maps of the expanding U.S. population since the 1790 census. Descriptions of other Graphis publications are also included in this edition. An index of designers and artists, art directors, agencies and studios, clients and publishers is provided and the subject index includes the different types of diagrams. Although compiled as an aid to the professional graphic artist in solving particular design problems, this visually appealing volume is also accessible to the lay reader who wishes to understand graphically presented information and to the novice illustrator or brochure designer.

CONTENTS
Editor's foreword
   Walter Herdeg
Introduction
   Leslie A. Segal
Subject index
Chapter 1: Comparative statistical diagrams
Chapter 2: Flow diagrams, organization charts, etc.
Chapter 3: Diagrams visualizing functions, processes
Chapter 4: Tabulations, timetables, etc.
Chapter 5: Cartographic diagrams, decorative maps
Chapter 6: Diagrams used as design elements, computer-plotted diagrams
Index to artists and designers

Index to art directors
Index to agencies and studios
Index to clients and publishers
Abbreviations used for countries of origin (in captions and indexes)

207 pp. 7 chapters. Drawings, photographs, charts, maps, graphs, subject index, color graphics. ISBN 3-85709-410-9.

Herot, Christopher F.

overview

Spatial Data Management Systems
1979-83

This series of papers by Herot and his associates describes the development and implementation of a database management system using graphics techniques and direct manipulation of information by the user. Spatial database management systems are based on the observation that the cognitive organization of some kinds of information may resemble mapping operations in which data is stored in an approximation of its spatial and temporal occurrence in the environment. If a database is organized and accessed in ways which make "spatial" sense to its users, they will find it easier to learn and later manipulate in their work. In the research described here, this approach was applied to the development of a system which permits naval personnel to locate and call up data on the ships of the Soviet and United States navies. The system requires several screens on which data is displayed. Users move around in the system using joysticks although standard keyboard access is available as well. Information is presented using a combination of text and iconic representation. Herot has presented summaries of this and similar work in his several recent publications. The interested reader may want to consult his papers in the *ACM Transactions on Database Systems*, vol. 5, 1981; *Automated Tools for Systems Design*, 1982 (North Holland Publishing Company); and *Human Factors and Interactive Computer Systems*, Yannis Vassiliou, ed., 1984 (Ablex Publishing Corp.).

137
Herot, Christopher F.

technical report

Spatial Management of Data
1979

(Computer Corporation of America; sponsored by Defense Advanced Research Projects Agency; March 1979)

Reports on the development and implementation of a prototype system of database management consisting of Graphical Data Space (GDS) positioning for the organization and retrieval of information.

The Spatial Database Management System (SDMS) described in this report was developed in response to the perceived need for growing numbers of people to retrieve information from database management systems (DBMS) without formal training in the use of such systems. This overview describes the SDMS concept and its various features, its advantages over a conventional DBMS, and the implementation of the SDMS prototype. In contrast to a conventional DBMS, in which the user employs formal query language, information on SDMS is presented graphically and the user accesses data via a color raster scan display. By manipulating a joystick, the user locates areas of interest on the "world-view" map of the data surface and can zoom in for more detail. Information is more readily available and its structure more apparent in this system than in a symbolic DBMS, allowing for retrieval of data without prior knowledge of the system. Information available to the user through SDMS can come from numerous sources. This report describes the storage of data on an optical videodisk, in a symbolic DBMS, and as images stored as bit-arrays on a digital disk. Features of the system defining the relationship between symbolic and graphical representation of data are examined. At the time of this report the implementation of SDMS was still in process and consisted of approximately 40,000 lines of code. The work is not overly general, but is written at a level accessible to the serious student or professional involved in programming, data structuring, and database development. While the original report illustrated the graphic displays with color plates, the public release version is only available in black and white photocopy form.

CONTENTS

1: INTRODUCTION

2: EXAMPLE

2.1: Retrieval of Data

2.2: Creation of the Graphical Data Surface
    2.2.1. Icon class description
    2.2.2. The association statement

3: CONTRASTS TO CONVENTIONAL DBMS

3.1: Motion Controls

3.2: The Graphical Data Space as Its Own Data Dictionary

3.3: Browsing

3.4: Using Icon Position to Convey Information

3.5: Graphic Representations

3.6: New Data Types

4: OPTICAL VIDEODISK

5: DEFINING GRAPHICAL VIEWS

5.1: Dual Representation of Data
    5.1.1. Entities and icons
    5.1.2. Specific associations
    5.1.3. Class associations

5.2: Icon Classes

5.3: Using INGRES Data

5.4: Sub-Icons

5.5: SQUEL - The Query Language of SDMS

6: SDMS PROTOTYPE IMPLEMENTATION

6.1: System Environment

References

34 pp. 6 chapters. Photographs, figures, tables, references.

138
Friedell, Mark
Kramlich, David
Herot, Christopher F.
Carling, Richard

Spatial Data Management System
1979

technical report

(Computer Corporation of America; sponsored by Defense Advanced Research Projects Agency; 31 August 1979)

Reports upon the work completed on the prototype Spatial Data Management System (SDMS) for the Graphical Data Space (GDS) which allows users without formal training to access graphically represented information via a color raster scan display.

This report: provides an overview of the current icon creation mechanism and two new icon creation features—a secondary data mechanism and a subicon mechanism; proposes extensions to icon creation for geographical representation of aggregate information that can be built upon these new icon creation features; describes new blinking and framing features which expand the Spatial QUEry Language (SQUEL); and describes two new text viewing features in SDMS—an anti-aliased text font and a procedure for rapid transit through texts. Icon creation, the graphical representation of symbolic data, is an icon class descriptor (ICD), processor, or mapping rule which operates on symbolic data. Secondary data facilities of Icon Class Description Language (ICDL) allow multiple relations to be presented on a single icon. Subicon facilities allow a portion of an icon to appear independent of the parent icon. Blinking and framing features allow modification of selected icons' graphical data space (GDS) so that they are visually distinctive. Zooming in on special icons (text port displays) which appear with a table of contents, if available, allows rapid transit through text material. The report includes a process chart. The syntax of commands is included in several sections, and comments relevant to implementation are provided. The material is written at a level accessible to serious students or professionals involved in programming, data structuring, and database development.

CONTENTS

1: INTRODUCTION

2: GRAPHICAL DISPLAY OF DATA

2.1: SQUEL Commands
    2.1.1. DISPLAY command
    2.1.2. ASSOCIATE command

2.2: Icon Class Descriptions

2.3: Icon Creation Overview
    2.3.1. SQUEL monitor
    2.3.2. SQUEL interpreter
    2.3.3. Association processor
    2.3.4. Integrity maintenance daemon
    2.3.5. Icon creation
    2.3.6. Icon manager

2.4: Secondary Data
    2.4.1. Functional description of secondary data
    2.4.2. Implementation of secondary data

2.5: Subicons
    2.5.1. Functional description of subicons
    2.5.2. Implementation of subicons

2.6: Extentions: Aggregate Data Display
    2.6.1. Modifications to the implementation

3: BLINKING AND FRAMING

3.1: Function

3.2: Implementation
    3.2.1. SQUEL
    3.2.2. Modification process
    3.2.3. Blinker

3.3: Data Structures

4: VIEWING TEXT IN SDMS

4.1: Anti-Aliased Text Font

4.2: Rapid Transit in Text

5: REFERENCES

44 pp. 5 sections. Figures, references.

139
Kramlich, David
Herot, Christopher F.
Carling, Richard
Friedell, Mark

technical report

Spatial Data Management System
1979

(Computer Corporation of America; sponsored by Defense Advanced Research Projects Agency; 30 November 1979)

Reports on the work completed upon the prototype Spatial Data Management System (SDMS) for the organization and retrieval of geographically represented information via a color raster scan display.

The report provides the following updated information: a new DISASSOCIATE statement in the modified query language of the underlying DBMS which allows a user to undo the effects of a previous ASSOCIATE statement; extensions to the graphical editor (PAINT); extensions to the module, Icon Manager, which manages objects in the Graphical Data Space (GDS); and a terminal emulator to provide a text interface to SDMS. An ASSOCIATE statement produces an icon, as described in the previous quarterly report. The DISASSOCIATE statement allows for the deletion of the icons of ASSOCIATE. The graphical editor (PAINT) now supports the invocation of subprocesses that allow functionally related commands to be grouped in one process. An administrative mode now allows the user to create and manipulate icons and ports. A template mode permits the grouping of related icons. Several new commands have been added to prepare for extensions to the administrative mode of the graphical editor. The interface between the Icon Manager and the SDMS componments are also discussed. A terminal editor, which uses the Lexidata display system, has also been added and the user's terminal interactions with SDMS are managed with this emulator. A list of commands is included. The material is written at a level accessible to serious students or professionals involved in programming, data structuring, and database development.

CONTENTS

1: INTRODUCTION

2: ENHANCEMENTS TO SQUEL

3: PAINT EXTENTIONS

3.1: ADMIN Mode

3.2: Template Mode

4: ENHANCEMENTS TO THE ICON MANAGER

4.1: New Features for Templates

4.2: New Features for ADMIN Mode

4.3: Interface
    4.3.1. Icon manager command summary

5: TERMINAL EMULATOR

5.1: Design

5.2: SDMS Architecture

6: REFERENCES

38 pp. 6 sections. Figures, references.

140
Herot, Christopher F.
Carling, Richard
Friedell, Mark
Kramlich, David

technical report

Spatial Data Management System: Final Report
1980

(Computer Corporation of America; sponsored by Defense Advanced Research Projects Agency; 30 December 1980)

Final report on the implementation and training phases of the prototype Spatial Data Management System (SDMS). This system is used to organize and retrieve information via a color raster scan display. The SDMS was developed for implementation on the Navy ship, the *USS Carl Vinson.*

This work: adds information to previous SDMS reports on the transfer of the SDMS from the development environment to the demonstration and development facility of DARPA's Cybernetics Technology Office; enumerates adaptations of the SDMS to allow higher levels of functionality; and describes training methods used for the tactical decision makers who used the SDMS. Product integration consisted of the creation of "an SDMS data surface, providing relevant images at various points on the data surface, and arranging for the activation of the specific products associated with the different images selected" by the zoom-in feature. The report provides a list of products integrated with the SDMS system and describes them briefly. Computer-aided training of Tactical Attack Officers (TAOs) is also described and evaluated. Computer-based simulation involved recreation of a portion of the TAO's environment—antisubmarine warfare—using personal computers connected via telephone lines, allowing low cost practice on a portable system. Additional training involved generating a minimal, comprehensive set of problems for practice where each problem tested specific pieces of knowledge the students had learned previously. The report presents a brief, two-level model of the integrated system in the form of a structured diagram, with textual explanation. The material is written at a level accessible to serious students or professionals involved in programming, data structuring, database development, and computer assisted instruction.

CONTENTS

1: INTRODUCTION

2: SDMS/CTO PRODUCT INTEGRATION

2.1: Physical Transfer of SDMS

2.2: Hardware and Software Enhancement

2.3: Location and Correction of Errors

2.4: CTO/DDF Staff Training and Support

2.5: Product Integration

3: COMPUTER-AIDED TRAINING OF TACTICAL DECISION MAKERS

3.1: Problem

3.2: Solution

3.3: Example Session

3.4: System Model
    3.4.1. Present lesson
    3.4.2. Generate scenarios
    3.4.3. Play SSN

3.5: Conclusions

4: BIBLIOGRAPHY

29 pp. 4 sections. Figures, bibliography.

141
Herot, Christopher F.
Barnett, Jane
Carling, Richard
Friedell, Mark
Kramlich, David
Rosenberg, Ronni L.

USS Carl Vinson SDMS: Final Report
1983

technical report

(Computer Corporation of America; sponsored by Advanced Research Projects Agency; monitored by Office of Naval Research; June 1983)

Contains a detailed example of how to use the prototype Spatial Database Management System (SDMS) installed in the Intelligence Center of the *USS Carl Vinson* (CVN 70) and describes the system environment. SDMS consists of Graphical Data Space (GDS) positioning for the organization and retrieval of information.

The SDMS is being used to "access information about Allied and Soviet platforms, including their positions, characteristics, and armaments." The report gives an example of how SDMS is used as an interface to the *USS Carl Vinson* database information about platforms. Data are viewed through color displays that show flat surfaces on which pictorial representations are arranged. The Graphical Data Space (GDS) is a collection of all the data surfaces. "The GDS consists of all the pictures the user can access." Users can traverse data surfaces or zoom in on an image to gain detail without use of a keyboard. A query language is also used. The system encourages browsing, and by retaining a spatial framework, requires less prior knowledge of the structure and contents of the database. Retrieval can occur without specifying it precisely or knowing its exact location in the database. Interaction with the database at the user station takes place through a set of three color displays. The world view or high-level view shows all the categories of data that can be accessed through the system when the user first starts SDMS. The user employs a joystick to traverse the data surface or moves to a location quickly by touching the location on the world or high-level view. Detailed views are shown on the center display screen. Information, menu, and map displays are available to the user. Pictures, diagrams, charts, and maps are included to clarify the text. The material is written at a level accessible to serious students or professionals involved in programming, data structuring, database development, and training.

CONTENTS
1: Introduction
2: Using SDMS
    2.1. Ispace display
    2.2. Menu display
    2.3. Map display
3: System Environment
4: Bibliography
5: Glossary
6: Acronyms and Abbreviations

45 pp. 6 sections. Figures, bibliography, glossary.

142
Hess, Stanley

The Modification of Letterforms
Art Directions, 1972

Describes and illustrates the principles of graphic design that relate to the construction of alphanumeric characters. Focusing on the shaping of letters, this book traces the evolution of the Latin alphabet and examines the techniques used in fashioning different styles of print.

Each page of text is accompanied by a full page of illustrations on the facing page to provide examples of the principles discussed. Brief notations in the margin outline the work's main points. The author considers historical developments in letter design ranging from the twentieth century B.C. (Sinai inscriptional letters) to the twentieth century A.D. (Gothic lettering). Included in this period are Phoenecian lapidary letters and Roman and Venetian characters. He compares and contrasts various letter styles as he discusses ways to enhance legibility and techniques to elicit desired effects. Practical methods and rules of letter design reveal the basic skills involved in establishing the appropriate height and width of letters or achieving visual equality between small and capital letters. More technical terminology, such as optical anamorphosis, introduces the student of graphic design to advanced concepts of lettering and layout. This book is easy to read, making it suitable for anyone who wishes to learn more about the subject.

CONTENTS
The modification of letterforms
Shape
Illusion
Image
Continual proportionals
Small letter proportionals
Space
Pattern
Equality
Slope
Surface
Prospect
Glossary

149 pp. 12 chapters. Drawings, figures, glossary. ISBN 0-910158-03-7.

143
Hildreth, Ellen C.

The Measurement of Visual Motion
The MIT Press, 1984

(from the *ACM Distinguished Dissertations* series)

Provides both theoretical analysis and experimental validation of computer-based techniques for measuring and understanding visual phenomena in the human eye. Selected for publication in the *ACM Distinguished Dissertation* series, this book has been recognized for its high quality and its substantial contribution to computer-related science and engineering.

Written by a Ph.D. candidate at the Massachusetts Institute of Technology, this dissertation focuses on the human visual system and how it reconstructs a three-dimensional representation of the world from the two-dimensional image projected onto the retina. The author maintains that this reconstruction depends largely upon the analysis of movement in the changing image. This investigation of motion analysis follows a computational approach, depicting the human system as an information processor that performs computations on internal symbolic representations. Algorithms are used to test the adequacy of the computational theory upon which this study is based. This study also aims to reveal the particular assumptions about the physical world which serve to influence perception. Theory from psychophysics, perceptual psychology, and neurophysiology is also incorporated. While much of the material presented is highly technical, perceptual researchers and experimental psychologists will find this book to be relevant and informative. Several appendices provide additional propositions and proofs which further demonstrate the applicability of the computational approach.

CONTENTS

1: Introduction
    1.1. The problem and approach
    1.2. The measurement of visual motion
    1.3. The computation of surface boundaries from motion
2: Background
    2.1. Two processes in human vision
    2.2. The measurement of visual motion
3: Computation of the Velocity Field
    3.1. The constant velocity constraint
    3.2. Rigid motion in the image plane
    3.3. The smoothness constraint
    3.4. Deriving additional constraint from the changing image
    3.5. Summary
4: An Algorithm to Compute the Velocity Field
    4.1. The discrete formulation
    4.2. Satisfying the image constraints exactly
    4.3. Satisfying the image constraints approximately
    4.4. Examples of the smoothest velocity field
    4.5. The convergence of iterative methods
    4.6. Summary

5: The Computation of Motion Discontinuities
  5.1. Related work on discontinuity detection
  5.2. The early detection of discontinuities
  5.3. Limitations of a primitive detection algorithm
  5.4. Translation versus rotation
  5.5. Possible algorithms for detecting motion discontinuities
6: Perceptual Studies of Motion Measurement
  6.1. The measurement of motion along zero-crossing contours
  6.2. The smoothness assumption
  6.3. Deriving further motion constraints from eye movement
  6.4. Tracking localizable features
  6.5. Short range and long range motion processes
  6.6. The use of multiple channels for motion measurement
  6.7. The independence of motion measurement and interpretation
7: The Psychophysics of Discontinuity Detection
  7.1. Contributions of previous work
  7.2. The localization of boundaries in random dot patterns
  7.3. Velocity versus more primitive measurements
  7.4. Size versus displacement
  7.5. Future psychophysical experimentation
8: Neurophysiological Studies of Motion
  8.1. The retina- $\nabla^2 G^*I$ and its time derivative
  8.2. Visual cortex—the measurement of $v \perp (s)$ along zero-crossings
  8.3. Higher cortical areas- the velocity field and its discontinuities
9: Summary and Conclusions
Appendix I
Appendiix II
Appendix III
Appendix IV
Appendix V
References
Author Index
Subject Index

241 pp. 9 chapters. Drawings, photographs, figures, graphs, algorithms, abstract formalisms, author index, references, appendices. ISBN 0-262-08143-1.

144
Hills, Philip
(ed.)

collection

The Future of the Printed Word: The Impact and the Implications of the New Communications Technology
Greenwood, 1980

Specialized readings which consider the place of printed media in the future of communications.

Experts from the fields of publishing, library and information science, computing, and education consider electronic display, microfiche, film, and computer printouts as well as the prime focus, traditional forms of "print." The papers are easily accessible to the nonspecialist reader and cover a variety of topics, including: the nature of information needs in the coming decade; the role of various media in the learning process; the design of visual displays for disseminating public information, using both traditional and new technologies; design principles for computer-generated output; electronic publishing, particularly of scientific information; a review of printing techniques; publication in reduced format (microfilm, microform); and videodiscs. In conclusion, two papers consider the future of print, one from a socioeconomic standpoint, and one which suggests trends in scientific and technological publishing. This cogent collection presents a positive outlook for the continuing, if changing, importance of words on paper and directs readers toward an integration best described by Patricia Wright: "The old and the new technologies can be seen not only as rivals but as mutually supportive."

CONTENTS

Preface

1. Future methods and techniques
   John M. Strawhorn
2. Some questions concerning the unprinted word
   Maurice B. Line
3. The place of the printed word in teaching and learning
   P.J. Hills
4. The design of official information I—gobbledygook?
   Patricia Wright
5. The design of official information II—the new technologies
   Patricia Wright
6. Designing for the new communications technology
   Linda Reynolds
7. Electronic alternatives to paper-based publishing in science and technology
   Donald W. King
8. Euronet DIANE—a precursor to electronic publishing
   Franco Mastroddi, Serge Lustac
9. Present and future printing techniques
   Yuri Gates
10. Microform publication
    S. John Teague
11. A note on videodiscs
    Yuri Gates
12. The future of the printed word: economic and social factors
    A.J. Meadows
13. Scientific and technical publishing in the 1980s
    A.J. Kent

Learn with BOOK
   R.J. Heathorn

172 pp. 13 chapters. Drawings, figures, tables, references. ISBN 0-313-22693-8.

145
Hollister, Walter M.
(ed.)

collection

Advancement on Visualization Techniques
AGARD, 1980

(report number AGARD-AG-255 of the North Atlantic Treaty
Organization Advisory Group for Aerospace Research and
Development)

A NATO sponsored collection which covers recent developments in
research technology and applications in the field of visualization and
display in aircraft cockpits, particularly military cockpits.

Several articles describe, evaluate, and compare a variety of displays.
One article describes advantages of the pictorial displays resulting from
the use of cathode ray tubes (CRTs) instead of traditional flight
instruments. A number of articles focus on newly developing display
techniques, especially flat panel displays including liquid crystal, gas
plasma, electroluminescent, light emitting diode, electrochromic,
electrophoretic, ferroelectric, and magnetic particle displays. Some
disadvantages of CRTs are identified, specifically their bulk, high
voltage power needs, and lack of suitability for the bright, ambient
lighting typical of cockpits. Advantages of flat panel displays include
lower space requirements, power requirements, and life-cycle costs and
greater reliability, flexibility, and ease of retrofitting. Also discussed are
parameters of importance for designing helmet-mounted displays
including size, weight, eye relief, field of view, distortion, and image
quality. The remaining articles cover other aspects of cockpit display,
including cockpit design, special needs of control configured vehicles,
advances in optical infinity lenses, and tactical and map display. These
articles are technical, but the editor of the collection asserts that this
work should be of value to newcomers in the field as well as experts.
The articles are accompanied by nicely produced graphs, charts, figures,
and photographs.

CONTENTS
Preface
W.M. Hollister
The presentation of static information on air traffic control displays
R.J.G. Edwards
Flat panel display technology overview
*J. Brindle, B. Gurman, J. Redford, E. Schlam, W. Mulley, P.
Soltan, G. Tsaparas, K.B. Urnette, J. Coonrod, W. Melnick,
J. Mysing*
The electro-optical display/visual system interface: human factors
considerations
J. Laycock, R.A. Chorley
Integration of sensors with displays
A.C. Wesley, I.T.B. Blackie
Liquid crystal displays
A.J. Hughes
Cathode ray tubes and plasma panels as display devices for aircraft
displays
S. Woodcock

Large area gas discharge displays
 J.P. Michel
Optical infinity lens developments for flight simulator visual
displays
 W.B. Albery, J.A. LaRussa
Evolution of tactical and map displays for high performance
aircraft
 W.H. McKinlay
Helmet mounted displays: design considerations
 H.L. Task, D.F. Kocian, J.H. Brindle
An advanced electronic cockpit instrumentation system: the
coordinated cockpit display
 D.L. Baty, M.L. Watkins
The influence of visual requirements on the design of military
cockpits
 J.W. Lyons, G. Roe
Display concepts for control configured vehicles
 R.W. Klein, W.M. Hollister
Experiments using electronic display information in the NASA
terminal configured vehicle
 S.A. Morello

*220 pp. 14 papers. Drawings, photographs, figures, tables, abstract
formalisms, references. (ISBN 92-835-1371-1)*

Hopgood, F. Robert A.   *SEE UNDER ID 105*

146
Hubbard, Stuart W.   **The Computer Graphics Glossary**
Oryx Press, 1983

reference

Provides descriptions of approximately 800 terms, all directly pertinent
to computer graphics.

The author has attempted to construct a complete glossary, while
recognizing the impossibility of creating an all-inclusive glossary for a
field as dynamic as computer graphics. The glossary includes listings of
product names with sources for all products whose manufacturers
granted Hubbard permission for inclusion. The glossary listings are
descriptive, not prescriptive, and offer multiple definitions where a term
has more than one meaning in use. The most common usage is listed
first. Hubbard provides short, clear descriptions of terms. The format is
highly readable because terms are printed in a large, bold type with
ample space between items. A number of useful photographs and figures
are included; the photographs depict various equipment used in
computer graphics—a photoplotter, a Compuscanner, a sensing pen—
while figures usually show a typical output for a particular computer
system. *The Computer Graphics Glossary* is designed for use by
computer-aided design professionals and computer-aided manufacturing

professionals, but would also be appropriate for people outside the computer graphics industry who are interested in learning about the technology.

95 pp. Photographs, figures. ISBN 0-89774-072-6.

147
Huggins, A.W.F.
Getty, David J.

Display-Control Compatibility in Three-Dimensional Displays: Final Report
1984

technical report

(report number BBN-5584; Bolt Beranek and Newman, Inc.; sponsored by Office of Naval Research; 29 February 1984)

The final report of a research project which examined human perceptual performance in relation to three-dimensional display-control compatibility issues.

In this series of experiments, researchers at Bolt, Beranek and Newman (BBN) have examined various aspects of human factors influences pertinent to the application of three-dimensional display technology. Basis research questions involved the accuracy of operator perception of display items and the contribution of the third dimension to the performance of tasks monitored through the 3-D display. Experimental work utilized SpaceGraph, a display developed by BBN which is truly three-dimensional rather than stereoscopic in nature. Summarized in this document, the research program was organized into three phases, which are discussed in four earlier reports (*Display-Control Compatibility in 3-D Displays 1: Effects of Orientation; 2: Effects of Cue Symmetry; 3: Perception of Direction*; and *4: Perception and Control of Motion*).In the initial phase, the authors studied how the orientation of a rotating object (a cube) to a fixed control (a cubical response box) affected the speed and accuracy of operator decisions regarding the object. Phase two was concerned with the accuracy of an operator's ability to identify and project an object's trajectory based on its orientation. Using a real-time control task, phase three experiments were designed to measure the relative utility of each of the three dimensions of the display, exploring the observation that the depth dimension was less quickly and accurately perceived than the other two. Implications for further research are discussed and the bibliography of project publications presented. Display designers and perceptual psychologists will find this an interesting and important series. Readers interested in detailed information regarding the rationale, experimental procedures, and references of the individual project phases should consult the individual reports.

23 pp. Bibliography.

148
Huggins, William H.
Entwisle, Doris R.

Iconic Communication: An Annotated Bibliography
Johns Hopkins University Press, 1974

reference

Motivated by work on computer-generated films, the authors have collected selected references which focus on how graphic icons communicate to human beings.

The authors synthesize information collected from psychology, social anthropology, education, computer graphics, and perception studies. The emphasis is on how visual images, particularly certain shapes which move and change, may communicate information, especially quantitatively organized information of a technical or scientific nature. Seven short chapters introduce the major areas covered by the references which include: the basic nature of iconic communication; how iconic recognition has evolved in a complex world; the relationship of iconics to linguistics, education, and psychology; imagery research; and the application of iconics in computer-generated film, "dynamic symbols," computer pantomimes, face mnemonics, and Weaver's stimuli. References are abstracted for content, and brief reader's comments are sometimes included. While specifically related to the authors' original work in computer-generated film, the references have value to a variety of disciplines and research areas, including students, researchers, and professionals in art, cognitive psychology, education, linguistics, and computer graphics. The major fault of the book is the lack of an updated reference list covering the vigorous activity which has occurred in the field since 1974.

CONTENTS

Preface

Iconic Communication

Iconics and Evolution

Relation of Iconics to Linguistics

Iconics and Education

Iconics and Psychology

Research on Imagery

Applications of Iconics
Computer-generated files
Testing of "dynamic symbols"
Computer pantomimes
Face mnemonics
Weaver's stimuli

References—Format and Description
330 entries, listed by last name and date of publication, abstracted and discussed

Index

171 pp. Drawings, figures, charts, graphs, models, general index. ISBN 0-8018-1528-2.

149
Hurlburt, Allen

Layout: The Design of the Printed Page
Watson-Guptill, 1977

This concise text, well designed and well illustrated, is highly recommended for anyone involved in the visual display of information and ideas.

Based on his own interest in the broad psychological aspects of perception, illusion, and paradox, Hurlburt has written this book for practicing designers and design students. In the introduction he stresses the importance of the multidisciplinary nature of design, a process which draws on the creativity of architects, artists, and sculptors as well as industrial, interior, and graphic designers. The book is divided into four chapters, the first of which examines style. Hurlburt confines himself to the twentieth century and examines the influence that the great movements in painting and architecture have had on graphic design. In the second chapter he traces the roots of symmetrical form back to classical Greece and the roots of twentieth century asymmetrical form back to Japanese modular systems. From asymmetry he progresses to the importance of balance and contrast and looks at signs and symbols, perspective, isometric dimension, and grids, all of which play their part in the design process. The third chapter deals with content, photography, humor, and the importance of typography to convey the message. The author emphasizes the need for totality of design. In the final chapter Hurlburt looks at the communication between the graphic artist and his reader. In his conclusion the author emphasizes how essential perception and response are to visual communication. This is a very readable text.

CONTENTS

Introduction
1: Style
    Style: roots of design
    Prelude: Art Nouveau
    Cubism sets the stage
    Futurism
    Dada breaks the mold
    Surrealism
    Russian revolutionary design
    El Lissitzky
    Alexey Brodovitch
    Art Deco
    De Stijl
    The Bauhaus
    After the Bauhaus
    Summary: a measure of style
2: Form
    Form: defining structure
    Symmetry: the classic ideal
    Asymmetry: the oriental order
    Asymmetry moves west
    The Mondrian influence

Balance
Contrasts of value and color
Contrast of size
The design trilogy
Free form
Signs and symbols
Dimension: perspective
Dimension: isometric
Angles and diagonals
The Modulor: Le Corbusier's design system
Grids and systems
Summary: filling the void
3: Content
Content: word and image
The design synthesis
The creative concept
Typography: the visual language
Typography: serifs and simplicity
Typography: style and legibility
Photography: camera and image
Photographic effects
The designer as photographer
Illustration
The designer as illustrator
Graphic illustration
Humor
Summary: the total effect
4: Response
Response: the significant exchange
Perception: Gestalt psychology
Illusion: the changing view
The visual paradox
Conclusion: The Measure of a Design
Bibliography
Index

159 pp. 4 chapters. Drawings, photographs, general index, bibliography. ISBN 0-8230-2655-8.

150
Hurlburt, Allen

The Grid: A Modular System for the Design and Production of Newspapers, Magazines, and Books
Van Nostrand Reinhold, 1978

This concise summary of the grid as used in newspaper, magazine, and book design provides a useful bridge between the graphic arts and computer-aided design.

This book explores the grid as a basis for graphic design. It is divided into three chapters dealing with newspapers, magazines, and books. There is also a short introduction which treats the history of the grid from the Renaissance artists to Le Corbusier's Modulor and the work of Josef Müller-Brockmann who, like Hurlburt, sees the grid as "an aid, not a guarantee." The first chapter summarizes the changes that have taken place in newspaper design since the 1930s, with particular emphasis on the revitalization that took place both in Europe and the U.S. in the 60s and 70s. Chapter two deals with the changes that have occurred as magazines have changed their emphasis from visual content to text/picture combinations. Hurlburt emphasizes the sense of order and proportion that the use of the grid brings to the best modern magazine publications. The third chapter looks at the grid in book design from the Gutenberg Bible to Jan Tschichold's work for Penguin. It also looks ahead to the rapidly increasing computerization of book design. Included are: a technical appendix on the use of the computer and the ways in which it is particularly suited for the modular approach to page design; a glossary of computer terminology; a bibliography; and an index. Although this book is short—eighty pages of text with many illustrations—the scope of the text is broad. While some of the technical changes that he anticipates have already occurred, Hurlburt provides a historical perspective which summarizes the grid with authority. This book is particularly recommended for those who work with computer-aided design.

CONTENTS

Introduction:
With grids by Le Corbusier, Paul Rand, Massimo Vignelli, Josef Müller-Brockmann, and Otl Aicher

Part One:
Newspapers:
With grids by Edwin Taylor, Massimo Vignelli, Frank Ariss, and Alan Fletcher

Part Two:
Magazines:
With grids by Massimo Vignelli, Willy Fleckhaus, Will Hopkins, Karl Gerstner, and Walter Bernard

Part Three:
Books:
With grids by Jan Tschichold, Bradbury Thompson, Ed Day, and Louis Silverstein
Technical appendix
Glossary of computer technology
Bibliography
Index

96 pp. 3 chapters. Drawings, photographs, general index, bibliography, glossary, appendix. ISBN 0-442-23598-4.

151
IBM Human Factors
Center

Human Factors of Workstations with Visual Displays (3ed.)
IBM, 1984

(IBM technical manual G320-6102)

Discusses human and VDT characteristics to be considered in the design of VDTs and their implementation in the work environment.

The third edition of this technical manual, issued by the IBM Human Factors Center, covers many of the human factors to consider when developing, selecting, or implementing a VDT workstation. The subjects discussed fall into three categories: the physical aspects of VDTs, human characteristics, and workstation design for proper VDT use. Though the orientation is toward CRT displays, most of the material is applicable to all display technologies. Due to the dominant role vision plays in VDT operation, this report covers the visual factors of VDT use more thoroughly than other aspects of VDT use. The optical characteristics of the eye, and the eye's common impairments, receive extensive treatment. A section on VDT technology focuses on the criteria used to make VDTs appropriate for the human optical system. Brief discussions of radiation safety, the keyboard, workstation configuration, and acoustic noise are also included. This manual's strength lies in its succinct review of human factors related to the design and implementation of VDTs. Though other publications on this subject go into greater depth, this manual provides an excellent overview of many of the topics related to the human/VDT interface. Many charts and figures enhance the text. Office managers, systems managers, VDT designers, and ergonomic engineers would be interested in this report. Useful references supplement the essentially introductory nature of the report.

CONTENTS

INTRODUCTION

RADIATION SAFETY

Ionizing Radiation

Non-ionizing Radiation

Standards

Light Emissions

THE HUMAN OPTICAL SYSTEM

Optical Characteristics of the Eye
    The eye muscles
    Pupil size and acuity
    Pupil size and field luminance
    Pupil size and accommodation
    Rate of change of pupil size

The Retina
Visual Acuity
Contrast Sensitivity
Peripheral Contrast Sensitivity
Spectral Sensitivity
Color Vision
Color Mixing
Color Vision Anomalies
Common Disorders
    Hyperopia
    Myopia
    Phoria
    Aniseikonia
    Presbyopia
Frequency of Visual Disorders
Zones of Visual Comfort
Eyewear
    Flat-top bifocals
    Full-width bifocals
    Progressive-addition bifocals
    Trifocals
Visual After-Effects
VISUAL DISPLAY CONSIDERATIONS
Monochromatic Displays
    Raster scan CRT
    Stroke character CRT
    Storage tube CRT
    Plasma panels
    Liquid crystal displays
    Light emitting diodes
    Electroluminescent displays
Multicolor Displays
    Three-primary raster scan
    Beam penetration
CRT Selection
Phosphor Selection
Persistence
Refresh Rate and Technique
Image Instability
Image Polarity
Display Brightness/Contrast Measurements
Resolution
Color
Surface Reflections
    Diffusing surface
    Screen orientation
    Anti-reflective coating
Contrast
    Contrast-enhancement filters
    Other contrast-enhancement devices

Contrast Specification

Character Size

Character Size Measurement

THE KEYBOARD

Keyboard Layout

Key Mechanism

Keytops and Spacing

Keyboard Packaging

Pointing Methods
  Cursor control keys
  Light pens
  Other techniques

WORKSTATION CONFIGURATION

Seated Work Position

Work Surfaces

Display Location

LIGHTING

Measurement of Light
  Lux
  Candlefoot
  Millilambert
  Footlambert

Luminance Level and Acuity

Workstation Light Level

Luminance Balance

Disability Glare

Discomfort Glare

Age and Discomfort Glare

Transient Adaption Factor (TAF)

Other Considerations

ACOUSTIC NOISE

Decibel

Range of Hearing

Noise Ratio Curves

REFERENCES

BIBLIOGRAPHY

READER COMMENT FORM

64 pp. 7 chapters. Figures, graphs, bibliography, references.

**International Organization
for Standardization (ISO)**   *SEE UNDER ID 102*

152
Itten, Johannes

The Elements of Color
Van Nostrand Reinhold, 1970

(study edition of Itten's *The Art of Color,* 1961, edited by Faber Birren, translated by Ernst van Hagen)

Presents the color theory of Johannes Itten.

This work is a condensation and simplification of Itten's major work, *The Art of Color* published in German in 1961. Here, the author presents his aesthetic color theory, a theory based foremost on the author's experience and intuition as a painter. Itten states that colors are forces which can affect people positively or negatively and we can study the effects that colors have visually, emotionally, or symbolically. Color effects may be intensified or weakened by contrast; visual judgments proceed on the basis of comparisons. He has developed seven categories of color contrasts to account for the impact of color: hue, light-dark, cold-warm, complementary, simultaneous, saturation, and extension. Each is illustrated and discussed in terms of visual, emotional, and symbolic value. The impact of individual colors is also analyzed, but Itten stresses that color is always modified by its context. This is an information-rich volume, packed with color illustrations, examples from art history, exercises for the student, quotes from famous artists, advice to painters and art students, notes on the physics of color, and formal theory and practical observations regarding color mixture, composition, and more. Itten traces the history of color use in art, displaying extensive knowledge of color application in other periods and cultures. Well-translated from German, the author's style displays a near reverence for the qualities and effects of color. Considered to be one of the greatest modern teachers of color theory, Itten taught at the Bauhaus in Weimar. He also directed schools for textile design in Germany and Switzerland as well as founding the Museum Reitberg in Switzerland. This volume is written to appeal to both the student of color theory and the professional artist or designer.

CONTENTS

Foreword and Evaluation
    Faber Birren
Introduction
Color Physics
Color Agent and Color Effect
Concord of Colors
Subjective Timbre
Theory of Color Design
The Twelve-Part Color Circle
The Seven Color Contrasts
    Hue
    Light-dark
    Cold-warm
    Complementary
    Simultaneous

Saturation
Extension
Color Mixing
The Color Sphere
Color Harmony
Form and Color
Spatial Effects of Color
Theory of Color Impression
Theory of Color Expression
Composition
Postscript

95 pp. 17 chapters. Figures, color plates. ISBN 0-442-24038-4.

153
Jarett, Irwin M.   **Computer Graphics and Reporting Financial Data**
John Wiley and Sons, 1983

A basic handbook on the use of computer graphics in design, display, and interpretation of financial data.

This handbook of computer graphics is for use as a sourcebook in the design of a graphics management information system (GMIS). The author begins by defining GMIS and discusses business computer graphics, MIS vs. GMIS, financial graphics standards, and how to design a GMIS. A thorough discussion of charts, their types and functions, and which chart to use for a specific purpose is included. The book also covers the application of GMIS to cash control, accounts receivable, inventory, fixed assets, accounts payable, long term debt, net worth, equity, sales/COGS/gross margin, purchases, and payroll. The book is intended for financial managers, CPAs, controllers, EDP operators, programmers, and DP and MIS designers, as an aid to the more effective presentation of financial data by using computer graphics. This is not a book on the technology of computer graphics, but a book on how to use display design to present information effectively, efficiently, and clearly. For such purposes it is very thorough and easy to understand.

CONTENTS
1. Business computer graphics
2. MIS vs. GMIS
3. Financial graphic standards
4. How to design a graphic management information system
5. Graphic financial statement sequences
6. Cash control
7. Accounts receivable
8. Inventory
9. Fixed assets
10. Accounts payable

11. Long-term debt
12. Net worth: equity
13. Sales/COGS/gross margin
14. Purchases
15. Payroll
16. Key indicators and the graphic management instrument panel
17. Presentation graphics
Bibliography
Index

360 pp. 17 chapters. Figures, charts, graphs, tables, models, general index, bibliography. ISBN 0-471-86761-6.

154
Jarosz, Christopher J.
Rogers, Steven P.

technical report

Evaluation of Map Symbols for a Computer-Generated Topographic Display: Transfer of Training, Symbol Confusion, and Association Value Studies
1982

(report number DAVAA-TR-81-0089-5; Anacapa Sciences, Inc.; sponsored by U.S. Army Communications-Electronics Command; monitored by U.S. Army Avionics R&D Activity; December 1982)

Describes research in which sixty-nine topographic and tactical symbols were developed for use on a computer-generated topographical display (CGTD), and then evaluated.

Map symbols conventionally used on paper maps are not suitable for display screens because the matrix of display units (pixels) on the screen does not permit a sharp enough resolution. This study utilizes a set of guidelines to develop symbols possibly suitable for use on a CGDT to be used by army aviators. Two questionnaire booklets were administered to thirty-three military personnel in an attempt to evaluate the symbols. The first booklet measured transfer of the symbols and symbol confusion. The transfer of training task required subjects to match the new symbols to the familiar paper-map symbols and thus determine the similarity of symbols in the two sets. The symbol confusion task required subjects to compare symbols within the new set to one another so that symbols which were too similar within the symbol set could be identified. The second booklet measured association value of the new symbols through a procedure in which symbols were matched with verbal definitions. Each new symbol was assigned a score based on its evaluation across the three tasks. This evaluation procedure succeeded in distinguishing the effectiveness of the symbols and in identifying classes of symbols that required more or less modification. For example, military unit symbols had poor transfer of training, higher potential for confusion, and lower association value and so require extensive modification, while standard alphanumeric symbols met the evaluation criteria and required little modification. Appendices to the report reproduce the contents of the two survey booklets and show the response distributions for the three tasks. This research report is clearly written and well organized. The study is not complex, and an audience having a basic understanding of experimental methods should be able to comprehend the report.

CONTENTS

FOREWORD

SECTION 1: INTRODUCTION

Background
    Army aviation tasks
    Map use in Army aviation
    Difficulties in map use
    The computer-generated topographic display
    Map display resolution problems

Map Symbol Design Requirements
    Transfer of training
    Symbol confusion
    Association value

Research Objectives

Organization of This Report

SECTION II: MAP SYMBOL DEVELOPMENT

Applicable Coding Techniques

Previous Research in Map Symbol Development

Symbol Development for the CGTD
    Symbol size
    Content
    Distinctiveness
    Similarity
    Numerosity

Evaluation of Candidate Symbol Effectiveness

SECTION III: STUDY ONE: TRANSFER OF TRAINING AND SYMBOL CONFUSION

Method
    Survey tasks
    Survey participants

Results
    Task one: transfer of training
    Task two: symbol confusion

SECTION IV: STUDY TWO: SYMBOL ASSOCIATION

Method
    Survey task
    Survey participants

Results
SECTION V: DISCUSSION
Transfer of training
Symbol Confusion
Association Value
SECTION VI: SUMMARY AND RECOMMENDATIONS
REFERENCES
APPENDIX 1: SURVEY BOOKLET FOR STUDY ONE
(Transfer of Training and Symbol Confusion Tasks)
APPENDIX 2: RESPONSE DISTRIBUTIONS FOR TRANSFER OF
TRAINING TASK
APPENDIX 3: RESPONSE DISTRIBUTIONS FOR SYMBOL
CONFUSION TASK
APPENDIX 4: SURVEY BOOKLET FOR STUDY TWO
(Symbol Association Study)
APPENDIX 5: RESPONSE DISTRIBUTIONS FOR SYMBOL
ASSOCIATION TASK

106 pp. 5 sections. Photographs, maps, tables, mathematical formulae, references, appendices.

155
Johnsson, Bengt
Andersson, Bertil

technical report

**The Human-Computer Interface in Commercial Systems:
Investigations of Dialogue Design Factors and Usability with
Alphanumeric Display Terminals**
1981

(report number LSST-58; Department of Electrical Engineering,
Linkoping University, Sweden; 1981)

This report explores considerations of cost versus efficiency when
computers in the commercial world are used by non-computer
specialists. To address this problem Johnsson and Andersson conducted
an extensive study incorporating both on-site investigation and
controlled experimentation.

The study consists of four parts: a literature survey, a questionnaire and
interview, controlled experimentation, and, finally, conclusions and
recommendations. The survey-interview portion of the study was
conducted with two purposes in mind: problem formation and
information dispersal. Among the questionnaire results obtained by the
authors were: the appropriate number of function keys, desired length of
response times, task specifications, and dialogue methods. Controlled
experimentation was conducted to determine the effects of syntax,
response time, sequence of information, user environment, and amount
of information per frame on the computer user's performance and
satisfaction. The results obtained from the experiments showed that:
form filling resulted in fewer mistakes; normal response time was
preferred; customer guidance produced fewer mistakes (although

computer guidance was faster); comfort was preferred over stress, especially when handling complex criteria; and a large amount of information per frame was generally preferred. Although written with some technical detail, this study will be of interest to anyone working in the design of interactive computer systems.

CONTENTS

PREFACE

PART I: INTRODUCTION AND BACKGROUND

1: Introduction

2: Dialogue Design

3: Experimental Research in Man-Computer Communication

PART II: QUESTIONNAIRE

1: Purpose

2: Method and Extent

3: Results
    3.1. System
    3.2. Machine
    3.3. Terminalists
    3.4. Man computer dialogue
    3.5. Miscellaneous

4: Summary of Results
    4.1. Facts about Swedish systems
    4.2. Identified problem areas

PART III: EXPERIMENTS

1: Introduction

2: Problem Description and Delimitation

3: Criteria and Dependent Variables

4: Definitions of Experimental Conditions
    4.1. Task
    4.2. Terminalists
    4.3. Customer
    4.4. Terminalist environment
    4.5. Customer environment
    4.6. Computer system

5: Definitions of Experimental Factors
    5.1. Syntax
    5.2. Computer system response time
    5.3. Sequence of information handling
    5.4. Terminalist environment
    5.5. Amount of information per frame

6: Experimental Design
    6.1. Plans
    6.2. Models

7: Experimental Procedure
    7.1. The Dialogue laboratory
    7.2. Activities
    7.3. Experimental methods
    7.4. Measurements

8: Evaluation Procedure
    8.1. General
    8.2. To measure, decide and compare attitudes
9: Results Concerning Experimental Conditions
    9.1. Terminalist
    9.2. Customer
    9.3. Computer system
10: Results Concerning Experimental Factors
    10.1. Related to terminalists
    10.2. Related to customers
11: Discussion
    11.1. Experimental conditions
    11.2. Experimental factors
PART IV: CONCLUSIONS AND FUTURE RESEARCH
1: Conclusions
    1.1. Background
    1.2. Questionnaire
    1.3. Experiments
2: Future Research
APPENDICES:
Appendix 1. "Task Sheets." Examples
Appendix 2. Display frame layouts
Appendix 3. Attitude Test Form. Example
REFERENCES

315 pp. 20 chapters in 4 parts. Figures, graphs, tables, references, appendices.

156
Jonassen, David H. (ed.)

collection

The Technology of Text: Principles for Structuring, Designing, and Displaying Text
Educational Technology Publications, 1982

Papers collected in response to a growing need for a more systematic application of research-supported principles, focusing on the effective presentation of written discourse.

Intended for a wide audience of educators, typographers, and designers, this volume is a comprehensive treatment covering not only the sequencing, structuring, designing, and laying-out of the printed page, but the electronic representation of written discourse as well. Chapters are arranged in four sections. The first is concerned with the basic structure of prose and how its arrangement, organization, and sequence can enhance textual meaning. Section two focuses on basic techniques for displaying or signaling the structure of text. The most significant material, presented in section three, deals with the "specific problem in constructing and displaying text electronically." These issues have broad applications as information transfer becomes increasingly computer-controlled and video display a widely accepted, effective, and efficient medium. A final section addresses individual differences in the perception of textual media. Though theoretically oriented, the textual display techniques presented here have many practical applications for a variety of professionals, including text users, editors, designers, product developers, and teachers. Contributors represent research from the disciplines of neuropsychology, perception, learning, memory, reading, and typography; a synthesis of these diverse topics provides guidelines for systematically designing text.

CONTENTS

Preface

Section One: Implicit Structures in Text

1. Introduction to section one: implicit structures in text
   David H. Jonassen
2. Analyzing and describing the structure of text
   Ann Jaffe Pace
3. Getting started: pattern notes and perspectives
   Alan Fields
4. Writing and evaluating textbooks: contributions from instructional theory
   I. Fulya Sari, Charles M. Reigeluth
5. Brain functions during learning: implications for text design
   James D. Hand

Section Two: Explicit Techniques for Structuring Text

6. Introduction to section two: explicit techniques for structuring text
   David H. Jonassen, Paul A. Kirschner
7. Text as diagram: using typography to improve access and understanding
   Robert Waller
8. Textual display techniques
   Philippe C. Duchastel
9. Designing instructional text
   James Hartley
10. Programmed instruction revisited
    David H. Jonassen
11. Structured outline representations for procedures or algorithms
    Paul F. Merrill
12. Advance organizers in text
    David H. Jonassen
13. Design principles for diagrams and charts
    William Winn, William Holliday
14. Affecting instructional textbooks through pictures
    Phillip J. Brody
15. A user-oriented approach to the design of tables and flowcharts
    Patricia Wright
16. Structured writing and text design
    Robert E. Horn
17. Printing: the next stage: discourse punctuation
    Richard Showstack

Section Three: Electronic Text
18. Introduction to section three: electronic text
    David H. Jonassen
19. Computer aids for writing text
    Ester U. Coke
20. Displaying text on microcomputers
    Paul F. Merrill
21. Display problems for teletext
    Linda Reynolds
Section Four: Individual Differences and Learning from Text
22. Individual differences and learning from text
    David H. Jonassen
Index

478 pp. 22 papers in 4 sections. Drawings, photographs, figures, charts, tables, general index, references, biographical data. ISBN 0-87778-182-6.

157
Judd, Deane B.
Wyszecki, Gunter

Color in Business, Science and Industry (3ed.)
John Wiley and Sons, 1975

(from the *Wiley Series in Pure and Applied Optics*, Stanley S. Ballard, series ed.)

The revised third edition of Judd and Wyszecki's classic text on color optics discusses how the eye works, lists the tools available to assist in color measurement, and shows how to select the best tool for a given color-measuring job.

This book includes: information on new techniques in color measurement; new standards for colorimetry (illuminants, artificial sources, reflectance factor, colorimetric observer, uniform color spacing, and degree of metamerism) as established by the International Commission on Illumination; and reports on research that has yielded new insights into the nature of color vision. New information on industrial color problems such as color formulation, color tolerance and acceptability, color rendering of light sources and colorimetry of fluorescent materials is also included. The book supplies the businessman and technologist with information which will reduce industrial waste by increasing production efficiency and sales. Over half of the book is devoted to such topics as spectrophotometers and colorimeters, color standards and color seals. The book concludes with a short chapter, "Physics and Psychophysics of Colorant Layers," covering gloss, opacity, Kubelka-Munk analysis, and colorant formulation. While many of the topics are treated mathematically, the authors' explanations are clear and numerous examples are presented which make the material interesting and easy to understand. The detailed table of contents makes it easy to locate information. All of the material is made relevant by discussions in the context of color problems encountered in business, science, and, especially, industry.

CONTENTS

INTRODUCTION

1: BASIC FACTS

The Eye
    Focusing elements
    Sensitive elements
    Eye pigments
    Interpretive elements
    Some open questions in the physiology of color vision

Fundamental Aspects of Color
    Chemical—pigments and dyes
    Physical—radiant energy and the spectrum
    Psychological—the customer's angle
    Psychophysical—how to predict what the average customer will see

Color Matching
    Addition of color stimuli
    Rapid succession of color stimuli
    Mixture of colorants

Color Deficiencies
    Classification of visual systems
    Causes of color blindness
    Types of color vision in the normal eye
    Tests of color blindness

Theories of Color Vision

2: TOOLS AND TECHNIQUES

Spectrophotometry
    Selecting a spectrophotometer

Fundamental Standards of Colorimetry
    Standard illuminants and sources
    Standard of reflectance factor
    Standard illuminating and viewing conditions
    CIE 1931 standard colorimetric observer
    CIE 1964 supplementary standard colorimetric observer
    Calculation of tristimulus values and chromaticity coordinates
    CIE supplementary standard observer versus CIE 1931 standard observer
    Color temperature and correlated color temperature
    Dominant wavelength and purity
    Metamerism

Colorimeters
    Visual colorimeters
    Photoelectric colorimeters

Colorimetry by Difference

Colorimetry of Fluorescent Materials

Reproduction of Pictures in Color

Color Standards
    Systematic sampling of the color solid
    Colorant-mixture systems
    Color-mixture systems
    Screen-plate printing color systems
    Color-appearance systems

Two-dimensional color scales
One-dimensional color scales
Nonsystematic and incomplete sampling of the color solid
Uniform Color Scales
Uniform lightness scale
Uniform chromaticness scales
Combined lightness and chromaticness scales
Color tolerances
Dark and Light Adaption—Chromatic Adaption
Color Rendering of Light Sources
Object-Color Perception in Complicated Scenes
Color Languages
Basic or psychological color terms
Psychophysical color terms
Colorant terms
Color names
Color Harmony
3: PHYSICS AND PSYCHOPHYSICS OF COLORANT LAYERS
Gloss
Fresnel reflection
Types of gloss
Connection between gloss and color
Opacity or Hiding Power
Kubelka-Munk Analysis
The exponential solution
The hyperbolic solution
Simple numerical analysis
Colorant Formulation
Identification of colorants
Color-patch predictions
APPENDIX
REFERENCES
AUTHOR INDEX
SUBJECT INDEX

553 pp. 3 parts. Drawings, figures, charts, graphs, tables, mathematical formulae, algorithms, author index, subject index, references, glossary, appendix. ISBN 0-471-45212-2.

158
Julesz, Bela

Foundations of Cyclopean Perception
University of Chicago Press, 1971

Traces a decade of psychological research on visual perception with emphasis on the author's own findings about Cyclopean perception obtained by use of computer-generated visual stimuli.

This work examines research by the author and others in the field of visual perception. Because most experiments are demonstrated, the visualization of complex surfaces is presented for psychologists, natural scientists, mathematicians, and designers. The relatively new computer-produced random-dot correlogram (purified of all monocular depth and familiarity cues) is the technique that underlies this stereopsis research and the resulting advances in monocular and binocular perception. The majority of reported experiments are accompanied by the actual correlogram, collected in a high quality, color appendix of analgraphs (effects are seen when the reader uses the special glasses provided with this volume). The author uses the term Cyclopean "to denote a *central* processing stage inside the brain having a concrete neuroanatomical existence." The basic aspect of Cyclopean perception is the tracing of the information flow in the visual system. This is accomplished by studying perceptual output as a function of stimuli input (correlograms). Additional experiments in visual perception, including optical illusions, simultaneous contrast phenomena, and aftereffects of movement and depth, further demonstrate the separation of retina processes from cerebral ones. The main findings of Cyclopean perception are reviewed within the context of neuroanatomical and neurophysiological evidence. The author considers his perceptual methodology an active discipline and outlines many clinical applications. Julesz is head of the sensory and perceptual processes department of Bell Telephone Labs.

CONTENTS

Preface

1: Introduction

2: Foundations of Cyclopean Perception
    2.1. Human visual perception and the "Cyclopean mind"
    2.2. Separation of peripheral and central processes
    2.3. Two classes of Cyclopean stimulation
    2.4. Monocular, binocular, and Cyclopean stimulation
    2.5. Classical versus Cyclopean perception: three outcomes
    2.6. Outcome 1: Cyclopean phenomenon identical to classical phenomenon
    2.7. Outcome 2: Only classical phenomenon exists
    2.8. Outcome 3: Only Cyclopean phenomenon exists
    2.9. Some limitations of Cyclopean techniques
    2.10. An example of studying brightness-contrast with Cyclopean techniques
    2.11. Auditory versus visual Cyclopean stimulation

3: Cyclopean Stimulation and Physiological Psychology
    3.1. Perception as a hierarchy of pattern matchings
    3.2. Perception versus scrutiny
    3.3. Hierarchy of neural feature extraction in visual perception
    3.4. Psychological studies of feature extraction
    3.5. Further classes of Cyclopean stimulation based on Emmert's Law and color phenomena
    3.6. Localization of vernier acuity perception
    3.7. Localization of stroboscopic movement perception
    3.8. Perception of local and global levels
    3.9. Monocular local versus binocular global information
    3.10. Monocular global versus binocular local information

4: Figure and Ground
    4.1. The first questions of the "twenty questions" game
    4.2. The perception of moving clusters
    4.3. Perception of connected clusters under rigid transformations
    4.4. Clusters in visual texture discrimination
    4.5. Perception of clusters having the same binocular disparity
    4.6. Perception into figure and ground
    4.7. Perception of symmetries
    4.8. Perceptual operators of two kinds
    4.9. Perception and selective attention: parallel versus serial
    4.10. Ambiguous figure ground reversal of Cyclopean stimuli

5: Binocular Depth Perception
    5.1. Random-dot stereograms and binocular depth perception
    5.2. Some anatomical, physiological, and psychological facts about binocular depth perception
    5.3. Local versus global stereopsis
    5.4. Textures in visual perception
    5.5. Complex versus simple stereograms
    5.6. Removal of monocular depth cues
    5.7. A new paradigm: stereopsis and ambiguities
    5.8. Hysteresis in binocular depth perception
    5.9. The role of convergence
    5.10. Dynamic phenomena in stereopsis

6: A Holistic Model
    6.1. Ambiguous surfaces in three-dimensions
    6.2. Ambiguously perceivable random-dot stereograms
    6.3. Perception time of stereopsis
    6.4. Effect of increased disparity
    6.5. A model of binocular depth perception
    6.6. Extension of the model to perceptual learning
    6.7. Implications of the model for the neurophysiology of binocular fusion and rivalry

7: Classical and Cyclopean Procedure
    7.1. Cyclopean phenomena revisited
    7.2. Localization of optical illusions
    7.3. "Cyclopean depth" sensation
    7.4. Localization of eidetic memory
    7.5. Cyclopean movement detectors
    7.6. Pulfrich phenomenon without monocular cues
    7.7. Cyclopean contours and closure phenomena
    7.8. Perception of undetermined areas
    7.9. Cyclopean aftereffects

8: Miscellaneous Uses of Cyclopean Methods
    8.1. Objective tests for stereopsis
    8.2. Clinical uses of random-dot stereograms
    8.3. Neurophysiological probing during Cyclopean stimulation
    8.4. Toward the automation of binocular depth perception
    8.5. Three-dimensional reconstruction from two-dimensional brightness distribution
    8.6. How to set up Cyclopean research facilities

9: Invariance and Form Recognition
    9.1. Problems of semantics
    9.2. Binocular and monocular perceptual invariances
    9.3. Klein's Erlanger program and perception
    9.4. Cooperative phenomena and perceptual constancies
    9.5. Toward a psychophysics of form
10: Cyclopean Perception in Perspective
    10.1. Other psychoanatomical techniques
    10.2. Unsolved problems of Cyclopean research
    10.3. The role of Cyclopean perception in psychology
    Appendix: Some comments on the viewing of the anaglyphs and
    other practical matters
    Anaglyphs
    References
    Name index
    Subject index

406 pp. 10 chapters. Drawings, photographs, figures, tables, mathematical formulae, models, author index, subject index, references, appendix, anaglyphs. ISBN 0-226-41527-9.

159
Kantowitz, Barry H.
Sorkin, Robert D.

Human Factors: Understanding People-System Relationships
John Wiley and Sons, 1983

Designed as a one-semester, introductory text for college seniors and first year graduate students interested in the human factors discipline, the emphasis is on concepts enabling students to learn how human factors professionals solve problems.

Many theoretical models are presented but every chapter highlights applications to real-world events. Although not a handbook, much detail is presented in the appendices at the ends of chapters. Each chapter begins with examples of familiar events (from taking showers to airplane crashes) in which human factors are critical and ends with a concise summary of material covered in the chapter. The importance of optimizing balance between economic goals and human welfare is discussed throughout the text. The twenty chapters of text are divided into five major sections. The introductory section covers systems and people, error, and reliability. The Human Capabilities section includes: hearing and signal detection theory, vision, psychomotor skill, and human information processing. Section two concludes with an overview of the concerns of the remaining three sections. Human-Machine Interfaces discusses: visual displays, auditory and tactile displays, speech communication, controls and tools, and data entry. In Human-Machine System Properties the areas covered are: feedback and control, human factors in computer programming, decision making with applications to inspection and maintainability, and workplace design. The last section, Environment, deals with: noise, microenvironments, macroenvironments, environmental stressors, and legal aspects of human factors. The text is well written with boldfaced subheadings in the margin to make locating information easy.

CONTENTS

Preface

PART ONE: INTRODUCTION

Chapter 1: Systems and People
    Person-machine systems
    Models
    Engineering economics
Summary
Appendix

Chapter 2: Error and Reliability
    Human error
    Error, codes, and information theory
    Reliability
Summary
Appendix

PART TWO: HUMAN CAPABILITIES

Chapter 3: Hearing and Signal Detection Theory
    Sound waves and hearing
    Signal detection theory
Summary
Appendix

Chapter 4: Vision
    The visual stimulus
    Structure of the visual system
    Sensitivity of the eye
    Target detection and identification
    Color
    Size and distance perception
Summary
Appendix

Chapter 5: Psychomotor Skills
    Reaction time
    Information theory and reaction time
    Motor control
Summary
Appendix

Chapter 6: Human Information Processing
    The information-processing approach
    Memory
    Attention
Summary

PART THREE: HUMAN-MACHINE INTERFACES

Chapter 7: Visual Displays
    J.R. Buck
    Communications and displays
    Visual displays: distinctions, space, and types
    Information integration and aiding

Summary

Chapter 8: Auditory and Tactile Displays
   Auditory displays
   Tactile displays

Summary

Chapter 9: Speech Communication
   Speech production and perception
   Channel intelligibility and quality
   Speech technology

Summary

Chapter 10: Controls and Tools
   Types of control
   Control features
   Control design
   Control-display relationships
   Tools

Summary

Chapter 11: Data Entry
   H.E. Dunsmore
   Introduction
   Data entry device features
   Text editors

Summary

PART FOUR: HUMAN-MACHINE SYSTEM PRIORITIES

Chapter 12: Feedback and Control
   B.H. Kantowitz, J.R. Buck
   The feedback model
   Practical control systems
   Behavioral control theory
   Task management and supervisory control

Summary

Chapter 13: Human Factors in Computer Programming
   H.E. Dunsmore
   Experimental problems
   Programming techniques
   Programming languages

Summary

Chapter 14: Decision Making with Applications to Inspection and
Maintainability
   J.R. Buck, B.H. Kantowitz
   Decision making
   Some necessary mathematics
   Human decision making
   Decision making in inspection
   Troubleshooting and maintainability

Summary

Chapter 15: Workspace Design
   Engineering anthropometry
   Design layout
   Design applications

Summary

Appendix

PART FIVE: ENVIRONMENT

Chapter 16: Noise
    Physical description of noise
    Noise-induced hearing loss
    Effects of noise on performance
    Measurement of environmental noise

Summary

Chapter 17: Microenvironments
    Personal space
    Room design
    Illumination

Summary

Chapter 18: Macroenvironments
    Transportation
    Cities

Summary

Chapter 19: Environmental Stressors
    Stress
    Temperature
    Stressors
    Stress and work
    Aftereffects

Summary

Chapter 20: Legal Aspects of Human Factors
    Product liability
    Occupational Safety and Health Act
    Equal employment opportunity

Summary

References

Author Index

Subject Index

699 pp. 20 chapters in 5 parts. Photographs, figures, charts, graphs, tables, mathematical formulae, models, author index, subject index, references, appendices. ISBN 0-471-09594-X.

Kazan, Benjamin

overview

Advances in Image Pickup and Display
Academic Press, 1974-83

Issued in series between 1974 and 1983, these six volumes review the technical status of image pickup and display devices. Benjamin Kazan, editor for the series, notes that the field of electronic imaging "is characterized by an unusual diversity of devices, technologies and applications." The great variety of industrial, military, research, and commercial applications for imaging techniques will continue to create an atmosphere in which technical advance will be rapid. Individual volumes are devoted to a particular type of device and its associated technology and applications. The reviews, by experts in their fields, were written specifically for this series. Considering the speed with which the field is advancing, the earlier volumes in this series are dated, but will continue to be useful basic references.

160
Kazan, Benjamin
(ed.)

collection

Advances in Image Pickup and Display, Volume 1
Academic Press, 1974

A synthesis of information from the diverse disciplines, both pure and applied, which have contributed to the fast-growing field of imaging technology.

The first paper reviews developments in channel electron multiplication, particularly the use of finely microchanneled tubes in place of one photomultiplier tube. Schlagen explains spatial information retention, gain exploitation, and covers performance characteristics and manufacturing techniques of the channel plates themselves. Fisher and Martinelli's paper handles the more experimental field of tubes using negative electron affinity (NEA). Besides comparing NEA with conventional emitters, the authors explain the surface properties of semi-conductors necessary to create the dipole layer that allows electrons to escape easily, emphasizing work on NEA photocathodes and TSE (transmission secondary emission) dynodes, including unpublished results by the authors. NEA transmitters used for low-light applications such as IR are also discussed here. In the the third paper Hutter covers electron optics, or "the state of the art of deflection." For early color systems designers, defocusing and distortion created difficulties in beam convergence and color purity. The advent of computers fast enough to carry out the calculations required by existing electron optics theories made possible more rigorous design of beam deflection systems. He also discusses the behavioral requirements and characteristics of various beam structures, including electrostatic yokes and special problems of multiple beam (color TV), orthogonal beam and double deflection (electron microscope) systems. The final paper deals with light-valve devices, which can modulate high intensity or coherent light in systems such as very large screen TV projection, including a discussion of the "Pockels effect." The French group presenting this paper have been in the forefront of exploiting this effect for large-screen images, storage, differentiation and subtraction of images as well as conversion of incoherent to coherent light in image-processing applications. The paper discusses crystals appropriate for use in Pockels effect devices, along with electron beam and optically-addressed devices.

CONTENTS

List of Contributors

Preface

Dedication

Image Tubes with Channel Electron Multiplication
  P. Schagen
  I. Introduction
  II. The principle of channel electron multiplication
  III. The performance characteristics of channel plates
  IV. Channel plate technology
  V. The application of channel electron multiplication to image conversion
  VI. The application of channel electron multiplication to image intensification
  VII. Other applications of channel image intensification
  References

Negative Electron Affinity Materials for Imaging Devices
  Dennis G. Fisher, Ramon U. Martinelli
  I. Introduction
  II. Comparison between NEA and conventional emitters
  III. NEA surface properties
  IV. NEA photocathodes
  V. Transmission Secondary Emission (TSE) dynodes
  VI. NEA image devices
  VII. Summary
  References

The Deflection of Electron Beams
  Rudolf G.E. Hutter
  I. Introduction
  II. Basic electrostatic and magnetostatic deflection systems
  III. Methods for increasing deflection sensitivity and/or reducing deflection power requirements
  IV. Systems for high-frequency deflection
  V. Deflection defocusing and corrective measures
  VI. Electrostatic deflection yokes
  VII. Special deflection problems
  VIII. Concluding remarks
  References
  General bibliography

Pockels-Effect Imaging Devices and Their Applications
  G. Marie, J. Donjon, J.-P. Hazan
  I. Introduction
  II. Single crystals usable in Pockels-effect imaging devices
  III. Electron-beam-addressed devices
  written in cooperation with R. LePape and B. Monod
  IV. Optically addressed devices
  written in cooperation with M. Grenot, S.A. Massiot-Philips, and J. Pergrale
  V. Large screen display applications
  VI. Image-processing applications in noncoherent light
  part of this section written in cooperation with F. Dumont

VII. Image and data processing applications in coherent light
References
Subject Index

308 pp. 4 papers. Photographs, figures, graphs, tables, mathematical formulae, abstract formalisms, models, subject index, references. ISBN 0-12-022101-2.

161
Kazan, Benjamin (ed.)

collection

Advances in Image Pickup and Display, Volume 2
Academic Press, 1975

Covers several technologies that began to attract serious research interest in the 1970s.

The idea of a laser beam TV system is an obvious one; laser systems offer the high resolution and spectral purity necessary for large screen displays. In the first paper suitable laser types are discussed, along with the light modulation and beam deflection components of the system. The second paper covers thin-film doped ceramics, dubbed "ferpics" and "cerampics," depending upon whether they operate in the birefringence or scattering mode. The properties of the photoconductive layers themselves are considered, along with the possibilities for use in alphanumeric display. The single pickup tube television camera is the subject of the final paper. Offering reduced cost and bulk and eliminating the problem of beam convergence, the singe tube camera still presents problems in color encoding. Time division and space division (vertical stripe) multiplexing are discussed as color encoding systems, along with carrier system options.

CONTENTS
Preface
Contents of Volume I
Laser Displays
  Manabu Yamamoto, Teiichi Taneda
  I. Introduction
  II. Historical summary
  III. Description of system
  IV. Preliminary considerations on resolution
  V. Coherent light sources
  VI. Light modulation
  VII. Beam deflection
  VIII. An 1125-scanning-line laser color-TV display
  IX. Applications of scanned beam techniques
  X. Concluding remarks
  Appendix: Acoustooptic imaging with a pulsed laser
  References
Display Applications of PLZT Ceramics
  J.R. Maldonado, D.B. Fraser, A.H. Meitzler
  I. Introduction
  II. Birefringence-mode, strain-biased, image storage and display devices—ferpics
  III. Scattering-mode image storage and display devices—cerampics

IV. Summary of the performance of display devices

V. Alphanumeric display devices

VI. Transparent conductive and photoconductive films for ceramic image storage and display devices

VII. Concluding remarks

References

Striped Color Encoded Single Tube Color Television Camera Systems
J.J. Brandinger, G.L. Fredendall, D.H. Pritchard

I. Introduction—color encoding background

II. Frequency division—amplitude modulation strip filter encoding systems

III. Index systems—spatial frequency encoding

IV. Summary

Appendix I. Systems evaluation considerations

Appendix II. 1-H delay comb filter fundamentals

Appendix III. Spectral characteristics of stripe filters

References

Subject Index

253 pp. 3 papers. Drawings, photographs, figures, charts, graphs, tables, mathematical formulae, models, subject index, references. ISBN 0-12-022102-0.

162
Kazan, Benjamin
(ed.)

collection

Advances in Image Pickup and Display, Volume 3
Academic Press, 1977

Covers imaging devices which sparked new research interest because they applied new concepts to previously insoluble problems.

Pyroelectric materials, which polarize spontaneously upon heating, are being applied to infrared detection and medical thermographic systems. In this volume the first article discusses the advantages of the pyroelectric vidicon, especially the elimination of bulky and expensive cooling systems. The growing of pyroelectric crystals, construction and performance of pyroelectric vidicon tubes, and applications such as forest fire mapping are included. Gas-discharge panels, though conceived of in the 1920s, required prohibitively complex driver systems to fire the gas cells. The Burroughs SELF-SCAN® panel, described in the second paper, circumvented this problem by priming display cells to reduce voltage requirements and the number of driver stages. Primarily an alphanumeric display device, the SELF-SCAN® panel represents "the application of an ingenious idea to a very old and well-known technology." The final and most extensive paper summarizes 1970s state-of-the-art solid-state imagery. The authors, from naval research laboratories, include a thorough, theoretical treatment of the charge-coupled concept, which vastly improved image quality and eliminated the need for X-Y addressed arrays. The review contrasts design considerations of surface channel and buried channel devices, responsivity of both CCD and CID devices, and surveys promising military and commercial applications for color cameras and surveillance systems.

CONTENTS

Preface

Contents of Previous Volumes

Theory and Performance Characteristics of Pyroelectric Imaging Tubes
  B. Singer
  I. Introduction
  II. Pyroelectric materials and simple detectors
  III. Pyroelectric vidicon
  IV. Performance of pyroelectric vidicons
  V. Methods of obtaining improved performance
  VI. Applications
  VII. Conclusion
  Appendix
  References

Gas Discharge Panels with Internal Line Sequencing (SELF-SCAN® Displays)
  R. Cola, J. Gaur, G. Holz, J. Ogle, J. Siegel, A. Somlyody
  I. Historical perspective
  II. Basic properties of gas discharge cells
  III. Basic SELF-SCAN® display principles
  IV. Panel design and processing
  V. Typical characteristics
  VI. Drive circuitry
  VII. Displays with increased character capacity
  VIII. Continuous tone imaging
  IX. Phosphors in SELF-SCAN® displays
  X. Concluding remarks
  References

Imaging Arrays Using the Charge-Coupled Concept
  D.F. Barbe, S.B. Campana
  I. Introduction
  II. Device theory and design
  III. Two-dimensional self-scanned arrays
  IV. Mechanically scanned arrays
  V. Applications
  VI. Summary and conclusions
  References

Subject Index

302 pp. 3 papers. Drawings, photographs, figures, graphs, tables, mathematical formulae, abstract formalisms, subject index, references. ISBN 0-12-022103-9.

163
Kazan, Benjamin
(ed.)

collection

Advances in Image Pickup and Display, Volume 4
Academic Press, 1981

This fourth volume in Kazan's series updates research on liquid crystal
technology, reviews the somewhat neglected field of cathodochromics,
and introduces new methods of bilevel digital display for computer
output.

Liquid crystals, common in watch and calculator displays, are valued
for their low power requirements and viewability under ambient light.
But the search for the ultimate tiny TV inevitably has led to adapting
liquid crystals to more complex graphic and television images. The first
paper here, from Hitachi Labs in Japan, describes techniques for
overcoming the "crosstalk voltages" that reduce image contrast in
conventional X-Y addressing. The paper concentrates on techniques for
matrix addressing, including field-effect transistor (FET) switching.
Multicolor liquid crystal displays and other future possibilities are
considered. Cathodochromic materials, which turn opaque
when struck by an electron beam, were incorporated into radar screens
during World War II but have since fallen into disuse except for certain
storage oscilloscope applications. Primarily of historic interest, this
paper from RCA thoroughly covers the physical properties underlying
cathodochromic phenomena and the chemical characteristics of chromic
materials, particularly halides. It also outlines the construction of
various tube types. Future applications especially suitable for
cathodochromics such as radar, narrow-bandwidth image transmission
systems, and buffer storage are considered. Bilevel digital display, the
subject of the final paper (from Bell Labs), is the simplest way to handle
on-off computer output and still produce apparent gray scale
(pseudogray) in the resultant image. Several algorithms are discussed
here for achieving gray scale tones using a fixed size display site, along
with algorithms for brightness and contrast control and for coding and
elimination of data redundancy. A section on bilevel image system
design is included; the author's purpose is the improvement of
computer data output as a "window into electronic information banks"
for the nonprofessional user.

CONTENTS
Preface
Contents of previous volumes
Liquid-Crystal Matrix Displays
Eiji Kaneko
I. Introduction
II. Operating principles and characteristics of liquid-crystal devices
III. Amplitude-selective *X-Y* addressed liquid-crystal matrix
displays
IV. Matrix displays using special addressing techniques
V. Nonlinear elements for improved addressing of matrix displays
VI. Field-effect transistor (FET) switching elements for matrix
addressing
VII. Multicolor liquid-crystal displays
VIII. Concluding remarks

References

Cathodochromics: Their Properties and Uses in Display Systems
  Brian W. Faughnan, Philip M. Heyman, Istvan Gorog, Igal Shidlovsky
  I. Introduction
  II. Physical aspects of cathodochromic materials
  III. Preparation and chemical properties of cathodochromic sodalite
  IV. Detailed properties of cathodochromic materials
  V. Cathodochromic tubes
  VI. Cathodochromic systems
  VII. Conclusions
  References

Processing Images for Bilevel Digital Displays
  C.N. Judice, R.D. Slusky
  I. Introduction
  II. Algorithms
  III. Modifications of basic algorithms
  IV. Bilevel image representation and data reduction
  V. Animation of pseudogray scale images
  VI. Bilevel imaging system design
  VII. Concluding remarks
  References
  Index

237 pp. 3 papers. Drawings, photographs, figures, graphs, tables, mathematical formulae, algorithms, general index, references. ISBN 0-12-022104-7.

164
Kazan, Benjamin (ed.)

collection

Advances in Image Pickup and Display, Volume 5
Academic Press, 1982

Covers several techniques developed for information display, with emphasis on electroluminescent properties of materials.

The electronic printer is surveyed in the first article, with a theoretical description of the impact printer. Electrostatic, ink-jet, and laser-scanning printers are included. The second article, which discusses ion-insertion electrochromic displays, contains a thorough discussion of the properties of suitable materials, particularly iridium oxide and tungsten trioxide. Although researchers hope that ECDs will overcome some of the difficulties of LCDs, such as limited viewing angle, this technology is still highly experimental. This paper also discusses fabrication of the films and the problems inherent in addressing displays of this type. A paper from IBM research labs on electroluminescent films also concentrates on the physical properties of the phosphor materials. Of particular interest is the memory effect or hysteresis, which allows maintenance of a high degree of brightness. While still highly experimental, EL technology holds promise for high-resolution flat panel displays, due to the high voltage threshold and simpler addressing. A discussion of film preparation is included. Vacuum fluorescent displays (VFDs), with their bright blue-green display, have gained acceptance in the market as character display devices. The final article discusses developments and applications, concentrating on phosphors used, construction of the cathode elements, manufacture of baseplates and VFD films, and address drivers. A thorough overview of a familiar technology.

CONTENTS

Preface

Contents of Previous Volumes

A Survey of Electronic Printing Technologies
   Ulf Rothgordt
   I. Introduction
   II. Mechanical printers
   III. Nonimpact printers
   IV. Concluding remarks
   References

Ion-Insertion Electrochromic Displays
   G. Beni, J.L. Shay
   I. Introduction
   II. Tungsten trioxide
   III. Li^+ and Na^+ insertion in WO_3
   IV. Solid phosphotungstic acid
   V. Anodic iridium oxide films
   VI. Sputtered iridium oxide films
   VII. Matrix addressing
   VIII. Organic ion-insertion electrochromics
   IX. Conclusion
   References

Physical Phenomena in ac Thin-Film Electroluminescent Phosphors
   A. Onton, V. Marrello
   I. Introduction
   II. Thin-film materials
   III. Key physical phenomena
   IV. Hysteresis phenomena
   V. Probe layer measurements of EL excitation and the memory effect
   VI. Display attributes
   VII. Conclusions
   References

Vacuum Fluorescent Displays
   T. Nakamura, K. Kiyozumi, S. Mito
   I. Background and history
   II. Construction of VFDs and their operating principle
   III. Phosphors for low-energy electrons
   IV. Cathode element
   V. Manufacturing processes for VFDs
   VI. Driving methods
   VII. Some examples of VFDs and their characteristics
   VIII. Brief reviews of different types of flat-panel displays
   IX. Conclusions

References

Index

288 pp. 4 papers. Drawings, photographs, figures, graphs, tables, mathematical formulae, models, general index, references. ISBN 0-12-022105-5.

165

Kazan, Benjamin (ed.)

collection

Advances in Image Pickup and Display, Volume 6
Academic Press, 1983

Updates of previous topics, primarily relating to consumer TV applications.

The first paper, from Mitsubishi, updates consumer color TV, which, although constantly refined because of competitive market pressures, has experienced no major breakthroughs. The author explains the physical principles and engineering limitations behind improvements in brightness, contrast, focus, and reliability. While emphasizing shadow-mask tubes for industrial (CRT) and consumer applications, the author includes developments in deflection yokes, in-line gun systems, smaller tube necks, and fine-pitch shadow-mask tubes. This paper provides an overview of the industry from the Japanese point-of-view. The Burroughs SELF-SCAN® panel for alphanumeric display was thoroughly treated in Volume 3; this volume includes a paper from NHK (Nippon Hoso Kyokai) Research Labs describing efforts coordinated by the Japanese Broadcasting Company to produce a gas-discharge panel with resolution sharp enough for large-screen television. Studies of filling gases, phosphors, and cell designs, aimed at producing adequate gray-scale for television, are included. Two experimental designs are detailed, a planar-positive column (PPC) panel and a thin-center-sheet (TCS) panel. The TCS is employed in the largest flat color TV panel to date. The last paper updates the previous review of solid-state imaging. Japanese firms in particular have concentrated on developing a single-chip color camera. Significant development areas include refinement of the old X-Y address system and development of a new "virtual-phase" CCD system. A hybrid CCD scanner combines silicon with a photoconductive overlay, reducing blooming and spurious signals. Performance characteristics of various sensors, and specialized scientific applications, particularly in astronomy, are included.

CONTENTS

Preface

Contents of Previous Volumes

Recent Advances in Color Picture Tubes
Yutaka Takano
I. Introduction
II. Shadow-mask tubes for consumer applications
III. Shadow-mask tubes for industrial and special applications
IV. Miscellaneous color picture tubes

V. Future trends and conclusions
References

Gas-Discharge Panels for Displaying Color Television Images
Display Devices Research Group of NHK
I. Introduction
II. Basic studies associated with the development of gas-discharge panels
III. Ten-inch planar positive-column panel and TV display system
IV. Sixteen-inch color TV panel with two-line-at-a-time driving and associated display system
V. Conclusions
References

Image Sensors for Television and Related Applications
Paul K. Weimer, A. Danforth Cope
I. Introduction
II. Photosensitive elements for solid-state scanning
III. Solid-state sensors employing X-Y address buses for scanning
IV. Solid-state sensors based on internal charge transfer
V. Nonsilicon sensors for visible light imagers
VI. Performance characteristics of solid-state sensors
VII. Image sensors for particular applications
VIII. Alternative approaches to silicon imagers
IX. Conclusions
References

Index

261 pp. 3 papers. Drawings, photographs, figures, charts, graphs, tables, mathematical formulae, models, general index, references. ISBN 0-12-022106-3.

166
Keates, J.S.

Cartographic Design and Production
John Wiley and Sons, 1973

A textbook of cartography focused on graphical and technical aspects of making maps. Collection of data and metrical aspects of cartography are excluded from the book.

The author discusses principles and applications of cartography, stresses the importance of understanding the basic principles, and emphasizes the importance of not confusing principles and applications. He believes that cartography should be understood as an integrated, consistent whole, not as a series of unrelated techniques. Division of cartography into topographic and thematic categories is also viewed as being counterproductive. The text has three parts. Part one deals with the graphical aspects of cartography, particularly how maps are designed to communicate information effectively and how this can and should be accomplished within the framework of traditional graphic representations. Part two covers the technology of map making, a topic the author considers to be of increasing importance and one which seldom receives the kind of independent consideration provided in this text. Part three, devoted to applications, focuses on map production. The author stresses the use of the same map producing principles for a variety of forms of maps. This useful and thorough textbook is designed for use by students of cartography, cartographers, and others with a serious interest in cartography. Many helpful figures contribute to the reader's comprehension of the ideas and techniques presented. The approach to cartography taken by the author reflects a general approach to topographic science developed at the University of Glasgow, where he is a senior lecturer in the Department of Geography.

CONTENTS

Preface

PART ONE: THE GRAPHICAL BASIS OF CARTOGRAPHY

Chapter One: Vision and Perception
Visual perception
Vision
Light
Colour characteristics and description
Graphic symbols and perceptual limitations

Chapter Two: Cartographic Symbols
Symbol types
Graphic variables
Form, dimension, and colour
Texture
Symbols and representation
Topographic maps
Representation and locational information
Classification and generalisation
The practice of generalisation

Chapter Three: Map Design
General design problems
Principles of cartographic design
Design of map symbols

Chapter Four: The Representation of Relief
Elevation
Contours
Hypsometric colours
Slope
Hachures
Shading
Combined systems

Chapter Five: The Representation of Physical Features
Hydrography
Coastline
Surface characteristics
Surface composition
Ice and permanent snow
Vegetation

Chapter Six: The Representation of Artificial Features
Point, line, and area symbols
International boundaries
Boundaries in rivers

Chapter Seven: Special-Purpose and Special-Subject Maps
    Point, line, and area symbols
    Lines of constant value
    Bounding lines and areas
    Special subjects and base maps

Chapter Eight: The Representation of Place Names
    Place names
    Place names within a country
    Foreign names
    Standardisation of place names

PART TWO: THE TECHNICAL BASIS OF CARTOGRAPHY

Chapter Nine: The Physical Structure of the Graphic Image
    Definitions
    Chromatic and achromatic images
    Continuous-tone, half-tone, and tint
    Image form and position
    Image-forming systems
    Deposition, removal and transformation
    Creation, duplication, combination, and modification
    Selection and separation
    Colour
    Multiplication

Chapter Ten: Base Materials
    Stability, transparency, receptivity
    Opaque and translucent materials
    Plastics

Chapter Eleven: Process Photography
    The photographic process
    Process camera
    Contact copying
    Sources of illumination
    Photographic emulsion
    Sensitometry
    Line, continuous-tone, and half-tone
    Half-tone and half-tone tint
    Half-tone screens
    Colour reproduction and colour correction
    Photographic image modification
    Unsharp masking
    Electronic scanning
    Tint screens
    Reversal of image form
    Combination
    Miniaturisation

Chapter Twelve: Non-Photographic Systems
    Ferric salts processes
    Dichromated colloids
    Diazo compounds
    Other dye images
    Photopolymerisation
    Infrared and thermographic systems
    Electrostatic processes

Chapter Thirteen: Multiple Reproduction Processes
> Intaglio, relief and planographic processes
> Offset photolithography
> Printing plates for offset lithography
> Letterpress
> Gravure and collotype

Chapter Fourteen: Printing Paper and Ink
> Paper
> Base materials
> Manufacture
> Characteristics
> Sizes
> Ink
> Pigments
> Drying methods
> Ink and colour reproduction

Chapter Fifteen: Proofing Processes
> Proofing systems
> Photomechanical processes
> Electrostatic proofing
> Ink transfer
> Colour diazo
> Offset-litho proof presses

Chapter Sixteen: Automation of Image Formation
> Automation and cartography
> Scanning
> Line plotting
> Plotting machines
> Formation of line images
> Optical exposure devices
> Point symbols
> Lineprinter

PART THREE: MAP PRODUCTION

Chapter Seventeen: Production Planning
> Technical considerations
> Quality, durability, convenience
> Technical factors in production
> Register
> Checking
> Sequence of operations
> Organisation of the map space
> Single sheets
> Maps in books and atlases
> Specification

Chapter Eighteen: Compilation
> Types of compilation
> Derived maps and basic maps
> Sources of information
> Evaluation of source material
> Construction of the map framework
> Changing scale
> Compilation procedure

Name arrangement
Chapter Nineteen: Automation of Map Compilation
Data acquisition
Digital data base
Digitising
Image-following methods
Cartographic digitisers
Scanning
Compilation procedures and problems
Interactive control
Interpolation
Chapter Twenty: The Line Image
Positive line images
Point and quantitative symbols
Negative line images
Scribing
Line patterns
Chapter Twenty-One: Lettering
Lettering methods
Type
Type characteristics
The use of type on maps
Production of type image
Photo-lettering
Type stick-up
Automatically-controlled lettering
Chapter Twenty-Two: Tint and Tone
Tint
Masks
Tint construction
Tint selection and control
Tone
Drawing for hill shading
Working procedures
Highlights
Chapter Twenty-Three: Organisation of Production
Flow diagram
Terminology
Production procedures
Work schedule
Estimating
Output and work load
Cost control
Chapter Twenty-Four: Revision
Types of revision
Revision information
Revision policy
Technical execution of revision
References
Index

240 pp. 24 chapters in 3 parts. Drawings, photographs, figures, graphs, tables, general index, references. ISBN 0-470-46235-3. (ISBN 0-470-15106-4)

167
Kim, Scott

Inversions: A Catalog of Calligraphic Cartwheels
BYTE Books, 1981

Illustrates and discusses inversions, word-forms which are crafted to be read in more than one direction, often incorporating an element of wit.

Many of the words in this book were "meant to be seen, not read." They illustrate the characteristics of symmetry or inversion. Some "read the same upside down, some read the same in a mirror, some repeat off to infinity." Artistic, often brilliant, inversions occupy roughly two-thirds of the book. The remaining third explores perceptual and philosophical issues related to symmetry, vision, and letter forms. Kim's fascination with inversions stems from his belief that "working within the limits of pure symmetry is an excellent means to new discoveries." He suggests that the "sleights of mind" that allow inversions to work can give clues about the brain's strategies of perception. Drawing upon examples used in the book, Kim illustrates some of the procedures used to create inversions. His guidelines for designing inversions could serve as a creative procedure for all design problems. Short discussions of symmetry in music, wordplay, and art are also included. An introduction by Douglas Hofstadter provides illuminating anecdotal material on both the author and the subject. This book will appeal to a wide audience, but those concerned with artificial intelligence would be particularly interested in the insight offered on perception and pattern recognition, and designers of graphic displays will find the chapter on processes to be informative and applicable.

CONTENTS
> Foreword
>> *Douglas Hofstadter*
> Introduction, Acknowledgements

Images
> Words—short
> Words—describing symmetries
> Words—long
> Variations—on *Gödel, Escher, Bach*
> Variations—on calligraphic themes
> Names—contemporary
> Names—historical
> Names—personal

Text
> Background—symmetry
> Background—vision
> Background—letterforms
> Experiences—processes
> Experiences—examples

Associations—music
Associations—wordplay
Associations—art
List of images, Bibliography
Backword

125 pp. 2 parts. Figures, general index, bibliography. (ISBN 0-07-034546-5)

168
King, Jean C.   **The Designer's Guide to Text Type**
Esposito, Tony   Van Nostrand Reinhold, 1980

reference

This guide for designers presents large text samples of fifty-one frequently used typefaces, in 6 through 12 point and in 14 point. Handsomely produced, the volume complements the numerous works available which present display typefaces, but which seldom give leaded showings of the text typefaces.

CONTENTS
Introduction
Facts about the VIP
Copyfitting
ITC American Typewriter: Light, Medium and Bold
Aster: Standard, Italic and Bold
ITC Avant Garde Gothic: Book, Book Italic, Demi, Demi Italic, Medium, Medium Italic, Bold, and Bold Italic
Baskerville: Standard, Italic, Bold, and Bold Italic
Bembo: Standard, Italic, Bold, and Bold Italic
ITC Benguiat: Book, Book Italic, Bold, and Bold Italic
Bodoni: Book, Book Italic, Bold, and Bold Italic
ITC Bookman: Light, Light Italic, Demi, Demi Italic, Medium, Medium Italic, Bold, and Bold Italic
Caledonia®: Standard, Italic, Bold, and Bold Italic
Caslon: 540, 540 Italic, Bold 3, and Bold 3 Italic
Century: Expanded, Expanded Italic, Bold, Bold Italic, Old Style, Old Style Italic, Old Style Bold, Schoolbook, Schoolbook Italic, and Schoolbook Bold
ICT Cheltenham: Light, Light Italic, Bold, and Bold Italic
Clarendon: Standard, Light and Bold
ICT Clearface: Regular, Regular Italic, Heavy, and Heavy Italic
Cloister: Standard, Italic and Bold
ICT Eras: Light, Book, Demi and Bold
Friz Quadrata: Standard and Bold
Garamond 3: Standard, Italic, Bold, and Bold Italic
ITC Garamond: Book, Book Italic, Bold, and Bold Italic

Goudy: Old Style, Old Style Italic, Bold, and Extra Bold

Helvetica®: Light, Light Italic, Bold, Bold Italic, Standard, Italic, Heavy, and Heavy Italic

Janson: Standard and Italic

ITC Kabel: Book, Medium, Demi and Bold

Kennerly: Standard, Italic, Bold, and Bold Italic

ITC Korinna: Standard, Italic, Extra Bold, and Extra Bold Italic

Melior®: Standard, Italic, Bold, Bold Italic

Memphis: Light, Light Italic, Bold, Bold Italic, Medium, Medium Italic, Extra Bold, and Extra Bold Italic

Optima®: Standard, Italic, Bold, and Bold Italic

Palatino®: Standard, Italic, Bold, and Bold Italic

Perpetua: Standard, Italic, Bold, and Bold Italic

Plantin: Standard, Italic, Bold, and Bold Italic

Primer®: Standard and Italic

Sabon: Standard, Italic and Bold

ITC Souvenir: Light, Light Italic, Demi-Bold, Demi-Bold Italic, Medium, Medium Italic, Bold, and Bold Italic

Spartan®: Light, Light Italic, Heavy, Heavy Italic, Medium, Medium Italic, Black, and Black Italic

Times Roman®: Italic, Bold, and Bold Italic

Trade Gothic®: Light, Light Italic, Bold, and Bold Italic

Trump: Standard, Italic, Bold, and Bold Italic

Univers: Light 45, Light Italic 46, Bold 65, Bold Italic 66, 55, Italic 56, Black 75, and Black Italic 76

Walbaum: Standard, Italic, Bold, and Bold Italic

Weiss: Standard, Italic, Bold, and Extra Bold

ITC Zapf International: Light, Light Italic, Demi, and Demi Italic

320 pp. General index. (ISBN 0-442-25425-3)

169
Kmetz, A.R.
von Willisen, F.K.
(eds.)

collection

Nonemissive Electrooptic Displays
Plenum, 1976

(based on the fourth Brown Boveri Symposium; Baden, Switzerland; 29-30 September 1975)

Thirteen technical, detailed review papers cover the materials, phenomena, and technologies of the nonemissive display field as applied to practical display systems.

The review papers are supplemented by short contributed papers and comments from chaired technical sessions. Ninety-six invited participants from diverse scientific disciplines and many countries attended this symposium. The first day was devoted to liquid crystal displays while the second day included sessions on electrochromic, ferroelectric, and flat panel displays. The underlying philosophy of this symposia series is a close working relationship between engineering and the basic sciences; the topics selected for review papers and the strong emphasis on display applications follow this guideline. This specialized volume is for scientists and engineers.

CONTENTS

Foreword
Preface
List of participants
Session 1: Display Engineering and Electrooptics
Chairman: A.P. Speiser
Requirements on modern displays
J. Kirton
Discussion
Session 2: Liquid Crystal Display Effects
Chairman: W. Helfrich
Electrical and optical properties of twisted nematic structures
D.W. Berreman
Discussion
Cholesteric texture and phase change effects
E.P. Raynes
Discussion
Liquid crystal color displays
T.J. Scheffer
Discussion
Short communication: spectrum of voltage controllable color
formation with nematic liquid crystals
H. Mada, S. Kobayashi
Session 3: Liquid Crystal Materials and Technology
Chairman: F.J. Kahn
Chemical composition and display performance
D. Demus
Discussion
Anchoring properties and alignment of liquid crystals
E. Guyon, W. Urbach
Discussion
Short communication: measurement of alignment tilt in twisted
nematic displays
K. Toriyama, T. Ishibashi
Discussion
Session 4: Electrochromic Displays
Chairman: C.J. Gerritsma
Principles of electrochromism as related to display applications
H.R. Zeller
Electrochromic and electrochemichromic materials and phenomena
I.F. Chang
Short communication: Mechanism of electrochromism in WO_3
G.E. Weibel
Electrochromic display devices
J. Bruinink
Joint discussion

Session 5: Alternative Non-Emissive Displays
    Chairman: R. Engelbrecht
    Electrophoretic displays
        J.C. Lewis
    Discussion
    Ferroelectric displays
        K.H. Härdtl

Session 6: Display Systems
    Chairman: S. Kobayashi
    Matrix addressing of non-emissive displays
        A.R. Kmetz
    Short communication: temperature dependence of multiplexed
    twisted nematic liquid crystal displays
        F.J. Kahn, R.A. Burmeister, Jr.
    Short communication: scanning limitations of twisted nematic
    display devices
        C.J. Gerritsma, P. van Zanten
    Discussion
    Integrated electrooptic displays
        T.P. Brody
    Discussion
    Short communication: progress toward TFT-addressed TNLC flat-
    panel color television
        A.G. Fischer

Concluding Remarks
    C. Hilsum
    Author index
    Subject index

360 pp. 19 papers in 6 sessions. Drawings, photographs, figures, graphs, tables, mathematical formulae, author index, subject index, references. ISBN 0-306-30957-2.

170
Knuth, Donald E.

TEX and METAFONT: New Directions in Typesetting
Digital Press, 1979

(a revised edition of part 1 entitled *The TEXbook* is now available from Addison-Wesley; a revision of part 2 *The METAfontbook* is scheduled for publication in late 1985)

Introduces and provides user information for innovative new systems of computer typesetting and alphabet design.

In TEX, Knuth offers a standard language for computer typography which allows any word-processing system, typewriter, computer-based editor, or TEX system editor to be used as an input device for typesetting. TEX is capable of handling various formats and languages and is promoted as user-extendable to virtually all applications. TEX and METAFONT (Knuth's system for computer design of character shapes) gained impetus from his frustration with the poor quality of printing and symbol design in mathematical journals and books. Hypothetically, an author using Knuth's systems could design his or her own book from style of typeface to overall format, thus creating an attractive and accurate publication ready for the public in less time and at less expense than most current publications. In part one of the book, Knuth explains his research in mathematical typography which led to T$_E$X and METAFONT. This section was originally delivered as the 1979 Josiah Willard Gibbs Lecture and is reprinted from the *Bulletin of the American Mathematical Society*, March 1979. Part two and part three of the book consist of user manuals for T$_E$X and METAFONT, respectively. T$_E$X is described as conceptually "a big paste up job" consisting of boxes and glue, terms that describe Knuth's basic units of page construction. METAFONT is presented in terms of pen settings and eraser strokes. A device-independent system of computer programs for each character shape, METAFONT contains 20 parameters which the user can manipulate to vary the style of type. New symbols can also be added. Numerous examples illustrate the author's discussion of good and bad typeface. Knuth presupposes the reader's familiarity with a computer text editor. He recommends his book to non-mathematicians and most of the text is, in fact, accessible without sophisticated mathematical knowledge. Progressively more difficult exercises test the reader's comprehension of materials covered while "dangerous bend signals" warn of rough going in the manuals. A conversational style of writing and a wry sense of humor help to sustain the reader throughout. The author has recently expanded his discussions of each of these topics and has separated them into two new publications, *The T$_E$Xbook* and *The METAFONTbook*. *The T$_E$Xbook* is treated elsewhere in this publication; at the time of printing, *The METAFONTbook* was not yet available. However, based on previews of the first five chapters (of a projected twenty-seven), this version of METAFONT will be substantially revised; the version described in *T$_E$X and METAFONT* is now referred to as METAFONT79. It is clear from the preview chapters that Knuth considers the new version of METAFONT to be far superior to the original, and readers interested in implementing this method would do well to base their work on the new version, which is projected for publication in the winter of 1985. The author is professor of both computer science and electrical engineering at Stanford University.

CONTENTS

Part 1: Mathematical Typography

Part 2: T$_E$X, a System for Technical Text
1. The name of the game
2. Book printing versus ordinary typing
3. Controlling T$_E$X
4. Fonts of type
5. Grouping
6. Running T$_E$X
7. How T$_E$X reads when you type
8. The characters you type
9. T$_E$X's standard roman fonts
10. Dimensions
11. Boxes
12. Glue

13. Modes
14. How T$_E$X breaks paragraphs into lines
15. How T$_E$X makes lists of lines into pages
16. Typing math formulas
17. More about math
18. Fine points of mathematics typing
19. Displayed equations
20. Definitions (also called macros)
21. Making boxes
22. Alignment
23. Output routines
24. Summary of vertical mode
25. Summary of horizontal mode
26. Summary of math mode
27. Recovery from errors
A. Answers to all the exercises
B. Basic T$_E$X format
E. Examples of a book format
F. Font tables
H. Hyphenation
I. Index
S. Special notes about using T$_E$X at Stanford
X. Recent extensions to T$_E$X

Part 3: METAFONT, a System for Alphabet Design
1. The basics
2. Curves
3. Pens and erasers
4. Running METAFONT
5. Variables, expressions, and equations
6. Filling in between curves
7. Discreteness and discretion
8. Subroutines
9. Summary of the language
10. Recovery from errors
A. Answers to all the exercises
E. Example of a font definition
F. Font information for text
I. Index

351 pp. 3 parts. Figures, mathematical formulae, general index, references, appendices. ISBN 0-932376-02-9.

171
Knuth, Donald E.

The T$_E$Xbook
Addison-Wesley, 1984

A highly readable book on a computer typesetting language specifically designed for books that contain a great deal of mathematics.

In the twenty-seven chapters and ten appendices, Knuth leads the reader through the principles of this computer language in an accessible and entertaining manner. The first five chapters of this work introduce the user to the computer keyboard, different typesets, and grouping. Chapters six through twenty-four are devoted to "learning by doing."

The final three chapters of the book consist of the formalized and concise presentation of the T$_E$X language; however, Knuth suggests that the student not read chapters twenty-four through twenty-six until the language user needs to ascertain how the inside of a computer functions. This multilevel text allows the reader to learn at his or her own speed. Specifically, the author provides straightforward information and exercises on both an elementary and a more difficult and esoteric level. Thus, once the student becomes more proficient at T$_E$X, he or she can reinforce this knowledge by returning to the more challenging exercises. Stimulating and clearly written, this material is appropriate for all students regardless of their prior knowledge of computers.

CONTENTS
1. The name of the game
2. Book printing versus ordinary typing
3. Controlling T$_E$X
4. Fonts of type
5. Grouping
6. Running T$_E$X
7. How T$_E$X reads what you type
8. The characters you type
9. T$_E$X's roman fonts
10. Dimensions
11. Boxes
12. Glue
13. Modes
14. How T$_E$X breaks paragraphs into lines
15. How T$_E$X makes lines into pages
16. Typing math formulas
17. More about math
18. Fine points of mathematics typing
19. Displayed equations
20. Definitions (also called macros)
21. Making boxes
22. Alignment
23. Output routines
24. Summary of vertical mode
25. Summary of horizontal mode
26. Summary of math mode
27. Recovery from errors

Appendices
A. Answers to all the exercises
B. Basic control sequences
C. Character codes
D. Dirty tricks
E. Example formats
F. Font tables
G. Generating boxes from formulas
H. Hyphenation
I. Index
J. Joining the T$_E$X community

483 pp. 27 chapters. Drawings, figures, mathematical formulae, general index, appendices. (ISBN 0-201-13448-9)

172
Kolers, Paul A.
Wrolstad, Merald E.
Bouma, Herman
(eds.)

proceedings

Processing of Visible Language 1
Plenum, 1979

(proceedings of the conference of the same name, sponsored by the Institute for Perception Research [IPO]; Eindhoven, The Netherlands; 5-8 September 1977)

Tutorial and research papers by psychologists, graphics designers, and engineers examining graphic communication, including: writing systems; visual presentation and its interpretation; text processing; reading research, including eye movements and skill acquisition; symbol design; and diverse subtopics related to this broad, interdisciplinary field.

CONTENTS

Eye Movements in Search and Reading
    Introduction
        P.A. Kolers
    The control of eye movements in reading (tutorial paper)
        Ariane Levy-Schoen, Kevin O'Regan
    On the role and control of eye movements in reading
        George W. McConkie
    Moment to moment control of eye saccades as a function of textual parameters in reading
        Kevin O'Regan
    Eye movements in reading: eye guidance and integration
        Keith Rayner
    Understanding the reading process through the use of transformed typography: PSG, CSG and automaticity
        Dennis F. Fisher
    Reading and searching through geometrically transformed text
        Lester A. Lefton
    Reading eye movements, macro-structure and comprehension processes
        Wayne L. Shebilske, L. Starling Reid
Design of Graphic Language
    Introduction
        M.E. Wrolstad
    A schema for the study of graphic language (tutorial paper)
        Michael Twyman
    Typography: a technique of making a text 'legible'
        Wim Crouwel
    Making maps easy to read—a summary of research
        Richard J. Phillips
    Typographic access structures for educational texts
        Robert H.W. Waller
    The use of visual cues in text
        Jeremy J. Foster
    Relations between the qualifications of different groups of readers and different aspects of text
        Mogens Jansen

Word Perception and Its Role in Reading
Introduction
    H. Bouma
Word recognition in reading (tutorial paper)
    Alan Allport
Facilitation in word recognition: experiments causing change in the Logogen model
    John Morton
Word knowledge and letter recognition as determinants of word recognition
    Don G. Bouwhuis
Orthographic regularities in English words
    Richard L. Venezky
Rule-governed and wholistic encoding processes in word perception
    Alexander Pollatsek, Thomas H. Carr
Spelling patterns, letter cancellation and the processing of text
    Philip T. Smith, Anne Groat

Perceiving and Producing
Introduction
    P.A. Kolers
Reading and listening (tutorial paper)
    Dominic W. Massaro
Working memory and reading
    A.D. Baddeley
A direct access from graphics to meaning: a study of the Stroop effect in sentences
    Shulamit S. Reich, Colin Cherry
Reading by eye and writing by ear
    Uta Frith
A comparison of explicit and implicit knowledge of an alphabet
    Lee Brooks, Amina Miller
The perception of language cohesion during fluent reading
    L.J. Chapman
When two no's nearly make a yes: a study of conditional imperatives
    P. Wright, P. Wilcox
Styles and strategies in silent reading
    A.K. Pugh

Technological Media Designed for Visual Presentation
Introduction
    H. Bouma
The design of technological displays (tutorial paper)
    Robert I. Rosenthal
Electronic paperwork processing in the office of the future
    W. Hoekstra
Television text: first experience with a new medium
    Richard Jackson
Non-serial language
    N.E. Wiseman, C.A. Linden
Paragraphs of pictographs: the use of non-verbal instructions for equipment
    Tony Marcel, Philip Barnard

Computer aided design of graphic symbols
> *Arthur O. Eger*

Name Index

Subject Index

537 pp. 33 papers in 5 sections. Figures, tables, author index, subject index. ISBN 0-306-40186-X.

173
Kolers, Paul A.
Wrolstad, Merald E.
Bouma, Herman
(eds.)

proceedings

Processing of Visible Language 2
Plenum, 1980

(proceedings of the conference of the same name, sponsored by the University of Toronto, the Ontario Institute for Studies in Education, the NATO Scientific Affairs Division, the International Reading Association, and Communications Canada; Niagara-on-the-Lake, Ontario, Canada; 3-7 September 1979; vol. 13 in the *NATO Conference Series on Human Factors*)

Papers by psychologists, engineers, and graphics designers emphasizing the design aspects of language display, including a historical overview. Some of the topics include graphs, calligraphy, cartography, and graphic literacy; writing systems; textual literacy, including the perception and representation of text; electronic display, human-computer interaction, pictorial recognition, and the ergonomics of VDT design; and a special section of theoretical papers on topics ranging from representation to research surveys.

CONTENTS

Writing Systems
> Introduction
>> *M.E. Wrolstad*
> Principles of writing systems within the frame of visual communication (tutorial paper)
>> *I.J. Gelb*
> English shorthand systems and abbreviatory conventions: a psychological perspective
>> *P.T. Smith, H.M. Pattison*
> Remarks on ancient Egyptian writing with emphasis on its mnemonic aspects
>> *E.S. Meltzer*
> The Korean writing system: an alphabet? a syllabary? a logography?
>> *I. Taylor*

Graphic Systems
> Introduction
>> *M.E. Wrolstad*
> A structure for nontextual communication (tutorial paper)
>> *J.Doblin*
> The syntax of pictorial instructions
>> *K.P. Szlichcinski*

Making newspaper graphs fit to print
H. Wainer
Some problems of illustration
H.E. Paine
Islamic calligraphy: meaning and symbol
A. Welch

Textual Literacy
Introduction
P.A. Kolers
Usability: the criterion for designing written information (tutorial paper)
P. Wright
Wholistic models of feature analysis in word recognition: a critical examination
L. Henderson
Developmental trends in the perception of textual cohesion
L.J. Chapman, A. Stokes
Structuring an internal representation of text: a basis of literacy
W.L. Shebilske
Graphic aspects of complex texts: typography as macro-punctuation
R.H.W. Waller

Graphic Literacy
Introduction
P.A. Kolers
Pictures and the real thing (tutorial paper)
D.N. Perkins
The influence of texture gradients on relief interpretation from isopleth maps
J.D.M. Underwood
The acquisition and processing of cartographic information: some preliminary experimentation
M.W. Dobson
Graph reading abilities of thirteen-year-olds
B.V. Roller
Interpreting directions from graphic displays: spatial frames of reference
M.J. Sholl, H.E. Egeth

Textual Technology
Introduction
H. Bouma
The presentation of text and graphics (tutorial paper)
R.A. Myers
Spacing of characters on a television display
W.C. Treurniet
Optimal segmentation for sentences displayed on a video screen
J. Pynte, G. Noizet
Text enhancement and structuring in computer conferencing
A. Baer, M. Turoff
Towards an electronic journal
N. Moray
Human performance in computer aided writing and documentation
L.T. Frase, S.A. Keenan, J.J. Dever

Graphic Technology
  Introduction
    H. Bouma
  Human-computer interactive systems: a state-of-the-art review
  (tutorial paper)
    R.M. Baecker
  Simultaneous speech transcription and TV captions for the deaf
    R.G. Baker, A.C. Downton, A.F. Newell
  Pictorial recognition and teaching the blind to draw
    C.N. Vincent
  Telidon Videotex and user-related issues
    H. Brown, C.D. O'Brien, W. Sawchuk, J.R. Storey,
    W.C. Treurniet
  Human factors and VDT design
    A.E. Çakir
Theory of Representation
  Introduction
    P.A. Kolers
  Theory of representation: three questions (tutorial paper)
    V.A. Howard
  Textual literacy: an outline sketch of psychological research on
  reading and writing
    P. Wright
  Anaphoric relations, comprehension and readability
    J.T. Dutka
  Communicating with computers
    R.L. Venezky, N. Relles, L.A. Price
  Towards a model for picture and word processing
    J.G. Snodgrass
  The basic test of the graph: a matrix theory of graph construction
  and cartography
    J. Bertin
Subject Index
Name Index

616 pp. 36 papers in 7 sections. Photographs, figures, tables, author index, subject index, references. ISBN 0-306-40576-8.

Kramlich, David   *SEE UNDER ID 139*

174
Kronauer, Richard

Quantification of Interference and Detectability Properties of Visual Stimuli for Optimal Display Design
1983

technical report

(report number AFOSR-TR-83-1015; Division of Applied Sciences, Harvard University; sponsored by Air Force Office of Scientific Research; 19 May 1983)

An initial report covering the first eight months of a three year study, this paper outlines the initial stages of research designed to "measure the detectability of a sinusoidal traveling-wave grating in the presence of a mask of band-limited spatiotemporal noise."

Describes the initial work which extended the study of coherent masking to three-spectral dimensions and improved estimates of the number of discrete components necessary to simulate randomness in any finite three-dimensional spectral band. The development of a computer generated noise mask is detailed. These studies are intended to be preliminary to more complicated (12 parameter) experiments in incoherent masking; it is expected that the greatest success for reducing interference in continuous information transfer will be achieved when an incoherent mask is fully developed. Two appendices present the progress report and informal scientific reports from earlier phases of this project. The topics and experiments presented here are for specialists in computer-generated display, and the style of writing does little to expand the report's accessibility beyond these experts; however, the concepts presented will be of great interest to that highly specialized group.

26 pp. Figures, graphs, references, appendices.

175
Küppers, Harald

Color: Origin, Systems, Uses
Van Nostrand Reinhold, 1973

(translation by F. Bradley of Küppers' *Farbe: Ursprung, Systematik, Anwendung,* 1972)

Designed for a broad-based readership, this book is a comprehensive effort to coordinate the various theories of color into a single model, the rhombohedral system.

In developing his rhombohedral model, the author begins with general considerations of color as a problem in such varied disciplines as chemistry, printing, theology, philosophy, psychology, and poetry. To indicate the depth of the problem the author cites the dispute between the theoreticians and practitioners about even the "right" names for colors. The physiology that allows a gray, achromatic world to be seen in color is then explored—how electromagnetic vibrations become the red of a tulip or the green of its stem. Also treated here are visual defects, optical illusions, and the range of the eye's adaptive capabilities.

Moving through physical and technical matters such as the light spectrum, emission and reflectance curves, metameric colors (those of identical appearance but different spectral composition), and measurement of color density, the author reviews other color systems— the color cube, Hickethier's color code, Ostwald's Pyramid, the CIE System, and DIN 6164, concluding with a critical assessment of their value. Finally, the detailed system of color arrangements in the rhombohedron model is discussed, leading to a set of specific conclusions and a new law of integrated mixtures. This theory, a natural progression from the other color solids examined, will interest printers, artists, color researchers, and photographers, as well as those working in television, computer graphics, or any of the screen-generated color media. This rhombohedral color solid satisfies the author's requirements that a color theory must be: logical; simple to use; in compliance with the physical principles which produce color and the physiological functions of the eye in perceiving color; a proper illustration of the laws of additive and subtractive mixture; and able to represent relations mathematically.

CONTENTS
    List of illustrations
General Section
    Our many-colored environment
    'Color' as a problem
    Color and language
    Which color names are 'right'?
Physiological Section
    Everything is really gray
    The process of vision
    Visual defects
    Optical illusions
    Adaptation and simultaneous contrast
Physical and Technical Section
    The family of electromagnetic vibrations
    The light spectrum
    Emission and reflectance curves
    Metameric colors
    Spectrum analysis and color temperature
    Polarization and interference
    Properties of body colors
    Color saturation and measurement of color density
Systematic Section
    Primary colors and the color circle
    Complementary colors
    Additive mixture
    Subtractive mixture
    Simultaneous additive and subtractive mixture
    Possibilities of modifying a color
    Possibilities of mixing two colors
    The color cube
    Hickethier's color code
    Ostwald's Pyramid (double cone)
    The CIE System

DIN 6164
Critical assessment of the color systems

The Rhombohedral System
The rhombohedron as a geometrical body
Arrangement of the colors in the rhombohedron
Saturation planes of the rhombohedron
Color tone planes of the rhombohedron
Planes of equal color value (brightness planes)
The achromatic planes
Division of the colors into groups
The system of arrangements in the rhombohedron

Conclusions
A new law of mixtures: the integrated mixture
Laws of color harmony
Hardly anything is final
Points to remember
Bibliography

155 pp. 6 chapters. Figures, charts, bibliography, color graphics. ISBN 0-442-29985-0.

176
Lachman, Roy
Lachman, Janet L.
Butterfield, Earl C.

Cognitive Psychology and Information Processing: An Introduction
Lawrence Erlbaum Associates, 1979

A new and unique account of the metatheory, assumptions, intellectual background, and values of information-processing psychology.

The thesis of the book is that sense can be made out of any research science by grasping aspects of its paradigm. Features of the paradigms are given and their applications to other sciences discussed. The literature of the various subfields of cognition are organized and interrelated, and the significant aspects of the cognitive literature are covered in depth. Particular attention has been paid to the language of the text so that it is readable by the nonspecialist. The book assumes no professional expertise and, although it is intended primarily for the student, the material will be valuable to the professional and the researcher. The objective is to provide a knowledge and perspective of the content of cognitive psychology. The final chapter examines criticisms of the paradigm, cites one current effort to launch an alternative approach, and offers a cautious prognosis for the information-processing paradigm and the field of cognitive science. Chapters begin with a complete abstract and contain summaries and/or conclusions. The contents are: the characteristics of the paradigm and the contributions of other disciplines to its attainment, a summary of experiments about attention as consciousness and attention as processing capacity, distinctions between semantic and episodic memory, a discussion of multistore models, factual and paradigmatic conclusions drawn from twenty years of psychological research on syntax, a description of the convergence of research and theory concerning permanent memory and psycholinguistics, a discussion of discourse processing and global models of comprehension, and a chapter on pattern recognition guest authored by James F. Juola.

CONTENTS

Preface

1: Science and Paradigms: The Premises of This Book
    Abstract
    I. Introduction
    II. Cognitive psychology as an experimental science
    III. Characteristics of paradigms
    IV. Paradigms, information processing, psychology, and society

2: Psychology's Contribution to the Information-Processing Paradigm
    Abstract
    I. How do antecedents shape a paradigm?
    II. The contribution of neobehaviorism
    III. The contributions of verbal learning
    IV. The contributions of human engineering

3: Contributions of Other Disciplines to Information-Processing Psychology
    Abstract
    I. Introduction
    II. The contributions of communications engineering and information theory
    III. The contributions of linguistics

4: The Information-Processing Paradigm
    Abstract
    I. Introduction: the concept of intelligent action
    II. The influence of computer science on cognitive psychology
    III. An information-processing system
    IV. The information-processing paradigm

5: Reaction Time: The Measure of an Emerging Paradigm
    Abstract
    I. Introduction
    II. Preview: a brief history of reaction-time research
    III. Information theory
    IV. Engineering psychology
    V. Decomposing mental processes
    VI. Speed-accuracy trade-off
    VII. Signal detection theory
    VIII. Serial or parallel processing?
    IX. The status of CRT in 1979

6: Consciousness and Attention
    Abstract
    I. Introduction
    II. Attention as consciousness
    III. Memory processes in selective attention
    IV. Attention as processing capacity
    V. Reprise

7: Some Structural Features of Human Memory: The Episodic Memory System and Its Parts
    Abstract
    I. Introduction
    II. Three memory stores
    III. Experimental reasons for positing a sensory register
    IV. Characteristics of the short-term store
    V. Differentiating the long-term store from the short-term store
    VI. A reminder

8: Flexibility in the Episodic Memory System: New Directions for Multistore Models
    Abstract
    I. The current status of multistore models
    II. Alternatives to multistore models of human episodic memory
    III. Extensions of multistore models
    IV. Conclusions

9: Semantic memory
    Abstract
    I. Introduction
    II. Formation of the field of semantic memory
    III. The normal-science study of semantic memory
    IV. Two models of semantic memory
    V. Word production
    VI. Comparison of word production and sentence verification studies

10: Psycholinguistics
    Abstract
    I. Introduction
    II. Neobehavioristic and information-theory approaches to language
    III. The influence of the linguist Noam Chomsky
    IV. The psychology of syntax
    V. Semantics and pragmatics
    VI. Case grammar
    VII. Summary

11: Comprehension from the Psycholinguistic Viewpoint
    Abstract
    I. Overview
    II. The concept of the synthesized code
    III. The form of the synthesized code
    IV. Content of the synthesized code
    V. A model of conversational comprehension

12: Discourse Processing and Global Models of Comprehension
    Abstract
    I. Introduction
    II. Discourse processing
    III. Comprehensive theories in general
    IV. Some particulars of four theories
    V. Where the theories stand on some major issues
    VI. Summary of comprehensive theories

13: Pattern Recognition
James F. Juola
Abstract
I. Information processing and pattern recognition
II. Some sensory physiology
III. Theories of pattern recognition
IV. Speech perception research
V. Visual perception and reading research
VI. Theoretical overview

14: Epilogue: Critiques of the Paradigm
Abstract
I. Introduction
II. Normal science and narrowing of focus
III. Critiques

References

Author Index

Subject Index

573 pp. 14 chapters. Figures, graphs, tables, author index, subject index, references. ISBN 0-89859-131-7.

177
Leavitt, Ruth
(ed.)

collection

Artist and Computer
Harmony Books, 1976

A collection of essays by artists who use computers as the principal means of communicating their visual ideas.

Ruth Leavitt, herself an artist who works with computers, has done an excellent job of putting together the work and ideas of American, European, and Japanese artists, some of whom have worked with computers since the early sixties. Some of the artists replied to a series of questions compiled by the author; others simply wrote a statement about their work. The result is a multi-faceted perspective on why some artists have chosen this particular medium and how they work with the computer. Because the state of computer art changes almost as rapidly as the technology advances, some of the techniques described in this collection have been superseded. However, this book includes essays by a number of artists who are still involved with computer-generated display. The entire range of computer uses is represented, from computer-as-idea-tool to computer-assisted design, simulations of large scale projects, and finally work generated entirely on the computer. Patsy Scala writes of computer art as "the catalyst which [will change] both the art world and the computer community." This statement encapsulates the reasons why this profusely illustrated collection of essays should be of interest to both artists and computer scientists, and in particular those scientists who are concerned with visual display.

CONTENTS
Preface
   Ruth Leavitt
The following artists contributed essays to this volume:
   Ann H. Murray
   Robert Mallary
   Aldo Giorgini
   Aaron Marcus
   Collette and Charles Bangert
   Ben F. Laposky
   Leslie Mezei
   Tony Longson
   Peter Struycken
   Edward Ihnatowicz
   Vera Molnar
   Laurence Press
   Manuel Barbadillo
   Patsy Scala
   William J. Kolomyjec
   Edward Zajec
   Edward Manning
   Duane M. Palyka
   Kenneth Knowlton
   Joseph Scala
   Karen E. Huff
   Miljenenko Horvat
   John Whitney
   Herbert W. Franke
   Charles Csuri
   Christopher William Tyler
   Manfred Mohr
   Ruth Leavitt
   Kurt F. Lauckner
   Vicky Chaet
   Lillian Schwartz
   Larry Elin
   Hiroshi Kawano
   Roger Vilder
   Jacques Palumbo

120 pp. 35 chapters. Drawings, photographs, figures, tables, references, color plates. ISBN 0-517-52787-1. (ISBN 0-517-52735-9)

178
Levens, Alexander
Chalk, William

Graphics in Engineering Design (3ed.)
John Wiley and Sons, 1980

(second edition published under the title *Graphics, Analysis and Conceptual Design,* 1968)

A comprehensive textbook which provides an introduction to the concepts of engineering design and graphics for the undergraduate student.

This textbook provides practical information on the use of graphics in engineering design. The material is organized into three main parts—introduction, application, and implementation. The introduction describes the design process and the role of graphics, discusses freehand sketching and layout drawings, details the phases and steps of the design process, and examines the fundamental principles of orthogonal projection. The section on applied graphics focuses on the fundamental principles of orthogonal projection, intersections in design, vector quantities and diagrams, pictorial representation, graphical representation and design data, graphical solutions and computations, and computer graphics. The discussion of graphics for design implementation includes specific ideas for communicating technical information through graphics, writing, and oral presentation. The authors have arranged the material in a logical and understandable fashion and have included specific suggestions for the use of this text in a variety of courses. Three workbooks are available which include basic information, but each emphasizes different areas covered to reinforce Each chapter concludes with several exercises designed to reinforce concepts presented. A series of nine appendices provides invaluable reference material in table or dictionary form. This volume would be useful as a reference tool for professionals and as a textbook for undergraduate students in design engineering.

CONTENTS

Part 1: Introduction to Design and Fundamentals of Engineering Graphics
    Chapter 1. Introduction
    Chapter 2. Sketching for technical design
    Chapter 3. Layout drawings
    Chapter 4. Design process: phases and steps
    Chapter 5. Fundamental principles of orthogonal projection

Part 2: Applied Graphics for Design, Analysis, and Communication
    Chapter 6. Applications of the fundamental principles of orthogonal projection
    Chapter 7. Developments and intersections in design
    Chapter 8. Vector quantities and vector diagrams
    Chapter 9. Pictorial representation
    Chapter 10. Graphical representation and significance of design data
    Chapter 11. Graphical solutions and computations
    Chapter 12. Computer graphics

Part 3: Graphics for Design Implementation
Chapter 13. Technical drawings: sections and conventional practices; fasteners and joining; machine elements
Chapter 14. Technical drawings: dimensions and specifications; detail and assembly drawings
Chapter 15. Technical reports; design documentation; patents
Appendices
Appendix A: Line conventions; lettering; and geometric constructions
Appendix B: English unit and metric unit tables
Appendix C: Abbreviations and symbols
Appendix D: First and third angle arrangment of views
Appendix E: Mathematical (algebraic) solutions of space problems
Appendix F: Graphical solutions of differential equations
Appendix G: Useful technical terms and human factors
Appendix H: Strength of materials; coefficients of friction; rolled steel structural shapes (inch and metric units); beam diagrams; and solid conductors
Appendix I: Metric practice and conversion tables
Index

736 pp. 15 chapters in 3 parts. Drawings, photographs, figures, tables, abstract formalisms, general index, appendices. ISBN 0-471-01478-8.

179
MacGregor, Annette J.

Graphics Simplified: How to Plan and Prepare Effective Charts, Graphs, Illustrations, and Other Visual Aids
University of Toronto Press, 1979

A concise guide on the use of legible graphics in an educational environment. Definitely a how-to book, the emphasis is on when to use legible charts and graphs and how to design them to convey information most effectively.

This small paperback handbook was written by a professor and medical illustrator at the University of Saskatchewan for her colleagues: teachers and scientists. Chapter one discusses the selection of graphic representations (bar, column, line, semi-logarithmic, and pie and frequency distribution charts) with suggestions for when, and when not, to use them. The second chapter tells how to prepare charts and graphs and discusses scales, legends, tones, and word legibility. It is interspersed with graphic maxims, e.g., "lower case letters are easier to read than uppercase letters." While good graphic design involves the same elements in all media, each medium has its own requirements; these special needs are discussed in chapter three. Chapter three ends with a list of materials useful in chart and graph preparation. Photographic illustrations are dealt with in chapter four. Amply illustrated, this book is easily understood and could be used by anyone interested in designing graphics for a variety of media on any subject.

CONTENTS
Introduction
1. Charts and graphs
2. Preparing charts and graphs
3. Media specifications and artists' aids
4. Choosing illustrations
5. Selected references
Index

64 pp. 5 chapters. Drawings, charts, graphs, tables, general index, references. (ISBN 0-8020-6363-2)

180
Mandelbrot, Benoit B.

The Fractal Geometry of Nature
W.H. Freeman, 1982

(revised edition of *Fractals,* 1977)

Based on his technical papers and the previous edition of this book, Mandelbrot presents an overview of the origins, development and applications of fractal geometry.

As a field of study, fractal geometry had its formal origins in 1975. It evolved out of the author's work on a mathematics for describing irregular and fragmented patterns and forms. Mandelbrot asserts that natural phenomena exhibit a level of complexity that Euclidean geometry, in which objects may have only one, two, or three dimensions, cannot describe with any degree of resolution. To quote Mandelbrot, "Clouds are not spheres, mountains are not cones, coastlines are not circles, and bark is not smooth, nor does lightning travel in a straight line." In fractal geometry, dimensionality is continuous and thus allows the description and generation of irregular, complex, and amorphous patterns such as turbulence, galactic clusters, trees, river deltas and coastlines, soap bubbles, crystal lattices, and economic price scaling. Calling the book a scientific essay, the author deliberately adopts an idiosyncratic style which allows him to wander as he pleases through the field of study he developed. This essay illustrates the power and beauty of fractal geometry in the diversity of analyses and applications it permits. For example, fractal-based modeling and simulation techniques for computer graphics have led to display imagery which is difficult to distinguish from a photograph. The book is very well illustrated, but many figures do not appear with the explanatory text or are referred to in several places; turning pages back and forth to look at them is distracting. Despite the personal style and often wry digressions, the book requires focus and the attention of the reader. The mathematics is not rigorous, but Mandelbrot assumes at least a basic knowledge of modern science and math. Aimed at an audience composed of general scientists, mathematicians, and educated laymen, this is a difficult but rewarding book.

CONTENTS

I: Introduction
1. Theme
2. The irregular and fragmented in nature
3. Dimension, symmetry, divergence
4. Variations and disclaimers

II: Three Classic Fractals, Tamed
5. How long is the coast of Britain?
6. Snowflakes and other Koch curves
7. Harnessing the Peano monster curves
8. Fractal events and Cantor dusts

III: Galaxies and Eddies
9. Fractal view of galaxy clusters
10. Geometry of turbulence; intermittency
11. Fractal singularities of differential equations

IV: Scaling Fractals
12. Length-area-volumes relations
13. Islands, clusters, and percolation; diameter-number relations
14. Ramification and fractal lattices

V: Nonscaling Fractals
15. Surfaces with positive volume, and flesh
16. Trees; scaling residues; nonuniform fractals
17. Trees and the diameter exponent

VI: Self-Mapping Fractals
18. Self-inverse fractals, Apollonian nets, and soap
19. Cantor and Fatou dusts; self-squared dragons
20. Fractal attractors and fractal ("chaotic") evolutions

VII: Randomness
21. Chance as a tool in model making
22. Conditional stationarity and cosmographic principles

VIII: Stratified Random Fractals
23. Random curds: contact clusters and fractal percolation
24. Random chains and squigs
25. Brownian motion and Brown fractals
26. Random midpoint displacement curves

IX: Fractional Brown Fractals
27. River discharges; scaling nets and noises
28. Relief and coastlines
29. The areas of islands, lakes, and cups

A Book-within-the-Book, in Color
30. Isothermal surfaces of homogeneous turbulence

X: Random Tremas; Texture
31. Interval tremas; linear Lévy dusts
32. Subordination; spatial Lévy dusts; ordered galaxies
33. Disc and sphere tremas: moon craters and galaxies
34. Texture: gaps and lacunarity; cirri and succolarity
35. General tremas, and the control of texture

XI: Miscellany
36. Logic of fractals in statistical lattice physics
37. Price change and scaling in economics
38. Scaling and power laws without geometry
39. Mathematical backup and addenda

XII: Of Men and Ideas
    40. Biographical sketches
    41. Historical sketches
    42. Epilog: the path to fractals
List of References
Index of Selected Dimensions
Index of Names and Subjects

460 pp. 42 chapters in 12 parts. Drawings, mathematical formulae, abstract formalisms, general index, references, color plates. ISBN 0-7167-1186-9.

181
Marr, David

Vision: A Computational Investigation into the Human Representation and Processing of Visual Information
W.H. Freeman, 1982

Presents a new framework for the study of vision, and introduces computational theories for specific visual processes predicated on the assumption that visual perception is primarily an information-processing problem.

This posthumous book (a synopsis of the author's research at the M.I.T. Artificial Intelligence Lab) is an introduction to the computational theories of the human visual system which argue that vision is the computation of a description and, thus, ultimately reproducible by a machine. A central tenet of the author is that any information-processing task involves three different levels of explanation—computational, algorithmic, and implementational—and that to understand the workings of the information-processing task of vision one must consider all these levels of abstraction. How these levels relate to one another is a significant feature of the approach and a basis for the research. The book is divided into three parts. The multi-level framework, along with a philosophical discussion and historical overview, is presented first. The second section (Chapters 2-6) contains the analysis of specific visual processes and the results achieved at the three levels. Critical issues revolve around the way in which images are presented (Marr's concept of the "primal sketch," the two-and-a-half-D sketch, and the three-D sketch). The last section contains a defense, involving questions and answers, set up as a conversation between Marr and an informed critic. *Vision* is seen as a milestone in the history of the subject. A reviewer notes, "even if no single one of Marr's detailed hypotheses ultimately survives, which is unlikely, the questions he raises can no longer be ignored."

CONTENTS
PART 1: INTRODUCTION AND PHILOSOPHICAL PRELIMINARIES
General Introduction
Chapter 1: The Philosophy and the Approach
    Background
    Understanding complex information-processing systems
    A representational framework for vision

PART 2: VISION

Chapter 2: Representing the Image
    Physical background of early vision
    Zero-crossing and the raw primal sketch
    Spatial arrangement of an image
    Light sources and transparency
    Grouping processes and the full primal sketch

Chapter 3: From Images to Surfaces
    Modular organization of the human visual processor
    Processes, constraints, and the available representations of an image
    Stereopsis
    Directional selectivity
    Apparent motion
    Shape contours
    Surface texture
    Shading and photometric stereo
    Brightness, lightness, and color
    Summary

Chapter 4: The Immediate Representation of Visible Surfaces
    Introduction
    Image segmentation
    Reformulating the problem
    The information to be represented
    General form of the 2 1/2-D sketch
    Possible forms for the representation
    Possible coordinate systems
    Interpolation, continuation, and discontinuities
    Computational aspects of the interpolation problem
    Other internal computations

Chapter 5: Representing Shapes for Recognition
    Introduction
    Issues raised by the representation of shape
    The 3-D model representation
    Natural extensions
    Deriving and using the 3-D model representation
    Psychological considerations

Chapter 6: Synopsis

PART 3: EPILOGUE

Chapter 7: A Conversation
    Introduction
    A way of thinking

Glossary

Bibliography

Index

397 pp. 7 chapters in 3 parts. Drawings, photographs, figures, graphs, tables, mathematical formulae, algorithms, general index, bibliography, glossary. ISBN 0-7167-1284-9. (ISBN 0-7167-1567-9)

182
Marsh, Patrick O.

Messages That Work: A Guide to Communication Design
Educational Technology Publications, 1983

This work presents a message design model for effective communication based on the socioeconomic and informational needs of our rapidly changing, electronic-media oriented society.

Professor Marsh identifies current socioeconomic conditions and needs, including accelerating patterns of employment mobility and increasing print illiteracy, and, with such factors in mind, constructs his communications design model to be applicable to various message types. A long introduction discusses the author's theoretical model of communication, which is based largely on classical rhetoric, McLuhan's media theories, mathematical information theory, and cognitive psychology. He explains the application of this theory—the construction of messages that work—in the book's four main parts. In part one the author's model achieves message information control by means of an "obscurity index" and by quantifying information load. Part two analyzes the control of message complexity. The model classifies data from cognitive psychology into six interactive elements of complexity, which makes the construction of message complexity profiles possible. Part three examines the generation and blueprint of an information- and complexity-controlled message. Such a blueprint (or message plan) allows the designer to determine what is needed to make the message work and also allows him to visualize the whole message. Part four provides a succinct conceptual review of the model's design process as well as exercises to reinforce the precepts of effective message design. The work concludes with a defense of the author's theory-then-research method and a formal statement of his "Axiomatic Theory of Message Design." This is a lucid exposition of an adaptable and effective communication model for the electronic age, richly supplemented by helpful figures and tables, and including three extensive appendices that facilitate its use both as a textbook for students and as a professional manual. A detailed work on effective message design which should be of interest to systems designers, analysts, and cognitive psychologists.

CONTENTS
List of steps in design process
Table of matrices
Introduction and context
Part I: Controlling the Informational Content
Chapter 1. Committing to the purpose statement
Chapter 2. Discovering support tactics
Chapter 3. Determining information load and body structure
Part II: Controlling Message Complexity
Chapter 4. Creating the contextual atmosphere
Chapter 5. Refining the message within receiver-imposed constraints
Chapter 6. Achieving desired response styles
Part III: Manifesting the Message
Chapter 7. Integrating the message design
Chapter 8. Implementing the message design

Part IV: Applications of the Design Process
    Chapter 9. Applications of the design process: some exercises for internalizing the process
    Chapter 10. Applications in research: a formal theoretical statement
Appendices
    Appendix A. Theoretical refinement
    Appendix B. Less common usages
    Appendix C. Extended examples
References
Index

458 pp. 10 chapters in 4 parts. Drawings, figures, graphs, tables, general index, references, appendices. ISBN 0-87778-184-2.

183
Massaro, Dominic W.
Taylor, Glen A.
Venezky, Richard L.
Jastrzembski, James E.
Lucas, Peter A.

Letter and Word Perception: Orthographic Structure and Visual Processing in Reading
North-Holland, 1980

(vol. 4 in the *Advances in Psychology* series, G.E. Stelmach, P.A. Vroon, series eds.)

Presents the work of five disparate researchers investigating how spelling rules (orthography) are used in letter and word perception.

This monograph is an outgrowth of the National Institute of Education's funding priorities in basic skills research, particularly word recognition. It was believed that such research might yield results usable in elementary grades to assess visual word recognition abilities of both good and poor readers and, if fundamental differences were found, to suggest appropriate remediation methods. The specific question addressed is how the reader's higher-order knowledge (orthographic structure) of the language interacts with visual feature analysis in recognizing words. Each chapter begins with introductory remarks and ends with a summary. Using an already developed and tested information processing model, the first chapter describes in detail the mechanisms of reading. The chapter is comprehensive, accessible to the lay reader (most highly technical information is relegated to appendices), and provides an excellent introduction to the remaining five chapters. After two chapters devoted to the early research and current understanding of visual information and orthographic structure, a lengthy fourth chapter lists a variety of experimental studies and their results. The fifth chapter summarizes perceptual recognition and overt judgment data reported in the experimental studies. The final, brief chapter consists of summaries and conclusions, the most significant being that a reader's search for a target letter was found to be dependent on featural similarities between that letter and others in the test string. The book should be of interest to educators, psychologists, students, and researchers in the field of orthography and letter and word perception.

CONTENTS

PREFACE

1: READING AND INFORMATION PROCESSING

An Information Processing Model of Reading

2: VISUAL INFORMATION

Early Work

Feature Analysis

Letter Features

3: ORTHOGRAPHIC STRUCTURE

Statistical Redundancy

Phonologically Based Descriptions

Rule-Governed Regularity
    Phonological constraints
    Scribal constraints
    Morphemic features
    Psychological assumptions
    Dichotomy issue

An Initial Algorithm for Rule-Governed Regularity

4: EXPERIMENTAL STUDIES

Massaro et al. 1979 Studies

Study 1: Initial Replications
    Procedure
    Orthographic structure
    Similarity effects
    Target-catch differences

Information Processing Model

Study 2: Precue Versus Postcue
    Orthographic structure
    Similarity effects
    Target versus catch trials
    Information processing model

Study 3: Mixed-Case
    Orthographic structure
    Similarity effects

Study 4: Limited Viewing Time
    Similarity effects
    Target versus catch trials
    Discussion

Study 5: Speeded RT Task with Good Visual Information
    Procedure
    Orthographic structure

Study 6: Speeded RT Task with Poor Visual Information
    Procedure
    Orthographic structure

Study 7: High-Accuracy RT Task with Poor Visual Information
    Procedure
    Orthographic structure

Summary of Accuracy and Reaction Time Experiments

Overt Judgments

Study 8: Typicality Ratings

Study 9: Positional-Frequency Ratings

Study 10: Regularity Versus Positional-Frequency Judgments

Summary of Overt Judgment Experiments

Appendix 4.1: Details of Method, Procedure, and Results of Study 1: Initial Replication

Appendix 4.1A: Rules for the Selection of Orthographically Regular and Irregular Strings

Appendix 4.1B: The 200 Stimulus Items Used in Studies 1-10

Appendix 4.2: Details of Method, Procedure, and Results of Study 2: Precue Versus Postcue

Appendix 4.3: Details of Method, Procedure, and Results of Study 3: Mixed-Case

Appendix 4.4: Details of Method, Procedure, and Results of Study 4: Limited Viewing Time

Appendix 4.5: Details of Method, Procedure, and Results of Study 5: Speeded RT Task with Good Visual Information

Appendix 4.6: Details of Method, Procedure, and Results of Study 6: Speeded RT Task with Poor Visual Information

Appendix 4.7: Details of Method, Procedure, and Results of Study 7: High-Accuracy RT Task with Poor Visual Information

Appendix 4.8: Details of Method, Procedure, and Results of Study 8: Typicality Ratings

Appendix 4.8A: The Pseudowords Used in Study 8

Appendix 4.8B: Directions for Typicality Ratings without Words and for Typicality Ratings with Pseudowords

Appendix 4.8C: Directions for Typicality Ratings with Words

Appendix 4.9: Details of Method, Procedure, and Results of Study 9: Positional-Frequency Ratings

Appendix 4.9A: Directions for Positional-Frequency Ratings

Appendix 4.10: Details of Method, Procedure, and Results of Study 10: Regularity Versus Positional-Frequency Paired-Judgments

Appendix 4.10A: Regularity Instructions for Paired-Judgments

Appendix 4.10B: Positional-Frequency Instructions for Paired-Judgments

5: STRUCTURAL DESCRIPTIONS

Descriptive Measures

Type Versus Token Counts

Scale of Frequency

Position-Sensitive Versus Position Insensitive Counts

The Most Effective Frequency Measure

Frequency Versus Regularity

Within Class Analysis

Word Frequency

Multiple Regression

Summary

Appendix 5.1: Stimulus Items and Results

Appendix 5.2: Single-Letter Positional Frequencies
    Three-letter words
    Four-letter words
    Five-letter words
    Six-letter words
    Seven-letter words

Appendix 5.3: Bigram Positional Frequencies
    Three-letter words
    Four-letter words
    Five-letter words
    Six-letter words
    Seven-letter words

6: SUMMARY AND CONCLUSIONS

REFERENCES

GLOSSARY

AUTHOR INDEX

SUBJECT INDEX

278 pp. 6 chapters. Figures, algorithms, models, author index, subject index, references, glossary, appendices. ISBN 0-444-85493-2.

184
McCormick, Ernest J.
Sanders, Mark S.

Human Factors in Engineering and Design (5ed.)
McGraw-Hill, 1982

The fifth edition of this ergonomics text surveys the human factors field; its thrust is that designers of features, facilities, equipment, and procedures in our environment should pay careful attention to the human use of these products in order to best meet human needs.

The text has five major divisions. In "Information Input" the authors discuss the capabilities of human sensory systems and speech communication, and point out how these capabilities must be considered when designing effective sensory displays and speech transmission systems. In "Human Output and Control" the authors discuss the design of hand and foot controls, data entry devices, and hand tools, and suggest how these devices should be designed based upon the sensory, psychomotor, and anthropometric characteristics of intended users. In "Workspace and Arrangement" the emphasis is on the relationship between the design and arrangement of physical facilities and comfort and performance. In "Environment" factors such as light, atmospheric condition, noise, and motion are considered. Finally, "Selected Topics" presents examples of investigations in specific areas that demonstrate the effects of design features on human performance and welfare. Selected references enable readers to delve further into fields only introduced by this text. This book is designed for first year human factors engineering students, is well written and easy to understand, and uses everyday examples to illustrate human factors concepts. It is a comprehensive survey of ergonomics, full of valuable information.

CONTENTS

Preface

Part 1: Introduction
    1. Prologue
    2. The data base of human factors

Part 2: Information Input
    3. Information input and processing
    4. Visual displays
    5. Auditory, tactual, and olfactory displays
    6. Speech communications

Part 3: Human Output and Control
    7. Human activities: their nature and effects
    8. Human control of systems
    9. Controls
    10. Hand tools and devices

Part 4: Work Space and Arrangement
    11. Applied anthropometry and work space
    12. Physical space and arrangement

Part 5: Environment
    13. Illumination
    14. Atmospheric conditions
    15. Noise
    16. Motion

Part 6: Human Factors: Selected Topics
    17. Application of human factors data
    18. The built environment
    19. Transportation and related facilities
    20. Selected aspects of work-related human error

Appendixes
    A. List of abbreviations
    B. Control devices
    C. Selected references

Indexes
    Name index
    Subject index

615 pp. 20 chapters in 6 parts. Photographs, figures, graphs, tables, author index, subject index, references, appendices. ISBN 0-07-044902-3.

McKay, Lucia   *SEE UNDER ID 106*

185
McLean, Ruari

The Thames and Hudson Manual of Typography
Thames and Hudson, 1980

(from *The Thames and Hudson Manuals* series, W.S. Taylor, general ed.)

Serves as an excellent introduction to typography for anyone who wishes to communicate by means of the visible word.

Although McLean is concerned primarily with the word as it appears on the printed page, much of what he has to say about readability, legibility, and attractiveness is just as applicable to the design of computer screen display as to the design of books. The historical outline of typography, which opens the book, covers the major developments from Gutenberg to the computerization of typesetting. McLean then discusses basic equipment and lighting for the studio. A chapter on legibility stresses the fact that "the designer must know *what* is to be read, *why* it is to be read, *who* will read it, and *when* and *where* it will be read," and explores modifications for specific purposes such as signage, diagrams, isotypes, and logarithms. A short chapter on calligraphy and the use of lettering as design is followed by chapters on typefaces and methods of composition. The concise text and excellent illustrations combine to create essential reading for anyone interested in communicating with words and letters. McLean demonstrates the different results that are achieved by using the same typeface with different film-setting systems: Monotype, Compugraphic, Photon, Monophoto, Linotron, and IBM Composer. He also discusses fonts, the point system, and the measurement of letters using *ems*. The second half of the book is concerned with paper, book design, the parts of a book, jobbing typography, and typography for newspapers and magazines, information applicable to any visual medium. This beautifully illustrated book offers a fine overview of typography and concludes with a comprehensive bibliography. Provides an overview of typography for typographers, printers, graphic artists, and book designers, but is also of interest to those involved in computer-generated display.

CONTENTS

Introduction

1: Historical Outline
    Origins
    The first printed books in the West
    From Plantin to Bodoni
    The Nineteenth Century
    The Twentieth Century

2: Studio and Equipment
    Furniture
    Lighting
    Basic equipment
    Stationery
    Special equipment
    Reference material

3: Legibility
  Three rules of legibility
  Legibility research
4: Lettering and Calligraphy
  Letter shapes
  Italic
  Lettering as design
5: Letters for Printing
  Description and classification
  Classification of typefaces
  Sans-serif type
  A font of type
  The point system and measurement of letters
  The parts of a letter
  Set
6: Methods of Composition
  Hot-metal machine composition
  Cold-metal (strike-on) setting
  Filmsetting
  Computers
  Word-processing systems
7: Paper
  What is paper?
  Qualities of paper
  A brief history of papermaking
  The raw materials
  The finishes of paper
  Watermarks
  Paper kinds and terms
  Paper sizes
  The weight of paper
  Paper and designers
8: Cast-Off and Layout
  The layout
  Copy mark-up and preparation
9: Book Design
  It begins with words
  Typographic style
  Centered or asymmetric typography?
  Originality
  House styles
  Margins
  Page size and shape
  Grids
  Treatment of illustrations
  'Bleeds'
10: The Parts of a Book
  Prelims
  Main text
  Captions
  Appendices
  Bibliography

Index
End-papers
Case
Jackets
11: Jobbing Typography
Working with clients
Designing stationery: letterheads
Other stationery
Tables
Programmes and menus
Calendars
Ambiguity
Posters
12: Newspaper and Magazine Typography
Newspaper design
Magazine design
Notes on the Text
Appendix 1: List of Suppliers
Appendix 2: British Standards Institution
Glossary of Filmsetting Terms
Further Reading
Index

216 pp. 12 chapters. Drawings, photographs, tables, general index, bibliography, appendices, endnotes. ISBN 0-500-67022-6.

186
McLendon, Charles B.
Blackistone, Mick

Signage: Graphic Communications in the Built World
McGraw-Hill, 1982

A well-written, well-illustrated comprehensive handbook for all those interested in the relatively recent field of signage; an intelligent synthesis by two leading American consultants.

During the 1970s, while the authors were involved with a General Services Administration (GSA) project to evaluate the concepts, techniques, and materials used for graphic communication in federal facilities, they realized that, while a professional may have expertise in his or her field, there is generally a lack of communication when it comes to solving the problems that arise when cooperation is needed to produce a unified signage program. This handbook emphasizes the importance of a total team concept in the design of signs. The book is divided into four parts. The first identifies various professional disciplines and defines their roles in the total team concept. The second deals with the concept of a total signage system, breaking it down into its various components from bidding and specifications to design drawings and layouts. The authors discuss not only the usual graphic units of form, space, color, and typography, but also the more practical aspects of materials and mounting hardware, as well as design guidelines for symbols and symbol signs. This part of the book concludes with a catalogue of signs for different facilities and stresses the importance of identifying the potential readers. The third part lists the GSA's contracting procedures. There are also useful chapters on: how to prepare cost estimates, design drawings for each sign type, and on technical specifications. The book concludes with a brief evaluation of each of the ten government facilities that were involved in the Federal Signage Demonstration Program, along with a summary of the results. This work offers a thoroughly professional synthesis of the requirements for effective environmental graphic communication, and would be of value to practitioners in any of the disciplines which participate in building and designing signs. A book for those involved with the design and construction of signs in the built environment: managers, architects, engineers, landscape architects, graphic designers, psychologists, building contractors, and sign fabricators and installers.

CONTENTS
Foreword
Preface
Part One: Program/Project Organization
One. The team concept
Two. Data base summary, vocabulary of terms, and classification of sign types
Part Two: The Systems Concept and How to Use It
Three. The first step
Four. The systems concept in action
Five. The next step: components of the system
Six. Design guidelines for symbols and symbol-signs
Seven. Catalog of signs
Part Three: Procurement: The Last Step
Eight. Elements of a contract package
Nine. Design intent drawings
Ten. Technical specifications
Part Four: Appendix
Digest of the data base
Tying down some loose ends
Notes and bibliography
Acronym glossary
Index

146 pp. 10 chapters in 4 parts. Drawings, figures, general index, bibliography, appendix, acronym glossary. ISBN 0-07-005740-0.

Mezrich, Joseph J.   *SEE UNDER ID 53*

187
Monkhouse, Francis J.
Wilkinson, Henry R.

Maps and Diagrams: Their Compilation and Construction (3ed.)
Methuen Inc., 1971

Teaches how to produce maps and diagrams through a focus on cartographic principles and techniques, the handling of data, and the acquisition of drawing skills.

The text opens with a lengthy chapter on the materials and techniques of map making. Drawing instruments and media are described as well as numerous techniques such as shading, color use, lettering, reproduction, and use of scales. The five chapters that comprise the main body of the text cover specific types of maps and diagrams: relief, climatic, economic, population, and settlement. Sources of data for these various figures are discussed as well as different techniques and diagram styles that can be used for producing each map and diagram type. The authors conceive of maps and diagrams as intimately related and regard diagrams as important for portrayal of geographic data. An appendix discusses statistical methods in geography. This third edition, published in 1971, has been updated to "give students some idea of the novel and exciting developments in tools, materials, techniques and methods (notably in the realms of quantification, mechanization, and automation)." This detailed text includes 237 well-drawn illustrations that provide useful examples of map and diagram types and techniques for the reader. Exercises are incorporated into the text throughout, and ample references are provided. These exercises and other material in the text have been tested over time in cartography courses at the University of Liverpool. Written primarily for serious students of geography, the book will, according to the authors, also be useful for historians, economists, and others who produce and handle maps. While this text presents the fundamental principles of cartography in an original and coherent fashion, it will be of interest to computer map-making professionals only as a reference. The rapid technological changes which have occurred since the publication of the third edition limit its usefulness to designers working with computer displays.

CONTENTS
Preface to the First Edition
Preface to the Second Edition
Preface to the Third Edition
Illustrations
1: Materials and Techniques
    Drawing instruments
    Inks and colours
    Drawing media
    Map compilation
    Scales and scale-lines
    Frames and panels
    Point-symbols
    Graphs and diagrams
    Chorochromatic maps

Chorographic compage maps
Isopleths and choropleths
Shading and stipples
Colour
Lettering
Reduction and enlargement
Map duplication and reproduction
Measurement of area and distance
Automated cartography
Models
Topological maps
2: Relief Maps and Diagrams
The depiction of relief
Morphometric analysis
Profiles
Gradient and slope
Intervisibility
Regression curves and scatter diagrams
Landscape drawing and field-sketching
Block-diagrams
Geological maps
3: Climatic Maps and Diagrams
Data
Isopleth maps
Columnar diagrams
Line-graphs
Wind-rose diagrams
Sunshine record and other duration diagrams
Rainfall dispersion diagrams
Climographs
Arrows
Symbols
Schematic diagrams
4: Economic Maps and Diagrams
Data
Non-quantitative maps
Isopleth maps
Choropleth maps
Quantitative symbols
Graphs
Columnar diagrams
Divided rectangles and circles
Star-diagrams
Flow-line maps
5: Population Maps and Diagrams
Data
Non-quantitative maps
Choropleth maps
Quantitative symbols
Isopleths
Divided circles
Columnar diagrams
Pyramids

Divided rectangles
Star-diagrams
Information diagrams
Three dimensional diagrams
Arrows
Graphs
Centrograms
Stereograms
Automatic population mapping
6: Maps and Diagrams of Settlements
Data
Facsimiles
Chorochromatic maps
Traces
Symbols
Choropleth maps
Isopleth maps
Columnar diagrams and divided rectangles
Special diagrams
Graphs
The use of computer graphics
Other aspects
Appendix: An Introduction to Numerical and Mechanical Techniques
R.G. Barry
Sampling
Mechanical methods
The statistical treatment of data
Note: symbols used in the appendix
Index

522 pp. 6 chapters. Maps, graphs, tables, mathematical formulae, footnotes, general index, appendix. ISBN 0-416-07440-5. (ISBN 0-416-07450-2)

188
Monmonier, Mark S.

Maps, Distortion, and Meaning
Association of American Geographers, 1977

(number 75-4 of the *Resource Papers for College Geography Series*, Salvatore Natoli, series ed.)

One of a series of resource papers produced by the Commission on College Geography of the Association of American Geographers, this paper offers a discussion of the theory of maps and map-making techniques, along with the skills necessary for effective map-reading.

Aimed at the undergraduate geography student, the book stresses that map-reading skills are as important as map-making skills. The emphasis is on the concept of cartographic communication, and particularly on how easily that communication can be distorted. Beginning with the underpinnings of maps—scale, projection, and symbol—the paper proceeds with a discussion of information theory as it pertains to map-making. The possibilities for distortion are detailed; for instance, use of great circle instead of straight line projections gives an entirely different impression of the relationship between destination and distance. The construction of maps to convey specific statistical information is thoroughly discussed, including the transformation of stepped statistical surfaces into choroplethic maps. The necessity of avoiding inclusion of extraneous information ("author noise" or "designer noise") is emphasized, along with methods intentionally used to skew the perception of information. Provides insight for the map-reader with some formal map skills, and alerts the designer of cartographic displays to some common pitfalls.

CONTENTS

Preface and User's Guide

I: Elements of a Map
    Projection
    Scale and generalization
    Symbolization

II: Cartographic Communication
    Major factors of map communication
    Information theory
    A model of cartographic communication

III: Projections and Pragmatism
    The Mercator mystique
    Area cartograms
    Distance transformations
    Stepped statistical surfaces

IV: Classification and Choroplethic Maps
    Classification error
    Pattern and perception
    Cartographic correlation
    Information overkill

V: Purpose and Distortion
    Route planning and route following
    Maps for data processing
    Advocacy, research, and mapping
    Maps and advertising
    Information and misinformation

VI: Concluding Remarks

Bibliography

51 pp. 6 chapters. Figures, maps, bibliography. (ISBN 0-89291-120-4)

189
Monmonier, Mark S.

Computer-Assisted Cartography: Principles and Prospects
Prentice-Hall, 1982

This book focuses on how computers store, retrieve, analyze, and display geographic information.

The emphasis is on how computers can make maps and how computers will eventually change the nature and appearance of maps. The first two chapters "explain how computers, programs, and data files can serve as archives for massive amounts of map information and plot tailor-made maps in seconds." The following four chapters analyze the interaction of map symbols, automated map analysis, and vector and raster digital map data. Chapter seven discusses the importance of organization among data files for the fulfillment of various mapping objectives. Examples of how the computer assists the designer to make a thorough analysis of the data and its possible applications are presented in the last chapter. The book looks briefly at hardware for storing and displaying map data and treats the two mapping programs, CMAP and SYMAP in some detail. An appendix lists sources of contact for additional information about current hardware and software developments. Common cartographic and mathematical terms are defined in the glossary. Well-organized and highly readable, with illustrations on almost every page, this basically non-technical work does require some knowledge of algebra and trigonometry. Written by a geographer, and primarily for geographers and cartographers, this work will also be useful to others who use computer-produced maps (geologists, foresters, planners, landscapers, architects, demographers, environmental scientists, computer scientists, civil engineers, and land surveyors) would find it useful too.

CONTENTS

Preface
1: AN INTRODUCTION
Computer Hardware for Graphic Display
An Historical Perspective
Implementation and Planning
2: COMPUTERS AND ALGORITHMS
Memory and Logic
Computers and Generable Behavior
Algorithms and Programming
    Programming languages
    An example in FORTRAN
    Mapping on the line printer
    Advanced developments
3: RASTER SYMBOLS AND SURFACE MAPPING
Uses and Limitations of Raster Symbols
Raster-Mode Surface Mapping
    The SYMAP program
    Trend surface maps
    Packages
    Some electives in SYMAP
    Grid interpolation

Cartographic Responsibilities and Decisions
4: RASTER-MODE MEASUREMENT AND ANALYSIS
Overlay Analysis
    Polygon-to-grid conversion
    Areal aggregation
    Set theory and land analysis
    Local operators
Graphic Display
    Hill shading
    Grid-to-vector conversion
Analysis of Satellite Imagery
    Radiometric classification
    Geometric adjustment
    Color composite maps
    Interactive systems
5: VECTOR SYMBOLS
Mathematical Basics
    Point transformations
    Matrix operators
    Windowing and clipping
Symbol Generation
    The railroad symbol
    The circle
    Shaded circles
    Shaded polygons
    Contour threading
    Label placement
6: CARTOMETRY AND MAP PROJECTIONS
Cartometry
    Deflection angles
    Area
    Centroids
    Point-in-polygon matching
    Overlay analysis
Projections and Transformations
    Conventional projections
    Cartograms
    Reprojection for clarity
Stereoscopic Views
Oblique Views
    Oblique projections
    Hidden line removal
7: CARTOGRAPHIC DATA STRUCTURES
Basic Concepts
    Addressing and memory
    Cartographic data manipulation
    An example
    Networking and information display
Topological Considerations
    DIME features
    Topographic data

8: COMPUTER-ASSISTED MAP DESIGN

Geographic Content
    Meaningful areal aggregation
    Data reduction
    Atlas layout

Map Layout

Planning Color Maps

Classification and Mapped Pattern

Generalization
    Feature selection
    Line smoothing
    Feature shifting
    Generalization and intelligence

Selected Readings

Sources of Additional Information

Glossary

Index

214 pp. 8 chapters. Drawings, photographs, figures, maps, graphs, mathematical formulae, algorithms, footnotes, general index, glossary, selected readings. ISBN 0-13-165308-3.

190
Moore, Martha V.
Nawrocki, Leon H.

technical report

The Educational Effectiveness of Graphic Displays for Computer Assisted Instruction
1978

(report number ARI-TP-332; U.S. Army Research Institute for the Behavioral and Social Sciences; sponsored by Office of the Deputy Chief of Staff for Personnel; September 1978)

Reviews the literature on instructional graphics and discusses the implications of the research finding in terms of graphic displays for computer-assisted instruction (CAI).

Computer-based instruction is especially important to the military because of its commitment to education and training. This paper is concerned with the military training applications of sophisticated graphic displays which can be modified to meet specific needs. This capability is of particular importance for use with CAI systems. The cost of interactive CAI systems, especially terminals, necessitates thorough consideration of display requirements. Important considerations in selecting graphic display systems include: display sophistication; motion portrayal requirements; drawing accuracy; and the complexity of rotation and size changes. Graphics requirements contribute greatly to the cost of a terminal. This report reviews the literature on the instructional effectiveness of graphics, discusses CAI research with graphics, and suggests a framework for individual differences. The authors conclude that assumptions about the inherent value of graphics for instructional purposes have no basis in empirical evidence and situations in which instructional graphics are effective need to be determined. "Intended for sponsors of R&D tasks and other research and military agencies" and for educators interested in CAI.

CONTENTS

Introduction

Where Are We?
    Perceptual efficiency
    Realism
    Learner preference and motivation
    Multiple sensory input
    Visuals and instructional media
    Individual differences
    Overview

CAI and Graphics
    Graphic studies
    Instructional strategies: reinforcement and sequencing
    Summary

Where Do We Go?
    The definitional problem
    Research framework

References

Distribution

52 pp. 3 parts. Figures, references.

191
Moore, Martha V.
Nawrocki, Leon H.
Simutis, Zita M.

technical report

The Instructional Effectiveness of Three Levels of Graphics Displays for Computer-Assisted Instruction
1979

(report number ARI-TP-359; U.S. Army Research Institute for the Behavioral and Social Sciences; sponsored by Office of the Deputy Chief of Staff for Personnel; April 1979)

Compares the instructional effectiveness of three types of graphics displays for computer-assisted instruction (CAI).

In an earlier paper in this series, Moore and Nawrocki reported that there is little empirical evidence to support a belief in the effectiveness of graphics in CAI. This paper reports experiments designed to explore the instructional effectiveness of computer graphics. Subjects "manipulated three different levels of computer graphics: high (animations plus line drawings), medium (line drawings alone), and low (schematic representations and boxed alphanumerics)." For the experiments, three groups of thirty subjects were given a CAI lesson on the psychophysiology of audition, differing only in the level of graphics presented. Four types of performance tests were administered: acquisition and use of principles; identification of structures; definitions and use of terminology; and memory of specific facts. From these four tests, information on the role of computer graphics for acquisition of specific knowledge categories could be gathered. Results from this experiment indicate "that the type of graphics used during the CAI lesson did not affect lesson completion time or final performance on the retention tests." Intended for researchers in CAI and computer graphics.

CONTENTS

Introduction

Method
    Subjects
    Design
    Lesson materials
    Graphics levels
    Attitude survey
    Dependent measures
    Apparatus
    Procedures

Results
    Performance measures
    Aptitude and performance
    Attitude toward CAI

Conclusions

References

Distribution

List of Tables

List of Figures

27 pp. 3 parts. Drawings, figures, tables, references.

192

Moroze, Michael L.

technical report

The Ability to Process Abstract Information
1983

(report number AFIT/CI/NR-83-51T; Department of Industrial Engineering and Operations Research, University of Massachusetts; sponsored by Air Force Institute of Technology; September 1983)

Investigates the capacity of the human operator to process information and describes the design implications of human performance capacities on man-machine systems.

The investigation uses head-up display (HUD) in aircraft as its research example. The head-up display presents information on a transparent glass which permits the pilot to access displayed data without leaving the visual plane of the exterior environment. HUD was developed to aid pilots, especially those in high workload and crisis situations such as landing, weapons delivery, and terrain following. In actual use, however, the HUD may be most intrusive in the very situations it was created for; pilots, in fact, prefer to turn it off and use the traditional cockpit displays. The author discusses the design errors which lead to these problems and addresses the research needed to increase the effective application of technology to human needs. Included in the thesis is an excellent review of the literature, detailing work that has already been performed and applying it to ongoing research. A useful reference list follows the text. Three appendices—tables summarizing results, a subject breakdown, and sample questionnaires—conclude the report. This thesis addresses issues that will interest designers involved with any high technology area which relies on the man-machine interface (including designers of visual displays, graphics, and management programs), in addition to its direct relevance to military aircraft display design.

CONTENTS

INTRODUCTION

CHAPTER I: REVIEW OF THE LITERATURE

Stress
    Stressor
    Perception
    Physiological responses
    Psychological responses

Information Processing
    Filter theories
    Controlled and automatic processing

Workload

Human Performance Considerations
    General considerations of the head-up display

Possible problems of HUD Use

Stress
    Information processing
    Mental workload
    Symbology

II: RESEARCH DESIGN AND METHOD

Research Design
    Purpose
    Definition

Method
    Subjects
    Apparatus
    Procedure
    Training
    Testing
    Measures

III: RESULTS AND DISCUSSION

Results
    Training and testing analysis
    Percent correct digital sequences
    Questionnaire analyses

Discussion
    Observations
    Recommendations

REFERENCES
APPENDIX A
APPENDIX B
APPENDIX C

83 pp. 3 chapters. Photographs, figures, graphs, tables, models, references, appendices.

193
Muckler, Frederick A. (ed.)

collection

Human Factors Review: 1984
Human Factors Society, 1984

Provides an overview of current trends in human factors research by presenting critical reviews and discussions of technical literature in eight broad areas of interest to the human factors community.

This is the long-awaited first volume in a projected series from the Human Factors Society. The present volume includes critical discussions of research and available literature on human vigilance and reliability; human factors in terminal and workstation design; human factors in voice technology; dialogue design; learning and instructional strategies in computer education and training; military and civilian applications of team research and team training from 1955-1980. The eight notably well-organized essays are critically focused, succinct, and informative. Each begins with an abstract and concludes with abundant recent and historically important references. A promising beginning for what should be an indispensable critical reference series for information scientists, cognitive psychologists, anthropologists, and all who are involved in disciplines affecting—or affected by—human factors.

CONTENTS
Preface
1. Research relevance and the information glut
   Robert R. Mackie
2. Human reliability
   David Meister
3. An evaluation of human factors research on visual display terminals in the workplace
   Martin G. Helander, Patricia A. Billingsley, Jayne M. Schurick
4. Human factors in voice technology
   Michael E. McCauley
5. Dialogue design considerations for interactive computer systems
   Beverly H. Williges, Robert C. Williges
6. Interfacing learning strategies and instructional strategies in computer training programs
   Eleanor R.N. Robinson, Frederick G. Knirk
7. Computer applications to instruction
   Ray Eberts, John F. Brock

8. Team research and team training: a state-of-the-art review
   Jean L. Dyer
Author index
Subject index

345 pp. 8 chapters. Figures, tables, author index, subject index, references.

194
Muehrcke, Phillip

Thematic Cartography
Association of American Geographers, 1972

(vol. 19 in the *Commission on College Geography Resource Paper* series)

A brief description of the state of thematic cartography, designed for use as a supplement to available undergraduate texts.

The author makes the distinction between primary mapping, in which original data is acquired, interpreted, and used to create maps, and thematic cartography, in which specialized maps are created using available information. He also distinguishes between map making (the physical process of producing maps) and cartograpy (the "conceptual, problem oriented research directed at formalizing the *science* underlying the *art*"). In doing so he examines the importance of objectivity and communication between the two fields, emphasizing the relations of data collection, cartographic processing, and map usage to each other. The advent of computers and automation in cartography are viewed as having "revitalized and reoriented a discipline founded upon convention" because a greater understanding and control of these relationships is possible. A novel (though dated) approach to thematic mapping, this research paper will be of interest to anyone significantly involved with data collection for cartographic applications, the processing of cartographic data, or map utilization.

CONTENTS
I: INTRODUCTION
II: DATA COLLECTION
1: Automation
2: Type of Data
3: Scale
4: Sampling and Prediction
5: Measurement
6: Preprocessing
III: MAPPING
1: Production Efficiency
    (a) Automation
    (b) Equipment and materials
    (c) Task reduction
2: Product Effectiveness
    (a) Symbolic representation
    (b) Scientific model building

IV: IMAGE PROCESSING
1: Visual Analysis
2: Quantitative Map Analysis
3: Optical Analysis
4: Tactual Map Reading
V: THE OUTLOOK
REFERENCES AND SELECTED READINGS
66 pp. 5 chapters. Figures, maps, references.

195
Müller-Brockmann, Josef

Grid Systems in Graphic Design: A Visual Communication Manual for Graphic Designers, Typographers and Three Dimensional Designers
Arthur Niggli, 1981
(text in both German and English, with the German title of *Raster systeme für die visuelle Gestaltung: Ein Handbuch für Grafiker, Typografen und Ausstellungsgestalter*)

Offers the typographer and visual display designer an introduction to and survey of the functions and applications of grid systems for solving visual problems of two and three dimensions.

The work includes detailed explanations of the essential points of grid design and its numerous applications, and provides the designer with a practical reference tool which will facilitate the solving of visual problems. The author begins with a succinct but comprehensive survey of prominent typefaces from the past and present, followed by an examination of the advantages and disadvantages of various column widths and margin proportions. The central portion of the work consists of a thorough discussion of grid construction and the problems associated with producing an aesthetically coherent and functionally effective grid, including the use of photographs and illustrations in complex grid fields. An extensive section of useful examples illustrates these themes. This is followed by discussions of: grid applications for business; the advantageous use of grid systems in three-dimensional design; and systematically designed exhibitions. The work concludes with an historical survey of ancient and modern mathematical forms of order, situating the grid in its historical context. Throughout the work, copious illustrations and photographs from a variety of international sources complement the well-organized and informative text. This book will serve as an excellent introductory and reference work for beginner and advanced professional alike, and is limited only by the brevity of its bibliography. Josef Müller-Brockmann has written a book of interest to beginning students of graphic design, typographers, photographers, and graphic designers.

CONTENTS
Foreword
The book
Grid and design philosophy
The typographic grid
What is the purpose of the grid?

Sizes of paper
The typographic measuring system
Typeface alphabets
Width of column
Leading
Margin proportions
Page numbers
Body and display faces
Construction of the type area
Construction of the grid
Type and picture area with 8 grid fields
Type and picture area with 20 grid fields
Type and picture area with 32 grid fields
The photograph in the grid system
The illustration in the grid system
Solid tint in the grid system
Practical examples
The grid system in corporate identity
The grid in three-dimensional design
Examples of exhibitions
Systems of order in ancient and modern times
Concluding remarks
Bibliography
List of artists

176 pp. 25 chapters. Drawings, photographs, bibliography, list of artists.
ISBN 3-7212-0145-0.

196
National Research Council.   **Video Displays, Work, and Vision**
Committee on Vision   National Academy Press, 1983

(prepared for the National Institute for Occupational Safety and Health
[NIOSH] by the Panel on Impact of Video Viewing on Vision of
Workers, Edward J. Rinalducci, chair)

The concise text of an authoritative report which reviews scientific
studies pertinent to the vision problems encountered in occupational
video viewing.

This report is an investigation of the problems related to the use of
video display terminals (VDTs) in the workplace. Through a review of
the current state of knowledge it covers: 1) the current level of
understanding of the visual factors and underlying mechanisms that
produce discomfort in video viewing; 2) problems of definition of such
terms as "eyestrain" and the relationship of physiological, subjective,
ergonomic, and performance measures to such concepts; 3) the questions
of whether adequate standards for display characteristics can be
established based on existing knowledge in such areas and whether there
is an adequate basis for standardizing viewing conditions; 4) how VDT
problems relate to a substandard environment and how many such
conditions would remain even under ideal conditions; 5) the relative

roles of visual, ergonomic and psychosocial factors in vision problems encountered; 6) a possible relationship between vision symptoms and more general stress responses; 7) a comparison of vision problems with VDTs related to vision problems in comparable non-VDT tasks; and 8) the question of whether there are radiation hazards associated with the use of VDTs. The twelve panel members were chosen for their expertise in ophthalmology, optometry, oculomotor function, physiological optics, epidemiology, occupational health, radiation biophysics, display technology, illumination engineering, human factors, and industrial and organizational psychology. All members reviewed the literature, consulted with additional experts, wrote draft chapters, critically reviewed and discussed all other panel members' chapters, and then revised their chapters based on all the above inputs. The resulting collaborative effort is this published report. With a thirty-page list of references, it stands as the most up to date and authoritative attempt to deal with issues of VDT uses and standards.

CONTENTS

Preface

EXECUTIVE SUMMARY

1: SUMMARY OF FINDINGS

Introduction
Background
Focus of the study
Organization of the report
The literature base
The nature of VDT work

Field Studies of VDT Workers and Workstations
Studies of radiation emission from VDTs
Cataracts
Field surveys based on self-reports of VDT operators

Equipment and Workstation Design
VDT design and display quality
Lighting and reflections
Human factors

The Concept and Study of "Visual Fatigue"

Job Design and Psychosocial Stress

Design, Practice, and Standards
Principles of good design and practice
Public education
Standards and guidelines for VDT use

Research Needs

2: CRITIQUE OF SURVEY METHODOLOGY

Introduction

Survey of VDT Users
Adequacy of theory
Adequacy of research design
Adequacy of measurement
Adequacy of sampling
Unanswered questions

Research Design Considerations
   Control and choice in studies of VDT physical parameters
   Practical considerations
3: RADIATION EMISSIONS AND THEIR EFFECTS
Types and Levels of Radiation Emitted by VDTs
   Studies of emission levels
   Radiation safety standards
   VDT emissions and ambient radiation
Biological Effects of Radiation
   Ionizing radiation
   Nonionizing radiation
   Skin rashes
VDT Use and Cataracts
   Prevalence and causes of cataracts
   The evidence regarding VDT use and cataracts
   Methods of studying whether there is a relationship between VDT
   use and cataracts
   Conclusions about radiation hazards
4: DISPLAY CHARACTERISTICS
Effects of CRT Display Variables
   Luminance
   Contrast and contrast polarity
   Raster structure
   Resolution
   Jitter and temporal instability
   Refresh rate and persistence
   Color
   Reflection characteristics
   A summary measure: modulation transfer function
Display Measurement: Techniques and Problems
   Measurement techniques
   Measurement of various parameters
   Standardization
Flat-Panel Displays
   Dot-matrix display variables
   Dot-matrix display quality measures
   Advantages and disadvantages of flat-panel displays compared with
   CRTs
Filters for VDTs
   Kinds of filters
   Evaluation of filters
5: LIGHTING AND REFLECTIONS
Illumination
   Transient adaption
   Reflections
   Glare
Review of VDT Studies
   Field surveys of VDT workers
   Field surveys comparing VDT and non-VDT work
   Laboratory studies

6: ANTHROPOMETRY AND BIOMECHANICS IN VDT
APPLICATIONS

Postural Strain

Overview of Biomechanical Factors
    Work posture
    Muscular load
    Joint angles
    Anthropometry

Workstation Design
    Effects of chair design features on the spine
    Effects of working height on postural strain
    Effects of display position on postural strain

7: VISUAL TASKS, FUNCTIONS, AND SYMPTOMS

Visual Issues in VDT Studies
    Field surveys
    Experimental field and laboratory studies of visual functions in
    VDT work
    The need for job and task analysis
    Are there unique features of VDT tasks?
    The special task of reading
    The problematic concepts of "visual fatigue" and "eyestrain"
    Refractive errors and visual difficulties
    Myopia

Oculomotor Factors Affecting Visual Performance
    Eye movements
    Blinking
    Triadic near reflex: combined focusing, convergence, and aperture
    mechanisms

Summary and Conclusions

8: JOB DESIGN AND ORGANIZATIONAL VARIABLES

Introduction
    Workers' complaints and job structures
    Defining psychosocial stress and strain

A Framework for Studying Psychosocial Stressors in VDT Work
    Person-environment fit
    Objective and subjective fit

Stressors for Study in VDT Work
    Control
    Participation
    Predictability and controllability
    Complexity
    Role ambiguity
    Threat of unemployment
    Quantitative workload
    Prescription for overload—deadline plus delay
    Responsibility for persons
    Role conflict
    Social support

Discussion and Conclusions

9: DESIGN, PRACTICE, AND STANDARDS FOR VDT EQUIPMENT AND WORK

Principles of Good Design and Practice
> Image quality and display design
> Lighting and reflections
> Systematic design of VDT workstations
> Job design and organizational variables

Standards and Guidelines for VDT Design

10: RESEARCH NEEDS

Effects of Displays on Visual Activity
> Objective correlates of visual complaints
> Relating display characteristics to workplace conditions
> Effects of image instability
> Distinguishing specific effects of VDTs

Psychosocial Stressors

APPENDICES

A: A Review of Methodology in Studies of Visual Functions During VDT Tasks
> *John O. Merritt*

B: Review of a Preliminary Report on a Cross-Sectional Survey of VDT Users at the *Baltimore Sun*
> *R. Van Harrison*

C: Dissent
> *Lawrence W. Stark*

D: Biographical Sketches of Panel Members and Staff

REFERENCES

273 pp. 10 chapters. Photographs, figures, charts, graphs, tables, references, appendices. (ISBN 0-309-03388-8)

National Technical Information Service

overview

Citations from the NTIS and Department of Energy Databases
1982-83

These citation collections from the NTIS and Department of Energy databases contain a significant set of the technical literature on display devices and systems between the years 1951 and 1983. *Signs and Display Systems*, from the NTIS database, consists entirely of technical reports from the United States and some European researchers. Most of these citations refer to military research relating to human factors and display design but there is also work on map and symbol design. The collections on *Interactive Display Devices* from the NTIS and DOE databases include both technical reports and journal literature from North American, Japanese, European, and Russian research communities. Both collections also include a subject term index. Although these collections focus on the development and applications of interactive graphics systems rather than display design per se, they do provide useful references for the designer. In particular, the collection for the Department of Energy database includes user's manuals and descriptions of design packages which are useful in assessing the state of the art.

3 reports.

197
National Technical Information Service

technical report

Signs and Display Systems: Graphic Design and Human Engineering (Citations from the NTIS Database, 1964-March 1982)
1982

(National Technical Information Service; June 1982)

CONTENTS
  Bibliographic information
  Ordering reports
  Prices of reports
  Sample citation
  Technical Application Center
  About NTISearches
  Citations

247 pp. 245 citations.

198
National Technical Information Service

technical report

Interactive Display Devices: Citations from the NTIS Database (June 1970-September 1983)
1983

(National Technical Information Service; September 1983)

CONTENTS
  Bibliographic information
  Ordering reports
  Sample citation
  About the data base
  About published searches
  Title list
  Citations
  Subject term index

164 pp. 227 citations. Subject index.

199
National Technical Information Service

technical report

Interactive Display Devices: Citations from the U.S. Department of Energy Database (June 1976-August 1983)
1983

(National Technical Information Service; August 1983)

CONTENTS
  Bibliographic information
  Ordering reports
  Sample citation
  About the data base
  About published searches

Title list
Citations
Subject term index

262 pp. 278 citations. Subject index.

200
Nawrocki, Leon H.

Alphanumeric versus Graphic Displays in a Problem-Solving Task
1972

technical report

(report number TN-227; U.S. Army Behavior and Systems Research Laboratory; sponsored by U.S. Army Combat Developments Command; September 1972)

This is a comparison of performance on a problem-solving task when the task was explained using alphanumeric symbols as opposed to "graphic" (pictorial) symbols. The study also examined the influence of memory requirements and information complexity on performance of the problem-solving task.

The problem-solving task used in the study was a military problem in which subjects were required to write orders that would direct the movement of military units from one configuration to another based upon updated displays. The unit configurations were displayed using either alphanumeric or graphic symbols. The subjects were either given access to both configurations as they worked out the problem or else forced to work the problem from memory, after the original configuration was removed following a ten minute study period. Four levels of complexity of information were presented in the tables. Display format and memory requirement were between-subjects variables, while information complexity was a repeated measure or within-subjects variable. Eighty enlisted men participated in the study and these men were randomly assigned to the four (between-subjects) experimental conditions. Each subject worked a series of problems at each of the four levels of information complexity. The measures of task performance examined by the experimenter were accuracy (percentage of correct responses), speed (median time to solve problems), and type of errors (percentage errors of omission versus commission). An error of commission "occurred when a unit was correctly selected but the number moved or the relocation was incorrect." Errors of omission involved "failures to include a unit type which required movement." The results of this study showed no difference between type of display format when memory was required. When memory was not required fewer errors of omission were committed under the alphanumeric display format than under the graphic display format. Some interactions between memory requirement and information complexity were also found. The research reported in this paper is methodologically sound and well written. It is important to note that the displays investigated in this study were displays on an 8" x 10" piece of paper rather than computer displays. This research was conducted for the express purpose of finding means to improve speed and accuracy in the processing of military information, particularly for making tactical decisions. The research does, however, have relevance for individuals outside the military who are interested in display format.

CONTENTS

Background

Objectives

Method
    Task and apparatus
    Design
    Subjects
    Procedure
    Dependent variables

Results
    Accuracy
    Speed

Implications

Appendix

Distribution

DD Form 1473 (Document Control Data - R&D)

30 pp. 5 chapters. Graphs, tables, footnotes, appendix.

201
Nelson, Roy P.

The Design of Advertising (3ed.)
Wm C Brown, 1977

A basic text on layout for students of advertising.

This book, written by a professional designer who also teaches layout at the college level, is intended to help advertising students master the basic elements of advertising layout. Since the purpose of advertising is generally to sell a product, a service, or an idea, this book offers a particular and central point of view which may only be touched upon in other works on design and layout. Its purpose is to teach advertising students the basic principles of design which will allow them to produce successful, visually pleasing designs. The book is divided into sixteen well-organized chapters, starting with graphics and creativity and proceeding through typography, production, layout, and color to the design of posters and long-term design of the kind used in trademarks, logotypes, record covers and packages. Four separate chapters deal with the different approaches that must be used in newspapers, magazines, television, and direct-mail advertising. This is a very basic, yet comprehensive, textbook. The book includes a series of assignments for each chapter, a glossary of advertising and editorial terms and a very extensive bibliography. It is recommended as a good overall introduction to the art of visual persuasion. (Note: A fourth edition of this work was published in 1981, but was not available for bibliographic verification.)

CONTENTS

INTRODUCTION

Advertising Layout: What It Is

Advertising Layout: Who Does It

Style and Taste

Working with the Professional Designer

CHAPTER 1: GRAPHICS AND THE CREATIVE PROCESS

The Creative Person: Who He Is

Creativity: What It Is

The Matter of Style

    The changing face of style

    Style and restriction

    The designer in defense of his choices

The Purpose of the Ad

Facing the Assignment

Facing Client Stipulations

Visualizing the Ad

Avoiding "Adiness"

Seeing the Ad in Context

Creativity and the Designer

    Is there a "right" answer?

    Is there a "right" approach?

Levels and Stages of Creativity

Stimulating Creativity

    Reading and observing

    Research

    Experimentation

    Using the "swipe file"

Letting Go

Facing "Designer's Block"

CHAPTER 2: PUTTING IT INTO WORDS

Kinds of Advertising

Institutional Advertising

Where Advertising Originates

Media of Advertising

Advertising's Job

The Challenge of Copy

The Mechanics of Copy

The Research Phase

The Theme

    Hanging it on a news peg

Putting Yourself in the Reader's Place

    Involving the reader

Writing Style

    Guidelines for copywriters

Naming Names

Ad Talk

The Headline
    Functions of a headline
    Kind of headlines

Slogans

Anthropomorphic Selling

Humor in Advertising

Copyreading and Proofreading

Copy for Broadcast
    The "design" of a radio commercial
    Who produces radio commercials
    Slanting the commercial
    The mechanics
    Radio style

The Logic of Advertising

The "New Advertising"

Restraints upon Advertising

Truth in Advertising

CHAPTER 3: ELEMENTS TO ARRANGE

The Basic Element

Moods in Line

Optical Illusions

Advertising Elements

Peripheral Elements

Arranging the Elements

Indicating the Elements
    Headlines
    Copy
    Art
    The logotype

CHAPTER 4: TOOLS TO DO THE JOB

Primary Tools and Supplies

Other Materials to Consider

Care and Treatment

CHAPTER 5: WHAT THE DESIGNER SHOULD KNOW ABOUT PRODUCTION

The Printing Process
    Letterpress
    Offset lithography
    Gravure
    Stencil printing
    Some comparisons

Reproducing the Pictures
    Line reproduction
    Halftone reproduction

Setting the Type
    Hot type
    Cold type
    Is hot type dead?

How Production Affects the Designer

The Pasteup
    Pasteup supplies
    The procedure

CHAPTER 6: LAYOUT STAGES AND FORMATS

Layout Stages
    Thumbnails
    Rough layouts
    Comprehensives
    Pasteups

The Matter of Size

Nine Basic Formats
    Mondrian layout
    Picture-window layout
    Copy-heavy layout
    Frame layout
    Circus layout
    Multipanel layout
    Silhouette layout
    Type-specimen layout
    Rebus layout

Using the Alphabet as a Base

CHAPTER 7: APPLYING THE PRINCIPLES OF DESIGN

Design Defined

Order and Beauty: The Relationship

Design and Layout: The Difference

The Ingredients of Design

The Principles of Design
    Balance
    Proportion
    Sequence
    Unity
    Emphasis

Beyond the Principles

The Test of a Good Layout

CHAPTER 8: WORKING WITH TYPE

Where Our Letters Come From

The Form of the Letters
    Type with serifs
    Type without serifs
    Type that slants
    Effects of handwriting on type
    Modern influences

Supergraphics

The Point System

Categories of Type
    Subcategories
    The variety of faces
    Type moods to consider
    Other considerations

On Mixing Types
The Case for Readability
Body Type
    Shape of the copy block
    Picture captions
Display Type
    Calligraphy
    Punctuation in display type
    Word emphasis
Copyfitting
    The square-inch method
    The column-inch method
Spacing
Lettering Headlines
    The guidelines
    Optical spacing
    Letter strokes
    Observing letters
CHAPTER 9: WORKING WITH ART
Relevancy
The Logic of Art
The Value of Vagueness
Pictures that Lie
What to Watch for in Pictures
    Size
    Scale
The Variety of Renderings
Art Styles
    Commercial art vs. fine art
    Stock art
The Coming of Photography
    Model releases
Amateurism
Editing Pictures
Cropping
Arranging Pictures
Handling Pictures
Indicating Art
The Presentation
CHAPTER 10: WORKING WITH COLOR
The Case for Black
Why Use Color?
    Color's relationship to shape
    Color and passivity
The Dimensions of Color
Primary and Secondary Colors
The Color Wheel
Appropriate Colors
    The symbolism of color
    The unusual in color

The Production of Color
Cutting the Cost of Color
    Substitutes for process color
    "Posterizing" the colors
    Color that's free
Color in Newspapers
    ROP color
    Rotogravure color
    Comic-section color
    The cost
Choosing a Second Color
Indicating Color on the Layout
CHAPTER 11: NEWSPAPER ADVERTISING
The Newspaper as an Advertising Medium
    Overcoming the limitations
Serving Local Advertisers
Nature of Retail Advertising
    Establishing a graphic style
    Who does the ads
    Koehler's "Seven Deadly C's"
    The question of quality
    Illustrations vs. photographs
The Mat Services
    Mats from manufacturers
    Editing mats
    Using borders
    The unified look
Roughing in the Ad
    The focus
    The theme
    Procedure
    Size and shape of the ad
    Special layout sheets
    Keeping production costs down
The Ad in Place
CHAPTER 12: MAGAZINE ADVERTISING
The Other Magazine Category
Statistics in Magazines
Serving the Advertiser
The Local Advertiser and Magazines
Magazine Formats
The Advantages of Magazines
Magazines and TV
The Challenge of Magazine-Ad Design
CHAPTER 13: TELEVISION ADVERTISING
Nature of the Audience
Who uses TV
Kinds of Commercials
Lengths of Commercials
Ways of Presenting Commercials

Animation

Planning the Commercial

The Storyboard
Designing the storyboard
The elements you work with
The variety of shots
Transitions
A summary of advice

Producing the Commercial
The costs

Restrictions

CHAPTER 14: Direct-Mail Advertising

Direct Mail: What It Is

The Pre-Design Phase

Direct Mail and the Designing Process

Form

Production Aspects
Paper stock
Printing processes

In-Plant Printing
Duplicators
Copiers
Ways to cut costs

CHAPTER 15: POSTERS AND DISPLAYS

Those Burma-Shave Signs

The Ecology Thing

A Bit of History

The Poster as Art

Outdoor Advertising
Outdoor as local advertising
Production

Doing the Comp
Some basic rules

The Poster Idea
Outdoor classics

Transit Advertising

Point-of-Purchase Advertising
First came signs
The forms are endless
P-O-P design and production

CHAPTER 16: LONG-TERM DESIGN

Trademarks
Trademark terminology
What trademarks do
Where trademarks are used
Symbology

Designing the Trademark
    Versatility in trademarks
    Shape
    Precautions to take
    Redesign
    Factors beyond the designer's control
Legal Considerations
    "Weak" and "strong" trademarks
Corporate Identity Programs
The NBC Affair
Logotypes
Book Jackets
    The five panels
    Production decisions
Record Covers
Packages
    Packages and the ecology
    Decisions to be made
    Shape and design of the package
    When packages change
ASSIGNMENTS
GLOSSARY
BIBLIOGRAPHY
INDEX

337 pp. 16 chapters. Drawings, photographs, footnotes, general index, bibliography, glossary. ISBN 0-697-04327-4.

202
Neurath, Otto

International Picture Language/Internationale Bildersprache
Department of Typography, University of Reading, 1980

(a facsimile reprint of the 1936 English edition with a German translation by Marie Neurath)

A classic work in the field of graphics for public instruction, by a pioneer in the field of international symbols.

Recently, there has been renewed interest in Otto Neurath's work in visual communication, particularly in those areas studied under the acronym ISOTYPE (International System Of TYpographic Picture Education), upon which internationally-familiar symbols are based. This facsimile reprint of work originally published in 1936 is Neurath's extensive explanation of the principles of ISOTYPE work. The text is printed in English at the top and German at the bottom of each page. It is a summary of pictorial-statistical methods used to develop an international picture language and is directed toward the field of public instruction. Neurath used this foundation for later work in instructional design and visual education. The text is in Basic English, a core vocabulary reduced to 850 words. Because of this constraint, the reader may notice awkward usage, language, and typographical peculiarities. The original illustrations, though dated, represent principles of graphic methods that still apply in visual communication and public instruction. Clearly, this volume is a historical document of special interest to researchers and practitioners in the fields of instructional design, visual communication, and visual education.

CONTENTS
> Editorial introduction
> Dedication
> *International picture language*

70 pp. Drawings, graphs. ISBN 0-7049-0489-6.

203
Newcomb, John

The Book of Graphic Problem-Solving: How to Get Visual Ideas When You Need Them
Bowker, 1984
(from *The Bowker Design Series*)

Teaches a systematic approach to solving graphics problems creatively and effectively.

A good portion of the book describes the Bite method for developing creative graphics. In the Bite system an author's or editor's working title (or other short statement) is thoroughly analyzed in a prescribed and work oriented way to obtain the various meanings and implications of the title. The ideas generated in this way can then be transferred into visual forms. The author stresses the importance of producing visual messages that complement written messages. Another section of the book discusses the "conversation" that takes place between a publication and its readers and describes ways to create an entertaining publication. The author presents a number of helpful tips for the aspiring graphics artist and a seven-stage sequence for attacking graphics problems. The ideas presented in this chapter are derived from interviews the author conducted with experts in the graphics design field. A final chapter discusses ways to produce good graphics on a low budget. Over 250 photographs and sketches provide convincing demonstrations of the techniques the author advocates. This book developed out of a seminar on the creative process given by the author for Folio Magazine's Face-to-Face publishing seminar series. Especially intended for students, art directors, designers, and illustrators, this work could also be useful for anyone doing creative work, such as editors, copywriters, and playwrights.

CONTENTS

Preface

Introduction

Why Is This Book Needed?
> The importance of using words and pictures to create effective communication
> The designer's function and the skills that are needed
> Artists, writers, and editors: the integrated creative team
> Starting the creative process with words

The Bite System: A Reliable Starting Point
   A word-oriented method for creating visual solutions
   Dissecting the problem and creating more graphic "handles" for
   verbal/visual display
   Three applications of the Bite System
   A portfolio of problems and solutions: the Bite System in action
Shaping Your Conversation With the Reader
   Pace, variety, and excitement within a format discipline
   The "body language" of a publication and creating a personality for
   your magazine
   The twelve basic tools for surprising and entertaining the reader
   Style and function in magazine formats
Train Yourself to Be an Effective Design Thinker
   Great idea makers and their products
   How top designers attack graphic problems: mental strategies and
   creative work procedures
   How to make the most of your ability to find solutions to
   communications problems
   Long-term training and maintenance for your graphic imagination
Low Budgets: Champagne Design with Beer Money
   Communicative excellence with limited art budgets: ways to cut
   costs and still get good graphic results
   Your future as a professional graphic designer
Picture Credits
About the Author

259 pp. 5 chapters. Drawings, photographs. (ISBN 0-8352-1895-3)

204

Newman, Richard L.

technical report

**Operational Problems Associated with Head-Up Displays during
Instrument Flight**
1980

(report number AFAMRL-TR-80-116; Crew Systems Consultants;
sponsored by Air Force Aerospace Medical Research Laboratory;
October 1980)

Problems confronting pilots using Head-Up Display (HUD) units are
considered in this study. HUDs are intended to assist pilots in landing
their aircraft during inclement weather by projecting the flight
instruments upon the frontal windscreen in the direct sightline of the
pilot.

Newman's study utilized a questionnaire that was sent to both military
and civilian pilots (primarily military) whose aircraft are equipped with
this technology. The questionnaire addressed basic issues which
included: problems of perception in changing flight conditions;
symbology; accuracy and stability; brightness; clutter; pilot confidence in
HUD; vertigo and disorientation; training and usage; frequency of use
according to weather and flight phase; and presentation of desired data.
The author found that pilots reported persistent problems with

disorientation and vertigo, excessive brightness of display for night use, poor placement of HUD relative to preferred pilot seating height, and poor production quality of some devices. It was also found that pilots whose HUD system included ILS presentation did not want this feature. In addition, the author raised important points in his conclusion about the haphazard way pilots are introduced to HUD, the use of HUD in training undergraduate pilots, and different approaches to the dynamics issue. This report includes three appendices which present the original questionnaire, a format for follow-up interviews, and a bibliography. This is a readable, informative study concerning a highly complex and vital technology.

CONTENTS

ABBREVIATIONS

BACKGROUND

Historical HUD Developments

Potential for All-Weather Landings

Present Day Operational HUDs

Operational Problems with HUDs

HUD Training Assessment

HUD Survey

Problems Addressed

Pilots Surveyed

Responses Received
    Degree of use of the HUD
    Operational problems
    Symbology problems
    Vertigo/disorientation
    Optical problems
    Stability/accuracy issues
    Clutter
    Pilot confidence in the HUD
    The data desired in a HUD
    Training and procedural issues
    Previous HUD experience
    General comments

Additional Questionnaires

A REVIEW OF HUD TRAINING

Monitoring of Pilots During Initial HUD Flying

Current Training Techniques

Effect of Pilot Experience of HUD Survey

A REVIEW OF HEAD-UP DISPLAY CHARACTERISTICS

General Arrangment of HUDs
    Source of the image
    Optical design
    Brightness
    Significant properties of HUDs

HUD Classification

Data Displayed in HUDs

HUD PROBLEMS UNCOVERED IN SURVEY

Summary

Brightness

Field-of-View

Design of Reference Position

Display Motion

Disorientation or Vertigo Inducement

ILS-Related Problems

Detection of HUD Status

Unresolved Issues
    Vertigo/disorientation
    Information presented on HUD
    Display dynamics
    ILS interpretation
    Procedural issues

TRAINING ISSUES

Organizational Attitudes

Flight Control with the HUD
    Use of the velocity vector
    Operational procedures

Instrument Cross-Check

Specific HUD Training

STANDARDIZATION

Vocabulary
    Velocity vector
    Flight path angle
    Pitch symbol
    Pitch ladder
    Roll index

Primary Symbols

Scales

Other Data
    Navigational data
    Performance information
    Systems data

Summary
FORMAT FOR HUD FOLLOW-UP INTERVIEWS
Choice of Pilots to Be Interviewed
ILS Approach Questions
Data Presentation Questions
Velocity Vector Questions
Disorientation Questions
Additional Questionnaires
CONCLUSIONS
Operational Problems
    Display motion
    Pilot disorientation
    ILS presentation
    Display brightness
    Design eye reference position
Procedural Issues
Use of HUD in Training
Approaches to the Dynamics Issue
Need for Standardization
RECOMMENDATIONS
Improve HUD Data Base
    Follow-up interviews
    Additional questionnaires
    Continue training review
Develop Dynamic Correlation
    Obtain dynamic response data
    Experiment to evaluate response
    Definition of accuracy requirements
Measure the Pilot's Ability to Detect HUD Discrepancies
    Instrument errors in solid IMC
    Pilot reaction to subtle HUD errors
    Pilot detection of gross problems
Evaluate the Effect of a HUD in Spatial Disorientation
Develop HUD Training Program
    Effect of HUD experience
    Develop HUD syllabi
Modifications to HUD Specifications
    Location of design eye reference point
    Minimum brightness level
    Standardization
APPENDIX A - ORIGINAL QUESTIONNAIRE
APPENDIX B - FORMAT FOR FOLLOW-UP INTERVIEW
APPENDIX C - BIBLIOGRAPHY
REFERENCES

231 pp. 11 chapters. Figures, tables, author index, subject index, bibliography, references, appendices.

205
Newman, William M.
Sproull, Robert F.

Principles of Interactive Computer Graphics (2ed.)
McGraw-Hill, 1979

(from the *McGraw-Hill Computer Science Series*, Harold S. Stone, series ed.)

Provides a well-integrated discussion of interactive computer graphics with exercises and examples.

The text organization emphasizes a sound understanding of basic principles, with each new topic related to the theme of systems design presented after the basic chapters. This structure makes the work particularly useful as a textbook; the five introductory chapters, along with parts two and three on graphics packages and interactive graphics, make a complete introductory course, while the sections on raster graphics and three-dimensional graphics can be added for a more comprehensive course. Three final chapters on advanced topics are suitable for graduate level work and discuss display processors, device-independent graphics systems, and user interface design. The only prerequisite for understanding is some programming experience and familiarity with machine organization and data structures. There are exercises with each chapter. Program examples are written in Pascal. The included line illustrations were produced using an interactive graphics system. This extensively updated revision of the first (1973) edition reflects the rapid advances in this field and contains substantial new material. Intended for hardware and software systems designers, readers interested in basic algorithms and techniques, as well as those interested primarily in applications.

CONTENTS

Preface

PART ONE: BASIC CONCEPTS

Chapter 1: Introduction
    1.1. The origins of computer graphics
    1.2. How the interactive-graphics display works
    1.3. Some common questions
    1.4. New display devices
    1.5. General-purpose graphics software
    1.6. The user interface
    1.7. The display of solid objects

Chapter 2: Point-Plotting Techniques
    2.1. Coordinate systems
    2.2. Incremental methods
    2.3. Line-drawing algorithms
    2.4. Circle generators

Chapter 3: Line-Drawing Displays
    3.1. Display devices and controllers
    3.2. Display devices
    3.3. The CRT
    3.4. Inherent-memory devices
    3.5. The storage-tube display

3.6. The refresh line-drawing display

Chapter 4: Two-Dimensional Transformations
    4.1. Transformation principles
    4.2. Concatenation
    4.3. Matrix representations

Chapter 5: Clipping and Windowing
    5.1. A line clipping algorithm
    5.2. Midpoint subdivision
    5.3. Clipping other graphic entities
    5.4. Polygon clipping
    5.5. Viewing transformations
    5.6. The windowing transformation

PART TWO: GRAPHICS PACKAGES

Chapter 6: A Simple Graphics Package
    6.1. Ground rules for graphic software design
    6.2. Functional domains
    6.3. Graphic primitives
    6.4. Windowing function
    6.5. Miscellaneous functions
    6.6. Example: a graph-plotting program
    6.7. Implementation of the functions
    6.8. The transformation processor
    6.9. The display-code generator

Chapter 7: Segmented Display Files
    7.1. Segments
    7.2. Functions for segmenting the display file
    7.3. Posting and unposting a segment
    7.4. Segment naming schemes
    7.5. Default error conditions
    7.6. Appending

Chapter 8: Display File Compilation
    8.1. Refresh concurrent with reconstruction
    8.2. Free storage allocation
    8.3. Display-file structure
    8.4. Display files for storage-tube terminals

Chapter 9: Geometric Models
    9.1. A simple modeling example
    9.2. Geometric modeling
    9.3. Symbols and instances
    9.4. Implementation of instance transformations

Chapter 10: Picture Structure
    10.1. Defining symbols by procedures
    10.2. Display procedures
    10.3. Boxing
    10.4. Advantages and limitations of display procedures
    10.5. Structured display files

PART THREE: INTERACTIVE GRAPHICS

Chapter 11: Graphical Input Devices
    11.1. Pointing and positioning devices
    11.2. The mouse
    11.3. Tablets
    11.4. The light pen
    11.5. Three-dimensional input devices
    11.6. Comparators

Chapter 12: Graphical Input Techniques
    12.1. Introduction
    12.2. Positioning techniques
    12.3. Pointing and selection
    12.4. Inking and painting
    12.5. On-line character recognition
    12.6. Conclusion

Chapter 13: Event Handling
    13.1. Introduction
    13.2. Polling
    13.3. Interrupts
    13.4. The event queue
    13.5. Functions of handling events
    13.6. Polling task design
    13.7. Light-pen interrupts

Chapter 14: Input Functions
    14.1. Dragging and fixing
    14.2. Hit detection
    14.3. On-line character recognizers
    14.4. Conclusion

PART FOUR: RASTER GRAPHICS

Chapter 15: Raster Graphics Fundamentals
    15.1. Introduction
    15.2. Generating a raster image: the frame buffer display
    15.3. Representing a raster image
    15.4. Scan converting line drawings
    15.5. Displaying characters
    15.6. Speed of scan conversion
    15.7. Natural images

Chapter 16: Solid-Area Scan Conversion
    16.1. Geometric representations of areas
    16.2. Scan-converting polygons
    16.3. Priority
    16.4. The Y-X algorithm
    16.5. Properties of scan conversion algorithms

Chapter 17: Interactive Raster Graphics
    17.1. Updating the display
    17.2. The painting model
    17.3. Moving parts of an image
    17.4. Feedback images

Chapter 18: Raster-Graphics Systems
    18.1. Representations
    18.2. Raster manipulation functions
    18.3. Systems using raster representations
    18.4. Systems using geometric representations
    18.5. Conclusion

Chapter 19: Raster Display Hardware
    19.1. Raster display devices
    19.2. Frame buffers
    19.3. The random-access frame buffer
    19.4. Real-time scan conversion
    19.5. Other encoding schemes

PART FIVE: THREE-DIMENSIONAL GRAPHICS

Chapter 20: Realism in Three-Dimensional Graphics
    20.1. Techniques for achieving realism
    20.2. Modeling three-dimensional scenes
    20.3. Modeling and realism

Chapter 21: Curves and Surfaces
    21.1. Shape description requirements
    21.2. Parametric functions
    21.3. Bezier methods
    21.4. B-spline methods
    21.5. Displaying curves and surfaces
    21.6. Conclusion

Chapter 22: Three-Dimensional Transformations and Perspective
    22.1. Transformations
    22.2. Transformations in modeling
    22.3. Transformations in viewing
    22.4. The perspective transformation
    22.5. Three-dimensional clipping
    22.6. Three-dimensional graphics packages
    22.7. Examples

Chapter 23: Perspective Depth
    23.1. The screen coordinate system
    23.2. Properties of the screen coordinate system
    23.3. Homogeneous coordinate representations of projective transformations
    23.4. Summary

Chapter 24: Hidden-Surface Elimination
    24.1. Two approaches
    24.2. The depth-buffer algorithm
    24.3. Geometric computations
    24.4. Scan-line coherence algorithms
    24.5. Area-coherence algorithms
    24.6. Priority algorithms
    24.7. Choosing an algorithm
    24.8. Sorting and coherence

Chapter 25: Shading
    25.1. A shading model
    25.2. Applying the shading model
    25.3. Special effects
    25.4. Conclusions

PART SIX: GRAPHICS SYSTEMS

Chapter 26: Display Processors
26.1. The simple refresh line-drawing display
26.2. Random-scan storage-tube displays
26.3. High-performance displays
26.4. The unbuffered high-performance display
26.5. The buffered high-performance display

Chapter 27: Device-Independent Graphics Systems
27.1. Device independence
27.2. The programmer's model of the output process
27.3. Graphics system design
27.4. Function set design
27.5. Conclusion

Chapter 28: User Interface Design
28.1. Components of the user interface
28.2. The user's model
28.3. The command language
28.4. Styles of command language
28.5. Information display
28.6. Feedback
28.7. Examples
28.8. Conclusion

APPENDICES

Appendix I: Vectors and Matrices

Appendix II: Homogeneous Coordinate Techniques

Bibliography

Index

541 pp. 28 chapters in 6 parts. Drawings, photographs, figures, mathematical formulae, algorithms, models, general index, bibliography, appendices. ISBN 0-07-046338-7.

206
NIOSH

technical report

Potential Health Hazards of Video Display Terminals
1981

(report number 81-129; Hazard Evaluation and Technical Assistance Branch, NIOSH; sponsored by National Institute for Occupational Safety and Health; June 1980)

Describes the findings of a field investigation conducted at the request of three labor unions.

This study entailed four phases: radiation measurements, industrial hygiene sampling, a survey of health complaints and psychological and mood state, and ergonomics and human factors measurements. Radiation and hygiene sampling showed acceptable conditions by current legal limits. Psychological and ergonomic studies identified rectifiable problems. Health complaints and psychological mood state in VDT operators and a comparison group of nonoperators were evaluated using a multifaceted questionnaire. The ergonomics and human factors evaluation was conducted by examining several workplace and VDT characteristics. The questionnaire survey indicated that a higher percentage of VDT operators reported more visual complaints at two of the three sites studied, more muscular complaints at one site, and more emotional complaints at all sites. The ergonomic evaluation of the VDT workstations indicated that the measured illumination levels were generally acceptable; however, glare was a problem at a number of workstations. Some problems were noted with the physical dimensions of the workstations, including excessive keyboard height and VDT screen height. This report provides general recommendations concerning work/rest regimens, testing of operator's visual functions, and ergonomic factors. Contains extensive tables and forty references.

75 pp. 4 sections. Tables, references.

207
Okoshi, Takanori

Three-Dimensional Imaging Techniques
Academic Press, 1976
(revised translation by the author of his *Sanjigen Gazo Kogaku,* 1972)

A history and description of three-dimensional imaging techniques, both holographic and non-holographic.

When Okoshi began his research on three-dimensional imaging in 1967, he discovered that there were no books available on the topic; this is his response to that deficiency. He traces the development of the field from the introduction of the first stereoscopic viewer in 1838 to the present and extrapolates to three-dimensional television of the future. After a quick explanation of the physiology and psychology of depth perception, the book proceeds with a detailed and technical description of the applications and theories of lens-sheet three-dimensional pictures (including integral photography and lenticular sheet three-dimensional imaging), projection type three-dimensional displays, and holography. These are all techniques for producing truly three-dimensional spatial images which reveal different aspects of the subject as the observer changes perspective. Techniques for binocular stereoscopic imaging also produce three-dimensional images which offer much less information than autostereoscopy but are still useful for some applications. Concluding chapters treat information reduction techniques, possible future applications of three-dimensional imaging, and describe techniques including computer output displays and x-ray imaging. The work emphasizes holographic techniques for the reconstruction of spatial images. Published in Japanese in 1972, this book was revised and translated into English in 1974 and constitutes a well-organized, comprehensive summary of the field to that date.

CONTENTS
Preface
1: Introduction
    1.1. History of information media
    1.2. Definition of three-dimensional imaging
    1.3. Classification of three-dimensional imaging techniques
    1.4. Organization of this book

2: History of Three-Dimensional Imaging Techniques
    2.1. Prehistory
    2.2. Stereoscopes
    2.3. Parallax barriers
    2.4. Integral photography (IP)
    2.5. Lenticular-sheet three-dimensional pictures
    2.6. Holography
    2.7. Projection-type three-dimensional displays
    2.8. Three-dimensional movies
    2.9. Summary
    References
3: Physiology and Psychology of Depth Perception
    3.1. Introduction
    3.2. Human eyes
    3.3. Physiological and psychological cues of depth perception
    3.4. Some recent studies on depth perception
    References
4: Lens-Sheet Three-Dimensional Pictures
    4.1. Introduction
    4.2. Recording of lens-sheet three-dimensional pictures
    4.3. Optimum design of lenticular-sheet pictures
    4.4. Optimum design of integral photography
    4.5. Beaded-plate integral photography
    4.6. Future engineering tasks related to lens-sheet three-dimensional
        pictures
    4.7. Summary
    Appendix: Aberration in spherical/cylindrical lens systems
    References
5: Projection-Type Three-Dimensional Displays
    5.1. Introduction
    5.2. Principles of projection-type three-dimensional displays
    5.3. Classification of direction-selective screens
    5.4. Inversions between orthoscopic and pseudoscopic images using
        an autocollimating screen
    5.5. Optimum design of a projection system
    5.6. Diffuser-backed lenticular screens
    5.7. Triple-mirror screen and curved triple-mirror screen
    5.8. Summary
    Appendix: Derivation of reflection matrices and reflection ray
        vectors of a CTM screen
    References
6: Holography
    6.1. Introduction
    6.2. Principle of holography
    6.3. Various holography techniques
    6.4. Theory of imaging in a holographic system
    6.5. Interference fringes formed in a hologram
    6.6. Image reconstruction from a volume hologram
    6.7. Efficiency of holography
    6.8. Resolution of holography
    6.9. Noise in holography
    6.10. White-light recording of a hologram
    6.11. White-light reconstruction of an image from a hologram

6.12. Image holography

6.13. Color holography

6.14. Light sources

6.15. Hologram recording materials

6.16. Summary

Appendix I: Analysis of a Fourier-transform hologram with lens

Appendix II: Analysis of the resolution of an image reconstructed from a finite hologram

Appendix III: Derivation of the speckle-noise formula

References

7: Information Recorded in Three-Dimensional Images and Its Reduction

7.1. Introduction

7.2. Basic properties of focusing of a light beam in image space

7.3. Sampling point number of a hologram

7.4. Sampling point number in integral photography

7.5. Sampling point number in multiple photography

7.6. Summary of computations of P and M

7.7. Information reduction in integral photography

7.8. Information reduction in holography

7.9. Summary

References

8: Miscellaneous Three-Dimensional Imaging Techniques

8.1. Introduction

8.2. Computer-generated holograms

8.3. Computer-generated integral photograph

8.4. Binocular stereoscopic display of computer outputs

8.5. Varifocal mirrors

8.6. Three-dimensional X-ray imaging

8.7. Holographic screen

8.8. Binocular stereoscopic television

8.9. Autostereoscopic three-dimensional television

8.10. Other three-dimensional imaging techniques

References

9: Conclusion

Index

403 pp. 9 chapters. Drawings, figures, tables, mathematical formulae, abstract formalisms, general index, references. ISBN 0-12-525250-1.

208
Overheim, R. Daniel
Wagner, David L.

Light and Color
John Wiley and Sons, 1982

A textbook intended as a comprehensive introduction to the physics of light and color for undergraduates who have a minimal math and science background.

The goal of this text is to provide students from a wide range of academic backgrounds with a basic understanding of the physical nature of light and its practical applications. The first chapter provides a concise historical perspective of theories from Pythagoras to Einstein. The difference between geometrical optics and the true physical nature of light is also discussed. The next four chapters investigate color phenomena. The connection is made between the spectral composition of light and perceived color. The application of color concepts to television, printing, pigments, and stage lighting brings the theory to a practical level. Colorimetric systems from Newton to CIE are then discussed, followed by a study of the progression of vision theory. The final chapters consider geometric and wave optics, both theoretical and applied, in telescopes, projectors, cameras, lasers, and holograms; the last chapter deals with light and color in nature. All chapters have an introduction and most have a concise conclusion. There are problems and exercises at the end of each chapter and four appendices, including a bibliography. An instructor's manual is available.

CONTENTS

Preface

1: THE PHYSICAL NATURE OF LIGHT

1.1: Early Ideas

1.2: The Speed of Light

1.3: The Origin of Color

1.4: Waves

1.5: The Wave-Particle Controversy

1.6: The Transverse Wave Theory of Light

1.7: Electric and Magnetic Fields

1.8: The Photon Theory of Light

1.9: Light and Energy

In Conclusion

Problems and Exercises

2: THE ORIGIN OF COLOR

2.1: The Terminology of Illumination
   Physical units
   Luminous units

2.2: Continuum Sources
   Blackbody radiation

2.3: Bright-Line Sources

2.4: Reflectance

2.5: Transmission

2.6: Absorption

2.7: Primary Colors
   Additive primaries
   Subtractive primaries

2.8: Application of Color Concepts
   Color television
   Color printint
   The mixing of pigments
   Oils
   Watercolors
   Interior decorating and fashion design
   Stage lighting

In Conclusion

Problems and Exercises

3: COLORIMETRY—DESCRIBING AND MEASURING COLOR

3.1: Newton's Colorimetric System

3.2: The CIE System
   Metamerism
   The laws of color matching
   The XYZ system
   Chromaticity coordinates
   Use of the CIE chromaticity diagram
   Dominant wavelength and purity
   The analysis of surfaces
   A word of caution

3.3: The Munsell Color Notation System

3.4: The Ostwald Color System

In Conclusion

Problems and Exercises

4: COLOR VISION

4.1: Basic Features of Color Vision
   Trichromacy
   Color constancy
   Contrast effects
   Afterimages
   Color blindness
   Lightness constancy

4.2: Early Theories
   Newton
   Young

4.3: Theories of the Late Nineteenth Century
   Hemholtz
   Hering

4.4: Current Theories of Color Vision
   Details of the visual system
   The zone theory
   The retinex theory
   The importance of edges
   Kuffler units

In Conclusion

Problems and Exercises

5: THE APPEARANCE OF OBJECTS

5.1: Reflection from Opaque Surfaces
   Metals
   Nonmetallic surfaces

5.2: Transparent Colorants
   Single colorant: effect of thickness and concentration
   Transparent colorant mixtures

5.3: Opaque Colorants
   The pigment particles
   The support
   The outer surface
   Colorant mixtures

5.4: The Use of Color in Painting
Problems and Exercises
6: GEOMETRIC OPTICS
6.1: Reflection
6.2: Plane Mirrors
6.3: Curved Mirrors
6.4: Refraction
6.5: Refraction by Lenses
6.6: Chromatic Aberration
6.7: Lens Equations
In Conclusion
Problems and Exercises
7: APPLIED GEOMETRICAL OPTICS
7.1: The Reduced Eye
7.2: Adaptation
7.3: Defects of Vision
    Chromatic aberration
    Spherical aberration
7.4: The Camera
    Telephoto lenses
    Sensitivity to light
    Intensity of the camera image; *f*-numbers
    Exposure times; film speed
    Depth of field
    Chromatic aberration
    Spherical aberration
7.5: Other Optical Devices
    The magnifier
    The compound microscope
    Telescopes
    The reflecting telescope
    The slide projector
Problems and Exercises
8: WAVE OPTICS
8.1: Young's Two Slit Experiment
8.2: The Diffraction Grating
8.3: Single Slit Diffraction
8.4: The Laser
    The hologram
    Other laser uses
8.5: Polarization
In Conclusion
Problems and Exercises
9: LIGHT AND COLOR IN NATURE
9.1: Rainbows and Halos
    Rainbows
    Halos

9.2: Interference Phenomena
    Oil spots and soap bubbles
    Coating on glass
    Irridescence

9.3: Scattering Effects
    Rayleigh scattering
    Scattering by large particles

9.4: Mirages

9.5: The Aurora

In Conclusion

Problems and Exercises

Appendix A: Calculation of the CIE Tristimulus Values

Appendix B: The Spectrophotometer

Appendix C: Sine Functions

Appendix D: Annotated Bibliography

Index

269 pp. 9 chapters. Drawings, photographs, figures, graphs, mathematical formulae, general index, bibliography, appendices, color plates. ISBN 0-471-08348-8.

Pachella, Robert G.

Cognitive Studies of Complex Displays
1977-81

overview

These papers describe experimental work done by Robert Pachella and his students at the University of Michigan's Human Performance Center. Although the reports do not form an integrated series, they all focus on the perceptual dimensions of complex visual displays. The reports authored by Pachella, Somers, and Cheng develop a theory of dimensional integrality in which the physically independent dimensions of a stimulus become perceptually fused. The reports by Pachella and Benjamin examine the effect of stimulus complexity on the perception of multidimensional displays. Progress reports on this work appear in several of the proceedings from the Human Factors Society Annual Meetings; the reader may want to refer to these papers for a more integrated view of this research. The reader is also referred to the overviews for Cohen, "Image Descriptors for Displays," and Synder, "Visual Performance in Display Design," for other studies of displays and visual perception.

209
Somers, Patricia
Pachella, Robert G.

technical report

Interference among Sources of Information in Complex Integrated Displays
1977

(report number HPC-58; Human Performance Center, University of Michigan; sponsored by Engineering Psychology Program, Office of Naval Research; February 1977)

Types of dimensional nonseparability are examined, masking and distraction distinguished from interference and combination, and a method presented for measuring combination.

Examines previously developed concepts of integrality and studies the various causes of interference in complex displays. The authors trace a brief history of perceptual psychology, explain similarity scaling, discuss the City-Block metric model and the Euclidean metric model, and describe related research on integrality. Integrality is defined as "the phenomenon of physically independent dimensions appearing fused into a single perceptual attribute such that the physically separable dimensions are not perceptually separable." Dimensions are specified as the physical aspects of a stimulus while attributes are the subjective aspects of a stimulus. Integrality is distinguished from masking and distraction and divided into combination and interaction of stimulus dimensions. When two stimulus dimensions interact, perception of one dimension varies systematically with the level of the other dimensions, and yet these dimensions can be separated by subjects given a filtering task with no pressure to respond quickly. When two dimensions cannot be separated under any conditions, they are considered to be a combination. This research develops a method of measuring combination by requiring that the subject filter out the influence of irrelevant stimuli in pair-wise judgments of similarity. A demonstration experiment is described and the method developed found to be sensitive to the influences of an irrelevant dimension on judgments of similarity. Individual differences were found in the filtering abilities of the ten subjects, indicating that integrality is not strictly a stimulus characteristic, but a product of interaction between stimulus and perceiver. Comparisons of performance on speeded and unspeeded filtering tasks can be used to distinguish between interaction and combination. Implications for multidimensional display design are briefly discussed; depending on the nature of user tasks, dimensions should interact in some cases and combine in others. This is important research for the display designer as well as those working in perceptual psychology.

43 pp. Figures, tables, references.

210
Somers, Patricia

technical report

Perceptual Interaction between Stimulus Dimensions as the Basis of Dimensional Integrality
1978

(report number HPC-61; Human Performance Center, University of Michigan; sponsored by Engineering Psychology Program, Office of Naval Research; September 1978)

Describes and tests the author's psychological theory of dimensional integrality.

One of a series of papers, this dissertation describes and tests a new psychological theory of dimensional integrality. In integrality, physically independent, separable dimensions appear fused into a single, nonseparable perceptual attribute. Somers proposes that while all stimuli perceived are combinations of perceptually independent dimensions, in integral stimulus sets the perceptual dimensions and physically independent dimensions do not correspond. "Integrality," states Somers, "is demonstrated psychophysically by interaction in psychological similarity space between physically independent dimensions." Her theory is described in detail and contrasted to more traditional views of integrality. The results and predictions of other research are reviewed. Experimental methods and results are reported from three experiments designed to test the theory's predictions on speeded classification of interactive and noninteractive stimulus sets. The psychophysical structure of the stimulus sets was concluded to be the best predictor of speeded classification performance. This report will be of interest to other researchers and practitioners in psychological and perceptual studies.

CONTENTS

List of Figures

List of Appendices

Chapter I: Introduction
    The psychophysics of integrality
    Operational definitions of integrality

Chapter II: Experiment I
    General method
    Experiment Ia: Interacting dimensions
    Experiment Ib: Non-interacting dimensions
    Experiment Ic: Combined set

Chapter III: Experiment II
    Method
    Results and discussion

Chapter IV: Experiment III
    Method
    Results
    Discussion

Chapter V: General Discussion

Appendices

References

147 pp. 5 chapters. Figures, graphs, tables, references, appendices.

211

Pachella, Robert G.
Somers, Patricia
Hardzinski, Mary

A Psychophysical Approach to Dimensional Integrality
1980

technical report

(report number HPC-64/014523-7-T; Human Performance Center, University of Michigan; sponsored by Engineering Psychology Program, Office of Naval Research; March 1980)

Describes integrality, explains the manner and conditions under which it operates and presents the theoretical basis of this research program.

Part of an extensive effort to examine the nature and characteristics of dimensional integrality, this report summarizes the theoretical foundations of the research in this series. Dimensional integrality is defined as the "property of the mapping of a physical specification of complex stimulation into the multidimensional psychological characteristics of the stimulation as perceived." Their approach, labelled by the authors as "psychophysical compatibility," is compared to other theoretical positions on integrality. This paper discusses the historical precedents of Gestalt psychology, W.S. Torgerson's work on multidimensional scaling, W.R. Garner's work on the nature of integrality, and unsolved problems in integrality research. Experimental data are presented in support of the authors' position and their definition of integrality validated using information processing tasks involving speeded clarification. The authors state that their approach explains how integrality results in filtering decrements and how redundancy leads to gains in performance—rather than using these results to define integrality. Limitations of the psychophysical approach are discussed. This report is a draft version of a chapter which will appear in *Auditory and Visual Pattern Recognition*, edited by D. Getty and J. Howard.

42 pp. Figures, references.

212

Benjamin, Moshe
Pachella, Robert G.

The Effect of Complexity in Integrated Multidimensional Displays
1980

technical report

(report number HPC-TR-66; Human Performance Center, University of Michigan; sponsored by Engineering Psychology Program, Office of Naval Research; December 1980)

This study explores the effect which irrelevant information has on the ability of observers to ignore it or be affected by it when their task is to form judgments about the relevant information being displayed.

Moshe Benjamin and Robert G. Pachella admit that integrated multidimensional displays are a great aid to the presentation of complex information. However, the authors conducted an experiment which showed that problems do exist because distinctive irrelevant information can interplay with the relevant information displayed, affecting the perception of the observer. The authors conducted an experiment to determine "whether or not the judgments of the relevant features were systematically affected by the amount and nature of the irrelevant information." Benjamin and Pachella exposed twenty-seven paid volunteers from the University of Michigan to a computer drawn schematic face utilizing four different shapes of facial outlines and three possible irrelevant dimensions of eyebrows, mouths, and pupils of the eyes. The slant of the eyebrows, the shape of the mouth, and the placement of the pupils gave two values to each face. Twenty of the twenty-seven subjects were exposed to stimuli pairs which consisted of stimuli with no irrelevant features, stimuli with two irrelevant features, and stimuli with three irrelevant features. The other seven subjects were exposed to stimuli consisting of the twenty-four faces which had common features. The subjects were asked to judge the similarity of the pairs before and after the irrelevant information was added. The experiment exhibited two results: despite being instructed not to let irrelevant information sway them, the subjects' perceptions of the relevant information was affected due to the interaction between the irrelevant and relevant information changing the appearance of the information; and the appearance of the information displayed is again altered because of an attraction of the subject's attention due to the prominent distinctiveness of some irrelevant information. The report is a clear and interesting addition to the work being done on conveying information through computerized graphical devices and as such will interest display designers as well as perceptual psychologists.

23 pp. Figures, graphs, references.

213
Cheng, Patricia W.

A Psychophysical Approach to Form Perception: Incompatibility as an Explanation of Integrality
University Microfilms International, 1980

(Ph.D. dissertation, University of Michigan, 1980)

This dissertation offers support for psychophysical incompatibility theory as an explanation of stimulus integrality.

Observing that lawful patterns will not emerge if a researcher fails to identify the pertinent independent and dependent variables, Cheng announces her intentions of carefully assessing the variables employed in research on the visual phenomenon of integrality. Previous conceptualizations of integrality are critically reviewed and problems with the psychophysical view of integrality are summarized. Cheng proposes that the lack of correlation between proximal stimulation and perception (a problem in "traditional" psychophysical theory) may be due to the incorrect selection of variables. She proposes a new interpretation of the psychophysical compatibility theory (Pachella, Somers, and Hardzinski, 1980). This theory assumes that, "regardless of what physical variables are manipulated, people always encode stimuli in psychological dimensions," dimensions which should be separable since they can be attended to selectively. To the extent that these dimensions are not separable, incompatibility between physical and psychological dimensions is postulated to account for integrality. Cheng discusses other work in this series of research papers and, in four experiments, sets out to solve some problems encountered by Somers (1978) and to challenge the definition of integrality developed by Garner (1974). This work, prepared as Cheng's 1980 doctoral dissertation in psychology, is strongly recommended to those interested in this subject, and for those working on any facet of integrality.

CONTENTS

List of Appendices

Chapter I: Introduction
    Integrality and separability
    Garner's theory
    A psychophysical approach
    The psychophysical compatibility theory
    Previous results

Chapter II: Experiment I: A Validation
    Selection of task
    Selection of stimuli
    The experiment

Chapter III: Experiment II: A Test of the Sufficiency of Rectangularity and a Case of Degree of Integrality
    Method
    Results and discussion
    Conclusion

Chapter IV: Experiments III and IV: Tests of the Necessity of Rectangularity: An Explanation of Asymmetric Integrality and an Issue of Selective Attention
    Experiment III
    Experiment IV

Chapter V: General Discussion and Summary
    Types of representation
    New criteria for distinguishing integral and separable dimensions
    Summary

Appendices

References

150 pp. 5 chapters. Figures, tables, references, appendices.

214

Pachella, Robert G.

technical report

The Development and Utilization of Integrated Multidimensional Displays: Final Report
1981

(report number HPC-67; Human Performance Center, University of Michigan; sponsored by Engineering Psychology Program, Office of Naval Research; February 1981)

Summary of work from a four and one half year research project on dimensional integrality, including the development of research methodologies and theoretical framework.

The purpose of this research was to establish "basic facts about the nature of complex integrated multidimensional displays and their compatibilities with human perceptual abilities." The research led to the development of a comprehensive theory of multidimensional integrality as well as techniques for measuring aspects of integrality. In this report, work performed under the contract is summarized and placed in perspective. Four major headings of research are identified: preliminary analysis of dimensional integrality, methodological developments, empirical findings and development of theory, and work still in progress at the time of this report. This research was described in nine technical reports (two more are in preparation) and sixteen presentations at meetings and conferences. A bibliography of these reports is included. Perceptual psychologists and those involved in display design will find this work of great interest.

13 pp. Bibliography.

215

Pankove, Jacques I. (ed.)

collection

Display Devices
Springer-Verlag, 1980

(vol. 40 in the *Topics in Applied Physics* series)

Presents thorough discussions of some popular display devices and surveys of other important techniques in (circa 1980) display device technology.

This collection of seven papers provides detailed coverage of primary display devices, including light-emitting diodes, plasma displays, liquid-crystal displays, electrochromic displays, and electrophoretic displays. An introductory chapter presents brief discussions of other, less common, devices, and a concluding chapter discusses display devices in a more general, philosophical context. The book's organization moves from devices which emit light to those which modulate it; for each type of display the general principles and characteristics are described, along with discussions of device technology and performance. A highly technical and mathematical but very well-illustrated work, intended for practicing engineers and graduate students.

CONTENTS

INTRODUCTION
By J.I. Pankove (with 19 figures)

1.1: Characterization of Displays
1.1.1. Luminance or brightness
1.1.2. Color
1.1.3. Contrast and gradation
1.1.4. Directional visibility
1.1.5. Driving power
1.1.6. Efficiency
1.1.7. Speed
1.1.8. Memory and storage
1.1.9. Degradation
1.1.10. Resolution and size
1.1.11. Addressability

1.2: Psychophysical Factors

1.3: Technical Discussion of Display Devices
1.3.1. Light-Emitting Diodes—LED
1.3.2. Plasma panel
1.3.3. Electroluminescence
1.3.4. Incandescent display
1.3.5. Cathodoluminescent displays
1.3.6. Liquid-Crystal Displays—LCD
1.3.7. Electrochromic Displays—ECD
1.3.8. Electrophoretic Displays—EPID
1.3.9. Electroplating cell
1.3.10. Light valves
1.3.11. Electro-optic modulators

1.4: Applications

References

2: LIGHT-EMITTING DIODES—LEDS
By C.J. Nuese and J.I. Pankove (with 41 figures)

2.1: Carrier Excitation
2.1.1. Photoluminescence
2.1.2. Cathodoluminescence
2.1.3. Injection electroluminescence

2.2: Recombination Processes
2.2.1. Band-to-band radiative recombination
2.2.2. Radiative recombination via impurities
2.2.3. Nonradiative recombination

2.3: Materials for LEDs
2.3.1. Brightness considerations
2.3.1. Binary compounds
2.3.3. Ternary alloys
2.3.4. Quaternary alloys

2.4: Metallurgical Considerations
2.4.1. Crystal defects
2.4.2. Lattice mismatch
2.4.3. Optical losses
2.4.4. Series resistance
2.4.5. Degradation

2.5: LED Technology
    2.5.1. Vapor-phase epitaxy
    2.5.2. Liquid-phase epitaxy
    2.5.3. Impurity diffusion
    2.5.4. Glow-discharge decomposition
    2.5.5. Device structures
2.6: Applications
References
AC PLASMA DISPLAY
    By T.N. Criscimagna and P. Pleshko (with 41 figures)
3.1: Background Information
    3.1.1. Historical evolution
    3.1.2. Modes of operation
    3.1.3. Basic cell operation
    3.1.4. Cell light emission
3.2: Panel Materials and Processing
    3.2.1. Substrate
    3.2.2. Conductors
    3.2.3. Dielectric films
    3.2.4. Overcoat materials and gas mixtures
    3.2.5. Seals, spacers, and backfill
3.3: Voltage-Transfer Characteristics of a Cell
    3.3.1. Wall charge and wall voltage
    3.3.2. Stable discharge sequences
    3.3.3. Voltage-transfer-characteristic curve
    3.3.4. Writing operation
    3.3.5. Erase operation
3.4: Nonhomogeneous Cell Characteristics in a Panel
    3.4.1. Cell-to-cell interaction
    3.4.2. Physical parameters and their effects
3.5: Write, Erase, and Sustain Margins
    3.5.1. Panel operating-voltage margins
    3.5.2. Image test patterns
3.6: Drive Waveforms
    3.6.1. Sustain waveforms
    3.6.2. Write waveforms
    3.6.3. Erase waveforms for selected cells
3.7: Panel Operating Drive Systems
    3.7.1. Sustain drive
    3.7.2. Half-select pulses
    3.7.3. Half-select cancellation pulses
    3.7.4. Full-select pulses
    3.7.5. Panel drive systems
3.8: Panel Limitations and Extendibility
    3.8.1. Resolution
    3.8.2. Color
    3.8.3. Image
3.9: Summary
References
4: LIQUID-CRYSTAL DISPLAYS, LCD.
    By D.J. Channin and A. Sussman (with 10 figures)

4.1: Background Information

4.2: Device Physics
    4.2.1. Nematic LCD
    4.2.2. Field-effect LCD
    4.2.3. Electrohydrodynamic LCD
    4.2.4. Optical characteristics of LCD

4.3: Large-Scale Displays
    4.3.1. Addressing techniques for large-scale displays
    4.3.2. Multiplexing theory

4.4: Device Performance
    4.4.1. Dynamic scattering
    4.4.2. Twisted-nematic field-effect display

4.5: Manufacturing Technology

4.6: Final Comments

References

5: ELECTROCHROMIC DISPLAYS BASED ON WO_3
    By B.W. Faughnan and R.S. Crandall (with 9 figures)

5.1: Background Information
    5.1.1. Electrochromic displays
    5.1.2. Historical outline
    5.1.3. Nature of EC in WO_3

5.2: Principles of Electrochromism in WO_3
    5.2.1. Basic phenomenon of the EC effect in WO_3
    5.2.2. Dynamics of coloring and bleaching
    5.2.3. Optical properties

5.3: Material Preparation and Characterization
    5.3.1. Preparation
    5.3.2. Film characterization

5.4: Device Technology
    5.4.1. Introductory remarks
    5.4.2. Liquid-solid devices
    5.4.3. All-solid state devices

5.5: Device Performance
    5.5.1. General considerations
    5.5.2. Switching speed
    5.5.3. Constant-current operation
    5.5.4. Power requirements
    5.5.5. Device lifetime and degradation mechanism

5.6: Conclusions

Appendix A

References

6: ELECTROPHORETIC DISPLAYS
    By A.L. Dalisa (with 16 figures)

6.1: Principles of Operation
    6.1.1. General characteristics
    6.1.2. Electrical addressing of EPID devices

6.2: Device Technology
    6.2.1. Colloidal-suspension technology
    6.2.2. Device design
    6.2.3. Device fabrication

6.3: Device Performance

    6.3.1. Optical characteristics

    6.3.2. Electrical characteristics

    6.3.3. Matrix-addressed devices

    6.3.4. Lifetime and environmental effects

6.4: Conclusions

References

7: ELECTRONIC DISPLAYS

    By E.O. Johnson (with 4 figures)

7.1: Basic Functions

7.2: Display-Element Classes

    7.2.1. Photon-generator elements

    7.2.2. Ambient-photon-control elements

    7.2.3. Display element summary

7.3: Addressing

7.4: Conclusion

References

ADDITIONAL REFERENCES WITH TITLES

SUBJECT INDEX

252 pp. 7 chapters. Drawings, figures, graphs, tables, mathematical formulae, subject index, references. ISBN 0-387-09868-2.

216
Park, Chan S.

Interactive Microcomputer Graphics
Addison-Wesley, 1985

Presents an introduction plus treatment of some more complex topics in the production of graphics on microcomputers. Mathematical components, programming techniques, and some application areas are covered in the book.

The author's purpose in writing this book was to survey, unify and present some of the latest advances in microcomputer graphics for management and practicing engineers, including the math and programming necessary to "generate reasonable graphics images on a low-cost microcomputer." The first part of the book examines the hardware characteristics and graphics capabilities of the IBM PC and IBM PC XT microcomputers. A program for a simple method for creating pictures provides an introduction to graphic programming. This introduction demonstrates the author's emphasis throughout the book on hands-on learning. Part two presents the mathematical components of microcomputer graphics, including coverage of two- and three-dimensional geometric transformations and the removal of hidden edges and surfaces. Part three applies the basic concepts presented in part two to designing a simple graphics package. These chapters develop a number of programs including "interfacing graphics input data with any graphics routine"; two-dimensional plotting; and transformations. The final section presents applications of graphics programming. An appendix presents sample programs in statistical graphics. Programs are written in BASIC for use on the IBM PC, but should be fairly adaptable to other languages and microcomputers. A software disk containing the programs presented is available from the publisher. This work is suitable as a textbook in introductory computer graphics or as a supplementary text in courses in advanced computer programming, engineering graphics, CAD/CAM, or management science. Includes exercises and a reference list for each chapter. Prerequisites for understanding the text are knowledge of BASIC, programming experience, and knowledge of linear algebra. This is an attractive book, amply enhanced with figures, examples, and graphics.

CONTENTS

PART ONE: GRAPHICS CHARACTERISTICS OF THE IBM PC

Chapter One: The Microcomputer and Its Graphics Capabilities
    1.1. Microcomputer graphics applications
    1.2. The IBM personal computer
    1.3. Characteristics of the color/graphics adapter
    1.4. Summary
    References
    Survey articles
    Selected computer graphics journals
    Selected computer journals or magazines with occasional computer graphics articles
    Selected magazines for personal computers

Chapter Two: Graphics Programming
    2.1. Memory-mapped graphics in text mode
    2.2. Memory-mapped graphics in graphics mode
    2.3. IBM PC graphics BASIC commands
    2.4. Advanced graphics programming
    2.5. Summary
    Exercises
    References

PART TWO: MATHEMATICAL ELEMENTS FOR COMPUTER GRAPHICS

Chapter Three: Mathematical Elements in 2-D Computer Graphics
    3.1. Transformation of points
    3.2. Transformation of lines and objects
    3.3. Homogeneous coordinate systems
    3.4. Sequential 2-D transformations
    3.5. Viewport planning of 2-D graphics
    3.6. Screen display for 2-D graphics on IBM PC
    3.7. Summary
    Exercises
    References

Chapter Four: Mathematical Elements in 3-D Graphics
    4.1. Coordinate systems
    4.2. Transformation matrix
    4.3. Viewing in three dimensions
    4.4. Perspective depth
    4.5. Viewport planning for 3-D graphics
    4.6. Screen display of 3-D graphics

4.7. Summary
Exercises
References

Chapter Five: Hidden Line and Surface Removals
5.1. The visibility of single convex object
5.2. The visibility of several objects
5.3. Program development of drawing two convex objects
5.4. The masking technique
5.5. The image space algorithms
5.6. Summary
Exercises
References

PART THREE: USER INTERFACE DESIGN

Chapter Six: Interactive Data Editor
6.1. Design principles
6.2. Computer programming logic
6.3. Description of data editor
6.4. Editing examples
6.5. Summary
References

Chapter Seven: Interactive 2-D Plotter
7.1. Plotting features envisioned
7.2. Design principles
7.3. Computer programming logic
7.4. Case example
7.5. Description of 2-D plotter
7.6. Plotting examples
7.7. Cubic spline interpolation
7.8. Summary
References

Chapter Eight: Interactive Computer-Aided Design
8.1. Using the computer as a designer's aid
8.2. Design principles
8.3. Menu-driven commands
8.4. Mode selection
8.5. Graphics commands
8.6. Utility commands
8.7. Status messages
8.8. Multilayered drawings
8.9. Summary
References

Chapter Nine: Interactive 3-D Plotter
9.1. Projection method adopted
9.2. Program design
9.3. Creating a data file for a 3-D plotter
9.4. Description of commands
9.5. Drawing a 3-D function
9.6. Summary
References

PART FOUR: GRAPHICS APPLICATIONS IN MANAGEMENT
DECISION MAKING

Chapter Ten: Interactive Forecasting System
    10.1. Model development
    10.2. Measure of performance criteria
    10.3. Description of the Winters' program
    10.4. Summary
    Exercises
    References

Chapter Eleven: Multiple Regression Analysis
    11.1. Multiple regression model
    11.2. Statistical properties of the regression model
    11.3. Measure of model adequacy
    11.4. Description of the multiple regression program
    11.5. Summary
    Exercises
    References

Chapter Twelve: Economic Analysis Under Risk
    12.1. Risk analysis
    12.2. Selecting input probability distributions
    12.3. Generating random variables
    12.4. Description of risk simulation program
    12.5. Replication and precision of results
    12.6. Summary
    Exercises
    References

Appendix A: Hexadecimal Conversion Table
Appendix B: Statistical (Business) Graphics
    B.1. Program to plot 3-D histograms
    B.2. Program to plot 3-D stacked bar charts
Index

458 pp. 12 chapters in 4 parts. Photographs, figures, tables, mathematical formulae, algorithms, abstract formalisms, models, general index, appendices. ISBN 0-201-05541-4.

217
Pavlidis, Theo

Algorithms for Graphics and Image Processing
Computer Science Press, 1982

An examination of pictorial information processing by computers, covering computer graphics, computer image processing, and pictorial pattern recognition.

This book deals with image generation from nonpictorial information. Interactive computer graphics refers to devices and systems which accept user input and produce an appropriate display from such information. Image processing denotes situations where both input and output are pictures. Image processing includes contrast enhancement of photographs, altering illumination levels, and the creation of new images from a set of other images. Pictorial pattern recognition starts with a picture and transforms it into an abstract description of numbers, using symbols or a graph. Further processing results in the assignment of the original picture into one of several classes. Examples include automatic mail sorters which identify postal codes written on envelopes and automated medical diagnostic machinery for detection of certain anomalies on radiographs. The book's seventeen chapters cover topics including: gray scale images, reconstruction techniques, data structures, processing bilevel images, algorithms for graphics and image processing, curve and surface fitting, and generation of graphic displays. Intended for junior, senior or graduate level computer science, engineering, mathematics, or physical science majors.

CONTENTS

Preface

CHAPTER 1: INTRODUCTION

1.1: Graphics, Image Processing, and Pattern Recognition

1.2: Forms of Pictorial Data
   1.2.1. Class 1: Full gray scale and color pictures
   1.2.2. Class 2: Bilevel or "few color" pictures
   1.2.3. Class 3: Continuous curves and lines
   1.2.4. Class 4: Points or polygons

1.3: Pictorial Input

1.4: Display Devices

1.5: Vector Graphics

1.6: Raster Graphics

1.7: Common Primitive Graphic Instructions

1.8: Comparison of Vector and Raster Graphics

1.9: Pictorial Editor

1.10: Pictorial Transformations

1.11: Algorithm Notation

1.12: A Few Words on Complexity

1.13: Bibliographical Notes

1.14: Relevant Literature

1.15: Problems

CHAPTER 2: DIGITIZATION OF GREY SCALE IMAGES

2.1: Introduction

2.2: A Review of Fourier and Other Transforms

2.3: Sampling
   2.3.1. One-dimensional sampling
   2.3.2. Two-dimensional sampling

2.4: Aliasing

2.5: Quantization

2.6: Bibliographic Notes

2.7: Relevant Literature

2.8: Problems

Appendix 2.A: Fast Fourier Transform

CHAPTER 3: PROCESSING OF GREY SCALE IMAGES

3.1: Introduction

3.2: Histogram and Histogram Equalization

3.3: Co-occurrence Matrices

3.4: Linear Image Filtering

3.5: Nonlinear Image Filtering
    3.5.1. Directional filters
    3.5.2. Two-part filters
    3.5.3. Functional approximation filters

3.6: Bibliographic Notes

3.7: Relevant Literature

3.8: Problems

CHAPTER 4: SEGMENTATION

4.1: Introduction

4.2: Thresholding

4.3: Edge Detection

4.4: Segmentation by Region Growing
    4.4.1. Segmentation by average brightness level
    4.4.2. Other uniformity criteria

4.5: Bibliographic Notes

4.6: Relevant Literature

4.7: Problems

CHAPTER 5: PROJECTIONS

5.1: Introduction

5.2: Introduction to Reconstructive Techniques

5.3: A Class of Reconstruction Algorithms

5.4: Projections of Shape Analysis

5.5: Bibliographic Notes

5.6: Relevant Literature

5.7: Problems

Appendix 5.A: An Elementary Reconstruction Program

CHAPTER 6: DATA STRUCTURES

6.1: Introduction

6.2: Graphing Traversal Algorithms

6.3: Paging

6.4: Pyramids or Quad Trees
    6.4.1. Creating a quad tree
    6.4.2. Reconstructing an image from a quad tree
    6.4.3. Image compaction with a quad tree

6.5: Binary Image Trees

6.6: Split-and-Merge Algorithms

6.7: Line Encodings and Line Adjacency Graphs

6.8: Region Encodings and the Region Adjacency Graph

6.9: Iconic Representations

6.10: Data Structures for Displays

6.11: Bibliographic Notes

6.12: Relevant Literature

6.13: Problems

Appendix 6.A: Introduction to Graphs

CHAPTER 7: Bilevel Pictures

7.1: Introduction

7.2: Sampling and Topology

7.3: Elements of Discrete Geometry

7.4: A Sampling Theorem for Class 2 Pictures

7.5: Contour Tracing
    7.5.1. Tracing of a single contour
    7.5.2. Traversal of all the contours of a region

7.6: Curves and Lines on a Discrete Grid
    7.6.1. When a set of pixels is not a curve
    7.6.2. When a set of pixels is a curve

7.7: Multiple Pixels

7.8: An Introduction to Shape Analysis

7.9: Bibliographic Notes

7.10: Relevant Literature

7.11: Problems

CHAPTER 8: CONTOUR FILLING

8.1: Introduction

8.2: Edge Filling

8.3: Contour Filling by Parity Check
    8.3.1. Proof of correctness of algorithm 8.3
    8.3.2. Implementation of a parity check algorithm

8.4: Contour Filling by Connectivity
    8.4.1. Recursive connectivity filling
    8.4.2. Nonrecursive connectivity filling
    8.4.3. Procedures used for connectivity filling
    8.4.4. Description of the main algorithm

8.5: Comparisons and Combinations
8.6: Bibliographic Notes
8.7: Relevant Literature
8.8: Problems
CHAPTER 9: THINNING ALGORITHMS
9.1: Introduction
9.2: Classical Thinning Algorithms
9.3: Asynchronous Thinning Algorithms
9.4: Implementation of an Asynchronous Thinning Algorithm
9.5: A Quick Thinning Algorithm
9.6: Structural Shape Analysis
9.7: Transformation of Bilevel Images into Line Drawings
9.8: Bibliographic Notes
9.9: Relevant Literature
9.10: Problems
CHAPTER 10: CURVE FITTING AND CURVE DISPLAYING
10.1: Introduction
10.2: Polynomial Interpretation
10.3: Bezier Polynomials
10.4: Computation of Bezier Polynomials
10.5: Some Properties of Bezier Polynomials
10.6: Circular Arcs
10.7: Display of Lines and Curves
    10.7.1. Display of curves through differential equations
    10.7.2. Effect of round-off errors in displays
10.8: A Point Editor
    10.8.1. A data structure for a point editor
    10.8.2. Input and output for a point editor
    10.9: Bibliographic Notes
    10.10: Relevant Literature
    10.11: Problems
CHAPTER 11: CURVE FITTING WITH SPLINES
11.1: Introduction
11.2: Fundamental Definitions
11.3: B-splines
11.4: Computation with B-splines
11.5: Interpolating B-splines
11.6: B-splines in Graphics
11.7: Shape Description and B-splines
11.8: Bibliographic Notes
11.9: Relevant Literature
11.10: Problems
CHAPTER 12: APPROXIMATION OF CURVES
12.1: Introduction
12.2: Integral Square Error Approximations
12.3: Approximation Using B-splines
12.4: Approximation by Splines with Variable Breakpoints
12.5: Polynomial Approximations

12.5.1. A suboptimal line fitting algorithm
12.5.2. A simple polygon fitting algorithm
12.5.3. Properties of algorithm 12.2

12.6: Applications of Curve Approximation in Graphics
12.6.1. Handling of groups of points by a point editor
12.6.2. Finding some simple approximating curves

12.7: Bibliographic Notes

12.8: Relevant Literature

12.9: Problems

CHAPTER 13: SURFACE FITTING AND SURFACE DISPLAYING

13.1: Introduction

13.2: Some Simple Properties of Surfaces

13.3: Singular Points of a Surface

13.4: Linear and Bilinear Interpolating Surface Patches

13.5: Lofted Surfaces

13.6: Coons Surfaces

13.7: Guided Surfaces
13.7.1. Bezier surfaces
13.7.2. B-spline surfaces

13.8: The Choice of a Surface Partition

13.9: Display of Surfaces and Shading

13.10: Bibliographical Notes

13.11: Relevant Literature

13.12: Problems

CHAPTER 14: THE MATHEMATICS OF TWO-DIMENSIONAL GRAPHICS

14.1: Introduction

14.2: Two-Dimensional Transformations

14.3: Homogeneous Coordinates
14.3.1. Equation of a line defined by two points
14.3.2. Coordinates of a point defined as the intersection of two lines
14.3.3. Duality

14.4: Line Segment Problems
14.4.1. Position of a point with respect to a line
14.4.2. Intersection of line segments
14.4.3. Position of a point with respect to a polygon
14.4.4. Segment shadow

14.5: Bibliographic Notes

14.6: Relevant Literature

14.7: Problems

CHAPTER 15: POLYGON CLIPPING

15.1: Introduction

15.2: Clipping a Line Segment by a Convex Polygon

15.3: Clipping a Line Segment by a Regular Rectangle

15.4: Clipping an Arbitrary Polygon by a Line

15.5: Intersection of Two Polygons

15.6: Efficient Polygon Intersection

15.7: Bibliographic Notes

15.8: Relevant Literature

15.9: Problems

CHAPTER 16: THE MATHEMATICS OF THREE-DIMENSIONAL GRAPHICS

16.1: Introduction

16.2: Homogeneous Coordinates
 16.2.1. Position of a point with respect to a plane
 16.2.2. Intersection of triangles

16.3: Three-Dimensional Transformations
 16.3.1. Mathematical preliminaries
 16.3.2. Rotation around an axis through the origin

16.4: Orthogonal Projections

16.5: Perspective Projections

16.6: Bibliographic Notes

16.7: Relevant Literature

16.8: Problems

CHAPTER 17: CREATING THREE-DIMENSIONAL GRAPHIC DISPLAYS

17.1: Introduction

17.2: The Hidden Line and Hidden Surface Problems
 17.2.1. Surface shadow
 17.2.2. Approaches to the visibility problem
 17.2.3. Single convex object visibility

17.3: A Quad Tree Visibility Algorithm

17.4: A Raster Line Scan Visibility Algorithm

17.5: Coherence

17.6: Nonlinear Object Descriptions

17.7: Making a Natural Looking Display

17.8: Bibliographic Notes

17.9: Relevant Literature

17.10: Problems

AUTHOR INDEX

SUBJECT INDEX

ALGORITHM INDEX

416 pp. 17 chapters. Drawings, figures, mathematical formulae, algorithms, author index, subject index, references, algorithm index. ISBN 0-914894-65-X.

Petersen, Rohn J. *SEE UNDER ID 284*

218
Phillips, Arthur H.

Handbook of Computer-Aided Composition
Marcel Dekker, 1980

(vol. 31 in the *Books in Library and Information Science* series, Allen Kent, series ed.)

Presents a comprehensive survey of the various techniques and of the hard- and software employed in electronic composition, editing, and publishing; a thorough reference work by an expert in the field.

This is a lengthy manual on the different methods and kinds of equipment used for electronic composition and publishing. The work offers historical background on the development of electronic printing techniques in order to stress the greater freedom of composition and design which the new technologies afford. The author dedicates the majority of the book to the variety of electronic composition techniques, their areas of application, and the requisite hard- and software. This is done in nine well-organized, instructive chapters covering: conventional and improved computer keyboards and their uses; word-processing systems and equipment; the use of optical character recognition and video-display systems in text-editing; the applications of various hard- and software systems to the composition, editing, printing, and publishing of books and journals (including scientific and technical works); the use of particular software systems in newspaper and magazine composition; and text composition photocomposers and equipment (including trends in their development). The book concludes with a chapter on prospective uses and effects of electronic composition systems in the near future, including a discussion of the impact these technologies may have on creative writing, text-translation, and the printed word itself. An extremely informative and useful work, suitable either as introductory text on electronic composition techniques or as a handbook for the professional writer, editor, publisher, printer, or systems designer.

CONTENTS

Preface

1: Defining the Problem
　Definition of computer-aided composition
　Aim and development of computer-aided composition
　Categories of composition
　Functions of typographer and programmer
　References

2: Printer's Typefaces and Fonts
　Printer's type design
　Printer's measurements
　Linecaster type font measurements
　Computer accessibility of type fonts
　Summary of photosetter font facilities
　References

3: Monotype and Linecaster Mechanical Composition
   Line justification
   Monotype justification
   Linecaster mechanism and justification
   Teletypesetting tape and code
   Computer control of the linecaster
   Summary of computer-aided hot-metal composition
   References

4: Computer Text Input Keyboards
   Conventional and improved keyboards
   Computer input codes for text processing
   Keyboard design for computer-aided composition
   Design factors of electronic text keyboards
   Video display input keyboards
   Keyboard-computer-photosetter interface
   Keyboard development summary
   References

5: Word Processing
   Definition of word processing
   Automatic direct-impression equipment
   Summary of non-VDU typescript-oriented word processors
   Video display word-processing systems
   Summary of video display word-processing systems
   Word-processing interfaces
   General summary of word processing
   References

6: Optical Character Recognition of Text
   Optical bar code readers
   OCR fonts
   OCR correction methods
   OCR input to computer-aided composition systems
   OCR equipment
   Summary of OCR text input systems
   Reference

7: Technical and Scientific Book and Journal Composition
   Computer-generated and composed tables
   Use of video display systems in book composition
   General-bookwork tabular composition
   Computer-aided mathematical composition
   The editorial processing center
   Bookwork page makeup
   References

8: Bookwork Correction, Editing, and Retrieval
   Development of automated text correction
   Proof stages in computer-processed text composition
   Computer batch processing of corrections
   Video display systems for text correction and editing
   Dedicated text input correction and editing equipment
   Information retrieval
   Summary of bookwork correction and updating methods
   References

9: Newspaper and Magazine Computer Systems
    The automated newsroom
    Wire service input
    Development of newspaper composition systems
    Computer manufacturers' composition software
    Newspaper systems from composition equipment manufacturers
    Editing and composition systems by software houses
    CRT terminals for display advertisement setting
    Line and tone illustration in computer composition
    Facsimile communications systems
    Newspaper and magazine page makeup
    Summary of newspaper computer systems
    References
10: Nonscanning Text Composition Photocomposers
    Development of the text composition photocomposer
    Design principles of the nonscanning photocomposer
    Recorded input nonscanning photocomposers
    The direct-entry photocomposer
    Summary of development trends
    References
11: The Scanned Image Photocomposer
    Design of the CRT photocomposer
    Graphic arts laser technology
    Summary of scanned image photocomposer development
    References
12: Perspective and Prospect
    Automated news and magazine production
    Database composition
    Computer-aided book production
    Prospects of computer-aided composition
    New contestants for information media
    Conclusions
    References
Index

434 pp. 12 chapters. Drawings, photographs, figures, general index, references. ISBN 0-8247-6963-5.

219
Piantanida, Thomas P.

technical report

Perception of Spatial Features with Stereoscopic Displays
1981

(report number N14-0742-81C-0002; SRI International; sponsored by Engineering Psychology Programs, Office of Naval Research; 30 November 1981)

This short technical report presents a detailed description of the experiments and apparatus used in the study of human perception of three-dimensional displays.

The experiments were specifically concerned with form, depth and motion-in-depth perception as well as the interaction between the observer and the display. The levels of measurement used in the experiment involved both subjective measurements as reported by the observer and the objective measurements made by observing the eye movements of the observer. The report suggests that the form perception and depth perception mechanisms treat the same retinal image differently. Thus, "edges are critical to the production of static depth and in-motion-depth, but the description of a retinal image edge provided by the form-perception mechanism may vary from that perceived by the depth perception mechanism." The report is specialized and aimed at the interested reader in the fields of vision and visual perception.

CONTENTS

List of Illustrations

I: Rationale

II: Methods

III: Results

IV: Discussion

V. Dissemination of Information

Appendices

      A. Accurate three-dimensional eyetracker

      B. Three-dimensional visual stimulus deflector

30 pp. 5 chapters. Drawings, figures, graphs, appendices.

220
Poulton, E.C.

Tracking Skill and Manual Control
Academic Press, 1974

A synoptic survey and critical reconsideration of research in tracking and motor skills.

The book is divided into two parts. Concerned with methodology and research design, the first contains specific chapters dealing with the measurement of tracking performance and ill-advised methods of measurement. Research performed in the late '50s and early '60s is surveyed, analyzed, and the empirical results summarized in the second part. This section includes work on tracking with single steps, with many steps, ramp tracks, and sine wave tracks. Tracking with pursuit and compensatory displays is also compared. In later chapters, there is an extensive discussion on types of control displays, including non-visual and augmented displays. These chapters end with short summaries of human factors considerations helpful to design engineers, as well as specific design recommendations. Specialists in the field will already be acquainted with much of the material. However, it is clearly written and presented, making it readily accessible to the interested non-specialist. The book's greatest utility appears to be as an introductory but comprehensive coverage of the subject for upperclass undergraduates or beginning graduate students. Engineering psychologists, human factors experts, and manual control design engineers might also find it interesting, but, as indicated above, much of the research discussed is at least twenty years old.

CONTENTS
Preface
PART 1: INTRODUCTION AND METHOD
Chapter 1: Tracking Skills
  Summary
  Choice and action
  True motion and relative motion
  Tracking along a contour
  Target acquisition
  Tracking by eye and by voice
  Paced and selfpaced tracking
  Control systems of various orders
  The engineering variables
  Memory for tracking skills
  Differences between aircraft pilots and nonpilots
Chapter 2: The Design and Evaluation of Experiments
  Summary
  Controlling for transfer
  The minimum number of people
  A typical experiment
  Evaluation of experimental results
  Recommended experimental design and evaluation
Chapter 3: Recommended Methods of Scoring
  Summary
  Errors in position at reversals
  Reponse amplitude analyzed by frequency
  Errors in time
  Errors in phase
  Overall measures of error
  Overall pattern analysis
  Recommendations on scoring
Chapter 4: Not Recommended Methods of Scoring
  Summary
  Overall estimates of high frequencies
  Frequency analyses involving the error
  Autocorrelation of the error
  Overall average time lags
  Time on target
  Consistency
  Subjective estimates of difficulty
PART 2: TRACKING
Chapter 5: Tracks with Single Steps
  Summary
  Step tracking
  Speed of quick movements
  Size of quick movements
  Speed of movements and accuracy
  Visual guidance of quick movements
  Reaction time for a correction
  Aiming by successive approximation and by monitoring
  Control sensitivity and acquisition time
  Recommended control sensitivity

Chapter 6: Tracks with Many Steps
    Summary
    Tracking many steps
    Interactions between responses to pairs of steps
    Difficulties of interpretation
    The range effect for sizes of step
    The range effect for times of step
    The range effect for directions of step
    Strategies with fully predictable steps
Chapter 7: Ramp Tracks
    Summary
    Tracking at a constant rate
    First responses to velocity ramps
    Response frequency and rate matching
    Average error and rate of ramp track
    Lag and lead errors with ramp tracks
    Side to side errors with velocity ramp tracks
    Tracks with multiple ramps
Chapter 8: Sine Wave Tracks
    Summary
    Tracking an object whose rate varies
    Amplitude of sine wave tracks
    Frequency of sine wave tracks
    Lag and lead errors with single sine wave tracks
    The irregularity of tracks with 2 or more sine waves
    Response frequencies with sine wave tracks
    Human describing functions
    Human remnants
Chapter 9: Pursuit and Compensatory Displays
    Summary
    Tracking with pursuit and compensatory displays
    Display mode with step tracks
    Display mode with ramp tracks of constant velocity
    Display mode in predicting and learning single sine wave tracks
    Display mode in predicting and learning irregular sine wave tracks
    Display mode in learning and monitoring the control system
    Errors due to misunderstanding compensatory displays
    Displays intermediate between pursuit and compensatory displays
    Asymmetrical transfer between pursuit and compensatory displays
    Experimental comparisons between pursuit and compensatory displays
    Compensatory displays, high order control systems, and low frequency tracks
    Magnifying pursuit and compensatory displays
    Recommended display mode
Chapter 10: Augmented Displays
    Summary
    The need for augmented displays
    Kinds of augmented displays
    Rate augmented displays
    Quickened displays
    Disadvantages of quickened displays
    Predictor displays

Preview of track ahead
Recommended augmented displays

Chapter 11: More Display Variation
Summary
Kinds of display variation
Magnified displays
Nonlinear displays
Delayed displays
Filtered displays
Noisy visual displays
Simulated displays
Compatible displays
Integrated displays
Recommended display variations

Chapter 12: Display Sampling
Summary
Kinds of display sampling
Intermittent displays
Stepped displays
Sampling 2 displays
Sampling 4 displays
Sampling many displays while flying
Tracking with an additional task
Blinking
Recommendations for display sampling

Chapter 13: Displays Using Alternative Visual Dimensions
Summary
The need for alternative sensory dimensions
Direction and rate of flash
Rate and brightness of flash
Rate of movement
Movement versus flash in peripheral vision
Brightness
Direction and brightness
A supplementary display when 2 conventional displays are at different distances
Recommended alternative visual dimensions

Chapter 14: Nonvisual Displays
Summary
Available nonvisual sensory dimensions
A 3 state display of the direction of sound
Direction and rate of interruption of sound
Direction and intensity of sound
Pitch of sound
Pitch and rate of interruption of sound
Integrated auditory displays
Correlated audiovisual tracks
Vibration on the skin
Electric shock on the skin
Felt acceleration and tilt
Forced response guidance
Recommended nonvisual displays

Chapter 15: Controls
Summary
Kinds of control variation
Stylus versus joystick
Joystick versus joyball
Joystick versus 2 controls
Lever versus crank
Compatability of control with display
Thumb, hand, and forearm controls
Control by eye
Spring centered controls
Friction in a control
Viscous damping and inertia in a control
Control loading to prevent accidental operation
Power operated and hand operated control systems
Backlash in a control
Deadspace in a control
Recommended controls

Chapter 16: Orders of Control Systems
Summary
Available orders of control systems
Aided and quickened control systems
Asymmetrical transfer between orders of control system
Order of control system with step tracks
Order of control system with velocity ramp track
Order of control system with sine wave tracks and pursuit displays
Order of control system with sine wave tracks and compensatory displays
Rate control systems, compensatory displays, and low frequency tracks
Acceleration aiding with accelerating tracks
Adaptive training devices
Interference between simultaneous orders of control system
Recommended orders of control system

Chapter 17: Other Control System Variations
Summary
Kinds of control system variation
Optimum control gain and maximum output of a rate control system
Nonlinear control systems
Stepped inputs to control systems
Control system lags
Oscillating control systems
Crosscoupled control systems
Sudden changes in control systems
Recommended variations for control systems
References
Index

427 pp. 15 chapters in 2 parts. Figures, graphs, tables, general index, references. ISBN 0-12-563550-8.

221
Prueitt, Melvin L.

Art and the Computer
McGraw-Hill, 1984

A visually-oriented report on the nature, problems, solutions, and applications of computer art.

In this vibrantly illustrated volume, Prueitt examines the potential of computer art. Deeming the computer the new tool of the artist, a tool that allows the artist direct expression of the mind without using the hand as an intermediary, Prueitt proclaims an approaching revolution in the art world as significant as the Renaissance. He emphasizes the aspects of computer graphics which make this revolution possible. Through the use of the computer, the artist can manipulate each element of the work, changing perspective, lighting, or color, as well as the size, shape, or position of any item in the picture. Graphics packages for home computers extend the possibility of creation to those without skills in drawing or painting. Computer art is enduring; the program can always be rerun and the image reproduced photographically. In a very readable text, Prueitt briefly discusses problems and approaches in the creation of graphic designs on a computer, and covers such items as shading, anti-aliasing techniques, input methods, and animation. This book sees the computer both as a tool for the development of displays in areas such as chemistry, mathematics, and cartography, and as an artist's tool. Illustrations include a computer model of a virus, a simulation of erosion, and a graphic presentation of a probability statement. Featuring an introduction by Carl Sagan, this volume is written for both the professional artist and the novice. The work should appeal to anyone with an interest in using the computer to generate creative graphics. Over 300 pictures, most in color, demonstrate the range and versatility of the computer as a tool for artistic expression.

CONTENTS

Foreword
 Jennifer Mellen
Preface
Introduction
 Carl Sagan
PART ONE: THE SUBJECT
 From computer to human
 From human to computer
 Perspective
 Shading
 A different viewpoint
 The program
 Creating perspective pictures
 Hidden-line and hidden-surface removal
 Shading and shadowing
 Ray tracing

Anti-aliasing
Motion pictures
Animation
Computer-aided design
Home computer art
The computer as designer
The computer artist
Everlasting art
Color intervals
The substance of beauty
Visual mystique
Computer as a teacher
New art forms
Exploring the images
A new vision
Maintaining appreciation
The eye and mind of the beholder
The future

PART TWO: THE GALLERY
Line drawings
Perspective mesh plots
Symmetry
Asymmetry
Science
Topography
Erosion
Mathematics
Landscapes
Computer caverns
Still lifes
Computer sculptures
Outer space
Lighting effects
Errors
Home computers
Pictures from Japan
Realism
Patterns and designs
Abstractions
Eye pieces
Electronic flowers

Indexes
Artist index
Subject index

246 pp. 2 parts. Subject index, color graphics, artist index. ISBN 0-07-050894-1. (ISBN 0-07-050899-2)

222
Reading, Veronica M.
(ed.)

collection

Visual Aspects and Ergonomics of Visual Display Units
University of London. Institute of Ophthalmology, 1978

Thirteen papers prepared for use in coursework at the Institute of
Ophthalmology, London.

This collection presents European (especially British) investigations of
health issues related to the use of visual display terminals (VDTs). The
material does not include the results of the many studies conducted
since 1978, the year of original publication. Nevertheless, display
designers will find these papers interesting for their straightforward
discussions of visual acuity, glare, luminance, optimum character
display, teletext typography, and CRT engineering principles. Because
the collection was designed for use in a college level course, most papers
are written at an accessible, introductory level. Topics range from the
physiology of the eye to the design of workstations. The novice to the
field might find the work of particular value if an understanding of
European work on health-related issues in VDT design and use is
desired.

CONTENTS
The contribution of various parts of the eye to visual acuity
R.F. Fisher
A simple screening technique for visual assessment
B. Whycer
Visual factors I
V.M. Reading
Visual factors II
R.A. Weale
Typography for teletext
G. Shaw
Postural stress in sedentary work
J.D.G. Troup
Work station design
M. Ballantine
Discomfort glare and VDUs in a multi-purpose environment -
introduction
W.G. Taylor
Discomfort glare and VDUs in a multi-purpose environment
J.G. Levitt
Basic engineering principles of cathode ray tubes
D. Faulkner
Radiation: the non-hazards of VDUs
F. Harlen
Eyestrain
J.M. Heaton
In-house studies
R.A. Weale

128 pp. 13 papers. Figures, graphs, references.

223
Refioglu, H. Ilhan
(ed.)

collection

Electronic Displays
IEEE Press, 1984

(from the *IEEE Press Selected Reprint Series*, sponsored by the IEEE
Circuits and Systems Society, M.G. Morgan, series ed.)

Gathers together selected reprints of papers on display technologies
previously published in professional engineering journals.

Contributors to this publication include engineers employed by IBM,
Bell Laboratories, Rockwell International, Philips Laboratories,
Burroughs Corporation, RCA, and Sharp Corporation, among others. A
number of Japanese engineers are also represented. Divided into seven
sections, this collection features 103 papers that provide descriptive
analyses of the structure and function of the various types of electronic
display systems. Following a general introduction to display
technologies, detailed discussions are presented covering liquid crystal
displays, electrophoretic and electrochromic displays, electroluminescent
displays, gas discharge displays, cathode ray tube displays, and light-
emitting diode displays. Numerous tables, graphs, and drawings
augment the discussion. Appearing initially in such publications as the
Society for Information Display Digest, Applied Physics Letters, and
various publications of the IEEE, these papers are addressed to
designers and users of electronic displays as well as to researchers in the
field.

CONTENTS

PREFACE

PART I: INTRODUCTION TO ELECTRONIC DISPLAYS
Recent advances in display technologies
I.F. Chang
Alphanumeric display
G.F. Weston
Flat-panel displays: a critique
L.E. Tannas, Jr., W.F. Goede

PART II: LIQUID CRYSTAL DISPLAYS

Section II-A: Basic Principles and Properties
Voltage-dependent optical activity of a twisted nematic liquid
crystal
M. Schadt, W. Helfrich
Liquid crystal displays: an experiment in interdisciplinary research
that worked
G.H. Heilmeier
Liquid-crystal orientational bistability and nematic storage effects
G.D. Boyd, J. Cheng, P.D.T. Ngo
A display device using the depolarization in a twisted nematic
liquid-crystal layer
T. Uchida, Y. Ishii, M. Wada

Section II-B: Display Devices and Systems
Reflective mode, 40 character, alphanumeric twisted-nematic liquid crystal displays
F.J. Kahn
An 80-character alphanumeric liquid crystal display system for computer terminals
K. Odawara, T. Ishibashi, K. Kinugawa, H. Sakurada, H. Tanaka
A radial format LCD/semiconductor system for analog watch applications
R.L. Gruebel, B.W. Marks, R.T. Noble, P.A. Penz, K.H. Surtani
Double-layered-electrode LCDs
T. Kamikawa
A single-polarizer twisted nematic display
A.R. Kmetz
Bright dichroic guest-host LCDs without a polarizer
T. Uchida, H. Seki, C. Shishido, M. Wada
Liquid crystal matrices for TV and colored graphic displays
J. Robert, F. Clerc
LCD pocket TV developments in Japan
G. Labrunie
Section II-C: Light Valves and Laser Addressed LCD's
A new television projection light valve
A.D. Jacobson, J. Grinberg, W.P. Bleha, L.J. Miller, L.M. Fraas, D.D. Boswell
Photoactivated birefringent liquid-crystal light valve for color symbology display
J. Grinberg, W.P. Bleha, A.D. Jacobson, A.M. Lackner, G.D. Myer, L.J. Miller, J.D. Margerum, L.M. Fraas, D.D. Boswell
A new color-TV projector
A.D. Jacobson, D.D. Boswell, J. Grinberg, W.P. Bleha, P.G. Reif, B. Hong, S.G. Lundquist, J.H. Colks
A 2000-character thermally-addressed liquid crystal projection display
A.G. Dewey, J.T. Jacobs, B.G. Huth, G.T. Sincerbox, G.J. Sprokel, A. Juliana, R.W. Koepcke
Laser-addressed liquid-crystal multifunction light valve
A. Sasaki, M. Inoda, T. Ishibashi
Application of the liquid crystal light valve to a large screen graphics display
B.S. Hong, L.T. Lipton, W.P. Bleha, J.H. Colles, P.F. Robusto
Section II-D: Displays with On-Substrate (Integrated) Control
A thin-film-transistor-controlled liquid-crystal numeric display
J.C. Erskine, P.A. Snopko
A thin-film transistor for flat panel displays
F.C. Luo, I. Chen, F.C. Genovese
A liquid crystal display device with thin-film transistors
M. Matsuura, Y. Takafuji, K. Nonomura, F. Funada, T. Wada

Amorphous silicon thin-film transistor for liquid crystal display panel
> *S. Kawai, N. Takagi, T. Kodama, K. Asama, S. Yangisawa*

Thin film polysilicon devices for flat-panel display circuitry
> *A. Juliana, S.W. Depp, B. Huth, T. Sedgwick*

A liquid-crystal display panel using an MOS array with gate-bus drivers
> *K. Kasahara, T. Yanagisawa, K. Sakai, T. Adachi, K. Inoue, T. Tsutsumi, H. Hori*

A liquid crystal TV display panel with drivers
> *T. Yamazaki, Y. Kawahara, S. Motte, H. Kamamori, J. Nakamura*

2" × 5" Varistor-controlled liquid crystal matrix display
> *D.E. Castleberry, L.M. Levinson*

The optimization of metal-insulator-metal nonlinear devices for use in multiplexed liquid crystal displays
> *D.R. Baraff, J.R. Long, B.K. MacLaurin, C.J. Miner, R.W. Streater*

PART III: ELECTROPHORETIC AND ELECTROCHROMIC DISPLAYS

Section III-A: Electrophoretic Displays

Electrophoretic image display (EPID) panel
> *I. Ota, J. Ohnishi, M. Yoshiyama*

An electrophoretic bar graph display
> *R. White*

High resolution electrophoretic display with photoconductor addressing
> *S.F. Blazo*

Section III-B: Electrochromic Displays

Performance characteristics of electrochromic displays
> *I.F. Chang, W.E. Howard*

A refreshed matrix-addressed electrochromic display
> *A.G. Arellano, G.S. Keller, P.J. Melz, M.D. Shattuck, C.V. Wilbur*

A multicolor electrochromic display
> *M.M. Nicholson, R.V. Galiardi*

Iridium oxide electrochromic seven-segment digit display
> *W.C. Dautremont-Smith, L.M. Schiavone, G. Beni, J.L. Shay*

An integrated electrochromic data display
> *D.J. Barclay, C.L. Bird, D.H. Kirkman, D.H. Martin, F.T. Moth*

Electrochromic displays for watches
> *T. Miyoshi, K. Iwasa*

PART IV: ELECTROLUMINESCENT DISPLAYS

Section IV-A: Overview

Electroluminescent display technologies and their characteristics
> *W.E. Howard*

EL powder technology for the eighties
> *A. Vecht*

Section IV-B: ac Electroluminescent Displays
Stable high-brightness thin-film electroluminescent panels
T. Inoguchi, M. Takeda, Y. Kakihara, Y. Nakata, M. Yoshida
TV imaging system using electroluminescent panels
S. Mito, C. Suzuki, Y. Kanatani, M. Ise
Inherent memory effects in ZnS:Mn thin film EL devices
Y. Yamauchi, M. Takeda, Y. Kakihara, M. Yoshida, J. Kawaguchi, H. Kishishita, Y. Nakata, T. Inoguchi, S. Mito
Character display using thin-film EL panel with inherent memory
C. Suzuki, Y. Kanatani, M. Ise, E. Misukami, K. Inazaki, S. Mito
Electron-beam switching of thin film ZnS electroluminescent devices
W.E. Howard, P.M. Alt
ACTFEL displays
L.E. Tannas, Jr., D.A. Treadway
Low-voltage-driven AC thin-film electroluminescent devices
H. Kozawaguchi, J. Ohwaki, B. Tsujiyama, K. Murase
Feasibility of a dual-color ACTFEL display
R.E. Coovert, C.N. King, R.T. Tuenge
Section IV-C: dc Electroluminescent Displays
Direct-current electroluminescence in zinc sulphide: state of the art
A. Vecht, N.J. Werring, R. Ellis, P.J.F. Smith
An operating 36-character DC electroluminescent alphanumeric display
A.L. Mears, J. Parker, R.W. Sarginson, R. Ellis
Performance of DC EL coevaporated ZnS:Mn, Cu low voltage devices
M.I. Abdalla, J. Thomas, A. Brenac, J.-P. Noblanc
Hermetically sealed high contrast EL display
M.K. Kilcoyne, A.F. Cserhati, D.L. Armijo, I.S. Santha, B. Garcia
DCEL dot matrix displays in a range of colors
A. Vecht, M. Higton, J. Mayo, J. Blackmore
Section IV-D: Displays with On-Substrate (Integrated) Control
High display viewability provided by thin-film EL, black layer, and TFT drives
K.O. Fugate
Thin-film transistor switching of thin-film electroluminescent display elements
Z.K. Kun, F.C. Luo, J. Murphy
High resolution thin-film EL TV display system
R.D. Ketchpel, S.P. Graves, M.K. Kilcoyne, T.C. Lim, D.L. Armijo, I.S. Santha, B. Garcia
MOS-EL integrated display device
K. Oki, Y. Ohkawa, K. Takahara, S. Miura
PART V: GAS DISCHARGE (PLASMA) DISPLAYS
Section V-A: Overview
Gas-discharge displays: the state of the art
A. Sobel

Section V-B: ac Plasma Displays
  AC plasma display technology overview
    P. Pleshko
  A planar single-substrate AC plasma display with capacitive vias
    G.W. Dick, M.R. Biazzo
  Self-shift plasma display panels with meandor electrodes or meandor channels
    S. Andoh, K.-I. Oki, K. Yoshikawa, Y. Miyashita, T. Shinoda, S. Sato, T. Sugimoto
  A high-resolution shift panel
    J.R. Beidl, F.C. Campagna, T.N. Criscimagna
  Electron transport shelf-shift display using an AC plasma panel
    P.D.T. Ngo, S.R. Maliszewski
Section V-C: dc Plasma Displays
  Panaplex II®: a low cost digital display
    T.C. Maloney
  Sixteen-inch gas-discharge display panel with 2-lines-at-a-time driving
    T. Kojima, R. Toyonaga, T. Sakai, T. Tajima, S. Sega, T. Kuriyama, J. Koike, H. Murakami
  A Self-Scan® imaging display panel
    T.C. Maloney
  Self-Scan® II panel displays—a new family of flat display devices
    D.E. Miller, R.A. Cola
  A flat-panel TV display system in monochrome and color
    Y. Amano
  An improved performance Self-Scan® I panel design
    D. Miller, J. Ogle, R. Cola, B. Caras, T. Maloney
  A high resolution DC plasma display panel
    Y. Amano, K. Yoshida, T. Shionoya
  Lamp phosphors and color gamut in positive-column gas-discharge cells for TV displays
    R.G. Kaufman
  A positive-column discharge memory panel without current-limiting resistors for color TV display
    Y. Okamoto, M. Mizushima
PART IV: CATHODE RAY TUBE (CRT) DISPLAYS
Section VI-A: CRT Displays
  History and development of the color picture tube
    E.W. Herold
  Color picture tube design trends
    A.M. Morrell
  An in-line gun for high resolution color display tubes
    H.-Y. Chen
  Quadrupole post-focusing shadowmask CRT
    M. van Alphen, J. van den Berg
  A dipole-quadrupole focus mask for color picture tubes
    E.F. Hockings, S. Bloom, C.A. Catanese
  Magnetic post-focusing in shadowmasks for color picture tubes
    J. Verweel
  Magnetic focusing for CTV tube masks
    J. Verweel

Performance of penetration color CRTs in single-anode and dual-anode configurations
  G.R. Spencer
Comparative evaluation of high-resolution color CRTs
  J. Brun
Projection television
  W.E. Good
Recent advance in high-brightness and high-resolution color light-valve projectors
  T.T. True
Contemporary large screen displays
  R.E. Thoman
Self-converged, three-CRT projection TV system
  R. Hockenbrock, W. Rowe
Section VI-B: Flat Panel CRT Displays
A digitally addressed flat-panel CRT
  W.F. Goede
Flat cathode-ray-tube display
  W.C. Scott, W.C. Holton, W.G. Manns, D.F. Weirauch, M.R. Namordi, F. Doerbeck, J.E. Gunther
Matrix-array cathode ray tube
  M.D. Sirkis, H.I. Refioglu, I. Kaufman, G.E. Huling
Large-screen flat-panel television: a new approach
  T.L. Credelle
The channel electron multiplier CRT: concept, design and performance
  A. Woodhead, D. Washington, A. Knapp, J. Mansell, C. Overall
Section VI-C: Vacuum Fluorescent Displays
Flat panel multi-digit fluorescent display
  K. Kiyozumi, M. Masuda, T. Nakamura
A 240-character vacuum fluorescent display and its drive circuitry
  K. Kasano, M. Masuda, T. Shimojo, K. Kiyozumi
Flat VFD TV display incorporating MOSFET switching array
  S. Uemura, K. Kiyozumi
Vacuum fluorescent display for TV video images
  M. Iwade, K. Kasano, M. Masuda, T. Nakamura
High resolution vacuum fluorescent display with 256×256 dot matrix
  M. Uchiyama, M. Masuda, K. Kiyozumi, T. Nakamura
PART VII: LIGHT EMITTING DIODE DISPLAYS
Section VII-A: Overview
Recent developments in light emitting-diode-technology
  M.G. Craford
Section VII-B: Display Devices and Systems
Large high-density monolithic XY-addressable arrays for flat-panel LED displays
  B.L. Frescura, H. Luechinger, C.A. Bittmann
Limitations on the size of monolithic XY addressable LED arrays
  B.L. Frescura
A GaP monolithic numeric display with internal reflection facets
  M. Inoue, H. Yamanaka, T. Uragaki, I. Teramoto

An LED numeric display for the aircraft cockpit
R.N. Tyte, J.H. Wharf, B. Ellis, T.F. Knibb, R.G. O'Rourke, R.M. Gibb
A high-brightness GaP green LED flat panel device for character and TV display
T. Niina, S. Kuroda, H. Yonei, H. Takesada
Multi-mode matrix LED display program
K.T. Burnette, W. Melnick

Author Index

Subject Index

Editor's Bibliography

467 pp. 108 papers in 8 parts. Drawings, photographs, figures, charts, graphs, tables, mathematical formulae, author index, subject index, references. ISBN 0-87942-169-X.

224
Rehe, Rolf F.

Typography: How to Make It Most Legible (rev. ed.)
Design Research International, 1984

A good basic introduction to typography, with clear illustrations and an accessible style.

This sixty-two page booklet is a master's thesis that is currently in its sixth reprinting since its first publication in 1972. It is a good basic summary of typography and particularly of legibility research. Professor Rehe, Director of Design Research International, a group specializing in typographic design, research, and consultation, reduces all the essentials of type size and face, numbers, color and design to little more than a page each. For this reason the volume should be regarded as a primer for the totally uninitiated. Well-chosen, well-designed illustrations help make the author's points dramatically, and the overall appearance of the book is in itself a good argument for his design principles. There is also a 184-entry bibliography, consisting largely of journal articles from the *Journal of Typographic Research* (now *Visible Language*) and from the *Journal of Applied Psychology*, that is very thorough and well worth the price of the booklet.

CONTENTS

1: The Need for a Functional Typography
The technological-typographical revolution
Scientific investigation of typography appears
The importance of effective typography
The typographer as mass communicator
The role of the typographer

2: Research Methods and Approach
How the eye perceives the printed word
The methods of measuring legibility
Selection of studies
The recommendations

3: Research Findings and Recommendations
Legibility of individual letters
Type size
Line width
Leading
Kinds of type
Serif or sans-serif type?
Justified or unjustified typography?
Lowercase or uppercase typography?
Alternatives: spaced-unit, square-unit
Newspaper typography
Ligatures and legibility
Television typography
Numbers
Mathematical material
Color and background
Type in reverse
Writing style and typography
Simplification of design units
Unit spacing
Legibility of children's books
The Initial Teaching Alphabet
Miscellaneous findings
Congeniality
General findings
4: Research Applications in Design and Production of Booklet
The type
The design approach
Conclusions and outlook
Credits
Glossary
Bibliography
Index

80 pp. 4 chapters. Drawings, figures, general index, bibliography, glossary.

225
Resnick, Elizabeth

Graphic Design: A Problem-Solving Approach to Visual Communication
Prentice-Hall, 1984

(from The Art and Design Series)

A well-illustrated text introducing the concepts and techniques of graphic design, with an emphasis on the creative use of topography.

This volume describes the principles and processes of graphic design. Each chapter offers a brief discussion of a design concept and then assigns a specific teaching exercise to illustrate it. Chapters consist primarily of graphic designs created by the author's own students in response to these exercises, and the author's analysis of each design's visual impact. The reader learns important terminology and the basics of selecting materials and approaching a design problem. Principles of design such as balance, emphasis, and unity; the figure ground relationship of shapes; and letters and form, movement, and texture are covered. Seven of the ten chapters deal with the visual characteristics and potential range of expression of typographic forms. Other chapter assignments explore the representation of a tool and examine the poster as a form of visual communication. Unfortunately, none of the designs are reproduced in color and this seems to detract particularly from the discussion of poster design. The reader may choose more advanced reading from the references cited at the end of each chapter. Aimed primarily at the beginning design student, this text can easily be read by anyone interested in becoming acquainted with the field.

CONTENTS
Foreword
Introduction
One. The letterform collage
Two. The relationship of letters
Three. Letterform progressions
Four. Word action progression
Five. Word play typography
Six. Self-promotion typography
Seven. The simple tool
Eight. The quote poster
Nine. The vegetable poster
Ten. The country poster
Bibliography
Index

148 pp. 10 chapters. Drawings, photographs, general index, bibliography, references. ISBN 0-13-363267-9. (ISBN 0-13-363259-8)

226
Reynolds, Linda
Simmonds, Doig

Presentation of Data in Science
Martinus Nijhoff, 1981

(third printing, 1983)

Provides the basic knowledge of the principles and skills necessary for the production of successful illustrations.

This practical and richly illustrated handbook is modeled after a studio started by Simmonds in 1975 at the Royal Postgraduate Medical School to train lecturers and writers in the sciences and medicine to illustrate their own work. Designed to aid other authors or teachers who have knowledge but lack the skills to provide informative illustrations to accompany their work, this book covers the skills needed to produce a variety of visual aids. Methods are outlined for producing professional-looking tables, graphs, charts, and diagrams. Other topics include graphic standards for publications, slides, posters, overhead transparencies, synchronized tape-slide presentations, and television. All material is presented clearly along with outlines and details of the techniques and supplies needed for effective and efficient production of illustrations from planning through completion. A valuable work for any scientist who, in the interest of speed and economy, prepares his own illustrations to accompany his publications or lectures.

CONTENTS

LIST OF ILLUSTRATIONS

FOREWORD
   James Calnan, FRCS, FRCP

INTRODUCTION

1: THE LEGIBILITY OF TYPE

1.1: Introduction

1.2: Investigating Legibility
     1.2.1. The reading process
     1.2.2. Methods of research

1.3: Type Forms
     1.3.1. The basic anatomy of type
     1.3.2. Typeface
     1.3.3. Type weight
     1.3.4. Italics
     1.3.5. Capitals versus lower case
     1.3.6. Numerals

1.4: Type Size

1.5: Line Length

1.6: Line Spacing

1.7: Letter and Word Spacing

1.8: Justified versus Unjustified Setting

1.9: Margins

1.10: Single- versus Double-Column Layouts

1.11: Paper and Ink

2: THE PRESENTATION OF TEXT

2.1: The Visual Representation of Information 'Structure'

2.2: Continuous Text
     2.2.1. Headings
     2.2.2. Paragraphs

2.3: Bibliographies and References

2.4: Indexes

3: THE PRESENTATION OF TABLES

3.1: Structure

3.2: Layout and Typography
     3.2.1. General principles
     3.2.2. Horizontal emphasis
     3.2.3. Vertical emphasis
     3.2.4. Headings
     3.2.5. Lettering

4: THE PRESENTATION OF GRAPHS, CHARTS AND DIAGRAMS
4.1: The Relative Merits of Different Kinds of Illustration
4.2: The Content of Illustrations
4.3: General Principles of Presentation
    4.3.1. Layout
    4.3.2. Framing
    4.3.3. Visual emphasis
4.4: The Presentation of Graphs and Charts
    4.4.1. Data points
    4.4.2. Standard errors
    4.4.3. Lines linking data points
    4.4.4. Scale calibrations
    4.4.5. Axes
    4.4.6. Labelling of axes
    4.4.7. Keys
    4.4.8. Headings
5: PRINTED PUBLICATIONS
5.1: Introduction
5.2: Graphic Standards for Graphs, Charts and Diagrams in Printed Journals
    5.2.1. Instructions to authors
    5.2.2. Reproduction ratios
    5.2.3. Size of drafts and artwork
    5.2.4. Formulae
    5.2.5. Character style
    5.2.6. Character spacing
    5.2.7. Space between lines of text
    5.2.8. Tones and shading
    5.2.9. Positive versus negative images
    5.2.10. Contrast
    5.2.11. Oversize artwork for publication
    5.2.12. Compatibility with standards for slides
5.3: Guide Lines for Camera-Ready Copy
    5.3.1. Copy for journals or proceedings of meetings
    5.3.2. Copy for reports
5.4: Original Artwork versus Copies
    5.4.1. Reasons for copying artwork
    5.4.2. Copying methods
5.5: Overlays and Cover Sheets
5.6: Marks of Identification
5.7: Sending Artwork to the Publisher or Printer
6: SLIDES
6.1: Introduction
6.2: Planning a Slide Presentation
    6.2.1. The use of 'introduction' and 'conclusion' slides
    6.2.2. The body of the presentation
    6.2.3. Constructing a story-board
    6.2.4. Rehearsal
6.3: The Content of Slides
    6.3.1. Word slides
    6.3.2. Data slides
    6.3.3. Headings for data slides

6.4: Graphic Standards for Slides
    6.4.1. Originals
    6.4.2. Slide formats
    6.4.3. Size of drafts and artwork
    6.4.4. Line thickness
    6.4.5. Character height
    6.4.6. Character style
    6.4.7. Character spacing
    6.4.8. Layout for word slides
    6.4.9. Tones and shading
    6.4.10. Positive versus negative images
    6.4.11. Contrast
6.5: The Use of Colour
    6.5.1. Black-and-white versus coloured artwork
    6.5.2. The use of coloured images
    6.5.3. The use of coloured backgrounds with black lettering
6.6: Testing Slides
6.7: Projection of Slides
6.8: The Design of Lecture Theatres
7: POSTERS
7.1: Introduction
7.2: The Content of Posters
    7.2.1. General principles
    7.2.2. The structure of the poster
    7.2.3. Headings
7.3: Useful Equipment for Poster Production
7.4: Graphic Standards for Posters
    7.4.1. Poster formats
    7.4.2. Size of drafts and artwork
    7.4.3. Character height
    7.4.4. Character style
    7.4.5. Layout of text
    7.4.6. Illustrations
    7.4.7. Poster layout
    7.4.8. The use of colour
7.5: Packing and Transporting Poster Displays
8: OVERHEAD PROJECTION TRANSPARENCIES
8.1: Introduction
8.2: Graphic Standards for Transparencies
    8.2.1. Originals
    8.2.2. Format and size
    8.2.3. Line thickness
    8.2.4. Character height
    8.2.5. Layout
    8.2.6. The use of colour
8.3: Techniques in the Use of OHP Transparencies
    8.3.1. Overlays
    8.3.2. Reveals
    8.3.3. Masking

8.4: Testing OHP Transparencies

9: TAPE-SLIDE PROGRAMMES

9.1: Introduction

9.2: Planning a Tape-Slide Programme

9.3: Writing the Script

9.4: Graphic Standards

9.5: The Recording

10: TELEVISION

10.1: Introduction

10.2: Graphic Standards for Television
    10.2.1. Format
    10.2.2. Size of drafts and artwork
    10.2.3. Line thickness
    10.2.4. Character height
    10.2.5. Tones and shading
    10.2.6. Contrast
    10.2.7. The use of colour

11: MATERIALS, EQUIPMENT AND WORKING COMFORT

11.1: Introduction

11.2 Basic Essentials for Black-and-White Artwork
    11.2.1. Paper
    11.2.2. Pencils
    11.2.3. Inks
    11.2.4. Pens
    11.2.5. Rulers and set squares
    11.2.6. Templates and stencils
    11.2.7. Erasers
    11.2.8. Scalpels
    11.2.9. Burnishers
    11.2.10. Adhesives
    11.2.11. Drafting tape
    11.2.12. Drawing boards

11.3: Other Useful Items for Black-and-White Artwork
    11.3.1. Self-adhesive tapes
    11.3.2. Dry-transfer symbols and lettering
    11.3.3. Tone sheets
    11.3.4. 'Pounce' powder
    11.3.5. Fixatives and varnishes

11.4: Additional Materials for Colour and OHP Work
    11.4.1. Self-adhesive colour sheets
    11.4.2. Paints
    11.4.3. Brushes
    11.4.4. Cells and foils (acetate sheets)

11.5: Working Comfort
    11.5.1. Organisation
    11.5.2. Furniture
    11.5.3. Lighting

12: BASIC TECHNIQUES

12.1: Care and Preparation of Paper

12.2: Ink Work

    12.2.1. Use of technical drawing pens

    12.2.2. Blotting

    12.2.3. Drawing ink lines

    12.2.4. Finishing-off ink lines

    12.2.5. Use of templates and stencils

    12.2.6. Short cuts

12.3: Correcting Errors in Ink Work

    12.3.1. General comments

    12.3.2. Cut-and-stick corrections

    12.3.3. Edge-crossing

    12.3.4. Correcting with a knife

    12.3.5. Correcting with paint

12.4: Use of Dry-Transfer Materials

    12.4.1. Lettering

    12.4.2. Tones

    12.2.3. Making corrections

12.5: Use of Self-Adhesive Tones and Colours

    12.5.1. Methods of application

    12.5.2. Trapped air bubbles

    12.5.3. 'Windows'

12.6: Simple Object Drawing of Line Diagrams

    12.6.1. General principles

    12.6.2. Basic shapes

    12.6.3. Lighting

    12.6.4. Special effects

    12.6.5. Making symmetrical shapes

    12.6.6. Observation of objects

13: WORKING METHOD

13.1: Planning the Illustration

    13.1.1. Choice of media

    13.1.2. Summary of standards

13.2: Making the Draft

    13.2.1. Rough sketches

    13.2.2. The use of graph paper for drafts

    13.2.3. The use of typewriter grids

13.3: Using the Draft

    13.3.1. Fixing the draft to the artwork or drawing board

    13.3.2. Transferring information from the draft to the final artwork

13.4: Making the Final Artwork

13.5: Making Additions to the Artwork

GLOSSARY

LITERATURE

SUBJECT INDEX

209 pp. 13 chapters. Drawings, photographs, figures, charts, graphs, tables, subject index, bibliography, glossary. ISBN 90-247-2398-1. (ISBN 90-247-3054-6)

227
Robinson, Arthur H.
Sale, Randall D.
Morrison, Joel L.
Muehrcke, Phillip C.

Elements of Cartography (5ed.)
John Wiley and Sons, 1984

This revised fifth edition of a text first published in 1953 seeks to provide a balanced treatment of cartographic theory and cartographic practice during a time of transition and change in the field.

The first part of this comprehensive text is introductory, discussing basic characteristics of maps and charts—their function, scale, range, scope, and focus (geometric, technologic, presentation, artistic, and communication), as well as the history and the current status of the discipline. The communication focus is used in this text to organize and present material because it is the most inclusive approach, and because the sciences, engineering, and humanities use maps as tools for expressing concepts. The second and third sections review the theory and practice of cartography. Map scale, coordinate systems, reckoning, projections, color, pattern, typography, and lettering are covered. Also covered are remote sensing, mapping with point, line, and area symbols, and the portrayal of land-surface form. The final part of the text is an extensive review of worksheets, databases, digitizing, data file manipulation, and other technical and non-technical aspects of modern mapmaking. Designed for use in a wide range of academic situations, from introductory to advanced levels, this revision has added much new material, including a chapter on land surface representation. It has also increased coverage of image manipulation of cartographic data and added a glossary of relevant terms from related sciences. While computer-generated maps are not covered in detail, the brief section which describes digitizing, data file manipulation, and databases as tools for preparation of a basic compilation worksheet will be helpful. In addition, the solid principles of cartography presented here will serve anyone working on cartography, whether they are using a computer or paper and pencil.

CONTENTS

Part One: Introduction to Cartography
1. The nature of cartography
2. The history and the profession of cartography
3. Technology of cartography

Part Two: Theoretical Principles of Cartography
4. The spheroid, map scale, coordinate systems, and reckoning
5. Map projections
6. Processing and generalizing geographical data
7. Graphic perception and design
8. Color and pattern
9. Typography and lettering the map

Part Three: The Practice of Cartography: Data Manipulation and
Generalization
   10. Remote sensing and data sources
   11. Simplification and classification processes
   12. Symbolization: mapping with point symbols
   13. Mapping with line symbols
   14. Mapping with area symbols
   15. Portraying the land-surface form
Part Four: The Practice of Cartography: Production and Reproduction
   16. Compilation and credits
   17. Map reproduction
   18. Map production
Appendix
   A. Useful dimensions, constants, formulas and conversions
   B. Geographical tables
   C. Glossary of technical terms
Index

*544 pp. 18 chapters in 4 parts. Photographs, figures, maps, graphs,
tables, general index, references, glossary, appendices. ISBN 0-471-
09877-9.*

228
Rock, Irvin

The Logic of Perception
The MIT Press, 1983

A cognitive theory of perception exploring the thought-like, problem-
solving nature of the perceptual process.

Experimental evidence, much of it his own, convinced the author to
modify his earlier views on the nature of perception and to conclude
that perception is the result of intelligent operations. Formerly an
advocate of Gestalt theory, Rock here espouses the essence of the theory
the Gestaltists rejected. In an impressive consolidation of experimental
evidence, including more than 250 references, the author formulates a
comprehensive theory of perception and suggests that the study of
perception may lead to new knowledge about thought itself. In his
theory, perception, while constrained by the proximal stimulus,
demonstrates thought-like qualities including reasoning, decision-
making, learning from experience, sudden insight, and the development
and utilization of internalized categories. The book describes four kinds
of cognitive processes and their role in perception: form construction, or
perception of shape; problem solving, based on a process of hypothesis
generation; relational determination, culminating in a description; and
inference, the process of deduction from a rule. The book opens with
explanations of other theories of perception (stimulus theory and
spontaneous interaction, or Gestalt, theory) and recounts the arguments
against the author's own cognitive theory. From here the author begins
the delineation of his position. Writing for a wide audience, Rock has
made a point of defining his terms and has avoided an overly technical

style. Numerous examples and illustrations augment the text and offer the reader direct experience of perceptual problems.

CONTENTS
Preface
1. Introduction
2. Characteristics and theories of perception
3. Form perception based on a process of description
4. Perception as problem solving. I: Solution finding
5. Perception as problem solving. II: Solution acceptance
6. Perception as problem solving. III: The preference for certain solutions
7. Perception as problem solving. IV: Case studies
8. Perception governed by stimulus relationships
9. Unconscious inference
10. Perceptual interdependencies
11. Knowledge and perception
12. Criticisms, clarifications, and conclusions
References
Index

365 pp. 12 chapters. Drawings, figures, tables, references. ISBN 0-262-18109-6.

229
Rogers, David F.

Procedural Elements for Computer Graphics
McGraw-Hill, 1985

This companion volume to *Mathematical Elements for Computer Graphics* discusses and demonstrates the mathematics of creating computer graphics, with an emphasis on raster scan graphics.

This volume is a decade newer than its companion and for the most part covers different material. The only substantial overlap is in the first chapter; both books cover computer graphics hardware and include photographs of relevant graphics devices. Chapter one in the present volume emphasizes cathode ray tube displays and interactive hardware. Later chapters cover: raster scan graphics, discussing at length procedures of line and circle drawing and filling polygons so that they appear solid as well as antialiasing algorithms for portraying lines without jagged edges; clipping, including two- and three-dimensional; hidden line and hidden surface algorithms for determining what parts of an object are visible from a specific observation point; and rendering, creating real-appearing pictures through the use of illumination, texture, shadow, transparency, and color effects. This chapter includes glossy color plates showing the outcome images of various rendering algorithms. The author uses the same method of presentation that was employed in *Mathematical Elements for Computer Graphics*. Various topics are discussed followed by the presentation of a detailed algorithm, a working example, or both. The algorithms are presented in "pseudocode" that can easily be translated into the reader's choice of common computer languages. The pseudocode is discussed in an appendix. Exercises for each chapter are included at the back of the book. Prerequisites for the use of the book are a background in college mathematics and working knowledge of a higher level computer language. This book was designed for use as an introductory text for use in computer graphics courses at the advanced undergraduate and graduate levels.

CONTENTS

Preface

Chapter 1: Introduction to Computer Graphics
    1.1. Overview of computer graphics
    1.2. Types of graphics devices
    1.3. Storage tube graphics displays
    1.4. Calligraphic refresh graphics display
    1.5. Raster refresh graphics displays
    1.6. Cathode ray tube basics
    1.7. Color CRT raster scan basics
    1.8. Video basics
    1.9. Interactive devices
    1.10. Summary
    1.11. References

Chapter 2: Raster Scan Graphics
    2.1. Line drawing algorithms
    2.2. Digital differential analyzer
    2.3. Bresenham's algorithm
    2.4. Integer Bresenham's algorithm
    2.5. General Bresenham's algorithm
    2.6. Circle generation—Bresenham's algorithm
    2.7. Scan conversion—generation of the display
    2.8. Real-time scan conversion
    2.9. Run-length encoding
    2.10. Cell encoding
    2.11. Frame buffers
    2.12. Addressing the raster
    2.13. Line display
    2.14. Character display
    2.15. Solid area scan conversion
    2.16. Polygon filling
    2.17. Scan-converting polygons
    2.18. A simple ordered edge list algorithm
    2.19. A more efficient ordered edge list algorithm
    2.20. The edge fill algorithm
    2.21. The edge flag algorithm
    2.22. Seed fill algorithms
    2.23. A simple seed fill algorithm
    2.24. A scan line seed fill algorithm
    2.25. Fundamentals of antialiasing
    2.26. Simple area antialiasing
    2.27. The convolution integral and antialiasing
    2.28. Halftoning
    2.29. References

Chapter 3: Clipping
    3.1. Two-dimensional clipping
    3.2. Sutherland-Cohen subdivision line clipping algorithm
    3.3. Midpoint subdivision algorithm
    3.4. Generalized two-dimensional line clipping for convex boundaries
    3.5. Cyrus-Beck algorithm
    3.6. Interior and exterior clipping
    3.7. Identifying convex polygons and determining the inward normal
    3.8. Splitting concave polygons
    3.9. Three-dimensional clipping
    3.10. Three-dimensional midpoint subdivision algorithm
    3.11. Three-dimensional Cyrus-Beck algorithm
    3.12. Clipping in homogenous coordinates
    3.13. Determining the inward normal and three-dimensional convex sets
    3.14. Splitting concave volumes
    3.15. Polygon clipping
    3.16. Reentrant polygon clipping—Sutherland-Hodgman algorithm
    3.17. Concave clipping regions—Weiler-Atherton algorithm
    3.18. Character clipping
    3.19. References
Chapter 4: Hidden Lines and Hidden Surfaces
    4.1. Introduction
    4.2. Floating horizontal algorithm
    4.3. Roberts algorithm
    4.4. Warnock algorithm
    4.5. Weiler-Atherton algorithm
    4.6. A subdivision algorithm for curved surfaces
    4.7. z-buffer algorithm
    4.8. List priority algorithm
    4.9. Scan line algorithms
    4.10. Scan line z-buffer algorithm
    4.11. A spanning scan line algorithm
    4.12. Scan line algorithms for curved surfaces
    4.13. A visible surface ray tracing algorithm
    4.14. Summary
    4.15. References
Chapter 5: Rendering
    5.1. Introduction
    5.2. A simple illumination model
    5.3. Determining the surface normal
    5.4. Determining the reflection vector
    5.5. Gouraud shading
    5.6. Phong shading
    5.7. A simple illumination model with special effects
    5.8. A more complete illumination model
    5.9. Transparency
    5.10. Shadows
    5.11. Texture
    5.12. A global illumination model using ray tracing
    5.13. A more complete global illumination model using ray tracing

5.14. Recent advances in rendering

5.15. Color

5.16. References

Appendixes

Appendix A: Pseudocode

Appendix B: Projects

Index

433 pp. 5 chapters. Drawings, photographs, figures, charts, tables, mathematical formulae, algorithms, models, general index, references, appendices. (ISBN 0-07-053534-5)

230
Rogers, David F.
Adams, J. Alan

Mathematical Elements for Computer Graphics
McGraw-Hill, 1976

A cohesive introduction to the mathematical theories and concepts required to utilize computer graphics techniques.

An introduction to the text presents an overview of current computer graphics technology, including numerous photos of graphics devices. Four chapters discuss representation and transformation of points and lines, three-dimensional objects, two-dimensional curves, and three-dimensional curves. Among the topics covered are manipulation and display techniques for graphical computer output; rotation, translation, and scaling techniques; and procedures for defining curves. Chapter six discusses mathematical descriptions of surfaces. Throughout the text mathematical techniques are emphasized rather than procedural techniques. Three lengthy appendices cover graphics primitives and graphics elements; rules of matrix algebra; and instructive computer algorithms for database manipulations and transformations (in BASIC). This textbook does not present new mathematical material, although it does feature some new material on presentation. Previously, this material had not been collected and presented in a unified manner, using one notation. This book grew out of an introductory course in computer graphics and is intended as a textbook for such classes or as a supplementary text for advanced courses in mathematics and computer programming. The book should also be useful for professional programmers. Most of the material assumes the equivalent of one year of college mathematics.

CONTENTS

Foreward

Preface

Chapter 1: Introduction to Computer Graphics Technology

1.1. Overview of computer graphics

1.2. Representing pictures to be presented

1.3. Preparing pictures for presentation

1.4. Presenting previously prepared pictures

1.5. Interacting with the picture

1.6. Description of some typical graphics devices
1.7. Classification of graphics devices
References
Chapter 2: Points and Lines
2.1. Introduction
2.2. Representation of points
2.3. Transformations and matrices
2.4. Transformation of points
2.5. Transformation of straight lines
2.6. Midpoint transformation
2.7. Parallel lines
2.8. Intersecting lines
2.9. Rotation
2.10. Reflection
2.11. Scaling
2.12. Combined operations
2.13. Transformations of a unit square
2.14. Arbitrary 2×2 rotation matrix
2.15. Two-dimensional translations and homogeneous coordinates
2.16. Points at infinity
2.17. Two-dimensional rotation about an arbitrary axis
References
Chapter 3: Three-Dimensional Transformations and Projections
3.1. Introduction
3.2. Three-dimensional scaling
3.3. Three-dimensional shearing
3.4. Three-dimensional rotations
3.5. Reflection in three dimensions
3.6. Translation in three dimensions
3.7. Three-dimensional rotations about an arbitrary axis
3.8. Elements for the general rotation matrix
3.9. Affine and perspective geometry
3.10. Axonometric projections
3.11. Perspective transformations
3.12. Techniques for generating perspective views
3.13. Points at infinity
3.14. Reconstruction of three-dimensional information
3.15. Stereographic projection
References
Chapter 4: Plane Curves
4.1. Introduction
4.2. Nonparametric curves
4.3. Parametric curves
4.4. Nonparametric representation of conic sections
4.5. Nonparametric circular arcs
4.6. Parametric representation of conic sections
4.7. Parametric representation of a circle
4.8. Parametric representation of an ellipse
4.9. Parametric representation of a parabola
4.10. Parametric representation of a hyperbola
4.11. A procedure for the use of conic sections
4.12. Circular arc interpolation
References

Chapter 5: Space Curves
    5.1. Introduction
    5.2. Representation of space curves
    5.3. Cubic splines
    5.4. Normalized parameters
    5.5. Boundary conditions
    5.6. Parabolic blending
    5.7. Bezier curves
    5.8. B-spline curves
    References
Chapter 6: Surface Description and Generation
    6.1. Introduction
    6.2. Spherical surfaces
    6.3. Plane surfaces
    6.4. Curved surface representation
    6.5. Bilinear surface
    6.6. Lofted or ruled surfaces
    6.7. Linear Coons surfaces
    6.8. Bicubic surface patch
    6.9. The F-patch
    6.10. Bezier surfaces
    6.11. B-spline surfaces
    6.12. Generalized Coons surfaces
    6.13. Conclusions
    References
Appendix A: Computer Graphics Software
    A.1. Computer graphics primitives
    A.2. Computer graphics elements
    A.3. Canonical space
Appendix B: Matrix Operations
    B.1. Terminology
    B.2. Addition and subtraction
    B.3. Multiplication
    B.4. Determinant of a square matrix
    B.5. Inverse of a square matrix
Appendix C: Computer Algorithms
    C.1. An algorithm for two-dimensional translations
    C.2. A two-dimensional scaling algorithm
    C.3. A two-dimensional reflection algorithm
    C.4. A general two-dimensional rotation algorithm
    C.5. A three-dimensional scaling algorithm
    C.6. An algorithm for three-dimensional rotation about the x-axis
    C.7. An algorithm for three-dimensional rotation about the y-axis
    C.8. An algorithm for three-dimensional rotation about the z-axis
    C.9. An algorithm for three-dimensional reflections
    C.10. An algorithm for three-dimensional translation
    C.11. An algorithm for three-dimensional rotation about any arbitrary axis in space
    C.12. An axonometric projective algorithm
    C.13. A dimetric projective algorithm
    C.14. An isometric projective algorithm
    C.15. An algorithm for perspective transformations
    C.16. Three-dimensional reconstruction algorithms

C.17. A stereo algorithm
C.18. An algorithm for a nonparametric circle
C.19. An algorithm for a parametric circle
C.20. Parametric ellipse algorithm
C.21. An algorithm for a parametric parabola
C.22. Algorithms for parametric hyperbolas
C.23. An algorithm for a circle through three points
C.24. An algorithm for generating cubic splines
C.25. An algorithm for parabolic blending
C.26. A Bezier curve algorithm
C.27. A B-spline curve algorithm
C.28. An algorithm for a bilinear surface patch
C.29. An algorithm for a linear Coons surface
C.30. An algorithm for a bicubic surface patch
C.31. Bezier surface generation algorithm

Index

239 pp. 6 chapters. Drawings, photographs, figures, graphs, tables, algorithms, abstract formalisms, general index, appendices. (ISBN 0-07-053527-2)

231
Rookledge, Gordon
Perfect, Christopher

reference

Rookledge's International Typefinder: The Essential Handbook of Typeface Recognition and Selection
Sarema Press, 1983

This concise handbook comments briefly on the individual characteristics of most international typefaces.

Written as a thorough reference work for professional designers and design students, this handbook presents numerous international typeface specimens and defines their characteristics. The authors examine both text and decorative (non-continuous) typefaces, introducing a new typeface classification system based on the grouping of typefaces according to specific design features. A brief explanation of sixteen general type categories (eight text, eight decorative) precedes examples drawn from smaller groups within each category based on more specific design features. The work lists typefaces in the normal weight of type for text setting. Due to the great number of decorative typefaces, the author's selection offers a survey of the more commonly used designs. Well designed, with excellent reproductions and succinct commentary, this work will be a useful tool for the working designer and will also help the student to evaluate type design using the type feature classification presented here.

CONTENTS

Preface
Herbert Spencer

Introduction

PART ONE: TEXT TYPEFACES

    Explanation of categories

      1. Sloping e-bar (Venetian serif)
      2. Angles stress/oblique serifs (Old style serif)
      3. Vertical stress/oblique serifs (Transitional serif)
      4. Vertical stress/straight serifs (New transitional serif)
      5. Abrupt contrast/straight serifs (modern serif)
      6. Slab serif
      7. Wedge serif (Hybrid serif)
      8. Sans serif

    'Earmark' tables

PART TWO: DECORATIVE (NON-CONTINUOUS TEXT) TYPEFACES

    Explanation of categories

      1. Flowing scripts
      2. Non-flowing scripts (including Blackletter & Uncial)
      3. Unmodified (formal text shape)
      4. Fat & thin face (modified & unmodified)
      5. Ornamental
      6. Modified serif
      7. Modified sans serif
      8. Modified outrageous

Appendix

Bibliography

Index of Typefaces

288 pp. 16 chapters in 2 parts. Bibliography, appendix, index of typefaces. ISBN 0-85331-468-3. (ISBN 0-85331-469-1)

232
Rosenfeld, Azriel
Kak, Avinash C.

Digital Picture Processing (2ed.) 2 vols.
Academic Press, 1982

(from the *Computer Science and Applied Mathematics* series, Werner Rheinboldt, series ed.)

Presents a comprehensive survey of the various concepts, algorithms, techniques and uses of computer image processing. A thorough, informative, and well-organized survey of a rapidly expanding field.

Rosenfeld and Kak offer a thorough treatment of the concepts, algorithms, and theories behind the various techniques and uses of computer picture processing. Of interest to advanced display and systems designers, this two-volume second edition includes extensive revision and expansion of the original as well as completely new material which considers the latest developments in the field of digital picture processing. The authors organize their survey into twelve lucid and detailed chapters. An introductory chapter that concludes with a useful guide to the literature leads to a thorough presentation of the mathematics necessary to process images digitally. The authors' somewhat restricted treatment of human visual perception and its relationship to computer imaging dispenses with discussion of the anatomy and physiology of the human visual system and proceeds from the "black box" standpoint of perception psychology. Following chapters discuss computer picture processing techniques, with emphasis on: picture sampling; computer techniques for picture compression and the enhancement of low-quality pictures; the use of filtering theory in image restoration; the mathematics of image reconstruction, imaging geometry, and pixel classification; and representation schemes and their application to geometric property measurement. The final chapter presents an analysis of picture descriptions at various structural levels and a discussion of how to construct models appropriate to a given picture analysis task. Throughout the book pictures, illustrations, and figures complement the text. An additional useful feature is the presentation of various exercises which apply the text's numerous mathematical formulae and thus clarify their functions.

CONTENTS

VOLUME ONE
  Preface
  Contents of volume 2
Chapter 1: Introduction
  1.1. Picture processing
  1.2. Scenes, images, and digital pictures
  1.3. A guide to the literature
  References
Chapter 2: Mathematical Preliminaries
  2.1. Linear operations on pictures
  2.2. Discrete picture transforms
  2.3. Random variables
  2.4. Random fields
  2.5. Vector space representation of images
  References
Chapter 3: Visual Perception
  3.1. Brightness and contrast
  3.2. Acuity and contour
  3.3. Color
  3.4. Pattern and texture
  3.5. Shape and space
  3.6. Duration and motion
  3.7. Detection and recognition
  References
Chapter 4: Digitization
  4.1. Sampling using an array of points
  4.2. Sampling using orthonormal functions
  4.3. Quantization of picture samples
  4.4. Bibliographic notes
  References

Chapter 5: Compression
    5.1. Transform compression
    5.2. Fast implementation of KL compression
    5.3. Fourier, Hadamard, and cosine transform compression
    5.4. Bit allocation in transform compression
    5.5. Predictive compression
    5.6. Block truncation compression
    5.7. Error-free compression
    5.8. More on compression techniques
    5.9. The rate-distortion function
    5.10. Bibliographic notes
    References

Chapter 6: Enhancement
    6.1. Quality
    6.2. Gray scale modification
    6.3. Sharpening
    6.4. Smoothing
    6.5. Bibliographic notes
    References

Chapter 7: Restoration
    7.1. The *a priori* knowledge required in restoration
    7.2. Inverse filtering
    7.3. Least squares filtering
    7.4. Least squares filtering: the discrete case
    7.5. Constrained deconvolution
    7.6. Recursive filtering
    7.7. Some further restoration methods
    7.8. Bibliographic notes
    References

Chapter 8: Reconstructon
    8.1. Methods for generating projection data
    8.2. The Fourier slice theorem
    8.3. The filtered-backprojection algorithm for parallel projection data
    8.4. Aliasing artifacts in reconstructed images
    8.5. Noise in reconstructed images
    8.6. Reconstruction from fan projections
    8.7. Algebraic reconstruction techniques
    8.8. Bibliographic notes
    References
    Index

VOLUME TWO
    Preface
    Contents of Volume 1

Introduction
    Picture processing
    Scenes, images, and digital pictures
    A guide to the literature
    References

Chapter 9: Matching
    9.1. Imaging geometry
    9.2. Registration
    9.3. Geometric transformation
    9.4. Match measurement
    9.5. Bibliographical notes
    Appendix: Analysis of time-varying imagery
    References
Chapter 10: Segmentation
    10.1. Pixel classification
    10.2. Edge detection
    10.3. Feature detection
    10.4. Sequential segmentation
    10.5. Iterative segmentation: "relaxation"
    10.6. Bibliographical notes
    References
Chapter 11: Representation
    11.1. Representation schemes
    11.2. Conversion between representations
    11.3. Geometric property measurement
    11.4. Bibliographical notes
    References
Chapter 12: Description
    12.1. Properties
    12.2. Models
    12.3. Bibliographical notes
    Appendix: Analysis of three-dimensional scenes
    References
    Index

784 pp. 12 chapters in 2 volumes. Drawings, photographs, figures, graphs, tables, mathematical formulae, algorithms, abstract formalisms, models, general index, references. ISBN 0-12-597301-2.

233
Rosinski, Richard R.

Effect of Projective Distortions on Perception of Graphic Displays: Final Report
1982

technical report

(report number TR-82-1; University of Pittsburgh; sponsored by Office of Naval Research; April 1982)

Discusses the basis and effects of geometric distortion on perception of graphic displays.

Only when viewed from the geometric center does a graphic display accurately illustrate three-dimensional space; viewing the image from other positions results in virtual space distortions. Despite this fact, such distortions are not always perceived by the viewer. Rosinski analyzes the geometric basis for virtual space distortions and recounts recent experiments on the perception of geometric distortion in pictorial displays. This raises the fundamental issue of the relationship between visual stimulation and perceptual experience. Experiments are described that test for the effects of distortion when familiar, unfamiliar, and moving objects are viewed. Slant, depth, internal depth, height, and width serve as the geometric controls to test the effects of distortion. Experimental evidence indicates that the perceptual process can actively compensate for spatial distortion under some conditions. In unfamiliar or irregular objects, geometric distortion of graphic display determines spatial perception, but pictorial representations of regular or familiar objects are less subject to perceived distortion. Studies with perception of moving objects reveal results comparable to those found in static object studies. Distortion in moving objects had similar effects on perception as the objects viewed in static gradients. Implications for graphic design are discussed briefly, though the report deals mostly with matters relevant to display design. Students and researchers in display design and visual perception will find the report interesting. The interested reader may also wish to consult an earlier report from this same project, *Observer Compensation for Projective Distortion of Graphic Displays.*

CONTENTS
>   Introduction
>   Distortion of unfamiliar objects
>   Effects of familiarity
>   Insensitivity to distortions
>   Extension to motion-carried information
>   Implications
>   References

16 pp. 6 sections. Figures, tables, abstract formalisms, references.

234
Samet, Michael G.

technical report

Development of Innovative Graphic Symbology for Aiding Tactical Decision Making
1983

(report number PFR-1103-83-10; Perceptronics, Inc.; sponsored by Office of Naval Research; October 1983)

Presents the development and evaluation of a new system of tactical symbology in which graphic overlays allow the user to call up information selectively.

This report summarizes the results of work performed in the design, implementation, and evaluation of an experimental user-responsive situation display system for supporting tactical decision making. Tactical symbology has not changed for decades and traditional symbols have translated inefficiently to computer-generated displays. The display screen is often cluttered with inappropriate levels of detail, making it hard to comprehend tactical information. This work develops new tactical symbols and presents a system of automated overlays and map backgrounds which allow the user to selectively call up desired information while studying a particular situation. The system was tested using Marine Corps officers who were presented with a tactical scenario and asked to use these overlays to answer tactical questions. User acceptance of the system was high. Users selected overlays which would minimize display clutter, in general adding information incrementally to the situation display. The quality of answers to the tactical questions was analyzed in relation to the pattern of overlay selection and this information used to determine performance-base procedure guidelines, allowing more efficient and effective use of the system. The author cites as a significant by-product of this work the demonstration of a performance-based approach to system design and discusses the use of the call-up system as a tool in cognitive research. Graphic display designers, human factors practitioners, and military personnel involved in these areas would benefit from the information in this report.

CONTENTS

1: Overview

2: Program Objectives
    2.1. Research problem
    2.2. Specific objectives

3: Summary of Work Accomplished
    3.1. Research setting
    3.2. System description
    3.3. Experimental studies
    3.4. Research results
    3.5. Research conclusions
    3.6. Future research

4: Technical Reports

5: Scientific Personnel

24 pp. 5 chapters. Tables.

235
Schachter, Bruce J. (ed.)

collection

Computer Image Generation
John Wiley and Sons, 1983

Presents a detailed analysis of computer image generation (CIG) intended for CIG workers and anyone interested in sophisticated computer graphics presentations. Readers should have a basic knowledge of computer graphics to benefit fully from this book.

This book discusses topics including: descriptions of algorithms and architectures for major CIG devices on the market; photographs of these systems including block diagrams of the architecture of the devices; a review of some of the better known techniques in computer generated graphics applicable to simulation; database design; special effects generation; VLSIC approaches to computer image generation; CIG systems for military and civilian training including their effectiveness and cost; and future architectures for image generation.

Much of this book is devoted to the analysis of visual training simulators, one of the most successful applications of CIG technology. Other potential uses of CIG include manufacturing, entertainment, medicine, the military, the arts and sports. The book is attractively designed with a clear typeface and numerous examples of scenes of aircraft, terrain, and landing strips in both color and black and white generated using CIG.

CONTENTS

Preface
1. Introduction
Bruce J. Schachter

Techniques and Systems
2. Computer-generated graphics
William S. Bennett
3. Factors affecting the design of CIG systems
Bruce J. Schachter
4. Computer image generation systems
Bruce J. Schachter
5. Digital image anomalies: static and dynamic
Nicholas S. Szabo
6. Data-base design
Bruce J. Schachter
7. Generation of special effects
Bruce J. Schachter

VLSIC Approaches to Computer Image Generation
8. The role of LSI/VLSI in computer image generation
Thomas R. Hoffman
9. VLSIC architectures for image generation
Richard Weinberg

Training
10. An overview of military training-system development
Allen Collier
11. Reaping the benefits of flight simulation
Jesse Orlansky, Joseph String
12. The army's counterattack on training costs
Jerome A. Pogorzelski
13. Flight simulation in air-combat training
Richard C. Needham, Bernell J. Edwards, Jr., Dirk C. Prather
14. Training centers for business aircraft
Bruce J. Schachter
Bibliography
Author index
Subject index

236 pp. 14 papers in 3 parts. Photographs, figures, charts, graphs, algorithms, author index, subject index, bibliography, color plates. ISBN 0-471-87287-3.

236
Schiekel, Manfred
Süssenbach, Helmut
Schwedes, Wilhelm
Keiner, Hildegard
Peppel, Günter
Hellwig, Wolfgang
Knoll, Anton
Rettich, Renate
Unbehaun, Rüdiger

Rasteranzeigeschirm in Gasentladungstechnik
1982

technical report

(report number BMFT-FB-T82-039; AEG-TELEFUNKEN,
Geschäftsbereich Elektronische Bauelemente, Fachbereich Technische
Röhren; sponsored by Bundesministerium für Forschung und
Technologie; March 1982)

This German-language report examines the technology of matrix display
panels in gas-discharge technique (plasma display panels or PDP) and
concentrates on the development of flat gas-discharge display panels in
stacked-tube technique for color picture presentation.

This lengthy technical report (written in German) from the Electronic
Components Division of AEG-Telefunken discusses the development
and application of matrix display panels (PDP). The report offers a brief
survey of the current state of research on PDPs, their use as television
screens, and their increasing use as text-processing displays. Stressing
the advantages of dc-PDP matrix display screens over conventional
cathode ray tube screens, the authors develop a full-color dc-PDP
pulsed matrix display screen with an inherent memory characteristic
that eliminates earlier technical drawbacks and features improved
operational reliability, increased clarity and detail, enlarged format, and
heightened electro-optical effectiveness. The authors describe their
developmental procedures, results, and materials precisely and lucidly,
providing 101 pages of tables, figures, and illustrations to supplement
the highly specialized text. This report (which includes a brief abstract
in English) will interest electrical engineers and display designers with
an engineering background.

CONTENTS

1: Einleitung
    1.1. Derzeitiger stand der Technik
    1.2. Begründung und Zielsetzung
    1.3. Bemerkungen zur Methodik
    1.4. Ergebnis der Arbeiten

2: Physikalische Grundlagen
    2.1. Grundlagen impulsbetriebener Gasentladungs-Rasterschirme
        (GER)
    2.2. Prinzipielle Wirkungsweise von GER
    2.3. Physikalische Verhältnisse in der positiven Säule einer
        Niederdruckentladung
    2.4. Zündstatistik und Betriebsbereich

3: Technologie und Musterbau

    3.1. Aufbau von GER mit positiver Säule

    3.2. Aufbau von GER mit inhärentem Speicher

    3.3. Aufbau von GER mit negativem Glimmlicht

    3.4. Löt- und Aufbautechnik

    3.5. Siebdrucktechnik

    3.6. Leuchtstofftechnik

    3.7. Frontscheiben mit verschiedenen optischen Eigenschaften

4: Formier- und Messtechnik für GER

    4.1. Formiertechnik

    4.2. Messergebnisse an leuchtstoffbeschichteten GER mit positiver Säule als UV-Quelle

    4.3. Ermittlung der Betriebswerte von GER

5: Gerätebeschreibung

    5.1. Formiergeräte

    5.2. Konzeption neuer Endstufen

    5.3. Anzeigemodule GEZ 18/1 und GEZ 36/1

6: Schrifttum

7: Veröffentlichungen und Vorträge

8: Patente

9: Tabellen

10: Abbildungen

244 pp. 10 chapters. Drawings, photographs, graphs, tables, mathematical formulae, bibliography.

237
Schmid, Calvin F.

Statistical Graphics: Design Principles and Practices
John Wiley and Sons, 1983

Addresses the issue of design standards for statistical charts. After asserting that statistical graphics are a powerful form of visual communication the author develops a useful set of principles designed to develop expertise in chart design and improve chart quality.

Supplementing, as well as complementing, the author's earlier *Handbook of Graphic Presentation*, this work focuses on a variety of issues, problems, innovations, standards, principles, and practices related to chart design. After a thorough introduction which details the problems Schmid sees most frequently and deems most serious, solutions to these problems are outlined and developed. The use of statistical charts as presentive devices, rather than analytical tools, is stressed, although both applications are discussed. The chapters are organized by chart-type. Charts with similar purpose and function are grouped together and design principles are developed for the entire collection. While the book is written for those who actually produce statistical charts, its actual audience is much larger. Chart users in the fields of economics, demography, engineering, computer science, cartography, and probability analysis can benefit through use of this text. Application of quality charts in a task which requires graphic display improves the overall results. Schmid offers his reader an understanding of what a quality statistical chart is and which type works best for a given application. This is useful because, as Schmid notes, training and course work in chart design is rare. *Statistical Graphics* serves equally well as a reference work, a handbook for self-instruction, or a text for formal classroom use.

CONTENTS

Preface

1. Introduction: Basic issues, problems, principles, and practices of chart design
2. Rectilinear coordinate line charts: problems, principles, and standards
3. Bar and column charts: issues and problems
4. Miscellaneous graphic forms: techniques and standards
5. Semilogarithmic charts: their use and misuse
6. Choropleth maps: problems, principles, and practices
7. Two- and three-dimensional graduated point symbols: a perennial issue in statistical graphics
8. Projection techniques: pitfalls and problems
9. Pictorial charts: critique and guidelines
10. Presentation of errors in data: a neglected problem in statistical graphics

Name index

Subject index

212 pp. 10 chapters. Drawings, figures, charts, maps, graphs, footnotes, subject index, name index. (ISBN 0-471-87525-2)

238
Schmid, Calvin F.
Schmid, Stanton E.

Handbook of Graphic Presentation (2ed.)
John Wiley and Sons, 1979

reference

Designed "for all who are concerned with the clear presentation and interpretation of statistical data in graphic form," this comprehensive manual shows how to construct and use many different types of graphs.

After discussing the purposes of graphic presentation, the handbook explains design principles and techniques, then offers a detailed guide to drafting. The authors describe and evaluate many graphs, pointing out potential distortions and construction difficulties. Their graphical forms range from the popular pictorial chart to the specialized trilinear chart, from the frequently used bar and rectilinear charts to the less common ratio maps. Also covered are projection techniques, and the role of the computer in graphical depictions. This much expanded edition of the 1954 *Handbook* is richly illustrated with numerous graphs, charts, and maps. It promises to be a standard guide in the field of statistical presentation.

CONTENTS
1. Basic principles and techniques of chart design
2. Drafting techniques
3. Rectilinear coordinate charts
4. Bar and column charts
5. Semilogarithmic or ratio charts
6. Frequency graphs and related charts
7. Miscellaneous graphic forms
8. Statistical maps
9. Pictorial charts
10. Projection techniques in graphic presentation
11. Role of the computer in graphic presentation
Name index
Subject index

308 pp. 11 chapters. Photographs, charts, maps, graphs, tables, footnotes, author index, subject index. (ISBN 0-471-04724-4)

239
Schweitzer, Dennis L.

technical report

Interactive Surface Visualization Using Raster Graphics
`1983

(report number AFIT/CI/NR-83-31D; Department of Computer Science, University of Utah; sponsored by Air Force Institute of Technology, National Science Foundation, U.S. Army Research Office, and Office of Naval Research; August 1983)

This paper comprises a portion of a dissertation with the goal of discovering techniques for enhancing the display of three-dimensional forms by computer graphics.

Computer generated shaded images have evolved to the point that they are realistic enough to be easily confused with photographs of the objects they represent. The phenomena of light reflection, surface texture, shadows, and transparency have been major areas of computer graphics research in recent years. However, to provide for those applications in which the viewers are more interested in exact knowledge of the three-dimensional shape of a surface than a realistically shaded reproduction, this study investigated other interactive techniques. The author contrasts two approaches: naturalistic rendering of forms, and the use of visual perceptual cues (texture gradients, gradients of illumination, binocular stereopsis, and motion) to add information. These visual stimulations were investigated in an interactive environment in order to provide more information about and control over three-dimensional shaping of figures. The geometric principles behind depth perception and algorithms for artificial texturing are discussed. Both those involved in graphics design and psychologists working in the area of perception would find the information here of value.

CONTENTS

1: INTRODUCTION
1.1. Realism in Computer Graphics
1.2. Research in Visual Perception
1.3. Interactive Surface Visualization
2: DIRECT SHAPE VISUALIZATION
2.1. Introduction
2.2. Previous Work in Computer Graphics
2.3. Visualization of Depth and Surface Normals
    2.3.1. Depth
    2.3.2. Surface normals
2.4. Results
3: TEXTUAL GRADIENTS
3.1. Introduction
3.2. Visual Perception of Texture
3.3. Existing Algorithms
3.4. Artificial Texturing
    3.4.1. Texture size
    3.4.2. Texture shape
    3.4.3. Texture density
3.5. Implementation
    3.5.1. Texel projection
    3.5.2. Texel density
3.6. Results
4: GRADIENTS OF ILLUMINATION
4.1. Introduction
4.2. Perceptual Study of Shading
4.3. Realistic Rendering of Shade
    4.3.1. Shading algorithms
    4.3.2. Shadow algorithms
4.4. Visible Surface Shadows
4.4.1. Constraints
4.4.2. Implementation
4.5. Results
5: BINOCULAR STEREOPSIS
5.1. Introduction
5.2. Perceptual Analysis of Binocular Stereopsis
5.3. Binocular Images
5.4. Stereo Pairs from a Single Image
    5.4.1. Simulating disparity
    5.4.2. Providing retinal correspondence
    5.4.3. Depth filtering
5.5. Results
6: SHAPE PERCEPTION THROUGH HARDWARE
6.1. Introduction
6.2. Perceptual Analysis of Movement
6.3. Use of Motion in Computer Graphics
6.4. Multiple Frame Generation and Viewing
    6.4.1. Multiple frame viewing
    6.4.2. Multiple frame generation

6.5. Results
CONCLUSION
APPENDIX: FRAME BUFFER HARDWARE
REFERENCES

96 pp. 7 chapters. Drawings, photographs, figures, tables, mathematical formulae, references, appendix.

240
Scott, Joan E.

Introduction to Interactive Computer Graphics
John Wiley and Sons, 1982

Provides technical information about interactive computer graphics systems.

Scott presents a comprehensive introduction to interactive computer graphics which "combines in a single volume both technical information about graphic systems and practical knowledge concerning their use." The intent of this book is to explain technical concepts clearly, suggest applications in various fields, and provide help in getting graphics systems on-line. Technical terms are defined where they occur in the text, with definitions based on standard industry usage. Explanations are written in clear, non-mathematical English which is understandable by persons having no prior knowledge of interactive computer graphics. Illustrations appear throughout the text, line drawings explain the principles of the operation of hardware devices, and block diagrams clarify programming relationships. References for specialized topics beyond the scope of this book and a vendors' list are provided. The book's eleven chapters present information on topics including: work station input devices; interactive display devices; plots, hard copies, and photographs; graphic support equipment; a computer graphics model; interactive input techniques; and two- and three-dimensional graphics. Intended for business managers, draftsmen, engineers, architects, programmers and students. While not primarily designed as a textbook, it is suitable as an introductory college level text.

CONTENTS
PART ONE: HARDWARE
Chapter 1: Input Devices at the Work Station
    1.1. Light pens
    1.2. Digitizers
    1.3. Joysticks, trackballs, and dials
    1.4. Keyboards, buttons, and switches
    1.5. Voice data entry systems
    Vendor list
Chapter 2: Interactive Display Devices
    2.1. Stroke-writing screens
    2.2. Storage displays using stroke-writing screens
    2.3. Refreshed displays using stroke-writing screens
    2.4. Raster screens
    2.5. Character graphics systems

2.6. Plasma panel displays
Vendor list

Chapter 3: Lasting Results: Plots, Hard Copies, Photographs
3.1. Pen plotters
3.2. Electrostatic plotters
3.3. Vector to raster data conversion
3.4. Graphic film recorders
3.5. Alternative plotter equipment
3.6. Mode of operation
Vendor list

Chapter 4: Graphics Support
4.1. Computers
4.2. Communications
4.3. Storage

PART TWO: SOFTWARE

Chapter 5: Building the Computer Model
5.1. Command language
5.2. Association of graphic and nongraphic data
5.3. Program structure for interactive input
5.4. Logical input devices

Chapter 6: Interactive Input Techniques
6.1. Menu and menu alternatives
6.2. Macro commands
6.3. Accuracy
6.4. Sketching
6.5. Digitizing
6.6. Text
6.7. Dimensions
6.8. Three-dimensional input

Chapter 7: Viewing the Computer Model
7.1. Coordinate systems transformations
7.2. Clipping
7.3. Geometric transformations
7.4. The display file
7.5. Symbols

Chapter 8: Three-Dimensional Viewing
8.1. Extension of basic concepts
8.2. Perspective projection
8.3. Realistic-looking images
8.4. Hidden-line and hidden-surface removal
8.5. Illumination on surfaces

Chapter 9: Application Programs
9.1. Turnkey graphics systems
9.2. Graphics application products
9.3. Graphics packages
Vendor list

PART THREE: A PRACTICAL TOOL

Chapter 10: Management Concerns
    10.1. Application characteristics
    10.2. Turnkey system selection
    10.3. Personnel and procedures
    10.4. Economic justification
    10.5. Additional information
    Appendix: Graphics information source list
Chapter 11: Application Survey
    11.1. Architecture/engineering/construction
    11.2. Design/manufacturing
    11.3. Business management
    11.4. Cartography
    11.5. Health care
    11.6. Scientific research
    11.7. Art/entertainment/education
REFERENCES
INDEX

255 pp. 11 chapters in 3 parts. Drawings, photographs, figures, charts, mathematical formulae, general index, references. ISBN 0-471-05773-8. (ISBN 0-471-86623-7)

241
Sekuler, Robert
Tynan, Paul D.

technical report

Sourcebook of Temporal Factors Affecting Information Transfer from Visual Displays
1981

(report number TR-540; Department of Psychology, Northwestern University; sponsored by U.S. Army Research Institute; 1 June 1981)

This short book provides an overview of the time-dependent or "temporal" factors that influence human perception of visual displays.

This review covers the extensive literature on temporal human factors and offers recommendations for extrapolation of laboratory data to practical situations in the military and industrial workplace. Beginning their presentation with the applications section, the authors critique Military Standard 1472(A&B), which contains guidelines for display designers of military hardware, but does not sufficiently account for the influence of factors such as the length of time the operator fixes on each instrument. They suggest some rethinking of the way instruments like CRTs encode the real world. The perception of acceleration and deceleration, a much more difficult and subtle problem than the perception of motion itself, is discussed. Other chapters take up the possible influence of the classic motion "illusions" such as the motion aftereffect (MAE). The authors find the apparent motion literature to be deficient and point out some research gaps that need filling. Peripheral motion perception, flash and flicker sensitivity, perceived velocity, and absolute and differential motion thresholds are covered, along with eye-tracking errors responsible for distortion. An appendix details the several abstracts which serve as sources for the literature search. Intended for display designers and human factors engineers solving particular applications problems.

CONTENTS

Introduction

1: Applications and Recommendations for Applied Research

2: Extrapolations from Laboratory Data

3: Toward a Military Standard

4: The Absolute Threshold for Motion Perception

5: Suprathreshold Motion Perception

6: Illusions of Motion
     Motion aftereffect
     Apparent motion
     Induced motion

7: Motion Perception in the Periphery

8: Flash Sensitivity

9: Flicker Sensitivity

10: Suprathreshold Flicker Perception

11: Brightness Enhancement

12: Effects of Flash and Flicker on Visibility

13: Effects of Movement on Visibility
     Dynamic visual acuity
     Non-acuity measures
     Research in applied settings

14: Temporal Events Causing Distortion

Glossary

Appendix A

Appendix B

Appendix C

Bibliography

Author Index

Subject Index

182 pp. 14 chapters. Drawings, figures, graphs, tables, mathematical formulae, author index, subject index, glossary, appendices.

242
Shahnavaz, Houshang

VDU-Operators' Preferred Environmental Conditions in a Telephone Information Centre
1982

technical report

(report number TULEA-1982-11; Department of Human Work Sciences, University of Luleå; sponsored by Swedish Telephone Company; 1982)

An empirical study of the environmental conditions preferred by visual display unit (VDU) operators in a Swedish telephone information center.

General conditions of the workplace (lighting and dimension of the space) and conditions on the VDU screen (photometric and radiometric) were investigated. The subjects were twenty-six female and two male skilled operators between ages eighteen and fifty-four on both day and night shifts at a telephone information center in Televerket, Mälmo, Sweden. Workplace lighting was measured with a Hagner universal photometer and the video screen lighting was measured with a EG&G Photometer-Radiometer and an automatic spectroradiometer. Subjects' preferred environmental conditions were measured by actually having them adjust, to their satisfaction, the workplace station (table height, keyboard height, etc.), workplace lighting, and screen lighting and contrast. The results of the study showed the subjects' preferences in workplace station to correspond to ergonomic guidelines previously established by other researchers. Favored screen luminances and general workplace illuminances were far lower than levels reported in the literature. Age differences were a factor; older operators preferred brighter screens and workplace areas than younger operators. The study was conducted to provide data for further research investigating possible connections between visual impairments in VDU operators and environmental conditions. The writing is occasionally unclear, but many tables and figures aid the reader in achieving an understanding of the research and provide a thorough explication of the data. The report is technical, but should be accessible to a reader with a background in science and research methodology.

CONTENTS

Summary

Preface

1: Introduction

2: Method
    2.1. Subjects
    2.2. Apparatus
    2.3. Measurement procedure

3: Results of the Survey
    3.1. Workplace dimensions
    3.2. Ambient light conditions
    3.3. VDU-related factors (EG&G system measurements)

4: Discussion
Tables
References
Appendix
32 pp. 4 chapters. Drawings, graphs, tables, references, appendices.

243
Sherr, Sol

Electronic Displays
John Wiley and Sons, 1979

Presents comprehensive descriptions of present technologies in electronic displays and includes an excellent chapter on human factors for CRT screens.

Provides discussions for the reader with a minimal mathematical background, but also has enough analytical detail to satisfy the more advanced practitioner. This makes the book useful to the office manager interested in learning more about the technologies and equipment of electronic displays, as well as to industrial engineers, computer specialists, and students and educators in the field of electronics. This work can be used as a reference and selection guide as well as a general text. Chapters consider: human factors; technical features and performance characteristics of cathode ray, matrix, and alphanumeric devices; systems components and organization; groups of systems applications; and performance tests and evaluation. Many illustrations and tables aid in clarification, making this book a useful guide in the selection of electronic displays. Examples of how to evolve specifications, what range of performance to expect, and how to test and evaluate that performance are also given.

CONTENTS
Preface
Chapter 1: Perceptual Factors
Human factors and visual parameters and their significance to display-system performance.
Chapter 2: Cathode-ray Devices
Cathode ray tubes, scan converters, image-pickup tubes, special types; technology and applications.
Chapter 3: Matrix and Alphanumeric Devices
Light-emitting diodes, plasma, liquid crystal, EL, ferrolectric, electrochromic, electrophoretic, vacuum fluorescent, incandescent, and electromagnetic devices; technology and application data.
Chapter 4: Cathode-ray-tube Systems and Equipment
Alphanumeric and graphic terminals, analog and digital television, and large screen systems; technology and application data.
Chapter 5: Alphanumeric and Matrix Systems and Equipment
Numeric, alphanumeric, and dot matrix systems using devices of Chapter 3; technology and application data.

Chapter 6: Applications
   Business systems, control systems, graphics systems using CRTs; watches, calculators, and instruments using Chapter 3 devices; and matrix panel systems applications.
Chapter 7: Performance Evaluation
   Measurement techniques for determining performance of devices and systems.
Index

636 pp. 7 chapters. Drawings, photographs, figures, tables, mathematical formulae, general index. ISBN 0-471-02941-6.

244
Sherr, Sol

Video and Digital Electronic Displays: A User's Guide
John Wiley and Sons, 1982

An introductory and practical description of the technology, performance characteristics, and applications of electronic displays. Written to fill the gap between complex engineering texts and over-simplified popular literature.

This book, by an experienced display designer and well-known author in the field, is designed to familiarize the reader with the capabilities, limitations, and applications of available display technologies. It is also intended as a guide in selecting and evaluating a given system. The book has two sections, one describing equipment and the other offering practical application guidance. The first chapter defines electronic display systems, providing a foundation for the rest of the material. Another chapter examines human factors, particularly, the impact of the human visual apparatus on system design. Two chapters are devoted to cathode-ray tube (CRT) devices, both the common (television) and the elaborate (vector and raster computer graphics). Two more chapters describe non-CRT flat-panel displays (LEDs, LCDs, VFDs, plasma panels). Some parts require minimal knowledge of algebra and trigonometry, but most of the text consists of straightforward descriptions (using diagrams and photographs) of how the equipment works and device performance parameters. The second section deals with a variety of applications: numeric and alphanumeric readouts; query-response systems; word processing; management information systems (MIS); and computer graphics. Finally, system performance is covered in more detail (photometry, CRT, and flat-panel measurements). Many tables provide direct comparisons of the characteristics and capabilities of display devices along with advice on choosing the proper system for a particular application. The author mentions MIS managers, CAD specialists, and hobbyists among those who could benefit from reading this book.

CONTENTS
   Preface
   1. Electronic display systems
   2. Human factors or ergonomics
   3. Cathode ray tube systems: television or raster scan displays
   4. Cathode ray tube systems: vector and raster full graphics displays

5. Flat-panel displays: alphanumeric readouts
6. Flat-panel displays: alphanumeric and graphics
7. Applications: numeric and alphanumeric readouts
8. Applications: alphanumeric data systems
9. Applications: computer graphics
10. Performance evaluation
Index

252 pp. 10 chapters. Drawings, photographs, figures, tables, models, general index, references. ISBN 0-471-09037-9.

245
Sidner, Candace L.
Bates, Madeleine

technical report

Requirements for Natural Language Understanding in a System with Graphic Displays
1983

(report number BBN-5242; Bolt Beranek and Newman, Inc.; sponsored by Office of Naval Research; March 1983)

This short paper, from the Knowledge Representation and Natural Language Group at Bolt Beranek and Newman, describes an exercise in exploring user-system interchanges using a prototypical dialogue to modify a database and graphics display.

This paper explores the problems inherent in natural language interface design for those involved in the creation of an effective "intelligence" behind the system. The system described is designed to be an aid to the user and allow for a relatively natural expression of dialogue. The aspects of the study presented include: methodology used in the development and design of the interacting system, the analysis of the information obtained and the method used, and conclusions about the linguistic requirements of such a system. The data were obtained using two participants, joined by a datascreen, who carried out the protocols of scenarios, which were subsequently analyzed according to linguistic content with a view toward providing information for eventual systems design. The intended audience is systems designers, especially those involved in AI natural language study.

50 pp. 4 chapters. Drawings, figures, references, appendix.

246
Smith, Sidney L.
Mosier, Jane N.

Design Guidelines for User-System Interface Software
1984

technical report

(report number MTR-9420/ESD-TR-190; The MITRE Corporation; sponsored by Electronic Systems Division, Air Force Systems Command; September 1984)

This report, from an original project which develops guidelines for user interface software design, extends and expands upon a 1983 report by Smith and Arlene Aucella. New information was obtained for this report using results of a questionnaire included in earlier versions.

Although much of the material in this volume will seem familiar to readers of earlier versions of the report, the work has been significantly expanded and revised. A lengthy introduction reviews the rationale and background of this and the four previous versions (all sponsored by the MITRE Corporation). Guidelines are offered in six design areas: data entry, data display, sequence control, user guidance, data transmission, and data protection. These guidelines facilitate the design of user-efficient, user-friendly computer systems. A thorough index, a glossary, and a reference list allow novice as well as experienced designers to use the work effectively. Additionally, a form is provided at the end of the report so designers may suggest revisions to the current guidelines and submit new guidelines for consideration by the authors of future reports.

CONTENTS
INTRODUCTION
SECTION 1: DATA ENTRY
1.0: General
1.1: Position Designation
1.2: Direction Designation
1.3: Text
1.4: Data Forms
1.5: Tables
1.6: Graphics (No Entries)
1.7: Data Validation
1.8: Other Data Processing
1.9: Design Change
SECTION 2: DATA DISPLAY
2.0: General
2.1. Data Type
    2.1.1. Text
    2.1.2. Data forms
    2.1.3. Tables
    2.1.4. Graphics
    2.1.5. Combination

2.2: Density

2.3. Format

2.4. Coding

2.5. Generation

2.6: Framing

2.7: Update

2.8: Suppression

2.9: Design Change

SECTION 3: SEQUENCE CONTROL

3.0: General

3.1: Dialogue Type

    3.1.1. Question and answer

    3.1.2. Form filling

    3.1.3. Menu selection

    3.1.4. Function keys

    3.1.5. Command language

    3.1.6. Query language

    3.1.7. Natural language

    3.1.8. Graphic interaction

3.2: Transaction Selection

3.3: Interrupt

3.4: Context Definition

3.5: Error Management

3.6: Alarms

3.7: Design Change

SECTION 4: USER GUIDANCE

4.0: General

4.1: Status Information

4.2: Routine Feedback

4.3: Error Feedback

4.4: Job Aids

4.5: User Records

4.6: Design Change

SECTION 5: DATA TRANSMISSION

5.0: General

5.1: Data Types

5.2: Sending

5.3: Receiving

5.4: Transmission Control

5.5. Feedback

5.6: Queuing

5.7: Record Keeping

5.8: Design Change

SECTION 6: DATA PROTECTION

6.0: General

6.1: User Identification

6.2: Data Access

6.3: Data Entry/Change

6.4: Data Transmission

6.5: Loss Prevention
6.6: Design Change
REFERENCES
GUIDELINE TITLES
GLOSSARY
INDEX
460 pp. 6 sections. General index, references, glossary, index of guideline titles.

Snyder, Harry L.

overview

Visual Performance in Display Design
1976-84

Harry L. Snyder and his associates and students in the Human Factors Laboratory at Virginia Polytechnic Institute have produced an important body of research on human visual performance. The papers listed here represent a sample of that work relating visual performance and visual display parameters. The two reports by Snyder, *Human Visual Performance and Flat Panel Displays* and *Visual Search and Image Quality,* have become standard references. Snyder's contribution to Tanna's *Flat-Panel Displays and CRT's* (abstracted elsewhere in this collection) presents a current view of this work. Snyder and his students have presented much of their work at the Human Factors Society annual meeting and in the technical journal literature. Although the listing here does not reflect this, there are eight reports in the series on quality metrics and digitally derived imagery. Numbers I-III and VIII are available and have been abstracted for this collection. Numbers IV-VII have not been released, but Robert Beaton's dissertation, *A Human Performance Based Evaluation of Quality Metrics,* which is included here, is the basis of reports IV and VII. The reader interested in other experimental studies should refer to the overviews for Cohen, "Image Descriptors for Displays," and Pachella, "Cognitive Studies of Complex Displays."

247
Snyder, Harry L.

technical report

Visual Search and Image Quality: Final Report
1976
(report number AMRL-TR-76-89; Department of Industrial Engineering and Operations Research, Virginia Polytechnic Institute and State University; sponsored by Aerospace Medical Research Laboratory; December 1976)

Describes the effects of image quality and video noise on visual search patterns.

This paper is the final report in a series of experiments involving image search and visual quality. Subjects were asked to pick out target images from air-to-ground television film strips taken to provide two fields of view and two air speeds. These films were presented to the subjects in five different display quality set-ups. Using microphotometric techniques, image quality and video noise were measured independently at the display surface for each system and then correlated with the subjects' responses. As expected, decline of image quality and increase of video noise inhibited target identification. Snyder notes, however, that his independent measures of image quality show erratic correlation with the subjects' assessment of image quality, pointing to the need for continuing research in the area. No general summary of the research series is given; rather, results from previous work in the project are cited as they apply to the current experiment. For more information, the reader is referred to the earlier reports.

CONTENTS

Section I: Introduction
　MTFA concept
　Objective of this experiment
Section II: Method
　Experimental design
　Subjects
　Apparatus
　Targets and imagery
　Procedure
　Video system calibration
Section III: Results
　Target acquisition performance
　Image quality measures
Section IV: Discussion
　Target acquisition performance
　Photometric noise measurement
　Image quality
References
List of Tables

77 pp. 4 chapters. Figures, charts, graphs, tables, references.

248
Almagor, Maier
Farley, Willard W.
Snyder, Harry L.

technical report

Spatio-Temporal Integration in the Visual System
1979

(report number AMRL-TR-78-126; Department of Industrial Engineering and Operations Research, Virginia Polytechnic Institute and State University; sponsored by Aerospace Medical Research Laboratory; February 1979)

A report on the authors' "fast adaptation" theory of spatio-temporal integration, this work is primarily intended for researchers in human cognition and perception. However, the research also has implications for human factors engineering.

The report deals with the perceived failure of existing models of human perception to integrate the spatial and temporal dimensions. To remedy this deficiency a new model of visual perception is presented, tested, and shown to confirm the authors' proposed model: that both spatial and temporal integration work together in a fast adaptation system, a concept almost completely overlooked by existing theories of vision. The main conclusions of the report are: 1) that integration time is locally controlled in the retina and that its dyamics are very fast; and 2) as display luminescence increases integration time decreases and temporal bands decrease, evidencing a correlation between integration time and the length of the temporal bands. These conclusions carry with them a number of important applications in human engineering for the optimization of information display design (e.g., "head up" aircraft displays ought to be made as bright as possible.)

CONTENTS

I: INTRODUCTION

Temporal Information
    Nature of temporal sensitivity
    Previous temporal models
    Temporal integration
    Spatial integration and its relationship to temporal integration
    Temporal model description
    Direct predictions of the model

Spatial Information
    Spatial information processing
    Spatial model description
    Evidence consistent with the model

Purpose of This Research

II: METHOD

Rationale and Apparatus
    Integration time distribution
    Flicker experiment
    Temporal bands experiment

Procedures
    Integration time distribution
    Flicker experiments
    Temporal bands experiment

III: RESULTS

Integration Time Distribution

Flicker Experiment

Temporal Bands Experiment

Summary of Results

IV: DISCUSSION

V: APPLICATIONS OF THIS RESEARCH

VI: EXTENSIONS OF THIS RESEARCH

APPENDIX: EXPERIMENTAL DATA

REFERENCES

104 pp. 6 chapters. Drawings, figures, graphs, tables, references, appendix.

249
Snyder, Harry L.
Beamon, William S.
Gutmann, James C.
Dunsker, Eric D.

An Evaluation of the Effect of Spot Wobble upon Observer Performance with Raster Scan Displays
1980

technical report

(report number AMRL-TR-79-91; Department of Industrial Engineering and Operations Research, Virginia Polytechnic Institute and State University; sponsored by Aerospace Medical Research Laboratory; monitored by Wayne L. Martin, H. Lee Task, AFAMRL representatives; January 1980)

Describes two experiments designed to evaluate the effectiveness of spot wobble in improving the image quality of video displays.

The report begins with a brief summary of the history of the technique known as spot wobble. It was developed in England and experimentally applied by the British Broadcasting Corporation in the 1950s. In video, or raster-scan systems, the visibility of raster lines may detract from the clarity of the image being displayed. Spot wobble has been employed to reduce the prominence of the raster structure. The first experiment conducted in this study involved an air-to-ground target acquisition task. The second employed a static television display to test static target recognition. Both investigated the effects of spot wobble on observer performance in laboratory experiments with university students. This report describes the experimental designs and the results of these experiments. It would be useful to graphics designers, particularly those involved with raster scan hardware.

CONTENTS

INTRODUCTION

Spot Wobble

Other Raster Suppression Techniques

Research Purpose

METHOD: DYNAMIC TARGET ACQUISITION EXPERIMENT

Apparatus
    Video system
    Photometric apparatus and procedures
    System MTF determination

Target Acquisition Task
    Experimental design
    Apparatus
    Procedures

Observer Threshold Functions
    Experimental design
    Apparatus
    Observer threshold procedures

Modulation Transfer Function Area Calculations
    Procedures and apparatus

Observer Task Performance Evaluation
RESULTS: DYNAMIC TARGET ACQUISITION EXPERIMENT
Effect of Spot Wobble on Raster Modulation
System Modulation Transfer Functions
Observer Threshold Function
Target Acquisition Performance
    Number of correct responses
    Range for correct responses, WMEANS
    Range with minimums, WMINS
    Range with zeros, WZEROS
    Summary of target acquisition results
    Correlations of system parameters with observer performance data
METHOD: STATIC TARGET RECOGNITION EXPERIMENT
Experimental Design
Apparatus
Subjects
Procedure
Photometric Measurements
RESULTS: STATIC TARGET RECOGNITION EXPERIMENT
Target Recognition Performance
    Number of correct responses
    Search time
Spot Wobble Subjective Evaluation
    Ranking of spot wobble levels
    Subjective quality ratings by spot wobble level
MTFA Evaluation
    System MTF
    Threshold response curves
    MTFA calculations
DISCUSSION AND CONCLUSIONS
REFERENCES

129 pp. 6 chapters. Figures, graphs, tables, mathematical formulae, references.

250
Snyder, Harry L.

Human Visual Performance and Flat Panel Display Image Quality
1980

technical report

(report number HFL-80-1/ONR-80-1; Department of Industrial Engineering and Operations Research, Virginia Polytechnic Institute and State University; sponsored by Office of Naval Research; monitored by Gerald S. Malecki, ONR representative; July 1980)

Provides information intended to assist systems and human factors engineers in selecting flat panel display devices for particular applications.

Following a brief introductory section, section two describes a sequential analysis approach by which the engineer can select a display technology and estimate optimal design characteristics for that display. Section three presents an overview of current flat-panel display technologies: light emitting diodes, electroluminescence, liquid crystals, electrochromic displays, electrophoretic displays, and plasma displays. Each technology is examined in accordance with a list of thirteen descriptive parameters. Sections four and five focus on the visual capabilities and requirements of the human operator, noting the spatial, temporal, and chromatic capabilities of the normal human visual system and relating visual requirements to display evaluation. Section six summarizes the report and identifies data gaps and areas in which further research is needed.

CONTENTS

SECTION 1: INTRODUCTION

Purpose

Organization

SECTION 2: DESIGN APPROACH AND TECHNOLOGY SELECTION

Generalized Design Approach
    Display functional requirements definition
    Design requirements
    Technology selection

Airborne Displays
    Generic display requirements
    Technology selection

Displays for Amphibious Task Force Command and Control
    Generic display requirements
    Technology selection
    Summary

SECTION 3: TECHNOLOGY OVERVIEW

Parameter Definitions
    Physical size and configuration
    Power and voltage requirements
    Spectral emission
    Luminance
    Luminous efficiency

Element size, shape, density
Contrast and dynamic range
Uniformity
Temporal characteristics
Addressing/driving interfaces
Cost
Utility for display-type applications
Future technology projections

Technology Summaries
Cathode-ray tube (CRT)
Flat-panel CRT
Light-emitting diode (LED)
Electroluminescence (EL)
Plasma displays
Liquid crystal displays
Electrochromic displays
Electrophoretic displays

Technology Comparisons

SECTION 4: HUMAN OPERATOR VISUAL CAPABILITIES AND REQUIREMENTS

Spatial Discrimination
Classical approach
Contrast sensitivity function

Temporal Discrimination
Critical fusion frequency approach
Temporal sensitivity function approach
Application of temporal CFF to nonsinusoidal stimuli

Spatiotemporal Interaction

Chromatic Sensitivity and Discrimination
Colorimetry
Chromaticity discrimination
Chromatic sensitivity function approach
Temporal modulation of chromaticity gratings
Summary

SECTION 5: VISUAL REQUIREMENTS AND DISPLAY EVALUATION

Spatial Parameters
Resolution/density
Element size, shape, luminance distribution
Element spacing, continuity
Uniformity, noise, failure
Size, scale

Temporal Parameters
Rise and fall times
Refresh rate
Noise integration

Chromatic Parameters
Intrinsic chromatic contrast
Ambient effects
Chromatic adaption
Chrominance/luminance trade-offs

Unitary Metrics of Image Quality
    Spatially continuous monochrome displays
    One-dimensional spatially discrete monochrome displays
    Two-dimensional spatially discrete monochrome displays
    Chromatic displays

Information Transmission
    Alphanumeric displays
    Graphical displays

SECTION 6: SUMMARY AND CONCLUSIONS

Summary

Data Gaps and Needs
    Uniformity data needs
    Chrominance/luminance contrast tradeoffs
    Font, matrix requirements
    Resolution requirements
    Predictive model development

REFERENCES

442 pp. 6 chapters. Drawings, figures, graphs, tables, mathematical formulae, references.

251
Burke, James J.
Strickland, Robin N.

technical report

Quality Metrics of Digitally Derived Imagery and Their Relation to Interpreter Performance: I, Preparation of a Large-Scale Database
1982

(report number HFL-81-1; Department of Industrial Engineering and Operations Research, Virginia Polytechnic Institute and State University; sponsored by Air Force Office of Scientific Research; 1 April 1982)

This initial report of a several year U.S. Military sponsored research project provides a short overview of the project (which compares image quality and measured photointerpreter performance) and describes the development of a large imagery database to be used in the project.

Two versions of the same imaginary database were developed: a hard-copy, film version and a soft-copy, cathode-ray tube (CRT) digital version. The images were derived from high-quality low altitude aerial photographs that had a content typical of military tactical scenarios. Ten basic images were used and each image was degraded using five different degrees of blurring combined with five degrees of noise. Thus, a total of two-hundred and fifty degraded images were developed. (All two-hundred and fifty images are used in each of the hard-copy and soft-copy versions.) This report contains a summary of the actual development of the image sets and the description of the database, complete with detailed measures. The description is, for the most part, highly technical. The research presented here is intended primarily for military personnel working in the area of photointerpretation, but may be of interest to the wider scientific community. A reader interested in the database itself should look at this report, but anyone interested in the research project as a whole will find a later report more informative. The digital image database described here is available for use by other interested researchers.

CONTENTS

I: INTRODUCTION TO THE RESEARCH PROGRAM

Statement of the Problem

Overview of the Research Plan
    Research objectives
    Specific research tasks
    Program ground rules

II: OVERVIEW OF DATABASE DEVELOPMENT

Original Material and Photointerpretation Scenarios

Initial Selection of Equipment and Materials for Digitization

Final Preparation of Digital Database and Hardcopy Display

Summary Measures of Digital Database and Hardcopy Display

Availability of Database

III: SELECTION OF QUALITY DIMENSIONS OF DATABASE

Blur

Noise

Contrast

IV: GENERATING THE DIGITAL DATABASE FROM ORIGINAL POSITIVE TRANSPARENCIES

Format of the Digital Database

Image Identification Code, Order-of-Battle
    Scan characteristics of the Perkin-Elmer PDS microdensitometer

Grain Noise in Precision Photo Transparencies

Computer Production of Blurred, Noisy Images from Groundtruth Blur
    Blur
    Noise

Summary Measurements of Quality and Statistics of Digital Database
    Blur
    Noise
    Histogram-related statistics

V: GENERATING THE HARDCOPY DATABASE

Format of Hardcopy

Playback Characteristics of the Dicomed
    Resolution, MTF
    Noise
    Tone reproduction
    Generating transfer curves for playback

Summary Measures of Quality and Statistics of Hardcopy Database
    Blur
    Noise
    Histogram-related statistics, tone reproduction

VI: Discussion

REFERENCES

APPENDICES

A: NATO Imagery Interpretability Rating Scale
Definitions

B: Illustration of Database

C: Scan Characteristics and Setup Procedure for the PDS
Microdensitometer

D: Technical Specification Model D47 Digital Color Image Recorder

E: Additive Noise Produced by Film Recorder

F: Photographic Processing for Hardcopy

*103 pp. 6 chapters. Figures, graphs, tables, abstract formalisms,
references, appendices.*

252
Snyder, Harry L.
Turpin, James A.
Maddox, Michael E.

technical report

**Quality Metrics of Digitally Derived Imagery and Their Relation
to Interpreter Performance: II, Effects of Blur and Noise on
Hard-Copy Interpretability**
1982

(report number HFL-81-2; Department of Industrial Engineering and
Operations Research, Virginia Polytechnic Institute and State
University; sponsored by Air Force Office of Scientific Research;
1 January 1982)

Provides a first step in relating blur and noise content in digitally
derived imagery to information extraction performance of professional
photo interpreters.

The authors believe that an assessment program is needed to devise
procedures, techniques, and metrics of digital image quality. This report
compares image quality metrics for hard-copy images and addresses the
question of how photointerpretation performance is affected by
measurable physical properties of digitally derived imagery. To this end,
"trained photointerpreters performed an information extraction task
using images which were degraded by two known physical
characteristics common to digitalized imagery: blur and noise."
Conclusions from this study include: degradation of information
extraction performance attributable to noise is statistically significant;
analysis of variance indicates that the difference in information
extraction attributed to blur is not statistically significant; blur vs. noise
interaction is not statistically significant; and a high correlation exists
between scaling and information content which strongly suggests that
information extraction performance can be predicted from image rating
scores. The authors published a parallel experiment in 1981 which
assessed subjectively scaled quality of the same images. Intended for
military audiences and persons interested in photointerpretation.

CONTENTS

PREFACE

I: INTRODUCTION

Statement of the Problem

Overview of the Research Plan

Research Objectives

Specific Research Tasks

II: METHOD

Experimental Design

Photointerpreters

Apparatus
    Equipment
    Imagery

Essential Elements of Information (EEIs)

Procedure: Data Collection
    Task
    Instructions

Procedure: Scoring

III: RESULTS

Blur

Noise

Blur × Noise Interaction

Correlation with Scaling

IV: DISCUSSION

Effects of Image Variables

Scoring

Methodology

V: CONCLUSIONS

REFERENCES

APPENDIX

  A. Sample EEIS

  B. Instructions

LIST OF TABLES

LIST OF FIGURES

42 pp. 5 chapters. Figures, graphs, tables, references, appendices.

253
Snyder, Harry L.
Shedivy, David I.
Maddox, Michael E.

technical report

Quality Metrics of Digitally Derived Imagery and Their Relation to Interpreter Performance: III, Subjective Scaling of Hard-Copy Digital Imagery
1982

(report number HFL-81-3; Department of Industrial Engineering and Operations Research, Virginia Polytechnic Institute and State University; sponsored by Air Force Office of Scientific Research; February 1982)

Hard-copy imagery is examined to determine if altering the noise, blur, and scene content will affect the interpretability of 250 military scenes by trained Air Force photointerpreters.

This report is related to an earlier paper by Snyder, Turpin and Maddox (1980) dealing with digitally derived imagery. The authors' primary goals are to "conduct subjective quality scaling and information extraction studies on hard-copy images." Trained photointerpreters performed a subjective scaling task using characteristics common to digitalized aerial imagery. Experimental results show that noise, blur, and scene content can produce significant differential perceptions of interpretability. Additional conclusions reached by the authors include: "the main effects of blur and noise and the blur × noise interaction showed that digital images, like analog images, are poorer in subjective quality as the degree of blur or noise increases"; photointerpreters appear to evaluate available information in an objective manner; the optimal number of categories for an image interpretability scale is greater than ten (as many as sixty-two categories may be needed to accurately judge interpretability when examining well practiced photointerpreters); MDS is usable to represent the subjective dimensionality of a large imagery database; a high correlation exists between information extraction performance and scale values for digital imagery; and multidimensional scaling is usable for studying image quality, but it is of limited utility. In reviewing the literature, the authors conclude that "digital imagery did not appear to be greatly different from standard analog imagery in terms of subjective quality or interpretability." The report is intended for military audiences and photointerpretation specialists.

CONTENTS

PREFACE

I: INTRODUCTION

Overview of the Research Plan

Research Objectives

Specific Research Tasks

Background

    Noise effects

    Blur effects

    Subjective scaling and information extraction

    Multidimensional scaling

    Rating scales

II: SELECTION OF THE SCALING PROCEDURE
The Alternatives
The Most Feasible Alternative
III: PURPOSE OF THIS EXPERIMENT
IV: METHOD
Photointerpreters
Apparatus
Procedure
V: RESULTS
Analysis of Variance (ANOVA) on Ratings
 Blur
 Noise
 Order of battle
 Scene
 Blur × noise
 OB × blur
 OB × noise
 Scene × blur
 Scene × noise
 Scene × blur × noise
Optimal Number of Response Categories
MDS Analysis
Correlation with Performance
VI: DISCUSSION
Noise and Blur Effects
Number of Response Categories
MDS Analysis
Relationship between Information Extraction and Scaling
Digital Imagery Similarities
VII: CONCLUSIONS
REFERENCES
APPENDIX
A: The NATO Scale—An Image Interpretability Rating Scale
B: Scene MCT Results
C: Blur × Noise MCT Results
D: Scene MCT Results—Blur Level 40
E: Scene MCT Results—Blur Level 52
F: Scene MCT Results—Blur Level 84
G: Scene MCT Results—Blur Level 162
H: Scene MCT Results—Blur Level 322
I: Projections of MDS Analysis

72 pp. 7 chapters. Figures, graphs, tables, mathematical formulae, references, appendices.

254
Snyder, Harry L.

Quality Metrics of Digitally Derived Imagery and Their Relation to Interpreter Performance: VIII, Final Report
1983

technical report

(report number HFL-83-1; Department of Industrial Engineering and Operations Research, Virginia Polytechnic Institute and State University; sponsored by Air Force Office of Scientific Research; 30 June 1983)

This final report summarizes a five-year research project sponsored by the U.S. military. The project compared human responses to varying quality and type of digital images with quality metrics of the images.

This report provides an overview of all phases of the research project, providing information about methodology and results as well as drawing general conclusions. The coverage of each phase of the project is limited in detail in this summary report and the reader interested in specifics and subtle results should refer to previous reports. Appendix B to this report provides references for all technical reports, conference papers, and archival publications related to the total research project. This research project first developed two identical sets of two hundred and fifty images on film hard-copy and cathode ray tube soft-copy with the images degraded to varying degrees of noise and blur. One study examined the effects of noise and blur degradation on subjective evaluations of image quality and on actual ability to extract information from the images. Another segment of the research project identified a set of system quality metrics and image dependent quality metrics for describing images. These quality metrics were correlated with the measures of human responses to the images (subjective evaluations and information extractable from the images). In brief, the results showed that while soft-copy images were *perceived* as better than hard-copy images, information extraction was better for hard-copy images than for soft-copy images. Processing of CRT images modified these findings, however. Correlations were high between some of the *system quality* metrics and human responses to the images. This report, like the earlier ones in the series, is highly technical and will be of use primarily to professionals working in this area.

CONTENTS
PREFACE
I: INTRODUCTION
Overview of the Research Plan
Research Objectives
Specific Research Tasks
II: METHODOLOGY
Database Preparation
    Hard-copy image preparation
    Soft-copy image display
    Summary of blur and noise levels
Hard-Copy Experiments
    Information extraction
    Subjective quality scaling

Soft-Copy Experiments
    Information extraction
    Subjective quality scaling
Processed Soft-Copy Experiments
    Information extraction
    Subjective quality scaling
Quality Metric Evaluation
IV: RESULTS
Hard-Copy Subjective Quality Scaling
Hard-Copy Information Extraction
Soft-Copy Subjective Quality Scaling
Soft-Copy Information Extraction
Comparison of Hard-Copy and Soft-Copy Results
    Subjective image quality
    Information extraction performance
Processed Soft-Copy Subjective Quality Scaling
    Contrast modification
    Deblurring processes
    Noise removal processes
    Deblurring and noise removal
    Control condition
Processed Soft-Copy Information Extraction
Quality Metric Evaluation
    System image quality metrics
    Image-dependent quality metrics
V: DISCUSSION
Scenario Realism
Hard-Copy vs. Soft-Copy Interpretation
Processed vs. Nonprocessed Soft-Copy Interpretation
Metrics of Image Quality
VI: CONCLUSIONS

94 pp. 6 chapters. Graphs, tables, references, appendices.

255
Abramson, Sandra R.
Snyder, Harry L.

technical report

Operator Performance on Flat-Panel Displays with Line and Cell Failures
1984

(report number HFL-83-3; Department of Industrial Engineering and Operations Research, Virginia Polytechnic Institute and State University; sponsored by Office of Naval Research; January 1984)

This research report investigated the effects of cell failures, character font, and character case on readability of flat-panel plasma displays.

Three aspects of cell failures were studied as within-subjects variables in this experiment. The total *percent of cells failed* varied from 0% to 20%, with six levels used. Three *types of cell failures* were examined: individual cells, cells in a horizontal line, and cells in a vertical line. *Failure mode* depended upon whether cells were mistakenly lit (on mode) or mistakenly darkened (off mode). Font style and character case were between-subjects variables. Three font styles (Lincoln/Mitre, Huddleston, and the style used on the HP262IA computer terminal) were compared in upper case and mixed upper and lower case. The sixty college students who participated in the study were tested at all levels of each of the three cell failure (within-subjects) factors, and were randomly assigned to one of the six font style × character case (between-subjects) experimental conditions. Readability of the display was measured using a modification of the Tinker Speed of Reading Test. Accuracy and response speed in identifying errors provided the two dependent variables. The results cover: which cell failures were more detrimental to readability; reading performance based on type of cell failures; response times based on case of characters; the most readable font style; and how results are tempered by interactions with other independent variables in this study. This report does a good job of describing a complex set of findings; however, a good understanding of experimental design and statistics will be helpful. Several recommendations for flat-panel display designs are offered by the researchers. The experiment reported here was methodologically sound. The investigation of readability reported here will be of general interest to designers of all types of displays; those working with flat-panel displays will find the recommendations and analyses directly of value.

CONTENTS

Preface

I: Introduction
    Character font
    Matrix size
    Flat panel display failures
    Readability measurement
    Objectives of the experiment

II: Methodology
    Subjects
    Reading task
    Procedure
    Experimental design
    Creation of lower case fonts
    Equipment

III: Results
    Response time
    Response frequency

IV: Discussion
    Failure mode
    Failure type
    Percent failure
    Case
    Font

V: Summary and Design Recommendations
    Failures
    Case
    Font

References

Appendix A: Examples of Tinker Reading Passages

Appendix B: Instructions

45 pp. 5 chapters. Graphs, tables, references, appendices.

256
Beaton, Robert J.

A Human-Performance Based Evaluation of Quality Metrics for Hard-Copy and Soft-Copy Digital Imaging Systems
University Microfilms International, 1984

(Ph.D. dissertation, Department of Industrial Engineering and Operations Research, Virginia Polytechnic Institute and State University, 1984)

This dissertation reports on an ongoing, empirical study that is part of a U.S. Military sponsored research project; this particular study investigated the relationship between a number of quality metrics and human performance for two types of digital imaging systems—film and cathode ray tube.

A set of ten images, each degraded across five levels of noise combined with five levels of blurring (a total of two-hundred and fifty images), developed in an earlier phase of the research project were utilized in this experiment (see first report). Human performance was measured objectively through an information extraction measurement and subjectively through a "quality scaling procedure," both of which were described at length in an earlier report. Sixteen system quality metrics and twenty-one image dependent metrics were defined and examined in this study. The system quality metrics were based on the characterization of the physical components of the imaging system and included the modulation transfer function and human contrast sensitivity function. The image dependent metrics included five bivariate error statistics and sixteen metrics that corresponded to the system quality metrics except that the "displayed modulation spectrum of an image" was incorporated into the image dependent metric. Results showed system quality metrics superior to image dependent metrics in predicting human performance and that a signal-to-noise ratio metric was the best predictor. The experiment reported here is quite complex, and a good understanding of mathematics, statistics, and experimental design is required of the reader. This research will be useful to professionals working on developing high quality digital imagery.

CONTENTS
ABSTRACT
INTRODUCTION
SELECTED QUALITY METRICS
Background
System Quality Metrics
Image-Dependent Quality Metrics
Summary
METHOD
Empirical Modeling of Image Display Systems
    MTF of image digitizer
    MTF of blur filter
    MTF of image playback
    CRT display optimization and quantification
    MTF of composite imaging system
    CSF of human visual system
    Noise calculations
Digital Image Database
Human Performance Database
Computational Procedures
RESULTS AND DISCUSSION
System Quality Metric Evaluation
Image-Dependent Quality Evaluation
CONCLUSIONS
REFERENCES

115 pp. 4 chapters. Figures, graphs, tables, abstract formalisms, references.

Somers, Patricia   *SEE UNDER ID 209, 210*

257
Spencer, Herbert   **The Visible Word (2ed.)**
Lund Humphries, 1969

By linking reading efficiency and legibility research with typographic design, this volume seeks to relate research to practice.

In the introduction to this work, the author notes that although "they share a common objective, there has until now been remarkably little collaboration between the researchers and the producers of print." Beginning with comments on the continuing importance of printed text as a medium of information exchange and a review of the history of legibility research, he reports and illustrates some results of this research as they relate to typography, typographic composition, and type design. These comments include the relation between form and content, characteristics of type, and aspects of page layout. Noting that the standard Roman alphabet does not allow efficient representation of the sound systems of all those languages which use it, Spencer closes with an extensively illustrated section on the design of new or alternative alphabets including those intended for use in optical scanning and typesetting systems. A lengthy bibliography cites research from 1885 through 1967 and includes papers, research reports, and books from Germany, France, Great Britain, and the United States. More an extended essay than a book, there is little discussion or integration of research and design. Somewhat dated, the book also suffers from an excess of detail; 464 bibliographic entries are noted in 81 pages, three-fourths of which consist of illustrations. These illustrations, although carefully selected and reproduced, overwhelm the companion text. The book is worth its bibliography and is certainly a quick, painless introduction to legibility and typographic design, but the reader wanting more substance should refer to other works.

CONTENTS

Introduction

Investigating Legibility

Some Results of Research
    The relationship between content and form
    Capitals versus lower case
    Bold face types
    Italics
    Numerals
    Punctuation marks
    Type size, line length and leading
    Unjustified setting
    Paragraphs and indentation
    Margins
    Page size
    Non-horizontal alignment
    Paper and ink

Summary

Towards a New Alphabet

Glossary

Bibliography

107 pp. 5 chapters. Figures, bibliography, glossary.

258
Spoehr, Kathryn T.
Lehmkuhle, Stephen W.

Visual Information Processing
W.H. Freeman, 1982

(from *A Series of Books in Psychology*, R.C. Atkinson, G. Lindzey, R.F. Thompson, series eds.)

An introductory text for students beginning their studies of sensory and cognitive psychology. Aimed at those who are interested in the human visual processing phenomena and who wish to understand the visual system's individual parts and their interactions.

This text presents the visual system as an information processor and examines the processes and structures used in performing various tasks. Previous works in the field have failed to bridge the conceptual gap between the study of visual systems at the sensory and cognitive levels. In a single volume the authors present the concepts and methods of both approaches to the study of visual processing and present an integrated view of the visual processing system. An additional purpose is to acquaint readers with the methodology used to study visual processing. Numerous experiments are described so the reader can understand the scientific reasoning and logic behind their design. The first half of this work examines the component physical structures of the visual information processing system and the operations they carry out. Subjects covered include: mechanisms for the recognition of simple forms and pattern interpretation; mechanisms for the recognition of individual patterns or parts of patterns as whole objects; and the recognition and analysis of several patterns simultaneously. The second half of the book looks at the use of short- and long-term memory in visual processing. The authors examine how visual processing interacts with verbal skills during reading, visual memory representation and processing, and how language and visual information interact in abstract long-term memory.

CONTENTS

Preface
Chapter 1: Introduction
    The information processing approach
    Memory components in the information processing system
    The plan of this book
Chapter 2: Sensory Processes of the Visual System
    Structure of the visual system
    The response of single cells to light stimulation
    Pattern recognition
    Sensory considerations for pattern recognition
    Summary
    Suggested reading
Chapter 3: Pattern Recognition in Humans
    Template models
    Prototype models
    Feature models
    Pattern recognition by computers
    Summary

Suggested reading
Chapter 4: Organization and Visual Processing
    Gestalt principles of organization
    Hierarchical structure and global vs. local processing
    Dimensional structure and attention
    Summary
    Suggested reading
Chapter 5: Perceiving Several Patterns at Once
    Iconic store
    Processing stimuli in the iconic store
    Models of visual encoding
    Attention and scanning
    Summary
    Suggested reading
Chapter 6: Word Recognition
    Experimental findings
    Redundancy and word recognition
    Higher-order units
    Speech recoding and reading strategies
    Recognizing words in sentences
    Summary
    Suggested reading
Chapter 7: Picture Processing and Memory
    Recognizing a picture
    Attentional factors in picture processing
    Memory for pictorial information
    Recognition of faces
    Hemispheric specialization
    Summary
    Suggested reading
Chapter 8: Visual Imagery and Mental Representation
    Functional aspects of imagery
    Structural aspects of imagery
    Individual differences in imagery ability
    Cognitive maps
    Alternatives to the imagery theory
    Suggested reading
Chapter 9: Interactions Between Visual and Verbal Systems
    The Stroop effect
    Abstraction and generation in short-term memory
    Comparing sentences with pictures
    Accessing pictures and words in long-term memory
    Eyewitness testimony
    Suggested reading
Appendix A: Signal Detection Theory
    A typical detection experiment
    Assumptions of the theory of signal detectability
    Changing sensitivity and bias
    The receiver operating characteristic curve
    Summary

Appendix B: Analysis of Reaction Times
   Donders' subtraction method
   Additive stage durations
   Summary
References
Author Index
Subject Index

298 pp. 9 chapters. Drawings, figures, graphs, tables, models, author index, subject index, references, appendices. ISBN 0-7167-1373-X. (ISBN 0-7167-1374-8)

259

Steinbeck, Jürgen
Schiekel, Manfred
Unbehaun, Rüdiger
Herzog, Hans-Joest
Häberle, Gerhard
Biskupek, Rudolf

Flachanzeigeschirm mit Flussigkristallen
1980

technical report

(report number BMFT-FB-T-80-012; AEG-TELEFUNKEN, Serienprodukte AG, Geschäftsbereich Röhren und Baugruppen; sponsored by Bundesministerium für Forschung und Technologie; June 1980)

This report recounts the investigation and development of liquid crystal matrix display panels capable of projecting ninety scanned lines with two color representation or forty lines with four colors at the rate of fifty frames per second.

AEG-Telefunken presents a report (in German) on the development of liquid crystal matrix display panels which should be of interest to professional electrical engineers and display designers. Building on previous research, especially on the DAP-effect (Deformation Aufgerichteter Phasen, literally deformation of erect/upright phases), the authors investigate phase-deformation in cells with liquid crystals. The author's use of fluid crystals with a positive di-electric anisotropy in matrix display panels produces a color display that can represent various and complex data. The authors explain their examination of phase-deformation in well-organized but technically complex chapters, concluding with 74 pages of models, illustrations, charts, and graphs. The report includes an English language abstract. It will be of interest to researchers involved in matrix addressing in liquid crystal display panels.

CONTENTS

INHALTSVERZEICHNIS

1: ZUSAMMENFASSUNG

2: EINLEITUNG

2.1: Aufgabenstellung

2.2: Lösungsweg

3: PHYSIKALISCHE GRUNDLAGEN

3.1: Elektrooptisches Verhalten

    3.1.1. FK-Zellen mit elektrisch steuerbarer Doppelbrechung (DAP-Effekt Freèdericks-Effekt)

    3.1.2. Doppelbrechung

    3.1.3. Deformation der FK-Zelle im elektrischen Feld

    3.1.4. Einschaltverhalten

    3.1.5. FK-Zelle mit verdrillter Phase

    3.1.6. Schaltverhalten

3.2: Ansteuertechniken für FK-Rasterschirm

    3.2.1. Multiplexbetrieb

    3.2.2. Schaltung für die U/3-Ansteuerung von Flüssigkristall-Farbmatrizen

4: TECHNOLOGIE UND MATERIALUNTERSUCHUNGEN

4.1: Zellenaufbau

4.2: Orientierungsfragen

4.3: Flüssigkristallsubstanzen

4.4: Oberflächenuntersuchungen

    4.4.1. Elektronenmikroskopische Oberflächenuntersuchungen von bedampften Glassubstraten

    4.4.2. Abdruckuntersuchung an vollständig bedampften Glassubstraten

    4.4.3. Prüfung der einzelnen Schichten

    4.4.4. RHEED-Untersuchungen

    4.4.5. SiO$_2$-Schutzchicht auf ITO

    4.4.6. SiO-Schicht auf Glas

    4.4.7. Zusammenfassung

5: MESSERGEBNISSE

5.1: Hilfsmittel und Messmethoden

    5.1.1. Konoskopische Abbildung

    5.1.2. Spektroskopische Beobachtung bei Doppelbrechung

    5.1.3. Messung der Schichtdicke

    5.1.4. Messung der Schichtdickenänderung

    5.1.5. Messung der wirksamen Brechzahl

5.2: Winkelverteilung der Transmission in den Farben

5.3: Gangunterschiedskennlinien

5.4: Multiplexverhalten

5.5: Temperaturabhängigkeit

6: GERÄTEBESCHREIBUNG

6.1: Rasterschirm mit 32 × 32 Bildpunkten

6.2: Rasterschirm mit 80 × 80 Bildpunkten

6.3: Vorarbeiten für Rastershirm mit 256 × 256 Bildpunkten

6.4: Flachanzeige mit Farbschaltfilter

    6.4.1. Wirkungsweise der Anordnung

    6.4.2. Versuchsaufbau für eine 2-farbige Bildwiedergabe

7: SONSTIGES

7.1: Arbeiten anderer Stellen

    7.1.1. Allgemeines

    7.1.2. Geräte unde Prototypen Schaltungstechniken

    7.1.3. DAP-Effekt Rasterschirm

7.2: Literatur

7.3: Vorträge und Veröffentlichungen/Eigene Patente
    Abbildungen

167 pp. 7 chapters. Drawings, photographs, figures, graphs, tables, references.

260

Steinberg, Esther R.

Teaching Computers to Teach

Lawrence Erlbaum Associates, 1984

Offers a set of principles, procedures, and guidelines for developing effective computer-assisted instruction (CAI).

The principles and procedures presented here are based on two themes; the learner is the focus of CAI and the computer is merely a vehicle for instruction. The first seven chapters of the book present a three-phase plan for developing CAI. The first phase involves an initial planning of an entire lesson. The second phase entails implementing the Ripple Plan in which the program developer plans, programs, and evaluates one component of a lesson, before going on to the next component. The presentation and responses and feedback of one component are developed and then the component is evaluated and revised. Human-computer interactions and the flow of instruction are smoothed out within the component. In the third phase, the lesson as a whole is completed. The displays are designed and the individual components are pulled together into a cohesive whole by working out the flow of instruction between components, ordering the components, taking human factors into account, and adding introductory and concluding displays. Finally, the entirety of the lesson is evaluated and revised, utilizing review by experts and student performance as bases for evaluation. A sample lesson demonstrates this three-phase plan. Chapter eight discusses instructional conditions that promote the educational effectiveness of games, drills, and simulations (for example, insuring that a game is intrinsically instructional). The final chapter discusses efficiency in the development of CAI, implementation of the CAI in the classroom, and helping people learn how to learn. The actual process of programming the computer is not treated in this book. This clearly written, easy to follow book, developed as a text for the author's classes, will be useful to anyone who is designing or interested in learning about designing CAI.

CONTENTS

Preface

1: Getting Oriented
    Introduction
    Differences between CAI and traditional modes of instruction
    Rationale and guidelines for reviewing CAI lessons
    Procedures for reviewing lessons
2: Lesson Design: The Three-Phase Plan and the Ripple Plan
    Introduction
    The three-phase plan
    Initial planning: lesson level
    Sample lesson
    Ripple plan: unit level
    Overview of completion: lesson level
    Should the lesson author learn how to program?
3: Ripple Plan: Presentation
    Introduction
    Steps in the procedure
    Generate specific goals
    Choose the teaching techniques
    Write the script
    Ask questions
    Program and evaluate
    Sample lesson
4: Ripple Plan: Responses and Feedback
    Student responses
    Computer feedback
    Remediation
    Program and evaluate
    Sample lessons
5: Ripple Plan: Human Factors and Management
    Management under computer control
    Alternatives in assigning management
    Smoothing human-machine interaction
    Motivation
    Self-concept and anxiety
    Program and evaluate
    Sample lesson
6: Displays and Overall Lesson Structure
    Displays
    Overall lesson structure
7: Evaluation
    Evaluation measures
    Formative evaluation
    Summative evaluation
    Maintenance
    Documentation
8: Games, Drills, and Simulations
    Definitions
    Games
    Drills
    Simulations

9: Efficiency, Implementation, and Learning How to Learn
Efficiency
Implementation
Learning and learning how to learn
Bibliography
Index

185 pp. 9 chapters. Drawings, figures, charts, general index, bibliography. ISBN 0-89859-368-9. (ISBN 0-89859-453-7)

261
Stevens, Peter S.

Handbook of Regular Patterns: An Introduction to Symmetry in Two Dimensions
The MIT Press, 1980

reference

Both mathematicians and artists study plane symmetries. In a rigorous and visually delightful book, Stevens elegantly weds mathematical theory and design practice.

Using a system of commas to represent motifs, the author first defines symmetry and the four symmetry operations of reflection, rotation, translation, and glide reflection. He then moves on to the description and rich illustration of the three symmetry groups—point groups, line groups, and plane-filling groups. Classification of motif types are based on the crystallographer's notations for symmetry and symmetry operations, combined with symbols for representing band ornaments. Each section ends with a short set of exercises encouraging the reader to explore the material presented. The book concludes with a visual summary of each of the symmetry operations and groups. An appendix treats some of the formal geometry of space and addresses the limits of planar design. The illustrations represent diverse cultures and historical periods and are themselves aesthetically presented. In his commentaries on the motif types, Stevens notes that, despite the restrictions of plane space and geometry, symmetry operations are capable of producing a wealth of interesting and pleasing patterns. Like fugal compositions, these limits serve not to restrict, but to focus attention on, the possible. Little known Escher designs demonstrate many of the plane-filling groups. Stevens' prose has the clarity of the designs he presents. His book is accessible to the general reader, but has the depth and breadth to make it useful to technical audiences. The artist-designer can use the book as a catalogue of design motifs (it has more than a thousand examples). As a working manual, it provides extensive discussions of techniques for generating original designs. Since the mathematics can easily be used to generate algorithms, display designers can apply the principles directly to their work. Eminently practical and visually appealing.

CONTENTS
Preface
I: Symmetry Groups
  1. Basic operations
  2. How operations generate themselves

II: Point Groups
    3. Point groups
    4. The asymmetric motif: group 1
    5. Bilateral symmetry: group *m*
    6. Playing cards and walnuts: groups 2 and 2*mm*
    7. The triskelion and the green pepper: groups 3 and 3*m*
    8. The swastika and the Greek cross: groups 4 and 4*mm*
    9. Flowers and pentagrams: groups 5 and 5*m*
   10. Solomon's Seal and snowflakes: groups 6 and 6*mm*
   11. Stars and circles: point groups of higher order

III: The Seven Line Groups
   12. Ducks in a row: group *t*
   13. Friday's footprints: group *tg*
   14. Reflected reflections: group *tm*
   15. Reflected sails: group *mt*
   16. Grand right and left: group *t*2
   17. Reflected whirls: group *t*2*mg*
   18. Linear kaleidoscope: group *t*2*mm*
   19. Recapitulation

IV: The Seventeen Plane Groups
   20. Two nonparallel translations: group *p*1
   21. Two parallel glide reflections: group *pg*
   22. Two parallel mirrors: group *pm*
   23. A reflection and a parallel glide reflection: group *cm*
   24. Four half-turns: group *p*2
   25. A mirror and a perpendicular glide reflection: group *p*2*mg*
   26. Two perpendicular glide reflections: group *p*2*gg*
   27. Reflections in four sides of a rectangle: group *p*2*mm*
   28. Perpendicular mirrors and perpendicular glide reflections: group *c*2*mm*
   29. Three rotations through 120°: group *p*3
   30. Reflections in an equilateral triangle: group *p*3*m*1
   31. Reflections of 120° turns: group *p*31*m*
   32. Quarter-turns: group *p*4
   33. Reflections of quarter-turns: group *p*4*gm*
   34. Reflections in the sides of a 45°-45°-90° triangle: group *p*4*gm*
   35. Sixfold rotations: group *p*6
   36. Reflections in the sides of a 30°-60°-90° triangle: group *p*6*mm*
   37. Summary
Appendix: Derivations and the absence of group *p*5
Bibliography
Index

400 pp. 37 chapters in 4 parts. Drawings, photographs, mathematical formulae, general index, bibliography, appendix. ISBN 0-262-19188-1.

262
Stevenson, George A.

reference

Graphic Arts Encyclopedia (2ed.)
McGraw-Hill, 1979

A highly valuable reference, this work "consolidates all the most useful techniques, processes, concepts, and methods required in the graphic arts professions."

A purposeful and instructive text, *The Graphic Arts Encyclopedia* provides concise, understandable definitions and explanations of the key aspects of graphic design. The entries are alphabetically arranged and deal with the materials and tools necessary to form an image, types of images, surfaces on which images may be formed, and processes for image generation. This second edition contains a comprehensive revision of most entries, updated photographs and discussions of equipment, and new entries covering aspects of computer utilization in graphic arts professions. In addition to the main entries, the work is supplemented by a series of useful tables and three indices as well as an introductory bibliography to graphic arts and literature. Due to its emphasis on the clarification of basic concepts, this book is excellent for beginners, students, and professionals in fields related to, but not strongly associated with, graphic arts. This is a well-written reference which may easily be adapted for use as a text.

CONTENTS
    Preface
    How to use the encyclopedia
    Graphic Arts Encyclopedia
    Bibliography
    Product index
    Manufacturers' index
    Table 1. Metric conversion table
    Table 2. Paper sizes
    Table 3. Paper-cutting chart for booklets
    Table 4. Cover-paper cutting chart for booklets
    Table 5. Blotter-cutting chart
    Table 6. Greek alphabet
    Table 7. Useful mathematical rules
    Table 8. Constants and conversion factors
    Table 9. Numerals
    Table 10. Mathematical symbols
    Table 11. Decimal equivalents
    Table 12. Elements and symbols
    Table 13. Temperature conversion table
    Index

483 pp. Drawings, photographs, figures, charts, tables, general index, bibliography, product index, manufacturers' index. ISBN 0-07-061288-9.

263
Talcott, Noel A., Jr.

technical report

The Use of Interactive Graphic Displays for Interpretation of Surface Design Parameters
1981

(report number NASA-TM-81963; NASA Langley Research Center; sponsored by National Aeronautics and Space Administration; May 1981)

Details the Graphics Display Data (GDD) method developed for the rapid interpretation of surface design data.

Although it was initially designed for the optimization of flight vehicles (missiles, spacecraft, and cruise aircraft), researchers have realized the broader application of the GDD method to such disciplines as aerodynamic analysis, structural analysis, and experimental data analysis. An actual study of the GDD system used as "an interpretive tool for radiation equilibrium temperature distribution over the surface of an aerodynamic vehicle" is provided as an example and demonstrates the system's unique features. Most notable are features that distinguish the GDD method as user oriented: the application of the in-house design system by researchers doing related or similar work, the extension of the routines to other computer systems, and its status as "a way to organize the analysis codes, graphic tools, and utilities to allow the user or researcher a means of selecting his own path through the interactive analysis system." The displays can be changed, modified, and improved, allowing the user effective control. For greater detail and improved clarity, color graphic displays are also examined. Though color displays are an ideal extention for the GDD, Talcott stresses the need for more work to improve capabilities. The pictorial representation of data has many applications and the GDD system allows for rapid sorting and interpretation of large amounts of surface design data. Aerospace engineers and researchers as well as systems designers would find the information contained in this report interesting.

24 pp. Drawings, figures, charts, tables, references, color graphics.

264
Tannas, Lawrence E., Jr. (ed.)

collection

Flat-Panel Displays and CRTs
Van Nostrand Reinhold, 1985

A systematic and comprehensive survey of flat-panel and CRT display devices, organized as a tutorial, which also serves as a basic introduction to electronic information displays.

This collection of eleven essays on display technology offers a thorough review of the variety and performance characteristics of electronic display devices, with primary emphasis placed on flat-panel displays. After a useful introductory chapter on the history, classification, and nomenclature of all electronic displays, the following chapters examine in detail: the analysis of the display device within a larger system; the evaluation of image display quality; performance and utility of flat-panel displays, including emissive and nonemissive; a description of how the human vision system operates; a historical introduction to and review of CRT design and performance; the history and goals of flat-CRT technology as distinct from regular CRTs; the development and application of electroluminescent (EL) and light-emitting diode (LED) displays; the history, production, and application of plasma displays; and the theory, development, and construction of liquid-crystal (LC) displays, as well as other nonemissive technologies. An extremely well-organized, lucidly written series of essays, especially noteworthy for their attention to precise detail, historical background, rich documentation, and a comprehensive approach to current developments. This work is not intended to treat complex human factors, pattern recognition, or information theory issues; nevertheless, it should be of great use both as an introductory text for novice display designers and as a review manual for professionals in graphics hardware, systems analysis, and electrical engineering.

CONTENTS

PREFACE

1: INTRODUCTION
    L.E. Tannas, Jr.

1.1: History of Electronics for Displays

1.2: Electronic Displays
    1.2.1. Introduction
    1.2.2. Display categories
    1.2.3. Display technique
    1.2.4. Font
    1.2.5. The CRT challenge
    1.2.6. Definition of flat-panel displays
    1.2.7. Flat CRTs

1.3: Display Classifications
    1.3.1. Flat-panel display classifications

1.4: Display Nomenclature
    1.4.1. Electroluminescence vs. luminescence
    1.4.2. Gas discharge, or plasma panel
    1.4.3. Cathodoluminescence vs. vacuum fluorescence

1.5: Classification Nomenclature

1.6: Picture Element or Pixel

1.7: Display Array
    1.7.1. Duty factor
    1.7.2. Pixel contrast ratio

1.8: Addressing
    1.8.1. Direct addressing
    1.8.2. Scan addressing
    1.8.3. Grid addressing
    1.8.4. Shift addressing
    1.8.5. Matrix addressing

1.9: Display Device Development

1.10: Multidiscipline

1.11: Technology Impetus

1.12: Conclusion

References

2: SYSTEM REQUIREMENTS
   L.E. Tannas, Jr.

2.1: Introduction

2.2: System Classification

2.3: Display Installation Classification

2.4: Display Functional Classification

2.5: Systems Constraints
   2.5.1. Performance
   2.5.2. System design
   2.5.3. Environmental testing
   2.5.4. Standards

2.6: Display Subsystems
   2.6.1. Faceplate
   2.6.2. Bezel
   2.6.3. Interactors
   2.6.4. Electronics

2.7: Transillumination

2.8: Photometry
   2.8.1. Photometric measurements
   2.8.2. Photometric units

References

3: THE VISUAL SYSTEM: CAPABILITIES AND LIMITATIONS
   Harry L. Snyder

3.1: Introduction

3.2: Anatomy of the Visual System
   3.2.1. Overall organization
   3.2.2. Rod and cone characteristics

3.3: Spatial Vision

3.4: Temporal Vision
   3.4.1. Temporal CTF
   3.4.2. Other temporal psychophysical data

3.5: Color Vision
   3.5.1. Color systems and measurement
   3.5.2. The chromatic CTF

3.6: Summary

References

4: IMAGE QUALITY: MEASURES AND VISUAL PERFORMANCE
   Harry L. Snyder

4.1: Introduction
   4.1.1. Image measurement and specification
   4.1.2. Physical measures of image quality
   4.1.3. Behaviorally validated measures of image quality

4.2: The Modulation Transfer Function
    4.2.1. Concept and measurement
    4.2.2. Relation to vision
    4.2.3. Design utility of the MTF

4.3: Pixel Error Measures
    4.3.1. Measurement of pixel errors
    4.3.2. Relation to vision

4.4: MTF-Based Measures of Image Quality
    4.4.1. Equivalent passband, N_e
    4.4.2. Strehl intensity ratio
    4.4.3. Modulation transfer function area (MTFA)
    4.4.4. Gray shade frequency product (GSFP)
    4.4.5. Integrated contrast sensitivity (ICS)
    4.4.6. Visual capacity (VC)
    4.4.7. Discriminable difference diagrams (DDD)
    4.4.8. Displayed signal-to-noise ratio (SNR_D)
    4.4.9. Visual efficacy (VE)
    4.4.10. Information content (IC)
    4.4.11. Summary of the MFT-based metrics

4.5: Pixel Error Measures of Image Quality
    4.5.1. Nominalized mean square error (MSE)
    4.5.2. Point Squared Error (PSE)
    4.5.3. Perceptual MSE (PMSE)
    4.5.4. Image fidelity (IF)
    4.5.5. Structural content (SC)
    4.5.6. Correlation quality (CQ)

4.6: An Empirical Image Quality Model

4.7: Problems in Image Quality Measurement
    4.7.1. Lines, line pairs, and TV lines
    4.7.2. The measurement system
    4.7.3. What to measure and calculate
    4.7.4. Test pattern selection

4.8: Concepts Related to Image Quality
    4.8.1. Uniformity: large and small areas
    4.8.2. Shades of gray
    4.8.3. Resolution

References

5: FLAT-PANEL DISPLAY DESIGN ISSUES
    L.E. Tannas, Jr.

5.1: Introduction

5.2: Power Efficiency
    5.2.1. Emitters and nonemitters
    5.2.2. Ambient illumination
    5.2.3. Light losses
    5.2.4. Power loss
    5.2.5. Display system efficiency diagram
    5.2.6. Quantum efficiency
    5.2.7. Material efficiency
    5.2.8. Estimating display performance

5.3: Addressability
    5.3.1. Direct addressing
    5.3.2. Scan addressing
    5.3.3. Grid addressing
    5.3.4. Shift-addressing technique
    5.3.5. Matrix addressing
    5.3.6. Intrinsic matrix addressing
    5.3.7. Extrensic matrix addressing
5.4: Duty Factor
    5.4.1. Pixel dwell time
    5.4.2. Summary of dwell time effects
5.5: Gray Scale
5.6: Color
5.7: Cost
References for Section 5.1-5.7
5.8: Intrinsic Electronic Display Drive
    5.8.1. IC technology for high voltage display drivers
        Tom Engibous
References for Section 5.8
5.9: Extrinsic Electronic Display Addressing
    5.9.1. Fabrication and application of thin-film transistors to
        displays
        L.E. Tannas, Jr.
References for Section 5.9.1
    5.9.2. Extrinsic matrix addressing with silicon thin-film transistor
        arrays
        A.I. Lakatos
Reference for Section 5.9.2
6: THE CHALLENGE OF THE CATHODE-RAY TUBE
    Norman H. Lehrer
6.1: Introduction
6.2: Historical Origins of the CRT
6.3: Basic CRT Design and Operation
    6.3.1. Monochrome CRTs
    6.3.2. Color CRTs
6.4: Electron Optic Regions of the CRT
    6.4.1. The beam-forming region
    6.4.2. The focusing region
    6.4.3. The deflection region
    6.4.4. The drift region
6.5: Limitations on Electron-Gun Performance
    6.5.1. Optical analog of the electron gun
    6.5.2. Magnification
    6.5.3. Cathode loading
    6.5.4. Lens aberrations
    6.5.5. Thermal effects
    6.5.6. Space charge
    6.5.7. Final spot size
6.6: The Viewing System
    6.6.1. Cathodoluminescence
    6.6.2. Phosphors

6.7: CRT Resolution and Contrast
    6.7.1. Defining CRT resolution
    6.7.2. Contrast and gray scale in the CRT

6.8: The Life of the CRT
    6.8.1. Cathode life
    6.8.2. Phosphor life

6.9: Applications and Types of CRTs
    6.9.1. CRT applications
    6.9.2. Types of CRTs
    6.9.3. Examples of high performance CRTs

6.10: Driving the CRT
    6.10.1. CRT circuits
    6.10.2. CRT grid drive characteristics

6.11: Overview of CRT Performance

Reference

7: FLAT CATHODE-RAY TUBE DISPLAY
    Walter F. Goede

7.1: Introduction

7.2: Motivation and Goals

7.3: History

7.4: Functional and Technical Description

7.5: Cathodes for the Flat CRTs
    7.5.1. Single-point cathode
    7.5.2. Large-area thermionic-oxide-coated cathodes
    7.5.3. Large area nonthermic cathodes
    7.5.4. Cathode summary

7.6: Beam Positioning and Modulation Techniques
    7.6.1. Deflected-beam approaches
    7.6.2. Matrix-addressing approaches
    7.6.3. Modulation techniques
    7.6.4. Beam positioning and modulation summary

7.7: Brightness-Enhancement Techniques
    7.7.1. Multiple beam addressing
    7.7.2. Electron multipliers
    7.7.3. Internal-storage techniques

7.8: Phosphor Screens

7.9: Vacuum Envelope and Processing Techniques
    7.9.1. Vacuum envelope
    7.9.2. Processing

7.10: Technical Achievements
    7.10.1. Aiken tube and derivatives
    7.10.2. Banana tube
    7.10.3. Gabor tube
    7.10.4. Philips channel electron multiplier CRT
    7.10.5. Battelle flat CRT
    7.10.6. Digisplay
    7.10.7. Vacuum fluorescence
    7.10.8. RCA feedback and electron guide displays
    7.10.9 Zenith ion feedback display
    7.10.10. Arizona State active matrix display

7.10.11. Stanford Research Institute field emission display

7.10.12. Hybrid plasma/ CRT

7.11: Summary

References

8: ELECTROLUMINESCENT DISPLAYS

L.E. Tannas, Jr.

8.1: Introduction

8.1.1. Overview

8.1.2. Configuration definitions

8.2: History

8.2.1. Discovery of electroluminescence in polycrystalline films

8.2.2. First EL display activity

8.2.3. Thin-film EL

8.2.4. DC powder EL

8.2.5. TFT extrinsic EL drive

8.2.6. DMOS intrinsic EL drive

8.3: Theory of Operation

8.3.1. Status of theory

8.3.2. Differences in observed light generation mechanisms

8.4: AC Thin-Film EL

8.4.1. Physical structure

8.4.2. Performance

8.4.3. Discrimination ratio

8.4.4. Panel size

8.4.5. Temperature dependence

8.4.6. Life, aging, and burn-in

8.4.7. Light-generating process model

8.4.8. Fabrication techniques for AC thin-film EL

8.4.9. Transmission electron microscopy (TEM) of EL thin films

8.4.10. Electrode definition

8.4.11. Memory mode

8.4.12. Acoustical noise from AC thin-film EL panels

8.4.13. Failure modes

8.4.14. Color

8.5: AC Powder EL

8.5.1. Fabrication technique

8.5.2. Applications

8.5.3. Mechanism of light generation

8.5.4. Life and aging

8.5.5. Color in AC powder EL lamps

8.6: DC Powder EL

8.6.1. Fabrication

8.6.2. Theory of operation

8.6.3. Aging and failure mechanisms

8.6.4. Applications

8.6.5. Colors with DC powder EL phosphors

8.7: DC Thin-Film EL

8.8: Luminous Efficiency

8.9: Conclusion

References

9: LIGHT-EMITTING DIODE DISPLAYS

M. George Craford

9.1: Introduction

9.2: History of LED Display Devices

9.3: Basic LED Technology
    9.3.1. Radiative and nonradiative recombination
    9.3.2. Direct-indirect transition
    9.3.3. Nitrogen doping in $GaAs_1P_x$
    9.3.4. GaAlAs
    9.3.5. GaP:Zn, O
    9.3.6. Optical coupling efficiency

9.4: LED Performance—State of the Art
    9.4.1. Performance characteristics of different materials technologies
    9.4.2. Future performance improvement

9.5: LED Display Devices
    9.5.1. Overview
    9.5.2. Discrete emitter
    9.5.3. Bar-of-light displays
    9.5.4. Numeric displays
    9.5.5. Alphanumeric displays
    9.5.6. Numeric and alphanumeric displays with on-board integrated circuits
    9.5.7. Large-area x-y addressable LED arrays
    9.5.8. Large-area displays using a combination of LED products

9.6: LED Performance Parameters

9.7: Materials and Processes
    9.7.1. Substrate Preparation
    9.7.2. Epitaxial deposition
    9.7.3. Wafer fabrication

9.8: Summary and Conclusions

References

10: PLASMA DISPLAYS
    Larry F. Weber

10.1: Introduction

10.2: History
    10.2.1. History of gas discharges
    10.2.2. History of plasma displays

10.3: Basic Electro-Optical Characteristics of the Gas Discharge
    10.3.1. I-V characteristic
    10.3.2. Resistor load line technique
    10.3.3. External current-limiting requirement
    10.3.4. Luminous regions of a gas discharge
    10.3.5. Wavelength distribution

10.4: Gas Discharge Physics
    10.4.1. Gas discharge reactions
    10.4.2. Gas discharge feedback model
    10.4.3. Paschen curve
    10.4.4. Regions of the I-V characteristic
    10.4.5. Spatial regions of the normal glow discharge
    10.4.6. Priming
    10.4.7. Time-varying characteristics

10.5: Current-Limiting Techniques
10.5.1. DC current limiting
10.5.2. AC current limiting
10.5.3. Other current-limiting techniques

10.6: DC Plasma Displays
10.6.1. NIXIE tube
10.6.2. Segmented discharge displays
10.6.3. DC dot matrix displays
10.6.4. Self-Scan® display
10.6.5. Philips DC display

10.7: AC Plasma Displays
10.7.1. AC plasma display structures
10.7.2. Electrical characteristics of the AC display
10.7.3. Addressing
10.7.4. Drive-circuit considerations
10.7.5. Refreshed segmented AC plasma display
10.7.6. Refreshed dot matrix AC plasma display
10.7.7. AC shift panels

10.8: Hybrid AC-DC Plasma Displays
10.8.1. Self-Scan® memory panel
10.8.2. Sony AC-DC hybrid

10.9: Image Displays
10.9.1 Gray scale
10.9.2 Color plasma displays
10.9.3 Color television

10.10: Hybrid-Plasma CRT

10.11: Fabrication of Plasma Displays

10.12: Future of Plasma Displays

References

11: NONEMISSIVE DISPLAYS
P. Andrew Penz

11.1: Introduction
11.1.1. General characteristics of nonemissive displays
11.1.2. History
11.1.3. Definitions and acronyms

11.2: The Liquid-Crystal Phase
11.2.1. Liquid-crystal symmetry
11.2.2. Liquid-crystal materials
11.2.3. Physics of liquid-crystal displays
11.2.4. Liquid-crystal alignment

11.3: LCD Configurations
11.3.1. Dynamic scattering LCD
11.3.2. Dichroic dye LCD
11.3.3. Cholesteric-nematic LCD
11.3.4. Deformation of aligned-phase LCD
11.3.5. Twisted nematic LCD
11.3.6. Fluorescent LCD
11.3.7. Smectic LCD
11.3.8. Disclination display modes

11.4: Intrinsic Matrix Addressing of LCDs
    11.4.1. Fast-scan matrix addressing
    11.4.2. Two-frequency addressing
    11.4.3. Hysteresis multiplex addressing
    11.4.4. Thermal addressing
    11.4.5. Other intrinsic addressing models
    11.4.6. System considerations for intrinsic matrix addressing

11.5: Extrinsic Matrix Addressing of LCDs
    11.5.1. Ferroelectric addressing
    11.5.2. Varistor addressing
    11.5.3. Thin-film transistor addressing
    11.5.4. Bulk silicon addressing

11.6: Electrochromic Displays
    11.6.1. Introduction
    11.6.2. Nonstoichiometric ECDs
    11.6.3. Depositioned ECDs
    11.6.4. Other electrochromic mechanisms

11.7: Colloidal Displays
    11.7.1. Introduction
    11.7.2. Electrophoretic displays
    11.7.3. Dipolar suspension displays

11.8: Electroactive Solids
    11.8.1. Introduction
    11.8.2. Ferroelectric displays
    11.8.3. Ferromagnetic displays
    11.8.4. Surface deformation displays

11.9: Electromechanical displays
    11.9.1. Introduction
    11.9.2. Minielectric shutters
    11.9.3. Rotating ball displays
    11.9.4. Galvanometer displays

11.10: Conclusion
References
INDEX

468 pp. 11 chapters. Drawings, photographs, figures, tables, abstract formalisms, models, general index, references. ISBN 0-442-28250-8.

265
Teichner, Warren H.
Christ, Richard E.
Corso, Gregory M.

Color Research for Visual Displays
1977

technical report

(report number ONR-CR213-102-4F; Department of Psychology, New Mexico State University; sponsored by Office of Naval Research; June 1977)

Compares the effectiveness of color coding in visual displays with coding by achromatic letters, digits, and shapes.

An analysis of the literature is followed by a comparison of the effects on simple task performance of presenting information by these four methods. The authors conclude that color has no advantage over achromatic codes in simple tasks. Color is one dimension along which information can be presented. Part one presents ten general principles of information coding and concludes that color does not differ from other possible coding sets in that they all follow the same general principles. Part two presents detailed descriptions of the experimental methods for the fourteen experiments and the results obtained.

CONTENTS

LIST OF FIGURES

PART 1

Color and Visual Information Coding

Color as a Coding Dimension
    Principle 1. The principle of attensity
    Principle 2. The principle of identifiable code elements
    Principle 3. The principle of information
    Principle 4. The principle of input rate
    Principle 5. The principle of chunking
    Principle 6. The principle of redundancy, irrelevancy and
      compulsive encoding
    Principle 7. The principle of processing priority
    Principle 8. The principle of integrality
    Principle 9. The principle of temporal order
    Principle 10. The principle of practice

Review of Previous Reports

Multiple Task Experiments
    Experiment 1. Combined task I
    Experiment 2. Combined task II
    Experiment 3. Integrated task

Discussion and Conclusions

PART II

Experiment 1: Combined Task I
    Method
    Results
    Discussion

Experiment 2: Combined Task II
    Method
    Results
    Discussion

Experiment 3: Integrated Task
    Method
    Results

General Conclusions

References

117 pp. 2 parts. Figures, graphs, tables, references.

266
Teicholz, Eric
Berry, Brian J.L.
(eds.)

collection

Computer Graphics and Environmental Planning
Prentice-Hall, 1983

Introduces the use of graphics in environmental planning. Particular attention is given to geographic information systems and their contributions to the decision-making process.

The essays in this collection explore the development and use of computer graphics systems—called geographic information systems (GIS)—that can both visually display environmental data and subject the data to a number of analytic operations. The collection consists of four parts. The first part explores decision-making issues related to the environment. Examples include discussions of state-wide projects in New Jersey, South Carolina, and North Dakota. The second part focuses on the applications of computer graphics in regional policy analysis. Part three examines two case studies; a federal project on environmental pollution and a study of local government productivity in Philadelphia. The analytical abilities of geographic information systems are examined in part four. A site study for coal-fired power plants, mapping used for analysis of urban highway congestion patterns, and an analysis of the railroad industry serve as examples. A particularly interesting facet of this book can be found in the editor's analysis of what constitutes an ideal GIS. Using a matrix, they show how well the systems discussed in the book measure up to their ideal. This book serves as an excellent example of how computer graphics is shaping the expanding accumulation of raw data into forms that enhance communication and aid the decision-making process. Though the majority of essays focus on graphics in environmental planning, the applications have relevance to business managers, graphics engineers, city managers, urban planners, and database managers, as well as environmental planners.

CONTENTS

Contributing Authors

Preface

PART I: COMPUTER GRAPHICS IN ENVIRONMENTAL DECISION MAKING

Chapter 1: The CEQ Air Pollution Exposure Risk Model
    Kay H. Jones, Timothy L. Chapman, Randi Ferrari
    Abstract
    The air pollution problem
    Methodology for the air pollution-health risk model
    The role of computer graphics
    The CO health risk model
    Conclusions
    References

Chapter 2: A Statewide Mapping System for Generalized Planning Analysis
    Robert F. Mills
    Abstract
    Background
    Methodology
    Software
    Application and examples
    Conclusion
    State mapping systems—the next steps
    References

Chapter 3: Beyond Hardware and Software: Implementing a State-Level Geographical Information System
    David J. Cowen, Alfred H. Vang, Senator James M. Waddell, Jr.
    The demand for a geographical information system
    Creating a geographical information system: the ideal versus reality
    State-level approaches to geographical information systems
    References

Chapter 4: Program Evaluation and Policy Analysis with Computer Mapping
    Robert R. Bell, Gary C. Pickett, Joseph T. Scardina
    Mapping and programming analysis
    Requirements for mapping
    Description of the Tennessee Tech mapping system
    Method description
    Resources required
    Available mapping options
    Problems encountered
    Implications of the mapping project
    References

Chapter 5: A Graphics-Oriented Computer System to Support Environmental Decision Making
    H.V. Giddings
    Abstract
    Program definition
    The REAP computer system
    Functional definition
    The data base

BROWSE
QUERY
MAP
GAP
Integrated software
The master monitor
A set of tools
A typical example
Conclusion
References

PART II: COMPUTER GRAPHICS FOR REGIONAL POLICY
ANALYSIS

Chapter 6: Use of Computer Graphics in Policymaking
    Alan Paller
    Abstract
    The growth of computer graphics
    Examples of computer use by policymakers
    The principal role of graphic display in policymaking
    Action plan for the first computer graphics project

Chapter 7: Regional Environmental Analysis and Assessment Utilizing
the Geoecology Data Base
    R.J. Olson, J.M. Klopatek, C.J. Emerson
    Abstract
    Geoecology data base
    Applications of the geoecology data base
    Discussion
    References

Chapter 8: Selecting New Town Sites in the United States Using
Regional Data Bases
    Jack Dangermond
    The problem
    The methodology
    The role of computer graphics in solving the problem
    Examples of the computer graphics produced
    Some next steps in using this methodology
    References
    Appendix

Chapter 9: Cartographic Analysis of Deer Habitat Utilization
    C. Dana Tomlin, Stephen H. Berwick, Sandra M. Tomlin
    Problem
    Methodology and results
    Use of computer graphics
    Examples
    Retrospect
    References

PART III: TWO COMPUTER GRAPHIC CASE STUDIES: FEDERAL AND LOCAL GOVERNMENT

Chapter 10: Graphical Display Maps Foster Regulation Policy
    T.K. Gardenier
    Abstract
    Related quantitative methodology
    Computer graphics in identifying statistical association
    Illustrations of graphical maps for environment and health
    References

Chapter 11: The Influence of Computer Graphics on Local Government Productivity
    John Michael Hadalski, Jr.
    Abstract
    Mapping and land-data systems in local government, as portrayed by the city of Philadelphia
    The influence of computer graphics on local government productivity
    Technological issues in a local graphics program
    Policy and organization issues in local government computer graphics projects
    Conclusion: the future of computer graphics in local government
    References

PART IV: ANALYTICAL CAPABILITIES OF GEOGRAPHIC INFORMATION SYSTEMS

Chapter 12: Computer-Aided Siting of Coal-Fired Power Plants: A Case Study
    Dennis R. Smith, John H. Robinson
    Abstract
    Siting methodology and technique
    Site-selection criteria
    Site-selection analysis
    Conclusions

Chapter 13: Mapping Congestion Patterns on Urban Highway Networks
    J.B. Schneider
    Description of the problem
    Methodological approach
    Role of computer graphics
    Examples of displays from the CDS
    Next steps
    References

Chapter 14: The Princeton Railroad Network Model: Application of Computer Graphics in the Analysis of a Changing Railroad Industry
    Alain L. Kornhauser, Mark Hornung, Yehonathan Hazony, Jerome M. Lutin
    Abstract
    Major elements of the Princeton railroad network model
    The link-node network of U.S. railroads
    Demand data-carload waybill statistics
    FRA accident/incident file
    Models of shipper and railroad routing behavior
    Intracarrier route-generation model
    Intercarrier (quanta-net) route-generation model

Traffic assignment
Participatory value
Opportunity cost
Elementary traffic diversion
Advantages of graphics
References
INDEX

250 pp. 14 chapters in 4 parts. Figures, charts, maps, graphs, tables, models, general index, references. ISBN 0-13-164830-6.

267
Thiel, Philip

Visual Awareness and Design: An Introductory Program in Conceptual Awareness, Perceptual Sensitivity, and Basic Design Skills
University of Washington Press, 1981

Believing that the visual environment is "a slate on which we are continually writing messages to one another" and that professional designers are socially responsible for the impact of the messages they create, Thiel has written a program-textbook for the development of visual literacy and basic design skills.

His program involves a sequence of exercises in which the student is given progressively more challenging problems in design synthesis. The problems are intended to focus attention on specific sets of design issues so that students develop the capacity to handle the multiple requirements of design tasks. An anthology of quotations from artists, designers, scientists, philosophers, and historians has been set in column-form to accompany the text. This parallel mini-text provides additional information and commentary on specific issues; it also makes the book an excellent introduction to visual literacy and design for the non-professional. (Note and compare with Dondis, *A Primer of Visual Literacy*.) In addition to these quotes, an extensive discussion follows each exercise to direct attention to the issues raised by the exercise. Not simply practical guides to solving design problems, these discussions also integrate ethics, aesthetics and philosophy which keep in focus both the pragmatics of design and the social responsibilities of designers. Thiel is an architect; his book is biased in that direction. He assumes that it will be used in a classroom and so emphasizes the interaction of students with each other and an instructor as part of learning design skills. Even so, the exercises are useful outside this context. Perception of form, color, content and form, rhythmic patterning, texture, space, and scale all bear on the design of visual spaces. In the concentrated visual space of a display screen, mastery of these concepts is particularly important. Thiel's book is a significant step toward that mastery.

CONTENTS
Preface - A Word with the Instructor
Introduction
    A - Vision and environment
    B - Design and designers
    C - Program and procedure

Problems
1. Form perception
2. Basic pattern areas
3a. Texture archetypes: introduction
4. Form genesis
5. Aleatory form
6. Curvilinear form
7. Form and content
8. Visual organization
9. Color attributes
10. Color scales
11. Color analysis of scene
12. Color expression
13. Color and space
14. Color coding
15. Rhythmical organization
16. Rhythm and modulation
3b. Texture archetypes: conclusion
17. Texture, space, and scale

Postscript - A Valediction

Appendices
A - Film program
B - References
C - Quizzes

287 pp. 21 chapters in 3 parts. Drawings, photographs, charts, references, appendices. ISBN 0-295-95712-3. (ISBN 0-295-95786-7)

268
Tillitt, David N.
Petersen, Rohn J.
Smith, Robert L.

Performance and Design Requirements for a Graphics Display Research Facility
1982

technical report

(report number NUREG/CR-2711; EG&G Idaho, Inc.; sponsored by U.S. Nuclear Regulatory Commission; June 1982)

This report gives an overview of a graphics display research facility (GDRF) presently being planned by the U.S. Nucear Regulatory Commission. Performance requirements, design requirements, and implementation of the GDRF are the focus of this report.

Research sponsored by the Nuclear Regulatory Commission (NRC) but conducted through collaboration or by subcontracts with independent researchers often does not satisfy the needs of the NRC for timely research on specific topics relevant to regulatory decisions. A graphics display research facility (GDRF) is presently being designed by the NRC as a means to obtain better control of its research efforts and to obtain "objective data on man-machine relationships directly affecting the display of information and making of decisions in nuclear facilities." This GDRF is to be "an evolutionary, computer-based experimentation center for addressing long-term issues associated with automation, human performance, and risk in the operation of nuclear facilities." The authors of this report estimate that in time up to seventy percent of all NRC research in the area of human factors could be conducted at the GDRF. The facility will be designed for both laboratory and field research. The present report is a planning tool in which performance and design requirements of the GDRF are described and some aspects of implementation discussed. The report identifies the resources needed to create the facility, including hardware, software, personnel, and monetary resources. Budgetary information is discussed and GDRF objectives are identified. This publication is competently written, though its style is somewhat laborious. The report, which only considers major requirements of the facility, is written for the NRC and for research sponsors, facility designers, and researchers involved in the project. Other research facilities projects might find the requirements analysis described here useful in their own development.

CONTENTS

ABSTRACT

DEFINITION OF TERMS

PART I: GENERAL INFORMATION

1: Background

2: Scope

3: Purpose of Facility

4: Objectives—Measurable Research Targets

    4.1. Regulatory objectives

    4.2. Administrative objectives

5: Advantages of the GDRF

6: GDRF Effectiveness in Addressing Research Issues

PART II: PERFORMANCE REQUIREMENTS

1: Systems

    1.1. Control and measurement systems

    1.2. Man-machine interface systems

    1.3. Driver systems

    1.4. Analysis and communications systems

2: Agency and User

    2.1. Sponsor

    2.2. Researchers

    2.3. Developer

    2.4. Operators

3: Building

PART III: DESIGN REQUIREMENTS

1: General

    1.1. Architecture

    1.2. Standards

    1.3. Complexity

    1.4. Growth

2: Equipment

    2.1. Computing elements

    2.2. Man-machine interfaces

    2.3. Peripherals

    2.4. Networks

3: Software
    3.1. System software
    3.2. Applications software

4: Facility
    4.1. Operations and testing areas
    4.2. Electromechanical support facilities
    4.3. Security and protection facilities

PART IV: IMPLEMENTATION CONSIDERATIONS

1: Evolutionary Needs

2: Phased Implementation
    2.1. Strategy
    2.2. Resource requirements

3: Costing and Scheduling
    3.1. Costs
    3.2. Work breakdown structure
    3.3. Scheduling

REFERENCES

55 pp. 16 chapters in 4 parts. Figures, tables, models, references.

269
Tinker, Miles A.

Legibility of Print
Iowa State University Press, 1963

A detailed account of research conducted on the legibility of printed material. It is one in a series of volumes focusing on research topics in human communication.

Legibility, though often confused with readability, is defined as the coordination of shapes of letters and other symbols, characteristic word forms, and other typographical variables (type size, line width, leading, and print color) to facilitate ease and speed of reading. With improved technology and a departure from the primary concern about the aesthetics of print appearance, a scientific typography has slowly emerged. To formulate his more generalized definition, Tinker has summarized eight common techniques and methodologies used in the past to examine the legibility of print. These techniques are: speed of perception, perceptibility at a distance, perceptibility in peripheral vision, visibility, the Reflex Blink Technique, rate of work, eye movement, and fatigue in reading. Numerous tables and charts illustrate the concepts and the extensive bibliography details 238 sources. Supplementary and survey material is provided throughout the book. Though published in 1963, this book contains relevant information for the educator, practitioner, and the researcher concerned with improving communication through written text.

CONTENTS
    1. Introduction
    2. Methodology and definitions
    3. Legibility of letters and digits
    4. Kinds of type
    5. Size of type

6. Width of line
7. Leading and relationship of leading, type size, and line width
8. Spatial arrangements of the printed page
9. Color of print and background
10. Printing surfaces
11. Cumulative effect of combining nonoptimal typographical arrangements
12. Newspaper typography
13. Formulas and mathematical tables
14. Special printing situations
15. Illumination for reading
16. The hygienic reading situation
Bibliography
Index

329 pp. 16 chapters. Tables, general index, bibliography. ISBN 0-8138-2450-8.

270
Tinker, Miles A.

Bases for Effective Reading
University of Minnesota Press, 1965

Examines the psychological factors related to reading proficiency. Based upon thirty-two years of research at the University of Minnesota, this book provides a well-documented analysis of the reading process and suggests ways in which reading may be facilitated.

Part one explores the manner in which children and adults perceive words and comprehend meaning. This takes into consideration individual differences in mental abilities, as well as the degree to which the mechanics of reading have been mastered. Part two describes the mechanics of reading in relation to the dynamics of eye movement. The reading process is then shown to incorporate saccadic eye movements and fixation pauses. Part three considers typographical features such as size of type, line width, and their relation to the efficient reading of printed material. Part four focuses on lighting and its effect on visual efficiency, considering light color and intensity and suggesting ways to minimize visual fatigue. Part five reviews various methods for evaluating reading ability and diagnosing deficiencies. These include reading readiness tests, standardized survey tests, diagnostic tests, and tests of comprehension, vocabulary, reading speed, and reading interests. This book will be of special interest to reading teachers and researchers in the field, as well as to publishers and printers.

CONTENTS
Preface

Part One: About Reading, Perception, and Comprehension
1. Introduction
2. Perception in reading among adults
3. Perception in reading among children
4. Comprehension in reading

Part Two: Eye Movement in Reading
5. Nature and measure of eye movements
6. Time relations for eye-movement measures in reading
7. Variations of eye movements in reading
8. Eye movements in special reading situations
9. Role of eye movements in improving reading

Part Three: Scientific Typography: Printing for Easy and Efficient Reading
10. Nature of legibility
11. Legibility of type for adult books
12. Typography for children's books
13. Color and surfaces of printing paper
14. Newspaper typography
15. Spatial arrangement and position of the printed page
16. Special typographical arrangement

Part Four: Visual Functions and Illumination for Reading
17. Physiological factors influencing the hygiene of vision
18. Basic considerations in illumination and vision
19. Illumination for reading
20. The reading situation

Part Five: Appraisal of Reading Proficiency
21. Nature of reading appraisal
22. Techniques of appraisal
23. Appraisal in specific areas

Bibliography

Index

322 pp. 23 chapters in 5 parts. Figures, tables, general index, bibliography. ISBN 0-8166-0363-4.

271

Treurniet, W.C.

technical report

Display of Text on Television
1981

(report number CRC-TN-705-E; Communications Research Centre, Canada; May 1981)

Addresses technical and graphic design problems related to the display of information from central databases on color television receivers.

The ideal in presenting graphics and text on a television screen is an image that conforms to the average viewer's visual capabilities and preferences. This report briefly discusses certain aspects of North American television standards and presents experiments and demonstrations relevant to the display of static video imagery, mainly in terms of resolution and image flicker. The experiments, using a validated speed of reading test, examine the readability of upper versus lower case text, character and size spacing, placement of accents, proportional spacing of letters, width of the space character, and space between letters and lines. Additional discussion centers on the question of Red-Green-Blue versus composite video. In summary, the report lists specific recommendations regarding the display of text on a screen with 240 × 320 pixel resolution. The report is well organized and easy to read. Though slightly dated, it may be of interest to behavioral and social scientists, human factors engineers, and display design researchers. The report was originally prepared to propose standards for the Canadian Department of Communication's project to promote videotex services, and would be of interest to others working with videotex display.

CONTENTS

SUMMARY

ABSTRACT

INTRODUCTION

1: CURRENT TELEVISION STANDARDS

1.1: Resolution

1.2: Flicker

2: THE DISPLAY OF TEXT ON TELEVISION

2.1: Experiments Measuring Performance
  2.1.1. Upper case versus lower case
  2.1.2. Character size and spacing

2.2: Experiments Measuring Viewer Preference
  2.2.1. Placement of accents
  2.2.2. Proportional spacing of letters
  2.2.3. Width of the space character
  2.2.4. Space between letters and between lines

2.3: Red-Green-Blue (RGB) Versus NTSC Composite Video

3: CHARACTER SET DESIGN

4: CONCLUSIONS

5: ACKNOWLEDGEMENTS

6: REFERENCES

49 pp. 6 sections. Photographs, figures, tables, references.

272
Trumbo, Bruce E.

technical report

A Theory for Coloring Bivariate Statistical Maps
1980

(report number TR-44; Department of Statistics, Stanford University; sponsored by SIAM Institute for Mathematics and Society; December 1980)

Presents the development of a set of principles suggesting the effective color schemes to use in designing bivariate statistical maps.

Trumbo applies color theory to the goal of developing bivariate color maps which can be easily and accurately read without excessive reference to the key. He illustrates his work with reference to color schemes developed by the U.S. Bureau of the Census and to suggested improvements on these schemes. The types, purposes, and constraints of bivatiate maps are discussed, and other work in the area reviewed. Two models of color theory are summarized (Ostwald's and Hickethier's); hue, saturation, and brightness are briefly explained; and additive, subtractive, and partitive models of color mixing are discussed. Principles of color selection are developed based on the map's purpose and then reformulated in terms of the color models described. Specific types of color schemes are suggested by these principles; these are presented and their implications for empirical testing are discussed. In conclusion, the author suggests that, based on the theoretical considerations detailed in the report, certain map coloring schemes are more likely to produce good results than others in specific applications. It is regrettable that this work could not be illustrated in color, but it is clearly written and the diagrams are informative.

51 pp. Drawings, tables, references.

273
Tschichold, Jan

Asymmetric Typography
Faber and Faber, 1967

(translation by Ruari McLean of Tschichold's *Typographische Gestaltung,* 1935)

A classic work by one of the twentieth century's leading typographers.

This slim volume by one of the great craftsmen of typography was originally published in German in 1935. Although it was not translated into English for thirty years, Tschichold's translator states unequivocally that "the principles of asymmetric typography as stated by Tschichold in 1935 are still sound and true." In this classic work the master typographer's thesis is that the basic principle of centering, used consistently from Gutenberg until the 1920's, is only one of the possibilities open to the typographer (or the display designer). Tschichold treats briefly, and with authority, all of the major concerns: type sizes and forms, the importance of layout, use of space, richness of form, the use of color, and the possibilities raised by the merger of word and picture in photomontage. While the author was writing before the computer age, he has much to teach those who follow him. In his own words, "We can, today, develop the methods of the new typography, extend its use, and carry this activity into new areas." This work should be considered important reading by anyone concerned with the written word in any form.

CONTENTS
    Translator's foreword
    Introduction
        W.E. Trevett
    Author's note
    Historical survey
    Decorative typography
    The meaning and aim of the new or functional typography
    Types

Hand composition and machine composition
The word
The line
Emphasis on the line
Leading, length of lines and grouping
Indentation and line endings
Type sizes, headings and type mixtures
Jobbing work
The use of space
Tables
Rules
Colours
Paper
Posters
Richness of form
Abstract art
Typography, photography and drawings
The book today
Other books by the author in print

94 pp. Drawings, photographs, tables.

274
Tufte, Edward R.

The Visual Display of Quantitative Information
Graphics Press, 1983

This immensely practical and visually exciting book utilizes words, charts, graphs, and mathematical formulas to show how to improve the graphical communication of complex data.

The author first employs a historical analysis to illustrate types of errors in communicating data through graphs, and then proposes a theory of data graphics. The first part of the book covers: a historical analysis of the errors and missed opportunities to improve graphical communication; the principles which contribute to an outstanding display of graphic communication; the six points correcting the recurring problem of statistical bias; and the two rules for overcoming communication mediocrity by combining quantitative skill and reader respect. The second part of the work consists of six chapters presenting a theory of data graphics. These chapters cover: the five principles for creating a visually exciting and informationally competent data display; the methods used to avoid graphic artistry that detracts from the information displayed; the principles emphasizing graphic efficiency; the points on well designed graphics that can serve multiple functions; the principles for fitting the greatest amount of information in a small space; and an emphasis on combining visual beauty and pragmatic functionality in designing graphs. The central theme of this graphically well done and easily readable book is the responsibility of the data communicator to display complex, detailed information in a beautiful, clear, subtle, and simple manner.

CONTENTS

Part I: Graphical Practice
    1. Graphical excellence
    2. Graphical integrity
    3. Sources of graphical integrity and sophistication
Part II: Theory of Data Graphics
    4. Data-ink and graphical redesign
    5. Chartjunk: vibrations, grids, and ducks
    6. Data-ink maximization and graphical design
    7. Multifunctioning graphical elements
    8. Data density and small multiples
    9. Aesthetics and technique in data graphical design
    Epilogue: designs for the display of information

197 pp. 9 chapters in 2 parts. Drawings, photographs, maps, graphs, tables, mathematical formulae, footnotes, general index.

275
Turnbull, Arthur T.
Baird, Russell N.

The Graphics of Communication (4ed.)
Holt, Rinehart and Winston, 1980

This work provides a detailed introduction to the theoretical bases and practical applications of graphic communication. The text emphasizes the variety and use of electronic systems.

In this revised fourth edition of their standard graphics textbook, Turnbull and Baird present a comprehensive introduction to the theoretical bases and practical applications of graphic communication. The new edition stresses the impact of computer technology on information processing and its inseparable relationship with improved graphic communication methodologies. After a brief historical overview which covers the evolution of graphic communication from the development of the alphabet to the present, the authors turn to a succinct discussion of information theory and human information processing, concentrating on perceptual learning and cognitive structure. A detailed examination of graphic reproduction processes from the letter press to computerized graphics systems follows. Of special value is the authors' discussion of electronic graphics systems used by specific newspapers, magazines, ad agencies, and insurance companies, and the importance of matching particular systems to individual needs. The authors also survey the varied role of illustrations in graphic communications. Discussion of layout procedures and use of color precedes a treatment of design principles. Application of these principles to magazine, newspaper, and booklet design concludes the work. Numerous illustrations and photographs complement the authors' expansive textual survey. The text's usefulness is further enhanced by helpful checklists at the end of the more technical chapters, three appendices, and an extensive glossary. Though the bibliography is brief, this is an excellent introductory text that can also serve as a useful manual for display designers, editors, and publishers.

CONTENTS

Preface

1: Graphic Communication: Present and Past
Graphic communication today
Graphic communication yesterday

2: Why and How We Read: Human Information Processing
Reading and information
Human information processing

3: Graphic Reproduction Processes and Presses
Fundamentals of offset
Fundamentals of letterpress
Fundamentals of gravure
Fundamentals of screen printing
Photogelatin printing (collotype)
Fundamentals of flexography
Fundamentals of letterset (dry offset)
Fundamentals of thermography
Computerized imaging systems: jet and electrostatic printing
Duplicating and copying systems
Getting the job done: in office or at the printer
Checklist: Printer's specifications

4: Type and Typesetting
Typesetting terminology
Type and typesetting measurements
Type composition

5: Elements of Good Typography
Legibility
Appropriateness of type
Checklist: Typographical rules

6: Using Type Creatively
Visual syntax
Display legibility
The new typography
Symmetrical design
Assymmetrical design
Headline size
Initial letters
Conclusion

7: Electronic Copy Processing Systems
A little bit about bits
From bits to bytes
Computerized electronic copy processing systems
Some typical electronic systems
Tailoring systems to individual needs
In-house systems for ad agencies and PR offices
Other system uses
Wire service systems
Applications of remote terminals
Checklist: Electronic copy processing systems

8: Processing Copy Electronically
　　Working with electronic systems: some basics
　　Learning the VDT keyboard
　　Typewriters and optical character recognition as entry devices
　　Checklist: Electronic copy processing: some helpful hints
9: Preparing Words for Printing: Traditional Methods
　　Copy correction
　　Marking typesetting specifications
　　Copyfitting
　　Fitting display type to space
　　Electronics: a boon for copyfitting
10: Illustrations in Graphic Communication
　　The many functions and forms of illustrations
　　The production aspects of illustrations
　　Adding color to illustrations
　　Processing plates for full color reproduction
11: Preparing Illustrations for Production
　　Cropping photographs
　　Proportioning or scaling illustrations
　　Other methods of altering photo content
　　Processing line drawings
　　Color in illustrations
　　Marking illustrations for reproduction
　　Checklist: Reading proofs of illustrations
12: Preparing of Pasteups (Mechanicals)
　　Who does pasteups and why
　　What makes a good pasteup?
　　Tools needed for preparing camera-ready mechanicals
　　Getting the job done: commercial register work
　　Preparation of mechanicals: tight register work
　　Guidelines and dimension marks
　　Checklist: Mechanicals: some helpful hints
13: Color in Graphic Communication
　　The nature of color
　　Color dimensions in pigment
　　Psychological aspects of color
　　Functions of color
　　Types of color printing
　　The cost factor in color printing
　　Fidelity in process color
　　Checklist: Practical pointers in the use of color
14: Design: Combining Pictures and Words
　　Meaning in design
　　Design vocabulary
　　Putting it all together
　　Design principles
　　Making design articulate

15: Principles of Magazine Layout
   The first step: break-of-the book
   The dimensions of the stage: format
   Some theoretical bases for magazine design
   Achieving meaning through orderly presentation
   Balance and simplicity help create order
   Controlling direction
   Controlling contrast to achieve harmony and unity
   A word about special pages and problem pages
16: Newspaper Design and Layout
   Why newspapers have been "made up" and not designed
   Times are changing—and so are newspapers
   Changes in approach to newspaper page design
   The traditional approach to page layout
   Harmony in newspaper makeup
   Changing traditions
17: Designing Other Printed Literature
   Kinds of direct literature
   What kinds of printed pieces?
   Standard unit sizes `
   Special paper considerations
   Other design considerations
   Checking press sheets
18: Paper: Selection, Folding, Binding, Finishing
   Paper selection
   Basic kinds of paper
   Paper surfaces
   Paper weight and sheet sizes
   Imposition, binding, folding
Appendixes
   A. Some commonly used typefaces
   B. Specifications for this book
   C. Square-inch typefitting table
Bibliography
Glossary
Index

398 pp. 18 chapters. Drawings, photographs, figures, tables, general index, glossary, appendices. ISBN 0-03-021666-4.

276
Tzeng, Ovid J.L.
Singer, Harry
(eds.)
collection

Perception of Print: Reading Research in Experimental Psychology
Lawrence Erlbaum Associates, 1981

Attempts to integrate research from several fields into a usable and useful guide for reading instructors.

This work investigates both the acquisition and the skilled functioning of reading behavior, drawing on research from anthropology, artificial intelligence, linguistics, cognitive and educational psychology, neuroscience, and instructional technology. The papers address applications of instruction and examine experimental approaches to reading processes, including: the word recognition process; componential analysis used to evaluate individual differences in reading ability; speech recoding; orthography; and an interactive model of information processing. The aim of the book is to foster the practical application of diverse research to the specific problems of reading instruction and reading disability.

CONTENTS
Preface
Overview: Relevancy of Experimental Psychology to Reading Instruction
Ovid J.L. Tzeng
1. Teaching the acquisition phase of reading development: an historical perspective
Harry Singer
2. Integration processes in word recognition
Neal F. Johnson
3. Understanding word perception: clues from studying the word-superiority effect
James C. Johnston
4. Words and contexts
Philip B. Gough, Jack A. Alford, Jr., Pamela Holley-Wilcox
5. Processing words in context
Kathryn T. Spoehr, Richard E. Schuberth
6. Exploring the nature of a basic visual-processing component of reading ability
Mark D. Jackson, James L. McClelland
7. Recoding of printed words to internal speech: does recoding come before lexical access?
William P. Banks, Evelyn Oka, Sherrie Shugarman
8. Some aspects of language perception by eye: the beginning reader
Carol A. Fowler
9. What good is orthographic redundancy?
Marilyn Jager Adams
10. Language structure and optimal orthography
William S.-Y. Wang
11. Linguistic determinism: a written language perspective
Ovid J.L. Tzeng, Daisy L. Hung
12. Speech understanding and reading: some differences and similarities
Raymond S. Nickerson
13. Instruction in reading acquisition
Harry Singer
Author index
Subject index

323 pp. 13 chapters. Figures, charts, tables, footnotes, author index, subject index, references. ISBN 0-89859-154-6.

277
Ullman, Shimon

The Interpretation of Visual Motion
The MIT Press, 1979

(from *The MIT Press Series in Artificial Intelligence*, Patrick Henry
Winston, Mike Brady, series eds.)

This highly technical manuscript describes a study with a twofold goal:
"to investigate the process of interpreting visual motion"; and "to
illustrate the computational approach to the study of visual perception."

Two areas are distinguished by the author in this study of the visual
systems: the study of computation; and the study of the mechanisms
that support it. Ullman states: "The computational investigation
concerns the nature of the internal representations used by the visual
system and the processes by which they are derived. The study of the
mechanisms concerns, in the case of biological visual systems, the
neural circuitry in which they are implemented." Though recognizing
the dichotomy between these two areas, the author advocates examining
the task accomplished by the visual system in order to investigate the
computations performed. This approach differs from traditional
research regarding the nature of visual perception in that it allows for
distinct demarcation between the study of a process (vision) and the
study of the physical structure embodying this process (the brain).
Because of its technical and theoretical orientation, this book will be of
interest to that limited group of researchers in artificial intelligence
concerned with visual perception and its application in computer
technology. The author provides introductory comments about theory
and methodology as well as a nomenclature chart to denote
abbreviations in the text. Graphical and tabular representation is used
frequently to illustrate ideas and data.

CONTENTS

Introduction
PART I: THE CORRESPONDENCE PROBLEM
Chapter 1: The Basic Elements Problem
    1.1. Theoretical considerations
    1.2. The correspondence is not a grey level operation
    1.3. The correspondence tokens are not structured forms
Chapter 2: The Correspondence Process
    2.1. The general scheme
    2.2. Affinity
    2.3. Higher order interactions
    2.4. Applications of the competition scheme to examples
    2.5. Affinity and three dimensional interpretation
    2.6. A possible application to object concept incipiency
Chapter 3: The Minimal Mapping Theory of Motion Correspondence
    3.1. Introduction
    3.2. The optimal (independent) correspondence strategy
    3.3. Computational feasibility
    3.4. Computing the minimal mapping by a simple network
    3.5. Preference for one-to-one mappings
    3.6. Properties of the minimal mapping

3.7. The experimental determination of q(v)
3.8. Extensions
3.9. On the relations between chapters 2 and 3
PART II: THREE-DIMENSIONAL INTERPETATION
Chapter 4: The Interpretation of Structure from Motion
    4.1. Structure from parallel projection
    4.2. Criticism of past approaches
    4.3. Reflective constraints
    4.4. The structure from motion interpretation scheme
    4.5. The perspective case
    4.6. Psychological relevance
Chapter 5: The Perception of Motion from Structure
    5.1. The M.f.S. interpretation scheme
    5.2. Ames phenomena and the rivalry between the S.f.M. and the
    M.f.S. schemes
EPILOGUE
    Appendix 1. The structure from motion theorem
    Appendix 2. Structure from perspective projections
Footnotes
References
Index

229 pp. 5 chapters in 2 parts. Figures, graphs, tables, mathematical formulae, models, general index, bibliography, appendices. ISBN 0-262-21007-X.

278
Ullman, Shimon
Richards, Whitman
(eds.)

collection

Image Understanding 1984
Ablex, 1984

This edited collection of scholarly articles contains recent and important investigations into image understanding, otherwise known as computational vision.

This collection defines computational vision as the field of study "aimed at elucidating the computations that underly the extraction and use of visual information by both biological and artificial systems." An introduction describes the current field of computational vision, discussing various problems under investigation and providing an explanation of how each article in the collection fits into the field. The initial article is a reprint of a "classic" study by David Marr in which three levels of visual information processing are described: "incoming images," "visible surfaces," and "three-dimensional objects." Three of the articles in this collection address the "incoming image" level in which analysis focuses on intensity changes of the image. These include an expansion of the work on analysis of intensity changes at varying resolution scales for which Andrew Witkin received the best paper award at the 1983 International Joint Conference on Artificial Intelligence. The remaining six articles (and one note) address the "visible surface" level of analysis in which surface properties, material properties, and 3-D structure are extracted and represented. Four of these articles focus on extracting 3-D information from the image using "shape-from-shading," stereoscopic vision, and "recovery of structure from motion" techniques. The collection includes original work and classic published investigations. It is geared toward the professional or the advanced student in the area of image understanding although, with the help of the editor's thorough introduction, a well-educated reader with a research background could use the collection as an introduction to this complex field.

CONTENTS

Introduction
Shimon Ullman
Chapter 1. Early processing of visual information
David Marr
Chapter 2. Visual hyperacuity: spatiotemporal interpolation in human vision
M. Fahle, T. Poggio
Chapter 3. Scale space filtering: a new approach to multi-scale description
Andrew P. Witkin
Chapter 4. Photometric method for determining shape from shading
Robert J. Woodham
Chapter 5. A computational model of binocular depth perception
J.E.W. Mayhew, H.C. Longuet-Higgins
Chapter 6. Uniqueness and estimation of 3-D motion parameters and surface structures of rigid objects
Roger Y. Tsai, Thomas S. Huang
Chapter 7. Configurations that defeat the 8-point algorithm
H.C. Longuet-Higgins
Chapter 8. The interpretation of a moving retinal image
H.C. Longuet-Higgins, K. Prazdny
Chapter 9. On the reconstruction of visible surfaces
W.E.L. Grimson
Chapter 10. Multiresolution algorithms in computational vision
Demetri Terzopoulos
Author index
Subject index

268 pp. 10 chapters. Drawings, photographs, figures, algorithms, author index, subject index, references. ISBN 0-89391-254-9.

279
Ullner, Michael K.

Parallel Machines for Computer Graphics
University Microfilms International, 1983

(Ph.D. dissertation, California Institute of Technology, 1983)

Discusses parallel circuit applications for computer graphics.

After introducing general points of integrated circuit technology and computer graphics, this thesis discusses two graphics algorithms that benefit from parallel implementations. The first, the ray tracing algorithm, produces realistic computer images by simulating the interaction of light rays with planar surfaces. Though ray tracing is ordinarily a slow method, the required computation times can be reduced by using parallel processors. Three parallel devices exploiting this characteristic are discussed. The first uses a peripheral device to perform the primitive ray tracing computations. The second device uses a pipeline of surface processors to compute ray intersections with the model surface. The third consists of an array of processors; here the polygons are separated into disjoint regions, which are then processed simultaneously. Chapter three presents the second algorithm, which is designed for use on real-time machines. These devices create successive images so rapidly that no individual image is perceptible. The core of the discussion focuses on a scan-line tree, which uses information pipelines and leaf processors to produce segments of the image. Processors at the base of the tree make the final image available. Chapter four contains the author's observations on the potential applications and current limitations of the discussed algorithms. The text concludes with three appendixes, which include: discussions of the operations to evaluate device performance; a method for dividing a modeling space into a grid of subvolumes; and a programming language (Silicon) used for programming circuitry on special purpose chips. This thesis is notable for its clarity. Because both hardware and software considerations play a strong role in the topic, electrical engineers and circuit designers, as well as graphics programmers, would find this work of potential interest.

CONTENTS

ABSTRACT

1: INTRODUCTION

1.1: Integrated Circuit Technology

1.2: Computer Graphics

1.3: Overview

2: RAY TRACING MACHINES

2.1: The Ray Tracing Algorithm

2.2: Computations for Ray Tracing

2.3: A Ray Tracing Peripheral

    2.3.1. Host-peripheral interaction

    2.3.2. Operation of the peripheral

    2.3.3. Implementation of arithmetic

    2.3.4. Analysis

2.4: A Ray Tracing Pipeline
    2.4.1. Operation of the pipeline
    2.4.2. Implementation of arithmetic
    2.4.3. Communications requirements
    2.4.4. Analysis

2.5: Extensions

3: REAL-TIME MACHINES

3.1: Model Preparation

3.2: Previous Parallel Algorithms

3.3: A Scan Line Tree
    3.3.1. Transformation and clipping processors
    3.3.2. Scan conversion processors
    3.3.3. Merging processors
    3.3.4. The pixel conversion processor
    3.3.5. Analysis
    3.3.6. Extensions

3.4: Hidden Line Elimination

4: OBSERVATIONS AND CONCLUSIONS

APPENDIX A: IMPLEMENTING ARITHMETIC

A.1: Using Commercial Components

A.2: Using Custom Components

APPENDIX B: MOVING BETWEEN SUBVOLUMES

APPENDIX C: PROGRAMMING IN SILICON

C.1: Silicon Programming

C.2: Example: Inner Product

C.3: Example: PDP-8

C.4: Example: Convolution

C.5: Example: Self-Sorting Memory

C.6: Example: Two-Dimensional Graphics

C.7: Extensions

C.8: Implementation Overview

C.9: Dataflow Analysis

C.10: Folding

C.11: Size Determination

C.12: Functional Simulation

C.13: Bit Serial Implementation

C.14: Status of the Serial Implementation

C.15: Interactive Implementations

REFERENCES

227 pp. 4 chapters. Figures, graphs, mathematical formulae, algorithms, models, references, appendices.

280
University of Reading.
Department of Typography
and Graphic
Communication

Graphic Communication through ISOTYPE (2ed.)
University of Reading, Department of Typography, 1981

(published in connection with an exhibition recording the fiftieth anniversary of the foundation of the Gesellschafts- und Wirtschaftsmuseum in Wien; University of Reading, Reading, U.K.; May-October 1975; second revised edition)

This exhibit catalogue contains a brief, useful introduction to isotypes and provides important bibliographic references.

Although long out of print, this slim pamphlet has been of interest to students of Otto Neurath's work with universal symbols, or isotypes, and is now available again. Michael Twyman's essay provides an excellent introduction to Neurath's work and traces the history of isotypes. The two-part bibliography—one section of products and applications and one of theories and assessments—will serve to guide the reader to other works in the area. The catalogue of the exhibit, which provided the impetus for this publication, is of somewhat limited interest out of the context of the exhibition.

CONTENTS

The Significance of Isotype
   Michael Twyman
Catalogue of the Exhibition
   The Isotype Movement
   Principles of Isotype
   Working methods
   Products
   Before Isotype
   Influence of Isotype
   Range of work
An Isotype Bibliography
   Part 1: Products and applications
   Part 2: Theory and assessment

48 pp. 3 parts. Drawings, graphs, bibliography, references. (ISBN 0-7049-0480-2)

281
U.S. Joint Army-Navy-Air Force Steering Committee (eds.)

collection

Human Engineering Guide to Equipment Design (rev. ed.)
John Wiley and Sons, 1972

(prepared and edited by Harold P. Van Cott and Robert G. Kinkade of the American Institutes for Research; from the *Selected Government Publications* series)

One of the important "classic" works in the field of human factors engineering; collects extensive reference materials relevant to equipment design and use.

Van Cott and Kinkade chose articles which illuminate the application of human engineering, offering principles, data, and design practices. The opening two chapters review the logic and theories which link human engineering, systems engineering, and behavioral science. Thereafter the book presents materials more directly related to the practical demands of design problems. This material covers: the various forms of data presentation; the design of speech communication devices and human-monitored devices; data entry systems; the design of controls, individual workplaces, and multi-man-machine work areas; engineering anthropology; designing for maintainability; the design of training systems and devices; and the evaluation of human engineering projects. This book is intended for professionals in human engineering and equipment design. Its language, mathematics, and illustrations are advanced, and its references (listed after each article) are concise. Its contributors come from universities, research institutes, industry, and government (including the military). Each article begins with a brief abstract and outline.

CONTENTS
1. System and human engineering analyses
    Jerry S. Kidd, Harold P. Van Cott
2. Man as a system component
    Harold P. Van Cott, Melvin J. Warrick
3. Visual presentation of information
    Walter F. Grether, Charles A. Baker
4. Auditory and other sensory forms of information presentation
    Bruce H. Deatherage
5. Speech communication
    Karl D. Kryter
6. Man-machine dynamics
    George Frost
7. Data entry devices and procedures
    Robert Seibel
8. Design of controls
    Alphonse Chapanis
9. Design of individual workplaces
10. Design of multi-man-machine work areas
    Robert M. Thomson
11. Engineering anthropology
    H.T.E. Hertzberg

12. Designing for maintainability
    Billy M. Crawford, James W. Altman
13. Training system design
    Glenn L. Bryan, James J. Regan
14. Training device design
    Robert G. Kinkade, George R. Wheaton
15. Human engineering tests and evaluation
    Harold P. Van Cott, Alphonse Chapanis
Index

752 pp. 15 chapters. Drawings, photographs, figures, charts, graphs, tables, mathematical formulae, models, general index, references. ISBN 0-471-80011-2.

U.S. Nuclear Regulatory Commission

overview

CRT Display Evaluation
1981-83

These reports describe a series of studies performed to evaluate the effectiveness of the display systems used in nuclear reactor control rooms. Gauge and computer generated screen displays are examined from both an ergonomic and a systems perspective. The reports include checklists and rating sheets which can be adapted for use in evaluating most display systems. The authors emphasize that the evaluation of displays and display systems should be done in the context of the whole system in which they will be used. In the "whole system" they include the installation's purpose, the capabilities and constraints of its components (including its human elements and the physical workspace), and the integration of the components into a functioning unit. The interested reader may want to look at Banks et al., *Human Engineering Design Considerations for CRT Display,* Vols. I and II, and at Tillitt et al., *Performance and Design Requirements for a Graphics Display Research Facility.*

282
U.S. Nuclear Regulatory Commission

technical report

Human Factors Acceptance Criteria for the Safety Parameter Display System
1981

(report number NUREG-0835; Division of Human Factors Safety, U.S. Nuclear Regulatory Commission; October 1981)

This draft report proposes design review acceptance criteria to be used to assess the human factors aspects of computer-generated safety parameter display systems used in nuclear power plants.

The accident at Three Mile Island, along with subsequent investigations, revealed the need for improving systems designed to warn nuclear reactor operators of abnormal plant conditions. The Nuclear Regulatory Commission (NRC) has instructed each operating facility to develop a Safety Parameter Display System (SPDS) which provides information on at least a minimum number of plant parameters indicative of the safety status of the operation. The SPDS should allow swift and accurate identification of the source and location of any factor jeopardizing the safety of the plant. Anticipating that SPDS would be computer-driven CRT displays, this document specifies SPDS design review acceptance criteria which fall within the purview of human factors engineering. The human factors engineering review process is also described step by step. The criteria proposed would be used by the NRC in conducting its review; the findings could then be published in a special report.

CONTENTS

1.0: INTRODUCTION

2.0: SCOPE

3.0: GENERAL ACCEPTANCE CRITERIA FOR SPDS DISPLAYS

3.1: Detection of Abnormal Conditions

3.2: SPDS Data Display Format

3.3: Display Techniques
    3.3.1. Display patterns
    3.3.2. Scaling of displays
    3.3.3. Identification of displayed parameters
    3.3.4. Perceptual aids

4.0: SPECIFIC SPDS DESIGN REVIEW ACCEPTANCE CRITERIA

4.1: Functions
    4.1.1. Primary functions
    4.1.2. Secondary functions
    4.1.3. Future functions

4.2: Data Set
    4.2.1. Basis of parameter selection

4.3: Data Validation
    4.3.1. Real time validation
    4.3.2. Unvalidated data

4.4: Display
    4.4.1. Design principles
    4.4.2. Parameters displayed
    4.4.3. Pattern and coding
    4.4.4. Additional data
    4.4.5. Mode of operation

4.5: Location and Readability
    4.5.1. Display location
    4.5.2. Control board
    4.5.3. Display readability
    4.5.4. Display accessibility
    4.5.5. Control accessibility

4.6: Staff
    4.6.1. Control room staff
    4.6.2. Operator interaction

4.7: Procedures
    4.7.1. Failure recognition
    4.7.2. Technical specification

4.8: Audible Alarms

4.9: Design Criteria
    4.9.1. Functional qualification
    4.9.2. Backup displays
    4.9.3. Primary display, seismically qualified

5.0: HUMAN FACTORS ENGINEERING REVIEW PROCESS

6.0: REFERENCES

APPENDIX A: APPLICATION OF GENERAL CRITERIA TO DISPLAY PATTERNS

58 pp. 6 chapters. Figures, graphs, references, appendix.

283
Gertman, David I.
Blackman, Harold S.
Banks, William W.
Petersen, Rohn J.

technical report

CRT Display Evaluation: The Multidimensional Rating of CRT-Generated Displays
1982

(report number NUREG/CR-2942/EGG-2220; EG&G Idaho, Inc.; sponsored by Office of Nuclear Reactor Research, U.S. Nuclear Regulatory Commission; November 1982)

Describes the development of a multidimensional rating scale for CRT display formats which measures several aspects of operator preference.

The second report in a series examining various methods of evaluating the human factors aspects of CRT display formats. The display formats to be assessed are those utilized in nuclear power plants to apprise operators of plant safety status. This report summarizes the development of a multidimensional rating scale. Nuclear reactor control room operators rated various display formats on several physical and psychological dimensions. Using factor analysis and forced-choice techniques, the authors identified six cognitive dimensions: content density, content integration, format, cognitive fidelity, cognitive processing, and general acceptance. Two of the six dimensions proved successful in discriminating between the three formats used, and the instrument was found to be internally consistent with moderate test-retest reliability. Strength and limitations of the instrument are discussed and the scale is included in the report.

CONTENTS

Abstract

Foreword

Summary

Introduction

Methodology
    Overview
    Subjects
    Standardized instructions
    Apparatus

Results
>   Internal consistency measures
>   Test-retest reliabilities

Conclusions

References

Appendix A: SPD Formats

Appendix B: MDRS Rating Instrument

44 pp. 4 chapters. Figures, tables, references, appendices.

284
Petersen, Rohn J.
Smith, Robert L.
Banks, William W.
Gertman, David I.

An Empirical Examination of Evaluation Methods for Computer Generated Displays: Psychophysics
1982

technical report

(report number NUREG/CR-2916/EGG-2214; EG&G Idaho, Inc.; sponsored by U.S. Nuclear Regulatory Commission; September 1982)

Discussion of psychophysical methods of evaluating the effects of three different CRT display formats on operator performance.

The Nuclear Regulatory Comission (NRC) is concerned that computerized saftey systems should alert operators to possible hazardous conditions within nuclear power plants. This report is part of a larger effort to develop methods of evaluating the human factors considerations of safety parameter display systems (SPDSs). Overall, the program aims to study the interrelationships between various evaluative approaches and develop a protocol of reliable, cost-effective methods for evaluating the effectiveness of computerized displays. In this report, attention is focused on psychophysical methods of objectively assessing the effects of display format on the perceptual performance of plant operators. Operators were asked to identify or locate sources of plant abnormalities or to locate and report on the status of different plant parameters. Using a tachistoscope, very precise measurements were taken of time of display exposure in relation to operator accuracy. Information content was held constant while using three different CRT display formats. The evaluation methods examined in this study were found to be sensitive to performance changes elicited by variations in display format. Task content and operator familiarity with the display formats were also found to have an effect on the results. A valuable study for those concerned with the testing and evaluation of different display formats.

CONTENTS

ABSTRACT

SUMMARY

INTRODUCTION

Background

Objectives

EXPERIMENT 1: DETECTION

Method
    Subjects
    Apparatus
    Instructions to subjects
    Stimuli
    Subject training program
    Test procedure
    Design

Results

Discussion

EXPERIMENT 2: DETECTION

Method

Results

Discussion

EXPERIMENT 3: SPATIAL LOCALIZATION

Method

Results

Discussion

EXPERIMENT 4: PARAMETER RECOGNITION

Method

Results

Discussion

CONCLUSIONS

REFERENCES

APPENDIX A: A PRIMER ON THE THEORY OF SIGNAL DETECTION

APPENDIX B: MANOVA TABLES

44 pp. 6 chapters. Figures, graphs, tables, references, appendices.

285
Blackman, Harold S.
Gertman, David I.
Gilmore, Walter E.
Ford, Robert E.

Noninteractive Simulation Evaluation for CRT-Generated Displays
1983

technical report

(report number NUREG/CR-3556/EGG-2284; EG&G Idaho, Inc.; sponsored by U.S. Nuclear Regulatory Commission; December 1983)

Describes two experiments which are part of an ongoing research effort by the United States Nuclear Regulatory Commission to develop methods for evaluating different displays used in nuclear power plant control rooms.

The experiments tested four display formats (called STAR, BAR, METER, and P-T MAP) similar to actual safety parameter displays currently being developed. The dependent variables in the studies were: time to identify transients appearing on the display screen, confidence in identification of transients, and accuracy of identification of transients. Besides display format, two additional independent variables were used: transient difficulty and workload. The subjects were eighteen experienced nuclear power plant operators, and the two experiments differed only slightly in design. No differences were found in the four display formats. This was not a surprising result since all four formats had been carefully developed applying known information and ergonomic principles. The noninteractive method was determined to be useful in evaluating display capabilities for detection and recognition of transients; the noninteractive method was not found useful for evaluating display capabilities or in aiding operators to follow transients and take corrective actions. The noninteractive simulation method of evaluating computer displays was compared to other evaluation methods: a psychophysics approach, multidimensional scaling, a human factors checklist, and an interactive method. This well-written, technical report is intended for scientists interested in very specific questions, although any reader with a good background in scientific methodology can understand the report.

CONTENTS
ABSTRACT
SUMMARY
INTRODUCTION
PILOT STUDY
Design and Test Subjects
Method
Procedure
Scoring
Pilot Study Results and Discussion
EXPERIMENT I
Design
Test Subjects

Materials
    Safety parameter displays
    Transients
    Workload task
    Comprehension items
    Equipment and experiment work station
Experiment I Procedure
    Scoring
Results
Discussion of Experiment I
EXPERIMENT II
Design
Test Subjects
Materials
    Safety parameter displays
    Transients and comprehension items
    Equipment and experiment work station
Experiment II Procedure
    Scoring
Results
Discussion of Experiment II
GENERAL DISCUSSION
REFERENCES

28 pp. 4 parts. Drawings, figures, graphs, tables, references.

286
Blackman, Harold S.
Gertman, David I.
Gilmore, Walter E.

CRT Display Evaluation: The Checklist Evaluation of CRT-Generated Displays
1983

technical report

(report number NUREG/CR-3557/EGG-2285; EG&G Idaho, Inc.; sponsored by Office of Human Factors Research, U.S. Nuclear Regulatory Commission; December 1983)

Describes the development and testing of a checklist method for evaluating CRT display formats for use in a safety parameter display system (SPDS).

This is the third in a series of reports on a program directed toward developing multimethod evaluation procedures to determine the effectiveness of CRT safety parameter display systems (SPDS). Conducted for the Nuclear Regulatory Commission (NRC), the purpose of this program is to help set minimum standards and acceptance criteria to be used in reviewing the human factors aspects of licensee-developed display designs. This report discusses the development and testing of a checklist instrument. Nuclear reactor control room operators used the checklist to evaluate four display formats: bar, star, meter, and pressure-temperature map. Weights were developed for each scale item by a panel of nine judges using an equal interval Likert scale. Using a principle factoring method with iteration, four empirical factors were identified: display characteristics, information content, information format, and information quality. Data on validity and reliability are presented and the authors conclude that this instrument appears to be acceptable for use in display evaluation. The checklist is included in the report, and recommendations are made for its field use.

CONTENTS

Abstract

Summary

Introduction

Method of Checklist Development
  Item pool development—content validation
  Item review—content validation
  Weight development
  Judge selection
  Empirical validity

Experiment I
  Rationale
  Subjects
  Procedure

Results

Experiment II
  Rationale
  Subjects
  Procedure

Discussion

References

Appendix A: Human Factors Engineering Checklist for CRT Displays and Associated Weights

Appendix B: Description of Safety Parameter Displays

41 pp. 6 chapters. Photographs, figures, tables, references, appendices.

287
Uttal, William R.

A Taxonomy of Visual Processes
Lawrence Erlbaum Associates, 1981

An attempt to combine various theoretical views of perception into a unified metatheory which integrates physical and psychological views into a new taxonomy.

Convinced that the study of perception is dominated by disorderly and encyclopedic enumeration rather than by orderly arrangement and abstraction of general principles, Uttal attempts to organize the empirical data and current theories on visual perception into a unified scheme, a multilevel metatheory using several different kinds of explanation. He argues that much of what has been presented as neurophysiological theories of perception must be considered as metaphorical rather than as valid reductive explanation. This taxonomy uses a series of levels or stages at which the critical events for the individual perceptual processes occur, incorporating neurophysiological ideas as well as psychological concepts and descriptive phenomenology. While the present work examines visual perception, the author suggests that much of what he describes is also applicable to other forms of sensory perception. This volume should be of interest to researchers in the field of perception generally, as well as to visual researchers specifically.

CONTENTS

Preface

PART I: BASIC CONCEPTS

1: Introduction and Perspective
    A. The problem
    B. The issues
    C. The plan of the book

2: Theories of Perception
    A. Introduction
    B. Dimensions of perceptual theories
    C. Macrotheories of perception
    D. An interim summary

3: Foundations of Perceptual Science
    A. An introductory comment
    B. The nature of physical reality—a descent into the microcosm
    C. Photic energy as a stimulus
    D. The anatomy of the visual system
    E. Visual optics
    F. Transducer action in the photoreceptor
    G. A summary

PART II: A TAXONOMIC LEVEL THEORY OF VISUAL PERCEPTION

4: Prolog
    A. An introductory comment
    B. Empirical, logical, and conceptual obstacles to macrotheory development in perceptual science
    C. Attributes of the taxonomic level theory
    D. A comment

5: Level 0: Preneural and Prepsychological Processes Affecting Perception
    A. Introduction
    B. Perceptually significant environmental distortions of the stimulus
    C. Perceptually significant optical properties of the eye
    D. Perceptually significant properties of the ocular media— entophthalmic processes
    E. An interim summary

6: Level 1: Receptor Processes Affecting Perception
   A. Introduction
   B. Perceptual impact of the quantum catch
   C. Perceptual impact of wavelength-dependent absorption
   D. Perceptual impact of photochemical availability
   E. Perceptual impact of receptor and photochemical distribution
   F. Perceptual impact of receptor dynamics
   G. An interim summary

7: Temporal Interactions: A Multilevel Digression
   A. A comment
   B. Background
   C. Latency effects in visual perception
   D. Are there any perceptual effects of on and off transients?
   E. The duration of the visual experience
   F. Afterimages
   G. Visual persistence and short-term memory—iconic storage
   H. Sequential interactions of visual stimuli
   I. Subjective colors
   J. An interim summary

8: Level 2: Neural Interaction Processes Affecting Perception
   A. Introduction
   B. The perceptual impact of neural convergence
   C. The perceptual impact of lateral inhibitory interaction: masking of the third kind
   D. The perceptual impact of more complex network interactions
   E. Miscellaneous effects of neural interactions
   F. An interim summary

9: Mezzolog: On the Limits of Neuroreductionism—A Heretical View
   A. Introduction
   B. Some basic vocabulary
   C. Some current neuroreductionistic theories of perceptual phenomena
   D. A critique of neuroreductionistic theories of perceptual phenomena
   E. Counterindications to contemporary dogma in perceptual neuroreductionism
   F. An interim summary—a contemporary viewpoint

10: Level 3: Unidimensional Processes Affecting Prequantitative Spatial and Figural Organization
   A. Introduction
   B. Processes affecting the initial segregation of objects and fields
   C. Figural organization
   D. An interim summary

11: Level 4: Interdimensional Interactions Leading to Quantitative Perceptual Experiences—Perceptual Relativism
   A. Introduction
   B. Spatial context
   C. Temporal context
   D. Binocular interactions
   E. Multidimensional interactions
   F. An interim summary

12: Epilog: Emerging Principles of Visual Processing
    A. Introduction
    B. Metaprinciples of visual perception
    C. Some disappointments
    D. General principles
References
Author Index
Subject Index

1097 pp. 12 chapters in 2 parts. Drawings, photographs, figures, charts, graphs, tables, mathematical formulae, footnotes, author index, subject index, references. ISBN 0-89859-075-2.

288
Uttal, William R.

Visual Form Detection in Three-Dimensional Space
Lawrence Erlbaum Associates, 1983

(from the *John M. MacEachran Memorial Lecture Series*)

Describes the background, design, and results of a series of experiments involving the perception of form in stereoscopic space. Transcribed from a series of lectures, the presentation is addressed to psychologists and perceptual scientists.

The author provides a brief history of research and thought on form perception, reaching as far back as Plato and Aristotle. He characterizes his own approach as Neo-Gestaltian, emphasizing the importance of a wholistic analysis of perceptual processing. His goal in this study is to progress toward a general understanding of the ways in which humans perceive geometrical forms. The major portion of this book details the design and results of eighteen experiments testing perception of computer-generated stereoscopic stimuli viewed on a split screen oscilloscopic display. These experiments involve the detection of dot formations within a field perceived as a cubical space. Following a discussion of the results, the author proposes an autocorrelation model to explain his findings. Noting that he was able to perform only limited testing of this model due to time constraints, he draws the conclusion that some kind of autocorrelation-like mechanism exists in the visual nervous system.

CONTENTS

Preface
1: Form and Process
    Introduction
    What is a form?
    What is "form perception"?
    Earlier work in two dimensional form detection
    A brief history
2: The Experimental Paradigm
    General procedure
    Observers
    Apparatus
    The perceived cubical space

3: Experimental Design and Results
 Dots
 (Experiments 1-2)
 Lines
 (Experiments 3-6)
 Planes
 (Experiments 7-16)
4: Discussion
 Perceptual significance
 (Supplemental experiments 1-2)
 A formal model
 Final comments
References
 The author's publications
Author Index
Subject Index

163 pp. 4 chapters. Figures, graphs, tables, mathematical formulae, author index, subject index, references. ISBN 0-89859-289-5.

Van Deusen, Edmund   *SEE UNDER ID 107*

289
Vaughan, W.S., Jr.
Kinney, J.A.S.

technical report

Vision-Perception Research and Analyses Relevant to Display Design for Underwater Applications
1980

(Oceanautics, Inc.; sponsored by Engineering Psychology Programs, Office of Naval Research; November 1980)

Reviews and interprets research in the area of visual perception, focusing on how findings in this area can be applied to the design of displays for underwater use.

The report is organized according to issues of importance in underwater display design. Topics covered include: eye to console distance, symbol size, display luminance, peripheral location, and color. The vision-perception literature relevant to each topic is reviewed and pertinent issues discussed. Comparisons are made between design issues and specifications for air and underwater environments. Turbidity is repeatedly brought up as an important factor influencing design. Throughout the report applications of the research findings are discussed for: vehicle consoles, hand-held equipment, and underwater structures. The eye to console distance section of the report focuses on accommodation, the ability of the eye to focus on very close objects. Factors influencing symbol size include turbidity and luminance. In clear water symbol size requirements are less than in an air environment; usually turbidity is present and symbol size requirements are greater than for an air environment. The section on display luminance describes how to measure necessary luminance for dark and illuminated water and discusses the need to measure luminance underwater at the location of the onlooking eye. Issues covered under peripheral location include facemask design and refraction. The section on color compares functions of color in air and water environments. This research report has compiled data that is not easily available elsewhere. This is the first of two reports; the second report will provide display design recommendations for underwater environments. The report is definitely technical, though largely accessible to the nonspecialist. Many references are provided, although a substantial portion of them are to other work done by these authors. This work was originally performed for the U.S. Navy and would also be of interest to the designers of displays to be used with industrial and commercial devices for use underwater, and additionally will interest any student of human vision systems.

CONTENTS

SECTION I: INTRODUCTION

SECTION II: DATABASE OF VISION-PERCEPTION RESEARCH RELEVANT TO DISPLAY DESIGN ISSUES

A: Eye-to-Console Distance
    1. Human factor considerations
    2. Review of research and analyses
    a. Accommodation and age
    b. Eye-to-console distance and eye fatigue
    c. Eye-to console distance and peripheral visual functions
    3. References

B: Symbol Size
    1. Human factor considerations
    2. Review of research and analyses
    3. References

C: Display Luminance
    1. Human factor considerations
    a. Luminance is the measure of light energy appropriate to vision
    b. Luminance at the eye is the design objective
    2. Review of research and analyses
    Case A. Where the display will be viewed in dark water
    Case B. Where the display will be viewed in illuminated water
    3. References

D: Peripheral Location
    1. Human factor considerations
    2. Review of research and analyses
    a. Facemask structure limits the peripheral field
    b. Distortion of the visual image limits the peripheral field
    c. Turbid water limits the peripheral field
    3. References

E: Use of Color
    1. Human factor considerations
    2. Review of research and analyses
    a. Color as an aid to underwater search and detection
    b. Color as an aid to display legibility
    c. Color as an aid to detection of peripheral signals

d. Color as a coding technique
   3. References

56 pp. 5 chapters. Figures, graphs, tables, mathematical formulae, references.

290
Vickers, Douglas

Decision Processes in Visual Perception
Academic Press, 1979

(from the *Academic Press Series in Cognition and Perception*, Edward C. Carterette, Morton P. Friedman, series eds.)

A theoretical presentation of some of the fundamental mechanisms involved in the quantitative processing of visual information by human beings.

In three parts this book constructs "a general theory of perceptual activity in terms of the combination and interconnection of a single type of perceptual unit, distinguishable in terms of both structure and function, and capable of being given an elementary neurophysiological realization." Following basic principles of discrimination, identification, and self-regulation, it demonstrates how a general, adaptive decision module emerges from the multiple constraints that appear to operate in a variety of simple judgmental tasks. A tentative synthesis of traditional approaches to perception is offered, which attempts to clarify the crucial and pervasive role of these modules in the overall activity of perceptual organization. While the evidence considered is almost exclusively behavioral, the constraints used in constructing the theory include some consideration of the neurophysiological plausibility of the elementary mechanism, its potential for evolution, and its biological utility. The various theoretical notions are dealt with in a concrete, intuitive way, but abundant references are given to enable the reader to evaluate the argument in a more rigorous manner. This volume is intended for advanced undergraduates and researchers in experimental and cognitive psychology, particularly in the areas of perception, psychophysics, and human information processing. Anyone concerned with applications of human information processing in the fields of individual differences, human factors research, or the automatic processing of visual information will also find the work of interest.

CONTENTS

Preface

Part I: Simple Decision Processes
   1. Introduction
   2. Early models of discrimination
   3. Recent models of discrimination
   4. Models for three-category tasks and judgments of sameness and difference
   5. Signal detection
Part II: Confidence and Adaptation
   6. Confidence
   7. Adaptation

Part III: Complex Decision Processes
    8. The identification of stimuli
    9. Perceptual organization
    10. Further developments

References

Subject Index

406 pp. 10 chapters in 3 parts. Figures, charts, graphs, tables, abstract formalisms, models, subject index, references. ISBN 0-12-721550-6.

291
Waern, Yvonne
Rollenhagen, Carl

Reading Text from Visual Display Units
1982

technical report

(report number FOA-C-53006-H2; Department of Psychology, University of Stockholm; sponsored by Försvarets Forskningsanstalt; May 1982)

Reviews research data and attempts to identify all factors that contribute to the task of reading text from visual display units, with the eventual aim of evaluating the performance levels of readers.

This report views the reader both as a potentially powerful processor of information and as a human being, subject to an array of variables. By means of a task analysis the authors are able to examine the benefits and drawbacks of VDUs. They concentrate on: factors of situation, such as stress and fatigue; systems of presenting and using the text; text factors, which relate to purpose (task) and the prior knowledge of the reader; and personal factors, such as experience and memory; as well as dependent and independent variables. Emphasizing the concerns and needs of the individual reader, and recognizing those that are universal, the authors suggest a methodology for construction of a useful model. They point out, however, during the course of the article, that there are many areas of reading research which have not been sufficiently covered and could benefit from further study. A reference section provides seven pages of authors and titles in this relatively new area of research.

CONTENTS

ABSTRACT

INTRODUCTION

SITUATIONAL EFFECTS

Fatigue
    Display parameters
    Posture factors
    Environmental factors
    Personal factors
    Concluding remarks

The Stress Concept
Information Processing Psychology
STRESS AND PERFORMANCE
Sleep Deprivation and Its Effect on Performance
TASK ANALYSIS
Systems for Presenting and Handling the Texts
  1. Commands
  2. Presentation manner
  3. Keeping track of position within information
  4. The user as an active participant in the handling of
     information
Reading Purpose
Text Characteristics - Content and Form
ASPECTS OF READING AND METHODOLOGY
Processes during Reading
Reading Results
Metacognition
PSYCHOLOGICAL FRAME, OF REFERENCE
Metacognition
Processes during Reading
Reading Results
CONCLUSIONS FOR PLANNING RESEARCH
Important Independent Variables
  1. Situational factors
  2. System factors
  3. Text factors
  4. Personal factors
Important Dependent Variables
Modeling Reading Processes
REFERENCES
38 pp. References.

292
Wertheim, Alexander H.
Wagenaar, Willem A.
Leibowitz, Herschel W.
(eds.)

collection

Tutorials on Motion Perception
Plenum, 1982

(tutorials presented at the NATO Symposium on the Study of Motion
Perception; Veldhoven, The Netherlands; 24-29 August 1980; vol. 20 in
the *NATO Conference Series on Human Factors*)

Papers on factors which contribute to motion perception and
discussions of various types of motion perception.

The first chapter, written by veteran researcher in the field Hans
Wallach, discusses compensatory eye movements as they relate to
movements of the head in motion perception. The second chapter, by
another research pioneer, Gunnar Johansson, looks at the genetically
encoded neural "hardware" used in visual stimulus processing.

Subsequent chapters cover threshold measurement, stimulus uncertainty, the problem of visual localization, the perception of self motion, and neural components of motion perception. The final chapter explores practical aspects of research in the field, primarily specific problems of vehicle guidance and locomotion. Though chapters are preceded by either helpful summaries or introductions, the book was designed essentially as an advanced text and often includes complex mathematics. It is a comprehensive reference source for psychologists, neurologists, physicists, and other experienced researchers in the field of motion perception. The papers presented here represent substantially revised versions of the tutorials from the symposium; the research papers are published separately in *Acta Psychologica*, Vol. 48, 1981.

CONTENTS

EYE MOVEMENT AND MOTION PERCEPTION
    Hans Wallach

Summary

1: Three Stimuli for Motion Compared

2: Paths that Result from a Combination of Independent Motion Processes

3: Comparison of Three Stimuli for Motion Continued

4: Compensatory Eye Movement

5: Adaptation as Changed Evaluation of Compensatory Eye Movements

References

VISUAL SPACE PERCEPTION THROUGH MOTION
    Gunnar Johansson

Summary

Introduction

1: Proximal Stimulus as an Optic Flow
    1.1. About experimental policy and terminology

2: About the Perceptual Vector Analysis as Demonstrated in Object Motion Research
    2.1. Perception of self-motion and a stationary environment
    2.2. Wide angle simulation and perception of the environment
    2.3. About absolute visual measures of the environment

3: About Perception of the Environment as a Fundamental Frame of Reference for Visual Perception

4: Concluding Remarks

References

THRESHOLDS OF MOTION PERCEPTION
    Claude Bonnet

Introduction

1: A Classification of Motion Displays
    1.1. Single motion
    1.2. Oscillatory motion
    1.3. Frequency motion

2: Assumptions and Processes in Motion Detection
    2.1. Variables for thresholds
    2.2. Motion detection: two analysing systems

3: Experimental Findings
   3.1. Spatio-temporal sensitivity for motion detection
   3.2. Processing velocity vs. processing amplitude
   3.3. Further considerations
4: Effects of Retinal Eccentricity
   4.1. Psychophysical receptive fields and the magnification factor
   4.2. Effects of stationary marks and stationary positions
   4.3. The peripheral retina specialized for motion detection
   4.4. Self motion sensitivity
5: Conclusions
References

PSYCHOPHYSICS OF MOTION PERCEPTION
   Robert Sekuler, Karlene Ball, Paul Tynan, Joan Machamer
Summary
  1: Stimuli and Dependent Measures
  2: Elements of a Model
  3: Extensions to the Simple Model
  4: Studies of Stimulus Uncertainty
   References

VISUAL LOCALIZATION AND EYE MOVEMENTS
   Leonard Matin
1: Introduction
   1.1. The fundamental problem of visual localization
   1.2. Glossary
   1.3. Two types of failure of cancellation theories
   1.4. Brief statement of the main failure (type A) of cancellation
   theory and an important success
   1.5. Defining visual localization
2: Theories of Perceptual Stability
   2.1. Cancellation theories
   2.2. Information-theoretic or cognitive approaches
   2.3. Dual-suppression theory of spatial localization
3: Localization with Steady Gaze
   3.1. Normal observers
   3.2. Experimentally paralyzed observers
4: On Separating Visual Localization from Sensory/Motor Localization
5: Localization in the Presence of Saccadic Eye Movements
   5.1. Introduction
   5.2. Cancellation is not needed for stable visual localization in the
   presence of saccades in structured visual fields
   5.3. Three problems for perceptual stability in the presence of
   saccades
   5.4. Type B (Saccadic) suppression of visibility
   5.5. A failure of cancellation theory: saccades
   5.6. Spatiotemporal characteristics of EEPI used for visual
   localization in the presence of saccades in darkness
   5.7. Influence of visual persistence on visual localization in the
   presence of saccades
   5.8. Influence of visual background on visual localization in the
   presence of saccades
   5.9. Type B (saccadic) suppression for perception of displacement

5.10. Parametric adjustment and visual localization

6: Concluding Remarks
6.1. Unfinished business
6.2. Structured visual fields, sight on one's own body, and differences between visual localization in the horizontal and vertical dimensions

Footnotes

References

LINEAR SELF MOTION PERCEPTION
Alain Berthoz, Jaques Droulez

Introduction

1: Role of the Otoliths in Linear Self Motion Perception
1.1. Specific stimuli for the otolith receptors
1.2. Non-otolithic contribution to self motion perception in darkness
1.3. Threshold measurements
1.4. Interaxis differences
1.5. Dynamics of vestibular linear motion perception

2: Models of Linear Motion Perception of Otolithic Origin
2.1. Afferent processing
2.2. Central processing

3: The Perception of Self Motion Induced by the Visual System
3.1. Physical input of the retina during linear motion: "optic flow"
3.2. Linear vection
3.3. Modeling of linear vection

4: Visual Vestibular Interaction in Linear Self Motion Perception
4.1. Influence of otolithic stimulation on eye movements
4.2. Influence of linear acceleration on perceived image velocity
4.3. Modeling visual vestibular interactions

References

NEURAL SUBSTRATES OF THE VISUAL PERCEPTION OF MOVEMENT
Mark A. Berkley

Introduction

1: Definitions
1.1. Real movement
1.2. Apparent movement
1.3. Temporal response
1.4. Stimulus dimensions

2: Criteria for Establishing the Neural Substrates of Movement Perception
2.1. Direct methods
2.2. Indirect measurement methods

3: Experimental Data
3.1. Neurons that respond to moving stimuli
3.2. Neurons that respond to special classes of movement
3.3. Neurons that respond differentially to self-induced movement
3.4. Selective ablation studies

4: Conclusions

References

IMPLICATIONS OF RECENT DEVELOPMENTS IN DYNAMIC SPATIAL ORIENTATION AND VISUAL RESOLUTION FOR VEHICLE GUIDANCE

Herschel W. Leibowitz, Robert B. Post, Thomas Brandt, Johannes Dichgans

Introduction

1: The Two Modes of Processing Concept

2: The Multisensory Nature of Spatial Orientation

3: Anomalous Myopias and the Intermediate Dark-Focus of Accommodation

4: Some Implications for Selection, Licensing, and Training

    4.1. Night and space myopia

    4.2. Individual differences in the effectiveness of spatial orientation stimuli

    4.3. Contrast sensitivity function

    4.4. Fixational stability

    4.5. Visual vestibular interaction

    4.6. Aircraft simulation design

    4.7. Motor skills

References

INDEX

263 pp. 8 papers. Figures, graphs, tables, models, general index, references. ISBN 0-306-41126-1.

293
Weston, George F.
Bittleston, Richard

Alphanumeric Displays: Devices, Drive Circuits and Applications

McGraw-Hill, 1983

A guide to the design and operation of alphanumeric displays directed toward electronic engineers. It presents information on display technologies and how these relate to real applications.

Written by British research scientists, the book includes an abundance of schematic drawings, graphs, and tables. Theory and applications of display technology are detailed. Additional topics include: presentation of visual information, display requirements, addressing techniques, display techniques, scanned displays, matrix displays, drive circuits, and encoding and data organization. The purpose of the book is to inform engineers on the characteristics and applications of displays and drive circuits. A general survey of display technologies is amplified by extensive analysis of specific "scanned" and "matrix" displays, including CRTs, laser scan, LEDs, liquid crystals, gas discharge, electroluminescence, and incandescent filaments. Other concepts discussed are photometric parameters, legibility, and matrix multiplexing. The mix of human factors and theoretical discussions limits the book's usefulness as a reference for designers and theorists. A good bibliography is provided to guide readers to discussions of more depth.

CONTENTS

Preface

CHAPTER 1: PRESENTATION OF VISUAL INFORMATION

1.1. Introduction

1.2. Display Criteria

1.3. Photometric Parameters

    1.3.1. Luminous intensity

    1.3.2. Luminous flux

    1.3.3. Illuminance

    1.3.4. Luminance

    1.3.5. Luminous efficiency of radiation

    1.3.6. Colour

    1.3.7. Contrast ratio

1.4. Legibility

    1.4.1. Size and shape of the character

    1.4.2. Defects and blemishes

    1.4.3. Flicker and distortion

    1.4.4. Angle of view

1.5. Parameter Measurement and Performance Assessment

References

CHAPTER 2: DISPLAY REQUIREMENTS

2.1. Background

2.2. Applications

2.3. Display Specifications

CHAPTER 3: ADDRESSING TECHNIQUES

3.1. Introduction

3.2. Display Characteristics

    3.2.1. Luminance--voltage (L--V) characteristic

    3.2.2. L--IV characteristic

    3.2.3. I--V characteristic

    3.2.4. Optical and electrical rise and fall times

3.3. Addressing Methods

3.4. Direct Addressing

3.5. Multiplexing

    3.5.1. Operation of matrix multiplexing

    3.5.2. Real time multiplexing (light emitting displays)

    3.5.3. Optical requirements

    3.5.4. Contrast optimisation

    3.5.5. Matrix addressing limitations

    3.5.6. Real time matrix displays in other forms

    3.5.7. Multiple axis matrix multiplexing and storage

    3.5.8. Summary of matrix multiplexing

3.6. Scanning

CHAPTER 4: DISPLAY TECHNOLOGIES

4.1. Classification

4.2. General Survey

    4.2.1. Scanned displays

    4.2.2. Matrix displays

CHAPTER 5: SCANNED DISPLAYS

5.1. The Cathode Ray Tube

5.2. Flat Cathode Ray Tubes

5.3. Projection Systems

5.4. Storage C.R.T.s

5.5. Scanned Light Beam Displays

References

CHAPTER 6: MATRIX DISPLAYS

6.1. Introduction

6.2. Light Emitting Diodes

6.3. Electroluminescent Displays

6.4. Ferroelectric Displays

6.5. Liquid Crystals

6.6. Electrochromic Displays

6.7. Electrophoretic Displays

6.8. Gas Discharge Displays

6.9. Vacuum Fluorescent Displays

6.10. Incandescent Filaments

6.11. Other Displays

References

CHAPTER 7: DRIVE CIRCUITS

7.1. Classification of Drive Circuits

7.2. Light Emitting Diodes

    7.2.1. Multiplexing L.E.D.s

    7.2.2. Output stages

    7.2.3. Grey scale

7.3. Electroluminescent Displays

    7.3.1. A.C. powder

    7.3.2. A.C. thin film

    7.3.3. D.C. electroluminescent displays

7.4. Liquid Crystal Displays

    7.4.1. Multiplexing liquid crystal displays

    7.4.2. Active crosspoint drive

    7.4.3. Laser addressing

7.5. Gas Discharge Displays

    7.5.1. D.C. gas discharge

    7.5.2. A.C. gas discharge

7.6. Vacuum Fluorescent Displays

7.7. Filament Displays

7.8. Cathode Ray Tubes

References

CHAPTER 8: ENCODING AND DATA ORGANISATION

8.1. Introduction

8.2. The Display Subsystem

    8.2.1. Subsystem requirements

    8.2.2. Subsystem interfaces

    8.2.3. Data presentation

8.3. Non-multiplexed Displays

8.4. Matrix Displays

    8.4.1. Data memory

    8.4.2. Control characters and memory mapping

    8.4.3. Refresh circuits

    8.4.4. Interfacing with the display drive

    8.4.5. Software versus hardware

8.5. Other Facilities

8.6. High Resolution Displays

CHAPTER 9: APPLICATIONS

9.1. Introduction

9.2. The Pocket Calculator and Other Hand Held Instruments

9.3. The Digital Meter

9.4. Low Cost Data Terminal

9.5. Graphic Terminals

9.6. Full Page Editors

9.7. Conclusions

References

APPENDIX: LUMINANCE AND ILLUMINANCE CONVERSION TABLES

INDEX

194 pp. 9 chapters. Drawings, photographs, figures, charts, graphs, tables, general index, references, appendix. ISBN 0-07-069468-0.

294
White, Jan V.

Editing by Design: A Guide to Effective Word-and-Picture Communication for Editors and Designers (2ed.)
Bowker, 1982

A basic primer for magazine editors and designers. Its purpose is to combine the two normally separate functions of editing and design.

This work is a valuable tool for anyone whose business it is to transmit ideas and information visually. It is concise, well-written, and sufficiently comprehensive to expose the reader to all the relevant issues. This second edition of *Editing by Design* reproduces the information in the original text, updates information in light of changes in magazine making technology, and offers several new features. It differs from the first edition primarily in the addition of an analysis of the magazine as a physical object; how it is to be read and held affects the way that it is designed. There are also many new patterns for column grids, additional ways of handling pictures, and a section on what to do with pictures of people. There is also an expanded section on blending words with pictures. The author perceives the magazine (book, computer display printout) as a three-dimensional object, an approach that encourages continuity in style, design, and layout. This book discusses not only *how* to edit by design, but focuses on *why* certain approaches work and others don't. The book is divided into seven long chapters, each of which treats a specific part of the publication process, such as typography, illustrations, and color. Each part has a series of clearly defined subdivisions that enable the reader to find specific information quickly. There is also a useful glossary of printing terms. The book is profusely illustrated and the relationship between the illustrations and the text is excellent, showing that the author knows how to put the ideas he discusses into practice. Jan White has been responsible for designing and redesigning the formats of over 120 magazines, newletters, tabloids, and books, and is the author of a companion volume to this book, *Designing for Magazines: Common Problems, Realistic Solutions*. This book is highly recommended as a good basic introduction for those who wish to improve their understanding of design and layout.

CONTENTS

PREFACE

1: EDITING BY DESIGN

Editing

Design and the Designer

Layout and Styling
    Criteria for styling

2: THE MAGAZINE: OBJECT IN THREE DIMENSIONS

How We Hold the Product

How We Look At, Then Read, the Product
    Riffling the pages
    Reading the stories

Essential Equipment to Encourage Thinking in 3-D
    The working space
    Forms for planning the issue
    Assembling the issue in miniature

Exploiting the Third Dimension
    The spread
    The flow of spreads
    Horizontal alignment
    Horizontal modules
    Making the spread appear wider
    Typing pages together

Making the Most of the Scattered Pages
    Interrelationship of all editorial spaces
    Rhythmic repetition
    Graphic signals
    Deep head margins

3: THE PAGE: PATTERNS AND POTENTIALS

Margins

Columns

The Grid

Working with the Page
    White space
    Concentration of elements
    Contrasting elements
    Camouflaging
    Predetermined character

Unusual Devices

4: TYPE: THE PUBLICATION'S FABRIC

Principles of Effective Magazine Typography
    Restriction of typefaces
    Keeping in the family
    Standardization of column patterns
    Standardization of type specifications
    Consistent application of type
    The problem of type size

Some Do's and Don'ts in Type
    Type as tone of voice
    Italics: pros and cons
    All capitals: pros and cons
    Upper- and lowercase heads: cons
    Color and texture of type: justifying lines
    Color and texture of type: justifying columns
    Breaking up the text
    Neat columns
    Indenting
    Long headlines
    Restrained type in headlines
    Ragged-right setting
    Flush left feels right
    Captions
    Runarounds
    Breaking the rules

5: ILLUSTRATIONS: PHOTOGRAPHS AND PICTURES

Two Perils in Pictures
    Pictures show too much
    Pictures are not The Universal Panacea

What Is a Good Picture?

The Danger in Pretty Pictures

An Essential Investment in Time: The Story Conference

An Essential Investment of Money: Photostats

Choosing the Right Picture
    Seeing what is available
    Using the safe shot (or not)
    Just any old picture doesn't help much
    The grabbers
    The explainers
    Money and the hard-to-photograph

Seeing differently
Questionable quality
Symbolism in pictures
Mood shots
Picture files
Sizing the Picture
Size as indicator of importance
Size as a relative concept
Size as expression of story line
Bleeding pictures
Editing with Words and Pictures
Relationship of words to pictures
One picture, one message
The picture-caption presentation
Making the Most of the Available Material
Combining small elements into groups
Placement of the picture in imitation of the angle of the shot
The direction in which the people in the picture are looking
People Pictures
Sequences
The Horizon
Focusing Attention onto the Critical Area
By words
By cropping
By manipulating the image
Multisubject Pictures
Splitting the caption
Splitting the picture
Labeling the elements
Getting Extra Mileage from One Picture
Repetition of sections
Repetition and superimposition in varied sizes
Flopping left to right and upside-down
Dismembering into patterns
Using the Negative
Cutting the Picture into Strips
Pictures of Pictures
Partial Silhouetting
Silhouetting
Vignetting
Nonrectangular Shapes
Picture Frames
Rounded Corners and Photographic Realism
Blending Words with Pictures
Picture-Drawing Combinations
6: ILLUSTRATIONS: NONPICTORIAL
Charts and Graphs
Effectiveness
Simplicity
Headings and titles
Grids and graphics
Varieties

Pie charts, bar charts, graphs

Tables and Typographic "Illustrations"

Illustrations the Printer Can Supply
    Rules
    Borders
    Boxes
    Ornaments
    Initials and large type
    Free-floating sentences
    Headlines as "art"
    Variation of type size in body copy
    Variation of type color in body copy
    Floating subheads
    Repeated words
    Words and lines
    Text set in shapes
    Type as pictorial image

Illustrations Bought at the Store
    From the stationery store
    From the art supply store
    From the Post Office
    From the bank

No Illustration at All

Homemade Illustrations

Photomechanical Variations
    Halftone screens
    Dropout halftones
    Linecuts
    Line conversions and posterizations
    Photographic distortions

7: COLOR

Buildup

Color Used Functionally

How the Four Basic Functions Affect Color Choice
    Color as background tint
    Color as decoration
    Color as articulator of details
    Color as a tool for emphasis

Process Colors and Second Colors

How and Where to Use Color
    In pictures
    In words
    In panels
    In line art
    In charts, maps, graphs, plans, diagrams, tables
    In rules and decorative elements

GLOSSARY

INDEX

248 pp. 7 chapters. Drawings, photographs, figures, charts, graphs, general index, glossary. (ISBN 0-8352-1508-3)

295
White, Jan V.

Mastering Graphics: Design and Production Made Easy
Bowker, 1983

A very complete step-by-step graphic design guidebook which
anticipates publication problems and offers solutions.

With much detail the author presents many graphics design questions
and answers in areas such as format, typography, color use,
photography, paper selection, printing type, and binding. Some five
hundred illustrations and half-tones demonstrate logos, type face and
style, picture cropping and proportioning, headlines, mechanical layouts,
and some terminology. Technical terms and concepts are highlighted in
boldface type throughout the text. The book has an easy to follow
format and an attractive layout. Treatment of type and photography are
notable because they are both comprehensive and innovative.
Techniques to enhance a work's overall effectiveness by highlighting
central concepts are presented. These include the effective use of
cropping and framing, combining words with pictures, manipulating
images for symbolic purposes, and the use of color. Especially useful to
newsletter, newspaper, and magazine layout editors and students of
written communications and publication design.

CONTENTS

Introduction

1: Which Will You Choose: Newsletter, Magazine, Magapaper, Magtab,
or Tabloid?
    Newsletters
    Magazines
    Magapapers, magtabs, and tabloids

2: Make the Publication's Name Its Hallmark
    The difference between logo, nameplate, flag, and masthead
    Where to put your name on the page
    How to make the name impossible to miss
    Your name/your self: why you ought to personalize it
    How to make the name look different
    Enriching the name's effectiveness with color
    How to make your own special logo
    How to achieve the personalized look once the name is in type

3: How to Make the Most of Typewriter "Typography"
    Typewriter type, strike-on type, cold type: what they are
    How long should typewritten lines be?
    Should you use ragged-right or justified typewriter typing?
    How to reduce the scale of typewriter type
    Enlarging the paste-up to accommodate reduced typewriting
    The problem of creating emphasis in typewritten copy
    How to make headlines using your typewriter
    How to make sideheads on your typewriter
    How to make lists on your typewriter
    Big initials added to typewritten copy
    How to handle standing art with typewriters

4: Using Type Effectively
    Tone-of-voice typography
    What face to use?
    The confusion about names of typefaces
    Preparing copy for setting in type
    Specifying type: how to instruct the typesetter
    Type measurement
    Copyfitting: how much space will the words take in type?
    Copyfitting large-size type
    Proofs
    Body copy or text faces
    Sans serif vs. serif faces for body copy
    Line spacing, leading, interlinear spacing
    How long should the lines be?
    Should type be set justified or ragged?
    Display type
    Headlines
    How big should headlines be?
    What is the best place on the page to put your headline?
    A few technical terms about headlines
    Legibility of headlines: all cap, up-and-down style, or downstyle
    Decks and blurbs
    Captions, legends, cutlines
    Catch lines or boldface lead-ins
    Bylines
5: Tips to Help You Take Better Photos for Your Publication
    Move in as close as you can
    Use lenses that will move in close for you
    Having everything in focus is dull
    Put the center of interest elsewhere than plumb in the middle
    Make something dominant in every picture
    Compose your shots with an awareness of the lines of force
    Allow moving objects plenty of space
    Use the rectangle format to best advantage
    Enliven your picture with foreground interest
    Pick a background that explains the character of the personality
    Don't let the background become a nasty surprise
    Watch out for booby traps
    Check the edges of the picture in your viewfinder before you shoot
    Shoot people as the individuals they are
    Bunch people into tight groups
    Figure out fresh angles for cliché situations
    Sunlight is great, except that it makes strong shadows
    Flashbulbs create shadow monsters on walls
    Don't blind your subjects by shooting flash too close
    If you want animated reactions from people, be funny
6: People Pictures Don't Have to Be Boring
    The individual mug shot and how to make it more interesting
    Five common sense principles for using people pictures
    Make the best of those unavoidable catalog arrangements
    Cluster individual shots into close groupings

7: Tips to Make More Effective Use of Pictures
Option 1: Throw the ugly ones out
Option 2: Make the best of what you've got
The pretty picture: beguiling, but off the point
The awful picture: depressing, but informative and essential
Have the courage needed to use that unexpected image
How bleeds create an illusion of size
Interrupt the margin by bleeding pictures
How the reader interprets meaning through size
Why it is wise to crop the picture until it hurts
Crop to make pictures work together better
Crop for continuity of the horizon in neighboring pictures
Edit pictures so one image becomes dominant
Help pictorial scenes by cunning page arrangements
Cluster small, spotty pictures to give them greater visibility
Link images to create a cumulative impact
How to expose the sense of the story in pictures
Publish pictures of pictures
Bring attention to the important part of the image
Do things with the edges of the pictures
Manipulate the image for symbolic purposes
Use partial silhouetting to emphasize action
Combine words with pictures so $1 + 1 = 3$

8: Inescapable Technicalities about Pictures
Must all originals be black-and-white prints?
How can you tell that the picture is the right way 'round?
Why and how do you crop pictures?
How do you scale pictures to the size you want them to be?
How do you inform the cameraman about what you want?
What will the picture look like when it is reduced?
What is a halftone?
Who makes halftones?
What are photomechanical variations?
What is a linecut?
What is a line conversion?
What are screens and shading tints?

9: Illustrations and Their Substitutes: Where to Find Them, How to
Use Them
Custom-made art vs. existing art
Sources for photography: expensive, cheap, free
Old engravings in the public domain
Clip art: its uses and dangers
Transfer art and the easy way to become an "illustrator"
Handwritten notes: art at the end of your arm
Rubber stamps and the danger of being funny
Rules and how to use them to advantage
Boxes: what's in them for you?
Nonpictorial odds and ends as illustrations

10: Making Mechanicals: A Crash Course for the Uninitiated and Disinclined
   Taking the fear out of mechanicals and where to get advice
   The tools and materials you cannot work without
   The need to keep clean
   Working in miniature
   Making a rough dummy
   Practical tips on making mechanicals

11: How to Use Color Effectively (and Stay within Budget)
   Does the purpose for which color is used affect the choice of color?
   What is the difference between process color and second colors?
   What colors should you use?
   Flat color or spot color
   The difference between pictures with color tint and duotones
   Running type in color
   How color separations are made
   Proofs to check what you'll be getting
   Progressive proofs
   How to correct color proofs
   How to get more color for less investment

12: What You Need to Know about Paper
   How big is a piece of paper?
   Basis weight
   Bulking and thickness
   Show-through and opacity
   Brightness
   Shininess
   Finishes
   Colored stock
   Newsprint
   Envelopes

13: What You Absolutely Must Know about Printing, Folding, Binding, and Finishing
   Stenciling it yourself
   Mimeographing
   Photocopying and xerography
   Letterpress
   Offset
   Gravure
   Can you tell the difference between offset, letterpress, and gravure?
   What happens after printing?
   Paper has grain that affects its proper utilization
   How various ways of folding the sheet can be useful
   Binding
   Diecutting
   Perforating
   Laminating
   Mailing and distribution

Index

180 pp. 13 chapters. Drawings, photographs, general index. (ISBN 0-8352-1704-3)

296
White, Jan V.   **Using Charts and Graphs: 1000 Ideas for Visual Persuasion**
Bowker, 1984

A how-to manual and idea book for anyone who wants to learn about using charts and graphs.

This book looks at graphics as a language and teaches the reader how to communicate by visual means. An introductory chapter outlines types of charts and graphs and discusses requirements for making good diagrams (clear ideas, ample time) and characteristics of good diagrams (elegance, clarity, simplicity). The author devotes seven chapters to discussing, in detail, basic chart and graph forms including: pie charts, bar and column charts, dot charts, and maps. He discusses why, how, when, and where to use each different type of diagram and shows the richness of communication value and variety of form that each kind of diagram can produce. One chapter is devoted to understanding figures as symbols and utilizing symbolic meanings of figures in planning a diagram. Another chapter discusses how to combine chart forms into eye-catching hybrids, such as the combination of a pie chart and a bar chart, or the use of a column chart with a photograph. The chapter also discusses graphic tricks by which an artist can manipulate appearances to produce a desired impression. Other chapters describe the use of frames and boxes and discuss ways to physically create charts and graphs. Over 960 illustrations cleverly demonstrate the author's points. Jan V. White is the author of several books about graphics and has designed hundreds of magazines, tabloids, and books. This well-written, easy-to-use book is designed for editors, graphic arts professionals, and any interested laymen.

CONTENTS

1: Diagrams
  Technology and its limitations
  Imagination and its limitless breadth
  Types of charts and diagrams
  Why do we use charts?
  What is needed to make good diagrams?
  Characteristics of a good diagram

2: Pie Charts
  Using the pie chart format
  Comparing segments as pie charts
  Pie pictures
  Tipping the pie
  Three problems with pie charts

3: Bar and Column Charts
  Draftsmanship
  Field, background, grid, labeling
  Segmenting the whole
  Area comparison diagrams
  Step charts or histograms
  Divided bars and columns
  Floating range bars

Sliding bars
Soft columns
Diagonal bars
Pictograms
Comparing grouped columns
Comparing specifics and trends
Comparing complex statistics
Columns and bars in three dimensions
Bars at an angle
Comparing grouped bars in three dimensions
Sliding columns in three dimensions
Bars drawn in perspective
Bars in circles

4: Dot Charts
Graphic variations

5: Curve and Surface Charts
Differences between curve and surface charts
Axes
Plotting the dots
Lines or "curves"
Graphic enrichment of simple charts
Field or background
Logarithmic grids
Percentage comparison charts
Compound surface charts
Surface charts in three dimensions
Curve and surface charts combined
Circular charts
Frames and boxes

6: Flow Charts
Schematic diagrams
Organization charts
Verbal step-by-step diagrams
Process charts
Time lines
Time-and-activity charts

7: Maps
Maps as realistic pictures
Maps of the world seen as projections
World maps stylized
World maps distorted
Maps as background to statistics
Maps as background to movement
Maps as illustration

8: Tables
Verbal tables
Graphic tables
The problem of too many words in tables

9: Frames and Boxes
Combining frames and titles
Grouping frames

10: Graphic symbols
Index to visual interpretations
11: Hybrids
Combining charts with pictures
Combining charts with charts
Manipulating graphics
12: Techniques for Chartmaking
Prerequisite 1: the right physical conditions
Prerequisite 2: the right materials
To draw lines
To add colors and tints
To do the lettering
To subdivide a line into equal segments
To draw a chart at an angle
To draw a chart in perspective
To halve, quarter, or eighth a rectangle
To halve, quarter, or eighth a rectangle in perspective
To split a rectangle in perspective into unequal parts
To split a rectangle in perspective into horizontal layers
To draw an ellipse
To draw a spiral
To prepare charts for 35mm slides
To prepare charts for overhead projectors
To prepare charts for television screens
Index

202 pp. 12 chapters. Drawings, photographs, figures, charts, maps, graphs, general index. (ISBN 0-8352-1894-5)

297
Wickens, Christopher D.   **Engineering Psychology and Human Performance**
Charles E. Merrill, 1984

A much needed textbook which discusses some practical questions of system design from the perspective of theoretical research in cognitive experimental psychology and human performance.

Wickens focuses his study on the information processing capacities of human operators, and limits his discussion to the field of engineering psychology and the answers it holds for questions relating to system design. Wickens sees a close affinity between experimental psychology and the strong theoretical basis of engineering psychology as it has developed during the last thirty years. For him the laws of human behavior revealed through experimental psychology converge with the practical application goals of human factors to produce the field of engineering psychology. While system design solutions are proposed for some areas, the major purpose of the book is to provide a sound theoretical basis for derivation of specific and good human factors principles. Wickens intends to present a theory of human information-processing limitations as it applies to engineering psychology questions (and answers). He states that his work is not intended or organized as a handbook of human factors or engineering psychology. Rather, it is organized according to how the flow of information is processed by a human being. His stated audience includes: psychology students, who will see practical applications for their theoretical knowledge; engineering students, whose designs will benefit from the human limitations input available in the work; and actual practitioners in engineering psychology, human performance, and human factors engineering. With extensive chapter reference lists, supplemental sections in many chapters, a strong theoretical orientation, and Wickens' readable style, this should prove to be an important and valuable new textbook for a variety of courses.

CONTENTS

1: INTRODUCTION TO ENGINEERING PSYCHOLOGY AND HUMAN PERFORMANCE

Engineering Psychology and Human Factors

Human Performance

A Model of Human Information Processing

A Note on Organization

2: SIGNAL DETECTION AND ABSOLUTE JUDGEMENT

Overview

Signal Detection Theory

Applications of Signal Detection Theory

Vigilance

Absolute Judgement

SUPPLEMENT A: The ROC Curve and Information Theory (M)*
    The ROC curve
    Information theory

3: DECISION MAKING

Overview

Human Limits in Decision Making: Statistical Estimation

Human Limits in Decision Making: Statistical Inference

Values and Costs

Learning and Feedback: The Expert Decision Maker

Decision-Making Aids

How Optimal Is Decision Making?

4: PERCEPTION OF VERBAL MATERIAL

Overview

The Perception of Print

Comprehension

SUPPLEMENT B: Speech Perception (M,T)
    Representation of speech
    Units of speech perception
    Top-down processing of speech
    Applications

5: NONVERBAL PERCEPTION

Overview

Holistic Processing

Analog Perception

Space Perception, Maps, and Navigation

6: MEMORY

Overview

Codes in Information Processing

Time-dependent Processes in Working Memory

Long-term Memory

SUPPLEMENT C: Sensory Codes in Memory (T)
    The iconic code (short-term visual store)
    The echonic code (short-term auditory store)
    Iconic versus echonic memory
    Echonic memory versus the phonetic code

7: ATTENTION AND PERCEPTION

Overview

Selective Attention

Focused and Divided Attention

Practical Implications of Research on Focused and Divided Attention

SUPPLEMENT D: Attention and Perception: Theories and Experiments (T)
    Selective attention
    Focused attention
    Divided attention in perception

8: ATTENTION, TIME-SHARING, AND WORKLOAD

Overview

Time-sharing

Mental Workload

9: SELECTION OF ACTION

Overview

Variables Influencing Simple and Choice Reaction Time

Variables Influencing Choice Reaction Time

Departures from Information Theory

Is Information Theory Still Viable?

SUPPLEMENT E: Theories and Models of the Reaction Time Process (T)
    Models of choice reaction time
    Stages in reaction time

10: SERIAL REACTION TIME, TRANSCRIPTIONS, AND ERRORS

Overview

The Psychological Refractory Period

Serial Reaction Time

Errors in Performance

11: CONTINUOUS MANUAL CONTROL

Overview

Open-Loop Motor Skills

Tracking of Dynamic Systems

Multiaxis Control

Modeling the Human Operator in Manual Control

SUPPLEMENT F: Engineering Models of Manual Control (M)
    Frequency-domain representation
    Models of human operator tracking
    The optimal control model

12: PROCESS CONTROL AND AUTOMATION

Process Control

Automation

APPENDIX A: SOME VALUES OF d'

APPENDIX B: VALUES COMPUTED FROM THE FORMULA $A' = 1 - \frac{1}{4}\{P(FA)/P(H) + [1 - P(H)]/[1 - P(FA)]\}$

AUTHOR INDEX

SUBJECT INDEX
    *The material within each supplement is of two kinds. Fairly technical mathematical or quantitative treatments are indicated by M. Fairly theoretical analyses of certain topics with less direct potential applications are indicated by T.

513 pp. 12 chapters. Drawings, photographs, figures, graphs, author index, subject index, references, appendices. ISBN 0-675-20156-X.

298
Winkler, Robert E.

technical report

Readability of Electronic Displays
1979

(report number 79-237T; Department of Industrial Engineering, Kansas State University; sponsored by Air Force Institute of Technology; 1979)

Provides a brief assessment of the display design, human-machine interface, and environmental factors that influence readability of electronic displays and also provides an evaluation of several types of electronic displays.

Each of the display design, human-machine interface, and environmental factors is discussed in a separate section. The author defines each factor, discusses relevant research, and recommends parameters in which the factor should operate most effectively. The advantages and disadvantages of cathode ray tubes, light emitting diodes, liquid crystals, and gas discharge panels as displays are also discussed. All of the areas covered here are given very limited discussion. The literature review amounts to mention of a very small number of studies, with no information provided as to the methodologies used, and a one- or two-sentence summary of research findings; sometimes the study's findings are merely summarized in a table. The author makes his recommendations without providing the reader with the background necessary to evaluate his statements. For the reader wanting a quick outline of human factors relevant to readability of displays, this report will have some value. The reader seeking a thorough treatment will need to investigate further. The reproduction of this report is poor; the print is fuzzy, though readable, and some diagrams are illegible.

CONTENTS

Introduction
Display Design Characteristics
    Symbol size
    Resolution
    Percent active area
    Character generation
    Font
    Stroke width-to-height
    Symbol spacing
    Color
    Contrast
Man-Machine Interface
    Viewing distance
    Viewing angle
    Visual acuity
Environment
    Lighting
    Work area
Types of Displays
Conclusion

15 pp. 6 chapters. Figures, tables, mathematical formulae, references.

299
Wong, Wucius

Principles of Two-Dimensional Design
Van Nostrand Reinhold, 1972

This beginning textbook was written as an introduction to basic design for students with no prior experience in the field.

The principles set forth in this book originated as a series of lectures for a course in two-dimensional display design. The course was offered primarily for students with no design background whatsoever. Wong has produced a concise text accompanied by black-and-white illustrations. He sees good design as a very practical matter and breaks down its various elements into a visual language that even those new to the field will find easy to understand and to use. The four principle elements are conceptual, visual, relational, and practical. It is in their mastery and synthesis that the designer will progress to creative design. In its twelve chapters, this slim volume systematically approaches all the usual design concerns, including form, structure, anomaly, contrast, texture, and space. It distinguishes itself from other books on the subject with its no-nonsense, no-frills approach. Those who are used to the glossy, multi-colored texts that are the norm in this field might be tempted to overlook the understated confidence with which Wong analyzes a complex subject. This book, which is used as an introductory text in many design schools, will be useful for anyone who is looking for a direct approach to the basic problems of good design.

CONTENTS

Chapter 1: Introduction
Chapter 2: Form
Chapter 3: Repetition
Chapter 4: Structure
Chapter 5: Similarity
Chapter 6: Gradation
Chapter 7: Radiation
Chapter 8: Anomaly
Chapter 9: Contrast
Chapter 10: Concentration
Chapter 11: Texture
Chapter 12: Space

96 pp. 12 chapters. Drawings, figures, exercises. (ISBN 0-442-29565-0)

300
Wong, Wucius

Principles of Three-Dimensional Design
Van Nostrand Reinhold, 1977

This basic textbook introduces the novice to the elementary principles of solid geometry in design.

In this book, the author analyzes the problems of three-dimensional design using the same basic premises with which he approached two-dimensional design in his previous work (*Principles of Two-Dimensional Design*). He introduces a basic grammar of three-dimensional form which the reader can then use to generate a language with which to communicate design ideas in solid form. Once again, as in the earlier book, Wong treats his subject with deceptive simplicity. However, he again covers all the basic elements, which in this case include (among others) the plane, wall structures, prisms, polyhedral structures, triangular planes, and linear layers. There are ten chapters and each point is clearly illustrated, both with diagrams and with photographs of three-dimensional structures. This book provides a good basic introduction to the understanding of geometric solids.

CONTENTS

Chapter 1: Introduction
Chapter 2: Serial Planes
Chapter 3: Wall Structures
Chapter 4: Prisms and Cylinders
Chapter 5: Repetition
Chapter 6: Polyhedral Structures
Chapter 7: Triangular Planes
Chapter 8: Linear Framework
Chapter 9: Linear Layers
Chapter 10: Interlinking Lines

112 pp. 10 chapters. Drawings, photographs, figures. (ISBN 0-442-29561-8)

301
Wyszecki, Günter
Stiles, Walter S.

Color Science: Concepts and Methods, Quantitative Data and Formulae (2ed.)
John Wiley and Sons, 1982

(from the *Wiley Series in Pure and Applied Optics,* Joseph W. Goodman, advisory ed.)

This reference work collects detailed and technical information about many aspects of color science, including presentations of numerical information, mathematical algorithms, methodologies of color measurements, and color theory and concepts.

The book's opening chapter presents basic physical data important to color science, including information about radiant energy and optical filters. Later chapters cover: the eye, including data and formulas, with a focus on the part of the "visual process involved in deriving intermediate internal stimuli"; colorimetry, the numerical specification of colored stimuli, including the Commission Internationale de l'Eclairage's (CIE) system of color specification and the concept of trichromatic generalization; photometry, the operation involving matching brightness of colors; "notes on the methods, results, and laws of visual matching"; experimental data and theory on capabilities of the eye to distinguish color attributes such as brightness, hue, and chroma and the possibilities for developing scales for these attributes; visual thresholds; and a limited coverage of models and theories of color vision. The theories of color vision discussed include trichromatic theory, opponent-colors theory, and the zone theory (an integration of the first two). New or expanded topics in this second edition are: Maxwell's method of trichromatic matching, color matching, increment-threshold work, chromatic adaption, and work in color vision. Presentations are concise and quite technical, often including much mathematical discussion. A lengthy appendix provides detailed tables which include mathematical formulae and international standards. Specifically written for professionals in color research and color engineering and for advanced students of color science, this is not an introductory text, and excludes the type of material that would go into a basic work. It contains an extensive reference list and makes recommendations for further reading in topics not exhausted here.

CONTENTS

CHAPTER 1: PHYSICAL DATA

1.1: Basic Radiometric Quantities and Units

1.2: Sources of Radiant Energy

    1.2.1. The sun and daylight

    1.2.2. Thermal radiators

    1.2.3. Electric discharge lamps

    1.2.4. Electroluminescent sources

    1.2.5. Light-emitting diodes

    1.2.6. Lasers

    1.2.7. Sources of ultraviolet radiant energy

    1.2.8. Some photometric and colorimetric characteristics of sources of radiant energy

1.3: Optical Filters

    1.3.1. Absorption filters

    1.3.2. Glass filters

    1.3.3. Gelatin filters

    1.3.4. Liquid filters

    1.3.5. Absorption filters for special applications

    1.3.6. Miscellaneous absorption filters

    1.3.7. Interference filters

    1.3.8. Interference-filter wedges

    1.3.9. Beamsplitters

    1.3.10. Sheet polarizers

    1.3.11. Miscellaneous optical filters

1.4: Reflecting Materials

    1.4.1. Front-surface mirrors

    1.4.2. White reflectance standards

    1.4.3. Colored reflectance standards

    1.4.4. Black surfaces

    1.4.5. Building materials

    1.4.6. Natural objects

1.5: Monochromators

    1.5.1. Basic designs of monochromators

    1.5.2. Resolving power and transmitted radiant flux

    1.5.3. Slit-width correction

    1.5.4. Polarization

    1.5.5. Wavelength calibration

    1.5.6. Stray light

1.6: Physical Detectors of Radiant Energy

    1.6.1. Thermal detectors

    1.6.2. Photon detectors

CHAPTER 2: THE EYE

2.1: Preamble

2.2: The Structure of the Human Eye
  2.2.1. Cornea
  2.2.2. Lens
  2.2.3. Aqueous humor and vitreous body
  2.2.4. The fine-structure of the retina
  2.2.5. Main topographical features of the retina
  2.2.6. The fovea
  2.2.7. The photoreceptors

2.3: Specification of the External Stimulus
  2.3.1. Position in external field
  2.3.2. Radiometric specification
  2.3.3. Photometric specification

2.4: Factors in the Eye That Control the Internal Stimulus
  2.4.1. Image formation by the theoretical eye
  2.4.2. Eye axes and eye angles
  2.4.3. Chromatic aberration of the eye
  2.4.4. The Troland values of retinal illuminance
  2.4.5. Pupil size
  2.4.6. Light losses in the eye
  2.4.7. Fluorescent light in the eye

CHAPTER 3: COLORIMETRY

3.1: Preamble

3.2: Basic Colorimetric Concepts
  3.2.1. Trichromatic generalization
  3.2.2. Tristimulus space
  3.2.3. Basic colorimetric equations
  3.2.4. Imaginary color stimuli
  3.2.5. Colorimetric transformations

3.3: The CIE Colorimetric System
  3.3.1. The CIE 1931 Standard Colorimetric Observer
  3.3.2. The CIE 1964 Supplementary Standard Colorimetric Observer
  3.3.3. Development of the two CIE Standard Observers
  3.3.4. CIE standard illuminants
  3.3.5. CIE standard sources
  3.3.6. Standard of reflectance factor
  3.3.7. Standard illuminating and viewing conditions
  3.3.8. Calculation of CIE tristimulus values and chromaticity coordinates
  3.3.9. CIE uniform color spaces and color-difference formulae
  3.3.10. CIE Metamerism Index for Change in Illuminant
  3.3.11. CIE Color-Rendering Index

3.4: Dominant Wavelength, Excitation Purity, and Colorimetric Purity

3.5: Complementary Color Stimuli

3.6: Maximum Attainable Luminous Efficiency of Color Stimuli of Different Chromaticity

3.7: Optimal Object-Color Stimuli

3.8: Metameric Color Stimuli
    3.8.1. Definition of metamerism
    3.8.2. Methods of generating metamers
    3.8.3. Intersections of spectral reflectance curves of metamers
    3.8.4. Counting metamers
    3.8.5. Boundaries of mismatches of metamers
    3.8.6. Application of linear programming to miscellaneous colorimetric problems

3.9: Colorant Formulation

3.10: Specification of Color Tolerances

3.11: Distribution Temperature, Color Temperature, and Correlated Color Temperature

3.12: Colorimetric Instrumentation
    3.12.1. Spectroradiometers
    3.12.2. Spectrophotometers
    3.12.3. Spectrophotometry of fluorescent materials
    3.12.4. Propagation of random spectrophotometric errors
    3.12.5. Tristimulus-filter colorimeters

CHAPTER 4: PHOTOMETRY

4.1: Basic Photometric Quantities and Units

4.2: The Photometric Principle

4.3: The Standard Photometric System
    4.3.1. Historical note
    4.3.2. Standard photometric observers
    4.3.3. Photometric methods
    4.3.4. Measurement of total luminous flux
    4.3.5. Measurement of luminous intensity and illuminance
    4.3.6. Measurement of luminance

4.4: Calculation of Illuminance Produced by Lambert Sources of Different Shapes

CHAPTER 5: VISUAL EQUIVALENCE AND VISUAL MATCHING

5.1: Preamble

5.2: Classification of Matching Procedures
    5.2.1. Visual equivalence and visual match by strict substitution
    5.2.2. Asymmetric comparison and matching; quasi-symmetric matching
    5.2.3. Limited groups of asymmetric matching procedures
    5.2.4. Matching criteria
    5.2.5. Some particular matching or equivalence procedures

5.3: Maxwell's Method of Color Matching
    5.3.1. Historical note
    5.3.2. Basis of Maxwellian trichromacy
    5.3.3. Maxwell trichromacy and full trichromacy in quasi-symmetric matching
    5.3.4. Maxwell's method in nontrichromatic matching

5.3.5. Maxwellian matching as correlation of stimulus spaces

5.3.6. Maxwellian matching in the weaker sense

5.4: Precision of Color Matching for Normal Trichromats

5.4.1. MacAdam Ellipses

5.4.2. Brown-MacAdam Ellipsoids

5.4.3. Wyszecki-Fielder Ellipsoids

5.4.4. Repeatability of color matching ellipsoids for the same observer

5.4.5. Intercomparison of color-matching ellipses for different observers

5.4.6. Propagation of random errors in colorimetric transformations

5.5: Color-Matching Functions of Normal Trichromats

5.5.1. Two-degree data of Guild and Wright

5.5.2. Judd modification

5.5.3. Stiles two-degree pilot data

5.5.4. Stiles-Burch ten-degree data

5.5.5. ETL ten-degree data

5.5.6. Variations of color matching functions of different normal trichromats

5.6: Factors Modifying Color Matching

5.6.1. Filter pigments in the eye

5.6.2. Rod participation

5.6.3. Location of visual field

5.6.4. Size of visual field

5.6.5. High luminance level

5.6.6. Maxwell method versus maximum-saturation method

5.7: Luminous Efficiency Functions of Normal Trichromats

5.7.1. Matching or equivalence criteria and experimental procedures

5.7.2. Experimental data

5.8: Heterochromatic Brightness Matching of Complex Stimuli

5.8.1. Luminance of equally bright color stimuli

5.8.2. Additivity failures

5.9: Abney and Bezold-Brücke Effects

5.10: Hue Reversals: Brindley Isochromes

5.11: Stiles-Crawford Effect

5.12: Chromatic Adaptation

5.12.1. Asymmetric matching—basic concepts

5.12.2. Experimental procedures and data

5.12.3. A comparison of chromatic-adaption transforms

5.13: Chromatic-Response Functions

5.14: Color-Matching Properties of Color-Defective Observers

5.14.1. Normal and anomalous trichromats

5.14.2. Dichromats

5.14.3. Monochromats

5.15: Instrumentation for Color-Vision Research

5.15.1. Maxwellian view

5.15.2. Measurement of directional sensitivity and increment thresholds

5.15.3. The staircase methods

CHAPTER 6: UNIFORM COLOR SCALES

6.1: Preamble

6.2: Types of Scales and Scaling Methods

6.3: Brightness and Lightness Scales

6.4: Color Scales of Constant Lightness

6.5: Three-Dimensional Color Scales
    6.5.1. Principles of construction
    6.5.2. Color-difference formulae
    6.5.3. White. Whiteness formulae

6.6: Color-Order Systems
    6.6.1. Munsell color systems
    6.6.2. DIN color systems
    6.6.3. Swedish natural color systems
    6.6.4. OSA color systems

CHAPTER 7: VISUAL THRESHOLDS

7.1: Preamble

7.2: General Concepts
    7.2.1. Basic terms and definitions
    7.2.2. Quantum fluctuations and visual stimuli

7.3: Dark Adaptation and Absolute Thresholds
    7.3.1. Recovery of threshold sensitivity; dark-adaptation curves
    7.3.2. Threshold variation over the visual field
    7.3.3. Threshold sensitivity of fully dark-adapted eye
    7.3.4. Absolute threshold values for different conditions of measurement

7.4: Chromatic Adaptation and Increment Thresholds
    7.4.1. Two-color threshold methods
    7.4.2. Basic formulae
    7.4.3. Stiles' mean data
    7.4.4. Specific aspects of π mechanisms and later developments

7.5: Rod Saturation

7.6: Cone Saturation

7.7: Rod and Cone Interactions

7.8: Uniform Equivalence Fields
    7.8.1. Basic formulae

7.9: Spatial and Temporal Factors
    7.9.1. Distinctness of border
    7.9.2. Mach bands
    7.9.3. Flicker

7.10: Discrimination Thresholds
    7.10.1. Luminance differences
    7.10.2. Wavelength differences
    7.10.3. Purity differences
    7.10.4. Color-temperature differences
    7.10.5. Chromaticity differences
    7.10.6. Color-difference matches

CHAPTER 8: THEORIES AND MODELS OF COLOR VISION

8.1: Preamble

8.2: Visual Response Functions and the Spectral Properties of Visual Pigments

8.2.1. Principles of univariance

8.2.2. The visual-pigment layer

8.2.3. Dartnall's standard shape of visual pigment-absorption coefficient

8.2.4. Color-matching data and the spectral absorption curves of visual pigments

8.2.5. Dichromatism and the fundamental spectral sensitivities

8.2.6. Color-matching data and the pigment-bleaching model

8.3: Neural Models

8.3.1. Müller and Judd

8.3.2. Adams

8.3.3. Hurvich and Jameson

8.3.4. Guth

8.3.5. Ingling

8.4: Line Elements of Color Space

8.4.1. Basic concepts

8.4.2. Helmholtz

8.4.3. Schrödinger

8.4.4. Stiles

8.4.5. Trabka

8.4.6. Vos and Walraven

8.4.7. General construction of inductive line elements

APPENDIX OF EXTENDED TABLES AND ILLUSTRATIONS

REFERENCES

AUTHOR INDEX

SUBJECT INDEX

950 pp. 8 chapters. Figures, graphs, tables, mathematical formulae, abstract formalisms, models, author index, subject index, references, appendix. ISBN 0-471-02106-7.

Section II

Appendices

Appendix 1   Recommended Basic Library

The titles listed here form a starting library in display design. They provide the user with basic information on effective visual design.

ID	First Author	Title	Page
5	Angell, Ian O.	A Practical Introduction to Computer Graphics, 1981	12
8	Arnheim, Rudolf	Art and Visual Perception: A Psychology of the Creative Eye (rev. ed.), 1974	18
22	Bertin, Jacques	Semiology of Graphics: Diagrams, Networks, Maps, 1983	54
31	Brisson, David W.	Hypergraphics: Visualizing Complex Relationships in Art, Science and Technology, 1978	73
39	Card, Stuart K.	Psychology of Human-Computer Interaction, 1983	88
48	Chasen, Sylvan H.	Geometric Principles and Procedures for Computer Graphic Applications, 1978	111
54	Carlson, Curtis R.	Visibility of Displayed Information, 1978	124
55	Collins, Belinda L.	The Development and Evaluation of Effective Symbol Signs, 1982	127
69	Easterby, Ronald S.	Information Design: The Design and Evaluation of Signs and Printed Material, 1984	151
75	Fertig, Janet A.	An Inquiry into Effective Design of Graphicolingual Displays for Systems Engineering, 1980	158
79	Foley, James D.	Fundamentals of Interactive Computer Graphics, 1982	169
110	Gregory, Richard L.	Concepts and Mechanisms of Perception, 1974	241
131	Harvard University Laboratory for Computer Graphics and Spatial Analysis	How to Design an Effective Graphics Presentation, 1981	260
156	Jonassen, David H.	The Technology of Text: Principles for Structuring, Designing, and Displaying Text, 1982	294
159	Kantowitz, Barry H.	Human Factors: Understanding People-System Relationships, 1983	301
166	Keates, J.S.	Cartographic Design and Production, 1973	314
170	Knuth, Donald E.	TEX and METAFONT: New Directions in Typesetting, 1979	323
172	Kolers, Paul A.	Processing of Visible Language 1, 1979	327
173	Kolers, Paul A.	Processing of Visible Language 2, 1980	329
181	Marr, David	Vision: A Computational Investigation into the Human Representation and Processing of Visual Information, 1982	343
217	Pavlidis, Theo	Algorithms for Graphics and Image Processing, 1982	412
227	Robinson, Arthur H.	Elements of Cartography (5ed.), 1984	444
229	Rogers, David F.	Procedural Elements for Computer Graphics, 1985	446
230	Rogers, David F.	Mathematical Elements for Computer Graphics, 1976	449
244	Sherr, Sol	Video and Digital Electronic Displays: A User's Guide, 1982	471
250	Snyder, Harry L.	Human Visual Performance and Flat Panel Display Image Quality, 1980	480

267	**Thiel, Philip**	Visual Awareness and Design: An Introductory Program in Conceptual Awareness, Perceptual Sensitivity, and Basic Design Skills, 1981	518
274	**Tufte, Edward R.**	The Visual Display of Quantitative Information, 1983	526
291	**Waern, Yvonne**	Reading Text from Visual Display Units, 1982	553
301	**Wyszecki, Günter**	Color Science: Concepts and Methods, Quantitative Data and Formulae (2ed.), 1982	578

Appendix 2   Design Guidelines

The titles listed here contain design recommendations or requirements. Also included are reference works pertinent to screen displays.

ID	First Author	Title	Page
4	American Institute of Graphic Arts	Symbol Signs, 1981	10
11	Bailey, Robert W.	Human Performance Engineering: A Guide for System Designers, 1982	28
12	Banks, William W.	Human Engineering Design Considerations for Cathode Ray Tube-Generated Displays, 1982	33
13	Banks, William W.	Human Engineering Design Considerations for Cathode Ray Tube-Generated Displays, Volume II, 1983	35
37	Cakir, Ahmet	Visual Display Terminals: A Manual Covering Ergonomics, Workplace Design, Health and Safety, Task Organization, 1980	83
56	Conrac Corporation	Raster Graphics Handbook, 1980	129
57	Cornog, Douglas Y.	Legibility of Alphanumeric Characters and Other Symbols I: A Permuted Title Index and Bibliography, 1964	130
58	Cornog, Douglas Y.	Legibility of Alphanumeric Characters and Other Symbols II: A Reference Handbook, 1967	130
70	Elworth, Charles	Instructor/Operator Display Evaluation Methods, 1981	153
71	Engel, Stephen E.	Guidelines for Man/Display Interfaces, 1975	154
86	Galitz, Wilbert O.	Handbook of Screen Format Design (2ed.), 1985	184
96	Gorrell, E.L.	A Human Engineering Specification for Legibility of Alphanumeric Symbology on Video Monitor Displays (rev.), 1980	207
107	Van Deusen, Edmund	Graphics Standards Handbook, 1985	237
112	Hardesty, George K.C.	NAVSHIPS Display Illumination Design Guide, Section I: Introduction to Light and Color, 1973	245
131	Harvard University Laboratory for Computer Graphics and Spatial Analysis	How to Design an Effective Graphics Presentation, 1981	260
134	Heglin, Howard J.	NAVSHIPS Display Illumination Design Guide, Section II: Human Factors, 1973	261
146	Hubbard, Stuart W.	The Computer Graphics Glossary, 1983	279
168	King, Jean C.	The Designer's Guide to Text Type, 1980	320
185	McLean, Ruari	The Thames and Hudson Manual of Typography, 1980	351
218	Phillips, Arthur H.	Handbook of Computer-Aided Composition, 1980	419
224	Rehe, Rolf F.	Typography: How to Make It Most Legible (rev. ed.), 1984	436
241	Sekuler, Robert	Sourcebook of Temporal Factors Affecting Information Transfer from Visual Displays, 1981	467
246	Smith, Sidney L.	Design Guidelines for User-System Interface Software, 1984	473
262	Stevenson, George A.	Graphic Arts Encyclopedia (2ed.), 1979	502

274   **Tufte, Edward R.**   The Visual Display of Quantitative Information, 1983   526

281   **U.S. Joint Army-Navy-Air Force Steering Committee**   Human Engineering Guide to Equipment Design (rev. ed.), 1972   538

282   **U.S. Nuclear Regulatory Commission**   Human Factors Acceptance Criteria for the Safety Parameter Display System, 1981   539

286   **Blackman, Harold S.**   CRT Display Evaluation: The Checklist Evaluation of CRT-Generated Displays, 1983   545

Appendix 3   Graphics Standards

The titles listed here contain draft proposals for and background work on graphics standards.

ID	First Author	Title	Page
99	American National Standards Institute	Computer Graphics Metafile for the Storage and Transfer of Picture Description Information (draft proposal), 1984	213
100	American National Standards Institute	Graphical Kernel System (draft proposal), 1984	217
101	Computer Graphics	Computer Graphics: Status Report of the Graphic Standards Planning Committee, 1979	220
102	International Organization for Standardization (ISO)	Graphical Kernel Systems (GKS) Functional Description, 1984	223
103	Guedj, Richard A.	Methodology in Computer Graphics: Seillac I, 1979	227
104	Guedj, Richard A.	Methodology of Interaction: Seillac II, 1980	229
107	Van Deusen, Edmund	Graphics Standards Handbook, 1985	237

Appendix 4   Recommended Readings on VDT Health and Safety

In the titles listed here, current knowledge regarding the effects of VDTs on human health and workplace safety is presented and discussed.

ID	First Author	Title	Page
18	Bennett, John	Visual Display Terminals: Usability Issues and Health Concerns, 1984	47
20	Bergqvist, Ulf	Video Display Terminals and Health: A Technical and Medical Appraisal of the State of the Art, 1984	50
28	Boyce, P.R.	Lighting and Visual Display Units, 1981	69
37	Cakir, Ahmet	Visual Display Terminals: A Manual Covering Ergonomics, Workplace Design, Health and Safety, Task Organization, 1980	83
98	Grandjean, Etienne	Ergonomic Aspects of Visual Display Terminals, 1980	209
151	IBM Human Factors Center	Human Factors of Workstations with Visual Displays (3ed.), 1984	285
196	National Research Council. Committee on Vision	Video Displays, Work, and Vision, 1983	368
206	NIOSH	Potential Health Hazards of Video Display Terminals, 1981	392

Section III

Author Index

Author Index

The names listed here include both primary authors for all titles and contributing authors for such works as collections and proceedings. Because the names of authors, particularly in tables of contents for proceedings and collections, may appear in a variety of formats, it was not possible in every case to disambiguate between or among apparent variations on a single name. In most such instances, however, the editors were able to crosscheck multiple referents and to merge the appropriate references.

NOTE: Italicized numbers refer to document ID numbers, not to page numbers.

Abdalla, M.I. *223*
Abelson, H. *1*
Abramov, I. *42*
Abramson, S.R. *255*
Adachi, T. *223*
Adams, J.A. *15, 230*
Adams, M.J. *276*
Agrawal, D.P. *84*
Albers, J. *2*
Albery, W.B. *145*
Albonico, G. *98*
Alexander, C. *3*
Alexander, G.J. *69*
Alford, J.A., Jr. *276*
Allen, R.B. *10*
Allport, A. *172*
Almagor, M. *248*
Alt, P.M. *223*
Altman, J.W. *281*
Amano, Y. *223*
Anderson, D.C. *81*
Anderson, N.H. *88*
Andersson, B. *155*
Andoh, S. *223*
Angell, I.O. *5*
Anson, E. *104*
Anstis, S.M. *110*
Appel, A. *81*
Applegate, S.L. *6*
Arellano, A.G. *223*
Armijo, D.L. *223*
Arnheim, R. *7, 8*
Artwick, B.A. *9*
Asama, K. *223*
Attneave, F. *16*
Azzato, M. *90*
Baddeley, A.D. *172*
Badler, N.I. *93*
Badre, A. *10*
Baecker, R. *15, 81, 104, 173*
Baer, A. *173*
Bagnara, S. *98*
Bailey, R.W. *11*
Bair, J.H. *18*
Baird, R.N. *275*

Baker, C.A. *281*
Baker, R.G. *173*
Baker, W.E. *18*
Ball, K. *292*
Ballantine, M. *222*
Banchoff, T.F. *31*
Bangert, C.J. *177*
Bangert, C.S. *177*
Banks, W.P. *276*
Banks, W.W. *12, 13, 283, 284*
Baraff, D.R. *223*
Barbadillo, M. *177*
Barbe, D.F. *162*
Barclay, D.J. *223*
Barmack, J.E. *14*
Barnard, P. *69, 172*
Barnett, J. *141*
Barrett, R.C. *81*
Bartram, D. *69*
Bassani, G. *98*
Bates, M. *245*
Baty, D.L. *145*
Bauer, D. *98*
Beamon, W.S. *249*
Beaton, R.J. *256*
Beatty, J.C. *15*
Beck, J. *16*
Beidl, J.R. *223*
Belady, L.A. *17*
Bell, R.R. *266*
Beni, G. *164, 223*
Benjamin, M. *212*
Bennett, J. *18*
Bennett, W.S. *235*
Berbaum, K.S. *19*
Bergqvist, U. *20*
Bergström, S.S. *16*
Berkley, M.A. *292*
Berlyne, D.E. *41*
Berreman, D.W. *169*
Berry, B.J.L. *266*
Bersh, P.I. *69*
Berthoz, A. *292*
Bertin, J. *21, 22, 173*
Berwick, S.H. *266*

Biazzo, M.R. *223*
Biberman, L.M. *23, 24*
Billingsley, P.A. *193*
Binaschi, S. *98*
Bird, C.L. *223*
Birnbaum, M.H. *88*
Biskupek, R. *259*
Bittleston, R. *293*
Bittmann, C.A. *223*
Bjørset, H.H. *98*
Blackie, I.T.B. *145*
Blackistone, M. *186*
Blackman, H.S. *13, 283, 285, 286*
Blackmore, J. *223*
Blasgen, M.W. *17*
Blazo, S.F. *223*
Bleha, W.P. *223*
Blinn, J.F. *15, 25, 81*
Blommaert, F.J.J. *98*
Bloom, S. *223*
Bø, K. *103, 104*
Boff, K.R. *90*
Bohr, E. *69*
Bonar, J. *10*
Bonnet, C. *292*
Bono, P.R. *103*
Booth, K.S. *15*
Borgefors, G. *26*
Bosman, I.D. *27*
Boswell, D.D. *223*
Botden, P.J.M. *24*
Bouknight, W.J. *81*
Bouma, H. *98, 172, 173*
Bouwhuis, D.G. *172*
Boyce, P.R. *28*
Boyd, G.D. *223*
Boynton, R.M. *41, 43*
Braid, I.C. *33, 81*
Brandinger, J.J. *161*
Brandt, T. *292*
Braunstein, M.L. *29*
Brekke, B. *98*
Brenac, A. *223*
Bresenham, J.E. *81*
Brewer, J.A. *81*

Brindle, J.H. *90, 145*
Brinton, W.C. *30*
Brisson, D.W. *31*
Brisson, H.E. *31*
Britton, E.G. *32*
Brock, J.F. *193*
Brodlie, K.W. *33*
Brody, P.J. *156*
Brody, T.P. *169*
Brogan, J. *90*
Brooks, L. *172*
Brown, C.R. *98*
Brown, H.G. *173*
Bruening, R. *84*
Bruinink, J. *169*
Brun, J. *223*
Bryan, G.L. *281*
Buck, J.R. *159*
Buckler, A.T. *34*
Buffart, H. *88*
Buhmann, K. *98*
Burgess, P.R. *42*
Burke, J.J. *251*
Burmeister, R.A., Jr. *169*
Burnette, K. *27, 223*
Burnhill, P. *72*
Burtnyk, N. *15*
Buti, L.B. *98*
Butterfield, E.C. *176*
Bylander, E.G. *35*
Caelli, T. *36*
Cail, F. *98*
Cakir, A. *37, 173*
Campagna, F.C. *223*
Campana, S.B. *162*
Campbell, F.W. *110*
Campbell, J.O. *38*
Cane, V. *110*
Cantella, M.J. *24*
Canter, D.V. *69*
Caras, B. *223*
Card, S.K. *18, 39*
Carlbom, I. *40*
Carling, R. *138, 139, 140, 141*
Carlson, C.R. *51, 52, 53, 54*
Carpenter, L.C. *15*
Carr, J.W., III *81*
Carr, T.H. *172*
Carterette, E.C. *41, 42, 43, 44*
Case, D. *18*
Castleberry, D.E. *223*
Castner, H.W. *45*
Catanese, C.A. *223*
Catchpole, C.E. *24*
Catmull, E. *15, 46, 49, 81*
Cavonius, C.R. *98*
Chaet, V. *177*
Chalk, W. *178*
Chambers, J.M. *47*
Chan, P. *78*
Chang, I.F. *169, 223*
Chang, S.K. *84*
Channin, D.J. *215*
Chapanis, A. *281*

Chapman, L.J. *172, 173*
Chapman, T.L. *266*
Chasen, S.H. *48*
Chastain, G.D. *135*
Chen, H.Y. *223*
Chen, I. *223*
Cheng, J. *223*
Cheng, P.W. *213*
Cherry, C. *172*
Chorley, R.A. *145*
Christ, R.E. *69, 265*
Christensen, C. *81*
Christmann, M. *98*
Chung, W.L. *81*
Cicchella, G. *98*
Claridge, N. *98*
Clark, D.R. *49*
Clark, J.H. *15*
Clement, D.E. *44*
Clerc, F. *223*
Cleveland, W.S. *47, 50*
Cody, G.D. *52*
Cohen, B.G.F. *98*
Cohen, D. *81*
Cohen, R.W. *51, 52, 53, 54*
Coke, E.U. *156*
Cola, R. *162, 223*
Colks, J.H. *223*
Colles, J.H. *223*
Collier, A. *235*
Collins, B.L. *55*
Combée, B. *24*
Coonrod, J. *145*
Coons, S.A. *81*
Coovert, R.E. *223*
Cope, A.D. *24, 165*
Cornog, D.Y. *57, 58*
Corso, G.M. *265*
Cortili, G. *98*
Coulter, R.R., Jr. *81*
Cowen, D.J. *266*
Craford, M.G. *223, 264*
Crandall, R.S. *215*
Crawford, B.M. *281*
Credelle, T.L. *223*
Crestin, J.P. *103, 104*
Criscimagna, T.N. *215, 223*
Crouwel, W. *172*
Crow, F.C. *15*
Crowell, M.H. *24*
Cserhati, A.F. *223*
Csuri, C. *15, 177*
Cumming, G.D. *44*
Dainoff, M.J. *98*
Dalisa, A.L. *215*
Dallet, K. *41*
Damodaran, L. *59*
Dangermond, J. *266*
Dautremont-Smith, W.C. *223*
Deatherage, B.H. *281*
de Beaugrande, R. *60*
DeFanti, T. *49*
De Ma, S. *85*
Demus, D. *169*

de Nigris, F. *98*
Dent, B.D. *61*
Depp, S.W. *223*
Derefeldt, G. *62, 63*
Deutscher, M. *41*
De Valois, K.K. *43*
De Valois, R.L. *43*
Dever, J.J. *173*
Dewar, R. *69*
Dewey, A.G. *223*
Diamond, I.T. *42*
Dichgans, J. *292*
Dick, G.W. *223*
Dickerson, O.B. *18*
diSessa, A.A. *1*
Doblin, J. *64, 173*
Dobson, M.W. *173*
Dodwell, P.C. *43*
Doerbeck, F. *223*
Dondis, D.A. *65*
Donjon, J. *160*
Doran, D. *98*
Dowling, W.J. *41*
Downs, R.M. *66*
Downton, A.C. *173*
Drake, B.M. *98*
Droulez, J. *292*
Duce, D.A. *104, 105*
Duchastel, P.C. *156*
Dudek, C.L. *67*
Dumais, S.T. *10*
Duncan, K. *69*
Dunn, R.M. *103, 104*
Dunsker, E.D. *249*
Dunsmore, H.E. *159*
Dutka, J.T. *173*
Dyer, J.L. *193*
Dzida, W. *104*
Eades, C.A. *68*
Earhard, B. *41*
Easterby, R.S. *69*
Eastman, C. *81*
Eberts, R. *193*
Eckert, R. *104*
Edwards, B.J., Jr. *235*
Edwards, R.J.G. *145*
Eger, A.O. *172*
Egeth, H.E. *173*
Ehrenreich, S.L. *10*
Ehrlich, K. *10*
Eiloart, T.M.B. *110*
Elias, R. *98*
Elin, L. *177*
Ellis, B. *223*
Ellis, R. *223*
Ells, J. *69*
Elworth, C. *70*
Emerson, C.J. *266*
Encarnação, J. *103, 104*
Engel, F.L. *98*
Engel, S.E. *71*
Engelman, C. *104*
Enomoto, H. *84*
Entwisle, D.R. *148*

Erskine, J.C. *223*
Esposito, T. *168*
Estes, W.K. *44*
Evangelisti, C.J. *17*
Evans, R. *88*
Fahle, M. *278*
Farley, W.W. *73, 248*
Faughnan, B.W. *215, 163*
Faulkner, D. *222*
Feldman, L.A. *74*
Fertig, J.A. *75*
Feynmann, R.P. *15*
Fields, A. *156*
Firth, R. *41*
Fischer, A.G. *169*
Fisher, D.F. *172*
Fisher, D.G. *160*
Fisher, H.T. *76*
Fisher, R.F. *222*
Fleming, M.L. *77*
Foley, J.D. *15, 78, 79, 103, 104*
Føllesdal, D. *41*
Ford, R.E. *285*
Forrest, A.R. *33, 81*
Foster, D.H. *16*
Foster, J.J. *172*
Foster, R.J. *82*
Fowler, C.A. *276*
Fox, R. *90*
Fraas, L.M. *223*
Franke, H.W. *80, 177*
Frascara, J. *69*
Frase, L.T. *173*
Fraser, D.B. *161*
Fraser, S. *72*
Fredendall, G.L. *161*
Freeman, H. *81*
French, T.E. *82*
Frescura, B.L. *223*
Friedell, M. *138, 139, 140, 141*
Friedman, M.P. *41, 42, 43, 44*
Frith, U. *172*
Frost, G. *281*
Frutiger, A. *83*
Fu, K.S. *84*
Fugate, K.O. *223*
Fulton, D.L. *81*
Funada, F. *223*
Gagalowicz, A. *85*
Galiardi, R.V. *223*
Galitz, W.O. *86*
Gallop, J.R. *105*
Ganz, L. *43*
Garcia, B. *223*
Gardenier, T.K. *266*
Gates, D. *87*
Gates, Y. *144*
Gaur, J. *162*
Gear, C.W. *81*
Geissler, H.G. *88*
Gelb, I.J. *173*
Gelli, E. *98*
Gellman, L.H. *10*

Genovese, F.C. *223*
Gerbino, W. *16*
Gerritsma, C.J. *169*
Gerstner, K. *89*
Gertman, D.I. *12, 13, 283, 284, 285, 286*
Gervais, M.J. *88*
Getty, D.J. *90, 147*
Ghiringhelli, L. *98*
Gibb, R.M. *223*
Gibbons, A.S. *38*
Gibson, E.J. *16*
Gibson, J.J. *16*
Gibson, R.H. *42*
Giddings, H.V. *266*
Gilbert, J.C. *49*
Gilmore, W.E. *13, 285, 286*
Giloi, W.K. *84, 91*
Giorgini, A. *177*
Giudici, E. *98*
Giulieri, S. *81*
Glinert, E.P. *92*
Gnanamgari, S. *93*
Goede, W.F. *223, 264*
Goetze, G.W. *24*
Gogel, W.C. *44*
Gombrich, E.H. *94, 95*
Good, W.E. *223*
Gordon, J. *42*
Gorog, I. *51, 163*
Gorrell, E.L. *96*
Gorter, V. *108*
Gough, P.B. *276*
Gouraud, H. *81, 97*
Granda, R.E. *71*
Grandjean, E. *98*
Graves, S.P. *223*
Gray, S. *24*
Greenberg, D.P. *15, 108*
Greenspan, J. *10*
Gregory, R.L. *41, 44, 49, 109, 110*
Grether, W.F. *281*
Grieco, A. *98*
Grimson, W.E.L. *278*
Grinberg, J. *223*
Groat, A. *172*
Gruebel, R.L. *223*
Guedj, R.A. *103, 104*
Guidici, E. *98*
Gunther, J.E. *223*
Gurman, B. *27, 145*
Gutmann, J.C. *73, 111, 249*
Guyon, E. *169*
Haber, R.N. *41*
Haberle, G. *259*
Hackathorne, R.J. *81*
Hacker, W. *88*
Hadalski, J.M., Jr. *266*
Hagan, T.G. *81*
Haider, M. *98*
Hakiel, S.R. *69*
Hall, J.A. *24*
Hamlin, G., Jr. *81*
Hand, J.D. *156*

Hardesty, G.K.C. *112*
Härdtl, K.H. *169*
Hardzinski, M. *211*
Harker, G.S. *90*
Harlen, F. *222*
Harman, G. *41*
Harrington, S. *113*
Harrison, R.V. *196*
Hart, D.J. *37*
Hartley, J. *69, 72, 114, 156*
Harvey, L.O., Jr: *88*
Hayes, J. *104*
Hazan, J.P. *160*
Hazony, Y. *49, 266*
Heathorn, R.J. *144*
Heaton, J.M. *222*
Hecht, P.R. *69*
Heglin, H.J. *134*
Heilmeier, G.H. *223*
Helander, M.G. *193*
Helfrich, W. *223*
Hellwig, W. *236*
Hemingway, P.W. *135*
Henderson, L. *173*
Hendler, J.A. *10*
Henrion, M. *81*
Hensel, H. *42*
Herda, S. *104*
Herdeg, W. *136*
Hermans, E. *103*
Herold, E.W. *223*
Herot, C.F. *15, 137, 138, 139, 140, 141*
Hertzberg, H.T.E. *281*
Herzog, B. *81*
Herzog, H.J. *259*
Hess, S. *142*
Heyman, P.M. *163*
Higton, M. *223*
Hildreth, E.C. *143*
Hills, P.J. *144*
Hillyard, R.C. *33*
Hiraishi, H. *84*
Hochberg, J. *16, 41*
Hockenbrock, R. *223*
Hockings, E.F. *223*
Hodgman, G.W. *15, 81*
Hoekstra, H. *172*
Hoffman, T.R. *235*
Holley-Wilcox, P. *276*
Holliday, W. *156*
Hollister, W.M. *27, 145*
Holm, B.D. *81*
Holton, W.C. *223*
Holz, G. *162*
Hong, B. *223*
Hopgood, F.R.A. *103, 104, 105*
Hopkin, V.D. *72*
Hori, H. *223*
Horn, R.E. *156*
Hornung, M. *266*
Horridge, G.A. *42*
Horvat, M. *177*
Howard, I.P. *42*

Howard, V.A. *173*
Howard, W.E. *223*
Howe, J.A.M. *110*
Huang, T.S. *278*
Hubbard, S.W. *146*
Huchingson, R.D. *67*
Huff, K.E. *177*
Huggins, A.W.F. *147*
Huggins, W.H. *90, 148*
Hughes, A. *69*
Hughes, A.J. *145*
Huling, G.E. *223*
Hung, D.L. *276*
Hunt, G. *27*
Hünting, W. *98*
Hurlburt, A. *149, 150*
Huth, B.G. *223*
Hutter, E.C. *24*
Hutter, R.G.E. *160*
Hwang, R.C. *81*
Ihnatowicz, E. *177*
Ikebe, Y. *84*
Imai, S. *88*
Inazaki, K. *223*
Inoda, M. *223*
Inoguchi, T. *223*
Inoue, K. *223*
Inoue, M. *223*
Ise, M. *223*
Ishibashi, T. *169, 223*
Ishii, Y. *223*
Itten, J. *152*
Itzfeldt, W.D. *104*
Iwade, M. *223*
Iwasa, K. *223*
Izmailov, C.A. *88*
Jackson, M.D. *276*
Jackson, R. *172*
Jacobs, J.T. *223*
Jacobson, A.D. *223*
Jain, R. *84*
Jansen, M. *172*
Jarett, I.M. *153*
Jarosz, C.J. *154*
Jarvis, J.F. *15, 81*
Jastrzembski, J.E. *183*
Johansson, G. *292*
Johnson, E.O. *215*
Johnson, N.F. *276*
Johnson, T.E. *81*
Johnsson, B. *155*
Johnston, J.C. *276*
Johnston, P.G. *18*
Jonassen, D.H. *156*
Jones, K.H. *266*
Jordan, B.W., Jr. *81*
Judd, D.B. *157*
Judice, C.N. *15*
Juhasz, J.B. *69*
Julesz, B. *158*
Juliana, A. *223*
Kahn, F.J. *169, 223*
Kak, A.C. *232*
Kakihara, Y. *223*

Kalsbeek, J.H.W. *98*
Kamamori, H. *223*
Kamikawa, T. *223*
Kanatani, Y. *223*
Kaneko, E. *163*
Kanizsa, G. *16*
Kantowitz, B.H. *159*
Kasahara, K. *223*
Kasano, K. *223*
Kaufman, I. *223*
Kaufman, R.G. *223*
Kawaguchi, J. *223*
Kawahara, Y. *223*
Kawai, S. *223*
Kawano, H. *177*
Kay, A. *104*
Kazan, B. *160, 161, 162, 163, 164, 165*
Keates, J.S. *166*
Keele, S.W. *44*
Keen, P.G.W. *18*
Keenan, S.A. *173*
Keiner, R. *236*
Keller, G.S. *223*
Kent, A.J. *144*
Ketchpel, R.D. *223*
Kidd, J.S. *281*
Kilcoyne, M.K. *223*
Kim, S. *31, 167*
King, C.N. *223*
King, D.W. *144*
King, J.C. *168*
Kinkade, R.G. *281*
Kinneir, J. *69*
Kinney, J.A.S. *289*
Kinugawa, K. *223*
Kirkman, D.H. *223*
Kirschner, P.A. *156*
Kirton, J. *169*
Kishishita, H. *223*
Kiyozumi, K. *164, 223*
Klare, G.R. *69*
Klein, R.W. *145*
Kleiner, B. *47*
Klinger, A. *84*
Klint, P. *104*
Klopatek, J.M. *266*
Kmetz, A.R. *169, 223*
Knapp, A. *223*
Knapp, B.G. *10*
Knibb, T.F. *223*
Knirk, F.G. *193*
Knoll, A. *236*
Knowlton, K.C. *15, 49, 177*
Knuth, D.E. *170, 171*
Kobayashi, S. *169*
Kocian, D.F. *145*
Kodama, T. *223*
Koepcke, R.W. *223*
Koike, J. *223*
Kojima, T. *223*
Kolers, P.A. *172, 173*
Kolomyjec, W.J. *177*
Kornhauser, A.L. *266*

Kozawaguchi, H. *223*
Kraiss, K.F. *98*
Kramlich, D. *138, 139, 140, 141*
Krammer, G. *104*
Krause, W. *88*
Kronauer, R. *174*
Krueger, H. *98*
Kruger, L. *42*
Kryter, K.D. *281*
Kubala, A.L. *135*
Kubert, B. *81*
Kühl, W. *24*
Kulsrud, H.E. *81*
Kun, Z.K. *223*
Kundi, M. *98*
Kunii, T.L. *84*
Kuppers, H. *175*
Kuriyama, T. *223*
Kuroda, S. *223*
Labrunie, G. *223*
Labuda, E.F. *24*
Lachman, J.L. *176*
Lachman, R. *176*
Lackner, A.M. *223*
Lalich, N.R. *98*
Landauer, T.K. *10*
Lane, J.M. *15*
Laponsky, A.B. *24*
Laposky, B.F. *177*
LaRussa, J.A. *145*
Läubli, T. *98*
Lauckner, K.F. *177*
Laville, A. *98*
Laycock, J. *145*
Leavitt, R. *177*
Lederman, S.J. *42*
Lee, D.T. *84*
Lee, T.M.P. *81*
Leeuwenberg, E. *16, 88*
Lefton, L.A. *172*
Legault, R. *23*
Le Grand, Y. *43*
Lehmkuhle, S.W. *258*
Lehrer, N.H. *264*
Leibowitz, H.W. *16, 292*
Leighton, R.B. *15*
Lennon, W.J. *81*
Levens, A. *178*
Levie, W.H. *77*
Levinson, L.M. *223*
Levitt, J.G. *222*
Levitt, R. *24*
Levy-Schoen, A. *172*
Lewin, M.H. *81*
Lewis, J.C. *169*
Lim, T.C. *223*
Linden, C.A. *172*
Lindgren, C.E.S. *31*
Line, M.B. *144*
Lipton.L.T. *223*
Liu, P.S. *84*
Loeb, A.L. *31*
Long, J.R. *223*
Longson, T. *177*

Longuet-Higgins, H.C. *278*
Loutrel, P.P. *81*
Lubart, N.D. *98*
Lucas, M. *103*
Lucas, P.A. *183*
Lucido, A.P. *15*
Luechinger, H. *223*
Lundquist, S.G. *223*
Lunenfield, H. *69*
Luo, F.C. *223*
Lustac, S. *144*
Lutin, J.M. *266*
Lyons, J.W. *145*
MacGregor, A.J. *179*
Machamer, J. *292*
Machover, C. *15*
MacKay, D.M. *110*
Mackie, R.R. *193*
MacLaurin, B.K. *223*
Mada, H. *169*
Maddox, M.E. *252, 253*
Maguire, W. *16*
Maisano, R.E. *69*
Maldonado, J.R. *161*
Maliszewski, S.R. *223*
Mallary, R. *177*
Maloney, T.C. *223*
Mandelbrot, B.B. *180*
Manning, E. *177*
Manns, W.G. *223*
Mansell, J. *223*
Marcel, T. *69, 172*
Marcus, A. *108, 177*
Margerum, J.D. *223*
Margulies, F. *98*
Marie, G. *160*
Marks, B.W. *223*
Marks, L.E. *88*
Marr, D. *181, 278*
Marrello, V. *164*
Marsh, P.O. *182*
Marshall, E. *69*
Martin, D.H. *223*
Martinelli, R.U. *160*
Massaro, D.W. *172, 183*
Masterton, B. *42*
Mastroddi, F. *144*
Masuda, M. *223*
Matin, L. *292*
Matsuka, H. *84*
Matsuura, M. *223*
Mayhew, J.E.W. *278*
Mayo, J. *223*
McCauley, M.E. *193*
McClelland, J.L. *276*
McConkie, G.W. *172*
McCormick, E.J. *184*
McGee, J.D. *24*
McKay, L. *106*
McKinlay, W.H. *145*
McLain, D.H. *33*
McLean, R. *185*
McLendon, C.B. *186*
McNicol, D. *69*

Meadows, A.J. *144*
Mears, A.L. *223*
Meier, G. *27*
Meister, D. *193*
Meitzler, A.H. *161*
Melnick, W. *145, 223*
Meltzer, E.S. *173*
Melz, P.J. *223*
Meray-Horvath, L. *24*
Merluzzi, F. *98*
Merrill, P.F. *156*
Merritt, J.O. *90, 196*
Metelli, F. *16*
Metzger, W. *41*
Meyer, J.J. *98*
Mezei, L. *177*
Mezrich, J.J. *53*
Michaelis, P.R. *10*
Michel, J.P. *27, 145*
Miller, A. *172*
Miller, C. *110*
Miller, D.E. *223*
Miller, L.J. *223*
Miller, M.L. *10*
Miller, R.B. *69*
Mills, R.F. *266*
Miner, C.J. *223*
Misukami, E. *223*
Mito, S. *164, 223*
Miura, S. *223*
Miyamoto, S. *84*
Miyashita, Y. *223*
Miyoshi, T. *223*
Mizushima, M. *223*
Mohr, M. *177*
Molnar, V. *177*
Molteni, G. *98*
Monkhouse, F.J. *187*
Monmonier, M.S. *188, 189*
Montalvo, F.S. *15*
Moore, M.V. *190, 191*
Moran, T.P. *39, 104*
Moray, N. *110, 173*
Morelli di Popolo, M.R. *98*
Morello, S.A. *145*
Moretti, E. *98*
Morgan, H.L. *93*
Moroze, M.L. *192*
Morrell, A.M. *223*
Morrison, J.L. *227*
Morton, G.A. *24*
Morton, J. *172*
Moses, F.L. *10, 69*
Mosier, J.N. *246*
Moth, F.T. *223*
Motte, S. *223*
Muckler, F.A. *193*
Mudur, S.P. *104*
Muehrcke, P.C. *194, 227*
Muller-Brockmann, J. *195*
Mulley, W. *145*
Murakami, H. *223*
Murphy, J. *223*

Murray, A.H. *177*
Musselman, E.M. *24*
Myer, G.D. *223*
Myer, T.H. *15*
Myers, R.A. *173*
Myers, W. *15*
Mysing, J. *145*
Nakamura, J. *223*
Nakamura, T. *164, 223*
Nakata, Y. *223*
Namordi, M.R. *223*
Nawrocki, L.H. *190, 191, 200*
Needham, R.C. *235*
Neeland, R.P. *90*
Nees, G. *103*
Negroponte, N. *104*
Neighbors, M. *15*
Neill, W.T. *44*
Nelson, R.P. *201*
Neurath, O. *202*
Newcomb, J. *203*
Newell, A. *39, 173*
Newell, M.E. *15, 81, 103, 104*
Newell, R.G. *81*
Newman, R.L. *204*
Newman, W. *104*
Newman, W.F. *15*
Newman, W.M. *81, 205*
Ngo, P.D.T. *223*
Ni, L.M. *84*
Nicholson, M.M. *223*
Nickerson, R.S. *276*
Nievergelt, J. *104*
Niina, T. *223*
Ninke, W.H. *15*
Nixon, R.J. *81*
Noblanc, J.P. *223*
Noble, R.T. *223*
Noizet, G. *173*
Noll, A.M. *31*
Nonomura, K. *223*
Noro, K. *98*
Nudelman, S. *24*
Nuese, C.J. *215*
O'Brien, C.D. *173*
O'Rourke, R.G. *223*
Odawara, K. *223*
Ogle, J. *162, 223*
Ohkawa, Y. *223*
Ohnishi, J. *223*
Ohsuga, S. *104*
Ohwaki, J. *223*
Oka, E. *276*
Okamoto, Y. *223*
Oki, K.I. *223*
Okoshi, T. *207*
Olson, R.J. *266*
Onton, A. *164*
O'Regan, K. *172*
Orlansky, J. *235*
Östbcrg, O. *98*
Ota, I. *223*
Overall, C. *223*
Overheim, R.D. *208*

Pace, A.J. *156*
Pachella, R.G. *209, 211, 212, 214*
Paine, H.E. *173*
Paller, A. *266*
Palmer, S.E. *16*
Palumbo, J. *177*
Palyka, D.M. *177*
Pankove, J.I. *215*
Parducci, A. *88*
Park, C.S. *216*
Parke, F.I. *81*
Parker, J. *223*
Pattison, H.M. *173*
Pavlidis, T. *217*
Pennella, J.J. *90*
Penz, P.A. *223, 264*
Peppel, G. *236*
Pepper, R.L. *90*
Perfect, C. *231*
Perkins, D.N. *16, 173*
Perris, R. *98*
Petersen, R.J. *12, 268, 283, 284*
Petzold, P. *88*
Phillips, A.H. *218*
Phillips, R.J. *172*
Phillips, R.L. *15*
Phong, B.T. *15*
Piantanida, T.P. *90, 219*
Piccoli, B. *98*
Pickett, G.C. *266*
Pike, W.S. *24*
Pinson, E.N. *81*
Pirenne, M.H. *43*
Pirozzolo, F.J. *44*
Pisano, E.T. *98*
Pleshko, P. *215, 223*
Poggio, T. *278*
Pogorzelski, J.A. *235*
Pollatsek, A. *172*
Pooch, U.W. *15*
Porcu, T.A. *10*
Post, R.B. *16, 292*
Poulton, E.C. *110, 220*
Prather, D.C. *235*
Prazdny, K. *278*
Preiss, R.B. *15*
Press, L. *177*
Price, D. *27*
Price, L.A. *173*
Pritchard, D.H. *161*
Projector, T.H. *112*
Prueitt, M.L. *221*
Puffe, M. *88*
Pugh, A.K. *172*
Pynte, J. *173*
Quaas, P. *88*
Queinnec, C. *104*
Rabbitt, P. *44*
Radl, G.W. *98*
Rapagnani, N.L. *74*
Ratliff, F. *15*
Raymond, J. *81*
Rayner, K. *172*
Raynes, E.P. *169*

Reading, V.M. *222*
Redford, J. *145*
Redington, R.W. *24*
Reed, S.K. *44*
Refioglu, H.I. *223*
Regan, J.J. *281*
Rehe, R.F. *224*
Reich, S.S. *172*
Reid, L.S. *172*
Reif, P.G. *223*
Reigeluth, C.M. *156*
Relles, N. *173*
Resnick, E. *225*
Restle, F. *16*
Rettich, R. *236*
Rey, P. *98*
Reynolds, L. *69, 144, 156, 226*
Richards, W. *43, 278*
Richmond, J. *49*
Robert, J. *223*
Roberts, C.S. *81*
Roberts, J.O. *88*
Roberts, K. *41*
Roberts, T.D.M. *42*
Robinett, F.A. *69*
Robinson, A.H. *45, 227*
Robinson, E.R.N. *193*
Robinson, J.H. *266*
Robson, J.G. *43*
Robusto, P.F. *223*
Rock, I. *228*
Roe, G. *145*
Rogers, D.F. *15, 229, 230*
Rogers, S.P. *111, 154*
Rollenhagen, C. *291*
Ronchi, L.R. *98*
Rookledge, G. *231*
Rose, F.C. *57, 58*
Rosell, F.A. *23, 24*
Rosenberg, R.L. *141*
Rosenfeld, A. *16, 232*
Rosenthal, D.S.H. *104*
Rosenthal, R.I. *172*
Rosinski, R.R. *90, 233*
Ross, H.E. *110*
Rothgordt, U. *164*
Rottmayer, W. *41*
Rowe, W. *223*
Royce, J.R. *41*
Rozeboom, W.W. *41*
Rudolf, N. *110*
Rumsey, J.R. *81*
Sabin, M. *103*
Sabin, M.A. *33*
Sadasiv, G. *24*
Sahlin, C. *63*
Saigusa, K. *84*
Sakai, K. *223*
Sakai, T. *223*
Sakurada, H. *223*
Sale, R.D. *227*
Samet, M.G. *234*
Sancha, T.L. *81, 103, 104*
Sandelin, J. *18*

Sanders, M.S. *184*
Sandin, D. *49*
Sands, M. *15*
Santha, I.S. *223*
Sarginson, R.W. *223*
Sari, I.F. *156*
Sarris, V. *88*
Sasaki, A. *223*
Sasaki, M.K. *84*
Sasaki, T. *84*
Sato, S. *223*
Sawchuk, W. *173*
Scala, J. *177*
Scala, P. *177*
Scardina, J.T. *266*
Schachter, B.J. *235*
Schade, O.H., Sr. *23, 24*
Schadt, M. *223*
Schaefer, L.J. *81*
Schagen, P. *160*
Schaum, D.L. *98*
Scheffer, T.J. *169*
Schiavone, L.M. *223*
Schiekel, M. *236, 259*
Schlam, E. *145*
Schleidt, W.M. *42*
Schmid, C.F. *237, 238*
Schmid, S.E. *238*
Schmidt, A.H. *108*
Schmidtke, H. *98*
Schneider, J.B. *266*
Schneider, M.L. *10*
Schnitzler, A.D. *23, 24*
Schrack, G.F. *15*
Schuberth, R.E. *276*
Schumacker, R.A. *15*
Schumaker, L.L. *84*
Schurick, J.M. *193*
Schwartz, L. *177*
Schwedes, W. *236*
Schweitzer, D.L. *239*
Scott, J.E. *240*
Scott, W.C. *223*
Sedgwick, T. *223*
Sega, S. *223*
Seibel, R. *281*
Seki, H. *223*
Sekuler, R. *43, 241, 292*
Selfridge, K. *69*
Shackel, B. *18*
Shahnavaz, H. *242*
Shallcross, F.V. *24*
Shattuck, M.D. *223*
Shaw, A. *72*
Shaw, A.C. *104*
Shaw, G. *222*
Shay, J.L. *164, 223*
Shebilske, W.L. *172, 173*
Shedivy, D.I. *253*
Sherr, S. *243, 244*
Shidlovsky, I. *163*
Shimojo, T. *223*
Shinoda, T. *223*
Shionoya, T. *223*

Shishido, C. *223*
Shneiderman, B. *10*
Sholl, M.J. *173*
Shopland, C.D. *110*
Shoup, R.G. *15*
Showstack, R. *156*
Shugarman, S. *276*
Shumacker, R.A. *81*
Sidner, C.L. *245*
Siegel, J. *162*
Simmonds, D. *226*
Simpson, A. *59*
Simutis, Z.M. *191*
Sinaiko, H.W. *14*
Sincerbox, G.T. *223*
Singer, B. *162*
Singer, H. *276*
Sint, M. *104*
Sirkis, M.D. *223*
Slaby, S.M. *31*
Slottow, H.G. *15*
Slusky, R.D. *163*
Smith, A.R. *15*
Smith, C.S. *31*
Smith, D.R. *266*
Smith, M. *18*
Smith, M.J. *18, 98*
Smith, P.J.F. *223*
Smith, P.T. *172, 173*
Smith, R.L. *268, 284*
Smith, S.L. *69, 246*
Snodgrass, J.G. *173*
Snopko, P.A. *223*
Snyder, H.L. *23, 247, 248, 249,
    250, 252, 253, 254, 255, 264*
Sobel, A. *223*
Sokolov, E.N. *88*
Soloway, E. *10*
Soltan, P. *145*
Somers, P. *209, 210, 211*
Somlyody, A. *162*
Sorkin, R.D. *159*
Spencer, G.R. *223*
Spencer, H. *257*
Spencer, J. *72*
Spoehr, K.T. *258, 276*
Sprokel, G.J. *223*
Sproull, R.F. *15, 81, 104, 205*
Stammerjohn, L.W. *98*
Stark, L.W. *18, 196*
Stea, D. *66*
Stein, B.E. *42*
Steinbeck, J. *259*
Steinberg, E.R. *260*
Stevens, C.F. *42*
Stevens, P.S. *261*
Stevenson, G.A. *262*
Stewart, T.F.M. *37, 98*
Stifle, J. *81*
Stiles, W.S. *301*
Stokes, A. *173*
Storey, J.R. *173*
Strauss, C.M. *31*
Strawhorn, J.M. *144*

Streater, R.W. *223*
Strickland, R.N. *251*
String, J. *235*
Stroud, I.A. *33*
Struycken, P. *177*
Stuart, C. *15*
Stupp, E.H. *24*
Sugimoto, K. *84*
Sugimoto, T. *223*
Suppes, P. *41*
Surtani, K.H. *223*
Sussenbach, H. *236*
Sussman, A. *215*
Sutcliffe, D.C. *33, 105*
Sutherland, I.E. *15, 81*
Sutherland, N.S. *42*
Suzuki, C. *223*
Swezey, R.W. *69*
Szabo, J. *81*
Szabo, N.S. *235*
Szlichcinski, K.P. *69, 173*
Tajima, T. *223*
Takafuji, Y. *223*
Takagi, N. *223*
Takahara, K. *223*
Takama, J. *84*
Takano, Y. *165*
Takao, Y. *84*
Takeda, M. *223*
Takesada, H. *223*
Takeshita, T. *84*
Talbot, P.A. *81*
Talcott, N.A., Jr. *263*
Tanaka, H. *223*
Taneda, T. *161*
Tannas, L.E., Jr. *223, 264*
Task, H.L. *145*
Taylor, G.A. *183*
Taylor, I. *173*
Taylor, M.M. *42*
Taylor, W.G. *222*
Teague, S.J. *144*
Teichner, W.H. *265*
Teicholz, E. *266*
ten Hagen, P.J.W. *104*
Tennison, R.D. *17*
Teramoto, I. *223*
Terrana, T. *98*
Terzopoulos, D. *278*
Thanhouser, N. *81*
Thiel, P. *267*
Thoman, R.E. *223*
Thomas, J. *223*
Thomas, J.P. *43*
Thomas, K.B. *42*
Thomson, R.M. *281*
Tillitt, D.N. *268*
Timmers, H. *98*
Tinker, M.A. *269, 270*
Tisserand, M. *98*
Tjønn, H. *98*
Tomlin, C.D. *266*
Tomlin, S.M. *266*
Toriyama, K. *169*

Townsend, J.T. *88*
Toyonaga, R. *223*
Tozzi, C. *104*
Treadway, D.A. *223*
Treurniet, W.C. *173, 271*
Trevarthen, C.B. *42*
Triggs, T.J. *69*
Troup, J.D.G. *222*
True, T.T. *223*
Trumbo, B.E. *272*
Tsai, R.Y. *278*
Tsaparas, G. *145*
Tschichold, J. *273*
Tsuchiya, K. *98*
Tsujiyama, B. *223*
Tsutsumi, T. *223*
Tucker, H.A. *103, 104*
Tuenge, R.T. *223*
Tufte, E.R. *274*
Tukey, P.A. *47*
Turnbull, A.T. *275*
Turoff, M. *173*
Turpin, J.A. *252*
Tuttle, D.M. *38*
Twyman, M. *172, 280*
Tyler, C.W. *177*
Tynan, P. *241, 292*
Tyng, A.G. *31*
Tyte, R.N. *223*
Tzeng, O.J.L. *276*
Uchida, T. *223*
Uchiyama, M. *223*
Uemura, S. *223*
Ullman, S. *277, 278*
Ullner, M.K. *279*
Umbach, F.W. *98*
Unbehaun, R. *236, 259*
Underwood, J.D.M. *173*
Uno, S. *84*
Uragaki, T. *223*
Urbach, W. *169*
Urnette, K.B. *145*
Uttal, W.R. *90, 287, 288*
van Alphen, M. *223*
Van Cott, H.P. *281*
Van Dam, A. *79*
van den Berg, J. *223*
van den Bos, J. *104*
Van Deusen, E. *107*
Vang, A.H. *266*
van Nes, F.L. *98*
van Orden Roller, B. *173*
van Zanten, P. *169*
Vaughan, W.S., Jr. *289*
Vecht, A. *223*
Venezky, R.L. *172, 173, 183*
Verweel, J. *223*
Vicario, G.B. *16*
Vickers, D. *290*
Vickers, D.L. *15*
Vierck, C.J. *82*
Vigliani, E. *98*
Vilder, R. *177*
Vincent, C.N. *173*

Von Willisen, F.K. *169*
Vurpillot, E. *41*
Wada, M. *223*
Wada, T. *223*
Waddell, J.M., Jr. *266*
Waern, Y. *291*
Wagenaar, W.A. *292*
Wagner, D.L. *208*
Wainer, H. *173*
Walk, R.D. *44*
Walker, R.S. *81*
Walkowicz, J.L. *57*
Wallace, J.G. *110*
Wallace, V.L. *78*
Wallach, H. *292*
Waller, R.H.W. *156, 172, 173*
Wang, W.S.Y. *276*
Warman, E.A. *103*
Warren, R.M. *110*
Warrick, M.J. *281*
Washington, D. *223*
Watanabe, Y. *84*
Watkins, M.L. *145*
Weale, R.A. *222*
Webber, B.L. *93*
Weber, L.F. *264*
Webster, D.B. *42*
Weibel, G.E. *169*
Weimer, P.K. *24, 165*
Wein, M. *15*
Weinberg, R. *235*
Weinzapfel, G. *15*
Weirauch, D.F. *223*
Weiss, R.A. *81*
Weissenböck, M. *98*
Weisstein, N. *16*

Welch, A. *173*
Welford, A.T. *69*
Weller, D. *81*
Wendorf, J.W. *15*
Wenzel, B.M. *42*
Werring, N.J. *223*
Wertheim, A.H. *292*
Wertheimer, M. *41*
Wesley, A.C. *145*
Weston, G.F. *223, 293*
Wetherell, A. *69*
Weydert, J. *104*
Wharf, J.H. *223*
Wheatley, D.J. *98*
Wheaton, G.R. *281*
White, J.V. *294, 295, 296*
White, R. *223*
Whitney, J. *177*
Whitted, T. *15*
Whycer, B. *222*
Wickens, C.D. *297*
Wiggins, R.H. *10*
Wilbur, C.V. *223*
Wilcox, P. *172*
Wilkinson, H.R. *187*
Williams, M.C. *16*
Williams, R. *81*
Williges, B.H. *193*
Williges, R.C. *193*
Willson, R.H. *23*
Wilson, P. *59*
Winkler, R.E. *298*
Winn, W. *156*
Wiseman, N.E. *172*
Witkin, A.P. *278*
Wong, K.Y. *84*

Wong, W. *299, 300*
Woodcock, S. *145*
Woodham, R.J. *278*
Woodhead, A. *223*
Woon, P. *81*
Wright, P. *69, 72, 144, 156, 172, 173*
Wright, T.J. *81*
Wrolstad, M.E. *172, 173*
Wysotzki, F. *88*
Wyszecki, G. *157, 301*
Yajima, S. *84*
Yamaguchi, F. *81*
Yamaguchi, K. *84*
Yamamoto, M. *161*
Yamanaka, H. *223*
Yamauchi, Y. *223*
Yamazaki, T. *223*
Yanagisawa, T. *223*
Yangisawa, S. *223*
Yonei, H. *223*
Yonezaki, N. *84*
Yoshida, K. *223*
Yoshida, M. *223*
Yoshikawa, K. *223*
Yoshiyama, M. *223*
Yost, R.M. *41*
Young, T.Y. *84*
Yturralde, J.M. *31*
Zajec, E. *177*
Zanforlin, M. *16*
Zangwill, O.L. *110*
Zeller, H.R. *169*
Zoeke, B. *88*
Zwaga, H.J. *69*

Section IV

Subject Index

Subject Index

The subject index was designed to accommodate the several disciplines contributory to the design of computer-generated displays. Because both the language and the conventional indexing terminology for a given discipline may not necessarily be meaningful across disciplines, the emphasis here is on multiple entry points, which are intended to provide practitioners and researchers with familiar paths to perhaps unfamiliar subject matter.

The descriptors in this index are arranged in two levels. Primary descriptors appear in upper case and are distinguished by arrows. Lead-in terms have "see" instructions to the appropriate primary descriptors. The "see also" instructions refer the reader to related terms. Secondary descriptors are indented and appear in lower case.

NOTE: Italicized numbers refer to document ID numbers, not to page numbers.

►ALGORITHMS (see also ANIMATION AND MOVEMENT; FIGURE GENERATION ALGORITHMS; FRACTAL GEOMETRY; GRAPHIC GEOMETRY; SHADING AND TEXTURE ALGORITHMS; SIMULATION AND MODELING; SURFACE GENERATION ALGORITHMS; THREE-DIMENSIONAL GEOMETRY; TWO-DIMENSIONAL GEOMETRY)
color *79, 111, 229*
for computer-assisted cartography *189*
coordinate systems *240*
data structures *217*
fractal modeling *180*
holography *207*
hypergraphic displays *31*
for interactive graphics *113*
for microcomputer graphics *9, 216*
parallel processing techniques and real time computations *279*
set-up routines *5*
surface visualization techniques *239*
for text design *156*

►ANIMATION AND MOVEMENT
animation systems *15, 74, 81*
for microcomputers *9*
motion discontinuities *143*
motion dynamics *15*
ordered dither *15*
problems of *15*
techniques for *5, 15*
velocity fields *143*

►APPLICATIONS
architecture *15*
decision support systems *216*
economic analysis and forecasting *121, 126, 216*
education and research *74, 119, 130, 260*
environmental information systems *15, 117, 266*
information management systems *137, 138, 139, 140, 141, 153*
instructional materials *69*
military and defense systems *90*
programming languages *92*
remote sensing and resource mapping *118, 124, 129*
safety and hazard alerts *69*

►APPLIED GRAPHICS
for communication *178*
data analysis *178*
design and documentation *178*
technical drawings *178*

►APPLIED PSYCHOLOGY (see also COGNITIVE PROCESSES; ERGONOMICS; HUMAN ENGINEERING; HUMAN PERFORMANCE; PERFORMANCE EVALUATION)
39, 297

►AREA SYMBOLS (see also CARTOGRAPHIC SYMBOLS; CODES AND CODING; SYMBOLS)
form *45*
line *227*
orientation *45*
pattern *45*
point *227*
size *45*
texture *45*

►BIBLIOGRAPHIES AND CITATION COLLECTIONS *15, 57, 58, 132, 133, 148, 197, 198, 199*

►BILEVEL DIGITAL DISPLAYS
algorithms for *163*
animation *163*
image representation *163*
systems design *163*

►CARTOGRAPHIC DESIGN (see also AREA SYMBOLS; CARTOGRAPHIC SYMBOLS; CARTOGRAPHIC TECHNIQUES; MAP DESIGN; SYMBOLIC REPRESENTATION; SYMBOLS)
choropleth maps *61*
isarithmic maps *61*
pattern and perception *45*

scale *194*
semiotics and *194*
symbolic representation *61, 194*
thematic mapping *61*
typography for *61*

►CARTOGRAPHIC SYMBOLS (see also AREA
SYMBOLS; MAP DESIGN; SYMBOLIC
REPRESENTATION; SYMBOLS)
cartographic symbols *72, 76, 166, 227*
dot area symbols *45*
interpolated symbolisms *76*
pattern and perception *45*
semiotics and *194*
symbolic representation *61, 76, 194*
typography *61*

►CARTOGRAPHIC TECHNIQUES (see also
AREA SYMBOLS; CARTOGRAPHIC DESIGN;
MAP DESIGN)
cartographic design *61, 131, 166*
coordinate geometry and projections *61*
data collection and measurement *194*
spatial analysis *76*
thematic mapping *61, 76*

►CARTOGRAPHY (see also CARTOGRAPHIC
DESIGN; CARTOGRAPHIC SYMBOLS;
CARTOGRAPHIC TECHNIQUES; MAP DESIGN)
aesthetics *76*
cartographic communication *188*
cartographic data bases *116, 122, 227*
computer models in *125*
data models in *61*
language of cartography *76*
theory of *227*
types of maps *188, 227*

►CATHODE RAY TUBES
chromatic aberration and display
distortion *13*
color displays *111, 151, 165*
human factors design and evaluation
criteria *12, 13, 18, 151, 282, 283, 286*
large screen displays *223*
monochromatic displays *151*
operating principles and performance
limitations *165, 223, 243, 244, 264*
raster scan displays *244*
safety parameter displays *286*
visual ergonomics of *37*

►CATHODOCHROMIC SYSTEMS *163*

►CODES AND CODING (see also ICONIC
COMMUNICATION; ICONS; SYMBOLS)
code design *10, 11, 184*
coding methods *184*
color codes *62, 265*
design evaluation *62, 69*
echoic codes *297*
iconic codes *148, 297*
legibility *69*
natural language in *10*
for sensory input *184*
symbol associations *69*
use of abbreviations in *10*

►COGNITIVE ERGONOMICS (see also
HUMAN PERFORMANCE; VISUAL
PERFORMANCE; VISUOMOTOR INTEGRATION)
attention and workload *176, 297*
cognitive and performance modeling *39*
cognitive limits *11*
cognitive skills and complex information
processing *39, 297*
dialogue design *155*
interference and uncertainty *39, 228*
learning and memory *39*
psychomotor skills *297*
task acquisition and mastery *39, 297*

►COGNITIVE MAPPING *66*

►COGNITIVE PROCESSES
attention and workload *176, 297*
behavior modeling *39*
cognitive limits *11*
comprehension of multiple dimensions *31*
concrete and abstract data *192*
extraction of information *7, 176, 276*
imagination *7*
interference and uncertainty *39, 109, 228*
letter and word recognition *173, 276, 297*
pattern classification and inference *88,
154*
perceptual integration *7, 39*
reading style and strategy *60, 172, 173,
176, 276*
signal detection and judgment *109, 297*
task analysis and mastery *39, 66, 200,
297*
theories of representation *173*
visual and verbal interactions *258*
visualization *7*

►COLOR
algorithms for color displays *111*
color image processing *73*
color standards *157*
geometric optics and applications *208*
models for computer graphics *79*
natural color phenomena *208*
theories of *2*
wave optics *208*

►COLOR AND DESIGN
color and information coding *152, 265,
272*
color contrasts *2, 152*
display illumination *112*
form *152*
spatial effects *152*

►COLOR PHYSICS
color metrics *73*
color standards *157*
color terminology *157, 208, 301*
colorants *157, 208*
quantitative differentiation *76*
physics of color *152, 175, 208*
spectrophotometry *157*
spectroradiometry *73*

►COLOR PROPERTIES
absorption and transmittance *157, 208*
chromaticity *157*

color tolerance *157*
luminance *157*
mixing and modification *2, 152, 157, 175*
primary colors *175*
reflectance and opacity *157, 208, 301*
►COLOR SYSTEMS
　color atlas for computer graphics *63*
　color order systems *3, 63, 175, 208, 301*
　color scales *157, 301*
　color standards *157*
　complementarity and contrast *2, 152, 157, 175*
　mixing and modification *2, 152, 175*
►COLOR VISION
　chromatic adaptation *157*
　color blindness *157*
　color and brightness perception *232*
　models of *181, 301*
　perceptual color space *63*
　physiology of *43, 157, 175, 301*
　psychophysics of *43, 157*
　theories of *157, 208, 301*
►COLORIMETRY
　color temperatures and tolerances *157, 301*
　colorants *157, 208, 301*
　colorimetric instrumentation *301*
　complementarity *157, 301*
　metameric colors *301*
►COMMUNICATION
　cognitive models and strategies *182*
　context and content *182*
　information control *182*
　information load and complexity *182*
　sender-receiver parameters *182*
　symbol and sign systems *55*
►COMPOSITION *60, 156, 299*
►COMPUTER-AIDED DESIGN AND MANUFACTURE *17, 75, 84, 178*
►COMPUTER-ASSISTED CARTOGRAPHY
　algorithms for *189*
　cartographic databases *122, 189*
　graphic symbolisms *76, 189*
　multisubject mapping *76*
　value classing *76*
►COMPUTER-ASSISTED EDUCATION *77, 114, 190, 191, 260*
►COMPUTER ART (see also COMPUTER GRAPHICS)
　computer animation *108*
　gallery of *108, 221, 299*
　history of *80*
　intelligent systems for *84*
　interviews with artists *299*
　technical aspects *80, 221, 299*
　theory and aesthetics *80*
►COMPUTER GRAPHICS (see also GEOMETRY; GRAPHIC GEOMETRY; THREE-DIMENSIONAL GEOMETRY; TWO-DIMENSIONAL GEOMETRY)
　bibliography of *15*
　color order systems for *63*

control and syntactic structures *79, 104, 205*
engineering and scientific applications *74*
glossary for *146*
information management systems *153*
interactive techniques and practices *79, 104, 205, 240*
knowledge-based systems *104*
for microcomputers *9, 113, 216*
parallel processing and real time techniques *279*
survey of *15*
teaching facilities *49*
►CONTROL DEVICES (see also DISPLAY DEVICES; HUMAN FACTORS ENGINEERING; VISUOMOTOR INTEGRATION)
　control design and recommendations *159, 281*
　display-control systems *159*
　psychomotor compatibility *184*
　types of controls *184, 281*
►CONTROL SYSTEMS
　automation *297*
　design of *281*
　display-control compatibility *147*
　manual control systems *297*
　multiaxis and open loop systems *297*
►CORE SYSTEM
　ACM status report *101*
　graphics standards *103*
►CYCLOPEAN PERCEPTION
　Cyclopean methods and techniques *158*
　Cyclopean mind *158*
　mathematical data *48*
　peripheral versus central processes *158*
►DATA ANALYSIS
　CHART program *68*
　displaying equations *48*
　geographic information systems *266*
　graphic methods *47, 50*
　mathematical data *48*
►DATA GRAPHICS
　data density *274*
　data maximization *274*
　multifunctional elements *274*
　theory of *274*
►DATA MANAGEMENT
　cartographic databases *116, 122, 127, 189, 266*
　electronic composition *218*
　interactive data display and manipulation *6, 263*
　pictorial databases *84*
　statistical databases *122*
►DATA PRESENTATION
　comparisons *30, 238*
　default displays *93*
　drafting techniques *238*
　frequency plots *30, 238*
　graphic techniques *30, 47, 50, 179, 226, 237, 238*

projection techniques *238*
special purpose charts *30, 238*
time as a variable *30*
visual emphasis *226*

►DECISION MAKING
action selection *39, 176, 234, 297*
human limits *297*
learning and feedback *297*
perception and decision strategies *39, 147, 176*
reaction time *297*

►DEPTH PERCEPTION
computational theory of *181, 278*
depth representation *16*
form perception *90, 219*
illusions of motion *16, 29*
motion in depth *219*
rotary motion *29*
slant *29*
stereopsis *43, 90, 158, 181, 219*
three-dimensional imaging *207*

►DESIGN (see also DESIGN GUIDELINES AND
EVALUATION; DESIGN METHODS; DISPLAY
DESIGN; INFORMATION DESIGN; VISUAL
ARTS; WORK AND WORKPLACE DESIGN)
as adaptation and process *3*
design evaluation *11*
equipment design *281*
ergonomics of *18, 32*
experiments in interactive design *10*
graphic arts encyclopedia *262*
human-computer interaction *10, 32, 79*
information content of *182*
information delivery and packaging *38*
logical structure of *3*
methodology *2, 32, 150*
pattern in *3*
performance engineering and modeling
11, 39, 40, 250
for visual presentation *172*

►DESIGN GUIDELINES AND
EVALUATION
guideline evaluation *13*
health hazards of visual display terminals
206
human factors engineering *184, 281*
interface software *246*
symbols and symbol sets *4*

►DESIGN IN TWO AND THREE
DIMENSIONS *79, 299, 300*

►DESIGN ISSUES
coding *13*
research recommendations and summaries
13
screen organization and structure *13*
system feedback *13*

►DESIGN METHODS
analytical tools for *3*
anthropometrics *11, 281*
applied graphics *178, 203*
applied psychology for *39*
design for maintenance *281*

documentation and implementation *32,
86, 178*
grid systems *195*
human-computer interaction *10, 79*
interactive systems *10, 18, 32, 159*
mathematical analysis in *3*
performance modeling *40*
for visual awareness *267*

►DESIGN RESEARCH *268*

►DESIGN SYSTEMS *149*

►DISPLAY DESIGN (see also DESIGN ISSUES;
SCREEN CHARACTERISTICS; SCREEN DESIGN)
control configured systems *145*
display typology *75*
ergonomics of *10, 27, 283, 286*
format design *10, 71, 86, 284*
games and simulation *260*
graphicolingual displays *75*
natural language in *10*
perceptual and cognitive psychology in *14*
research facilities for *268*
research summaries and recommendations
12, 14
safety parameter displays *282, 284, 286*
tabular displays *72*
technical requirements *169*
visual research for *241*

►DISPLAY DESIGN CRITERIA
alert functions *284*
attention control *86*
back-up displays *282*
display accessibility and location *282*
display functions *282*
display parameters and tradeoffs *250, 282,
293*
frame content *71*
human factors design criteria *35, 71, 86,
282*
illumination guidelines for *112, 134*
information accessibility *10, 35, 284*
perceptually "perfect" images *54*
performance standards *35, 86, 196, 250,
282*
psychophysics for *284*
reduction of popping *19*
stimulus properties of visual displays *209*

►DISPLAY DESIGN EVALUATION (see
DISPLAY EVALUATION)

►DISPLAY DESIGN PARAMETERS (see also
SCREEN DESIGN)
code systems *69*
color *151, 196*
format design *10, 71, 86, 284*
image instability and polarity *151*
legibility *69, 96, 298*
luminance *96, 196*
machine prompts and menu systems *71,
86*
parameter tradeoffs *250*
persistence and refresh rate *151, 196*
phosphor selection *151*
reflectivity *151, 196*

resolution and contrast *151, 196*
symbol size *69*

►DISPLAY DEVICES (see also CONTROL
  DEVICES; IMAGE QUALITY; VISUAL DISPLAY
  TERMINALS)
  alphanumeric devices *244*
  color metrics *73*
  ergonomics of *18*
  head mounted displays *27, 204*
  human factors of *18, 244*
  illumination guidelines and specifications
    112, 134
  meters and scales *184*
  operating principles of *27, 215, 244*
  signal and warning devices *184, 281*
  visual characteristics of *27*
  workstation design *18*

►DISPLAY EVALUATION
  cognitive dimensions of *69, 283*
  display codes *69*
  display-operator performance evaluation
    70
  distracting and irrelevant information *212*
  experimental studies in *284*
  human factors in *10, 14, 282, 283, 286*
  information detection and recognition *10,
    69, 284*
  information format *71, 283, 286*
  information quality and complexity *212,
    286*
  methods *14, 69, 196, 283, 284, 286*
  multidimensional ratings in *283*
  performance standards *196, 283*
  safety parameter displays *69, 282, 284,
    286*
  symbol preference *135*
  technical information *69*

►DISPLAY RESEARCH FACILITIES *268*

►DISPLAY SYSTEMS
  color image processing *73*
  display-control systems *220*
  display photometry *147, 247*
  general system properties *14*
  human-display systems *51, 52, 53, 54,
    145*
  image quality and reproduction *23*
  integrated electro-optic displays *169, 223*
  menu-driven systems *86*
  modular systems *27*
  sensor-display integration *145*
  visual noise in *23*

►DISPLAY TECHNOLOGY
  color panels *165*
  data structures *293*
  electro-optic devices *162, 169, 215, 243*
  image sensors *165*
  integrated display control *223*
  ion insertion devices *164*
  performance measures *27*
  technical capabilities and potentials *27,
    161, 164, 215, 223, 293*

►DISPLAYS (see also VISUAL DISPLAYS)
  augmented displays *220*
  design guidelines *11, 35, 184*
  display-control systems *11, 90, 159*
  ergonomics of *244*
  human-display systems *51, 52, 53, 54*
  information integration and presentation
    159, 184, 281
  pursuit and compensatory displays *220*
  three-dimensional displays *90*
  types of displays *15, 90, 264, 281*

►ELECTROCHROMIC DEVICES *169, 215,
  223*

►ELECTROLUMINESCENT DEVICES *223,
  244, 264*

►ELECTROPHORETIC DEVICES *215*

►ELEMENTS OF DESIGN *201, 299*

►ENGINEERING GRAPHICS *178*

►ENVIRONMENTAL LIGHTING
  glare *151*
  luminance *151*
  for visual display terminals *28*

►ERGONOMICS (see also COGNITIVE
  ERGONOMICS; HUMAN ENGINEERING;
  HUMAN FACTORS; VISUAL ERGONOMICS)
  design methods *32*
  display performance and technology *243*
  human-display interfaces *145, 155*
  illumination for visual displays *112, 134*
  symbol design *154*
  system analysis and design *59*
  visual displays *37, 98, 242*

►ERGONOMICS OF DISPLAY DEVICES
  (see also SCREEN CHARACTERISTICS) *244,
  289*

►ERROR DETECTION AND ANALYSIS *71,
  159, 237, 297*

►EVALUATION
  display performance and reliability *49,
    243, 244, 283, 286*
  human engineering criteria *193, 281*
  image quality and visual performance *256*
  simulation and gaming *281*
  symbols and symbol sets *4, 69*
  three-dimensional display applications *90*
  type legibility testing *72, 275*

►EXPERIMENTAL STUDIES
  alphanumeric versus graphic displays *200*
  chromatic versus achromatic information
    coding *265*
  cognitive ergonomics in dialogue design
    147, 155
  depth perception and stimulus interaction
    90
  display design and evaluation *283, 284*
  dot and line detection in three-
    dimensional space *90*
  effects of line and cell failures on image
    quality *255*
  field studies in information design *10, 67*

graphicolingual displays *75*
health and safety issues of visual display
   terminals *20*
iconic communication systems *92*
information accessibility and recognition
   10, 284
object orientation and cue symmetry *147*
safety parameter displays *283, 284, 286*
stimulus properties of visual displays *209,*
   210, 211, 213
tracking and control operations *90, 249*
visual integration *248*
►FATIGUE
visual fatigue *196*
workload and stress in human-computer
   interaction *192*
►FIGURE GENERATION ALGORITHMS
aliasing *217*
edges *26, 79, 229*
Fourier transformations *217*
hidden lines *5, 81, 113, 229*
plane figures *205, 217, 229*
segmentation *217*
►FLAT PANEL DEVICES
design issues *264*
effects of cell and line failures on image
   quality *255*
technology of *244*
thin film transistor matrix devices *169*
visual parameters *250*
►FONT (see also TYPOGRAPHY)
letter shapes and design *185, 244*
Metafont *170*
typeface alphabets *87*
typeface classification *87, 185*
►FRACTAL GEOMETRY *180*
►FRAME DESIGN (see also SCREEN DESIGN)
294, 295, 296
►GEOGRAPHY *66*
►GEOMETRIC MODELING *33, 205*
►GEOMETRY (see also ALGORITHMS; GRAPHIC
   GEOMETRY)
relativity *1*
symmetry operations *261*
topology and hyperdimensional space *1*
►GRAPH SYSTEMS
graphic information processing *21*
image theory *22*
information levels in *21*
properties of *22*
rules of construction and legibility *22*
semiotics of *21*
►GRAPHIC ART
encyclopedia of *262*
principles of composition *273*
typography and graphic composition *142,*
   273
as visible language *136*
►GRAPHIC COMMUNICATION
color *275*
illustrations and picture-word
   combinations *275*

information processing in *275*
isotype *280*
visual syntax *275*
►GRAPHIC CONSTRUCTION *21*
►GRAPHIC DATA STRUCTURES *91*
►GRAPHIC DESIGN (see also GRAPHIC
   SCIENCE; INFORMATION DESIGN)
advertising *201*
color in *76, 201, 294*
design systems *149*
encyclopedia of *262*
flow charts and schematics *296*
graphic language and vocabulary *131,*
   136, 274, 295, 296
layout *149, 201, 294*
modular and grid systems *150, 195*
multifunctional elements *131, 136, 274*
symmetry and transformations *167, 225*
typography and composition *142, 201,*
   294, 295
visualization exercises *225*
wordplay *167*
►GRAPHIC GEOMETRY (see also
   ALGORITHMS; GEOMETRY;
   THREE-DIMENSIONAL GEOMETRY;
   TWO-DIMENSIONAL GEOMETRY)
algorithms for *33*
clipping and covering *5*
curves and conics *48, 97*
fractal modeling *180*
geometric transformations *5, 79, 113,*
   230, 240
for microcomputers *216*
projections *230*
set-up routines *5*
splines *48*
three-dimensional geometry *1, 5, 113,*
   230, 240
three-dimensional representations *79,*
   207, 229
two-dimensional geometry *1, 5, 229*
►GRAPHIC LANGUAGES *91*
►GRAPHIC METHODS
CHART system *68*
data collection and analysis *6, 30, 47, 179*
Design Pad *17*
general principles *22, 47, 50, 179, 237,*
   295, 296
grid systems *195*
logarithms *50*
multivariate data *6, 47, 50*
regression models *47*
time series *50*
►GRAPHIC SCIENCE
basic concepts *82, 179*
drafting techniques *64*
encyclopedia of graphic art *262*
graphic problem solving *82*
information analysis *22, 82, 179*

►GRAPHIC SIGN SYSTEMS (see also CODES
AND CODING; ICONS; SYMBOLS) *22*

►GRAPHICAL KERNEL SYSTEM
ANSI draft proposal *100*
graphics standards *105, 106*
introduction to GKS *105*
ISO draft for GKS *102*
primer for GKS *106*

►GRAPHICS HARDWARE *15, 84, 123, 128*

►GRAPHICS INTERFACES *17, 79, 99, 107,
113*

►GRAPHICS SOFTWARE
graphics programming *79, 81, 84*
graphics systems design *15*
raster displays *56*
software interfaces *103*

►GRAPHICS STANDARDS
Computer Graphics Metafile *99*
Core standards routines *113*
Core System status report *101*
Graphical Kernel System *105, 106*
graphics standards handbook *107*
for interactive graphics systems *104* `
ISO draft standard *102*
methods and specifications *103*
software interfacing *103*

►GRAPHICS SYSTEMS
algorithms for color displays *111*
automatic data presentation *93*
design and evaluation methods *40, 235*
display processing *205*
multifunction graphics *81*
Sketchpad *81*
spatial data management *137, 138, 139,
140, 141*
standards for *105, 106*

►GRAPHICS TECHNOLOGY *279*

►GRAPHS (see also GRAPH SYSTEMS; GRAPHIC
COMMUNICATION; GRAPHIC CONSTRUCTION;
INFORMATION DESIGN)
principles of graph construction *21, 50,
237, 274*
semiotics of *21*

►HEALTH AND SAFETY ISSUES OF
VISUAL DISPLAY TERMINALS
health hazards of visual display terminals
206
health issues *18, 20, 151*
human factors design criteria *18, 151, 282*
human factors evaluations *13, 18, 282*
visual fatigue *18*

►HUMAN COMPUTER INTERACTION
cognitive processes in *192*
communication guidelines *71, 79, 104,
155, 193*
design principles *79*
display-operator performance evaluation
70
ergonomics of *18*
graphics interfaces *137, 138, 139, 140,
141*

interactive techniques *78, 79*
research in *155*
software ergonomics *39*
task acquisition *39*
text as interface *60*
workload and stress *192*

►HUMAN ENGINEERING (see also
ERGONOMICS; HUMAN FACTORS; HUMAN
FACTORS ENGINEERING)
anthropometrics *184*
cognitive skills *39*
design applications and guidelines *184,
281*
for display devices *184*
display-control systems *11, 184*
illumination guidelines for visual displays
112, 134
operator variability *39*
performance modeling *11, 39, 184*
research methods in *184*
task analysis and design *11, 39, 59, 281*

►HUMAN FACTORS (see also ERGONOMICS;
HUMAN PERFORMANCE; VISUAL
PERFORMANCE)
engineering design and maintenance *12,
281*
equipment compatibility and selection *59,
159, 184*
human performance and reliability *11,
159, 281*
information flow *159, 184*
performance standards *11*
product liability *159*
research methods in *184*
task analysis and design *59*

►HUMAN FACTORS ENGINEERING
anthropometrics *184*
ergonomics of visual display terminals *98*
illumination guidelines for visual displays
112, 134
input-output systems *184*
operator-equipment compatibility *184*
research methods *184*

►HUMAN MOTIVATION *11*

►HUMAN PERFORMANCE (see also
COGNITIVE ERGONOMICS; FATIGUE; HUMAN
COMPUTER INTERACTION; VISUAL
PERFORMANCE; VISUOMOTOR INTEGRATION)
display design research *12, 13, 268*
display-control systems *70, 147, 204, 220*
display-observer interaction *219*
human beings as system components *184,
281*
job-task design *59, 196*
learning and memory *11, 39*
operator variability *39*
perceptual-cognitive integration and *11,
184*
performance modeling and evaluation *11,
39, 250*
problem solving and complex information
processing *11, 39, 192, 241*

psychosocial stresses *196*
reading text at visual display units *291*
symbol systems in performance
  enhancement *135, 234*
systems performance and reliability *11,
  59, 184*
target acquisition and tracking skills *204,
  220*
visual fatigue *196*
workstation design *196, 242*

►HYPERDIMENSIONALITY AND
  HYPERGRAPHICS *1, 31, 180*

►ICONIC COMMUNICATION
bibliography of *148*
in data management systems *137, 138,
  139, 140, 141*
ergonomics of *92*
experiments in *92*
iconic systems *92, 173*
iconic versus textual communication *92*
isotype *202, 280*
pictographs *92, 172, 173*
psychology of *148*

►ICONS
isotype *202*
as mnemonics *148*

►ILLUMINATION
ergonomics of *134*
input to luminance ratios *111*
internal illumination for display devices
  112
specifications for display devices *112, 134*
and visual function *270*

►IMAGE DESCRIPTORS
communication theory *51*
correlation fidelity *51, 52, 53, 54*
information capacity *51, 52, 53, 54*
perceived signal to noise ratio *51, 52, 53,
  54*
visual capacity *51, 52, 53, 54*

►IMAGE GENERATION *108, 180, 221, 235*

►IMAGE PERCEPTION *95, 288*

►IMAGE PROCESSING (see also COGNITIVE
  PROCESSES; VISUAL PROCESSING)
algebra and geometry of *232*
color digital image processing *73*
database preparation and digital imaging
  251
perceptually "perfect" images *54*
picture analysis and editing *84*
reconstruction and representation *232*
surface texture synthesis *85*
visual analysis *194*

►IMAGE QUALITY
contrast sensitivity *51, 52, 53, 54*
effects of cell and line failures on *255*
noise and image detection *23, 252, 253*
signal to noise ratios *51, 52, 53, 54*
visual performance and *23, 247, 251, 252,
  253, 254, 256*

►IMAGE REPRESENTATION
Gourand shading *97*
representational processes *181*

►IMAGE TRANSFORMATIONS *91*

►IMAGING *249*

►IMAGING DEVICES (see also DISPLAY
  DEVICES) *24, 27, 160, 162, 165, 243*

►IMAGING TECHNIQUES
algorithms for imaging *207, 239*
chamfer matching *26*
fractal modeling *180*
holography *207*

►INFORMATION DESIGN (see also
  CARTOGRAPHIC DESIGN; DISPLAY DESIGN;
  MESSAGE DESIGN; SCREEN DESIGN; TEXT
  AND TEXT DESIGN)
chromatic versus achromatic information
  coding *265*
cognitive models *182*
color schemes and models for *272*
data graphics *274*
field studies in *67*
graphic language and symbols *21, 131,
  172, 173, 274, 296*
graphic methods *21, 30, 50, 136, 173,
  179, 237, 238, 296*
iconic communication systems *92*
information delivery and packaging *38*
information load and redundancy *67, 182,
  184*
information mapping *114, 136, 173*
strategies of *61, 131, 182*
symmetry and transformations *167*
theory of *182, 184*
for visual presentation *131, 281*
wordplay *167*

►INFORMATION PRESENTATION
color models and schemes for *272*
data density and maximization *226, 274*
design and evaluation *69, 131, 226*
in drawings *72*
graphic data management *137, 138, 139,
  140, 141*
graphic language and vocabulary *274*
graphic versus linguistic information *75,
  226*
iconic communication *137, 138, 139, 140,
  141*
multifunctional elements *131, 274*
in text *60*

►INFORMATION PROCESSING (see also
  PERCEPTUAL PROCESSES; VISUAL
  PROCESSING)
attention and memory *297*
codes for *297*
graphic information processing *21, 75*

►INFORMATION TECHNOLOGY *144*

►INPUT DEVICES AND TECHNIQUES *12, 14, 71, 244, 281*

►INTERACTIVE GRAPHICS (see also COMPUTER GRAPHICS; GRAPHIC SCIENCE)
display architecture *79*
human factors of *15*
information display and review *6*
interactive techniques *79, 113, 239, 263*
parallel processing and real time techniques *279*
visual interfaces *15, 79*

►INTERACTIVE GRAPHICS SYSTEMS (see also GRAPHICS SYSTEMS) *56, 92*

►INTERACTIVE METHODS IN COMPUTER GRAPHICS *104*

►INTERFACE DESIGN
design studies *155, 193*
display-control systems *11, 184*
human factors guidelines *18, 78, 159, 298*
for interactive systems *104, 205*
software ergonomics *39, 246*
standards for *103, 107*

►INTERFACES
command language for *71*
Computer Graphics Metafile *99*
design studies *71, 155*
display and control systems *147*
human-machine systems *39, 78*
interactive techniques *79*
natural language interfaces in graphic displays *245*
visual interfaces *15, 159*

►ISOTYPE *202, 280*

►LASER DISPLAYS *161*

►LEGIBILITY CRITERIA
color and background *269*
page layout and alignment *226, 257, 269*
rules for typographic legibility *185, 226, 275*
for symbols *4*
test performance and specifications *96, 298*
type characteristics *226, 257, 269*

►LEGIBILITY PARAMETERS (see also SCREEN CHARACTERISTICS) *67, 298*

►LEGIBILITY RESEARCH (see also READING)
alphanumeric versus graphic displays in problem solving *200*
bibliography and index to *57, 58*
effects of cell and line failures on legibility *255*
human factors research *184*
methods *72*
perception and comprehension of print *257, 297*
typography and *224*

►LETTERFORMS *142, 167, 185, 225*

►LIGHT (see also COLOR; OPTICS; PHOTOMETRY) *112, 157*

►LIGHT-EMITTING DIODE DEVICES *35, 215, 223, 244, 264*

►LIGHTING AND ILLUMINATION (see also ENVIRONMENTAL LIGHTING; ILLUMINATION; VISUAL ERGONOMICS)
ergonomics of lighting for visual displays *112, 134*
input to luminance ratios *111*
International Committee on Illumination (CIE) Standards *157*

►LIQUID CRYSTAL DEVICES
color in *163, 169, 259*
large scale displays *215*
laser addressed devices *223*
operating principles and performance *35, 163, 169, 215, 223, 259*
special problems of *35, 169*

►MAP DESIGN
black and white in *76*
color in *61, 76, 227*
composition and legend design *61, 187*
evaluation methods *72*
figure-ground and surface-form relationships *61, 76, 166, 227*
general principles *166, 187, 188*
human factors in *72, 227*
multi subject mapping *22, 76*
pattern mapping *72, 227*
special purpose maps *166, 187*
surface transformations and distortions *61, 188*
thematic mapping *120*
typography and lettering *61, 227*
visual hierarchies in *61*

►MATHEMATICAL METHODS IN COMPUTER GRAPHICS AND DESIGN *25, 33, 46, 229, 230*

►MATRIX DISPLAY DEVICES
device characteristics *243*
effects of cell and line failures on image quality *255*
plasma panel color technology *236*

►MENTAL REPRESENTATION
symbol associations and evaluation *69*
visual imagery and *258*

►MESSAGE DESIGN
complexity and content control *77, 182*
conceptual learning and *77, 182*
design implementation and integration *182*
message structure and strategy *77, 182*
natural language in *10*
perceptual principles for *10, 77*
research in *182*

►MICROCOMPUTER GRAPHICS
animation *9*
coordinate systems *216*

display generation *9, 216*
interactive techniques *9, 216*
line and object transformations *216*
point transformations *216*
transformation matrices *216*
►MICROCOMPUTERS *9, 113, 216*
►MILITARY SYSTEMS *90*
►MOTION DETECTION
apparent motion *29, 36, 181, 292*
direction *147, 181*
eye movements and *292*
image sequences *143*
interpretation of motion *277, 278*
motion perception *36, 43, 158, 292*
psychophysics of *292*
rotary motion *29*
and spatial orientation *292*
three-dimensional motion *278*
tracking and trajectories *147*
transformation and analysis in motion
  perception *36, 277*
visual localization *292*
►MOTION MEASUREMENT *143, 277, 292*
►NON-EMISSIVE DEVICES *169, 264*
►OPTICS (see also LIGHT) *112, 157, 208*
►PATTERN RECOGNITION (see also
  COGNITIVE PROCESSES; PERCEPTUAL
  PROCESSES; VISUAL PROCESSING)
cognitive processing and *176*
color and shape as integral stimuli *53*
effects of chrominance and luminance *53*
figure-ground and form perception *158,
  232*
Gestalt psychology *16, 258*
metrical aspects of patterns *16*
pattern and pattern relationship
  perception *45, 88, 158, 232, 258*
picture perception *109*
symmetry *158*
texture discrimination *45, 158*
►PERCEPTION (see also DEPTH PERCEPTION;
  VISION; VISUAL PERCEPTION; VISUAL
  PROCESSING)
analog perception *297*
attention and vigilance *233, 297*
binocular interaction *16*
discrimination and decision processes *16,
  110, 290*
internal representations *16, 88*
legibility studies *96*
paradoxical perceptions and visual
  illusions *109, 110, 233*
perceptual ambiguity *109, 110*
perceptual construction *88, 109*
perceptual interdependence *88, 110, 228*
picture perception *109*
as problem solving *29, 110, 228*
psychophysics of perception *88, 297*
signal detection *297*
space perception *233, 297*
stimulus interactions *88, 210, 211, 213,
  228, 233, 290*

in three-dimensional displays *88, 233*
►PERCEPTUAL CODING *16*
►PERCEPTUAL INTERFERENCE
complex information *212, 290*
Cyclopean and paradoxical perception
  109, 158
distracting information *212*
interference patterns *109*
irrelevant information *212*
visual ambiguity *109*
►PERCEPTUAL ORDER *94*
►PERCEPTUAL PROCESSES
attention and vigilance *44, 297*
classification and inference *88*
feature processing *44, 88*
illusions and hallucinations *44*
information integration *88, 109, 297*
perceptual learning *44*
spatial problem solving and cognitive
  mapping *66*
stimulus ambiguity *44*
►PERCEPTUAL STUDIES
display complexity *212*
dot area symbols *45*
effects of irrelevant information on
  perception *212*
effects of pattern and texture *45*
legibility *96*
perceptual integration *7*
stimulus interactions *210, 211, 213, 233*
tracking and control operations *249*
visual assessment and demands *222*
►PERCEPTUAL SYSTEMS
analog perception *297*
attention and vigilance *297*
biology of perceptual systems *42*
models of perception *158, 297*
sensorimotor systems *42*
sensory adaptation and integration *11,
  297*
signal detection *297*
►PERFORMANCE EVALUATION
cell and line failures in matrix displays
  255
color preferences and color coding *62*
display-control systems *70, 147*
display-operator interactions *70*
displays and decision strategies *147*
graphicolingual displays *75*
information transmission in visual
  displays *200, 250*
legibility and screen parameters *114, 298*
performance modelling *40, 250*
processing concrete and abstract data *192*
symbol systems *55, 154, 234*
visual performance and flat panel displays
  250
►PERFORMANCE REQUIREMENTS
display research facility *268*
display systems *27*

►PERSPECTIVE *5, 64, 82, 109, 110, 167, 205, 261*

►PHOTOELECTRONIC IMAGING DEVICES *24*

►PHOTOMETRY (see also LIGHT; OPTICS) *23, 112, 247, 301*

►PICTURE LANGUAGES (see also ICONIC COMMUNICATION; ISOTYPE; SYMBOLS) *202, 280*

►PLASMA PANEL DEVICES
color technology *236*
operating principles *35, 215, 223, 244, 264*
special problems of *35*

►PRINTING TECHNOLOGIES *164*

►PRODUCT DESIGN AND LIABILITY *159*

►RASTER GRAPHICS *15, 56, 205, 229*

►RASTER SCAN DEVICES *23*

►READING (see also LEGIBILITY CRITERIA; LEGIBILITY RESEARCH; TEXT AND TEXT DESIGN; VISUAL PROCESSING)
experimental studies of *173, 183*
eye movements in *172, 270*
feature analysis *172, 173, 183*
graphic aspects of text *173*
lexical access *276*
and memory *172*
models of reading *183, 270*
orthographic structure *183, 276*
perception and comprehension of print *172, 173, 258, 270, 276, 297*
reading performance at visual display units *291*
style and strategy in *172, 276*
text design *172*
visual encoding *276*

►SCREEN CHARACTERISTICS
active area of screen *12, 298*
ambient light *12*
angle of view *12, 244, 271, 289*
character size and accents *12, 271, 289, 298*
color *12, 244, 289, 298*
font *67, 244, 298*
format *12, 244*
glare control *12*
image distortion and polarity *12*
line and column spacing *12, 271, 298*
luminance *12, 96, 289*
refresh rate and phosphor persistence *12, 298*
resolution and contrast *271, 298*
screen height and viewing distance *12*

►SCREEN DESIGN (see also DISPLAY DESIGN; INFORMATION DESIGN; READING)
attention control *67, 86*
character set design *271*
color in *86*
content and format *67, 86*
design standards and documentation *86*

message load *67*
sequencing *67*
symbol preferences *135*

►SEMIOTICS (see also CODES AND CODING; COMMUNICATION; ICONS; SYMBOLS) *21, 22*

►SHADING AND TEXTURE ALGORITHMS
contour filling *217*
illumination *229*
intensity *79*
shading and shadow *79, 97, 113, 205, 229*
texture *85, 229*
thinning *217*
transparency *229*

►SIGN SYSTEMS (see also SYMBOLS) *55, 69*

►SIGNAGE *67, 69, 186*

►SIGNS (see SYMBOLS)

►SIMULATION AND MODELING
fractal geometry and modeling *180*
image generation *79, 235*
mathematical modeling *48*
training systems *235*

►SOFTWARE ERGONOMICS
human performance *39*
interface software *246*

►STANDARDS
color standards *157*
control devices *281*
environmental lighting and visual display terminals *151*
Graphical Kernel System *105, 106*
graphics standards handbook *107*
human engineering guidelines *184*
human performance standards *11*
interface design standards *11*
International Committee on Illumination (CIE) Standards *157*
international graphics standards *105, 106*
visual ergonomic standards *243*

►SURFACE GENERATION ALGORITHMS
bilevel pictures *217*
curves *25, 33, 46, 81, 91, 113, 217*
free form surfaces *81*
hidden surfaces *46, 81, 91, 113, 205, 229*
projections *81*
splines *84, 217*
surface geometry *79, 91, 217, 230, 239*
visible surfaces *15, 239*

►SYMBOLIC REPRESENTATION
cartographic symbol generation *45, 189*
pattern and perception *45*
sign systems *55*

►SYMBOLS (see also AREA SYMBOLS; CODES AND CODING; ICONS; INFORMATION DESIGN)
advantages and limitations of sign systems *55*
character set design *271*
design guidelines *4, 55, 135, 154, 184, 234*
evaluation of sign systems *4, 55, 76, 154*

isotype *202*
proportional symbol mapping *61*
semiology of sign systems *22*
symbol interpretation *296*
symbol sets for visual communication *4, 76, 135, 296*
symbol systems for performance enhancement *234*
visual thinking *7*

►SYMMETRY
motifs *261*
perception of *158*
recursion *1*
symmetry groups *261*
symmetry operations *1, 261*
symmetry transformations *167, 261*

►SYSTEMS DESIGN
developmental planning and user analysis *59*
human beings as system components *159, 281*
message design *10, 281*
task analysis *59*
visual displays in *10*

►TEXT AND TEXT DESIGN (see also INFORMATION DESIGN; READING; TYPOGRAPHY; VISUAL DESIGN)
algorithms for text design *156, 218*
alphabet design *170*
character sets for optical display *271*
cognitive functions in *156*
composition research *60, 218*
enhancement and structuring *60, 156, 173, 257*
illustrations in *114*
modular and grid systems for *150*
text processing *60*
TEX system *170*
typographic variables *114, 156*

►THREE-DIMENSIONAL DISPLAYS
algorithms for *48, 217*
depth and motion perception *219*
evaluation of *90*
imaging techniques for *207*
perceptual research on *90, 233*
primitives *48*

►THREE-DIMENSIONAL GEOMETRY (see also ALGORITHMS; GEOMETRY; GRAPHIC GEOMETRY; TWO-DIMENSIONAL GEOMETRY)
contours *33*
coordinate systems *5, 113*
hidden lines and surfaces *5, 113, 205, 229*
holography *207*
mathematics for *217*
rotations and transformations *113, 205, 230*
three-dimensional construction *207, 229, 230*
visible surfaces *15*

►TWO-DIMENSIONAL GEOMETRY
clipping and covering *5, 113, 229*
geometry of space *261*

transformations of two-dimensional space *5, 229, 230*
windowing *113*

►TYPE (see also FONT; TYPEFACES; TYPOGRAPHY) *87*

►TYPEFACES (see also FONT; TYPOGRAPHY)
classification and terminology *185, 275*
design *83, 149*
font *185*
in graphic composition *83, 295*
guide to typefaces *87, 168, 231*
legibility *83, 231, 269*
letter shapes and design *185, 231*
for optical character recognition *83*
script *83*
type styles *87*

►TYPESETTING *170, 275*

►TYPOGRAPHY (see also FONT; TYPEFACES)
alphabet design *142, 170, 257*
characteritics of type *89, 224, 269, 294*
classification and terminology of type *185, 275*
composition with type *72, 83, 89, 149, 294, 295*
decorative typography *89, 231, 273*
effects of typographic arrangements *269*
evaluation of typographic format *72, 275, 294*
graphic composition with type *89, 142, 269, 273, 295*
grid systems for *195*
legibility rules *185, 270, 275*
logotype *83*
mathematics and *170*
optical effects of letterforms *142*
symmetry and letterforms *167, 225*
TEX and METAFONT *170*
word action progressions *225*

►VACUUM TUBE DEVICES *35, 244*

►VISIBLE LANGUAGE
alphabets for *257*
graphic design *136, 149, 179, 257*
text structure *257*
typographic design *87, 142, 149, 273*

►VISION (see also VISUAL PERCEPTION; VISUAL PROCESSING)
anatomy of the eye *151*
computational theory of *181*
contrast sensitivity *248, 250*
distortions of perceived space *233*
lighting requirements for visual function *151*
optical illusions *175*
psychophysics of *23, 43*
space perception *43, 233*
spatiotemporal integration *248*
visual acuity and sensitivity *151*
visual adaptation *175*
visual capabilities *43, 250*

►VISUAL ARTS (see also DESIGN) *65*

►VISUAL CODING *13, 281*

►VISUAL COMMUNICATION
    acquisition of graphic information *173*
    basic elements of *65, 203, 267, 296*
    character set design for optical display
      271
    composition as visual syntax *65, 267*
    graphic systems and literacy *173, 203*
    illustrations in *173*
    symbol sets for *4*
    visual techniques for *65, 203, 267, 296*
    writing systems *173*

►VISUAL DESIGN *267, 273*

►VISUAL DISPLAY TERMINALS (see also
    DISPLAY DEVICES)
    ambient light *196, 242*
    anthropometry *196*
    demands on the visual system *222*
    design principles *37, 222*
    evaluation of human factors research *193*
    job-task design *196, 242*
    operator preferences and psychosocial
      stress *18, 196, 242*
    reading performance and *291*
    symbol luminance *96*
    terminal configuration *37*
    visual fatigue *18*

►VISUAL DISPLAYS (see also DISPLAY
    DEVICES; DISPLAYS)
    character representation *184*
    chromatic aberration *13*
    color metrics *73, 184*
    display distortion *13*
    image and signal detectability *184*
    luminance changes *54*
    visual ergonomics of *37*

►VISUAL ERGONOMICS
    brightness *243, 244*
    character size *243, 244*
    color *243, 244, 275*
    contrast and resolution *37, 243, 244*
    design specifications for *243*
    flicker and jitter *243, 244, 271*
    glare and reflectance *37*
    illumination guidelines for visual displays
      112, 134
    luminance and illuminance *37, 242, 243,*
      244
    viewing angle *242, 243, 244*
    visual stimulus dimensions *209*
    visual syntax *275*

►VISUAL EXPERIENCE
    balance *8*
    dynamics and composition *8, 94*
    invention and discovery *94, 95*
    light and color *8*
    psychology of style *94*
    space *8*
    typography as visual expression *89*
    visual literacy *65*

►VISUAL FUNCTION *98, 143*

►VISUAL INTERFACES *15*

►VISUAL MOTION (see also MOTION
    DETECTION)
    computational analysis of *36, 143, 277*
    interpretations of motion and structure
      277
    measurement of *143*
    movement mapping *277*
    psychophysics of *36, 143*
    visual tracking *143*

►VISUAL PERCEPTION (see also DEPTH
    PERCEPTION; VISUAL PROCESSING)
    communication theory and information
      capacity *51*
    composition as visual syntax *65*
    computational analysis of *36*
    contrast sensitivity *51, 52, 53, 54*
    cue symmetry *147*
    and decision strategies *147*
    dimensional integrality and scaling *210,*
      211, 213, 233
    figure and ground perception *158*
    foundations of perceptual science *287*
    hyperacuity *278*
    interdimensional interactions and
      perceptual experience *13, 210, 287*
    modulation transfer functions *51, 52, 53,*
      54
    perceptual stability and visual persistence
      43
    selective attention *233*
    space and perspective *43, 109, 232, 233,*
      287, 288
    spatiotemporal interactions *43, 174*
    visual capacity *51, 52, 53, 54*
    visual distortions and ambiguity *90, 109,*
      233

►VISUAL PERFORMANCE (see also VISUAL
    PERCEPTION; VISUAL PROCESSING)
    advanced visualization techniques *145*
    applied research in *241*
    color preferences and color coding *62,*
      250, 265
    cue symmetry and stimulus orientation
      147
    effects of popping *19*
    effects of spot wobble *249*
    font and matrix requirements *250*
    image interpretation *251, 252, 253, 256*
    information theory and transmission *51,*
      250
    noise and image detection *23, 247*
    performance models and visual
      capabilities *250*
    reading performance at visual display
      units *291*
    spatiotemporal relations *241, 248, 250*
    target acquisition and recognition *247,*
      249
    threshold functions *248, 249*
    tracking and control operations *147, 220,*
      249

visual fatigue and stress *196*
visual tasks *196, 247, 301*
►VISUAL PROCESSING (see also COGNITIVE
    ERGONOMICS; COGNITIVE PROCESSES; IMAGE
    PROCESSING; READING; VISUAL PERCEPTION;
    VISUOMOTOR INTEGRATION)
    attention and vigilance *44*
    computational theory of *181*
    discrimination and decision processes *44,
        181, 290*
    geometric and three-dimensional forms
        288
    Gestalt organization in *109, 158, 258*
    image sampling *51, 54*
    interdimensional interactions *181, 287,
        290*
    letter and word perception *44, 172, 183,
        276*
    luminance information *54*
    perception versus scrutiny *95, 158*
    perceptual learning *44, 110*
    processes and constraints *110, 181*
    spatial problem solving *44, 66, 181*
    statistical properties of natural scenes *51*
    stimulus identification and differentiation
        44, 181, 290
    temporal interactions *181, 278, 287, 290*
    visual and verbal interactions *258*
    visual search *44*
    visualizing multiple dimensions *31*
►VISUAL SPACE
    design for *267*
    distortions of *233*
►VISUAL THINKING (see also COGNITIVE
    ERGONOMICS; COGNITIVE PROCESSES;
    PERCEPTION; PERCEPTUAL STUDIES)
    ambiguous structures *31*
    design for *267*

four-dimensional illusions *31*
graphic data analysis and display *50*
visible language *136*
visual design *89, 136*
visualizing complex relationships *1, 7, 31*
►VISUAL THRESHOLDS *301*
►VISUOMOTOR INTEGRATION (see also
    CONTROL SYSTEMS; DEPTH PERCEPTION;
    VISUAL PERCEPTION; VISUAL PERFORMANCE)
    alert functions *284*
    attention control *86*
    display-control systems *11, 184, 204*
    object detection and recognition *158, 232*
    perceptual-cognitive integration *11, 39, 42*
    psychomotor skills *297*
    reaction time *39, 71, 86, 147*
    sensory processing *11, 184*
    stimulus duration *232*
    target acquisition and tracking skills *39,
        220, 247*
    temporal factors in information transfer
        241
    visual tasks *196, 247*
►WORK AND WORKPLACE DESIGN (see
    also ERGONOMICS; HUMAN FACTORS
    ENGINEERING; PERFORMANCE EVALUATION;
    VISUAL DISPLAY TERMINALS)
    checklists for *59*
    environmental lighting *28*
    ergonomic requirements for visual display
        terminals *12, 37, 98*
    health and safety issues of visual display
        terminals *20, 206*
    interactive work areas *159, 281*
    job-task design *59, 196, 281*
    user support for *59*
    visual displays in *159*